More information about this series at http://www.springer.com/series/7409

Vincent G. Duffy (Ed.)

Digital Human Modeling and Applications in Health, Safety, Ergonomics and Risk Management

Posture, Motion and Health

11th International Conference, DHM 2020
Held as Part of the 22nd HCI International Conference, HCII 2020
Copenhagen, Denmark, July 19–24, 2020
Proceedings, Part I

 Springer

Editor
Vincent G. Duffy
Purdue University
West Lafayette, IN, USA

ISSN 0302-9743   ISSN 1611-3349   (electronic)
Lecture Notes in Computer Science
ISBN 978-3-030-49903-7   ISBN 978-3-030-49904-4   (eBook)
https://doi.org/10.1007/978-3-030-49904-4

LNCS Sublibrary: SL3 – Information Systems and Applications, incl. Internet/Web, and HCI

This Springer imprint is published by the registered company Springer Nature Switzerland AG
The registered company address is: Gewerbestrasse 11, 6330 Cham, Switzerland

Foreword

The 22nd International Conference on Human-Computer Interaction, HCI International 2020 (HCII 2020), was planned to be held at the AC Bella Sky Hotel and Bella Center, Copenhagen, Denmark, during July 19–24, 2020. Due to the COVID-19 coronavirus pandemic and the resolution of the Danish government not to allow events larger than 500 people to be hosted until September 1, 2020, HCII 2020 had to be held virtually. It incorporated the 21 thematic areas and affiliated conferences listed on the following page.

A total of 6,326 individuals from academia, research institutes, industry, and governmental agencies from 97 countries submitted contributions, and 1,439 papers and 238 posters were included in the conference proceedings. These contributions address the latest research and development efforts and highlight the human aspects of design and use of computing systems. The contributions thoroughly cover the entire field of human-computer interaction, addressing major advances in knowledge and effective use of computers in a variety of application areas. The volumes constituting the full set of the conference proceedings are listed in the following pages.

The HCI International (HCII) conference also offers the option of "late-breaking work" which applies both for papers and posters and the corresponding volume(s) of the proceedings will be published just after the conference. Full papers will be included in the "HCII 2020 - Late Breaking Papers" volume of the proceedings to be published in the Springer LNCS series, while poster extended abstracts will be included as short papers in the "HCII 2020 - Late Breaking Posters" volume to be published in the Springer CCIS series.

I would like to thank the program board chairs and the members of the program boards of all thematic areas and affiliated conferences for their contribution to the highest scientific quality and the overall success of the HCI International 2020 conference.

This conference would not have been possible without the continuous and unwavering support and advice of the founder, Conference General Chair Emeritus and Conference Scientific Advisor Prof. Gavriel Salvendy. For his outstanding efforts, I would like to express my appreciation to the communications chair and editor of HCI International News, Dr. Abbas Moallem.

July 2020   Constantine Stephanidis

HCI International 2020 Thematic Areas and Affiliated Conferences

Thematic areas:

- HCI 2020: Human-Computer Interaction
- HIMI 2020: Human Interface and the Management of Information

Affiliated conferences:

- EPCE: 17th International Conference on Engineering Psychology and Cognitive Ergonomics
- UAHCI: 14th International Conference on Universal Access in Human-Computer Interaction
- VAMR: 12th International Conference on Virtual, Augmented and Mixed Reality
- CCD: 12th International Conference on Cross-Cultural Design
- SCSM: 12th International Conference on Social Computing and Social Media
- AC: 14th International Conference on Augmented Cognition
- DHM: 11th International Conference on Digital Human Modeling and Applications in Health, Safety, Ergonomics and Risk Management
- DUXU: 9th International Conference on Design, User Experience and Usability
- DAPI: 8th International Conference on Distributed, Ambient and Pervasive Interactions
- HCIBGO: 7th International Conference on HCI in Business, Government and Organizations
- LCT: 7th International Conference on Learning and Collaboration Technologies
- ITAP: 6th International Conference on Human Aspects of IT for the Aged Population
- HCI-CPT: Second International Conference on HCI for Cybersecurity, Privacy and Trust
- HCI-Games: Second International Conference on HCI in Games
- MobiTAS: Second International Conference on HCI in Mobility, Transport and Automotive Systems
- AIS: Second International Conference on Adaptive Instructional Systems
- C&C: 8th International Conference on Culture and Computing
- MOBILE: First International Conference on Design, Operation and Evaluation of Mobile Communications
- AI-HCI: First International Conference on Artificial Intelligence in HCI

Conference Proceedings Volumes Full List

http://2020.hci.international/proceedings

11th International Conference on Digital Human Modeling and Applications in Health, Safety, Ergonomics and Risk Management (DHM 2020)

Program Board Chair: **Vincent G. Duffy, Purdue University, USA**

- Giuseppe Andreoni, Italy
- Mária Babicsné Horváth, Hungary
- Stephen Baek, USA
- André Calero Valdez, Germany
- Yaqin Cao, China
- Damien Chablat, France
- H. Onan Demirel, USA
- Yi Ding, China
- Ravindra Goonetilleke, Hong Kong
- Akihiko Goto, Japan
- Hiroyuki Hamada, Japan
- Michael Harry, UK
- Genett Jimenez-Delgado, Colombia
- Mohamed Fateh Karoui, USA
- Thorsten Kuebler, USA
- Noriaki Kuwahara, Japan
- Byung Cheol Lee, USA
- Kang Li, USA
- Masahide Nakamura, Japan
- Thaneswer Patel, India
- Caterina Rizzi, Italy
- Juan A. Sánchez-Margallo, Spain
- Deep Seth, India
- Meng-Dar Shieh, Taiwan
- Beatriz Sousa Santos, Portugal
- Leonor Teixeira, Portugal
- Renran Tian, USA
- Dugan Um, USA
- Kuan Yew Wong, Malaysia
- S. Xiong, South Korea
- James Yang, USA
- Zhi Zheng, USA
- Rachel Zuanon, Brazil

The full list with the Program Board Chairs and the members of the Program Boards of all thematic areas and affiliated conferences is available online at:

http://www.hci.international/board-members-2020.php

HCI International 2021

The 23rd International Conference on Human-Computer Interaction, HCI International 2021 (HCII 2021), will be held jointly with the affiliated conferences in Washington DC, USA, at the Washington Hilton Hotel, July 24–29, 2021. It will cover a broad spectrum of themes related to Human-Computer Interaction (HCI), including theoretical issues, methods, tools, processes, and case studies in HCI design, as well as novel interaction techniques, interfaces, and applications. The proceedings will be published by Springer. More information will be available on the conference website: http://2021.hci.international/.

General Chair
Prof. Constantine Stephanidis
University of Crete and ICS-FORTH
Heraklion, Crete, Greece
Email: general_chair@hcii2021.org

http://2021.hci.international/

Contents – Part I

Contents – Part II

Addressing Ethical and Societal Challenges

New Research Issues and Approaches in Digital Human Modelling

Posture and Motion Modelling in Design

Statistical Posture Prediction of Vehicle Occupants in Digital Human Modelling Tools

Erik Brolin[1]([⊠]) [iD], Dan Högberg[1] [iD], and Pernilla Nurbo[2]

[1] School of Engineering Science, University of Skövde, Skövde, Sweden
erik.brolin@his.se
[2] Ergonomics, Customer Experience Centre, Volvo Cars, Gothenburg, Sweden

Abstract. When considering vehicle interior ergonomics in the automotive design and development process, it is important to be able to realistically predict the initial, more static, seated body postures of the vehicle occupants. This paper demonstrates how published statistical posture prediction models can be implemented into a digital human modelling (DHM) tool to evaluate and improve the overall posture prediction functionality in the tool. The posture prediction functionality uses two different posture prediction models in a sequence, in addition to the DHM tool's functionality to optimize postures. The developed posture prediction functionality is demonstrated and visualized with a group of 30 digital human models, so called manikins, by using accurate car geometry in two different use case scenarios where the sizes of the adjustment ranges for the steering wheel and seat are altered. The results illustrate that it is possible to implement previously published posture prediction models in a DHM tool. The results also indicate that, depending on how the implemented functionality is used, different results will be obtained. Having access to a digital tool that can predict and visualize likely future vehicle occupants' postures, for a family of manikins, enables designers and developers to consider and evaluate the human-product interaction and fit, in a consistent and transparent manner.

Keywords: Digital human modelling · Vehicle ergonomics · Posture prediction

1 Introduction

Since most design work in industry is performed with the assistance of digital tools, such as computer aided design (CAD) and computer aided engineering (CAE) tools, it is imperative to be able to consider human factors also in the digital development process. This applies also to the very start of the design and development process, where many central design decisions are made that concerns human-product interaction aspects, such as fit, reach and visibility, which in turn influences the vehicle's ability to meet specified levels of accommodation [1]. Digital human modelling (DHM) tools provide designers and product developers with valuable decision support to consider human factors such as: health, comfort, safety, user diversity, and inclusion, in the design of environments, systems, products, and workplaces [2–4]. When designs are defined and tested in virtual worlds, DHM tools enable the incorporation of virtual test

© Springer Nature Switzerland AG 2020
V. G. Duffy (Ed.): HCII 2020, LNCS 12198, pp. 3–17, 2020.
https://doi.org/10.1007/978-3-030-49904-4_1

persons, so called manikins, to support that the items being designed meet different users' requirements related to ergonomics and user experience. When considering driver, passenger, and vehicle interior ergonomics in the automotive industry, it is important to be able to realistically predict the initial, more static, seated body postures of the vehicle occupants. There are several different models for posture prediction of driving and seated postures [5–15]. Among these models it is possible to identify two different methods for posture prediction: 1) postures are predicted through an optimization process by minimizing deviations from so called neutral comfort angles, or 2) through statistical regression equations that predicts coordinates for specific key positions on the human body or in the car interior [16]. Limitations with the optimization prediction method are that most of the published models do not include individual specific comfort joint angle values, neither equations for the prediction of comfort joint angle values based on anthropometric variables. Another issue or question relates to the prioritization of critical body joints to achieve comfort, which joints need to closer to their comfort values and which joints can deviate more? A limitation with the statistical prediction method is that there are few or outdated examples of implementation in DHM tools or similar software. An example of such an implementation is presented by Huston et al. [17] who have developed a parametric CAD accommodation model that provides geometric boundaries for equipped soldiers using driver and crew workstations in military ground vehicles.

This paper aims to demonstrate how statistical prediction models can be implemented in a DHM tool that has in-built optimization based posture prediction functionality. The overall objective of integrating the published statistical posture prediction models is to evaluate, and possibly improve, the overall posture prediction functionality in DHM tools. The paper describes how the statistical posture prediction models were implemented in a research version of the DHM tool IPS IMMA (Intelligently Moving Manikins) [18]. The paper focuses on posture prediction models for passenger cars specifically, even if a similar approach have been implemented also for trucks and buses.

2   Description of Methods

The IPS IMMA tool is able to generate manikin motions defined as quasi-static, generated by inverse kinematics, where a comfort function seeks to optimize comfort while fulfilling current constraints [19, 20]. An initial driving posture will be static as it does not include any motions, even if additional manikin motions can be added after the initial driving posture have been found. The seated driving posture prediction method initially used in this research was based on the IPS IMMA tool's functionality to optimize comfort, based on existing knowledge about postures in vehicles, i.e. comfortable joint angles for driver posture and minimization of joint torques, while not violating defined constraints, e.g. holding on to the steering wheel with both hands [21]. The implementation of the statistical posture prediction models in IPS IMMA uses positioned control frames that defines adjustment ranges (seat and steering wheel) as well as standard reference points [22] to make predictions of steering wheel, H-point [23], Mid-hip and Centre-eye position.

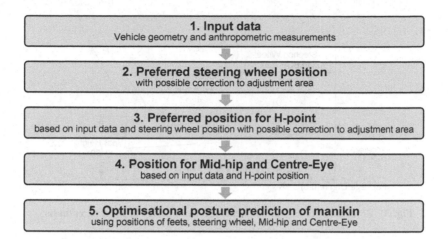

Fig. 1. Process of implemented posture prediction functionality

The posture prediction functionality uses two different posture prediction models in a sequence, in addition to the IPS IMMA tool´s functionality to optimize the posture (Fig. 1). The two posture prediction models are implemented in IPS IMMA through the embeddable scripting language Lua [24]. An initial script automatically generates necessary control frames to be placed manually at their correct positions in IPS IMMA (Fig. 2). Standard measurements are automatically calculated based on some of these control frames, e.g. the H30 measurement is automatically calculated as the vertical distance between the Ankle Heel Point (AHP) and the Seating Reference Point (SgRP) according to SAE J1100 [23] (Fig. 3). An additional script then uses the information from the control frames, together with information of each manikin, to predict the position and driving posture for all manikins within a pre-generated group of manikins, a so called manikin family. This prediction is done in three steps: 1) first a prediction of the steering wheel position is done, 2) followed by a prediction of the H-point position, 3) to eventually be able to predict the positions for the Mid-hip and Centre-eye points, which are used to position the manikins (Fig. 1).

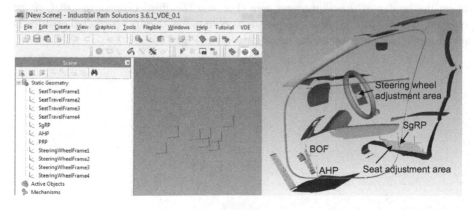

Fig. 2. Generated control frames manually placed at their correct positions in IPS IMMA

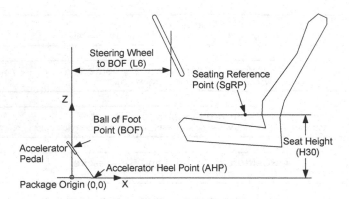

Fig. 3. Reference points and nomenclature from SAE J1100 in parenthesis

The prediction of the steering wheel location is done by using a model that was originally developed as an ordinal logistic regression to predict the distribution of subjective responses as a function of fore-aft steering wheel position (L6), seat height (H30) and driver stature [12]. In the study, subjective responses were measured on a rating scale that varied from 1 to 7. Response 1, 2, and 3 were counted as "too close" and response 5, 6, and 7 were counted as "too far" while response 4 were counted as "just right". In the implementation in IPS IMMA, the linear part of the logistic model is transformed and the subjective response of "just right", which was 4, is inserted to be able to predict the preferred fore-aft steering wheel location (L6) (mm) as

$$L6 = \frac{4 + 0.003441 \times \text{Stature} + 0.01854 \times \text{H30} - 0.00004958 \times H30^2}{0.021182} \quad (1)$$

The predicted preferred fore-aft steering wheel location (L6) is, in the current implementation in IPS IMMA, related to the set up steering wheel adjustment area (Fig. 4). The first case shows that, if the predicted fore-aft position (L6) is within the adjustment range and could be put on the mid-line of steering wheel adjustment area, the steering wheel height is put on that mid-line (Fig. 4). The second case shows that, if the preferred fore-aft position is outside the mid-line, then the steering wheel height is put on the border of the adjustment area (Fig. 4). The third case shows that, if the preferred fore-aft position is outside the adjustment range, then the predicted position is moved to the closest point of the adjustment area (Fig. 4).

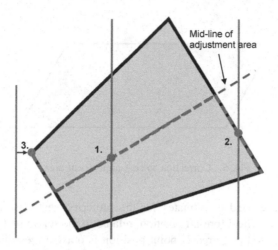

Fig. 4. Correction to steering wheel adjustment area

The predicted fore-aft steering wheel location (L6) is subsequently used to predict coordinates for the preferred seat position (H-point) (X, in relation to the Ball of Foot point (BOF), and Z, in relation to the ankle heel point (AHP)). Different posture prediction models for men and women using the Cascade Modeling Approach [14] are implemented as:

Female Driver Posture-Prediction of H-point (mm)

$$H-point_X = 678 + 0.284 \times S - 494 \times SHS + 2.33 \times BMI \\ - 0.388 \times H30 + 0.426 \times (L6 - 600) \tag{2}$$

$$H-point_z = 129 - 6.2 \times 10^{-2} \times S + 0.909 \times H30 - 4.65 \times 10^{-2} \times (L6 - 600) \tag{3}$$

Male Driver Posture-Prediction of H-point (mm)

$$H-point_X = -48 + 0.56 \times S + 1.39 \times BMI + 7.53 \times Age - 0.42 \times H30 \\ + 0.505 \times (L6 - 600) - 3.98 \times 10^{-3} \times S \times Age \tag{4}$$

$$H-point_z = 123.1 - 5.864 \times 10^{-2} \times S + 0.945 \times H30 \tag{5}$$

Note. S = stature (mm); SHS = sitting height/stature; BMI = body mass index (kg/m^2); H30 = seat height (mm).

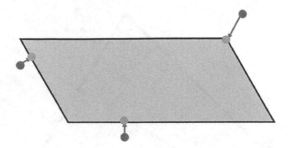

Fig. 5. Correction to seat adjustment area

The predicted preferred coordinates for the preferred seat position (H-point) is, similar to the steering wheel fore-aft position, related to the set up seat adjustment area (Fig. 5). If the predicted preferred H-point position is outside the adjustment area the H-point is moved to the nearest border. Coordinates for the Mid-hip and Centre-eye position are predicted in relation to the H-point position as:

Female Mid-hip Position in Relation to the H-point (mm)

$$Mid-hip_X = -162.3 + 358.3 \times SHS - 1.757 \times BMI \tag{6}$$

$$Mid-hip_z = 2238 - 1.26 \times S - 4719 \times SHS + 4.66 \times BMI - 6 \times Age - 5.3 \atop \times 10^{-2} \times BMI \times Age + 13.8 \times SHS \times Age + 2.54 \times S \times SHS \tag{7}$$

Female Centre-Eye Position in Relation to the H-point (mm)

$$Centre-eye_X = -364 + 7.64 \times 10^{-2} \times S + 540 \times SHS + 0.124 \times (L6 - 600) \tag{8}$$

$$Centre-eye_z = -461 + 0.163 \times S + 1445 \times SHS - 15.1 \times BMI + 3.61 \atop \times Age + 9.93 \times 10^{-3} \times S \times BMI - 6.54 \times SHS \times Age \tag{9}$$

Male Mid-hip Position in Relation to the H-point (mm)

$$Mid-hip_X = 196 + 7.38 \times 10^{-2} \times S - 552 \times SHS - 2.44 \times BMI \tag{10}$$

$$Mid-hip_z = 2269 - 1.39 \times S - 4615 \times SHS - 1.42 \times BMI \atop - 0.222 \times Age + 2.78 \times S \times SHS \tag{11}$$

Male Centre-Eye Position in Relation to the H-point (mm)

$$Centre-eye_X = -578 + 0.174 \times S + 706 \times SHS - 1.55 \times BMI \atop - 6.48 \times 10^{-2} \times H30 \tag{12}$$

$$Centre-eye_z = -498 + 0.361 \times Stature + 845 \times SHS \atop + 2.76 \times BMI - 0.175 \times Age \tag{13}$$

Note. S = stature (mm); SHS = sitting height/stature; BMI = body mass index (kg/m^2); H30 = seat height (mm).

The result of the scripted posture prediction functionality differs slightly depending on if the prediction is done on a whole manikin family or for a single manikin. For a single manikin the selected control points connected to the Mid-hip and Centre-eye position, together with the steering wheel, are automatically moved to the predicted positions and affects the posture of the manikin. For a manikin family the result is the predicted positions for the steering wheel, H-point, Mid-hip and Centre-eye for each manikin in the whole manikin family (Fig. 6). These positions can in an additional step be used to position and visualize the posture of a selected member of the manikin family.

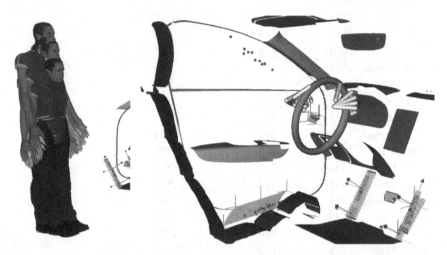

Fig. 6. Manikin family with predicted positions for steering wheel, H-point, Mid-hip and Centre-eye

3 Results

The developed posture prediction functionality is demonstrated and visualized with a manikin family consisting of 30 manikin cases, 15 male and 15 female cases (Table 1) based on anthropometric data from the ANSUR data set [25]. The 30 manikin cases are defined using two three dimensional boundary confidence ellipsoids calculated based on stature, sitting height, and waist circumference, three anthropometric measurements that describes a person's overall size as well as proportions [26–28]. For each confidence ellipsoid six axial cases, eight box cases and one centre case are defined [29]. All other necessary measurements are predicted based on these three key anthropometric measurements [30] except the age which was set to an arbitrary value of 45 years for all manikins.

The postures for each of the 30 manikin cases are predicted using accurate car geometry from a Volvo S90/V90 in two different use case scenarios (Fig. 7). In the first scenario, more generous adjustment ranges are defined, enabling more or less free positioning, which shows how the DHM tool with the posture prediction functionality can be utilized in early development phases as a specification tool, giving input to the design process. The second scenario uses the finally decided adjustment ranges to limit the positions of the manikins' positions, showing how the DHM tool can function as an evaluation tool in later development phases.

Table 1. 30 manikin cases used to demonstrate the posture prediction functionality. Cases italic have min or max values per measurement, marked in bold.

#	Sex	Stature (mm)	Sitting height (mm)	Waist circumference (mm)
1	Female	1629	851	725
2	Male	1755	913	839
3	*Female*	*1655*	*873*	***561***
4	Male	1800	938	662
5	Female	1691	818	720
6	Male	1823	878	839
7	Female	1585	793	591
8	Male	1723	855	675
9	Female	1775	896	664
10	Male	1917	959	797
11	Female	1555	768	780
12	Male	1671	827	880
13	Female	1793	940	789
14	Male	1745	871	854
15	Female	1866	930	1003
16	Male	1513	832	596
17	Female	1645	897	676
18	Male	1703	935	670
19	Female	1839	1000	798
20	Male	1483	807	786
21	Female	1593	868	882
22	Male	1673	910	859
23	Female	1788	971	1004
24	*Male*	***1924***	***1003***	*945*
25	Female	1603	830	889
26	*Male*	*1711*	*889*	***1017***
27	Female	1567	885	730
28	Male	1688	949	840
29	*Female*	***1464***	***762***	*661*
30	Male	1587	824	734

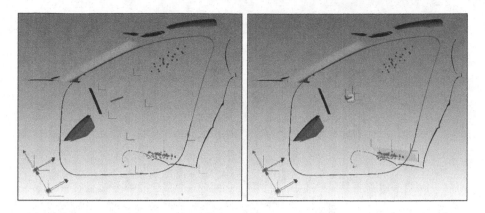

Fig. 7. Predicted positions for steering wheel (purple), H-point (red), Mid-hip (green) and Centre-eye (blue) for the 30 manikin cases for scenario 1 to the left and scenario 2 to the right (Color figure online)

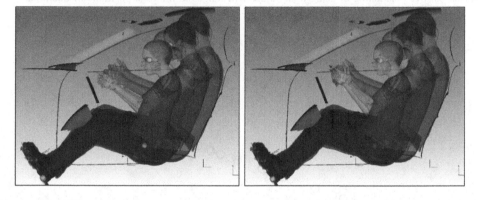

Fig. 8. Visualization of predicted postures for manikin cases #3, #24, #26, and #29 for scenario 1 to the left and scenario 2 to the right

Out of the 30 manikin cases, four manikin cases were selected, #3, #24, #26, and #29, to more easily portray the diversity in postures within the manikin family (Fig. 8). These four cases (italic in Table 1) were selected because they included the minimum and maximum values for the three anthropometric measurements, stature, sitting height, and waist circumference (bold in Table 1), used to define the two three dimensional boundary confidence ellipsoids. Further comparison of the results from this study indicates that smaller manikins reposition themselves further back when final decided adjustment areas of the seat and steering wheel is used in the simulation (Figs. 9, 10, 11, 12 and 13).

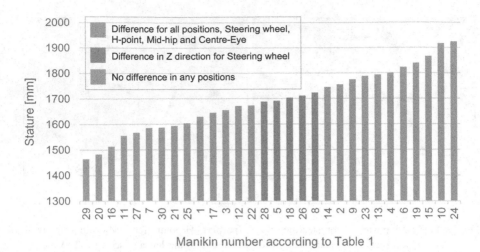

Fig. 9. Manikins sorted by stature and grouped by how many positions are different in the two scenarios: free positioning or using final adjustment ranges to limit the positions of manikins.

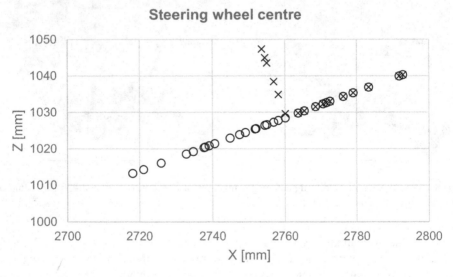

Fig. 10. Positions for steering wheel centre in first scenario, free positioning (circles) and second scenario, using final adjustment ranges to limit the positions of manikins (crosses)

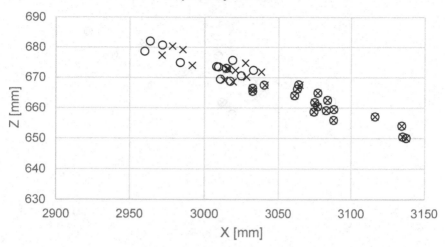

Fig. 11. Positions for H-points in first scenario, free positioning (circles) and second scenario, using final adjustment ranges to limit the positions of manikins (crosses)

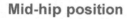

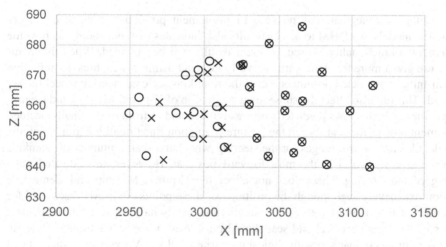

Fig. 12. Positions for Mid-hip in first scenario, free positioning (circles) and second scenario, using final adjustment ranges to limit the positions of manikins (crosses)

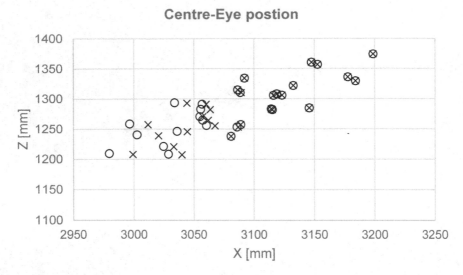

Fig. 13. Positions for Centre-eye in first scenario, free positioning (circles) and second scenario, using final adjustment ranges to limit the positions of manikins (crosses)

4 Discussion

The results illustrate that it is possible to implement previously published posture prediction models in a DHM tool. The results also indicates that, depending on how the implemented functionality is used, different results will be obtained. When the manikins were given more freedom, with an overly large adjustment area, thus not inflicting in their initially predicted posture, some of the manikins selected steering wheel further forward. This did also affect the subsequent prediction of H-point, Mid-hip and Centre-eye position, which shows predicted postures outside and in front of the finally decided adjustment area of the seat. When the posture prediction functionality is run, using the final decided adjustment ranges for the steering wheel and seat, a number of manikins have the steering wheel in the most forward position. However, this adjusted positioning of the steering wheel does not affect the H-point, Mid-hip and Centre-eye position extensively even though the positions of these points are moved backward for a number of manikins as well. These simulation results indicate that the adjustment ranges of the steering wheel and seat should be moved or extended slightly forward. However, initial comparison with clinical user trial results at Volvo Cars indicates that users of a real Volvo S90/V90 prefers to sit further back than what the posture prediction functionality shows. These contradictory results indicate that further evaluation and adjustments of the published statistical models is needed.

The developed posture prediction functionality is an initial implementation and needs further development. In its current state it predicts the most probable preferred posture. The statistical posture prediction models that is implemented also include the root mean square error (RMSE) which could be used to introduce a stochastic component to the posture prediction and thus imitate the postural diversity that exists within a population [31]. However, such additional functionality would also require a better or at least a different procedure to handle anthropometric diversity by randomizing also body size with a larger number of manikins. Imitating postural diversity and simulation with a large group of randomized manikins would create the possibility to quantify the overall accommodation level that is achieved by suggested design, i.e. what percentage of the target population that will be able to use the vehicle in an acceptable and comfortable way. The implemented functionality is realized through a 5-step process (Fig. 1) including a combination of two different statistical prediction models, first predicting steering wheel position and then H-point, Mid-hip and Centre-eye. This is a pragmatic approach toward implementing and testing published models, which needs to be investigated further. The implemented functionality also considers adjustment ranges and is able to force the manikin to position themselves within the predefined adjustment ranges. However, that process might need to be improved to better mimic how actual persons would behave when forced into smaller adjustment ranges. Also, additional constraints needs to be included in the posture prediction process such as the possibility to see out of the car, and not collide with roof and other parts of the interior, e.g. knee interference with lower part of dashboard.

Having access to a digital tool that can predict and visualize likely future vehicle occupants' postures, for a family of manikins, enables designers and developers to consider and evaluate the human-product interaction and fit, in a consistent and transparent manner. Appropriate predictions of an initial, more static, body posture is imperative in the automotive industry and needs to be investigated further in future research. In addition, it is also important for the automotive industry to be able to perform accurate simulations, covering both longer driving sequences and additional non-driving related activities. Today it is difficult to do more advanced and longer simulations in DHM tools, and also difficult to make objective assessments of longer simulation sequences. This applies also when considering driver, passenger, and vehicle interior ergonomics in the automotive industry. Simulation and assessment of additional non-driving related activities, like eating, texting, talking, relaxing etc., is assumed to be even more important in the near future with the introduction of highly automated or fully autonomous vehicles [32]. This is a future research endeavor.

Acknowledgements. This work has been made possible with the support from The Knowledge Foundation and the associated INFINIT research environment at the University of Skövde (projects: Virtual Driver Ergonomics, Synergy Virtual Ergonomics and ADOPTIVE), in Sweden, and SAFER - Vehicle and Traffic Safety Centre at Chalmers, Sweden, and by the participating organizations. This support is gratefully acknowledged.

References

1. Högberg, D.: Digital human modelling for user-centred vehicle design and anthropometric analysis. Int. J. Veh. Des. **51**(3/4), 306–323 (2009)
2. Duffy, V.G.: Handbook of Digital Human Modeling. CRC Press, Boca Raton (2009)
3. Wischniewski, S.: Delphi survey: digital ergonomics 2025. In: Proceedings of the 2nd International Digital Human Modeling Symposium. University of Michigan, Ann Arbor (2013)

4. Scataglini, S., Paul, G.: DHM and Posturography. Academic Press, London (2019)
5. Rebiffe, R.: An ergonomic study of arrangement of the driving positions in motorcars. In: Proceedings of Symposium on Sitting Posture, Zurich, Switzerland, pp. 132–147 (1969)
6. Grandjean, E.: Sitting posture of car drivers from the point of view of ergonomics. In: Grandjean, E. (Ed.), Human Factors in Transport Research, Part 1. Taylor & Francis, London (1980)
7. Krist. R.: Modellierung des Sitzkomforts - eine experimentelle Studie. Lehrstuhl für Ergonomie, Technical University Munich, Munich (1993)
8. Porter, J.M., Gyi, D.E.: Exploring the optimum posture for driver comfort. Int. J. Veh. Des. 19(3), 255–266 (1998)
9. Reed, M.P., Manary, M.A., Flannagan, C.A.C., Schneider, L.W.: A statistical method for predicting automobile driving posture. Hum. Factors 44(4), 557–568 (2002)
10. Reed, M.: Development of a new eyellipse and seating accommodation model for trucks and buses. University of Michigan, Transportation Research Institute. Report no. UMTRI-2005-30 (2005)
11. Hanson, L., Sperling, L., Akselsson, R.: Preferred car driving posture using 3-D information. Int. J. Vehicle Design 42(1/2), 154–169 (2006)
12. Reed, M.: Driver preference for fore-aft steering wheel location. SAE Int. J. Passeng. Cars-Mech. Syst. 6(2), 629–635 (2013)
13. Park, J., Ebert, S.M., Reed, M.P., Hallman, J.J.: A statistical model including age to predict passenger postures in the rear seats of automobiles. Ergonomics 59(6), 796–805 (2015)
14. Park, J., Ebert, S.M., Reed, M.P., Hallman, J.J.: Statistical models for predicting automobile driving postures for men and women including effects of age. Hum. Factors 58(2), 261–278 (2016)
15. Lee, S., Park, J., Jung, K., Yang, X., You, H.: Development of statistical models for predicting a driver's hip and eye locations. In: Proceedings of the Human Factors and Ergonomics Society Annual Meeting, vol. 61, no. 1, pp. 501–504 (2017)
16. Reed, M.P., Manary, M.A., Flannagan, C.A.C., Schneider, L.W.: Comparison of methods for predicting automobile driver posture. In: Digital Human Modeling for Design and Engineering Conference and Exposition, SAE Technical Paper Series 2000-01-2180, Dearborn, Michigan (2000)
17. Huston, F.J., Zielinski, G.L., Reed, M.P.: Creation of the driver fixed heel point (FHP) CAD accommodation model for military ground vehicle design. In: Proceedings of the 2016 Ground Vehicle Systems Engineering and Technology Symposium (GVSETS), Novi, Michigan (2016)
18. Högberg, D., Hanson, L., Bohlin, R., Carlson, J.S.: Creating and shaping the DHM tool IMMA for ergonomic product and production design. Int. J. Digit. Hum. 1(2), 132–152 (2016)
19. Bohlin, R., Delfs, N., Hanson, L., Högberg, D., Carlson, J.S.: Automatic creation of virtual manikin motions maximizing comfort in manual assembly processes. In: Hu, S.J. (ed.) Proceedings of the 4th CIRP Conference on Assembly Technologies and Systems, pp. 209–212 (2012)
20. Delfs, N., Bohlin, R., Hanson, L., Högberg, D., Carlson, J.S.: Introducing stability of forces to the automatic creation of digital human postures. In: Proceedings of DHM 2013, Second International Digital Human Modeling Symposium, USA (2013)
21. Bergman, C., Ruiz Castro, P., Högberg, D., Hanson, L.: Implementation of suitable comfort model for posture and motion prediction in DHM supported vehicle design. In: 6th International Conference on Applied Human Factors and Ergonomics (AHFE 2015), USA (2015)

22. Roe, R.W.: Occupant packaging. In: Peacock, B., Karwowski, W. (eds.) Automotive Ergonomics, pp. 11–42. Taylor & Francis, London (1993)
23. Society of Automotive Engineers: SAE J1100 – Motor Vehicle Dimensions. Society of Automotive Engineers, Inc., Warrendale, PA (2009)
24. Lua: Lua the programming language. https://www.lua.org/. Accessed 20 Feb 2020
25. Gordon, C.C., et al.: 1988 Anthropometric Survey of US Army Personnel: Methods and Summary Statistics. U.S. Army Natick Research, Development and Engineering Center, Natick, MA (1989)
26. Flügel, B., Greil, H., Sommer, K.: Anthropologischer atlas: grundla-gen und daten. Verlag Tribüne, Berlin (1986). (in German)
27. Speyer, H.: On the definition and generation of optimal test samples for design problems. Human Solutions GmbH, Kaiserslautern (1996)
28. Brolin, E., Högberg, D., Hanson, L.: Description of boundary case methodology for anthropometric diversity consideration. Int. J. Hum. Factors Model. Simul. 3(2), 204–223 (2012)
29. Bertilsson, E., Högberg, D., Hanson, L.: Using experimental design to define boundary manikins. Work J. Prev. Assess. Rehabil. 41(Suppl. 1), 4598–4605 (2012)
30. Brolin, E., Högberg, D., Hanson, L., Örtengren, R.: Adaptive regression model for prediction of anthropometric data. Int. J. Hum. Factors Model. Simul. 5(4), 285–305 (2017)
31. Parkinson, M.B., Reed, M.P., Kokkolaras, M., Papalambros, P.Y.: Optimizing truck cab layout for driver accommodation. ASME J. Mech. Des. 129(11), 1110–1117 (2007)
32. Yang, Y., Klinkner, J.N., Bengler, K.: How will the driver sit in an automated vehicle? – The qualitative and quantitative descriptions of non-driving postures (NDPs) when non-driving-related-tasks (NDRTs) are conducted. In: Bagnara, S., Tartaglia, R., Albolino, S., Alexander, T., Fujita, Y. (eds.) IEA 2018. AISC, vol. 823, pp. 409–420. Springer, Cham (2019). https://doi.org/10.1007/978-3-319-96074-6_44

Digital Human-in-the-Loop Framework

H. Onan Demirel[(✉)]

Oregon State University, Corvallis, OR 97331, USA
onan.demirel@oregonstate.edu

Abstract. Although there are numerous ergonomics assessment methods available for assessing safety, comfort, and performance of human-product interactions, there is a lack of comprehensive and widely available computational human-centered design framework that brings human factors principles into engineering design. In existing human-centered design approaches, computational assessment of human-product interaction is not explicitly considered as part of the early design phase, but rather it is addressed downstream in the design process through traditional human factors engineering strategies, often, includes physical prototyping and usability studies with extensive human-subject data collection. We hypothesize that digital human modeling can be utilized not only as an ergonomics evaluation tool but also as an engineering design methodology to embrace form and function during the early phases of the development. The digital human modeling approach has the potential to be a merger between the form and functionality aspects of product design by focusing on human needs, abilities, and limitations. This paper introduces a novel human-in-the-loop methodology which injects human factors engineering principles via digital human modeling into a computational design environment to assess the safety and performance of human-product interactions early in design.

Keywords: Digital human modeling · Human factors engineering · Engineering design

1 Introduction

The main objective of human factors engineering (HFE) is the design of optimal products and systems [1,2]. The domain is concerned about the interactions between humans and the entire system - including all entities that make up the system (e.g., products, machines, computers). At the core, HFE focuses on human needs, abilities, and limitations to sustain or improve human-system interactions. It is challenging to imagine any scientific discipline rather than HFE that has better overlapping interests and objectives with the human-centered design approach. Furthermore, HFE domain has a diverse knowledge base and supports a wide range of disciplines, including engineering design. It provides ergonomics assessment methods and tools, which are used for assessing safety, comfort, performance, and compatibility of products. However, there is a lack

ⓒ Springer Nature Switzerland AG 2020
V. G. Duffy (Ed.): HCII 2020, LNCS 12198, pp. 18–32, 2020.
https://doi.org/10.1007/978-3-030-49904-4_2

of comprehensive and widely available computational human-centered design framework that brings human factors principles into engineering design, particularly focusing on the early design phase of modern development. One of the advanced HFE methods that have the potential to create a paradigm shift in the engineering design domain is digital human modeling (DHM). It can bridge form and functionality aspects of product design with focusing on human needs, abilities, and limitations.

In this paper, DHM is proposed as a middle-ware to integrate engineering design, HFE, and systems engineering. The primary objective is to develop a human-centered design framework that introduces HFE principles early in the product design phase. Secondarily, the framework forms a holistic design scope by embracing emergent design methodologies and tools. In combination, the design framework contemplates on form and function aspects of the design process from conception to creation with human needs, abilities, and limitations are being central interests.

2 Background

2.1 What Is Digital Human Modeling

Complex functions of the human body, both physical and cognitive aspects, can be digitally represented, simulated, and analyzed through DHM tools [3,4]. DHM uses digital humans as representations of workers inserted into a simulation or virtual environment to facilitate the prediction of performance and safety. DHM includes visualizations of the human body with the mathematics and science in the background [4–8] (Fig. 1). It helps organizations design safer and efficient products while optimizing productivity and cost [9]. Engineering design practices that utilize DHM have the potential to enable engineers to incorporate HFE principles earlier in the design process [4,10–12]. One of the advantages of DHM applications is their integration flexibility with computer-aided engineering (CAE) packages and digital design technologies such as motion capture, eye-tracking, and virtual reality [4–6,13].

The U.S. military implemented one of the first DHM applications for cockpit design in which virtual drivers were used to assessing the safety and performance of the prototype vehicles. The use of DHM reduced the need for expensive and bulky physical mockups [10,14–16]. The popularity of DHM applications has increased in the past decade, and many companies have realized the effectiveness of DHM tools for early design ergonomics evaluation [17]. Recently, technological developments and advancement in the CAE software expanded the application areas of DHM [3,18]. There are multiple DHM platforms introduced as part of CAE packages, which include digital ergonomics and biomechanical assessment tools to evaluate the injury, safety, and comfort-related design attributes [19–21].

2.2 How Does Digital Human Modeling Provide an Integration

The proposed design framework not only integrates design, human factors, and systems engineering but also provides a systematic understanding of the human

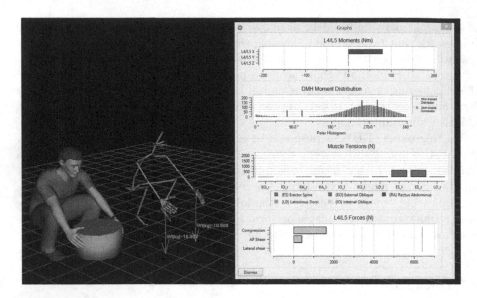

Fig. 1. DHM includes visualizations of the human with the mathematics and science in the background.

element inside the product development process. It embraces cross-functional knowledge and expertise through building connections with various disciplines (such as anthropometry, biomechanics, industrial engineering, mechanical engineering, industrial design, kinesiology, physiology, psychology, and others) [22]. This multidisciplinary approach allows modular integration to the second and third party design methodologies and technologies (Fig. 2).

One of the advantages of DHM applications is in their integration flexibility with concurrent engineering methodologies such as product lifecycle management (PLM), virtual product development (VPD), and CAE platforms [13]. Trial-and-error on physical prototypes may resolve some of the design complexions; however, it has a few limiting factors such as visualization, simulation, time, and cost. The time-to-market and cost of a product are critical for success in global competition [4]. These multi-faceted factors must be considered early in the design process to have a safe, efficient, and profitable product [23–25]. Designers must accomplish a competitive edge during the design, production, and marketing of products through reducing design timescales, overall cost, and time-to-market [10,12]. These complex goals need systematic product development strategies, which embrace the mechanics and aesthetics of the design process while considering manufacturing, marketing, management, and recycling phases of product development. In this context, absence or inadequate consideration of HFE principles can result in poor quality standards, which may lead to customer dissatisfaction, safety, and hazard concerns. Companies often end up in product recalls and lawsuits, which eventually result in reputation loss. Alternately, concurrent engineering tools provide an integrated platform to monitor

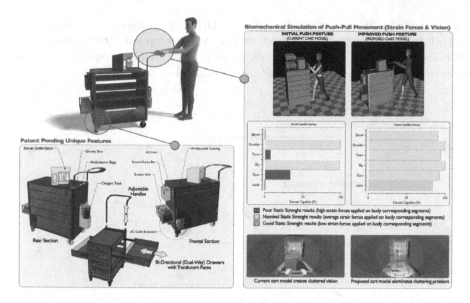

Fig. 2. DHM can be used not only as an ergonomics evaluation tool but also a method to embrace form and function during product development. A hospital code cart design study shows how biomechanics assessment process can be integrated to test product design alternatives. This approach integrates form aspects of industrial design with functional aspects of engineering design early in the product development phase.

technical and managerial aspects of the product development [26]; however, they fail to consider the human element early in the design process.

DHM integrated with concurrent engineering tools enable designers to assess whether people of different age, gender, size, and strength characteristics can safely and effectively perform tasks inside a computer simulation environment. Furthermore, virtual reality (VR) tools can be used along with DHM to provide a higher level of fidelity. Through the VR environment, user-product interactions can be assessed regarding comfort and safety without the need for full-scale physical prototypes [4,10,27]. A design platform that allows direct connections to DHM can assists designers to evaluate both aesthetics (visualizations - *concept sketching and rendering*) and functionality (mathematics - *simulation and analysis*) of product innovation. DMH can also provide a common medium to connect subjective judgment and divergent (inspirational) nature of industrial designers with the objective and convergent (structural) nature of the design engineers [22,28].

In theory, DHM forms an ideal medium for integrating industrial designers and mechanical engineers early in the design process. It also promotes a more holistic design approach by embracing emergent design methodologies and technologies, which can assist designers in considering the human element throughout the design-cycle. Thus, DHM can bring additional time and cost savings on top of the savings associated with concurrent design methodologies. Figure 3 shows cost associated with conventional, CAE, and DHM integrated engineering design methodologies. Because of its interdisciplinary focus, quantitative nature, and flexibility of integration with other design platforms, DHM becomes a potential problem-solving tool for various multidisciplinary design challenges.

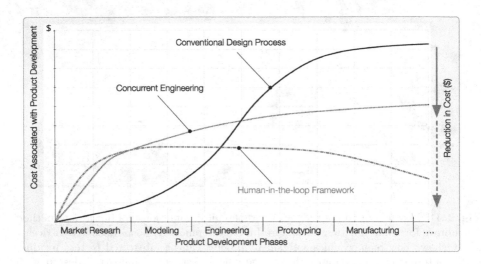

Fig. 3. DHM can reduce cost associated with physical prototyping or mockups [18]. In addition, identifying problems of human-product interactions early in design phase can reduce additional costs arises from product incompatibility.

3   Methodology

3.1   Fundamentals of Digital Human-in-the-Loop Design Framework

The Digital Human-in-the-loop (D-HIL) framework is a modified version of "Virtual Build" structure, which brings HFE design principles earlier to the product design process [8,11]. Previous VB studies focused solely on ergonomics evaluation and human factors assessment of products and systems [29,30]. The D-HIL framework focuses not only on ergonomics assessments but also on actual design processes including, but not limited to, concept development, structural integrity, and digital prototyping. It provides scientific insight (ergonomics, biomechanics) and artistic approach (rendering, visualization) on product-user interactions. In conventional design strategies, HFE design principles are often applied sequentially at later stages of product development as a post-evaluation method. This approach is associated with high costs and excessive time-to-market. In contrast, the D-HIL framework offers a non-sequential approach, which considers human-element early in the product development phase. Within the D-HIL framework, conceptual design ideas iteratively modified through DHM and CAE in a parallel sequence - before ever getting into the prototyping phase. This way, human needs, abilities, and limitations are considered early in the design process. Design errors or human-product incompatibilities can be captured before prototyping begins.

Data related to human attributes can come from manual or digital sources. For example, human posture data can either come from a manual anthropometric setup, or various digital systems (motion capture, eye-tracker, a motion prediction model). If manual methods are used, descriptive task parameters (e.g., push-pull distance, lift-lower height) are inserted manually to generate ergonomics evaluations. The CAD model can be updated parametrically, depending on the changes required after each ergonomic and structural assessment. The effects of variations on the CAD model in terms of ergonomics and structural integrity can be cross-checked simultaneously.

There are few variants of VB structure that bridge DHM and motion capture for ergonomic research [25,27,31]. Different than those studies that use DHM as a method of post-processing analysis tool, the D-HIL framework utilizes DHM to bring human needs, abilities, and limitations earlier into the design process. DHM is used as an actual product design tool rather than as a method of ergonomics evaluation executed at the very late stages of product development. At the micro-level, the framework functions similarly to the VB methodology. In contrast to VB, the D-HIL framework does not only functions as a post-processing ergonomics analysis tool. It is an integrated part of concurrent product design and development system (macro-level). This approach creates a holistic coverage of design entities while keeping human needs, abilities, and limitations at focus throughout the design process.

In this study, the human-centered design approach forms the foundation of the design strategy. It is composed of four product development phases (Understand, Conceptualize, Create and Realize) and four Constraints (Costumer Requirements, Human Capabilities and Limitations, Physical Requirements, and Process Requirements). Design flow works in clockwise (from Understand to Realize) and in ascending order (from quadrant 1 to 4), respectively, to establish a design hierarchy. This hierarchy provides a systematical process flow to understand customer requirements, generate concept ideas, then create digital models, and finally realize a high-fidelity digital model. The framework utilizes this hierarchical strategy to map user requirements with engineering constraints and find potential pathways to satisfy overall design goals (Fig. 4). Each building block acts as an individual part of an embedded system, where ascending blocks provide design decision filters to the information sent from lower blocks.

The D-HIL framework functions similarly to a Quality Function Deployment (QFD) system, where Customer Attributes (WHATs) are mapped to Engineering Requirements (HOWs) [32]. In QFD, WHATs provide customer needs, and HOWs provide engineering characteristics to satisfy (or ways to achieve) WHATs within available resources. These elements (WHATs and HOWs) eventually define the goals and constraints of the design system, which together form the available design space [33,34]. Goals are different than constraints. Goals define the ultimate design objectives (potential design alternatives), and constraints draw up the boundaries, which form the feasible design space. Not all initial goals can be achieved. In other words, what customers wish can sometimes be misleading or technically not feasible. Often, Engineering Requirements form the boundaries that shape up all feasible/alternative ideas. In this context, DHM defines human-aspects of Engineering Requirements. Without the use of DHM techniques, engineers utilize manual checklists or expert opinion, which often fail to generate a list of realistic Engineering Requirements systematically. How people interact with products, both physically and cognitively, goes beyond the scope of simple checklists and expertise. The use of DHM as a core member of the design cycle assists engineers in iterating various what-if scenarios parametrically without the need for extensive use of physical prototypes or mockups. Without such a design strategy, decision making during the design process would be misleading and erroneous, which often resulted in high costs, hazard, or dissatisfaction.

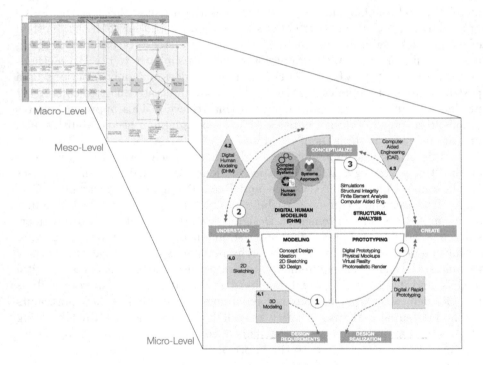

Fig. 4. Image shows extended overview of the D-HIL design framework, from macro-level to micro-level.

3.2   Phases of the Digital Human-in-the-Loop Design Process

Within the D-HIL framework, the product design process starts with identifying or understanding consumer needs, abilities, and limitations. Understanding the problem area is essential to create sound design requirements. After this step, engineering requirements are linked with a knowledge base where each requirement can guide designers to generate necessary design alternatives. Later, alternative (concept) models can be modeled and simulated to check various design specific what-if scenarios. The best model(s) from a pool of alternatives can be refined to create the most feasible prototype model(s) that meet engineering requirements while satisfying as much customer needs [32]. Finally, the concept product is selected, and beta products for manufacturing and production are finalized at the Realization stage. More information is provided below for each design phase.

- Understand: This is the initial product development phase where user needs, abilities, and limitations are identified and checked with the knowledge base. This phase is the most critical amongst other stages, which requires at most attention to identifying design challenges carefully. Designers often omit or ignore human aspects of the design process at the earlier stages of the design process, which ends up being a cost driver at the later stages of product development.

- Conceptualize: After design requirements are identified, concept models can be generated. These models should reflect the designers' creativity while satisfying design requirements. At the end of this phase, concept models should be filtered to obtain the prototype model(s), which represent the best models amongst a pool of design alternatives.

- Create: Prototype model(s) further go into more refinement process, which includes structural modeling and multi-physics simulations. If higher fidelity can not be achieved with available multi-physics simulations, physical prototyping, field tests, and experiments should be sought.

- Realize: At this stage final prototype should be further refined to meet manufacturing, maintenance, production, and packaging requirements. Depending on the complexity of a product or the nature of the design project, a final prototype can be a fully digital model, a physical prototype, or a combination of both.

3.3   Goals and Constraints

Within the D-HIL framework, upper blocks function as a filter for the lower blocks. In the Customer Requirements step, customer attributes are identified by designers. These attributes may exceed the physical and cognitive capabilities of users. Therefore, Human Capabilities and Limitations block acts as a filter for the design alternatives generated in the previous stage. This step only allows attributes that are capable of being performed by users. Later, qualified customer attributes are mapped to Physical Requirements, which are used to generate the form and functions associated with a conceptual design model. At this stage of the design process, only human-product interactions that are feasible pass to the next step. In Process Requirements stage, the concept model is further refined, and the working prototype is finalized. More information is provided below for each phase.

- Customer Requirements: The foundation of the design development is to understand customers' wants and needs. This step provides a vast number of customer needs and desires for a new product or modifications for an existing product. Human-centered products should be designed to reflect customers' needs while satisfying engineering requirements. This is also a critical step to define the design scope. Surveys show that poor product design definition is a factor in 80% of market delays [35].

- Human Capabilities and Limitations: This step filters customer requirements and provides a limitation to those that exceed human physiology and cognition (e.g., control button distance exceed the maximum reach of 75% male). Ignoring or omitting the human aspects of design is a costly mistake and should be avoided with all the costs. Products that do not reflect human capabilities and limitations are not appreciated by customers and result in compatibility issues, safety problems, and market failures.

- Physical Requirements: In this step, customer attributes and human needs are mapped to each other to provide a conceptual design that satisfies users' needs from a wide range of the population. Also, technical attributes such as form, functionality, and material selection are generated and checked with compatibility requirements.

- Process Requirements: After generating the conceptual models (or working prototypes), products are further refined by usability studies and experiments. In this step, available resources (suppliers, marketing) are mapped, and the working prototype is finalized for production.

4 How Does Human-in-the-Loop Framework Function?

At the core of the framework, DHM functions as an analytical design and analysis tool as well as a communication medium between contributors of each stage of the design. In this study, the HCD approach retains user needs, abilities, and limitations at sight throughout the design cycle. Goals and Constraints link HFE knowledge and methods with design requirements. Varying HFE methods and technology tools are added to adequate stages of product development through a modular approach. Variations and combinations of processes and technologies used inside the framework depend on the nature of the design study. A consumer product design may not require advance simulations. On the other hand, an aircraft design may demand multiphysics simulations, as well as extended physical experiments and prototyping. Thus, the domain of interest dictates what tools to be integrated into the framework. In either case, DHM blends form and function of aspects of products with humans at the center and builds connections with other design entities.

Human subject data either comes from digital libraries or collected through manual methods. Digital libraries include kinematics, anthropometrics, and posture related human attributes. If manual methods are used, attributes can be linked design framework through various data collection methods (motion capture, eye-tracker, sensors). Similarly, environment input could be a fully digital CAD model, an immersive VR environment, a physical prototype, or a hybrid model (a physical model with limited digital probes). DHM blends human data and environment input and generates analysis that constitutes mathematical (e.g., biomechanics) and visualization (e.g., rendering) outputs.

Within the D-HIL framework, concept model(s) go in a digital test that iteratively forces what-if design scenarios. This portion of the design framework uses multiphysics simulation tools to answer what-if scenarios. In case multiphysics tools are not capable of providing required answers to what-if questions asked by designers, physical experiments and field tests should be conducted for further understanding and refinement, if necessary. The need for physical prototyping often results due to the complexity of design projects where product or process requires higher levels of human-product interactivity [27]. At this stage, the designer should decide either to entirely rely on simulation tools or proceed with collecting human subject data through physical experiments. The choice of either method or degree of reliance on one method depends on the level of human product interaction that existed. If multiphysics simulation tools provide sufficient fidelity, then digital prototypes would be a sound strategy. At this stage, DHM can be utilized without the need for physical experiments or full-scale prototyping. When simulation tools lose the fidelity, then human subject experiments through physical models become an ideal path to follow (Fig. 5).

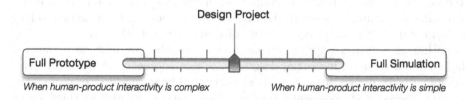

Fig. 5. The need for full-scale modeling or full-simulation in a design project is shown in a continuum [27]. The degree of the using either a full or a moderate simulation/prototyping depends on the nature of the design project.

The need for digital prototypes or full-scale models also defines the scope of the design project. Often, one can split design projects as either industrial design or engineering design-oriented. In the case where abstraction and conceptualization are concerned, industrial designers heavily involved with the generation of design ideas, which often require low fidelity models that rely on form aspects of

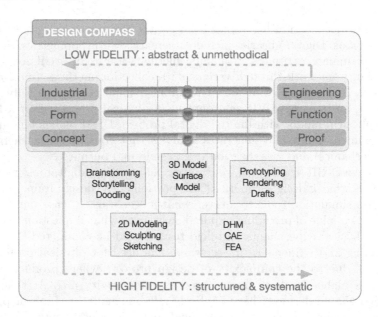

Fig. 6. Depending on the design study, either Industrial Design or Engineering Design can dominate each other. In product design studies, often Industrial Design or Engineering Design contribute equally. DHM can function either way by blending form and function aspects of design attributes centered at human needs, abilities and limitations.

design. In contrast, engineering design projects require high fidelity models that are based on the functionality of products with validation (proof). DHM has the advantage of working back-and-forth with either extreme and can accommodate the form and functionality requirements of design projects (Fig. 6).

Within the D-HIL approach, contributors to the product development, whether it's a group of industrial designers, design engineers, or managers, can interact with the design process at any given time. The framework connects technical (engineers) and non-technical experts (managers) as well as third party contributors (suppliers) together. It allows parametric modification of dimensions, tasks, and environments. Results due to changes in CAD models and CAE simulations can be simultaneously updated, and changes on ergonomics and structural evaluations can be monitored accordingly. This workflow creates opportunities for optimizing design alternatives through iterative changes (what-if scenarios). Also, holistic coverage of design disciplines and modular integration of various tools and technologies can provide unexplored spaces for creativity (Fig. 7).

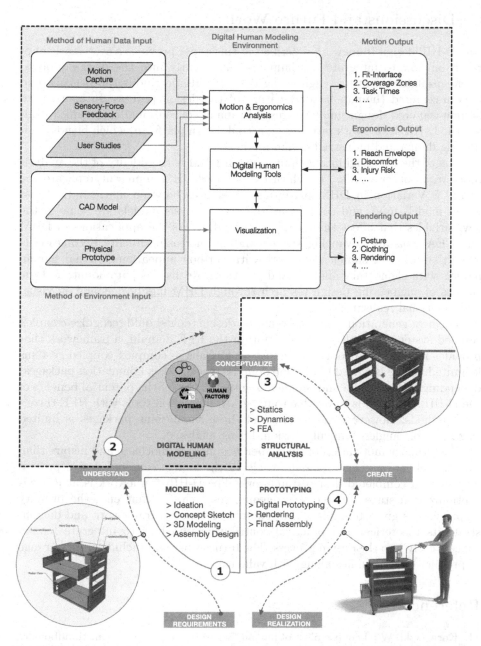

Fig. 7. The framework merges human subject data with a full scale CAD model and a low-fidelity physical prototype to generate three different outcomes: motion, ergonomics analysis and rendering. Through this approach human aspects of design data was integrated to realize a code cart that reflects user needs, abilities and limitations. DHM provided tools to validate ergonomics and visualization aspects of the human-product interactions.

5   Discussions and Future Work

The D-HIL design framework described in this paper provides a systematic approach on how to integrate the human element early into the design process. It encapsulates scientific (engineering design), artistic (industrial design), and human-centered (human factors) nature of the design process. In contrast to human-centered design guidelines used in many conventional ergonomics studies, the D-HIL framework provides an actual design platform, which blends engineering design and industrial design methods.

One of the most significant limitations in DHM is the fidelity of the analysis tools or, in other words, "to which extent does DHM represent/replicate the reality?" Variation in DHM platforms, differences between mathematical and visual models used, and coverage of different analysis models are some of the few variables that affect the fidelity of the DHM. As the applications of DHM and CEA tools are advancing and expanding, increasing fidelity becomes critical. It's no longer sufficient to work with cartoon appearance virtual human models with elementary analysis and functions. Realism is paramount, and the success of engineering design research through DHM highly depends on visual and functional realism.

The next generation of human-centered design tools should recognize complex coupled systems at multiple scales. Within the HFE domain, a framework that provides methods and tools for simulating humans in complex coupled systems is limited. There is a need to develop domain-specific tools (simulation packages) depending on the design and problem of interest. One of the potential benefits of the D-HIL approach is to be able to integrate simulation tools with HFE theory and methods. However, the coverage of these simulations packages is limited (e.g., comfort angles, binocular vision, lifting analysis).

The primary motivation of this paper was more to motivate and inspire than exhaustively cover every research article on the human-centered design process or present a completed design framework. The D-HIL framework is at its conceptualization stage and requires ongoing research. To that end, the primary emphasis was given to explain the general principles of framework and demonstrate its theoretical and practical contributions on how to integrate human aspects early into the design process. The future work will include a broad range of product design studies along with validation.

References

1. Karwowski, W.: The discipline of human factors and ergonomics. In: Handbook of Human Factors and Ergonomics, vol. 4, pp. 3–37 (2012)
2. Dul, J., et al.: A strategy for human factors/ergonomics: developing the discipline and profession. Ergonomics **55**(4), 377–395 (2012)
3. Sundin, A., Örtengren, R.: Digital human modeling for CAE applications. In: Handbook of Human Factors and Ergonomics, pp. 1053–1078 (2006)
4. Demirel, H.O.: Sensory feedback mechanism for virtual build methodology. Doctoral dissertation, Purdue University (2009)

5. Demirel, H.O., Duffy, V.G.: Applications of digital human modeling in industry. In: Duffy, V.G. (ed.) ICDHM 2007. LNCS, vol. 4561, pp. 824–832. Springer, Heidelberg (2007). https://doi.org/10.1007/978-3-540-73321-8_93
6. Demirel, H.O., Duffy, V.G.: Digital human modeling for product lifecycle management. In: Duffy, V.G. (ed.) ICDHM 2007. LNCS, vol. 4561, pp. 372–381. Springer, Heidelberg (2007). https://doi.org/10.1007/978-3-540-73321-8_43
7. Van de Poel, I., Goldberg, D.E.: Philosophy and Engineering: An Emerging Agenda, vol. 2. Springer, Dordrecht (2010). https://doi.org/10.1007/978-90-481-2804-4
8. Demirel, H.O.: Modular human-in-the-loop design framework based on human factors. Doctoral dissertation, Purdue University (2015)
9. Yang, J., Abdel-Malek, K., Farrell, K., Nebel, K.: The IOWA interactive digital-human virtual environment. In: ASME 2004 International Mechanical Engineering Congress and Exposition, pp. 1059–1067. American Society of Mechanical Engineers Digital Collection (2004)
10. Chaffin, D.B., Nelson, C., et al.: Digital human modeling for vehicle and workplace design. Society of Automotive Engineers Warrendale, PA (2001)
11. Demirel, H.O., Zhang, L., Duffy, V.G.: Opportunities for meeting sustainability objectives. Int. J. Ind. Ergon. **51**, 73–81 (2016)
12. Lämkull, D., Hanson, L., ÖrtengrenÖrtengren, R.: A comparative study of digital human modelling simulation results and their outcomes in reality: a case study within manual assembly of automobiles. Int. J. Ind. Ergon. **39**(2), 428–441 (2009)
13. Mark Porter, J., Case, K., Marshall, R., Gyi, D., neé Oliver, R.S.: 'Beyond Jack and Jill': designing for individuals using HADRIAN. Int. J. Ind. Ergon. **33**(3), 249–264 (2004)
14. Abdel-Malek, K.: Human modeling and applications special issue. Comput. Aided Des. **7**(39), 539 (2007)
15. Brown, P.: CAD: do computers aid the design process after all? Intersect Stanford J. Sci. Technol. Soc. **2**(1), 52–66 (2009)
16. Cappelli, T.M., Duffy, V.G.: Motion capture for job risk classifications incorporating dynamic aspects of work. SAE Trans., 1069–1072 (2006)
17. Smith, S.: Ergonomic software tools in product and workplace design: a review of recent developments in human modelling and other design aids-kurt landau (ed.): Ifao institut fur arbeitsorganisation, Stuttgart, Germany (2000). ISBN 3-932160-11-8. Appl. Ergon. **4**(33), 379 (2002)
18. Chaffin, D.B.: Human motion simulation for vehicle and workplace design. Hum. Fact. Ergon. Manuf. Serv. Ind. **17**(5), 475–484 (2007)
19. Freivalds, A.: Biomechanics of the Upper Limbs: Mechanics, Modeling and Musculoskeletal Injuries. CRC Press, Boca Raton (2011)
20. Konz, S.: Work Design: Occupational Ergonomics. CRC Press, Boca Raton (2018)
21. Ozkaya, N., Nordin, M., Goldsheyder, D., Leger, D.: Fundamentals of Biomechanics. Springer, Boston (2012). https://doi.org/10.1007/978-0-387-49312-1
22. Helander, M.G.: Forty years of IEA: some reflections on the evolution of ergonomics. Ergonomics **40**(10), 952–961 (1997)
23. Chandrasegaran, S.K., et al.: The evolution, challenges, and future of knowledge representation in product design systems. Comput. Aided Des. **45**(2), 204–228 (2013)
24. Hsu, W., Woon, I.M.Y.: Current research in the conceptual design of mechanical products. Comput. Aided Des. **30**(5), 377–389 (1998)
25. Duffy, V.G., Salvendy, G.: Concurrent engineering and virtual reality for human resource planning. Comput. Ind. **42**(2–3), 109–125 (2000)

26. Wickman, C., Söderberg, R.: Increased concurrency between industrial and engineering design using cat technology combined with virtual reality. Concurrent Eng. **11**(1), 7–15 (2003)
27. Duffy, V.G.: Modified virtual build methodology for computer-aided ergonomics and safety. Hum. Fact. Ergon. Manuf. Serv. Ind. **17**(5), 413–422 (2007)
28. Karwowski, W.: The discipline of ergonomics and human factors. In: Handbook of Human Factors and Ergonomics, vol. 3 (2006)
29. Tian, R.: Validity and reliability of dynamic virtual interactive design methodology. Ph.D. thesis, Mississippi State University (2019)
30. Wu, T.: Reliability and validity of Virtual Build methodology for ergonomics analyses. Mississippi State University (2005)
31. Chaffin, D.B.: Improving digital human modelling for proactive ergonomics in design. Ergonomics **48**(5), 478–491 (2005)
32. Burns, C.M., Vicente, K.J.: A participant-observer study of ergonomics in engineering design: how constraints drive design process. Appl. Ergon. **31**(1), 73–82 (2000)
33. Jansson, D.G., Smith, S.M.: Design fixationDesign fixation. Des. Stud. **12**(1), 3–11 (1991)
34. Hauser, J.R. Clausing, D., et al.: The house of quality (1988)
35. Ullman, D.G.: The Mechanical Design Process: Part 1. McGraw-Hill, New York (2010)

How Do We Sit When Our Car Drives for Us?

Martin Fleischer[⊠] and Si Chen

Chair of Ergonomics, Department of Mechanical Engineering,
Technical University of Munich, Boltzmannstr. 15, 85748 Garching, Germany
martin.fleischer@tum.de

Abstract. With increasing automation in the passenger vehicle, the role of the driver in the vehicle will change. The driver will spend more time and attention on the non-driving-related tasks (NDRTs). How the driver sits while conducting the NDRTs in a highly automated vehicle is investigated in this study. 25 participants were invited to an experiment in a vehicle mock-up, which simulates the highly automated vehicle on level 3 and level 4. Video recordings of their NDRTs and corresponding sitting postures were analyzed qualitatively and documented by encoding the positions within four body sections. The analysis shows the most common sitting postures for each NDRT. A higher number and more variations of the sitting postures were observed at level 4 than at level 3. A considerable effect of the automation levels was found in the torso position and leg position. Generous space in front of the seat enables the participant to perform a bigger range of movement and postures. The results of this study can be used as a reference for predicting NDRTs according to the performed sitting postures and vice versa. Moreover, this study contributes to the space management of interior design in the future.

Keywords: Automated driving · Postures · Non-driving related tasks

1 Introduction

Digital human models (DHMs) help to include necessary ergonomic and safety aspects early in the product development process. With the introduction of automated driving in SAE Levels 3 and 4 new challenges in automotive design arise and established DHMs need to adapt to new postures and tasks [1]. The driver becomes a passenger, thus new aspects in comfort [2] and safety [3] are researched. The posture of the participant in those study is often estimated after relevant tasks. The missing link between the task and the according posture in SAE level 3 and 4 automated driving [4] is evaluated in this study.

Since it is hard to conduct experiments regarding the passenger in real cars, studies were conducted in trains to gather first insights. Body postures were recorded through notes of the experimenter and later put into larger categories. The studies showed a huge variety in body postures [5, 6]. Since the new freedom of the passenger in a level 3 automation can be interrupted by a take-over request, [7] found that the take-over quality does not suffer under a more open knee joint angle of 133° (compared to 114° for conventional vehicles). A flatter backrest angle (38° compared to 24° in conventional vehicles) leads to a worse performance in the hands-on-time.

© Springer Nature Switzerland AG 2020
V. G. Duffy (Ed.): HCII 2020, LNCS 12198, pp. 33–49, 2020.
https://doi.org/10.1007/978-3-030-49904-4_3

2 Methodology

The study was approved by the ethics committee of the Technical University of Munich. The experiment was conducted at the Modular Ergonomic Mock-Up [8] at the Chair of Ergonomics of the Technical University of Munich, which is an automated multifunctional version of a seat mock-up and is based on a structure of parallel rail elements. The setup consisted of a car seat, pedals and the steering wheel. Two configuration were tested, the "Level 3" and the "Level 4" condition. Both are meant to represent a state according to SAE automated driving levels. For "Level 3" seat, pedals and steering wheel were configured in an SUV setting with an average H30 of 350 mm. The Backrest angle was fixed to 22°. It was prohibited to touch the steering wheel with either hand or objects during tasks. The participant was instructed to adjust the seat into a driving position, then the seat was moved backwards until the knee had an opening angle of 133° (see Fig. 1). This posture should allow an adequate take-over-performance as it is needed in a level 3 automated driving [7], while giving the passenger a little more space. For the condition "Level 4" the pedals and steering wheel were removed, thus representing a level 4 automated driving, where this could be feasible car environment.

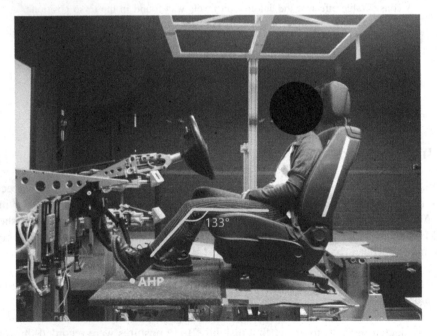

Fig. 1. Experimental setup

For those two conditions every participant was asked to perform the eleven tasks in Table 1 each for two minutes in a randomized order. The task "working with laptop" could not be conducted, because of the lack of space in the mock-up and was correspondingly dropped from the "Level 3" condition.

The postures chosen by the participants were filmed. The experimenter later classified the material with seven digits for four body regions; the head, the torso, the hands, the legs (see Fig. 2). The possible outcome for the digits are described in Tables 2, 3, 4 and 5 and were iteratively developed during the coding thus leaving little data unusable. Since some participants changed their posture during a task, it is possible that some participants contribute more postures to the dataset than others. A posture was classified after 4 s of holding, thus eliminating smaller tasks like fixing hair or scratching the nose.

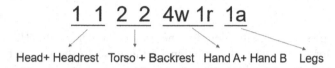

Fig. 2. Example coding for one posture

Table 1. NDRTs performed by the participants

Non-driving related task (NDRT)	Automation level	The required object
Reading a book	Level 3, Level 4	A book
Reading newspaper	Level 3, Level 4	Newspaper
Eating and drinking	Level 3, Level 4	Pretzel in a paper bag
Drinking	Level 3, Level 4	A bottle of water
Observing landscape	Level 3, Level 4	–
Talking to the co-driver	Level 3, Level 4	–
Relaxing	Level 3, Level 4	–
Using smartphone	Level 3, Level 4	Smartphone
Using Tablet	Level 3, Level 4	Tablet
Paperwork	Level 3, Level 4	Folder with A4 documents, pen
Making a phone call	Level 3, Level 4	Smartphone
Working with laptop	Level 4	Laptop

25 students and research associates owning a German driving license between the age of 21 to 30 years (M = 25.2; SD = 2.33) participated in the experiment for pay. The sample consists of 11 females and 14 males. The body height range extends from 1585 mm to 1900 mm.

Table 2 shows the classification for the body part head, containing head and headrest. For both there is the "difficult to detect" option, which was introduced after some tasks resulted in a constant moving of the head. "Straight" defines a head position where the participant is looking straight forward. As soon as the head was rotated sideways it was classified so ignoring the aspects of vertical orientation.

Table 2. Head classification

Body part	Position description	Code
Head	Downwards	1
	Straight	2
	Upwards	3
	Rotated	4
	Difficult to detect	*
Headrest	Free from headrest	1
	Against headrest	2
	Difficult to detect	*

Table 3 shows the classification for the torso. Similar to the Head one digit describes the torso itself the other relation of the torso to the backrest. A slightly reclined posture of the upper body against the backrest is defined as the start (neutral) position of the torso. So the neutral posture corresponds to a conventional vehicle design today, where torso angles of 22° to 25° are used. In reality those angles are observed to range from 5° to 35° [9]. Forwards and backwards an in relation to the neutral posture. A backwards leaning torso results from moving the hip forward out of the seat.

Table 3. Torso classification

Body part	Position description	Code
Torso	Forwards	1
	Start position(neutral)	2
	Backwards	3
	Rotated	4
	Inclined	5
Backrest	Free from backrest	1
	Against backrest	2

Table 4 shows the classification of the hands. Left- and right-handedness was ignored, by coding the hand dominating the task with "Hand A". For tasks, where an object is held in the hand, this hand was considered dominant. While the number gives the height of the hand, the letter gives information about the activity of the hand.

During the coding, a priority order is ensured, which means that a working hand is numbered prior to a resting hand. Also, a resting hand has priority over a hand supporting a body part, such as the example of "4w2s". In the case, that the two hands cannot be distinguished through dominance or status, the one with the lower position is then placed first, like the example of "2s4s" shows. This being a combination with repetition creates 91 possible combinations of hand postures.

Table 4. Hand classification

Body part	Position description		Code
Hand A/Hand B	On the thigh	Works	1w
		Rest	1r
		Supports body part	1s
	In front of the belly	Works	2w
		Rest	2r
		Supports body part	2 s
	In front of the chest	Works	3w
		Rest	3r
		Supports body part	3 s
	Over the shoulder	Works	4w
		Rest	4r
		Supports body part	4 s
	Straightened arm		5

Table 5 shows the classification for the legs, which differentiates mainly between the flexed/extended states. Knee joint angles seen from the side and below 90° are regarded as flexed, while above 110° was classified with extended.

Table 5. Leg classification

Body part	Position description		Code
Legs	Both legs flexed	With the knees forward	1a
		With crossed shanks	1b
		With closed ankle and the knees wide apart	1c
		With closed knees	1d
	Both legs extended	Extended slightly	2a
		Extended furtherly	2b
		Crossed	2c
	One leg extended; one leg flexed	Extended slightly	3a
		Extended furtherly	3b
	Legs crossed (ankle on knee)		4
	Legs crossed (knee over knee)		5

3 Results

Using this coding method a total of 1099 body postures were identified, 497 for the "Level 3" and 602 for the "Level 4" condition. 232 full body combinations were found for "Level 3" and 299 for "Level 4". Specifically less than 5 times (n < 5) occur 210 combinations in the "Level 3" condition and 278 in the "Level 4" condition. This is comparable to white noise in the data when looking at the whole body. Thus the data is analyzed for the four body regions separately for the two conditions in Sect. 3.1. Sect. 6 displays the results for every body region according to task and condition, which are explained in Sect. 3.2.

3.1 Condition Specific Results

Head

For the head the conditions were ignored as they had no visible effect. As per Table 6 the postures "11", "**", "21", "32" make up 84% of the data.

Table 6. Frequency of the task unspecific head postures

Head postures	**	11	21	22	31	32	41	42
Frequency	15%	49%	10%	3%	4%	10%	5%	3%

Torso

For the Torso the conventional driving posture "22" and the slouching posture "32", where the hip is moved forward from the neutral position, dominate the chosen postures. "22" makes up 77% and "32" makes up 12% of the total. The forward leaning posture "11" was chosen in 6% of the cases. When comparing "Level 3" and "Level 4" a slight increase in the postures differing from the neutral posture ("22") can be observed. The complete frequencies for every torso posture are displayed in Table 7.

Table 7. Frequency of the torso postures for the conditions "Level 3" and "Level 4"

Torso postures	22	32	11	52	12	42	41
Level 3	81%	10%	5%	2%	1%	1%	<1%
Level 4	74%	15%	7%	2%	1%	1%	<1%

Hands

Of the 91 combinations of possible hand postures 40 appear in the dataset. Since 30 of the occurring make up less than 2% of the total, only the top ten are reported in Table 8. The most frequent postures are "1w1w" and "1r1r". The comparison between "Level 3" and "Level 4" shows little shifts for the different conditions.

Table 8. Frequency of the top 10 hand postures for the conditions "Level 3" and "Level 4"

Hand postures	1w 1w	1r 1r	2w 2w	3w 3w	4w 1w	4w 1r	1w 2w	4w 3w	1w 1r	2w 3w
Level 3	21%	20%	13%	13%	8%	8%	5%	6%	3%	3%
Level 4	25%	18%	15%	8%	10%	7%	6%	4%	6%	2%

Legs

For the legs the comparison between "Level 3" and "Level 4" shows a big difference for the participant behavior. The distribution of the frequencies shifts towards postures taking up large space. In "Level 4" the frequencies are more evenly distributed. The complete frequencies for every leg posture are displayed in Table 9.

Table 9. Frequency of the leg postures for the conditions "Level 3" and "Level 4"

Leg postures	1a	2b	2a	2c	1c	3b	3a	1b	4	5	1d
Level 3	24%	27%	18%	2%	8%	13%	4%	2%	2%	0%	2%
Level 4	24%	7%	12%	20%	9%	5%	6%	5%	4%	5%	2%

3.2 Condition and NDRT Specific Results

The level and task specific frequencies for postures and tasks are reported in the following paragraphs. Two tables are generated for each of the two conditions. One contains the frequencies of postures taken while performing a certain task. The other displays the frequencies of tasks performed while holding a certain posture. A total of four tables exist per body region. An empty cell is equal to a frequency of 0. The more empty cells are present in the table the less different postures were chosen by the participants. The Tables 10, 11, 12, 13, 14, 15, 16, 17, 18, 19, 20, 21, 22, 23, 24 and 25 can be found in Sect. 6 and contain the described data. By assembling the body region postures with the highest probability the most relevant full body postures can be identified.

4 Discussion and Limitations

4.1 Data

Head

The posture of the head is mainly dominated by the objects held in the hands. The user needs visual feedback to operate. If nothing is held in the hands, the head usually moves a lot. Thus the head can be used as a predictor to decide between two states, task with object in use or task without object.

Torso

The data shows that the torso is likely to be in a normal driving state. This can be traced back to the fixed backrest, although the participants were allowed go into a slouch posture and often did not decided to do so.

Hands

The hands are the best predictor for a task when a posture is given. Similar to the head a clustering of tasks with similar properties is practicable. A difference between the two conditions is quite small. This hints that the given space at "Level 3" is already sufficient for most of the tasks. Working with the Laptop needs more space, because of size of the used object. The study did not include any supporting elements for the arms. This has a major influence on the posture as humans tend to adopt to their environment.

Legs

The posture of the legs does not allow any conclusion about what task is executed. From the opposite perspective human factors engineers or designers need to mind, that the users generally may take every leg position imaginable if they have enough space. This is the case for both of the conditions. As it is shown in the data the pedals in "Level 3" hinder the more extended postures.

4.2   Methodology

This study was conducted with 25 participants. Thus a descriptive statistic approach was used to identify big effects of the automation conditions. If done with a larger population the inferential statistics might be applicable. To keep the complexity of the experiment at a manageable level the backrest was fixed. This needs to be researched in future studies to understand the full scope of body positions in relation to NDRTs. The same applies to anthropology, time, vehicle dynamics and additional interior elements (e.g. footwell dimensions, doors or center tunnel). The coding system needs to be used by hand thus making data assessment time intensive. Depending on the research aim it might also be beneficial to make it more or less precise.

Being relevant for safety, comfort and ergonomic assessments this data has to be handled with care. The weighting of the tasks was kept equal here, but can have differing relevance depending on the use case of the car. Other studies show the magnitude of this factor [10–12].

5   Future Work

This study is among the first steps of the research to find the postures of drivers in automated cars, for designing the drivers place of future automated vehicles This is necessary since the state of the art methods of designing car interiors will find their limits in future applications.

Two studies need to be conducted in the near future. One to find preferred backrest angles of passengers during NDRTs and the other to make the connection between needed space and NDRTs.

6 Tables

Head

Table 10. Frequencies of head postures while performing certain tasks ("Level 3")

Task → Posture	**	11	21	22	31	32	41	42
Phonecall	100%							
Reading a book		85%	11%	4%				
Eating		32%	62%	3%		3%		
Drinking			12%		54%	35%		
Landschaft							72%	28%
Paperwork		100%						
Talk	100%							
Relax		3%	13%	23%		61%		
Using smartphone		93%	4%	4%				
Using tablet		100%						
Reading newspaper		96%	4%					

Table 11. Frequencies of task while holding certain head postures ("Level 3")

Posture → Task	**	11	21	22	31	32	41	42
Phonecall	50%							
Reading a book		17%	9%	10%				
Eating		9%	66%	10%		3%		
Drinking			9%		100%	31%		
Landschaft							100%	100%
Paperwork		18%						
Talk	50%							
Relax		1%	11%	70%		66%		
Using smartphone		18%	3%	10%				
Using tablet		18%						
Reading newspaper		18%	3%					

Table 12. Frequencies of head postures while performing certain tasks ("Level 4")

Task → Posture	**	11	21	22	31	32	41	42
Phonecall	100%							
Reading a book		100%						
Eating		37%	51%		2%	10%		
Drinking			7%		52%	41%		
Landschaft							54%	46%
Paperwork		100%						
Talk	100%							
Relax			21%	18%		61%		
Using smartphone		96%				4%		
Using tablet		100%						
Reading newspaper		96%		4%				
Laptop		100%						

Table 13. Frequencies of task while holding certain head postures ("Level 4")

Posture → Task	**	11	21	22	31	32	41	42
Phonecall	50%							
Reading a book		15%						
Eating		11%	74%		7%	14%		
Drinking			6%		93%	30%		
Landschaft							100%	100%
Paperwork		15%						
Talk	50%							
Relax			21%	86%		54%		
Using smartphone		15%				3%		
Using tablet		15%						
Reading newspaper		15%		14%				
Laptop		15%						

Torso

Table 14. Frequencies of torso postures while performing certain tasks ("Level 3")

Task → Posture	11	21	22	32	41	42	52
Phonecall	3%	3%	70%	9%	3%	3%	9%
Reading a book	4%		86%	11%			
Eating			100%				
Drinking			100%				
Landschaft			77%	20%			3%
Paperwork	29%		71%				
Talk			75%	16%		9%	
Relax			56%	44%			
Using smartphone	7%		89%				4%
Using tablet		8%	92%				
Reading newspaper	4%		89%	4%			4%

Table 15. Frequencies of task while holding certain torso postures ("Level 3")

Posture → Task	11	21	22	32	41	42	52
Phonecall	7%	33%	9%	10%	100%	25%	50%
Reading a book	7%		9%	10%			
Eating			10%				
Drinking			10%				
Landschaft			9%	20%			17%
Paperwork	67%		10%				
Talk			9%	17%		75%	
Relax			6%	40%			
Using smartphone	13%		9%				17%
Using tablet		67%	9%				
Reading newspaper	7%		9%	3%			17%

Table 16. Frequencies of torso postures while performing certain tasks ("Level 4")

Task → Posture	11	21	22	32	41	42	52
Phonecall	10%		62%	13%	3%	3%	10%
Reading a book	13%		70%	13%		3%	
Eating		4%	93%	4%			
Drinking			100%				
Landschaft		3%	66%	28%			3%
Paperwork	27%		70%	3%			
Talk			79%	17%		3%	
Relax			41%	56%			3%
Using smartphone	10%		72%	17%			
Using tablet	4%	4%	74%	19%			
Reading newspaper	7%		85%	7%			
Laptop	4%		96%				

Table 17. Frequencies of tasks while holding certain torso postures ("Level 4")

Posture → Task	11	21	22	32	41	42	52
Phonecall	17%		10%	9%	100%	33%	67%
Reading a book	17%		9%	7%		33%	
Eating		33%	11%	2%			
Drinking			11%				
Landschaft		33%	8%	15%			17%
Paperwork	39%		10%	2%			
Talk			10%	9%		33%	
Relax			5%	33%			17%
Using smartphone	13%		9%	9%			
Using tablet	4%	33%	8%	9%			
Reading newspaper	9%		10%	4%			
Laptop	4%		10%				

Hands

Table 18. Frequencies of hand postures while performing certain tasks ("Level 3").

Task → Posture	1w 1w	1r 1r	2w 2w	4w 1w	3w 3w	4w 1r	1w 2w	1w 1r	4w 3w	2w 3w
Phonecall						100%				
Reading a book	41%		10%		38%		10%			
Eating	14%		2%	24%	12%	8%	2%	18%	12%	10%
Drinking				57%				43%		
Landschaft		100%								
Paperwork	40%		44%		10%		6%			
Talk		100%								
Relax		100%								
Using smartphone	31%		31%		28%		3%		6%	
Using tablet	36%	2%	10%		12%		24%		5%	12%
Reading newspaper	35%		22%		35%		3%			5%

Table 19. Frequencies of tasks while holding certain hand postures ("Level 3")

Posture → Task	1w 1w	1r 1r	2w 2w	4w 1w	3w 3w	4w 1r	1w 2w	1w 1r	4w 3w	2w 3w
Phonecall						86%				
Reading a book	16%		6%		22%		16%			
Eating	9%		2%	43%	12%	14%	5%	43%	60%	42%
Drinking				57%				57%		
Landschaft		34%								
Paperwork	26%		46%		10%		16%			
Talk		34%								
Relax		30%								
Using smartphone	13%		21%		18%		5%		20%	
Using tablet	19%	1%	8%		10%		53%		20%	42%
Reading newspaper	17%		17%		27%		5%			17%

Table 20. Frequencies of hand postures while performing certain tasks ("Level 4")

Task → Posture	1w 1w	1r 1r	2w 2w	4w 1w	3w 3w	4w 1r	1w 2w	1w 1r	4w 3w	2w 3w
Phonecall						100%				
Reading a book	71%				16%		13%			
Eating	13%		2%	33%	6%	4%	2%	19%	15%	6%
Drinking				72%		7%			21%	
Landschaft		100%								
Paperwork	43%		49%				2%	2%		4%
Talk		100%								
Relax		96%	4%							
Using smartphone	53%		7%		27%		3%	10%		
Using tablet	42%		5%		5%		30%	14%		5%
Reading newspaper	38%	5%	13%		31%		5%	5%		3%
Laptop			93%				7%			

Table 21. Frequencies of tasks while holding certain hand postures ("Level 4")

Posture → Task	1w 1w	1r 1r	2w 2w	4w 1w	3w 3w	4w 1r	1w 2w	1w 1r	4w 3w	2w 3w
Phonecall						85%				
Reading a book	22%				17%		17%			
Eating	7%		2%	45%	10%	7%	4%	45%	57%	38%
Drinking				55%		7%			43%	
Landschaft		33%								
Paperwork	22%		41%				4%	5%		25%
Talk		34%								
Relax		30%	2%							
Using smartphone	16%		3%		27%		4%	14%		
Using tablet	18%		3%		7%		54%	27%		25%
Reading newspaper	15%	3%	8%		40%		8%	9%		13%
Laptop			41%				8%			

Legs

Table 22. Frequencies of leg postures while performing certain tasks ("Level 3")

Task → Posture	1a	1b	1c	1d	2a	2b	2c	3a	3b	4
Phonecall	13%	17%	8%		12%	9%		15%	10%	17%
Reading a book	8%	17%	8%	13%	9%	14%		15%	5%	
Eating	8%	17%	12%	13%	9%	6%	20%	8%	5%	17%
Drinking	8%		12%	13%	11%	7%		8%	5%	17%
Landschaft	10%		20%	13%	9%	8%		31%	5%	
Paperwork	14%		8%	13%	5%	8%			7%	17%
Talk	5%				14%	8%	20%	8%	20%	17%
Relax	5%	33%	8%		5%	16%	60%		22%	
Using smartphone	5%		16%	13%	9%	10%		8%	7%	
Using tablet	10%	17%	8%	25%	9%	7%			7%	17%
Reading newspaper	13%				9%	7%		8%	7%	

Table 23. Frequencies of tasks while holding certain leg postures ("Level 3")

Posture → Task	1a	1b	1c	1d	2a	2b	2c	3a	3b	4
Phonecall	29%	3%	6%		20%	23%		6%	11%	3%
Reading a book	19%	3%	6%	3%	16%	39%		6%	6%	
Eating	23%	4%	12%	4%	19%	19%	4%	4%	8%	4%
Drinking	23%		12%	4%	23%	23%		4%	8%	4%
Landschaft	25%		16%	3%	16%	22%		13%	6%	
Paperwork	39%		7%	4%	11%	25%			11%	4%
Talk	13%				27%	23%	3%	3%	27%	3%
Relax	11%	5%	5%		8%	38%	8%		24%	
Using smartphone	15%		15%	4%	19%	33%		4%	11%	
Using tablet	29%	4%	7%	7%	18%	21%			11%	4%
Reading newspaper	40%				20%	24%		4%	12%	

Table 24. Frequencies of leg postures while performing certain tasks ("Level 4")

Task → Posture	1a	1b	1c	1d	2a	2b	2c	3a	3b	4	5
Phonecall	12%	5%	17%	8%	6%	11%	12%	12%	10%	13%	5%
Reading a book	11%	5%	6%		8%		6%	12%		13%	11%
Eating	5%	10%	6%	15%	8%	7%	11%	4%		7%	5%
Drinking	4%	10%	6%	15%	6%	7%	11%	8%	5%	7%	5%
Landschaft	5%	10%	11%		6%	19%	12%	16%	20%		11%
Paperwork	9%	20%	3%	15%	14%	11%	4%	4%	5%		
Talk	15%		11%	8%	12%	15%	9%	12%	25%	13%	11%
Relax	4%	10%	14%		8%	11%	14%		15%	13%	
Using smartphone	6%	10%	17%		10%	7%	6%	8%	5%	7%	11%
Using tablet	11%	10%	8%	8%	10%	7%	4%		10%	13%	21%
Reading newspaper	9%	5%	3%		6%		5%	20%	5%	13%	21%
Laptop	11%	5%		31%	8%	4%	8%	4%			

Table 25. Frequencies of tasks while holding certain leg postures ("Level 4")

Posture → Task	1a	1b	1c	1d	2a	2b	2c	3a	3b	4	5
Phonecall	27%	2%	14%	2%	7%	7%	23%	7%	5%	5%	2%
Reading a book	37%	3%	7%		13%		17%	10%		7%	7%
Eating	17%	7%	7%	7%	14%	7%	31%	3%		3%	3%
Drinking	14%	7%	7%	7%	10%	7%	31%	7%	3%	3%	3%
Landschaft	13%	5%	10%		8%	13%	26%	10%	10%		5%
Paperwork	29%	13%	3%	6%	23%	10%	10%	3%	3%		
Talk	30%		8%	2%	12%	8%	16%	6%	10%	4%	4%
Relax	11%	6%	14%		11%	9%	34%		9%	6%	
Using smartphone	19%	6%	19%		16%	6%	16%	6%	3%	3%	6%
Using tablet	31%	6%	9%	3%	14%	6%	9%			6%	6%
Reading newspaper	30%	3%	3%		10%		13%	17%	3%	7%	13%
Laptop	38%	3%		14%	14%	3%	24%	3%			

Acknowledgements. This study was conducted in the context of the project INSAA funded by the Bundesministerium für Bildung und Forschung of Federal Republic of Germany.

References

1. Yang, Y., Fleischer, M., Bengler, K.: Chicken or egg problem? New challenges and proposals of digital human modeling and interior development of automated vehicles. In: Di Nicolantonio, M., Rossi, E., Alexander, T. (eds.) AHFE 2019. AISC, vol. 975, pp. 453–463. Springer, Cham (2020). https://doi.org/10.1007/978-3-030-20216-3_42

2. Bohrmann, D., Bengler, K.: Reclined posture for enabling autonomous driving. In: Ahram, T., Karwowski, W., Pickl, S., Taiar, R. (eds.) IHSED 2019. AISC, vol. 1026, pp. 169–175. Springer, Cham (2020). https://doi.org/10.1007/978-3-030-27928-8_26
3. Laakmann, F., Zink, L., Seyffert, M.: Neue Innenraumkonzepte für den Insassenschutz in hochautomatisierten Fahrzeugen. ATZ Automobiltech Z **121**(4), 54–59 (2019)
4. Taxonomy and definitions for terms related to on-road motor vehicle automated driving systems, SAE J3016 (2014)
5. Kamp, I., Kilincsoy, U., Vink, P.: Chosen postures during specific sitting activities (eng). Ergonomics **54**(11), 1029–1042 (2011)
6. Kilincsoy, Ü., et al.: Comfortable rear seat postures preferred by car passengers. In: Trzcieliński, S. and Karwowski, W. (eds.) Advances in human factors and ergonomics, 5th International Conference on Applied Human Factors and Ergonomics, Proceedings of the 5th AHFE Conference, vol. 20, 19–23 July 2014; 13, Advances in the Ergonomics in Manufacturing: Managing the Enterprise of the Future, AHFE Conference, Louisville, Ky, pp. 823–831 (2014)
7. Yang, Y., Gerlicher, M., Bengler, K.: How does relaxing posture influence take-over performance in an automated vehicle? In: Proceedings of the Human Factors and Ergonomics Society Annual Meeting, vol. 62, no. 1, pp. 696–700 (2018)
8. Bengler, K.: Modular Ergonomic Mockup (MEPS). http://www.lfe.mw.tum.de/en/research/labs/modular-ergonomic-mockup/. Accessed on 28 Jan 2020
9. Grünen, R.E., Günzkofer, F., Bubb, H.: Anatomische und anthropometrische Eigenschaften des Fahrers. Automobilergonomie. A, pp. 163–219. Springer, Wiesbaden (2015). https://doi.org/10.1007/978-3-8348-2297-0_4
10. Hecht, T., Darlagiannis, E., Bengler, K.: Non-driving related activities in automated driving – an online survey investigating user needs. In: Ahram, T., Karwowski, W., Pickl, S., Taiar, R. (eds.) IHSED 2019. AISC, vol. 1026, pp. 182–188. Springer, Cham (2020). https://doi.org/10.1007/978-3-030-27928-8_28
11. Susilo, Y.O., Lyons, G., Jain, J., Atkins, S.: Rail passengers' time use and utility assessment. Transp. Res. Rec. **2323**(1), 99–109 (2012)
12. Russell, M., et al.: What do passengers do during travel time? structured observations on buses and trains. JPT **14**(3), 123–146 (2011)

A Design Framework to Automate Task Simulation and Ergonomic Analysis in Digital Human Modeling

Mihir Sunil Gawand and H. Onan Demirel[✉]

Oregon State University, Corvallis, OR 97331, USA
{gawandm,onan.demirel}@oregonstate.edu

Abstract. Using Digital human modeling (DHM) early in design brings the advantage of reducing the time and resources committed to building full-scale physical prototypes. DHM also helps in minimizing efforts put on performing human subject data collection. However, majority of the repetitive two- and three-dimensional (2D/3D) object orientations and manikin adjustments in DHM are executed manually via point-and-click based keystrokes and precision mouse control, which correspond with increased user effort and time. Additionally, such manual adjustments often fail to mimic the actual postures with high fidelity; thus, injecting further user bias into the design. Due to lack of automation, engineers follow a much conservative approach via running a limited set of ergonomics simulations on select values in contrast to performing an exhaustive search for exploring an extensive set of anthropometry and postural variations. This study introduces an early design framework to automate manikin setup, task simulation, and ergonomic evaluations in DHM to provide concept design exploration capabilities. In this research work, a cockpit packaging design problem was explored to measure the reach gap values via the automation framework. Results suggest that the automation methodology has the potential to reduce the amount of time required to perform DHM simulations and helps in minimizing user bias. The automation framework generated ergonomic evaluations with high correlation values (>0.97) and provided approximately a 97.5% reduction in time when compared to manual simulations.

Keywords: Digital human modeling · Ergonomics · Human factors

1 Introduction

The motivation for this paper comes from the need to integrate human factors engineering (HFE) principles into the early design stage to evaluate ergonomics via computational models. This proactive approach helps designers to create concepts that include user needs, abilities, limitations as well as the engineering requirements, which has the potential to reduce not only the time but also the cost associated with prototyping.

© Springer Nature Switzerland AG 2020
V. G. Duffy (Ed.): HCII 2020, LNCS 12198, pp. 50–66, 2020.
https://doi.org/10.1007/978-3-030-49904-4_4

Considering human factors in the early stages of design is also significant for the market success of a product; however, the implementation is complex and not always systematic. To understand the needs of the users, traditionally, design teams conduct experiments via human subjects and develop numerous physical prototypes to study human-product interactions [6]. The process of employing human subjects and fabricating physical prototypes requires excessive time and resource commitments. With the advancements of computational design tools in the last two decades, modeling human-product interactions via computational design software has become an alternative method to evaluate ergonomics before building physical prototypes [10, 12, 25].

One of the software approaches developed in the HFE domain, digital human modeling (DHM), becomes a viable option for reducing the total design time and cost by diminishing the number of physical prototypes and the design iterations [13]. DHM offers the advantage of performing ergonomics analysis based on computer-aided design (CAD) or virtual prototypes [10], and allows designers to follow a proactive ergonomics approach before physical prototypes are built. Through DHM, one can create, manipulate, and control the movements of the virtual humans (manikins) to replicate human-machine interactions in a computer environment. Also, with the help of ergonomics analysis tools, designers can evaluate concept designs in terms of ergonomics adequacies and suggest improvements [12, 25]. Within DHM, human postures or motions are generated through the implementation of biomechanical and multi-physics theory, and computational algorithms are used to generate ergonomics analysis [25]. In addition to the ergonomics analysis tools, DHM provides anthropometric databases, posture libraries, and motion prediction packages. These functionalities help designers to check safety and ergonomics early in design which can reduce the overall time and cost required for physical prototype development [12, 14, 17, 19, 25].

Literature review shows that DHM is generally used in the later stages of the design process when most of the critical design decisions are taken and mock-ups are built [8, 14, 18, 20, 23, 24]. At that moment, many aspects of the design such as structure, material, and sub-assemblies are already finalized, and any further design change would require additional resources. This reactive approach often results in further iterations, re-designs, and sometimes a complete design overhaul, until the final design fits the ergonomic requirements. As such, a proactive approach through implementing computational based ergonomic analysis in the early phases of the design process is needed [7, 9].

This study introduces an early design framework to automate manikin setup, task simulation, and ergonomic analysis in DHM. In this research work, the automation framework was evaluated via a cockpit packaging study in terms of assessing accessibility requirements, mainly focusing on reach-gap measurements. The results from the automation methodology were compared with the manual setup method in terms of ergonomic accuracy, time, and user effort. The following section elaborates more on the automation framework proposed in this paper.

2   Background

Many DHM software consists of complex sliders, pop-up windows, and control interfaces dedicated to manipulating manikins and CAD objects that are often found to be non-intuitive and require expert knowledge and skill set [16]. Additionally, repetitive two- and three-dimensional (2D/3D) object manipulations performed to replicate human posture and movements are executed manually via precision mouse control which require significant designer effort and time. The lack of automation and the absence of quick simulation tools have been discussed in the literature as one of the limitations of DHM [7]. Using DHM for design space exploration (DSE) requires substantial designer efforts to build, set up, and execute simulations, which are reported as time-consuming as the tool needs user input and manipulations for every task [8]. There are few toolkits available to mitigate the disadvantages of performing manual operations; however, they often bring minor improvements [9,11,21]. For example, task simulation builder (TSB) builder in Siemens Jack platform implements posture and motion prediction modules [21,22], which aid designers in reducing the need for executing manual joint manipulations as the tool performs human movements automatically. The user selects the type of motion to be performed and the target/reference site as an endpoint for the motion. Although the advancements brought by such toolkits do help in reducing time spent on manual human manipulations, setting up simulations still takes much time and requires designers' manual effort to adjust each simulation element, including CAD models, human posture, and motion.

There is also the possibility of users introducing errors during the ergonomics analysis setup. However, only a minimal number of studies have been conducted to understand the challenges faced by the users and the errors caused due to manual DHM manipulations. Ziolek and Nebel (2003) discussed that the most common errors are related to the positioning and body manipulations of the manikins [26]. For example, while performing occupant packaging tasks for two manikins with different anthropometries, the position and posture used during simulation setup might slightly differ if a standard reference is not considered [26]. Another limitation occurs due to designers usually controlling the manikin movements based on intuition. Thus, task simulation becomes the designers' perspective of how one would accomplish a specific task. However, in reality, there might be variations in the way humans might perform these tasks.

Overall, the lack of DHM automation and the complexities associated with performing DHM simulations not only adds extra time and user effort but also causes engineers to follow a conservative approach. Focusing only on a limited set of ergonomics simulations rather than performing an exhaustive search limits DSE efforts. The practice of using a limited set of design variables results in a narrow DSE coverage and exploring only a few numbers of design alternatives [26]. Besides, relying on intuition increases the probability of injecting bias and errors, which can lead to the selection of erroneous or infeasible concepts. The next section elaborates more on how the framework functions.

3 Methodology

The automation framework proposed in this study uses Jackscript, a python-based scripting language, within Jack - a DHM software developed by Siemens that includes tool commanding language (Tcl) [4]. The main objective of the framework is to automate the ergonomic simulation process to increase the speed and accuracy of the simulation setup and ergonomic analysis. In this research, Jackscript and Tcl are used for creating automated sequences that help in reducing the effort required from the user to perform the ergonomic evaluations. The automation methodology provides real-time dynamic simulations of human motions, simultaneously performing ergonomic evaluations and storing data with minimal user effort.

The case study in this research is based on the design exploration research published by Ahmed et al. (2018), which focuses on the occupant packaging of a cockpit design [7] (See Fig. 1(b)). Figure 1(a) shows the data flow within the design exploration study. A total of 432 DHM simulations were run; each simulation consisted of numerous manual manipulations that included repetitive click-and-point keyboard strokes and precision mouse control. The entire process took around 108 h, with each simulation requiring around 20 min for manikin and object manipulation. Considering a typical eight-hour-long shift for five days a week, running these simulations approximately takes two weeks for a DHM expert to complete - considering there are no distractions.

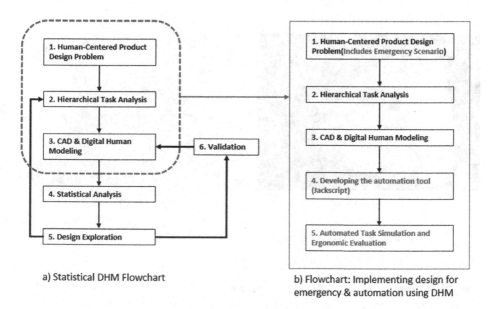

a) Statistical DHM Flowchart

b) Flowchart: Implementing design for emergency & automation using DHM

Fig. 1. Flowchart represents the DSE study introduced by Salman et al. (2018) and how the automation framework was integrated early in the design

If DHM simulations can be automated, a significant amount of time and human effort can be saved. Also, automation can aid designers to explore concept alternatives, which facilitates comprehensive DSE activities. In this study, we demonstrated our rationale by adding automation to generate cockpit packaging ergonomics based on the design study previously published by Salman et al. (2018). The next section will explain how the automation methodology works.

4   Simulation Setup: Case Study and Automation

This design problem focused on a fire/smoke emergency in a civilian aircraft cockpit. The DSE study was conducted to measure Reach Gap, which is referred to as the distance between the manikin's thumb tip and the target control. In this task, the manikin attempts to reach and operate the controls with its hand fully stretched from the shoulder in an upright posture.

4.1   Simulation Setup - Digital Human Modeling Environment

The CAD model for the cockpit packaging study was based on a Boeing 767 cockpit design. Figure 2 shows the exterior and interior configuration of the low-fidelity CAD replica, which was composed of multiple smaller sub-components, including front-facing instruments panel (main panel), central console with controls and displays, rudder pedals, yoke and pilots' seat.

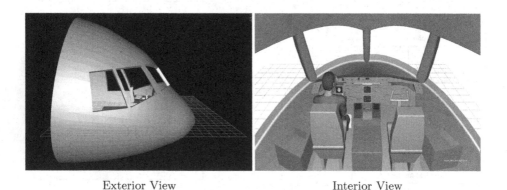

Exterior View   Interior View

Fig. 2. CAD representation of the Boeing 767 cockpit

4.2   Simulation Setup - Task Sequence

Hierarchical task analysis (HTA) was employed to identify what essential tasks had to be performed and the sequence in which these tasks must be executed. A six-step simplified HTA task sequence selected in this study was based on the checklists provided by the National Transport Safety Board (1996) [3]. The task sequence reflects what pilots are asked to perform in case of smoke build-up in a cockpit, which includes immediate descent or landing within 15 min of the fire being detected if possible [2].

Throughout this study, it was assumed that the smoke was detected in the cockpit, and the main pilot has put the oxygen mask on, as shown in Figs. 2b and 3. In the following step, the pilot sent a warning signal to the flight crew by activating the warning/caution alert lights using the warning button located at the front panel. In this particular case, it was assumed that the smoke/fire emergency was unmanageable, and pilots had to perform diversion or immediate landing. Thus, the next step performed by the pilot was to reach the vertical speed knob to identify and set the speed to descent. The third step included monitoring the engine indication and crew alerting system (EICAS) to check the status of the engine and any warning indicators from the enhanced ground proximity warning system (EGPWS) or traffic alert and collision avoidance system (TCAS) [1]. These tasks are not necessarily the steps that lead to immediate succession but a subset of tasks in an ascending order that the pilots should go through during fire/smoke emergencies. Also, these steps required DHM manikins to execute reach and visual monitoring tasks, which cover a wide range of cockpit volume and regions on the instrument panel. Based on the tasks identified via HTA, the sequence is as follows:

1. Look at the crew warning and alerting control
2. Reach the warning control
3. Look at the vertical speed indicator
4. Reach the vertical speed control
5. Look at the EICAS display screen
6. Reach the EICAS display screen.

4.3   Simulation Setup - Manikin Calibration and Reference Posture

Throughout the DHM simulations, a reference manikin was defined with a neutral posture for calibration and initialization. Figure 3 shows a side view of the neutral posture used in this study. A 50th percentile U.S. female represents a pilot positioned in the CAD environment, sitting in an upright posture and the legs comfortably reaching control pedals (Fig. 3). The comfortable upright posture was determined by using the Comfort Assessment toolbox in Jack's Occupant Packaging toolkit. The manikin was first positioned at the pilot seat, and the knee/ankle joints were adjusted such that the manikin's feet can reach the rudder pedals while maintaining comfort ratings. Sufficient space was also provided between the instrument panel, and the hands were located on the yoke. The oxygen mask was attached to the face of the manikin to represent the initial step of the fire/smoke emergency procedure. The neutral posture was used as a reference to eliminate any positioning-related errors during the automation and initiation of each simulation.

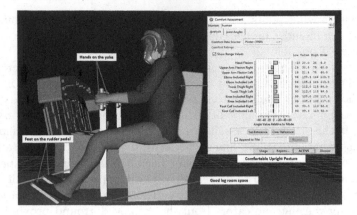

Fig. 3. The neutral posture setup used as a reference during simulation setup

5 Automation in Digital Human Modeling via Jackscript

In this step, the task simulation and ergonomic evaluation script were developed using Jackscript. The script can be written using any python-based integrated development environment like Spyder or PyCharm. Jackscript provides various manikin and object control functions such as *Move*, *Walk*, *Look At*, and *Reach*. Thus, one can implement the required tasks or interactions by calling these functions in Jackscript console. For example, if one wants to simulate a manikin looking at the display screen and reaching the radio control button, then the task sequence can be programmed as follows in Fig. 4. In the code below, "Task1" represents the manikin performs the task of looking at a predefined point (DisplayScreen) located at the front control display. Similarly, "Task2" represents that the manikin reaches the radio button (RadioButton). Other features can also be used, such as "DoTogether" to perform tasks simultaneously.

```
from js import *
def run():
        jack = CreateHuman()
        v = View()
        v.Attach(jack.bottom_head.sight)
        Task1 = jack.LookAt("h", DisplayScreen)
        Task2 = jack.ReachHold("right", RadioButton, jfrom = "shoulder", endeff = "forearm",
        reach_duration = 1, duration = 2, start = 1)
if __name__ == '__main__':
    run()
```

Fig. 4. A sample code written in the Jackscript language

Based on the tasks identified in HTA, each manikin went through the six-step task sequence (see Sect. 4.2), including three target sites located on the instrument panel, and performed *Reach* actions to activate crew warning, change vertical speed control, and reach EICAS display (Fig. 5). Each manikin was calibrated to perform *Reach* motions via "Locked Torso" inverse kinematics (IK) strategy, from the shoulder with the waist constrained (Fig. 6), which guaranteed no awkward postures by keeping joint angles within comfortable ranges.

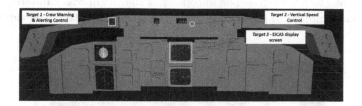

Fig. 5. Location of the three target sites on the instrument panel

5.1   Data Collection and Ergonomics Analysis

Along with performing task simulations listed above, the automation code was also executed for collecting Reach Gap data to perform occupant packaging study. The *thumb-tip* is often used as a standard end-effector for reach studies [15]. However, *"ReachHold"* function found in Jackscript only considers the *forearm* as the end-effector, which affected the *"ReachHold"* inverse kinematics (IK) scheme and resulted in awkward postures that were unrealistic to what humans would perform in reality. Thus, an alternate approach was identified by using the *forearm* end-effector with the *palm-center* site as the reference point (Fig. 6). As both sites represent a 3D vector, the Euclidean distance method was used to measure the distance between two vectors, as shown below.

$$d(A, B) = \sqrt{((x_a - x_b)^2 + (y_a - y_b)^2 + (z_a - z_b)^2)} \tag{1}$$

$$\text{where, Palmcenter: } A = (x_a, y_a, z_a)$$
$$\text{Target:} \quad B = (x_b, y_b, z_b)$$

Reach Gap analysis explained above was incorporated into the Jackscript code along with the automation algorithm that changes the manikin size and position. Once all the reach tasks were simulated, as the task sequence identified in Sect. 4.2, the ergonomic analysis was performed for the given anthropometry. Later, the manikin was scaled based on the corresponding anthropometry found in the anthropometry database. To ensure that each manikin was positioned according to its anthropometric scale, the neutral posture shown in Fig. 3 was kept as a reference, with heels of the manikin anchored to rudder pedals during scaling. This method ensured that while the manikin maintained the neutral posture, it also shifted in position as per the size of the manikin to provide proper access to the instrument panel and sufficient legroom space. For example, a 5th percentile Japanese female was positioned closer to the instrument panel due to the smaller stature. The manikin needed to be closer to the instrument panel for better accessibility (Fig. 7a). In contrast, a 95th percentile U.S. male was positioned farther from the instrument panel to provide functional legroom (Fig. 7b). In Fig. 7, the base of the pedal and the human lower torso sites are taken as references to show the differences in the positioning of two manikins.

Along with performing the ergonomic evaluations, Jackscript was also used for writing data to a CSV file. The automation algorithm was validated by comparing manual simulation results with data coming from automated simulations.

Fig. 6. Reach Gap: the distance from *palm-center* to vertical speed control

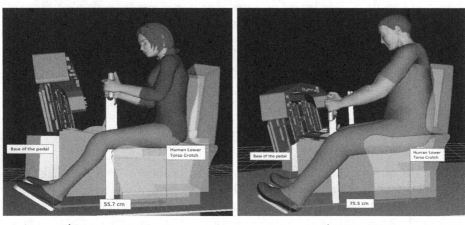

$5^{th}\%$ Japanese Female $95^{th}\%$ US Male

Fig. 7. Differences in the positioning of the manikins as per their anthropometry

5.2 Automated Task Simulation and Ergonomic Evaluation

After the Jackscript code was developed, it was imported to the DHM simulation interface via Tcl module, which enables Jack to take commands about what functions to perform once an option is selected from the graphical user interface

(GUI). A text file was created within the Tcl script, which commanded Jack to import and run the Python file containing the Jackscript code. Figure 8 shows how the automation structure functions within Jack. Additional features can be integrated into this toolbox, depending on the design requirements.

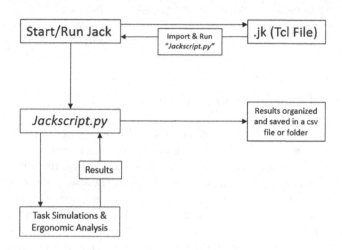

Fig. 8. Flowchart representing how the Jackscript code runs simulations in Jack

6   Simulation Study

The objective of this simulation study is to generate a design exploration study about the smoke/fire problem and provide a cockpit packaging assessment via automation capabilities integrated into DHM. In this study, each percentile within the anthropometric database was considered instead of applying a typically conservative approach of only running selective percentiles (e.g., 5th, 50th, 95th).

Jack's built-in anthropometric libraries contain stature (height and weight) for only specific percentiles, including 1th, 5th, 50th, 95th and 99th. With the help of Pennsylvania State University's Open Design Lab computational anthropometry tool (Data Explorer II), each percentile of anthropometry ranging from 1th to 99th in the U.S. ANSUR II library was extracted [5]. Then, the data was used to construct manikins, which were inserted into DHM simulations within the automation framework. The simulation study was composed of a total of 198 simulations. The experimental design is provided in the Table 1 below.

Table 1. Task conditions for the simulation study

Task conditions					Outputs
Target popullation	Anthropometry percentile	Gender	Type of movement	Target site	
US ANSUR II	1% to 99%	Male Female	Locked Torso	Target 1 Target 2 Target 3	Reach gap

7   Results and Discussions

The performance of the automation tool is analyzed in terms of (1) the accuracy of simulation outcomes, and (2) the time required to complete each simulation. A random sample set of ten population percentiles and five standard population (1th, 5th, 50th, 95th and 99th) percentiles from ANSUR II database were selected. A total of fifteen manikins (see Table 2) were used for generating task simulations and ergonomic evaluations manually via Jack's graphical user interface. Jack's human control interface was used for manipulating joint angles and neck positions. The reach gap was measured by using the "Measure Distance" tool in Jack. Data collected manually was compared with the corresponding values calculated by the automation algorithm. The time required to perform the entire simulation was recorded. During automated data collection, a standard was set for positioning the manikins. The location of the "Human Lower Torso" site for each manikin was identified from the "Seat Location" data collected by the automation tool. Thus, manikins were positioned exactly at the corresponding seat location, and the neutral posture was assigned at the beginning of each simulation (Fig. 3). This approach guaranteed in eliminating any discrepancies and errors due to differences in positioning. The following sections provide detailed information on the results and comparisons.

7.1   Comparison in Accuracy - Manual vs. Automated Simulations

One of the critical aspects of the automation methodology discussed in this study is the accuracy of the ergonomics results. This section provides data on the accuracy of the automation framework in terms of the ergonomic evaluation results when compared to results generated via the manual method. The Reach Gap calculation performed by the automation tool using the Euclidean distance method was compared by performing the same study manually. A total of fifteen manikins (see Table 2) were selected for comparison of the accuracy.

The majority of the reach gap values calculated by the automation tool were within 0.5 cm of the mean absolute error when compared to the values calculated using the manual simulation method. The difference in the results only differed for the Target 1 (2.2 cm), which is not an error in distance calculations but an inaccuracy due to the differences in the way Jack performs the dynamic motions. Jack follows a specific IK scheme when performing "Reach" function using the "Manipulate" option, as opposed to the IK scheme, followed when using the "ReachHold" function in Jackscript. It can be justified by the fact that the distance calculations for Targets 2 and 3 resulted in high accuracy, which indicates that the movement performed by the manikin for Target 1 is different. To check this justification, the Jackscript was used to perform the manikin movements using the "ReachHold" function, and the reach distances measured both via manual and automated methods were found to be similar, as shown in Table 2.

Table 2. Comparison of reach gap distances - manual versus automation method

Population (ANSUR II)	Target 1		Target 2		Target 3	
	Manual	Automation	Manual	Automation	Manual	Automation
Male - 86%	9.63	11.06	21.67	21.94	33.34	33.16
Male - 76%	8.83	10.25	21.30	21.63	32.65	32.54
Male - 55%	7.07	8.88	20.37	20.75	31.10	31.07
Female - 29%	2.34	5.79	18.70	18.50	26.91	26.31
Female - 59%	3.43	6.15	18.94	18.72	27.96	27.55
Female - 39%	3.00	5.85	19.04	18.43	27.65	26.94
Female - 76%	4.06	6.56	19.02	18.91	28.43	28.11
Male - 72%	8.84	10.27	21.34	21.66	32.67	32.58
Male - 92%	10.75	11.89	22.35	22.41	34.41	33.95
Male - 38%	6.23	8.25	20.02	20.43	30.38	30.40
Female - 1%	1.51	4.97	19.43	18.08	24.27	24.57
Female - 5%	1.84	5.08	19.39	18.05	26.35	24.97
Female - 50%	2.77	5.89	18.64	18.41	27.29	26.90
Male - 95%	11.49	12.79	22.75	22.98	34.98	34.77
Male - 99%	13.50	14.65	23.98	24.11	36.73	36.44
Avg. Diff. =	2.20		0.44		0.37	

One can see from Fig. 9, the Reach Gap values calculated by the automation tool follow the same trend-line as that of the values calculated using manual DHM simulations. Along with this, the Pearson correlation coefficients between manual and automated simulation results show a positive high-correlation with the coefficient values being 0.997, 0.971, and 0.995 for Target 1, 2, and 3, respectively (Table 4). The results show that the automation tool is accurate, with only minor improvements required in the simulation for hand movements while performing "Reach" motion. The majority of the values were within the absolute error of 0.5 cm except for the reach distances of Target 1, which can be accounted for the differences in the IK scheme. The automation tool is capable of simulating the dynamic human movements. Thus, which method to consider in terms of accuracy is arguable, especially for early design purposes (Table 3).

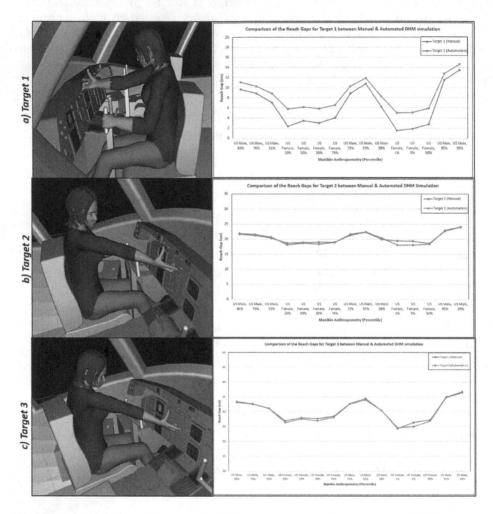

Fig. 9. Reach Gap trend-line comparisons between manual and automated DHM analysis for a) Target 1, b) Target 2, and c) Target 3

7.2   Comparison in Time - Manual vs. Automated Simulations

One of the key objectives for developing the automation framework was the need to reduce the time for running DHM simulation; thus, making the DHM-based design approach more natural to use for engineers in the early design. Specifically, when running HFE assessments for early purposes via DHM, one needs to consider multiple design concepts or alternatives, which require running numerous simulations. For example, as noted early, the study published by

Table 3. Descriptive statistics - manual versus automation for Reach Gap

	Target 1		Target 2		Target 3	
	Manual	Automation	Manual	Automation	Manual	Automation
Minimum	1.51	4.97	18.640	18.05	24.27	24.57
Maximum	13.50	14.65	23.98	24.11	36.73	36.44
Mean	6.35	8.56	20.64	20.33	30.34	30.02
Std. dev.	3.95	3.11	1.68	2.05	3.68	3.79
Median	6.23	8.25	20.02	20.42	30.38	30.40

Table 4. Pearson correlation - manual versus automation method for Reach Gap

	Target 1		Target 2		Target 3	
	Manual	Automation	Manual	Automation	Manual	Automation
Pearson correlation	0.997		0.971		0.995	

Salman et al. [7] uses manual DHM methods, which take around 15 min to execute simulations for a single manikin. As the number of simulations increases, the total simulation time and the effort required to generate ergonomics analysis becomes challenging to manage. In this study, one simulation consists of simulating all the tasks identified in Sect. 4.2 and performing ergonomic analysis for given human anthropometry. One manikin simulation includes eight tasks with the additional repetitive tasks of reach and head manipulations for Target 2 and Target 3; thus, resulting in a total of 16 tasks for a single simulation.

Table 5 provides a summary of the total-time required between manual and automated DHM simulations. Performing 16 tasks for one manikin took around 15 min and 50 s when executed manually by a DHM expert. In contrast, the automation tool performed these task simulations within 24 s. When considering the case of an exhaustive search approach or design exploration, such as the cockpit packaging analysis executed in this study, the total number of required simulations went up to 198 (99 manikins × 2 genders) for a single DHM environment. These simulations, when performed manually, took around 52 h and 15 min for an expert user. In contrast, the same set of simulations only took 1 h and 19 min when performed with the automation approach. The automation method in DHM provided around a 97.5% improvement in total simulation time. In other words, the time required for the DHM simulation is reduced by 97.5%. Thus, the automation approach not reduce down the simulation time but also eases the user effort.

Table 5. Total time required: manual DHM versus automated DHM

	Per anthropometry	Total time	Percent improvement
Manual simulation	15 min 50 s	∼52 h 15 min	Interval
Automated simulation	24 s	1 h 19 min	97.5 %

8 Conclusion

An automation framework for DHM-based simulation and ergonomics analysis was proposed in this study. The feasibility of this framework was assessed through a cockpit packaging study. Results show that the automation approach can result in reducing the expense in time without sacrificing for accuracy.

Although the proposed automation tool helps in saving significant user effort and time that is otherwise spend on performing the simulations manually in DHM, there are also disadvantages to using this tool. Manikin movements simulated by the automation tool are solely based on the path calculations performed by the IK scheme, which does not always reflect how humans behave while interacting with products. The majority of the DHM tools offer capabilities of integration with motion capture systems, in which case human subjects can be used to capture realistic postures. Another important observation is that a standard error exists within each computational approach since each computational model is an assumption of reality. The automation framework proposed in this study was specifically targeted to human-centered design studies that occur early in design, which often requires quick ergonomics analyses. Studies that focus on high precision and accuracy of human motion, such as kinesiology or biomechanics, might require actual human-subject data collection and experimentation for further validity check.

Overall, this automation tool offers a viable and quick solution when a design problem and task sequences are known for a design problem in which performing manual simulations won't be feasible. The next section talks about the future research directions.

9 Future Work

One of the limitations of this study was that the ergonomic evaluations were done by considering only the ideal conditions. Although the case study considered a fire/smoke in the cockpit emergency scenario, the study doesn't consider the actual effects of smoke on human performance (e.g., vision obscuration). The use of DHM for fire/smoke emergencies in the cockpit and evaluating pilot performance will be explored in the following studies.

Another limitation of this study is that it only considers a single design for ergonomics evaluation. The tool can be beneficial if the changes in the design environment can also be automated. We plan to implement this approach in the future, where the automation tool will be used for the design space exploration with multiple designs environments.

Additionally, programming using Jackscript is not a straight-forward option for novices. One needs to know and understand how Jackscript works and how various functions can be utilized to simulate human task. Future work in this area can focus on the development of graphical user interfaces similar to that of Jack's TSB interface, which will make it easier for the designer to use this tool for their purpose.

References

1. B767 flightdeck and avionics. https://www.scribd.com/doc/300085771/B767-Flightdeck-and-Avionics. Accessed 30 Aug 2019
2. In-flight fire: guidance for flight crews - skybrary aviation safety. https://www.skybrary.aero/index.php/In-Flight_Fire:_Guidance_for_Flight_Crews. Accessed 10 Aug 2019
3. In-flight fire/emergency landing, federal express flight 1406. Stewart International Airport, Newburgh, New York, 5 September 1996. https://www.ntsb.gov/news/events/Pages/Previous_Events.aspx. Accessed 31 Aug 2019
4. Jack. https://www.dex.siemens.com/plm/jack. Accessed 26 Aug 2019
5. Multivariate accommodation calculator: open design lab. http://tools.openlab.psu.edu/tools/explorer.php. Accessed 19 Aug 2019
6. Abras, C., Maloney-Krichmar, D., Preece, J., et al.: User-centered design. In: Bainbridge, W. (ed.) Encyclopedia of Human-Computer Interaction, vol. 37, no. 4, pp. 445–456. Sage Publications, Thousand Oaks (2004)
7. Ahmed, S., Gawand, M.S., Irshad, L., Demirel, H.O.: Exploring the design space using a surrogate model approach with digital human modeling simulations. In: ASME 2018 International Design Engineering Technical Conferences and Computers and Information in Engineering Conference, p. V01BT02A011. American Society of Mechanical Engineers (2018)
8. Bernard, F., Zare, M., Sagot, J.C., Paquin, R.: Using digital and physical simulation to focus on human factors and ergonomics in aviation maintainability. Hum. Factors **62**, 37–54 (2019). https://doi.org/10.1177/0018720819861496
9. Chaffin, D.B.: Improving digital human modelling for proactive ergonomics in design. Ergonomics **48**(5), 478–491 (2005)
10. Chaffin, D.B., Nelson, C., et al.: Digital Human Modeling for Vehicle and Workplace Design. Society of Automotive Engineers, Warrendale (2001)
11. Chiang, J., Stephens, A., Potvin, J.: Retooling jack's static strength prediction tool. Technical report, SAE Technical Paper (2006)
12. Demirel, H.O., Duffy, V.G.: Applications of digital human modeling in industry. In: Duffy, V.G. (ed.) ICDHM 2007. LNCS, vol. 4561, pp. 824–832. Springer, Heidelberg (2007). https://doi.org/10.1007/978-3-540-73321-8_93
13. Elkind, J.I., Card, S.K., Hochberg, J.: Human Performance Models for Computer-Aided Engineering. Academic Press, Cambridge (2014)
14. Karmakar, S., Pal, M.S., Majumdar, D., Majumdar, D.: Application of digital human modeling and simulation for vision analysis of pilots in a jet aircraft: a case study. Work **41**(Suppl. 1), 3412–3418 (2012)

15. Kennedy, K., Zehner, G.: Anthropometric accommodation in aircraft cockpits: a methodology for evaluation
16. Lämkull, D., Hanson, L., Örtengren, R.: A comparative study of digital human modelling simulation results and their outcomes in reality: a case study within manual assembly of automobiles. Int. J. Ind. Ergon. **39**(2), 428–441 (2009)
17. Lanzotti, A., Vanacore, A., Percuoco, C.: Robust ergonomic optimization of car packaging in virtual environment. In: Eynard, B., Nigrelli, V., Oliveri, S., Peris-Fajarnes, S., Rizzuti, S. (eds.) Advances on Mechanics, Design Engineering and Manufacturing. LNME, pp. 1177–1186. Springer, Cham (2017). https://doi.org/10.1007/978-3-319-45781-9_118
18. Mavrikios, D., Pappas, M., Kotsonis, M., Karabatsou, V., Chryssolouris, G.: Digital humans for virtual assembly evaluation. In: Duffy, V.G. (ed.) ICDHM 2007. LNCS, vol. 4561, pp. 939–948. Springer, Heidelberg (2007). https://doi.org/10.1007/978-3-540-73321-8_106
19. van der Meulen, P.A., DiClemente, P.: Ergonomic evaluation of an aircraft cockpit with RAMSIS 3D human modeling software. Technical report, SAE Technical Paper (2001)
20. Okimoto, M.L.L.R.: 21 digital human modeling in product evaluation. In: Human Factors and Ergonomics in Consumer Product Design: Methods and Techniques, p. 325 (2011)
21. Raschke, U., Kuhlmann, H., Hollick, M.: On the design of a task based human simulation system. SAE Trans. **114**, 760–766 (2005)
22. Reed, M.P., Faraway, J., Chaffin, D.B., Martin, B.J.: The humosim ergonomics framework: a new approach to digital human simulation for ergonomic analysis. Technical report, SAE Technical Paper (2006)
23. Stephens, A., Godin, C.: The truck that jack built: digital human models and their role in the design of work cells and product design. Technical report, SAE Technical Paper (2006)
24. Zhang, B., Álvarez Casado, E., Tello Sandoval, S., Mondelo, P.: Using ergonomic digital human modeling in evaluation of workplace design and prevention of occupational hazards onboard fishing vessels. In: Proceedings of the 8th International Conference on Occupational Risk Prevention, pp. 1–9 (2010)
25. Zhang, X., Chaffin, D.B.: Digital human modeling for computer-aided ergonomics. In: Handbook of Occupational Ergonomics, pp. 1–20. Taylor & Francis, CRC Press, London, Boca Raton (2005)
26. Ziolek, S.A., Nebel, K.: Human modeling: controlling misuse and misinterpretation. Technical report, SAE Technical Paper (2003)

CASRM: Cricket Automation and Stroke Recognition Model Using OpenPose

Tevin Moodley and Dustin van der Haar$^{(\boxtimes)}$

University of Johannesburg, Kingsway Avenue and, University Road,
Auckland Park, Johannesburg 2092, South Africa
{tevin,dvanderhaar}@uj.ac.za

Abstract. With the rapid changes within sport, specifically cricket, technology has been used to cater to the challenges faced within the domain. However, research within the field of study has shown that there is a gap to bridge in the way of establishing a cost-effective means to recognize different cricketing strokes. In our previous work, feature extraction methods such as Histogram of orientated gradients with support vector machines, K-nearest neighbor, and the AlexNet architecture were used to achieve cricket stroke recognition. While promising results were obtained, this article will attempt to exploit OpenPose skeleton keypoints, which will be used as a set of descriptive features that will be fed into the Long Short-Time Memory architecture for cricket stroke recognition. By applying the OpenPose skeleton to the dataset, the model can capture the pose keypoints of the cricket batsmen, whereby the body part locations and detection confidence are presented as a feature vector. The image dataset, which was compiled in a previous study, is used to ensure a fair measure of the proposed model. The strokes that will be addressed are as follows: *block*, *cut*, *drive* and *glance*. The Long Short-Time Memory architecture outperformed previously tested classifiers with a recorded model accuracy of 81.25%. The results suggest the model is capable of recognizing different cricket strokes. As a result, a human-computer interaction system can be developed to assist coaches and spectators to gain further understanding within the domain.

Keywords: Cricket stroke recognition · LSTM · Confusion matrix · ROC

1 Introduction

As computation becomes ubiquitous and the environments become enriched with new possibilities for communication and interaction, the field of human-computer interaction attempts to confront the challenges faced surrounding complex tasks, mediating networked interaction and managing the ever-increasing digital information [7]. Human-computer interaction systems have, in the past, been used to make contributions within various domains, and with the 2019 International Cricket World Cup completed, it was documented that 3 million

© Springer Nature Switzerland AG 2020
V. G. Duffy (Ed.): HCII 2020, LNCS 12198, pp. 67–78, 2020.
https://doi.org/10.1007/978-3-030-49904-4_5

people applied for the 650 000 spectators tickets available across the entire tournament. The increased use in technology has catered for the ongoing changes and rapid demand within the cricketing domain [10]. Perhaps one of the more successful systems used in the sport is a technology referred to as Hawk-eye. Hawk-Eye is a system, which tracks the trajectory of the ball so that it may aid umpires in the adjudication process of the leg before wicket [12].

Along with the successes, some believe there is still a gap to bridge in terms of establishing a cost-effective means to recognize different cricketing strokes [13]. According to Roopchand et al. certain areas have limited research dedicated to automated analysis. In our previous work, feature extraction methods such as Histogram of orientated gradients and more traditional classification methods that include support vector machines, K-nearest neighbor, and the AlexNet architecture were exploited in an attempt to achieve cricket stroke recognition [9]. In order to continue the research and obtain better results, the continued research will address OpenPose as a potential method to achieve cricket stroke recognition.

The OpenPose skeleton is a representation technique that has received a considerable amount of attention from developers of late [15]. To successfully gauge OpenPose, the same dataset created in a previous study is used, which analyses four different classes of strokes: *block*, *cut*, *drive* and *glance*. Section 2 and 2.1 will analyze the current problem areas and the current works within the domain. Section 3 will illustrate the manner in which the research was conducted and how the experiment was set up. Section 4 will highlight the results followed by a detailed discussion unpacking the results in Sect. 5.

2   Background

In cricket, the objective is to accumulate as many runs as possible. Eleven players play the game on each team, where both teams are provided the opportunity to bat and field. During each team's batting innings, the batsmen are required to accumulate runs [1]. The accumulation of runs is dependent on the batsman's ability to perform different cricketing strokes without being dismissed, as a dismissal of a batsman signals the end of their inning, where they are required to discontinue batting and leave the field immediately. Therefore, performing strokes using the correct technique may potentially lead to the accumulation of more runs, creating a higher chance of winning [1].

Performing cricket strokes can be a difficult task given that each stroke involves a variety of complex movements, which are dependent on the batsman's body placement of the head, hands, feet, and bat. These properties dictate the direction in which a ball travels after leaving the bat [3]. A study conducted by Carter in Education & Youth Ltd. establishes the fundamentals of batting and the mechanisms required to execute different strokes. The basic strokes highlighted in the research include the defensive block, the drive, cut, pull/hook, and leg glance. The defensive block is a stroke performed to prevent the batsman from being dismissed. The drive stroke is an extension of the block to obtain runs safely. The pull and cut strokes are performed to deliveries that are usually aimed toward the chest area of the batsman. Lastly, the leg glance is performed for deliveries that are directed into the batsman's legs [3]. The strokes identified by Carter cover the most basic strokes within the game and serve as justification for the strokes selected in this study.

With emphasis placed on performing cricket strokes and the increased use of technology to aid in the game. Creating a model that can recognize different cricket strokes may yield further contributions within the domain. Previous studies have been conducted to address the problem of creating a cost-effective means toward automated analysis, which will be discussed in the section to follow.

2.1   Related Works

Recent work conducted by Semwal et al. addresses the classification of the different types of the drive stroke. The system relies on pre-trained Convolutional Neural Networks (CNN) for extracting representations of auxiliary components using state-of-the-art saliency and optical flow techniques to bring out static and dynamic cues. The model performs exceptionally well by achieving an accuracy of 83.098% for right-handed batsmen while a less accurate score of 65.186% for the left-handed batsman [14].

Conventional computer vision methods have also been used in earlier studies. More specifically, research conducted by Karmaker et al. which argues that cricket stroke recognition can not be achieved using a single image [8]. The proposed model classifies cricket strokes using the motion vector detection for each frame with the integration of optical flow and transformation of vector angles with Spatio-temporal maximum average correlation height filter (MACH) to recognize actions [8]. The results achieved were promising. However, the overall accuracy of each stroke was poor, with the maximum accuracy score for the drive stroke of 63.57%.

Using CNNs, specifically AlexNet, along with conventional classification algorithms like support vector machines and k-nearest neighbors to determine the most suitable model for the domain. The research implemented AlexNet architecture to classify different cricketing strokes. The model achieved a 74.33% overall accuracy, and using metrics, the model proved to have a better balance between its precision and recall, thereby producing fewer false positives [9]. In order to produce more promising results, a different approach is realized whereby the OpenPose keypoint benefits are highlighted.

Researchers Phang and Lim recently exploited the OpenPose real-time system by proposing a real-time pipeline to address multi-person action recognition in a multi-camera setup using joint keypoint sequences from a detected person [11]. Using 14 keypoints from the human joints, Euclidean distance is applied from neck-to-pelvis on a standard person that is then fed into a Long Short-Time Memory (LSTM) recurrent network which achieved a 92% recognition accuracy rate. An attempt to exploit OpenPose by applying it to the cricketing domain, whereby the OpenPose skeleton keypoints will be used as a set of descriptive features, which will be fed into the LSTM classifier to establish a cost-effective means of cricket stroke recognition.

3   Proposed Model

This research aims to create a cricket stroke recognition model using OpenPose keypoint with the integration of a recurrent LSTM network in order to classify between different cricketing strokes and attempt to bridge the gap in creating a cost-effective means for automated analysis. The model proposed in Fig. 1 will provide a high-level view of the pipeline that will be followed throughout this research.

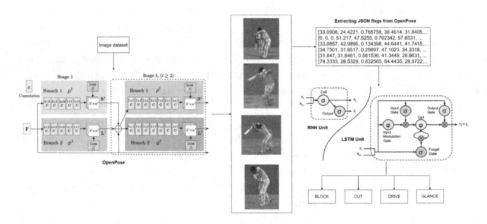

Fig. 1. A LSTM model to achieve cricket stroke recognition using OpenPose.

3.1   Capture

To ensure that the research is measured fairly, the same dataset will be used from previous works. The dataset was compiled using video highlights on International Test-Match Cricket, which was obtained from YouTube. Using OpenShot video editing software version *2.4.4*, the video was edited to create video snippets pertaining to the relevant information surrounding the cricket strokes. Once the video snippets were created, the frames in the snippets were extracted and labeled into their respective classes upon visual inspection. The image dataset compiled consists of 4 classes, namely; block, cut, drive, and glance. There are 480 images, where 400 images are reserved for the training set and 80 images for the testing set. The images are split using an 80:20 rule for training and testing. Images were tested and evaluated based on width and height. To ensure minimal distortion image aspect ratio chosen was set to *100(width)×150(height)*. The training class consisted of 4 classes where each class comprised of 100 images each, and the testing set contained 20 images in each class.

3.2 Feature Extraction

OpenPose is a library for real-time multi-person keypoint detection on C++ object-orientated programming with OpenCV and Caffe libraries. The OpenPose system is able to detect the human body, hand, and facial keypoint in single images [15]. OpenPose has the ability to output specific body keypoints in two alternative formats. OpenPose creates an array of keypoints containing body part locations and confidence. The coordinates produced by OpenPose are x and y that is normalized on a range between [0,1]–[0, source size] [2]. The specific keypoint with the corresponding human body part can be seen in Fig. 2.

Applying the OpenPose skeleton to the dataset, the model is able to capture the pose keypoint of the cricket batsmen, whereby the body part locations and detection confidence are represented as a feature vector. The feature vectors are labeled based on the class they represent to complete the data preparation process. Figure 2 illustrates how the OpenPose library was applied to each image within the dataset. The features extracted are then fed into a classifier, which will be discussed in the section to follow.

3.3 Classification

Long-Short Term Memory (LSTM) network has produced many successes, which models the dynamics and dependencies in sequential data within the 3D human action recognition field [16]. Recurrent neural networks (RNN) are used to infer a result using previously trained information. However, RNNs suffered from the vanishing gradient problem where an incorrect inference is made in the classification or prediction process. The introduction of LSTM and its advanced architecture partially overcomes the vanishing gradient problem as LSTM units allow the gradients to flow unchanged. However, it is not completely exempt from the gradient problem [16].

The LSTM architecture is made up of a cell, an input gate, an output gate, and a forget gate [6]. From Fig. 3, the cell may be viewed as the tracker that follows the dependencies between elements in the input sequence. The input gate is responsible for controlling the flow rate at which values proceed into the cell, and the forget gate controls the amount of time in which the values remain in the cells. The output gate controls how much the cell is used to compute the output activation of the LSTM unit [6]. Table 1 below is the layer type, the output shape, and the number of parameters identified at each of the layers.

The OpenPose-LSTM architecture has been defined, in order to gauge the model's ability to recognize different cricket strokes, a set of metrics are needed to draw the measure. The metrics used in the study are identified in the section below.

3.4 Benchmark Metrics

In order to determine the model's performance, different metrics will be used to assess the model proposed. The Receiver Operating Curve (ROC) calculates

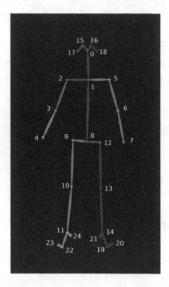 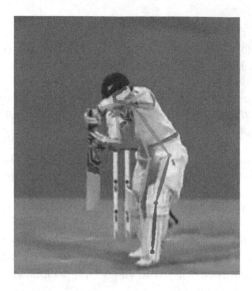

Fig. 2. On the left; the OpenPose output formatting based on the body parts of a human [2]. On the right; a representation of the block stroke image applied to the OpenPose library

both micro and macro averages. The micro-average computes the aggregate of all classes to determine the overall average. In contrast, the macro-average will compute each class independently and then calculate the average of each sum. To fully gauge the results, the ROC curve was computed, which is a graphical plot that is used to show the diagnostic ability of binary and multi-class classifiers. ROC curves plot the true positive rate, which is the number of true positives to the false positive rate that is the number of false positives [5].

Additional metrics were calculated to inspect the model. *Accuracy*, which is the ratio between correctly predicted observations to the total observations. *Precision* calculates the positive observations to the total predicted positive observations.

Table 1. The layer, output shape, and number of parameters at each layer for the LSTM architecture.

OpenPose-LSTM architecture		
Layer (type)	Output shape	Number of parameters
lstm_1	(None, 1, 128)	93696
time_distributed_1 (TimeDist)	(None, 1, 64)	8256
time_distributed_2 (TimeDist)	(None, 1, 32)	2080
time_distributed_3 (TimeDist)	(None, 1, 16)	528
flatten_1 (Flatten)	(None, 16)	0
dense_4 (Dense)	(None, 4)	68

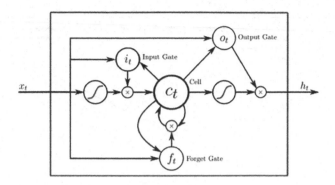

Fig. 3. Long-Short Term Memory unit with the cell, input gate, output gate, and the forget gate [6].

The *recall* is the ratio of correctly predicted positive observations to all the observations within that respective class. *F1-Score* is the weighted average between precision and recall.

4 Results

The study aims to create a model that can adequately recognize cricketing strokes. The model proposed in this research managed to achieve an 81.25% model accuracy.

From Fig. 4, the ROC curve for the OpenPose-LSTM architecture is illustrated, producing averages of 96% for the macro-average and 94% for the micro-average. For each class, the averages exceed 94%, contributing toward the model's ability to classify the strokes into their respective classes correctly. Each class is labeled as follows: block (class 0), cut (class1), drive (class2), and glance (class3). In an attempt to gain further understanding, a confusion matrix is calculated, highlighting the images that are falsely predicted.

Figure 5 shows the confusion matrix representing the OpenPose-LSTM algorithm. The confusion matrix indicates the number of false positives that are present within the test dataset. A heat map is provided to identify the classes that suffer from misclassification. There was a recorded total of fifteen misclassified images out of the eighty total images in the testing dataset. Class 0 produced the most false positives of eight, class 1 and 2 produced a mere total of two false positives each. Lastly, class 3 produced three false positives.

Table 2 is a representation of the metrics identified above. The table graphs each class within the test dataset. For each stroke, the accuracy, precision, recall, and f1-score is calculated. The results obtained in this research have been identified, which will be discussed in the next section.

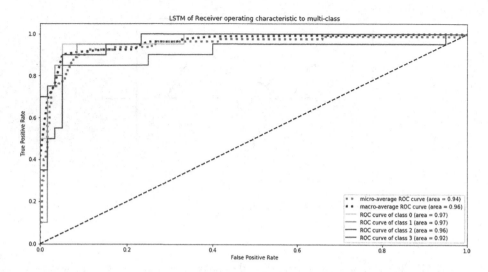

Fig. 4. The ROC curve illustrating the macro-average of 96% and the micro-average of 94%, the model performs well producing averages above 90% for each class.

Table 2. Performance metrics of the OpenPose combined with LSTM pipeline used to measure the model's accuracy.

Metrics			
Class	Precision	Recall	F1-Score
Block	92%	60%	73%
Cut	82%	90%	86%
Drive	75%	90%	82%
Glance	81%	85%	83%

5   Discussion and Critique

The ROC curve represented by Fig. 4 is the implementation of the OpenPose-LSTM architecture. The architecture is given the input shape followed by three dense layers beginning at 64 and ending at 16, as seen in Table 1. The model is then flattened and passed through the fully-connected layer. When computing the model's accuracy, the Keras sequential model is used, so that the first layer within the architecture can be set and the proceeding layers are shaped automatically [16]. The model accuracy is computed using the test dataset, which returned an accuracy of 81,25%. The high accuracy score indicates the model's ability to recognize different strokes. From the ROC curve in Fig. 4, each class performs well, exceeding scores above 94%.

In Fig. 5, the LSTM confusion matrix is shown. The confusion matrix is a table that is often used to describe the performance of a classification model on a

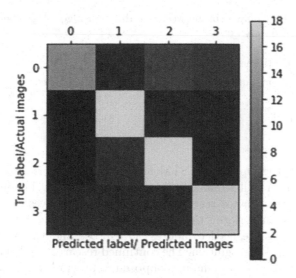

Fig. 5. Confusion matrix derived from the LSTM algorithm, illustrating the number of false positives that are produced within each class. The block class performing the worst with 8 false positives.

test dataset where the image labels are true [4]. The confusion matrix is displayed as a heat map, which highlights the classes that suffer from misclassification. Having noted the block class, which exhibits the most false positives, indicating the misclassification of images. Further motivations as to why misclassifications occur can be made using Table 2. While the block class has a precision score of 92%, the recall score of 60% demonstrates the model's inability to determine the ratio of correctly predicted positive observations to all the observations. While the precision score is significantly high, the class itself struggles to find a balance, which is motivated through the f1-score of 73%.

Inspecting the cut class using Fig. 5, the number of false positives recorded was two. As seen in the block class, Table 2 metrics validate the resulting confusion matrix with the recall score of 90%. The recall score demonstrates the manner in which the class can distinguish between true and false positives. The precision score of the cut class is less than that of the block class. However, the balance within the cut class is better, illustrating the cut class ability in making fewer misclassifications. The drive class also demonstrates a good balance with a recall score of 90%, but the precision score of 75% indicates that the additional class images are being classified as drive incorrectly. Further motivations through the use of the confusion matrix in that 4 images were incorrectly classified as a drive within the block class, suggesting that the block and drive classes may exhibit similar features that make it difficult to differentiate between the two. Difficulty in distinguishing between the two classes may hold true due to the nature in which the strokes are performed. Both strokes are similar except for the fact that the drive stroke is a continuation of the block where the batsman extends their arms. To highlight the contribution of the LSTM model within the domain, Table 3 below will illustrate the model that we used in previous works.

Table 3. Performance comparison between the different algorithms conducted in this study and a previous study.

Metrics used for performance comparison				
Algorithm	Accuracy	Precision	Recall	F1-Score
CNN	74.33%	74%	75%	75%
LSTM	81.25%	83%	81%	81%

Using Table 3, the OpenPose-LSTM architecture outperforms the AlexNet architecture, with a recall score of 81% as opposed to 75%. The model demonstrates its ability to balance true positives to false positives. The OpenPose-LSTM architecture outperforms the AlexNet architecture highlighted in Table 3. Therefore supporting the need to address OpenPose and LSTM as a suitable model for cricket stroke recognition. The continued research yielded more promising results within the cricket domain as opposed to previous work using the same dataset.

6   Conclusion

Creating a model that can recognize different cricket strokes will allow contributions within the environment, contributions ranging from coaching to helping a spectator understand the game. Understanding the stroke performed at a given moment will aid coaches in improving the techniques of a batsman, thereby allowing the batsman to enhance their skill level. Additionally, spectators are able to use the system to understand what strokes are performed the moment it is executed. Possibly, the greatest contribution being the gap bridged in developing a cost-effective means for automated analysis.

Semwal et al. conducted a study to recognize the different types of drive strokes. The study was successful in producing an accuracy of 83.098% for right-handed batsmen while a less accurate score of 65.186% for the left-handed batsman [14]. In their works, they have noted the lengthy process required to capture the dataset, which contained thousands of images. Having an abundance of images may potentially produce better results, in particular, the block stroke, which has a recall score of 60%, illustrating the class's inability to predict true positives from false positives. More data should be added in future works to make improvements within the domain.

Karmaker et al. argue that cricket stroke recognition cannot be achieved using a single image [8]. The model proposed classifies cricket strokes using motion vector detection for each frame. While promising research is shown, the current research does suggest that a single image may be used to classify different cricketing strokes. Producing a micro average of 96% and a model average 81.25%, the OpenPose-LSTM architecture is able to make classifications between different strokes adequately, and possible improvements are still achievable within the domain.

The outcome of any cricketing match is a team's ability to score runs and with the increased viewing audience, new and different pressures arise. Establishing a cost-effective means of automation to achieve cricket stroke recognition may potentially make future contributions within the domain. A human-computer interaction system that can enable coaches to analyze a batsman's technique to potentially infer suggestions to improve the skill level of the batsman or to provide knowledge to those who have minimal knowledge surrounding the game highlight the potential contributions. Future works will entail more data being captured to better train the model, which will be developed into an application that may be used to make the contributions highlighted within the domain.

References

1. Cricket (Australia). Salem Press Encyclopedia (2018)
2. Cao, Z., Hidalgo, G., Simon, T., Wei, S.E., Sheikh, Y.: OpenPose: realtime multi-person 2D pose estimation using Part Affinity Fields (2018). arXiv preprint arXiv:1812.08008
3. Carter, B.: Cricket. Education & Youth Ltd., London
4. Fawcett, T.: An introduction to ROC analysis. Pattern Recogn. Lett. **27**(8), 861–874 (2006)
5. Goutte, C., Gaussier, E.: A probabilistic interpretation of precision, recall and F-score, with implication for evaluation. In: Losada, D.E., Fernández-Luna, J.M. (eds.) ECIR 2005. LNCS, vol. 3408, pp. 345–359. Springer, Heidelberg (2005). https://doi.org/10.1007/978-3-540-31865-1_25
6. Graves, A., Mohamed, A.R., Hinton, G.: Speech recognition with deep recurrent neural networks. In: 2013 IEEE International Conference on Acoustics, Speech and Signal Processing, pp. 6645–6649. IEEE (2013)
7. Hollan, J., Hutchins, E., Kirsh, D.: Distributed cognition: toward a new foundation for human-computer interaction research. ACM Trans. Comput.-Hum. Interact. (TOCHI) **7**(2), 174–196 (2000)
8. Karmaker, D., Chowdhury, A., Miah, M., Imran, M., Rahman, M.: Cricket shot classification using motion vector. In: 2015 Second International Conference on Computing Technology and Information Management (ICCTIM), pp. 125–129. IEEE (2015)
9. Moodley, T., van der Haar, D.: Cricket stroke recognition using computer vision methods. In: Kim, K.J., Kim, H.-Y. (eds.) Information Science and Applications. LNEE, vol. 621, pp. 171–181. Springer, Singapore (2020). https://doi.org/10.1007/978-981-15-1465-4_18
10. Morgan, R.: Olympics top tv sport ahead of afl, comm. games & cricket (2018). http://www.roymorgan.com/findings/7508-top-sport-tv-viewing-december-2017-201803020101
11. Phang, J.T.S., Lim, K.H.: Real-time multi-camera multi-person action recognition using pose estimation. In: Proceedings of the 3rd International Conference on Machine Learning and Soft Computing, pp. 175–180. ACM (2019)
12. Rock, R., Als, A., Gibbs, P., Hunte, C.: The 5th umpire: Cricket's edge detection system. In: Proceedings of the International Conference on Scientific Computing (CSC). The Steering Committee of The World Congress in Computer Science, p. 1 (2011)

13. Roopchand, R., Pooransingh, A., Singh, A.: Bat detection and tracking toward batsman stroke recognition. In: 2016 8th International Conference on Computational Intelligence and Communication Networks (CICN), pp. 256–260. IEEE (2016)
14. Semwal, A., Mishra, D., Raj, V., Sharma, J., Mittal, A.: Cricket shot detection from videos. In: 2018 9th International Conference on Computing, Communication and Networking Technologies (ICCCNT), pp. 1–6. IEEE (2018)
15. Uddin, M.Z., Torresen, J.: A deep learning-based human activity recognition in darkness. In: 2018 Colour and Visual Computing Symposium (CVCS), pp. 1–5. IEEE (2018)
16. Zhang, S., Liu, X., Xiao, J.: On geometric features for skeleton-based action recognition using multilayer LSTM networks. In: 2017 IEEE Winter Conference on Applications of Computer Vision (WACV), pp. 148–157. IEEE (2017)

Development and Evaluation
of a Platform-Independent Surgical
Workstation for an Open Networked
Operating Theatre Using the IEEE 11073 SDC
Communication Standard

Okan Yilmaz[✉], Dario Wieschebrock, Jan Heibeyn,
Klaus Rademacher, and Armin Janß

Chair of Medical Engineering, RWTH University Aachen, Aachen, Germany
yilmaz@hia.rwth-aachen.de

Abstract. The modernization of the complex operating theatres comes along with new opportunities and challenges in particular in the areas of data processing, safety, Human-Machine-Interaction and interoperability.

With the funding of the BMBF (Federal Ministry of Education and Research), the OR.NET project (2012–2016) developed an approach of an open device connectivity within the operation room (OR) and the clinical environment. Within this approach, the open integration of medical devices from different manufacturers and the development of an international communication Standard family "IEEE 11073 Service-oriented Device Connectivity (SDC)" has been addressed [IEEE Standards Association 2019]. With the SDC standard, medical devices are able to communicate manufacturer-independently. To control medical devices and visualize parameters and function on the basis of the open interconnection approach, there is a need for a surgical and anaesthetic workstation. The aim of this research work has been the development of a cross-device and cross-platform software framework for a workstation at the Chair of Medical Engineering (mediTEC) at the RWTH Aachen University. The requirement analysis considers the functionalities of existing proprietary integrated OR systems (OR1 Neo, Core Nova, Tegris OR) and research projects for open networked OR systems (OR.NET, SCOT and OpenICE). Within the workstation, reusable and configurable components were developed, integrated and tested following the dialogue principles (DIN EN ISO 9241-110) to achieve a high degree of usability (DIN EN IEC 62366, DIN EN ISO 60601-1-6). The graphical user interfaces was integrated for 6 medical devices from different manufacturers for a mobile and a centralized workplace. To test the concept of the surgical workstation, 7 surgeons and 1 orthopedist from the Uniklinikum Aachen solved tasks, which were evaluated and discussed.

Keywords: Human-Machine-Interaction · Human factors · Usability evaluation · Integrated operating room · Open surgical workstation · Tablet control · Open communication standard IEEE 11073 SDC

V. G. Duffy (Ed.): HCII 2020, LNCS 12198, pp. 79–92, 2020.
https://doi.org/10.1007/978-3-030-49904-4_6

1 Introduction

Medical and technical developments are creating opportunities and numerous challenges in the operating room. Closed proprietary manufacturer systems are an obstacle here, as they complicate communication with potential network participants and do not permit unrestricted integration of third-party devices.

Closed systems such as OR1 NEO from Karl Storz, TEGRIS OR from Maquet and Core Nova from Richard Wolf offer a very wide range of functionalities, but none of these systems can fully integrate third-party devices.

In this work, third party medical devices are integrated on the basis of SDC into a surgical workstation with a high level of usability. Individual widgets for the user interfaces are developed, so that these can be reused and parts of the user interface can be generated dynamically.

A verification of the requirements and a comparison with an already implemented concept is performed. Additionally, interaction-centered usability tests with a representative user group are conducted in a usability laboratory and the results are statistically analyzed and discussed.

2 Materials and Methods

2.1 Comparison of Proprietary Manufacturer Solutions for Integrated Operating Systems

In this chapter, we list the functionalities of the closed proprietary manufacturer solutions. This includes optional features, which the manufacturers also offer for a higher price. The compared systems are OR1 NEO from Karl Storz, TEGRIS OR from Maquet and Core Nova from Richard Wolf.

Functions/Manufacturer	OR1 NEO	Core Nova	Maquet
Recording and streaming			
Image and video signals	Yes	Yes	Yes
Numeric Medical data	Yes	Yes	Yes
Video Streaming outside the operating theatre	Yes	Yes	Yes
Navigation			
Video recordings	Yes	Yes	Yes
Patient file or previous diagnoses	Yes	Yes	Yes
Connections to existing systems			
Hospital Information System (HIS)	Yes	Yes	Yes
Radiology Information System (RIS)	Yes	Yes	Yes
Picture Archiving and Communication System (PACS)	Yes	Yes	Yes

(*continued*)

(continued)

Functions/Manufacturer	OR1 NEO	Core Nova	Maquet
Health Level 7(HL7)	Yes	Yes	Yes
Digital Imaging and Communications in Medicine (DICOM)	Yes	Yes	Yes
Device integration			
Own equipment	Yes	Yes	Yes
Third-party manufacturers can add their own devices to the existing network	No	No	No
Selected manufacturers can integrate individual devices (after cooperation)	Yes	Yes	Yes
Integration of video signals from third-party devices	Yes	Yes	Yes
Control of integrated devices			
Central control module	Yes	Yes	Yes
Remote adjustment of values	Yes	Yes	Yes
Use of predefined settings	Yes	Yes	Yes
Devices can communicate with each other directly or using a central control module	Unknown	Yes	Unknown
Independent closed loop regulation through communication between devices	Unknown	Yes	Unknown
Planning of clinical workflows			
Creating checklists	Yes	Yes	Yes
Creation of process sequences (workflows)	Yes	Yes	Yes
Grouping functions of different devices	Yes	Yes	Yes

[Core nova 2019] [MAQUET Holding B.V. & Co. KG 2015; MAQUET Holding B.V. & Co. KG. 2019] [Karl Storz 2010, 2018, 2019].

After the tabular comparison of the key functions offered by the proprietary manufacturer solutions, it becomes clear that all three systems are very advanced and the range of functions is very similar to each other. No manufacturer was able to fulfill the point 'Third-party manufacturers can add their own devices to the existing network', which was to be expected, because those systems are proprietary, using a manufacturer-specific non-public communication standard. That is where this research starts, and contrary to existing systems, the goal is to fully integrate open networked third-party devices.

2.2   Requirements for the Surgical SDC Workstation

The requirements described below are intended to define the specific conditions for the development and the runtime environment for the software. In order to divide the desired features more precisely, they are split into functional and non-functional requirements.

Functional Requirements

- SDC supporting medical devices controllable within the network
- Integration of a user interface generating framework
- Navigation through control panels is possible
- Changes to the device are shown in the operating panel
- Simultaneously usage of operating panel from different devices
- Device alarms are visible on the operating panel
- Control panels for at least 3 medical devices

Non Functional Requirements

- Workstation runs on a 4:3 tablet and a 16:9 touchscreen
- Low latencies for adjusting values of medical devices
- Support of different resolutions
- Non-blocking behavior of the user interface
- Interception of errors during runtime
- Simplified maintainability through modularization
- Supported by different operation systems

2.3 Concept of the Surgical SDC Workstation

From the most commonly used web solutions of platform-independent systems (Rich Internet Application, Hybrid Application and Pure Web Application) the pure web application was selected as the client solution and Java bytecode as the server solution, so that the software architecture model is a client-server model. The advantage of a browser solution is especially the platform independence as well as the modern and efficient design of user interfaces. The decision for the programming language Java as server-side solution is based on the broad support of Java on different operating systems, well tested and available modules, as well as the secure and solid way the programs are executed. However, an implementation in C++ would also be possible.

The browsers provide the user interface and thus enable interaction with the devices. The server can communicate with the medical devices and receives requests from the browser and forwards them to the medical devices. With this approach, each client only needs to execute a single browser session to use all functions offered by the devices. This keeps the processor and memory requirements on the client side very low and provides furthermore independence for platform and device selection. Since this concept is based on a web browser as a client solution, this concept is from now on referred as **WebStation**. The workstation already developed by the Chair of Medical Technology (mediTEC) is referred as **Workstation** [Janß 2019].

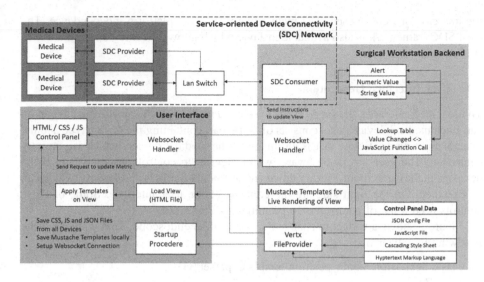

Fig. 1. WebStation structure

The concept of the WebStation is shown in Fig. 1 and consists of 4 parts:

– Service-oriented Device Connectivity (SDC) Network
– Medical devices
– Surgical Workstation backend (WebStation)
– User interface

The SDC framework enables network participants to exchange information, e.g. device settings, alarms and device identification with other SDC Network participants. The Library was provided by SurgiTAIX [Kasparick 2018; SurgiTAIX 2018]. Connected to each medical device is a SDC provider, who offers a service for information exchange in the network. The WebStation is built on top of a SDC consumer, who subscribes and uses all offered services from SDC Providers in the network, which are connected to medical devices. The SDC Consumer is part of the WebStation and the SDC Provider is part of the medical device.

The user interfaces each consist of an HTML, CSS and a JavaScript file. The HTML file contains the user interface, the CSS file contains the styles for the interface and the JavaScript file optionally contains the logic of the panel. These three files build the frontend and the control logic of the panel.

A configuration file in JSON format contains necessary information about the control panel, such as under which menu item the device should be displayed and the entire controller logic. As soon as the value of a metric changes (e.g. OR light is switched on), this document looks up which JavaScript function is to be called with which parameter and sends this via web sockets to the browser, which then execute the desired function.

Surgical Workstation Backend is the connection between the SDC network and the browser session. For the implementation of the backend, as already mentioned, the Java runtime environment is used. The main advantage is the platform independence. The used SDC framework is also available in Java, which allows the integration into a Java application.

2.4   User Interface Generation

To use a medical Panel, the surgeon has to select a medical device inside the navigation bar. Each medical device panel consists of a title bar, containing the device type and the manufacturer name. Below that is an image of the medical device, which is currently controlled. The user has to be aware, which device he controls remotely and if the device is in the same room. Further down are additional Settings and Presets, which can be executed. On the right side are the controls of the user interface. Some of those controls need a list of parameters to be initialized and used.

Figure 2 shows a widget to change the zoom of an endoscope. That widget has the following initializer list:

- Class: flexivision_zoom_position template_preset_view
- Title: Zoom
- Minimum value: 1
- Maximum value: 3
- List of possible values: 3.0 2.5 2.0 1.5 1.0
- SDC Metric Name: ZoomFactor
- SDC Provider EPR: Flexivision

To identify the widgets during the runtime, each widget type has an identifier class. In this case, the widget with 5 Buttons, a big blue number to show the actual value, a view of the current zoom value on the right, which can also be used to change the current value, is known as **template_preset_view.** So each HTML element with the initializer list above and the class **template_preset_view** will be rendered according to a template. The template, which has been used in this work is Mustache.js (http://mustache.github. com/). With Mustache you can define templates, leave placeholder for additional content and render it whenever and where you need. There are multiple different render engines for a web browser, so most render engines could be used here. It makes the maintenance easier by breaking the code up into smaller files, cause changes only need to be done once to be applied in the complete framework.

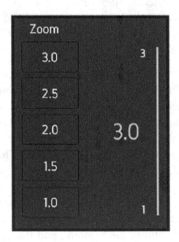

Fig. 2. Widget to change endoscope zoom

The individual control widgets were implemented on the basis of the guidelines from DIN EN ISO 9241-12 (Part 12: Information presentation) and DIN EN ISO 9241-110 (Principles of dialogue design).

2.5   Interaction Centered Usability Evaluation

In usability tests the newly implemented concept of the **WebStation** was compared with the currently available **Workstation**. A representative group of users carried out several tests and then completed a survey. The goal was to check the usability of the developed system taking into account the criteria effectiveness, efficiency, learnability and user satisfaction. With the interaction-centered evaluation of the UI revealing deficits and possible improvements of the user interface's operating concept should be identified.

In [Jakob Nielsen 2000] and [Laura Faulkner 2003], Nielson and Faulkner found that the more tests are performed, the higher is the detection percentage of errors in usability tests. According to Nielsen, five participants in studies are sufficient to detect 85% of all usability problems. The test participants consisted of employees of the University Hospital Aachen. A total of six neurosurgeons and one orthopedist took part in the tests, 5 of them male and 2 female surgeons. The mean age of the participants was 40 years, the average work experience was 11 years and the participants spent an average of 16 h per week in the operating theatre.

The tests are performed in the laboratory of the Chair of Medical Engineering (mediTEC) at RWTH Aachen University. There is a surgical workstation demonstrator, where various medical devices are available and connected (see Fig. 3).

The tests were performed on a 42" touchscreen monitor and an Apple iPad with the following device-software combinations:

- **Workstation** - Current Workstation on a 42" touchscreen
- **WebStation Desktop** - New WebStation concept on a 42" touchscreen
- **WebStation Mobile** - New WebStation concept on a 9.7" iPad

The standards DIN EN IEC 62366 [Deutsches Institut für Normung 2015b], DIN EN ISO 60601 [Deutsches Institut für Normung 2015a], ISO 9241-110 [Deutsches Institut für Normung e. V. 2006] serve as criteria for the present evaluation and in which the requirements of usability are defined as the degree to which a system, a product or a service can be used by certain users to achieve certain goals effectively, efficiently, in a learn-able and satisfactory way in a given context of use. According to these standards, the factors determining the usability are, in particular, the effectiveness, efficiency and satisfaction of the user when interacting with the tested system. These three main criteria are defined as follows:

- Efficiency describes the correlation between the results achieved and the resources used (time, human effort). In this work the efficiency is calculated by dividing the number of minimal steps per task by the number of steps needed. (E.g. The efficiency for a task where 1 step is needed to complete it but the participant used 4 steps is 1:4 = 25%). Additionally, the time to complete each task was measured, to have additional information to determine how fast each participant was.

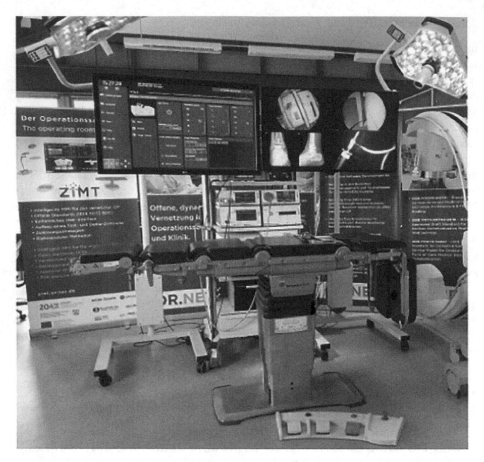

Fig. 3. Surgical workstation-demonstrator at the Chair of Medical Engineering, RWTH Aachen University

- Effectiveness measures the accuracy and completeness with which users achieve specific objectives, i.e. the degree to which objectives are achieved. In this work, a task is considered not fully completed if one of its sub-tasks is not completed. Since the degree of completion in this paper is very high, the inverse, the failure rate, is presented instead. The failure rate shows the percentage of users who could not complete a task. It is calculated by the following formula for each task individually: Number of tests failed/Number of tests
- Satisfaction refers to the individual's perceptions and reactions resulting from the use of a system, product or service. In the scope of this work, a short evaluation on a so-called Likert scale was performed after 3 of 5 executed tasks. A Likert Test presents an evaluation that is agreed or disagreed by a person on a scale of usually 5, 7 or 11 levels. The center value of the scale stands for "Neither agree nor disagree" [Statista 2019].

3   Results

As described in the evaluation methods in the previous section, the usability of the operating concept is evaluated using the criteria efficiency, effectiveness and satisfaction. Efficiency is measured in the user tests by using five tasks. Low efficiency is the result of too many operating steps being required to achieve the goal. A high efficiency, on the other hand, shows that the steps, which were carried out, were effective.

Figure 4 and Fig. 5 show the tasks on the X-axis and the efficiencies reached on the Y-axis. Figure 4 is more detailed, since it shows all recorded data as boxplots whereas Fig. 5 only shows the mean values.

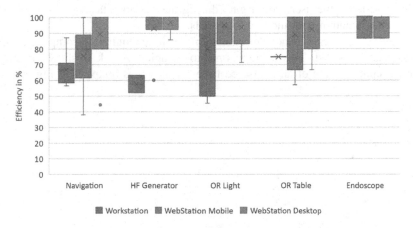

Fig. 4.   Efficiencies achieved per task

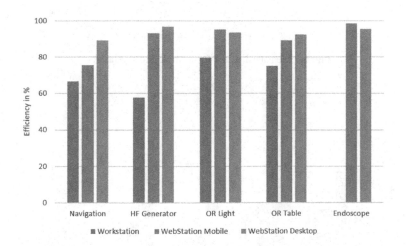

Fig. 5.   Average efficiencies per task

The efficiency of the Workstation is lower in all tasks compared to the WebStation Mobile and the WebStation Desktop. Many users have had difficulties using the workstation navigation because of the single and double clicking, which were partly necessary to open a menu item. The efficiency of the WebStation Mobile within the task navigation is about 75% and the workstation is evaluated with 67%. With the operating panel of the HF generator there were significant usage difficulties to navigate through the menu items of the selection of the modes because the arrow keys were partly too small. The efficiencies of the OR light and the OR table are quite high, but the WebStation concept shows better results than the Workstation. In the endoscope control panel the task was to perform 10 steps instead of 4–6 steps. Despite the high number of steps, the efficiency was the highest there. Reasons for this are on the one hand the experience the users could gain during the previous tasks and on the other hand the familiarization with the control panels.

For a more accurate efficiency determination, the time required to complete all steps of a task was measured. This average time to complete a task is shown in Fig. 7. A detailed representation of all measured times is shown as boxplots in Fig. 6.

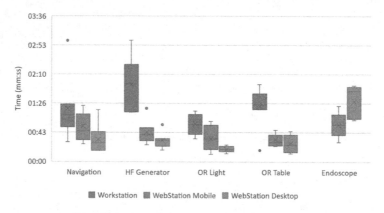

Fig. 6. Measured times for completing the tasks

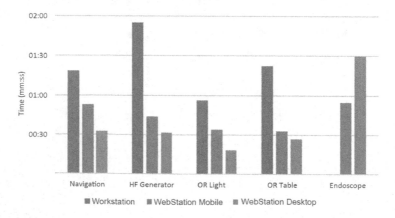

Fig. 7. Average time to complete the tasks

The operating time of the workstation was higher in all tests than the WebStation concept. Especially the time with the Workstation using the HF generator and operating table tasks is ~2.5 higher than of the WebStation Mobile and Desktop. This is due to the unclear labeling of the operating elements and the partly unintuitive control of the user interfaces. The completion time for the Workstation is also higher in the first 4 tasks, followed by the WebStation Mobile and the WebStation Desktop. Only for the last task, the users were faster with the mobile solution than with the desktop solution. There was no workstation solution for the last task, so there is no evaluation (bar) for the last task. The processing time is only compared within the intratasks and not the intertasks. Those are equally difficult and should take the same amount of time. The 1:30 min at the endoscope is therefore an extremely high value, but in the context of the task (10 steps instead of 6) a relatively good value.

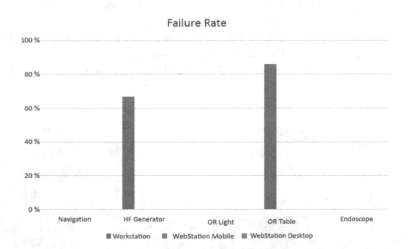

Fig. 8. Failure rate for each task in percent

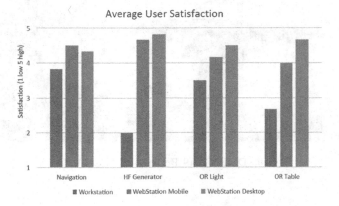

Fig. 9. Average user satisfaction for each task

The Failure rate is shown in Fig. 8. Because of identification and understanding problems, 2 tasks could not be completed. The only values differing from 0 within the failure rates are at the HF generator (70%) and at the operating table (86%). 5 of 7 persons could not complete the task at the HF generator and 6 of 7 could not complete the task at the operating table. This is reflected in efficiency (Fig. 4 and Fig. 5) and user satisfaction (Fig. 9).

4   Discussion and Conclusion

Developing a centralized surgical workstation, which uses the IEEE 11073 SDC standards, on basis of a server client model (web application as frontend, a java implementation backend) is possible. Controlling all medical devices within the SDC network was possible. Changes performed on those medical devices, were forwarded by the server and shown on each connected user-interface. It is possible, to navigate through the medical device panels and alarms executed by the medical devices, which are visible on the front end. All functional and non-functional requirements set were met. The Workstation was shown in the DMEA 2019 and the feedback of the clinical user and the suppliers (Fig. 10).

Fig. 10. DMEA 2019 Berlin [mediTEC 2019]

Furthermore we developed a user interface generating framework. By using the UI-Profiles developed by mediTEC [Janß et al. 2018], it was possible to implement re-useable frontend elements. This makes the verification process of the user interfaces easier. The usability tests shows, that the implemented workstation with its user-interfaces had a high degree of efficiency, effectivity and user satisfaction.

Acknowledgments. This research work has been funded within the project "ZiMT - Certifiable Integrated Medical Technology and IT Systems based on Open Standards in the Operating Room and Hospital" (State of North-Rhine Westphalia and the European Commission - European Regional Development Fund (EFRE); grant no.: EFRE-0800454).

References

Core nova. OP-Integration (2019)

Deutsches Institut für Normung.: Medizinische elektrische Geräte – Teil 1-6: Allgemeine Festlegungen für die Sicherheit einschließlich der wesentlichen Leistungsmerkmale – Ergänzungsnorm: Gebrauchstauglichkeit (IEC 60601-1-6:2010 + A1:2013); Deutsche Fassung EN 60601-1-6:2010 + A1:2015 (2015a)

Deutsches Institut für Normung.: Medizinprodukte – Anwendung der Gebrauchstauglichkeit auf Medizinprodukte (IEC 62366:2007 + A1:2014); Deutsche Fassung EN 62366:2008 + A1:2015 (2015b)

Deutsches Institut für Normung e. V.: Ergonomie der Mensch-System-Interaktion – Teil 110: Grundsätze der Dialoggestaltung (ISO 9241-110:2006); Deutsche Fassung EN ISO 9241-110:2006. (2006)

IEEE Standards Association.: 11073-20701-2018 - Health informatics–Point-of-care medical device communication - Part 20701: Service-Oriented Medical Device Exchange Architecture and Protocol Binding (2019). https://standards.ieee.org/standard/11073-20701-2018.html. Accessed 1 March 2019

Nielsen, J.: Why you only need to test with 5 users: user testomg (2000). https://www.nngroup.com/articles/why-you-only-need-to-test-with-5-users/. Accessed 15 March 2019

Janß, A.: ZiMT - Zertifizierbare integrierte Medizintechnik und IT-Systeme auf Basis offener Standards in Operationssaal und Klinik (2019). https://www.meditec.hia.rwth-aachen.de/de/forschung/aktuelle-projekte/zimt/. Accessed 19 January 2019

Janß, A., Thorn, J., Schmitz, M., Mildner, A., Dell'Anna-Pudlik, J., Leucker, M., Radermacher, K.: Extended device profiles and testing procedures for the approval process of integrated medical devices using the IEEE 11073 communication standard. Biomed. Tech. (Berl) **63**, 95–103 (2018). https://doi.org/10.1515/bmt-2017-0055

Karl Storz. OR1™ (2019). https://www.karlstorz.com/de/de/karl-storz-or1.htm

Karl Storz. OR1™ Neo -The new design of excellence (2010)

Karl Storz. OR1™ Neo -Der ultimative Operationssaal (2018)

Kasparick M (2018) Release der SDCLib/C 3.0.0 – die OSCLib mit neuem Namen und neuer API:55,76

Faulkner, L.: Beyond the five-user assumption: benefits of increased sample sizes in usability testing. Behav. Res. Methods Instrum. Comput. **35**, 379–383 (2003). https://doi.org/10.3758/BF03195514

MAQUET Holding B.V. & Co. KG.: TEGRIS – OP-Integration neu definiert Broschüre (DE) (2015)

MAQUET Holding, B.V. & Co KG.: TEGRIS OR Integration Management System (2019). https://www.maquet.com/int/product-articles/tegris-or-integration-management-system/. Accessed 14 March 2019

mediTEC - Chair of Medical Engineering (2019). https://www.meditec.hia.rwth-aachen.de/en/home

OR.NET e.V. ZiMT Projekt auf der DMEA

Statista. Likert-Skala - Definition (2019). https://de.statista.com/statistik/lexikon/definition/82/likert_skala/. Accessed 26 April 2019

SurgiTAIX. Release der SDCLib/C 3.0.0 – die OSCLib mit neuem Namen und neuer API (2018). https://surgitaix.com/wp/2018/02/09/release-der-sdclib-c-3-0-0-die-osclib-mit-neuem-namen-und-neuer-api/. Accessed 1 March 2019

Ergonomics and Occupational Health

Investigation on Heavy Truck Cab Ergonomics

Junmin Du[1(✉)], Weiyu Sun[2], Haoshu Gu[1], Xin Zhang[3], Huimin Hu[3], and Yang Liu[4]

[1] Beihang University, Beijing, China
dujm@buaa.edu.cn
[2] Hefei Hualing Co., Ltd., Hefei, China
[3] China National Institute of Standardization, Beijing, China
[4] Beijing Foton Daimler Automotive Co., Ltd., Beijing, China

Abstract. Cab ergonomics has an important impact on road safety and driver health, especially for heavy trucks, which is the main tool for long distance road transportation and usually result in more serious consequences than other types of vehicle if an accident occurs. However, for a long time, due to the poor design of the heavy truck cab, the situation of causing road risk and driver health problems have not been significantly improved. The understanding of the current ergonomic situation of the heavy truck cab will stimulate the design improvement. This paper investigated and analyzed the ergonomic problems and using experience of heavy truck cab installations, as well as the characteristics of professional driver groups and driving habits. The interviews and questionnaire survey on heavy truck drivers were used. The data was analyzed through statistical methods such as significance tests. It was found that the current truck cab components, including seat belts, seats, steering wheels, accelerators, brakes and clutch pedals, and shift levers, had varying degrees of ergonomic weakness. The research results provide reference for understanding the characteristics of heavy truck users, driving habits, user needs and existing design deficiencies, and improving of heavy truck cabs ergonomic design.

Keywords: Heavy truck driver · Cab ergonomics design · Investigation · Human machine interface

1 Introduction

Heavy trucks are the main tools for long-distance road transportation. Good cab ergonomic design is the foundation for guarantee of good driving experience, driver's health and road safety. Excellent cab ergonomic design can reduce driver's fatigue, distraction, misoperation rate and improve driving comfort. Based on this, the vehicle cab ergonomic design is more and more valued. Due to the differences in anthropometry and driving habits, there are different requirements for the size, layout and operation power of the various components inside the cab. However, in the current domestic design process, these differences were not recognized or comprehended enough in articulating its importance. The consideration of heavy truck cab ergonomics is insufficient, which results in inconveniences and high safety risks on road.

© Springer Nature Switzerland AG 2020
V. G. Duffy (Ed.): HCII 2020, LNCS 12198, pp. 95–105, 2020.
https://doi.org/10.1007/978-3-030-49904-4_7

According to the statistics published by Traffic Management Bureau of the Ministry of Public Security of China, in 2016, there were 50,400 truck-related road accidents nationwide, causing 25,000 deaths and 46,800 injuries, accounting for 30.5%, 48.23%, and 27.81% of the total car liability accidents, respectively. The number of truck accidents is much higher than that of trucks, and the consequences of heavy truck accidents are even more serious. The death rate and injury rate per vehicle for heavy trucks are much higher than for all types of vehicles (Mayhew et al. 2004). Fatigue is one of the important risk factors for major road traffic accidents in China (Liu et al. 2018). Poor ergonomic design of the cab can easily lead to driving fatigue. For instance, because of the unsuitable seat design, a large number of truck drivers feel tired and back uncomfortable very soon on road (Du et al. 2017). This kind of discomfort affects the drivers of heavy-duty trucks driving long distances even more seriously. In severe cases, it even impairs the driver's control of the vehicle.

In addition to road safety risks, another common risk among truck drivers is occupational injury. High rates of spinal disease, including neck and back pain, have been observed in professional drivers (Massaccesi et al. 2003; Okunribido et al. 2006; Okunribido 2016). Fatigue of the feet or other parts of the truck driver is also common (Du et al. 2017). The pain that causes occupational injuries may be caused by prolonged sitting, poor posture, body vibration, etc. (Robb et al. 2007). For example, poor seat design makes it easy for drivers to feel low back fatigue and discomfort. After a long period of accumulation of pain or fatigue, it may turn into chronic occupational musculoskeletal injury.

Strengthening the ergonomic design of the cab is an effective way to reduce driving fatigue and improve safety and health issues, while also improving the driving experience and satisfaction of the driver. Understanding the current situation of heavy truck cab ergonomic design will help to arouse people's attention to the ergonomics of the man-machine interface of the cab and solve the ergonomics problems in the design. Taking account of the driver's report and characteristics is an effective way to address the detailed defects of the ergonomic design in the truck cab.

Through interviews and questionnaire surveys with heavy-duty truck drivers, this paper obtains the characteristics of the professional heavy-duty truck drivers in China, their driving habits, and the detailed ergonomics design defects in the heavy truck cab. The research results are helpful to understand the group characteristics and needs of professional heavy truck drivers in China, as well as the current status of ergonomic design of heavy truck cabs, and provide references for targeted improvement of the human machine interface design of truck cabs.

2   Method

This study interviewed 9 heavy truck drivers firstly, and installed a driving recorder on the trucks of 6 of them to record their driving behavior for one day. Based on interviews and driving records, a questionnaire design was developed. Afterwards, in a logistics company in Beijing Daxing District and a heavy truck service area in Changping District, the quantitative questionnaire surveys were conducted using on-site questionnaires with one on one discussion. A total of 100 valid quantitative questionnaires were collected. Drivers participating in interviews and questionnaires must be professional heavy truck drivers with at least one year of driving experience in heavy trucks, and the truck weight must be at least 8 tons. Explain the purpose of the study to the driver before interviews and questionnaires to obtain their consent. The data used for analysis in this paper was from 100 questionnaires.

The primary topics in this investigation were as follows.

(1) Heavy truck driver group characteristics, including gender, age, height, weight, truck load, driving frequency, and driving mileage.
(2) Cab device ergonomics and driving experience, including seat belts (tightness, fix position), seat (height adjustment range, back and forth adjustment range, angle adjustment range, seat depth, width, back, headrest, lumbar support, seat hardness), pedals (pedal tilt angle, pedal step on depth, control force of pedal, the space between pedals), handles (the control force of handbrake and shift lever, the size of shift lever handle), steering wheel (outer diameter, grip diameter, height adjustment range, angle, feedback force, the block on the view field of the instrument panel), handbrake and shift lever (force of pulling, shifting handbrake and dimensions of shift lever handle), and others (mirror adjustment, blind spot area, entertainment system switch/adjustment button, air conditioning system switch/adjustment button, car lighting switch, glove box, first step height of stairs, distance between steps).

3 Results

3.1 Heavy Truck Driver Group Characteristics

The respondents of 100 valid questionnaires were all males. It also shows that among the participants of truck drivers, males have an absolute advantage in number. The age of the interviewed drivers was 34.6 ± 7.6 years, with young adults around 30 years old the most. Their response speed, strength, and bearing capacity were at the best level of human life. Increasing or decreasing with age, practitioners of truck driving became less.

The interviewed driver's height was 172.14 ± 4.86 cm. According to GB10000-88 "Chinese Adults Human Body Dimensions", adult males aged 18–60 have a P50 height of 167.8 cm and a P90 of 175.4 cm (GB10000-88 1988). Considering that the size of Chinese adults has increased in recent years, it can be judged that the height level of the respondents is medium to high.

The interviewed driver weighed 77.32 ± 9.22 kg. According to GB10000-88 "Chinese Adults Human Body Dimensions", adult males aged 18–60 have a P95 weight of 75 kg and a P99 of 83 kg (GB10000-88 1988). Considering that the body weight of Chinese adults has increased in recent years, it can be roughly judged that the respondents' weight level is medium to heavy.

Of the 100 respondents, the majority (88%) drove each day; 6% drove several times a week, 4% drove several times a month, and 2% drove several times a year. The mileage of more than 45,000 km in the past year accounted for nearly one-third, and the vast majority (99%) of the respondents had driven more than 5000 km in the past year, and only one had less than 5000 km. It can be seen that most of the respondents had high driving frequency and long mileage, and their views would be able to reflect the behavioral habits of truck drivers and the problems of heavy trucks.

3.2   Devices that Might Cause Fatigue or Discomfort

Overall Situation

Investigate devices that might cause fatigue or discomfort, such as seat belts, seats, truck driving and manipulation actuators. The main cab devices that respondents believed cause driving fatigue or discomfort were: seat belts (60%), seats (49%), accelerator pedal (11%), shift lever (8%), steering wheel (5%), brake pedal (3%), other devices (3%).

Seat Belts

Respondents mainly evaluated the using experience of seat belts based on tightness and upper fixed position. Total 79% of the respondents comment that seat belts were tight. 16% of the respondents felt the seat belts were so tight that make their neck uncomfortable; 63% of the respondents felt the seat belts were a little tight and they would be uncomfortable after wearing it for a long time.

Respondents were more satisfied with the position of the upper fixing point of the seat belt than tightness. Total 67% of the respondents indicated that the position of the upper fixing point of the seat belt was appropriate to ensure that the seat belt passed through the shoulder. But at the same time, 31% of the respondents felt that the position of the upper fixing point of the seat belt was too high and the seat belt pinched their neck; very few respondents (2%) felt that the position of the upper fixing point of the seat belt was too low to slip to the shoulder external.

Seat

Respondents evaluated seat satisfaction from seat shapes such as depth, width, seat back, headrest, waist back, and softness. More than half of the respondents were dissatisfied with the seat back for primary dissatisfaction on lumbar support (40%), seat hardness (24%), seat headrest (18%), seat back (14%), seat depth (13%), seat width (4%), others (4%).

Reasons for respondents' dissatisfaction with lumbar support included no lumbar support, the lumbar support was too concave, the support was insufficient, the back and waist (or shoulders and waist) could not lean on seat back simultaneously, the lumbar support was not adjustable or could not be adjusted to the correct position. These situation caused waist pain easily. Dissatisfaction with seat hardness was because the seat surface, seat back, and headrest are too hard. Dissatisfaction with the seat headrest was because the headrest's position was too far behind, the head was unstable on the headrest, the headrest's shape was too straight, cervical spine could not lean on, tired for neck hung up. Respondents were dissatisfied with the seat back because the seat back was too concave, the size was too small, the bottom was too backward, and the shoulders could not lean on the seat back when the waist lean on the seat back. Dissatisfaction with the seat depth was because the seat depth was too large or too small, could not sit to the end, waist was uncomfortable after long time sitting. Too narrow seat width had also caused dissatisfaction among a small number of respondents. Other dissatisfaction aspects included weak surrounding feeling, high seat height after airbag ventilation and could not be adjusted, stuffy and poor cab suspension.

In terms of seat adjustment range, 30% of the respondents indicated that the height adjustment range was small (the maximum adjustable height was not high enough or the minimum adjustable height was not low enough), and 39% of the respondents indicated that the front-to-back adjustment range was not appropriate (adjustable range is not big enough for forward and backward adjustment). Through the t-test, it was found that the respondent's evaluation of seat height, front-to-back adjustment range, and the height of the respondent had no significant relationship ($p > 0.05$). Because of the difference of individual body size and truck model, different respondents reported different reason for the same cab component. For example, the highest adjustable height of the seat is not high enough or the lowest adjustable height is not low enough. But no matter how the respondents evaluated, it reflected the mismatch between the size of the seat and the body of the respondent.

The Steering Wheel

Evaluations of the steering wheel's parameters (size, manipulation resistance force, adjustment range and position) were shown in Tables 1, 2, 3 and 4. It can be seen that, for the various parameters of the steering wheel, the respondents who evaluated the steering wheel as "appropriate" accounted for 3/5 to 4/5. The remaining respondents evaluated as "inappropriate", which mainly because they felt the outer diameter was oversized, the grip diameter was too small, manipulation resistance force was too heavy, and the height was not suitable.

Through the t-test, it was found that the respondents' evaluation of the opposite opinions on the outer diameter of the steering wheel had no significant relationship with the height of the respondents ($p > 0.05$). It also was found that the respondents' evaluation of steering wheel's grip diameter, manipulation resistance force, height adjustment range, forward and backward adjustment range had no significant relationship with respondents' height ($p > 0.05$).

Table 1. Evaluation of the steering wheel's size and manipulation force

Parameters	Evaluation		
	Appropriate	Oversized	Too small
Outer diameter	78%	17%	5%
Grasp diameter	61%	11%	28%
Manipulation resistance force	72%	23%	5%

Table 2. Evaluation of steering wheel's height adjustment range

Parameters	Evaluation			
	Suitable	Not high enough for maximum height	Not low enough for minimum height	Others
Height adjustment range	77%	9%	12%	2%

Table 3. Evaluation of steering wheel's forward and backward adjustment range

Parameters	Evaluation			
	Suitable	Not far enough from drivers' body	Not close enough from driver's body	Others
Forward and backward adjustment range	89%	6%	3%	2%

Table 4. Evaluation of steering wheel's position

Parameters	Evaluation				
	Suitable	Not suitable in relative position with pedal	Not suitable in relative position with seats	Not suitable tilt angle	Not Suitable height
Position	74%	2%	5%	6%	13%

Pedals

The evaluation indicators of the pedals included the pedal tilt angle, the pedal step on depth, the control force of pedal, and the space between pedals.

There were separately 83%, 86%, 89% respondents who were satisfied with accelerator, brake and clutch pedal. Detailed evaluation is shown in Table 5. There was no significant difference in the height of respondents in different evaluations for tilt angle of accelerator, brake and clutch pedal ($p > 0.05$).

Table 5. Evaluation of pedals tilt angle

Parameters	Evaluation		
	Suitable	Oversized	Too small
Accelerator pedal	83%	8%	9%
Brake pedal	86%	5%	9%
Clutch pedal	90%	8%	2%

Total 78%, 85%, and 84% of the respondents considered the three pedals of the accelerator, brake, and clutch to be suitable for step on, and a small number of respondents considered them inappropriate, as shown in Table 6. Respondents who gave different evaluations of accelerator, clutch and brake pedal step on depths had no significant difference in height (p > 0.05).

Table 6. Evaluation of pedals step on depth

Parameters	Evaluation		
	Suitable	Oversized	Too small
Accelerator pedal	78%	11%	11%
Brake pedal	85%	8%	7%
Clutch pedal	84%	12%	4%

The evaluation results of the distance between the accelerator pedal and the brake pedal showed that about 10% of the respondents thought the horizontal distance between the two was too small and about 10% of the respondents thought the height distance was too large. The rest of 80% respondents thought distance between accelerator and brake pedal was appropriate.

For the evaluation of the force on the three pedals of the accelerator, brake, and clutch, 13% of the respondents felt that the force on the accelerator pedal was too heavy, and 34% of them felt it was slightly heavy and felt uncomfortable when stepping on it frequently. Thence total 47% of the respondents felt that the force on the accelerator pedal was on heavy side. Nearly 40% of the respondents felt that the force on the brake pedal and clutch pedal was too heavy or slightly heavy, and among them, those who felt too heavy accounted for nearly 10%. Take the evaluation of "suitable" respondents as a benchmark, the t-test showed that there was no significant difference (p > 0.05) in driver's age between respondents who evaluated with "too heavy", "slightly heavy" and "suitable" on accelerator pedal force and clutch pedal force. There was significant difference (p < 0.05) in driver's age between respondents who evaluated on brake pedal force. Besides, on other aspects like driver's height, weight, and the truck weight, there were no significant difference (p > 0.05) between respondents who evaluated with "too heavy", "slightly heavy" and "suitable" on the three type of pedals. It indicated that the evaluation of the pedaling force (too heavy or slightly heavy) had no significant relationship with the respondent's physical characteristics and the weight of the truck. Significant difference in age on evaluation of brake pedal force was that age of respondents who evaluated with "too heavy" was 29.63 ± 4.60 years old, and age of respondents who evaluated with "suitable" was 34.66 ± 7.96 years old. As a result, young people tended to prefer pedals with less force.

Handbrake and Shift Lever
The Evaluation of the pull handbrake force, the shifting force and the dimension of shift lever handle are shown in Table 7.

It can be seen that the vast majority (96%) of the respondents reported that the force for pulling the handbrake was appropriate.

About 30% of the respondents reported that the shifting force of shifting lever was inappropriate and too heavy. By t-test, there was no significant differences in the weight and age of the respondents who evaluated the shifting forces as "large" and "suitable" ($p > 0.05$). However, there was significant difference in truck weight ($p < 0.001$) The truck weight was $18.36 \pm 7.60t$ for those who evaluated with "heavy". And the truck weight was $24.89 \pm 8.65t$ for those who evaluated with "suitable".

Table 7. Evaluation of handbrake and shift lever

Parameters	Evaluation		
	Suitable	Heavy	Light
Handbrake force	96%	2%	2%
Shift lever force	70%	28%	2%
Shift lever dimensions	86%	10%	4%

Relatively, fewer respondents evaluated the shift lever handle dimension as inappropriateness. A total of 14% of the respondents considered it inappropriate, of which 10% thought it was too large and 4% thought it was too small. Through t-test, there was no significant difference in the height of the respondents whose evaluation on the shift lever handle dimension was "too large" or "too small" compared with "suitable" respondents ($p > 0.05$).

Vision

In terms of internal vision, the steering wheel might obstruct the view of the dashboard. Regarding this issue, more than half (54%) of the respondents said that the steering wheel would cover the dashboard, and the other half (46%) said the steering wheel would not cover the dashboard.

In terms of external vision, more than half of the respondents (51%) indicated that there was a large blind spot, and the other half (49%) indicated that there was no large blind spot. The locations of the blind spots selected by the respondents who indicated there were larger blind spots are shown in Table 8. It can be seen that near the front wheels on both sides (zone A and B) were the most reflected blind spots. Among them, more than half of the respondents believed that there were blind spots near the right front wheels (zone A). In addition, about 10% of the respondents reflected there were blind spots at the rear (zone D) and front (zone C) of the truck.

Table 8. Position of external blind spots

Position	Zone A (near the right front wheel)	Zone B (near the left front wheel)	Zone C (directly in front of the truck)	Zone D (truck side rear)	Others
Schematic diagram					-
Respondent Number	56	19	11	14	5

4 Conclusions and Recommendations

According to the survey results of the truck driving experience of the interviewees, it could be concluded that the current truck cab components, including seat belts, seats, steering wheels, accelerators, brakes and clutch pedals, and shift levers, had varying degrees of ergonomic weakness. The main reasons were as following.

- tight seat belts, uncomfortable and stretched to the neck;
- uncomfortable lumbar support, hard seat surface, uncomfortable headrest and backrest, improper seat depth, small seat width;
- large outside diameter of steering wheel, small grip diameter, heavy steering resistance, inappropriate height;
- inappropriate tilt angle of the accelerator and brake pedal, inappropriate step on depth of the brake and clutch pedal, inappropriate distance between accelerator pedal and brake pedal;
- heavy shifting force, inappropriate dimension of the shift lever handle.

According to the proportion of problems feedback by respondents, the ergonomic design of the heavy truck cab should be optimized from the following aspects:

(1) the body size of truck drivers should be used as a design basis. Truck drivers are mainly young men, and the height and weight of the Chinese population have generally increased in recent years. These physical features should be considered seriously.

(2) Reduce the bondage force of the seat belt appropriately to avoid the over-tightening seat belt.

(3) The design of lumbar support, headrest (detachable), seat back, and seat depth should be adapted to the driver's body curve (especially the back curve) of different statures, and the adjustable range should be set to meet the needs of different drivers. widen the width of the seat. Increase the softness of the seat back and seat surface.

(4) Reduce the outside diameter of the steering wheel. Increase the grip diameter. At the same time, reduce the operating resistance, and increase the height adjustable range.
(5) Reduce the pedaling force of the accelerator, brake and clutch pedals, appropriately enlarge the horizontal distance and reduce the vertical height between accelerator and brake pedals, and consider both safety and comfort.
(6) Reduce the operating force of the shift lever and reduce the size of the shift lever handle appropriately.

In addition to the above issues that need to be improved, the respondents also put forward some open opinions and suggestions on the cab of the truck. The main appeals are as follows:

(1) Optimize the overall space layout of the cab, make the design more humane, and expand the cab space; increase the sleeping space, improve the bunk space, especially the upper bunk space; make the sleeping board folded to release more space when not in use for sleep.
(2) Make the operation be automatic, so as to let driving more effortless.
(3) In terms of environment, improve cab insulation, thermal insulation effect, reduce noise, and improve shock absorption effect (such as using suspension support or improving air bag).
(4) Need for auxiliary functions, including increasing the glove box in the truck (such as a glove box), adding on-board technology (such as car Bluetooth, driving recorder, mobile phone charging function), and improving the entertainment system.

Acknowledgement. This research was supported by National Natural Science Foundation of China (project number 71601007) and President Foundation of China National Institute of Standardization (project number 522018Y-5984).

References

Mayhew, D.R., Simpson, H.M., Beirness, D.J.: Report: heavy trucks and road crashes. Traffic Injury Research Foundation, Ottawa, Ontario, Canada (2004)
Du, J., Lu, H., Sun, W., Zhang, X., Hu, H., Liu, Y.: Investigation on driving habits of Chinese truck driver. In: Stephanidis, C. (ed.) HCI 2017. CCIS, vol. 713, pp. 526–531. Springer, Cham (2017). https://doi.org/10.1007/978-3-319-58750-9_73
GB10000-88: Chinese Adults Human Body Dimensions. State Bureau of Technical Supervision (1988)
Liu, G., et al.: Risk factors for extremely serious road accidents: results from national road accident statistical annual report of China. PLoS One 13(8) (2018)
Massaccesi, M., Pagnotta, A., Soccetti, A., Masali, M., Masiero, C., Greco, F.: Investigation of work-related disorders in truck drivers using RULA method. Appl. Ergon. 34(4), 303–307 (2003)

Okunribido, O.O., Magnusson, M., Pope, M.: Delivery drivers and low-back pain: a study of the exposures to posture demands, manual materials handling and whole-body vibration. Int. J. Ind. Ergon. **36**(3), 265–273 (2006)

Okunribido, O.O.: An investigation of posture and manual materials handling as risk factors for low back pain in delivery drivers. Ergon. Soc. S. Afr. **28**(2), 19–27 (2016)

Robb, M.J.M., Mansfield, N.J.: Self-reported musculoskeletal problems amongst occupational truck drivers. Ergonomics **50**(6), 814–827 (2007)

Design Methods for Human-Robot-Interaction

Nadja Fischer[1]([✉]) and Oliver Sträter[2]

[1] Volkswagen Group Components, Kassel, Germany
nadja.fischer@volkswagen.de
[2] University of Kassel, Kassel, Germany

Abstract. An experimental set-up was made to measure a human's reaction to a cooperating robot. The conclusion is a proposal of construction methods regarding layout, production planning and path planning of the robot.

1 Introduction

The recent generation of robots is enabled to renounce on the necessity of a safety fence and are hence capable of acting within the workspace of the industrial worker. For the implementation of human-robot-interaction (HRI) the use of small and light-weight robots is more common than the use of conventional industrial robots. The safety fence is replaced by a cluster of sensors that measure any interaction with and proximity to humans. What is the impact on the industrial worker?

This is the question that is assessed in this paper. As a theoretical basis, the characteristics of human-robot-interaction will be shown. The crucial characteristics will be selected and assessed during an experimental set-up with a statistically appropriate number of participants in interaction with a lightweight robot. Through both, objective and subjective measuring methods, the impact of distance, angle, and speed on humans is shown. The experimental set-up allows the separation and analysis of seven different directions of movements and their effect on the test subject. The highest level of attention is generated by movements towards the participants and any movement close to the subject.

The specific effect on the subject is measured via an eye-tracking system. The subject's eye movement allows the prediction of concentration, stress, and anxiety of the participants. In addition, the eye-tracking-system is guided by a questionnaire, specifically developed for the experimental set-up.

The conclusions of this paper are formed into recommendations for planning engineers' und robot programmers in order to optimize their HRI lay-outs. With a human-focused approach, the acceptance of HRI will be improved for the operators. To achieve a high level of acceptance, the movements of the robot must be perceived as predictable and familiar to the operator. This will reduce the additional stress and distraction that is caused by the proximity of a robot (Fischer 2019).

© Springer Nature Switzerland AG 2020
V. G. Duffy (Ed.): HCII 2020, LNCS 12198, pp. 106–118, 2020.
https://doi.org/10.1007/978-3-030-49904-4_8

2 Characteristics and Methods

First, the human-robot-interaction is subdivided into three components: the human, the robot and the surrounding workspace. Second, the particular characteristics of the human, such as the cognition of stress, concentration, and distraction, are further subdivided. Third, the relevant attributes of the robot are defined as direction, model and autonomy of its path planning. In addition, since the workspace connects the human with the robot, distance and angle with respect to the workplace's layout are considered.

The methods selected to gather information about those characteristics are a questionnaire and an eye-tracking system that measures eye- and pupil movements. An academic questionnaire consists of a systematic generation and recording disclosure (Döring and Bortz 2016, p. 398). Furthermore, the eye movement is selected insofar being a physiological characteristic of stress (Lysaght et al. 1989, p. 145). Specifically, the participant's attention is indicated by the eye-movement, which can be either deliberate or impulse-driven (Posner 1980, p. 21). Every kind of distraction delays attention and interrupts a current activity (Müller et al. 2015, p. 36). In this regard eye movement is considered as an indicator of human perception.

2.1 Definitions

The human-robot-interaction (HRI) consists of two participants that are brought together in a new environment, a new kind of an industrial workspace.

On the one hand, an HRI requires an industrial worker who is conventionally appointed in tasks that require a high amount of flexibility as well as a situational awareness.

On the other hand, a new generation of robots is needed for an HRI. In a classic industrial environment, a robot is placed behind a safety fence and is known as an automat that follows programmed control sequences in order to serve its mechanical work pattern (Duden 2017). The robot's advantages are speed, endurance, and precision.

When these two participants come together in a new industrial setting called human-robot-interaction, four different possibilities are permitted by international standardization (DIN EN ISO 10218 2012, p. 46). Most robots for HRI that are purchased on the industrial market, are usable for the third possibility of human-robot-interaction: the use of a robot with reduced speed and force. In this type of HRI physical contacts between human and robot is allowed under certain conditions. These are expressed by a draft for development (ISO TS 15066 2017).

This paper refers to a robotic system used with limited speed and force.

2.2 Characteristics

In order to analyze an HRI, it's three components, which are human, robot and workspace, are assessed individually. Furthermore, these three aspects are presented by their characteristics that can be used for description and as an adjusting screw (Fig. 1).

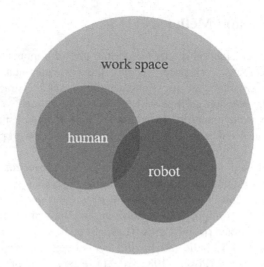

Fig. 1. Characteristics of a human-robot-interaction

The robots can be described by their technical execution, shape, availability and sensitivity.

In detail, the technical execution of a robot manipulator establishes a basis for the robot's field of application. Motor current control as well as several integrated sensors can control the robotic movements. Additional external sensors, such as photo-sensors or cameras can be used. The technical execution poses an immediate impact on the robot's level of sensitivity. Typical robots in human-robot-interaction consist of six or seven axes of movement. Moreover, the shape of the robot is an important factor for HRI (Bendel 2017, p. 31). The shape is defined by the color, the volume, the material, the similarity to a human's behavior and the robot gripper. In particular, the volume and the material have an impact on a co-working human. Robots for HRI usually are lightweight in comparison to their conventional relatives. Sometimes the outside of the robot is covered with a soft material, possibly with tactile or capacitive sensors (De Santis et al. 2007, p. 255). Furthermore, the similarity between robots and the human becomes important since cute and humanoid robots often achieve a higher level of acceptance among workers (Hinds et al. 2004, p. 174; Blume 2014, p. 73). In this context, the phenomenon of the uncanny valley should be taken into consideration (Mori 2012, p. 1).

The robot's gripper commonly presents a technological challenge. A gripper can be electrically or pneumatically powered, consists of two or more gripper fingers, a suction process by vacuum or another special and process-driven solution. The robot gripper is often considered the main component used to make close contact with the human. Therefore, it should be carefully chosen for an HRI implementation.

Particularly with regard to the human, a distinguished range of characteristics is to be considered. The human perceives a robot with all his sensory perceptions, for instance, the sense of sight, movement and hearing (Zühlke 2012, p. 227). This input of senses leads to the human's process of cognition and may result in a psychological reaction (Sträter 2005, p. 108; Thiemermann 2005, p. 19). The cognitive reaction is on a large scale contingent on the human's practical experience and memory. Accordingly, a negative experience with a (classical) robot is the most important factor that precludes an industrial worker from interacting with a robot in an HRI (Nomura et al. 2005, p. 2).

The human worker should always be treated according to his characteristics, by way of example, the age, educational background and physique (Rumsch et al. 2014, p. 20; European Commission 2012, p. 4). Within the scope of HRI manifold transformation in a job specification are possible, which can have influence over required qualifications, process quality and sequences of operations. Consequently, a social- and human-based integration of an HRI is obligatory (cf. Ortmann and Guhlke 2014, p. 1).

Notably, the communication between robot and human exerts influences on the human's sense of physiology, like his acceptance, motivation, and level of stress as well as his perceived control of the robot system (Holzträger 2012, p. 97; Reich and Eyssel 2013, p. 124; Nomura et al. 2005).

Both presented partners are brought together in a new environment, the industrial workspace. This workspace can be described by surrounding production conditions, for instance, temperature, noise, vibration and further industrial factors. Moreover, the workspace includes a multitude of characteristics to variegate and control the HRI.

Within the workspace, the relationship and extent of HRI are defined.

Through the geometry of the industrial layout, the distance between robot and human is controlled; and so is the likelihood of contact between the two partners (Arai et al. 2010). This characteristic should be regulated in direct conjunction with the kinetic behavior of the robot, for example, the speed, angle, and time of movement, direction of movement and autonomy of the robot (Thiemermann 2005, p. 47, 76).

In regard to this, the communication between robots and humans is existential. Notably, the robot's behavior should always be predictable and understandable to the human worker and at best possess a high level of usability (Thiemermann 2005, p. 46; Schmitz and Reckter 2019, p. 20). Moreover, the behavior of the human should be as well predictable to the robot and at its best perceived by sensors to avoid unnecessary contacts (Rüdiger and Reckter 2017, p. 18).

Above these characteristics, the safety and security of the complete human-robot-interaction is the crucial criterion (DGUV 2016, p. 2).

2.3 Methods

The experimental procedure, presented later in this survey, is designed to measure a participant's encroachment during the interaction with a robot. This experiment is likely suitable for an eye-tracking system and a questionnaire.

The eye-tracking system records the movement of the eye and therefore selected focal points, the so-called areas of interest (AOIs). The duration of fixation on an area of interest indicates the proband's concentration or distraction.

The eye-movements are classified into 'fixation' and 'saccades'. Fixation indicates a longer concentration on a fixed point, whereas saccades indicate short and erratic eye movements serving as an exploration of the environment or distraction by stimulus.

The duration of fixation on an area of interest indicates the participant's concentration or distraction. Throughout the saccades no concentration is possible.

Furthermore, the system collects data concerning the eye-blink response and pupil diameter. These three indicators can demonstrate the participant's strain during the experiment (Pfendler 1990, p. 159; Lysaght et al. 1989, pp. 144–145) by pointing out the participant's reaction to the robot.

The impartial measurement is accompanied by a questionnaire consisting of five categories. Two parts are to be answered before the experiment and the other three after the practical experience. The first part contains general information about the participant, for instance, his age, gender or status of employment. These are followed by questions regarding the participant's general experience in operating robots (Ortmann and Guhlke 2014, p. 20). After the procedure the NASA TLX (a well-established questionnaire) is used to gather information concerning the participant's stress and strain during the experiment (Pfendler 1993, p. 28). The fourth part of the questionnaire outlines the participant's opinion on robots. These questions are linked to the second part and should point out a change of mind caused by the experiment. A short fifth part of open questions concludes the questionnaire.

3   Test Phase

Prior to the actual survey, pilot surveys illustrate a significant degree of attention if the robot moves within the direct field of view. Movements in the peripheral perspective are causing a reduced degree of attention. Similarly, a reduction in the distance between the robot and the participant decreases the level of concentration. A recommended distance between human and robot is derived from the zones of interpersonal distances defined for human interaction (Hall 1966, p. 116).

For the main test phase, forty participants have been invited. The experimental set-up consists of a monitor screen, a model of a production line and a lightweight robot with a robot-gripper. The robot type is "KUKA LBR iiwa" with a payload of 14 kg.

The participants start their experiment by tapping a key on the monitor screen. Thereupon the production line starts its process, the filling of a box with small items. The process is composed of a separation, transportation on a flat conveyor, assembly and verification by an industrial camera. The participant's task is the supervision of the process.

After the camera inspection, the robot starts moving. Its first path heads directly to the machine, at a right angle to the participant. The robot picks up the work-piece and moves directly to the participants. The participant extracts the work-piece by a light push on the lower side of the robot-gripper. Following a short halt, the robot retracts back into its starting position.

The evaluation of the experiment identifies significant variances of the perception of the different robot movements. Specifically, the movement towards the participant, the waiting time until interaction with the participant and the halt after the interaction present a significant level of distraction.

As the speed of a robot movement is already extensively analyzed, the existing deliverables are integrated into the test concepts (Arai et al. 2010, p. 7; Koppenborg et al. 2013, p. 417). Moreover, the speed of the test robots is compliance with the excepted limits of speed and force (ISO TS 15066).

Both, the robot and the production line, equally draw the attention of the participant when they are in motion.

3.1   Pre-tests

A series of short pre-tests explores important factors of HRI in advance. These simple tests concentrate on only one characteristic. Whereby a definitive statement on the influence can be made.

All pre-testings' regard the participant's distraction. However, different impacts are tested. First, distraction is measured through a variety of angles and differences in distances between the robot and the human. These two characteristics are compared in a horizontal and vertical plane. The final pre-test studies an autonomic robot vehicle in a gear box production line.

The first comparison is about changing the distance and angle between the positions of robot and human. Three different positions point out an increasing distraction as a result of the decreasing distance and the peripheral robot motion. At the beginning of the experiment, the robot is located in the direct field of view of the participant (0°). The first step reduces the distance between the robot and the participant from a social distance to a personal distance (Hall 1966, p. 116). This change of distance leads to a slight increase in both, the fixation and the saccades. The second step relocates the robot outside the direct field of view in a peripheral angle to the participant (60°). Consequently, the saccades increase approximately to double the quantity.

These changes in distance and angle are solely located in one horizontal level. In a separate experimental setup, this contemplation is resolved with an observation of changing line-ups at a vertical level. Therefore, the head of the participant is defined as the center point of the setup. Accordingly, six different center points for a robot movement are tested. These points vary the distance between human and robot in the horizontal level from a personal distance to an intimate distance as well as the vertical level. In addition, the positions are classified in the direct vertical field of view. The examination of the eye-data demonstrates a distraction as a result of reduced distance at both levels. Nevertheless, the horizontal proximity of the robot leads to a stronger reaction than the reduced vertical distance.

The final pre-test shows a participant's reaction to an autonomous driving cleaning robot that is located in a production line. According to the autonomous navigation, the movement of the vehicle is sporadic and not predictable. Moreover, the workers' perception is intensified by the novelty of the robot as the test procedure was conducted on the date of the robot's integration and thus, is completely new to the industrial workers in the production line.

The experiment is subdivided into two parts. The first part was conducted directly after the implementation, while the second part was executed three hours after the robot was brought into service. During the first part, the average duration of fixations is 350 ms per fixation and the average number of saccades is 1,36 saccades per minute. In the second part of this testing, the average duration of fixation reduces to 200 ms per fixation and the average number of saccades increases to 2,88 saccades per minute. The comparison of these test parts shows two changes. While the average duration of fixations reduces by 41%, the number of saccades per minute increases by 53%. These outcomes do not allow an inference of the adaption during the two parts of the experiment. Nevertheless, the increase of saccades indicates that the participant's exercise control by an awareness of the robot's position. This assumption is supported by an impulse-driven eye-movement whenever the robot enters the participant's direct point of view. Moreover, the participant likely explores the last noted robot position notwithstanding the robot already moved. Due to the interrupted concentration during a saccade, a reduction of concentration on the assignment can be assumed for the participant.

Furthermore, the average number of fixations bears comparison with the other pre-tests wherein a six-axis robot manipulator is established.

These first experimentally obtained conclusions are the basis for the arrangement of the main test.

3.2   Main Test

The main experimental setup contains a seven-axis KUKA robot and the model of a small production line. Forty participant s participated in the test. The participants are of the approximate age of 38. Nine of them were female, and 31 were male. The work-space of 25 participants is located directly in a production area. The main occupational groups are maintenance, production planning and industrial working.

A schematic description of the main test can be found in the following Fig. 2:

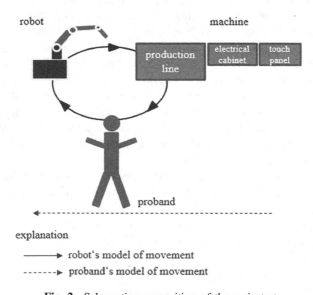

Fig. 2. Schematic composition of the main test

The beginning of the experiment is established by the participant pressing a button on the touch panel. Thereupon, different production steps, such as, decollating, hoisting and assembly occur. Depending on correct manufacturing and verification through an inspection camera the work-piece is presented for release. By reaching this position the work-piece triggers a photoelectric relay. Hence, a signal is sent to the robot through the programmable logic control (PLC) and the robot begins its movement across the participant and straight to the production line. After the work-piece is gripped by the robot, the robot moves frontal towards the participant and presents the work-piece for withdrawal. Through a light touch on the underside of the robot-gripper, the gripper opens its grab jaws. Thus, the participant takes over the work-piece. Subsequently, the robot closes its gripper fingers and moves backward until it eventually reaches its base position.

An illustration of the cycle of the robot's movement is clearly represented in Fig. 3:

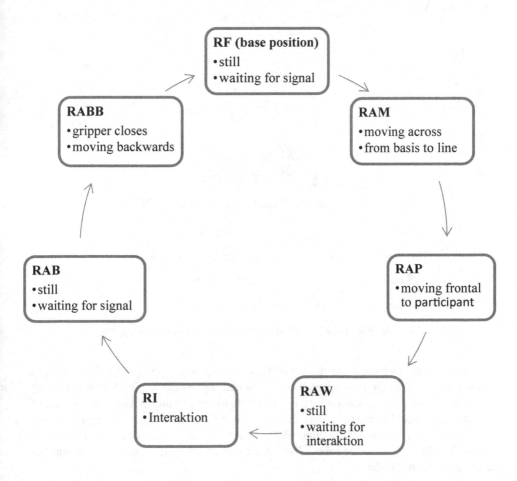

Fig. 3. Circle of the robot's movement

The evaluation of the pupil data compares all seven models of the robot's movement to each other. Therefore, the following charts present boxplots with the dispersion of the pupil data (duration of fixations on the y-axis) against the Areas of Interest (AOIs on the x-axis). For instance, two robot movements are presented in detail and compared to each other.

The robot's movement across the participant is chosen as a reference considering this movement appears neutral and comfortable to the participant. As shown in Fig. 4, this movement is characterized by a natural perception of the environment. Hence, the eye movement is apportioned among many AOIs and administered almost evenly across the AOIs.

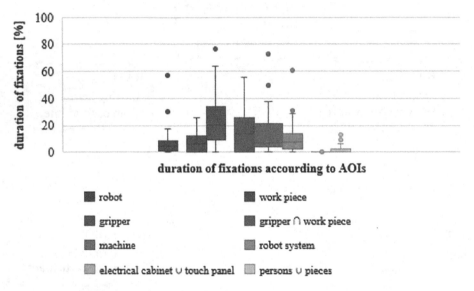

Fig. 4. Participant's AOIs during the robot's movement across

Hereinafter, in contrast to the robot's movement across the proband, the robot's movement towards the participant is contemplated. Specifically, Fig. 5 shows a highly concentrated eye movement on merely two AOIs as the distance between the robot and human decreases. For the most part, the participant focuses on the robot gripper and on the work-piece. This can be explained by a planning eye movement and the gripper being the closest part of the robot. The other areas of interest, such as the surrounding area, are circumstantial.

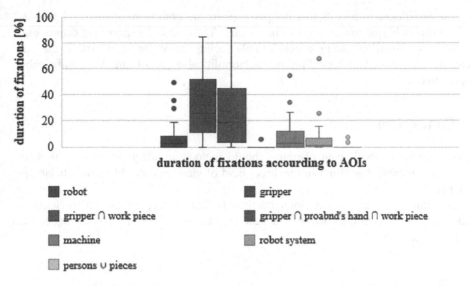

Fig. 5. Participant's AOIs during the robot's movement frontal

A statistical evaluation should classify the presented robot movements. More precisely, the test is carried out because a statistically relevant discrepancy concerning the duration of fixation is expected.

Therefore, the difference between the values are calculated and a paired comparison is realized. The critical t-value is 1,796 and the level of significance is $\alpha = 0,05$. The t-value of the robot movement towards the participant is 2,0868 and is thus above the critical t-value. This is confirmed by the comparison of the p-value to the level of significance. More precisely, a significant change in the duration of fixation of the robot's movement towards the participant is measured in comparison to the robot's movement across the participant.

Equally, the robot's waiting time before the interaction and the waiting time before the movement backwards as well as the movement backwards itself significantly diverge from the robot's movement across the participant.

While the robot is standing still and interacting with the human, the level of significance is comparable to the reference movement.

Anyhow, the participant's concentration on the moving work-piece during the production process is compared to the concentration on the robot manipulator moving towards the participant. Certainly, the work-piece gathers 90% and the moving robot 88% of the participant's concentration. With this in mind, the robot's attraction seems to refer to the movement itself.

As previously stated, the pupil diameter is measured and evaluated. The results of the test show that the diameter changes due to miosis and mydriasis. The approximately smallest diameter is measured while the robot is outside of the participant's field of view. And the approximately largest diameter is captured during the participant's preparation for interaction with the robot. Unfortunately, no statistically relevant change is gathered.

The questionnaire reveals that the participants are both technologically interested and positively biased towards robots in general. The practical experiment causes only minor stress. Notwithstanding a comfortable feeling during the experiment, the participants are discordant regarding the sociopolitical topic of the increasing robot population.

4 Conclusions

In conclusion, a robot's path planning should include an adequate distance from an interacting human, should run in the direct field of view and should include balancing distance.

In addition to this, the questionnaire reveals four characteristics that participants, with high acceptance rates towards a new robot system, inherit: young, male, low negative bias and tall.

5 Outlook

At the present time, human-robot-interaction is still a specifically case in an industrial environment (Schmitz and Reckter 2019, p. 21). Due to the changes in engineering standards, machine manufacturers and end-users are restrained by uncertainty. Moreover, the commercial consideration is difficult since the integration of an HRI is usually of a high payback period because soft facts can scarcely be consulted (Bauer et al. 2016, p. 22).

For a resoundingly success, the technical specifications concerning HRI must allow more flexibility regarding the robot's path planning (cf. Ostermann 2014, p. 12). Simultaneously, technical sensors should increase safety and security. This may lead to an autonomous path planning due to the robot's artificial intelligence (Siegert and Bocionek 1996, p. 97). A situation-based robot could move according to the human's distance, angle and a human's supposed future movements. However, the movement may not be unpredictable to the human.

Eventually, the robot will be an intelligent and comfortable coworker to the industrial worker.

Disclaimer. The results, opinions and conclusion of this thesis are not necessarily those of Volkswagen AG.

References

Arai, T., Kato, R., Fujita, M.: Assessment of operator stress induced by robot collaboration in assembly. CIRP Ann. – Manuf. Technol. **59**, 5–8 (2010)

Bauer, W., Bender, M., Braun, M., Rally, P., Scholtz, O.: Leichtbauroboter in der manuellen Montage - einfach einfach anfangen. Fraunhofer-Institut für Arbeitswirtschaft und Organisation IAO, Stuttgart (2016)

Bendel, O.: Co-Robots und Co. – Entwicklungen und Trends bei Industrierobotern. Netzwoche **09**, 30–31 (2017)

Blume, J.: Methoden und Anwendungen zur intuitiven Mensch-Roboter-Interaktion. Technischen Universität München, München (2014)

De Santis, A., Siciliano, B., De Luca, A., Bicchi, A.: An atlas of physical human-robot interaction. Mech. Mach. Theory **43**, 253–270 (2007). http://www.centropiaggio.unipi.it/sites/default/files/softarm-MMT.pdf. Accessed 20 Apr 2015

Deutsche Gesetzliche Unfallversicherung: DGUV-Information: Sicherheitsbezogene Betriebsarten an spanenden Werkzeugmaschinen der Metallbearbeitung. DGUV, Mainz (2016)

Deutsches Institut für Normung: DIN EN ISO 10218 Teil 1 und 2. Industrieroboter – Sicherheitsanforderungen. Beuth Verlag GmbH, Berlin (2012)

Deutsches Institut für Normung: ISO/TS 15066. Roboter und Robotikgeräte – Kollaborierende Roboter. DIN-Normenausschuss Maschinenbau, Vernier, Geneva (2017)

Döring, N., Bortz, J.: Forschungsmethoden und Evaluation in den Sozial- und Humanwissenschaften. Springer, Heidelberg (2016). https://doi.org/10.1007/978-3-642-41089-5

Duden: Duden: Roboter (2017). http://www.duden.de/rechtschreibung/Roboter. Accessed 30 Jan 2017

European Commission: Einstellung der Öffentlichkeit zu Robotern. Spezial Eurobarometer 382 (2012). http://ec.europa.eu/publicopinion/index.en.htm. Accessed 11 Sept 2015

Fischer, N.: Methoden zur Auslegung einer Mensch-Roboter-Kooperation. Universität Kassel, Kassel (2019)

Hall, E.T.: The Hidden Dimensions. Garden City. Anchor Books as Doubleday Anchor Books, New York (1966)

Hinds, P., Roberts, T.L., Jones, H.: Whose job is it anyway? A study of human-robot interaction in a collaborative task. In: Human-Computer Interaction, pp. 151–181. Lawrence Erlbaum Associates Inc., United States (2004)

Holzträger, D.: Gesundheitsförderliche Mitarbeiterführung - Gestaltung von Maßnahmen der betrieblichen Gesundheitsförderung für Führungskräfte. Rainer Hampp Verlag, Mering (2012)

Koppenborg, M., Lungfiel, A., Naber, B., Nickel, P.: Auswirkung von Autonomie und Geschwindigkeit in der virtuellen Mensch-Roboter-Kollaboration. In: Gesellschaft für Arbeitswissenschaft (ed.) Chancen durch Arbeits-, Produkt- und Systemgestaltung, pp. 417–420. GfA-Press, Krefeld (2013)

Lysaght, R., Hill, S.G., Dick, A.O.: Technical Report 851 - Operator Workload: Comprehensive Review and Evaluation of Operator Workload Methodologies. U.S. Army Research Institute, Fort Bliss, Texas (1989)

Mori, M.: The Uncanny Valley: The Original Essey by Masahiro Mori (translated by MacDorman & Minato). Robotics & Automation Magazine, June 2012. https://spectrum.ieee.org/automaton/robotics/humanoids/the-uncanny-valley

Müller, H.J., Krummennacher, J., Schubert, T.: Aufmerksamkeit und Handlungssteuerung - Grundlagen für die Anwendung. Springer, Heidelberg (2015). https://doi.org/10.1007/978-3-642-41825-9

Nomura, T., Kanda, T., Suzuki, T.: Experimental investigation into influence of negative attitudes toward robots on human-robot interaction. Springer, London (2005). http://citeseerx.ist.psu.edu/viewdoc/download?doi=10.1.1.59.6397&rep=rep1&type=pdf. Accessed 03 Jan 2019

Ortmann, U., Guhlke, B.: Konzepte zur sozial- und humanverträglichen Gestaltung von Industrie 4.0 (2014). http://www.unibielefeld.de/soz/las/TA/itsowl/. Accessed 04 Nov 2016

Ostermann, B.: Entwicklung eines Konzepts zur sicheren Personenerfassung als Schutzeinrichtung an kollaborierenden Robotern (2014). http://nbn-resolving.de/urn/resolver.pl?urn=urn%3Anbn%3Ade%3Ahbz%3A468-20140702-113540-2. Accessed 11 Sep 2015

Pfendler, C.: Zur Messung der mentalen Beanspruchung mit dem NASA-Task Load Index. Zeitschrift für Arbeitswissenschaft, 158–163 (1990)

Pfendler, C.: Vergleich der Zwei-Ebenen-Intensitäts-Skala und des NASA Task Load Index bei der Beanspruchungsbewertung während Lernvorgängen. Z. Arbeitswissenschaft **47**, 26–33 (1993)

Posner, M.: Orienting of attention. Q. J. Exp. Psychol. **32**, 3–25 (1980)

Reich, N., Eyssel, F.: Attitudes towards service robots in domestic environments: the role of personality characteristics, individual interests, and demographic variables. Paladyn – J. Behav. Robot. **4**(2), 123–130 (2013)

Rüdiger, A.: Was tun, wenn die Roboter kommen? CIOBRIEFING - Technology-Update für IT-Manager **8**, 18–21 (2017)

Rumsch, W.-C., Kruse, D.J., Köhler, F.: Technology Watch Studie: Roboter in Kooperation: Mensch - Roboter - Produkt. Innovationsgesellschaft für fortgeschrittene Produktionssysteme in der Fahrzeugindutsrie mgH, Berlin (2014)

Schmitz, W., Reckter, B.: Riskante neue Arbeitswelt. VDI Nachrichten **9**, 1(2019)

Siegert, H.-J., Bocionek, S.: Robotik: Programmierung Intelligenter Roboter. Springer, Heidelberg (1996). https://doi.org/10.1007/978-3-642-80067-2

Sträter, O.: Cognition and Safety - An Integrated Approach to Systems Design and Assessment. Ashgate, Hampshire (2005)

Thiemermann, S.: Direkte Mensch-Roboter-Kooperation in der Kleinteilemontage mit einem SCARA-Roboter. Jost-Jetter Verlag, Heimsheim (2005)

Zühlke, D.: Nutzergerechte Entwicklung von Mensch-Maschine-Systemen. Springer, Heidelberg (2012). https://doi.org/10.1007/978-3-642-22074-6

Research Project beyondSPAI - The Safe and Reliable Monitoring of Adaptive Safety Zones in the Proximity of Collaborating Industrial Robots Using an Intelligent InGaAs Camera System

Christof Hammer[✉] and Norbert Jung

University of Applied Sciences Bonn-Rhein-Sieg, Grantham-Allee 20,
53757 Sankt Augustin, Germany
{christof.hammer,norbert.jung}@h-brs.de
https://isf.h-brs.de

Abstract. Collaborative industrial robots are becoming increasingly costefficent for manufacturing companies. While these systems can be of great help for the human coworker, they simultaneously pose a serious health hazard, if safety measures are implemented inadequately. Conventional safety equipment like fences or light curtains offer very good protection, but such static safeguards are problematic in these new highly dynamic work scenarios. In this work, we present a prototypical interlocked, multi-sensor system for safeguarding dynamic zones around and close to industrial robots. The core of the system is a robust optical material classification method that can distinguish between skin and other materials (e.g. wood) using an intelligent InGaAs camera system. This feature is used to detect reliably human coworkers, consequently enabling a conventional robot to work as a person-aware cobot. The system is modular and can be easily extended with more sensors and different sensor types. It can be adapted to multiple brands of industrial robots and is quickly integrated into existing setups. The four safety outputs can - depending on the penetrated zone - either issue a warning, slow down the movement of the robot to a safe speed or safely stop the robot. Once all zones are identified as clear, the robot can speed up again to its original speed.

Keywords: Functional safety · Smart InGaAs camera-system · Skin detection · Collaborating industrial robots · Embedded system · Ultrasonic array · NIR-point sensor

1 Introduction

Technological advances nowadays, allow industrial robots to be used much more efficiently. However, for reasons of accident avoidance, most of these robots perform their work almost exclusively among themselves. In many cases, human

© Springer Nature Switzerland AG 2020
V. G. Duffy (Ed.): HCII 2020, LNCS 12198, pp. 119–131, 2020.
https://doi.org/10.1007/978-3-030-49904-4_9

operators are not allowed in predefined working areas, and are kept away by fences or the working speed of the robots is considerably reduced, which is not well suited for optimized production flow.

A relevant example scenario might be if, heavy parts were lifted and positioned by a robot, so its human colleague can perform tasks that are too difficult for the machine to carry out in a precise manner. This concept is an idea from the field of "Smart Production" which is one of the focuses of the German future-oriented project initiative "Industrie 4.0". To achieve the necessary interaction efficiently, safety measures like fences or access restrictions have to be replaced by other technical solutions. In essence, the collaborating robots are supposed to be able to interact safely with their human colleagues. Therefore, they have to react adaptively to the people around them.

To exploit the efficiency of collaboration and at the same time ensure the safety of employees, a multi-stage interlocked protection system with high reliability is required. In the presented research project such a system is designed, implemented as a prototype and evaluated in the field.

The general idea behind the project beyondSPAI is to merge different sensor technologies, for different predefined zones around the robot, together. With these merged and processed sensor inputs, the robot can recognize early enough the danger of coming too close to human beings. The systems only hard prerequisite for correct operation is, that some part of the human coworker's skin (hands, arm, face) has to be exposed, to be seen by the camera.

Depending on the distance, zone, and movement, the system either issues a warning, slows down the machine's work speed according to DIN EN ISO 13855 [1] or fully stops the robot to prevent harm. The robot starts up or speeds up again, as soon as the sensor or sensors that detected the initial stop condition indicate, that no more humans are in the hazardous working area.

2   Previous and Related Work

As the name suggests, beyondSPAI is the continuation of the previous research project SPAI[1,2]. The project was able to successfully prove, that an InGaAs camera system, monitoring the near-infrared spectrum, can reliably detect the presence of human skin over distances of several meters, indicating that a human being is present in the far range of a robot [2].

A related product to achieve safe camera-based supervision of the working area of a robot is the product SafetyEYE from Pilz [3]. SafetyEYE detects and reports objects that encroach into predefined zones, which can be freely defined. Depending on which zone was penetrated by the object, the working speed of the robot is either slowed down or the robot is safely stopped.

Using laser scanners the company SICK [4] offers a similar solution. Utilizing said scanners they monitor a defined area for obstacles, to either reduce the

---

[1] Sichere Personenerkennung im Arbeitsbereich von Industrierobotern - Safe and reliable detection of persons in the vicinity of industrial robots.

[2] SPAI was DGUV-funded Project No. FF-FP 0357.

robot's speed or to stop it completely. An advantage of the system is, that it can be attached to different types of robots and can be used as a mobile system.

A new product is introduced by the company Veo Robotics and is called FreeMove [5]. The working cell of an industrial robot is supervised by several 3D time-of-flight cameras. The data is used to construct a virtual 3D model, in which the robot, the workpieces, and humans can be identified by intelligent algorithms. If the robot comes to close to a point cloud that resembles a human being, the robot either slowed down or stopped completely.

Also closely related to the project is AIRSKIN by Blue Danube Robotics [6]. The AIRSKIN collision sensor is a comprehensive safety cover for robots and grippers. Robot and gripper are fully covered with soft AIRSKIN pads. If a collision between the robot and an object occurs, the collision sensor responds and instantly triggers an emergency stop. Additionally, the soft pads dampen the effects of the collision. Such a system can be used, if the robot speed is already sufficiently slow, as an additional safety measure to protect humans in the immediate proximity of the robot.

Combining different technologies the company Stäubli [7] offers a complete set of five modular SIL3-PLe safety functions (Safe limited speed, Safe Stop, Safe zones, Safe tool, and Safe touch). The offered TX2touch is a SIL3/PLe safety level certified cobot which can be configured to use any of their five safety products.

All currently available products are only limited to detect obstacles. Some solutions try to reconstruct persons or objects with computer vision algorithms, but none can distinguish between different materials (especially human skin as a reliable marker that a person is in the danger area). Therefore we want to address this important aspect with the research project presented in this work.

3   System Design

3.1   Adaptive Safety Zones

To obtain the highest flexibility while providing the best possible safety level, our system splits the working area of an industrial robot into three adaptive safety zones (or ranges). These are the far-zone which extends several meters around the robot, the middle-zone which is defined as 1 m around the robot arm and the close-range zone which is the area around the tool center point (TCP) of the robot. Adaptive denotes in our context, that the close-range and mid-range are seen from the robots perspective since the sensors are directly mounted on the robot and move and change directions accordingly.

The system supports three kinds of sensors: An NIR camera system for the far-zone, an ultrasonic array for the middle zone, and a NIR point sensor for the TCP. The data from all sensors is collected at a central control unit called beSafe-Hub, merged and evaluated. Depending on which zone was encroached, the control unit signals the robot to either slow down or perform a safe stop. Once the person has exited the zone(s), the robot is brought back to normal speed operation (Fig. 1).

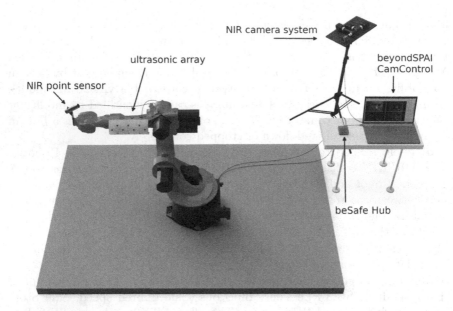

Fig. 1. Rendering of an industrial robot with the proposed system. The green rectangle on the bottom is a simplified representation of the far-zone, supervised by the camera system. (Color figure online)

Each zone is supervised by a primary sensor however, the hierarchy of the system allows the close and middle ranges to likewise be supervised by the sensor of a higher range. This adds additional safety and robustness to the detection. In the following, the principles of the three sensors are explained in detail.

3.2   Skin Detection Using NIR-Radiation

The skin detection technology is based on the distinction of material surfaces by their spectral signature. A spectral signature is defined as the reflection intensity at well-chosen, narrow and distinct wavebands located at 1020 nm, 1200 nm and 1550 nm in the near-infrared spectrum. In Fig. 3 the six skin types according to Fitzpatrick [8] are shown and Fig. 2 depicts the reflection intensities of different material surfaces and all skin types, which are united into a single "skin-corridor". The acquired signature is finally used as an input vector for a machine learning [9] classification model to distinguish between the two classes' skin and material. The NIR based skin detection has been used in previous research projects and proved to be very reliable, with a skin-type independent detection rate of 99.995% [10].

The images are taken sequentially with only one wavelength active and one additional image with no illumination. This capture procedure is known as field-sequential waveband capturing [11]. While this measurement method yields very good results, it has some shortcomings. The system needs special NIR illumination to produce images, which previously was realized by a NIR floodlight

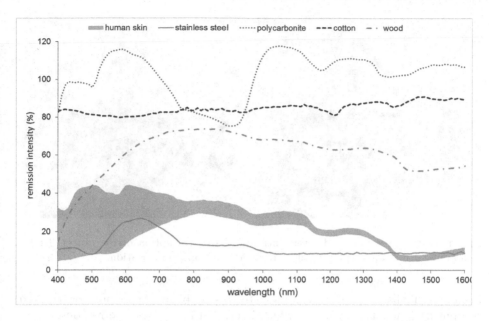

Fig. 2. Spectral remission intensities of skin and examples for relevant materials.

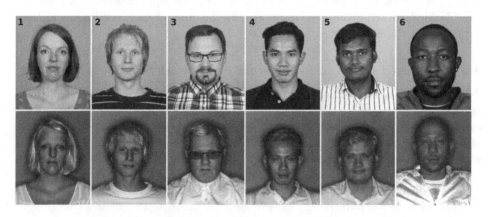

Fig. 3. Visual spectrum (RGB) and NIR portrait images of skin types I to VI according to Fitzpatrick [8].

consisting of high power LEDs with the wavelengths mentioned above. Furthermore the sequential capturing leads to a heavy reduction of the available frame rate.

The biggest challenge for this measurement method is introduced by moving objects, which are very important for the given robot application. Because of the sequential capturing of the three images, a (fast) moving object creates motion artifacts (see Fig. 4). Since the frames are no longer congruently with each other, it is not possible to calculate the needed spectral signatures. Although it has

Fig. 4. Left: Uncompensated errors introduced due to motion of the object. Right: Remaining errors after applying algorithms for motion compensation.

been shown, that algorithms can mediate this problem, the amount of required computing power is very high - which is critical for a real-time response - and the result can still produce errors at the edges of objects, which can cause false classifications that are problematic for safety-critical applications. Therefore it was decided to use a different approach in the project beyondSPAI, which is explained in the following sections.

3.3   Enhanced NIR-Camera System for Robust Skin Detection

The InGaAs camera technology is now enhanced to work without dedicated special NIR illumination. The initial idea of the project was to equip the sensor element of the InGaAs camera with a special NIR filter pattern, similar to the Bayer filter pattern used in state-of-the-art RGB cameras. Such a camera is available (OceanInsight PixelCam) [12], but due to export restrictions (ITAR) it was not possible to acquire. Therefore a system comprising of three cameras plus a dedicated optical system was developed and built, to simulate a single camera with such a pattern.

All cameras are connected optically by a relay optic to observe the same scene. The camera setup shown in Fig. 5 consists of three InGaAs cameras Allied Vision Goldeye-G033 (A), one changeable c-mount camera lens EHD Imaging EHD1614H1SW (B), four relay lenses Thorlabs AC254-060-C (C), two dichroic mirrors Thorlabs DMLP1180R and DMSP1500R (D), three bandpass interference filters Edmund Optics EO-85893, EO-85898 and EO-85903 (E) and tubing. All cameras share the same trigger, which is generated by a microcontroller system (F). Using this setup, we are able to capture the three images needed for the spectral signatures simultaneously, with frame rates up to 300 fps. Each camera delivers an image for one wavelength. A sophisticated control software combines the separate frames into on single "false color" image that is then used as input for the classification algorithm.

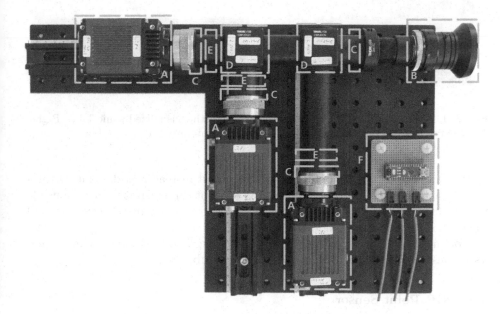

Fig. 5. The enhanced NIR camera setup used in the project

3.4   Ultrasonic-Array

The initial idea for the midrange supervision of the robot was to use ultrasonic holography, to recreate a virtual 3D image of the robot's environment and using machine learning for the detection of an obstacle. This was researched and successfully tested under laboratory conditions [13, p. 49]. However the number of needed sensors and computing power to fully cover the region of interest was not suitable for practical use, therefore it was decided to use conventional ultrasonic supervision with off the shelf automotive sensors [14]. These are cheap, robust and easily available. The reliability and performance level of the sensors were researched in an earlier project [15]. It could be shown, that the array with its chosen geometry and implemented self-testing methods achieves SIL2/PLd [16].

Since the prototypical control unit did not reach a sufficiently high performance level (PL), it was decided to design and build a new control unit for the ultrasonic array, that satisfies the requirements for SIL2/PLd. The unit's architecture is designed as a two-channel system with extensive monitoring capabilities. Its output signals can be user-customized for either open-drain mode or push-pull mode and are designed as a "No-Error" signal in compliance with the closed-circuit safety principle [17] (Fig. 6).

The array can operate in standalone mode or external mode. In standalone mode, the system's behavior is configured (i.e. distance to monitor) once and from that point on only generates a signal if the supervised safety zone is penetrated. Errors that are detected during the continuous self-tests immediately generate such a stop signal and are reported by LEDs. In external mode, the

Fig. 6. Left and middle: The ultrasonic array with the visualized sonic lobes Right: The 3D-printed prototype fitted with 18 sensors for mounting on the robot.

system does not create any autonomous signals but instead reports all its parameters to an external control entity (e.g. PC or Laptop) which is then responsible for all further actions. This mode is primarily designed for further research and should not be used during normal operation.

For the field tests, the ultrasonic array is configured in standalone mode and its signals are connected to the central beSafe-Hub.

3.5 NIR Point Sensor

The point sensor was originally developed to detect the presence of human skin in the vicinity of the blade a circular saw and is therefore optimized for short ranges up to 50 cm. The sensor technology uses the same wavelengths as the camera system but provides its illumination with built-in NIR-LEDs. The acquisition method, however, is very different. The sensor uses the Lock-In amplifier principle. All wavelengths are activated simultaneously but are pulsed on different frequencies. The pulsing light is captured by a single photodiode and digitized. The mixed frequency signal is then demodulated. The resulting three-wavelength signals are combined to obtain the spectral signature, which is evaluated by a classification algorithm running on the microcontroller. The sensor's response time is 1 ms. It operates in standalone mode, generating a dedicated signal if human skin is detected. This signal is routed to the central control unit of the beyondSPAI system and further processed (Fig. 7).

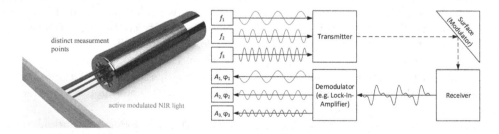

Fig. 7. Measurement principle of the NIR point sensor

3.6   beyondSPAI CamControl Software

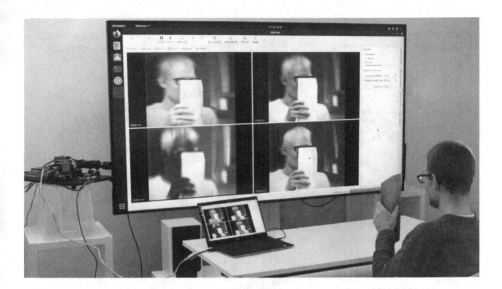

Fig. 8. beyondSPAI CamControl software

The beyondSPAI CamControl software captures and evaluates the images from the camera setup. The software implements complex image adjustment and correction algorithms and generates the false-color image needed for the skin classification. Therefore a single frame from each camera is simultaneously captured, individually adjusted, corrected, and combined into one single image (Fig. 8).

The skin classification is performed for each pixel in the image. The classifier was taught with several thousand different skin and material samples. The output of the classifier is a skin mask, that can operate in binary mode (skin, no skin) generating a black and white image overlay or in Gaussian mode, where the probability of a pixel being skin is displayed as a greyscale value from 0 to 255. The resulting skin mask is analyzed by a simple threshold algorithm. If the amount of skin pixels is higher than a user-selectable value, the software generates an alarm that is sent to the beSafe-HUB via USB.

3.7 BeSafe-HUB

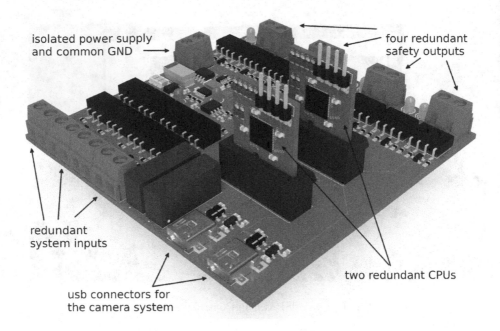

Fig. 9. Design of the beSafe HUB embedded system with two CPU boards attached

The central control unit for the beyondSPAI detection system is an embedded system called beSafe-Hub. It merges all signals from the individual sensors and generates the control signals for the robot. The system, depicted in Fig. 9, is designed completely redundant with two independent microcontrollers that perform the same tasks while controlling each other. All inputs are separately evaluated and both CPUs have to have the same result to generate the "All Clear" signal for the robot. The output(s) of the system use the same closed-circuit working technique as the ultrasonic array, to provide detection for cable errors or power failures.

Since the point sensor and the ultrasonic array are working in standalone mode, their signals are connected directly to the inputs of the beSafe unit. The information from the camera system is evaluated on i.e. a laptop or PC, to which the hub is connected by two independent USB ports.

Depending on the inputs, the four outputs which are connected to the robot's control unit, are set. The hubs logic also implements plausibility checks e.g. if the point sensor has detected the presence of skin, the camera should also have seen skin (or still seeing skin). Currently, the embedded system is being evaluated under laboratory conditions to test if the necessary redundancy and correct functional behavior have been reached.

4 Outlook and Future Work

In the current state of the project, it could be shown, that each sensor type is fully functional and correctly performing the needed supervision autonomously. Extensive test series have been completed with both point sensor and camera system. Over 80 different materials were measured at different distances. The false-color images were then used as training data for a J48 decision tree algorithm [18] and a multi-layer perceptron (MLP) algorithm with the WEKA [19] data mining software. To obtain a binary classification between skin and material, the different materials were united into one single class. Tables 1 and 2 show the conclusions for the camera system and the point sensor test series.

The results of the classifiers for the camera system are almost identical, but because of its much better computational performance, a threshold-based method derived from the data of the decision tree was implemented in the control software.

The results of the point sensor show very clearly that the sensor can reliably distinguish skin from the materials under consideration. The trained decision tree consists of only three leaves and therefore only a single threshold. The classes' skin and material can, therefore, be separated almost linearly. The classifier and its parameters are programmed to the sensor which will operate in standalone mode during the field tests.

The evaluation of the existing ultrasonic array indicated that the setup itself using its geometry and self-testing capabilities achieves performance level PLd, as required by the DIN EN ISO 10218-1 [20]. However this only applies not to the control logic, therefore an ongoing bachelor thesis is covering the redesign and implementation of the control unit to also satisfy the requirements for PLd.

Concurrently, the logic and safety features of the beSafe Hub are being implemented and tested in the laboratory. The next step will be the test of the system mounted on an industrial robot of type Kuka KR16 [21], which will be done in close cooperation with the Institute of Production (IFP) of the TH-Köln [22], in their laboratory different scenarios will be tested and evaluated afterward. The final project results are expected by the end of May 2020.

Table 1. Comparison of the MLP and J48 classifier results for the enhanced camera system

skin	material	
767573	20	classified skin
10	5608312	classified material
	1,30E-5	FNR
	3,57E-6	FPR

(a) MLP Algorithm

skin	material	
767575	10	classified skin
8	5608322	classified material
	1,04E-5	FNR
	1,78E-6	FPR

(b) J48-Algorithm

Table 2. Comparison of the MLP and J48 classifier results for the NIR point sensor

skin	material		skin	material	
360000	0	classified skin	360000	1	classified skin
0	661500	classified material	0	661499	classified material
	0	FNR		0	FNR
	0	FPR		1,51E-6	FPR

      (a) MLP Algorithm   (b) J48-Algorithm

Acknowledgments and Thanks. The project was funded by the German federal ministry for education and research in the funding program FHprofUnt, support code 13FH037PX5.

We want to thank K.A. Schmersal GmbH & Co. KG, Wuppertal [23] for the financial and technical support in the implementation of the research project.

Further, we thank the Institute for Occupational Safety of the German Social Accident Insurance, Sankt Augustin and the TH-Köln, Institute of Production (IFP) for the provided assistance and technical support.

References

1. DIN EN ISO 13855:2010–10, sicherheit von maschinen.- anordnung von schutzeinrichtungen im hinblick auf annherungsgeschwindigkeiten von krperteilen (ISO_13855:2010) deutsche fassung EN_ISO_13855:2010. https://doi.org/10.31030/1564348
2. beyondSPAI project website. https://www.h-brs.de/en/beyond-spai. Accessed 13 Jan 2020
3. Pliz GmbH website. https://www.pilz.com/en-INT/eshop/00106002207042/SafetyEYE-Safe-camera-system. Accessed 13 Jan 2020
4. Sick AG website. https://www.sick.com/us/en/safety-systems-and-solutions/safety-solutions/safe-robotics-area-protection-solutions/c/g513651. Accessed 13 Jan 2020
5. Veo Robotics website. https://www.veobot.com/freemove. Accessed 13 Jan 2020
6. Blue Danube Robots website. https://www.bluedanuberobotics.com/airskin/. Accessed 13 Jan 2020
7. Stäubli website. https://www.staubli.com/en-de/robotics/product-range/cobots/power-cobot/tx2touch-60/. Accessed 13 Jan 2020
8. Fitzpatrick, T.B.: The validity and practicality of sun-reactive skin types I through VI. JAMA Dermatol. **124**(6), 869–871 (1988)
9. Burkov, A.: The Hundred-Page Machine Learning Book. Andriy Burkov (2019). http://themlbook.com/
10. 8th International Conference Safety of Industrial Automated Systems - SIAS 2015. Deutsche Gesetzliche Unfallversicherung (DGUV) Glinkastr, Berlin, December 18–20 November 2015
11. Steiner, H.: Active Multispectral SWIR Imaging for Reliable Skin Detection and Face Verification. Cuvillier verlag göttingen, Universität Siegen (2016)
12. Oceninsight pixelcam website. https://www.oceaninsight.com/products/imaging/multispectral/pixelcam. Accessed 13 Jan 2020

13. 9th International Conference Safety of Industrial Automated Systems - SIAS 2018, 10–21 October 2018
14. Bosch mobility solutions website. https://www.bosch-mobility-solutions.de/de/produkte-und-services/pkw-und-leichte-nutzfahrzeuge/fahrerassistenzsysteme/baustellenassistent/ultraschallsensor/. Accessed 13 Jan 2020
15. Kirfel, A.: Konzeption und Realisierung eines sicheren Ultraschall-Sensorsystems zur Absicherung von Industrierobotern. Master's thesis, University of Applied Sciences Bonn-Rhine-Sieg (2012)
16. Hauke, M., et al.: IFA report 2/2017 Funktionale Sicherheit von Maschinensteuerungen - Anwendung der DIN EN ISO 13849. Zentralbereich des IFA, Referat Informationsmanagement (2017)
17. Börcsök, J.: Functional Safety: Basic Principles of Safety-Related Systems. Hüthig, Heidelberg (2007)
18. Decision tree algorithm short weka tutorial website. http://art.uniroma2.it/basili/MLWM09/002_DecTree_Weka.pdf. Accessed 13 Jan 2020
19. Witten, I., Hall, M., Frank, E., Holmes, G., Pfahringer, B., Reutemann, P.: The WEKA data mining software: an update. SIGKDD Explor. **11**, 10–18 (2009)
20. DIN EN ISO 10218–1:2012–01, industrieroboter_- sicherheitsanforderungen_- teil_1: Roboter (ISO_10218-1:2011); deutsche fassung EN_ISO_10218-1:2011
21. Kuka kr16 product website. https://www.kuka.com/de-de/produkte-leistungen/robotersysteme/industrieroboter/kr-cybertech. Accessed 13 Jan 2020
22. Institute of production at th-köln website. https://www.th-koeln.de/en/automotive-systems-and-production/institute-of-production_68082.php. Accessed 13 Jan 2020
23. A. Schmersal Holding GmbH & Co. KG website. https://www.schmersal.com/home/. Accessed 13 Jan 2020

Investigation of Clamping and Crushing Injuries with Electrically Height-Adjustable Therapy Beds

Elisabeth Ibenthal[✉], Saskia Sobkowicz, and Claus Backhaus

Zentrum für Ergonomie und Medizintechnik, FH Münster,
Bürgerkamp 3, 48565 Steinfurt, Germany
e.ibenthal@fh-muenster.de

Abstract. In the past, clamping and crushing injuries occurred exclusively in therapy beds with scissor or joint lifting systems. This suggests an increased application risk for this type. The aim of the presented study is the systematic-analytical investigation of the clamping and crushing risk for choice types of electrically height-adjustable therapy beds. To analyse the application situation, 41 work process analyses and 100 structured interviews with employees were carried out in ten physiotherapy practices. Following, clamping and crushing risks were examined for four therapy bed-types with qualitative fault tree analyses (DIN EN 61025). Therapy beds with scissor or joint lifting systems show an increased risk of clamp and crush injuries. Therapy beds with lifting column systems have the lowest risk but are rarely used in practice due to their limited usability and high procurement costs. Prospective, technical safety measures are particularly necessary for therapy beds with scissors or joint lifting systems. New goods should be equipped with capacitive contact sensors in the lifting mechanism. For existing therapy beds, it is recommended to develop a locking box with improved usability (e.g. RFID technology), a three-step switch as well as the reversal of the direction of movement in case of all-round switches.

Keywords: Risk assessment · Prevention · Hierarchy of controls

1 Introduction

Physiotherapists are exposed to high physical stress due to the daily treatment of patients, which can lead to musculoskeletal diseases [1, 2]. Therapy beds, whose working heights can be adjusted electrically or hydraulically, facilitate the treatment of patients. On the one hand, they enable the user to work in a back gentle manner by adjusting the working height to suit the user and the application. On the other hand, the height adjustment offers easy ascent and descent for patients.

V. G. Duffy (Ed.): HCII 2020, LNCS 12198, pp. 132–144, 2020.
https://doi.org/10.1007/978-3-030-49904-4_10

1.1 State of the Art

Electrically height-adjustable therapy beds differ in their lifting mechanisms, control units for operation and integrated safety measures to prevent unintentional operation of the height adjustment.

The lifting mechanism comprises the mechanism for raising and lowering the bed surface. In case of electrically height-adjustable therapy beds, this is operated by a control unit for hand or foot operation. Nevertheless, unintentional operation of the height adjustment can lead to serious clamping and crushing injuries with users, patients or third parties. For this reason, the German Federal Institute for Drugs and Medical Devices (dt. Bundesinstitut für Arzneimittel und Medizinprodukte, BfArM) has been recommending since 2004 that therapy beds be equipped with safety systems that fulfil the concept of integrated safety. Exemplary, so-called locking boxes or a two-hand circuit are mentioned [3].

Table 1 shows currently available designs of the therapy bed components "lifting mechanism", "control unit" and "safety system". The market distribution of lifting mechanisms results from 1,000 site inspections by the employers' liability insurance association for health services and welfare work (dt. Berufsgenossenschaft für Gesundheitsdienst und Wohlfahrtspflege, BGW) [4]. The estimation of the market offer of control units and safety systems is based on catalogue visits of five exemplary therapy bed manufacturers. Only those designs were included, that manufacturers offer in the basic equipment of therapy beds. The combination of different component designs results in different therapy bed types.

Table 1. Description and market distribution of different therapy bed components [cf. 5]

Component	Design	Description	Market distribution[a]/ offer[b]
Lifting mechanism	Scissor system	Height adjustment by changing the distances and angles between two articulated scissors	51%[a]
	Joint lifting system	Height adjustment by parallel articulated arms containing several joints	47%[a]
	Lifting column system	Height adjustment by one or two vertical lifting columns	2%[a]
Control unit	Hand-/ Footrail/All-round switch	Circumferential shift linkage under the bed surface or for foot operation. Depending on the model moving the bar to left/right or up/down raises or lowers the bed surface	Each: <5%[b]
	Hand/foot switch	Two push buttons for raising and lowering the bed surface	Hand: 32%[b] Foot: 62%[b]
	Push buttons	Stationary push buttons, usually integrated in the upper frame of therapy beds	<5%[2]
	Joystick	For foot operation. In addition to moving the bed surface up and down, also the can be changed	<5%[b]

(continued)

Table 1. (*continued*)

Component	Design	Description	Market distribution[a]/ offer[b]
Safety system	Directionally incompatible circuit	Only for all-round switches. Due to an inverse directional compatibility, therapy beds move up when the bar is pressed down and moves down when it is lifted	<5%[b]
	Locking box	A locking pin (key) disconnects the power supply of therapy beds. It can be integrated into the therapy bed or attached additionally	75%[b]
	Safety system in control unit	Additional device in the hand or foot switch to activate it. It can also be unlocked with a key	<5%[b]
	Spline	Motor stops as soon as the bed surface encounters resistance during lowering. The bed surface rests on the resistance with its own weight	<5%[b]
	Capacitive contact sensors	Sensor in the lifting mechanism. If this is touched, the height change is stopped	<5%[b]
	Rotary switch	On/off switch on therapy beds to activate the power supply (not recognised as a safety system)	<5%[b]
	Switch connector	External on/off switch between the power supply unit of therapy beds and the socket (not recognised as a safety system)	<5%[b]

[a]Market distribution as a result from 1,000 site inspections by the BGW [4].
[b]Market offer of five exemplary therapy bed manufacturers.

Compared to lifting column systems, which are only rarely represented with 2%, the scissor and joint lifting systems have a more stable bearing of the bed surface and can be moved more easily due to their lower dead weight. In addition, the procurement costs for lifting column systems are significantly higher.

In the basic equipment, 62% of therapy beds are offered with foot switches. However, the disadvantage of the foot switch is that it must be moved by changing treatment sides. In comparison, all-round switches offer the possibility to adjust the height of the bed surface from all therapy bed sides. The additional costs for an all-round switch are on average approx. € 250,-. The lower market offer of hand switches and handrails is due to an insufficient usability for two-handed treatments and treatments with oil.

75% of therapy beds are already offered with a locking box. To retrofit existing therapy beds locking boxes between € 90 and € 180 can be purchased, depending on the manufacturer [6].

1.2   Events with Therapy Beds

Despite a locking box, there were fatal accidents with therapy beds in 2016 and 2017 during cleaning work. While cleaning under the therapy bed, both cleaners unintentionally knelt on the all-round switch, which lowered the bed surface and trapped the cleaners. Due to jamming in the couch, cleaners couldn't remove their leg from the all-round switch [7].

Such events are subject to a legal reporting obligation. In the Federal Republic of Germany, the Federal Institute for Drugs and Medical Devices (BfArM) is responsible for these reports [8], in the United States the Food and Drug Administration (FDA) [9].

Since 2010, respectively nine and ten events of clamping and crushing injuries with therapy beds have been reported to the BfArM and the FDA [4, 10–19]. In addition, an incident is known from Australia in which an 18-month-old child was crushed by the lifting mechanism of a therapy bed [20].

6 of the 20 reported events have led to the death of a person, 3 incidents are foreign incarceration. All events occurred, as far as known, with therapy beds with scissor or joint lifting systems. This suggests an increased application risk for this type, accompanied by a limited occupational safety for users.

The aim of the presented study is the systematic-analytical investigation of the clamping and crushing risk for choice types of electrically height-adjustable therapy beds.

2   Method

2.1   Work Process Analyses in Physiotherapy Practices

To analyse the application situation in which the clamping and crushing events occurred, 41 work process analyses were carried out in ten physiotherapy practices. In addition, the existing therapy bed types were recorded.

Furthermore, 100 structured interviews with employees were carried out with the following guiding questions:

1. How many patients do you treat per day?
2. Are you aware of any accidents involving therapy beds, and if so, how many?
3. Have you received safety briefings for the use of electrically height-adjustable therapy beds and their risks?
4. Are your therapy beds equipped with safety systems to prevent unintentional height adjustments? If so, which ones and how often are they used?
5. If the safety system is a locking box, do you use it? If not, why?
6. How often and by whom is a therapy bed unintentionally operated?
7. How often is a height adjustment made during treatment?
8. Which control unit do you prefer?
9. Do you have any suggestions for improvements of the design of therapy beds, especially with regard to the safety systems?

The interviews were evaluated with a qualitative content analysis according to Mayring [21].

2.2   Choice of Therapy Bed Types

Based on the market offer and market distribution, four representative therapy bed types were chosen for which the risk of clamping and crushing injuries was examined. Each therapy bed type includes a lifting mechanism, a control unit and, if applicable, a safety system.

2.3   Risk Analysis of Clamping and Crushing Injuries

To examine the risk of clamping and crushing injuries for the chosen electrically height-adjustable therapy bed types a fault tree analysis (FTA) according to DIN EN 61025 were carried out [22]. The examined main event was "jamming in the lifting mechanism of an electrically height-adjustable therapy bed".

Based on the work process analyses, hazard situations were developed, which could lead to a clamping or crushing injury. These form the first level of all fault trees. On the second level follow the conditions necessary for the hazardous situations to occur. Subsequently, conditions were broken down in a top-down analysis into damage-causing sub-events and linked by logical operators (gates) [cf. 23]. These events were based on the identified incident reports as well as systematically-analytically by the investigation of possible defects of components and/or user interactions.

The fault trees were created in RAM Commander (Version 8.6, ALD Ltd.) and finally validated discursively assisted by a physiotherapist.

2.4   Risk Assessment of Clamping and Crushing Injuries

The probability of occurrence of clamping and crushing injuries was analysed qualitatively. For this purpose, Minimal Cut Sets (MCS) and orders were determined with RAM Commander (Version 8.6, ALD Ltd.). The MCS is the smallest set of events that must occur for the main event. The order of an MCS corresponds to the number of its events [24]. The probability of occurrence of the main event increases with the number of MCS and depends on its orders. The smaller the order, the higher the probability of occurrence for the main event.

In order to compare the probabilities of occurrence for clamping and crushing injuries with different therapy bed types, a weighted index was calculated depending on MCS and its orders (Eq. 1). The index is dimensionless and increases with growing probability of occurrence.

$$\text{Index-probability of occurrence} = \sum_{k=1}^{n} \text{No. MCS (k. order)} \times \frac{1}{k} \qquad (1)$$

The risk of clamping and crushing injuries arise from the probability of occurrence and the extent of damage [25]. Since the same main event with a fictitious extent of damage was examined for all therapy bed types, the risk depends directly on the probability of occurrence (or the calculated index of probability of occurrence).

Calculating the indices for each therapy bed type made it possible to rank them according to their risk of clamping and crushing injuries.

3 Results

3.1 Work Process Analyses in Physiotherapy Practices

27 therapy beds were inspected, 20 of which were equipped with a scissors and 7 with a joint lifting system. One therapy bed had a foot switch, the other 26 had an all-round switch for foot operation. Table 2 summarizes the answers of the structured interviews.

Table 2. Results of structured interviews ($n = 100$)

No.	Question	Answer
1.	How many patients do you treat per day?	On average, 18 ($\pm$ 3) patients are treated per day ($n = 100$)
2.	Are you aware of any accidents involving therapy beds, and if so, how many?	88% of respondents are not aware of any accidents. 12% have heard of one to three accidents ($n = 80$)
3.	Have you received safety briefings for the use of therapy beds?	45% of respondents have not received any safety briefings. 55% have taken part in a safety briefing ($n = 40$)
4.	Are your therapy beds equipped with safety systems? If so, which ones and how often are they used?	Locking boxes and switch connectors were mentioned. Warning signs and general "organisational measures" were also mentioned. Safety systems are rarely or never used
5.	If the safety system is a locking box, do you use it? If not, why?	The disuse of the locking box is due to poor positioning and an insufficient number of locking pins. Users often forget to remove the pin from the locking box after treatment
6.	How often and by whom is a therapy bed unintentionally operated?	Unintentional operation is carried out weekly to several times a week by users, patients and children
7.	How often is a height adjustment made during treatment?	The number of height adjustments depends on the treatment. In 11 examined processes an average of 8 ($\pm$ 1) height adjustments per treatment were recorded
8.	Which control unit do you prefer?	81% of respondents prefer all-round switches, 19% prefer foot switches ($n = 37$)
9.	Do you have any suggestions for improvements, especially with regard to safety systems?	Better accessibility to the locking box and a pressure or contact sensor in the lifting mechanism

3.2 Choice of Therapy Bed Types

Since in both scissor and joint lifting systems the angles of the articulated arms to one another change during height adjustments, both lifting mechanisms were equated for the risk analysis.

Four therapy bed types were chosen, consisting of:

1. Scissor or joint lifting system + hand switch + locking box,
2. Scissor or joint lifting system + all-round switch + locking box,
3. Scissor or joint lifting system + foot switch + locking box,
4. Lifting column system + foot switch.

3.3   Risk Analysis of Clamping and Crushing Injuries

Five hazard situations have been identified potentially leading to clamping or crushing injuries:

1. A height adjustment by an unauthorized person, after closing time and in the absence of the therapist (or the authorized person).
2. A height adjustment by an unauthorized person, during practice operation and in the absence of the therapist.
3. A height adjustment by an unauthorized person, during practice operation and in the presence of the therapist.
4. A height adjustment by an authorized person during practice operation.
5. A height adjustment due to a technical defect.

Figure 1 shows an exemplary section of the fault tree for the therapy bed with scissor or joint lifting system, foot switch and locking box. Hazard situation 2 is shown, divided into the conditions for the occurrence of the hazard situation and the first level of damage-causing events.

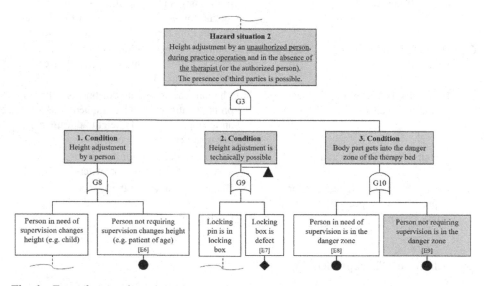

Fig. 1. Exemplary section of the fault tree for therapy beds with scissors/joint lifting system, foot switch and locking box

Events marked with a circle are basic events, which cannot be further differentiated. Events marked with a hash mark are not examined further in this fault tree analysis. The triangle refers to another position in the fault tree, where the event is also investigated (not shown in Fig. 1). Gates G8, G9 and G10 represent an OR operation, gate 3 an AND operation. Events marked in grey were taken from the incident reports of the BfArM and the FDA.

3.4   Risk Assessment of Clamping and Crushing Injuries

Table 3 shows the number of MCS, the orders as well as the index for probability of occurrence of the fault trees for the four examined therapy bed types. The last row of the table shows the risk ranking, resulting from the indices of the probability of occurrence. The therapy bed at rank 1 has the highest risk, the therapy bed at rank 4 the lowest risk of a clamp and crush injury.

Table 3. Minimal Cut Sets (MCS), orders, index-probability of occurrence and risk ranking of the examined therapy bed types

	Type 1: scissor/joint lifting hand switch locking box	Type 2: scissor/joint lifting all-round switch (foot) locking box	Type 3: scissor/joint lifting foot switch locking box	Type 4: lifting column footswitch
Number of MCS	76	70	87	24
Order 1	0	0	0	0
Order 2	0	0	0	18
Order 3	36	43	68	6
Order 4	39	27	19	0
Order 5	1	0	0	0
Index-probability of occurrence	22	21	27	11
Risk ranking	2	3	1	4

Therapy beds with joint or scissors lifting systems (type 1 to 3) have similarly high indices for the probability of occurrence of a clamping or crushing injury, while the calculated index for therapy beds with lifting column systems is noticeably lower.

4   Discussion

4.1   Work Process Analyses in Physiotherapy Practices

The therapy bed types captured in physiotherapy practices confirm the high market distribution of scissor and joint lifting systems and foot-operated all-round switches (see Table 1). This is also confirmed by the results of the interviews. The better usability of an all-round switch seems to compensate for the additional financial outlay in procurement.

On average, 18 (± 3) treatments per day with 8 (± 1) height changes per patient were determined for physiotherapy practice. This relatively high number of adjustments per day proves the necessity to make them safe for users, patients and third parties. Especially unintentional height adjustments are associated with a risk of accidents and must preferably be prevented as far as possible by technical measures. The interviews proved that unintentional operating errors occur several times a week. Particularly worrying is that people in need of supervision, such as children or people with cognitive impairments, also make these operating errors.

Only one in two of the surveyed employees received the legally required safety briefing for therapy beds. Furthermore, only 12% are aware of any events of clamping or crushing when using therapy beds. Therefore, users are insufficiently informed about the hazard of clamping and crushing injuries with therapy beds. This has a significant effect on the use of the existing locking boxes, which are rarely or never used. The reasons for this are the insufficient information and sensitisation of the employees as well as the poor usability of the locking boxes offered as a retrofit kit. These are often cumbersome to use, as they lie on the floor and are difficult to reach. In addition, there are often not enough locking pins, so that not every employee can carry them with him.

The insufficient information of users about the hazards of a therapy bed and the lack of ergonomic safety systems show the need and necessity for further preventive measures. For future measures, employees themselves recommended better accessibility to the locking boxes and a pressure or movement sensor in the lifting mechanism of the therapy bed.

Regarding new safety systems, the BfArM updated its recommendation for the conversion of therapy beds in September 2019. In future, therapy beds should be designed in such a way that "it is not possible for persons to become trapped in the adjustment mechanism with serious consequences" [cf. 26]. For this purpose, safety elements must be developed according to the current technical possibilities, acting on the level of the lifting mechanism.

4.2   Risk Analysis of Clamping and Crushing Injuries

Clamping and crushing injuries occur randomly in practice and can therefore only be recorded empirically to an insufficient extent. Therefore, the risk of a clamping and crushing injury was theoretically examined with a fault tree analysis. This method offers the advantage that causes of a single predefined event are examined, whereas other risk management techniques (e.g. Failure Mode and Effect Analysis) develop possible errors of all individual system components [cf. 27]. This made it possible to work out damage-causing events exclusively for clamp and crush injuries for four different therapy bed designs.

For the establishment of damage-causing events, the incident reports of the BfArM and the FDA were examined. A total of 20 events were reported, six of which resulted in death. However, a high number of unreported events can be assumed, especially for injuries with little or no physical damage. Furthermore, many users are not sufficiently aware of the legally prescribed reporting procedure probably, which is likely to result in a high number of unreported events involving crushing and clamping injuries.

4.3   Risk Assessment of Clamping and Crushing Injuries

Therapy beds with lifting column systems and foot switch have the lowest risk of clamping and crushing injuries. Followed by therapy beds with scissor or joint lifting systems, whose risks differ according to the control unit used. The highest risk is posed by therapy beds with scissor or joint lifting systems and foot switch.

However, therapy beds with lifting column systems are largely assessed unsuitable by users due to their low usability. Compared to therapy beds with scissors or joint lifting systems, they have a higher dead weight and less stability. Hence, manual shifting of those therapy beds is only possible to a limited extent. In addition, the cost of a therapy bed with lifting column system is many times higher than that of comparable systems with scissor or joint lifting systems.

Even foot switches have disadvantages compared to all-round switches. Especially the shifting of the switch with changing treatment sides is impractical in work routine. The higher usability of an all-round switch is shown by the willingness of physiotherapists to upgrade their therapy beds with it, despite the extra charge. 26 of 27 therapy beds recorded were equipped with an all-round switch, also mentioned as the preferred control unit in the interviews. The combination of a foot-operated all-round switch and a scissor or joint lifting system has the second lowest risk of clamping and crushing injuries.

As a result of the fault tree analysis, particularly therapy beds with scissor or joint lifting systems pose a hazard for users, patients and third parties. However, alternative therapy bed types are insufficiently available due to limited usability and higher procurement costs, merely. For this reason, the development of occupational safety measures is necessary to avoid clamping and crushing injuries in future. In this regard, the Working Condition Act requires the priority use of technical measures, followed by organizational and personal measures (hierarchy of controls) [28]. When developing measures, not only new therapy beds but also therapy beds already on the market must be considered (see Sect. 5).

4.4   Limitations

A limitation of the work results from the choice of the risk management technology. The construction of a fault tree is complicated by determining a consistent detail level. In order to ensure adequate comparability of all fault trees, events should not be presented too roughly, but also not too detailed. To improve the objectivity of analysis, all fault trees were developed by the same expert so that a comparable level of detail can be assumed. To ensure sufficient content validity, the created fault trees were validated by a physiotherapist.

Another difficulty was the risk quantification based on the qualitative probabilities of occurrence of the fault trees, which should allow a comparison of the four examined therapy bed types. Therefor it was required to determine the probability of occurrence as a function of the MCS number and the associated orders. For this purpose, a dimensionless, ordinal-scaled index was calculated, enabling the formation of a ranking of the probabilities of occurrence. However, the index does not allow statements about the relation of the calculated indices to each other. With this approach it is not possible to specify how many times the probability of occurrence of clamping and crushing injuries in therapy beds with scissor or joint lifting systems is greater. For a detailed investigation of probabilities of occurrence, reliability parameters for the damage-causing events are required, which do not sufficiently exist to date.

5 Conclusion and Recommendations

The results confirm the assumption that scissor and joint lifting systems have an increased risk of clamping and crushing injuries. Therapy beds with lifting column systems have the lowest risk but are rarely used in practice. Therefore, the development of technical occupational safety measures (engineering controls) for the prevention of clamping and crushing injuries is particularly necessary for therapy beds with scissor and joint lifting systems.

Based on the interviews conducted, in future, manufacturers should equip new therapy beds with (capacitive) contact sensors or comparable safety systems in the lifting mechanism.

To upgrade existing therapy beds, the development of a locking box with improved usability is recommended. For this purpose, the locking boxes should be ergonomically well designed and easily accessible on the therapy bed. The use of RFID technology (Radio-Frequency Identification) could be a possibility to improve the usability of locking boxes. Instead of a locking pin, the user carries an RFID card with him, activating the power supply for height adjustment if he is near the therapy bed. Further interactions are not necessary.

In addition, we recommend converting all-round switches to three-step switches. Level 1 is the neutral position in which the all-round switch is located without any user interaction. Level 2 is reached by operating the all-round switch with a defined force to adjust the height of the therapy bed. If this force is exceeded, level 3 is reached, in which the height adjustment is automatically stopped. In this way, clamping and crushing injuries can be avoided, which have occurred in the past due to a person being trapped (see events involving cleaning staff).

The reversal of the direction of movement of the all-round switch (viz. pressing down the bar raises the lying surface) represents another important measure for risk reduction.

The advent of the described technical prevention measures requires accompanying organisational measures (administrative controls). In addition to informing and sensi-tising users to the risk of clamping and crushing incidents, this also includes briefings in the safety systems available. Thus, increased awareness can be achieved when using therapy beds and user compliance for using safety systems can be improved.

Acknowledgments. The present study was funded by the Berufsgenossenschaft für Gesund-heitsdienst und Wohlfahrtspflege (BGW) in Germany.

References

1. Adegoke, B.O.A., Akodu, A.K., Oyeyemi, A.L.: Work-related musculoskeletal disorders among Nigerian physiotherapists. BMC Musculoskelet. Disord. 9(1), 112 (2008). https://doi.org/10.1186/1471-2474-9-112
2. Girbig, M., Deckert, S., Druschke, D., et al.: Arbeitsbedingte Belastungen, Beschwerden und Erkrankungen von Physiotherapeuten in Deutschland: Ergebnisse einer Fokusgruppendiskussion. Physioscience 9(2), 66–71 (2013). https://doi.org/10.1055/s-0033-1335476
3. Bundesinstitut für Arzneimittel und Medizinprodukte: BfArM-Bewertung bezüglich automatisch höhenverstellbarer Therapieliegen: Referenz-Nr.: 913/0704b (2004). https://www.bfarm.de/SharedDocs/Risikoinformationen/Medizinprodukte/DE/therapieliegen.html. Accessed 04 Sep 2019
4. Stößlein, E.: Therapieliegen: Risikobewertung des BfArM, St. Augustin (2019)
5. Gerhards, M., Mehringer, B.: Mechanische Gefährdungen an elektrisch verstellbaren Therapieliegen: Eine sicherheitstechnische Betrachtung (2019). https://www.bgw-online.de/DE/Arbeitssicherheit-Gesundheitsschutz/Gefaehrdungsbeurteilung/Therapieliegen/Therapiel iegen-Fachartikel.html. Accessed 04 Nov 2019
6. Medizina: Sperrbox für die Therapieliege zum Nachrüsten (2019). https://www.medizina.de/sperrbox-therapieliege-nachruesten.html. Accessed 18 Nov 2019
7. Berufsgenossenschaft für Gesundheitsdienst und Wohlfahrtspflege: Unfall bei Reinigungsarbeiten. BGW mitteilungen (2) (2017)
8. Perleth, M., Busse, R., Gerhardus, A., et al. (eds.): Health Technology Assessment: Konzepte, Methoden, Praxis für Wissenschaft und Entscheidungsfindung. Berliner Schriftenreihe Gesundheitswissenschaften. MWV Med. Wiss. Verl.-Ges, Berlin (2008)
9. U.S. Food & Drug Administration: Medical Device Reporting (MDR): How to Report Medical Device Problems (2019). https://www.fda.gov/medical-devices/medical-device-safety/medical-device-reporting-mdr-how-report-medical-device-problems. Accessed 04 Sep 2019
10. U.S. Food & Drug Administration: MAUDE Adverse Event Report: Patterson Medical Companies inc Performa Bar Activated 2-section Bobath Table, powered (2015). https://www.accessdata.fda.gov/scripts/cdrh/cfdocs/cfMAUDE/detail.cfm?mdrfoi__id=5044606&pc=INQ. Accessed 13 Nov 2019
11. U.S. Food & Drug Administration: MAUDE Adverse Event Report: Armedica MFG. Corp. Armedica Hi-Lo Treatment Table (2015). https://www.accessdata.fda.gov/scripts/cdrh/cfdocs/cfMAUDE/detail.cfm?mdrfoi__id=4663603&pc=INQ. Accessed 13 Nov 2019
12. U.S. Food & Drug Administration: MAUDE Adverse Event Report: Armedica MFG. Corp. Armedica Manufacturing Corp Hi-Lo Treatment Table (2015). https://www.accessdata.fda.gov/scripts/cdrh/cfdocs/cfMAUDE/detail.cfm?mdrfoi__id=4925834&pc=INQ. Accessed 13 Nov 2019
13. U.S. Food & Drug Administration: MAUDE Adverse Event Report: Armedica MFG. Corp. AMBA 240 (2015). https://www.accessdata.fda.gov/scripts/cdrh/cfdocs/cfMAUDE/detail.cfm?mdrfoi__id=5130875&pc=INQ. Accessed 13 Nov 2019
14. U.S. Food & Drug Administration: MAUDE Adverse Event Report: Armedica AM-BA Series Treatment Table (2015). https://www.accessdata.fda.gov/scripts/cdrh/cfdocs/cfMA UDE/detail.cfm?mdrfoi__id=4645290&pc=INQ. Accessed 13 Nov 2019
15. U.S. Food & Drug Administration: MAUDE Adverse Event Report: Armedica MFG. Corp. Armedica Hi-Lo Treatment Table (2014). https://www.accessdata.fda.gov/scripts/cdrh/cfdocs/cfMAUDE/detail.cfm?mdrfoi__id=4132582&pc=INQ. Accessed 13 Nov 2019

16. U.S. Food & Drug Administration: MAUDE Adverse Event Report: Patterson Medical Holdings Midland Hi-Lo Electric Table (2011). https://www.accessdata.fda.gov/scripts/cdrh/cfdocs/cfMAUDE/detail.cfm?mdrfoi__id=2384846&pc=INQ. Accessed 13 Nov 2019

17. U.S. Food & Drug Administration: MAUDE Adverse Event Report: DJO Global TRT 600 Spine Therapy Table Powered Traction Table (2011). https://www.accessdata.fda.gov/scripts/cdrh/cfdocs/cfMAUDE/detail.cfm?mdrfoi__id=2129740&pc=INQ. Accessed 13 Nov 2019

18. U.S. Food & Drug Administration: MAUDE Adverse Event Report: Midland MFG Co./Patterson Medical Electric Hi-Lo Treatment Table (2010). https://www.accessdata.fda.gov/scripts/cdrh/cfdocs/cfMAUDE/detail.cfm?mdrfoi__id=1634980&pc=INQ. Accessed 13 Nov 2019

19. U.S. Food & Drug Administration: MAUDE Adverse Event Report: Dynatronics Dynatron T3 Table Three Sectional Hi-Lo Treatment Table (2010). https://www.accessdata.fda.gov/scripts/cdrh/cfdocs/cfMAUDE/detail.cfm?mdrfoi__id=1617360&pc=INQ. Accessed 13 Nov 2019

20. Founten, L.: Clinic protocol blamed for infant crushed to death (2013). https://www.abc.net.au/news/2013-05-14/infant-massage-table-death-finding/4688060. Accessed 13 Nov 2019

21. Mayring, P.: Qualitative inhaltsanalyse. In: Mey, G., Mruck, K. (eds.) Handbuch Qualitative Forschung in der Psychologie, 1st edn, pp. 601–613. VS Verlag für Sozialwissenschaften (GWV), Wiesbaden (2010)

22. Deutsches Institut für Normung e. V.: Fehlerbaumzustandsanalyse 29.020(DIN EN 61025) (2007)

23. Himmelbauer, H., Treytl, A.: Fehlerbaumanalyse: Fault Tree Analyses (FTA) (1996)

24. Edler, F., Soden, M., Hankammer, R.: Fehlerbaumanalyse in Theorie und Praxis: Grundlagen und Anwendung der Methode. Springer, Heidelberg (2015). https://doi.org/10.1007/978-3-662-48166-0

25. Karrock, L.: Die Risikoanalyse: Analysieren, erfassen, bewerten, 1st edn. Books on Demand, Norderstedt (2010)

26. Bundesinstitut für Arzneimittel und Medizinprodukte: Aktualisierte Empfehlung des BfArM: Fall-Nr. 0785/03 (2019). https://www.bfarm.de/SharedDocs/Risikoinformationen/Medizinprodukte/DE/therapieliegen_update.html. Accessed 19 Nov 2019

27. Deutsches Institut für Normung e. V.: Medizinprodukte - Anwendung des Risikomanagements auf Medizinprodukte 11.040.01(DIN EN ISO 14971) (2009)

28. Gesetz über die Durchführung von Maßnahmen des Arbeitsschutzes zur Verbesserung der Sicherheit und des Gesundheitsschutzes der Beschäftigten bei der Arbeit: ArbSchG (1996)

Fitness Evaluation of Military Helmet Pad

Chia-Chen Kuo[1], Yu Shiau[1], Mao-Jiun Wang[2(✉)], and Jun-Ming Lu[1]

[1] Department of Industrial Engineering and Engineering Management,
National Tsing Hua University, No. 101, Sec. 2, Kuang Fu Road,
Hsinchu 30013, Taiwan, R.O.C.
[2] Department of Industrial Engineering and Enterprise Information,
Tunghai University, No. 1727, Sec. 4, Taiwan Boulevard, Xitun District,
Taichung 40704, Taiwan, R.O.C.
mjwang@ie.nthu.edu.tw

Abstract. Military helmets are designed specifically to protect soldiers' heads during combat. Poor helmet fit has been reported to decrease the helmet's comfort and the ability to provide safety protection. To increase the safety and comfort of soldiers wearing military helmets, the head size and pad design should be considered. Thus, the aim of this study is to evaluate the proper thickness of pad design for fit and comfort of military helmets. A total of 20 male participants were recruited in this study. A digital caliper and three-dimensional (3D) head scanner were used to measure participants' helmet standoff distance (SOD) with two pad thickness levels (10 and 20 mm) placed in the same helmet shell. A 3D head-scanning system was used to obtain the 3D head shape model and to measure the head dimensions. The CATIA software was used to calculate the SOD between the 3D head-scanning model and the military helmet to assess helmet fit. The SOD results showed that the contact pressures for the two pad thicknesses were significantly different in five regions. The pad with a thickness of 10-mm had less contact pressure. Thus, the pad with a thickness of 10-mm is recommended because it can provide better fit and comfort for a military helmet. The findings of this study provide useful references for designing and developing head-related products in the future.

Keywords: Helmet fitness · 3D head scanning · Head contact pressure

1 Introduction

Head shape and head characteristics are essential information for headwear product design. Good headwear product design, such as that for helmets, focuses on how to fit the shape of the head to provide comfort and safety [1]. Military helmets are designed specifically to protect soldiers' heads during combat. The most effective method of ensuring that headwear products fit human head shapes is to include head anthropometry in the headwear product design.

Traditionally, anthropometrical measurements of human body characteristics used direct measurement methods, such as digital tapes and calipers [2]. This method can obtain one-dimensional anthropometric data, such as length and thickness. The advantages of

© Springer Nature Switzerland AG 2020
V. G. Duffy (Ed.): HCII 2020, LNCS 12198, pp. 145–154, 2020.
https://doi.org/10.1007/978-3-030-49904-4_11

this method include ease of operation and low cost. However, accurately estimating three-dimensional (3D) anthropometric data using one-dimensional data is difficult [3].

Recently, with increasing improvements in computer-imaging technology, 3D laser-scanning technology has been widely used in many fields, including architecture [7], biological research [8], and medical research [9]. In addition, 3D laser-scanning technology can perform digitization to obtain the surface of the scanning objects' 3D point clouds [2]. Hence, 3D laser-scanning technology has been applied to 3D anthropometric data processing. Several studies used 3D laser-scanning technology to obtain 3D human body dimensions [1, 2, 4–6, 15]. The obtained 3D anthropometric data can be applied to human wear-related product designs, such as foot-related products [6] and head-related products [1].

Ideally, customized military helmets can provide the best fit and safety protection for each solider. However, customized military helmets may not be suitable for mass production [1]. Hence, several studies have been conducted to develop an anthropometric database based on different ethnic populations, such as the Civilian American and European Surface Anthropometry Resource (CAESAR) database [10], the National Institute of Occupational Safety and Health (NIOSH) head and face database [11], the SizeChina project database [12], and the Taiwan anthropometric database [13]. Significant differences exist in anthropometric data among the various ethnicities and populations [1]. For example, the Chinese (SizeChina) head type has a flatter rear head and forehead than the Caucasian (CAESAR) head type [12]. Hence, the Taiwanese military helmets would have significant differences when using Chinese or Caucasian anthropometric data for the Taiwanese head changes in the nutritional status also have a significant effect on anthropometric data. Kuo et al. [1] indicated that the differences in Taiwanese head anthropometric dimensions revealed a gradual increase comparing to the previous research in Wang et al. [13]. It is, therefore, necessary to update population anthropometric data.

Military helmet consist of shell, comfort pad, and retention system. Generally, the standard head length and head breadth have been critical to military helmet design [14]. The pad thickness was used to conform to the contours of head shape, providing a better custom fit. Poor helmet fit has been reported to decrease soldier safety protection. The term "helmet fit" is defined as the standoff distance (SOD) between the helmet and the skull. The SOD is used to provide a buffer zone and dissipate head heat [16]. A helmet is deemed to fit if the SOD is 12.5–19.1 mm [16, 17]. Thicker pads dissipate impact energy more but restrict the heat exchange from the head to the helmet [18, 19]. Hence, the pad thickness has significant effects on the soldiers' safety, stability, and comfort.

In addition, the mean absolute difference (MAD) is a common method to validate and compare measurement variations, such as accuracy and precision. Dekker [21] and Bradtmiller and Gross [22] revealed better accuracy with smaller MAD values. Lu and Wang [23] compared the accuracies of traditional and 3D scanning measurements and evaluated the precision of repeated measurements by MADs.

To increase the safety and comfort of soldiers wearing military helmets, the head size and pad design should be considered. However, there have been limited studies examining the correlation between pad thickness and military helmet fit. Thus, in this study, the proper thickness of pad design was evaluated for the fit and comfort of military helmets.

2 Methods

2.1 Participants

A total of 20 male participants were recruited in this study. The age of the participants ranged from 20 to 27 years old, and the mean age and standard deviation were 22.7 ± 1.42 years old, respectively. The mean and standard deviation of stature and body weight were 171.13 ± 6.38 cm and 68.77 ± 4.23 kg, respectively.

2.2 Apparatus

A 3D head-scanning system (INFOOT USB head-scanning system, HSU-01, I-Ware Laboratory Co., Ltd., Japan) and a digital caliper (Mitutoyo, Model CD-6″C) were used to measure the helmet SOD, as shown in Figs. 1a and 1b. The accuracies of the head scanner and digital caliper were both 0.01 mm. In addition, a 3D head-scanning system was used to obtain the 3D head shape model and helmet shell model.

An L-sized helmet was used in this study, as shown in Fig. 1d. The helmet shell was painted white for 3D modeling. The helmet was fitted for head circumferences between 580 and 600 mm. A retention system and a pad system were the basic elements of the helmet and provided optimal retention and fit. The easily adjustable four-point retention system included nape pad, adjustable tensioners on straps, chin cut, and buckle. Movable comfort pads provided impact protection and superior comfort by distributing the helmet's weight evenly. The seven-pad system fits most ground military helmets and includes one circular crown pad, two trapezoidal pads, and four oblong pads, as shown in Fig. 1e. The pad system has two thicknesses (10 and 20 mm).

The contact pressure was measured by a flexible pressure sensor (Parallax, Inc.), as shown in Fig. 1c. The accuracy of the pressure sensor was a linearity of ±3% of full scale. The minimum pressure that could be detected was 1 g/cm^2, and the sampling rate was 10 times per second.

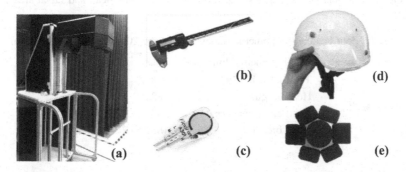

Fig. 1. Apparatus used in this study: (a) head-scanning system, (b) digital caliper, (c) flexible pressure sensor, (d) L-sized helmet, and (e) seven-pad system.

2.3   Experimental Design

A total of 20 male participants participated in this study. Each participant was involved in two levels of pad thickness (10 and 20 mm). The SOD and contact pressure were the two dependent variables and measured in the five regions: front, top, left side, right side, and occipital of the helmet. In addition to SOD, $MAD_{Accuracy}$ was used to evaluate the accuracy between caliper measurement and 3D measurement. $MAD_{Precision}$ was applied to evaluate the precision using repeated measurement. After each task was completed, a verbal survey and an interview were conducted to obtain the participant's subjective feelings about the just-completed task.

2.4   Experimental Procedure

Before the experiment, the study's purpose and procedures were introduced in detail to the participants. Then, they were requested to complete an informed consent form. First, to ensure scanning image quality, each participant placed a cotton cap on his head prior to the scan. During the scanning period, each participant's head and body needed to be stabilized. Each scan was repeated three times, and each took approximately 15 s to complete. Figure 2 shows the 11 markers' positions, and the references in ISO 7250 were followed [20]. Furthermore, four head dimensions were computed by the head-scanning system, as shown in Table 1.

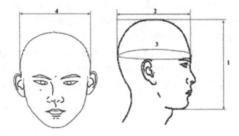

Fig. 2. Positions of 11 markers placed on the participant's head and facial area.

Table 1. Four head anthropometric dimensions of the 20 participants (unit: mm).

Anthropometric dimensions	Mean	SD
Total head height	238.69	3.74
Head length	188.21	4.18
Head circumference	588.31	7.35
Head breadth	168.75	2.26

Next, the participant followed standard wearing instruction to wear the L-sized helmet with two pad thicknesses. To ensure the fit of the helmet, the participant was requested to perform dynamic body movement, such as squatting and bending. Then, the participant's SOD was measured by a digital caliper. To make it possible to use a digital caliper probe to measure the distance between the helmet and skull, seven holes were drilled in the L-sized helmet (see Fig. 3). The measured result did not include the thickness of the helmet shell (10 mm) in the SOD value, and it was collected in five regions (front, top, left side, right side, and occipital areas) of the helmet. Each participant's SOD was measured three times.

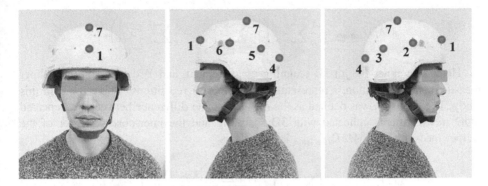

Fig. 3. Positions of the seven holes on the helmet.

Then, the participant wearing the helmet was scanned three times. Once the 3D scanning procedure was completed, Geomagic Studio (3D Systems, Inc.) software was used to align and map the scanned images. Deviation analysis was performed to compute the SOD in five regions between the helmet and skull by CATIA (Dassault Systèmes, S.A.) software, as shown in Fig. 4.

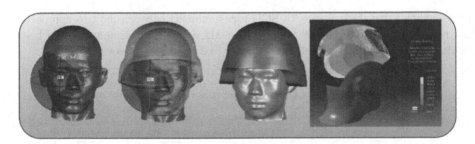

Fig. 4. Illustrations of 3D-scanned images and 3D SOD measurements.

After undergoing 3D scanning procedures, each participant was asked to wear the helmet with two pad thicknesses, and on each pad, a pressure sensor was mounted to collect the contact pressure in five regions (front, top, left side, right side, and occipital areas).

A 3-min rest period and a verbal survey and interview were scheduled between each task.

2.5 Statistical Analysis

The SOD and contact pressure results were analyzed using one-way analysis of variance (ANOVA) to evaluate how pad thickness affects SOD and contact pressures. The accuracy of two measurements was defined as the mean absolute difference ($MAD_{Accuracy}$). By referring to the ISO 20685 criterion [24], it can be determined whether the accuracy is acceptable. $MAD_{Accuracy}$ is defined as

$$MAD_{Accuracy} = \frac{1}{n}\sum\nolimits_{i=1}^{n}\left(\left|\frac{1}{r}\sum\nolimits_{j=1}^{r}X_{ij} - \frac{1}{r}\sum\nolimits_{j=1}^{r}Y_{ij}\right|\right). \tag{1}$$

Here, X_j denotes the jth 3D scanning measurement, and Y_j denotes the jth caliper measurement. In addition, r represents the number of repetitions, where $r = 3$ in this study. The precision was defined as the mean absolute difference between the repeated SOD measurements collected with 3D scanning and the inter-observer error of the caliper measurements. $MAD_{Precision}$ is defined as

$$MAD_{Precision} = \frac{1}{n}\sum\nolimits_{i=1}^{n}\left(\frac{\sum_{j=1}^{r}\sum_{k=1}^{r}|X_{ij} - X_{ik}|}{\left(\frac{r!}{2!(r-2)!}\right)}\right), j \neq k. \tag{2}$$

The paired T-test was used to verify the difference between the two approaches. The adopted statistical significance level was $\alpha = 0.05$. All statistical analyses were performed using SPSS Statistics v.22 software.

3 Results and Discussion

Table 2 shows that the precision of SOD measurements between the two approaches had no significant difference ($P > 0.05$). The 3D scanning measurements had better precision than the caliper measurements in all five regions, as shown in Table 2.

Table 2. Precision evaluation results between two measurement methods.

Measured region	P-value	MAD $_{Precision}$ (mm)	
		Caliper measurement	3D measurement
Front	0.11	0.42	0.32
Top	0.33	0.44	0.38
Left side	0.31	0.46	0.41
Right side	0.18	0.48	0.43
Occipital	0.08	0.56	0.46

The accuracy evaluation results are shown in Table 3. The accuracy of this study complied with the ISO 20685 criteria [24] and Meunier et al. [16] for all measured areas.

Table 3. Results of accuracy evaluations (unit: mm).

Measured region	This study	ISO 20685 [24]	Meunier et al. [16]
Front	1.21	2.00	4.00
Top	1.38	2.00	4.00
Left side	1.05	2.00	4.00
Right side	1.28	2.00	4.00
Occipital	1.88	2.00	4.00

The ANOVA results of SOD for two pad thicknesses are shown in Table 4. The results showed significant differences between the two pad thicknesses in five regions ($P < 0.05$). Figure 5 shows that the top and both sides had lower SOD for both the pad thicknesses. The SOD of 10-mm thickness was lower than that of the 20-mm thickness. The SOD of the 20-mm thickness in three regions (front, top, and occipital) exceeded the suggested range from 12.5 to 19.1 mm. In other words, the pad with a thickness of 20-mm had worse SOD results. According to the results of the interviews, most of the participants pointed out that the 20-mm pad thickness was too thick to wear, especially in the front and occipital regions. However, the 10-mm pad thickness had less stability at the front and occipital regions. This may explain why the front and occipital regions had higher SODs for the 10-mm pad thickness in this study.

Table 4. ANOVA results of SOD for pad thickness.

Variable	d.f.	Front	Top	Left side	Right side	Occipital
Pad thickness	1	0.03	0.02	0.02	0.03	0.03

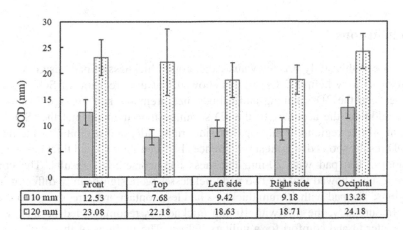

	Front	Top	Left side	Right side	Occipital
10 mm	12.53	7.68	9.42	9.18	13.28
20 mm	23.08	22.18	18.63	18.71	24.18

Fig. 5. Main effects of two pad thickness on SOD.

The ANOVA results for contact pressure of the two pad thicknesses are shown in Table 5. The contact pressures of the two pad thicknesses had significant differences among the five regions ($P < 0.05$). Figure 6 shows the variations in the contact pressure of the two pad thicknesses. The pad with a thickness of 10-mm had less contact pressure, except in the top region. The result was consistent with the SOD result that the 10-mm pad thickness had a higher contact pressure in the occipital region.

Table 5. ANOVA results of contact pressure for pad thickness.

Variable	d.f.	Front	Top	Left side	Right side	Occipital
Pad thickness	1	0.04	0.01	0.04	0.04	0.03

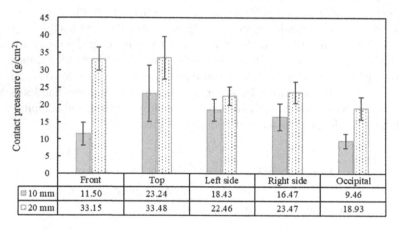

	Front	Top	Left side	Right side	Occipital
10 mm	11.50	23.24	18.43	16.47	9.46
20 mm	33.15	33.48	22.46	23.47	18.93

Fig. 6. Main effects of two pad thicknesses on contact pressure.

4 Conclusions

The purpose of this study was to evaluate the proper thickness of pad design for fit and comfort of military helmets. The results showed that the precision of SOD measurements between the 3D scanning and caliper measurements had no significant difference. In addition, the accuracy of the 3D scanning measurement met the ISO 20685 criteria in all five regions, front, top, left side, right side, and occipital of the helmet. The SOD results showed significant differences between the two pad thicknesses in the five regions. The pad with 20-mm thickness had worse SOD results. The contact pressure results showed that the two pad thicknesses were significantly different in the five regions. The pad with 10-mm thickness had less contact pressure, except in the top region. In summary, the pad with 10-mm thickness is recommended because it provides a better fit and comfort for a military helmet. The findings of this study provide useful information for designing and developing head-related products in the future.

References

1. Kuo, C.C., Wang, M.J., Lu, J.M.: Developing sizing systems using 3D scanning head anthropometric data. Measurement **152**, 107264 (2020)
2. Ball, R., Shu, C., Xi, P., Rioux, M., Luximon, Y., Molenbroek, J.: A comparison between Chinese and Caucasian head shapes. Appl. Ergon. **41**(6), 832–839 (2010)
3. Simmons, K.P., Istook, C.L.: Body measurement techniques: comparing 3D body-scanning and anthropometric methods for apparel applications. J. Fashion Mark. Manag. Int. J. **7**(3), 306–332 (2003)
4. Lu, J.M., Wang, M.J.J.: Automated anthropometric data collection using 3D whole body scanners. Expert Syst. Appl. **35**(1–2), 407–414 (2008)
5. Luximon, Y., Ball, R., Justice, L.: The 3D Chinese head and face modeling. Comput. Aided Des. **44**(1), 40–47 (2012)
6. Lee, Y.C., Wang, M.J.: Taiwanese adult foot shape classification using 3D scanning data. Ergonomics **58**(3), 513–523 (2015)
7. Dorninger, P., Pfeifer, N.: A comprehensive automated 3D approach for building extraction, reconstruction, and regularization from airborne laser scanning point clouds. Sensors **8**(11), 7323–7343 (2008)
8. Collard, M., O'Higgins, P.: Ontogeny and homoplasy in the papionin monkey face. Evol. Dev. **3**(5), 322–331 (2001)
9. Hennessy, R.J., Baldwin, P.A., Browne, D.J., Kinsella, A., Waddington, J.L.: Three-dimensional laser surface imaging and geometric morphometrics resolve frontonasal dysmorphology in schizophrenia. Biol. Psychiatry **61**(10), 1187–1194 (2007)
10. Robinette, K.M., Blackwell, S., Daanen, H., Boehmer, M., Fleming, S.: Civilian American and European Surface Anthropometry Resource (CAESAR), Final Report, 1. Summary. Sytronics Inc Dayton OH (2002)
11. Zhuang, Z., Bradtmiller, B.: Head-and-face anthropometric survey of US respirator users. J. Occup. Environ. Hyg. **2**(11), 567–576 (2005)
12. Ball, R.: Size China - A 3D anthropometric survey of the Chinese head (2009)
13. Wang, M.J., Wang, E.M.Y., Lin, Y.C.: Anthropometric Data Book of the Chinese People in Taiwan. Ergonomics Society of Taiwan, Hsinchu (2002)
14. Sohaimi, R., Zaidi, A., Abdullah, S.: Materials and design issues for military helmets. Adv. Mil. Text. Pers. Equip. **103**, 103–138 (2012)
15. Gross, M.E., Bradtmiller, B.: US Navy head anthropometry for helmet design. In: Proceedings of the Human Factors and Ergonomics Society Annual Meeting, vol. 43, no. 20, pp. 1070–1074. SAGE Publications, Los Angeles, September 1999
16. Meunier, P., Tack, D., Ricci, A., Bossi, L., Angel, H.: Helmet accommodation analysis using 3D laser scanning. Appl. Ergon. **31**(4), 361–369 (2000)
17. Li, Y.Q., Li, X.G., Gao, X.L.: Modeling of advanced combat helmet under ballistic impact. J. Appl. Mech. **82**(11), 111004 (2015)
18. Moss, W.C., King, M.J.: Impact response of US Army and National Football League helmet pad systems (No. LLNL-SR-464951). Lawrence Livermore National Lab CA (2011)
19. Pang, T.Y., Subic, A., Takla, M.: A comparative experimental study of the thermal properties of cricket helmets. Int. J. Ind. Ergon. **43**(2), 161–169 (2013)
20. ISO 7250: Basic human body measurements for technological design, in International Organization for Standardization. ISO, Switzerland (2001)
21. Dekker, L.D.: 3D human body modeling from range data. Ph.D. Dissertation, University College London, London, U.K. (2000)

22. Bradtmiller, B., Gross, M.E.: 3D whole body scans: measurement extraction software validation. In: Presented at the International Conference of Digital Human Modeling, Hague, The Netherlands (1999). 1999-01-1892
23. Lu, J.M., Wang, M.J.: The evaluation of scan-derived anthropometric measurements. IEEE Trans. Instrum. Meas. **59**(8), 2048–2054 (2010)
24. ISO 20685: 3D Scanning methodologies for internationally compatible anthropometric databases, in International Organization for Standardization. ISO, Switzerland (2005)

Ergonomic-Based Clothing Design
for the Elderly

Jingxiao Liao[✉] and Xiaoping Hu[✉]

School of Design, South China University of Technology,
Guangzhou, People's Republic of China
184740531@qq.com, hxp523@163.com

Abstract. With the population aging approaching, the life of the elderly has been paid more and more attention. The actual needs of the elderly are the starting point for the design of the clothing of the elderly. Ergonomics is an important means of coordinating the relationship between people and products, which helps humans to find the most suitable design for people's way of life. Clothing is the first in terms of food, clothing, living and traffics. In the design, the use of ergonomic principles can make clothing products more closely suited to the physiological structure of the elderly, in line with the living habits of the elderly. The experience of the elderly is the key to judge the quality of the clothing product design of the elderly. Therefore, the purpose of this study is to analyze the psychological and physiological needs of the elderly, and provide practical reference for the design of clothing styles for the elderly. Through data measurement and interview inquiry, the use of ergonomic principles, we can optimize the details of the design of clothing products for the elderly and provide the latest reference for the dimensional span positioning of older clothing styles.

Keywords: The elderly · Ergonomics · Clothing · Demands and needs

1 Introduction

Human life expectancy is being extended, population aging is getting increasingly attention. This trend of population aging is putting forward a deeper demand for the further improvement of the elderly clothing. Data from the sixth census released by the Guangzhou Bureau of Statistics in Guangdong Province, China, the proportion of the elderly over 65 years of age in Guangzhou was 6.672% [1]. The results of the 1% population sample survey in 2015 released by the Guangzhou Municipal Bureau of Statistics showed that the population aged over 65 in Guangzhou reached 7.915% [2]. From 2013 to 2015, the elderly population in Guangdong Province, China, grew significantly, and in the face of rising populations of the elderly, the demand for products for the elderly is also growing. It is particularly important to study the physical characteristics of the elderly, analyze the physiological and psychological needs of the elderly, and design the clothes that are more in line with the appearance of the elderly.

© Springer Nature Switzerland AG 2020
V. G. Duffy (Ed.): HCII 2020, LNCS 12198, pp. 155–166, 2020.
https://doi.org/10.1007/978-3-030-49904-4_12

This study takes the elderly women over 65 years of age as an example in Guangzhou, Guangdong Province, China. The main purpose of this study is to explore the physical structure characteristics of the elderly and their demand and needs of clothing, and to find out the color of clothing that conforms to the psychological characteristics of the elderly. By asking the elderly with the ability to live independently of their preference for clothing color, the psychological needs of the elderly are explored. Analyze the needs of older people by interviewing the styles they wear every day in winter. Measure the data of the elderly body as a reference for the classification of clothing plates and dimensions, and enrich the data of the elderly in southern China.

2   Research Methods

2.1   Anthropometry

Anthropometry is the most important step in the design of clothing for the elderly, and it is a significant prerequisite for the transformation of "human body to adapt to clothing" to "clothing adapts to the human body". The actual data obtained by human body measurement and use it to design, which is the key to more humane care of clothing products in the process of the design of clothing. China conducted a nationwide survey of adult size in the 1980s. In the 1980s, the GB10000-88 Human Dimensions of Chinese Adults was released, which is the basic body data in China [3]. With the time passing, China's material conditions and population age distribution has changed, today's standard clothing size cannot meet today's elderly consumer market. The lack of data on the body of the elderly also shows the need for human data measurement. The purpose of this measurement is to understand the true and effective body data of the elderly and provide some reference for the size of the clothing of the elderly.

Measure Objects and Time. A sample of elderly women with self-care abilities in various different regions of Guangzhou, Guangdong Province was randomly selected. The time is October 2019 to January 2020, in winter.

Methods and Tools. Measurements are made by hand. During the measurement, the subjects were required to wear close-fitting clothing, stand side by side with their feet, remain upright, arms naturally sagging, and breathing evenly. Measurement tools are: soft tape measure, height weight measuring instrument, Data recording instrument.

Measurement Program. The measured items were height, weight, neck circumference, shoulder width, waist, hips, whether the arm could be raised parallel to the thigh, and whether the bent arm could touch the ground. Measuring basic data for the elderly as necessary data for clothing style design, plate making and push pedal. Explore the physical toughness of the elderly over 65 years of age with basic self-care ability in order to judge their convenience for daily clothing wear.

2.2   Interview and Investigation

The interviewees were women over 65 years of age from different communities in Guangzhou, Guangdong Province, China, and asked about the needs of the elderly for their daily clothes. A total of 18 elderly people was drawn from the interview, from which 10 broadly representative elderly people were chosen. Here are the results of interviews with elderly people in the community:

Interviewee A, 70 years old. She said that she had injured her hand, could not lift her arm high, could not wear clothes that were too narrow, pullover style clothes were difficult to wear, and the zipper could not be pulled on by herself, but the buttons could. She doesn't buy clothes, she depends on her children, she doesn't like too bright colors, she likes dark brown, gray, and dark red. For winter clothing, as for the material of clothing, he likes light but very warm materials.

Interviewee B, 79 years old. She says she often buckles the wrong way, making it easier to use a zipper. She is more afraid of cold. She likes to buy loose clothes, but too loose jacket sleeves will be too large, revealing the warm clothes inside, she hopes the jacket can tighten the cuffs. She said that clothes with two pockets are enough. It doesn't need too much. Usually go to the market to buy clothes, the general price is about 50–60 RMB, will not buy too expensive clothes, like dark red. Compared to the high collar, she prefers the low collar, and she does not wear collared clothes in hot weather.

Interviewee C, 76 years old. She said that she likes to use more zippers than buttons. Buttons are prone to wrong buttons, and she doesn't like coats that are too long and too wide. Usually buy clothes, the price is 10-20RMB, children will also buy her clothes, the price will be slightly more expensive, but children often buy clothes that do not fit. Do not like the red and white and too fancy patterns. Regarding the material of the clothes, the interviewee stated that she likes comfortable fabrics.

Interviewee D, 76 years old. She said she likes the jacket with a zipper, is not old-fashioned, and is more convenient to wear. She does not like high-necked clothes because it is not comfortable, and she does not like too loose or too long clothes, because it is not too warm and fit is more important. She buys clothes more often than her children. In terms of color, she said that she did not like positive red, and she did not like white. White was dirty easily, and it was not easy to clean in winter.

Interviewee E, 82 years old. She said that when the weather is cold, she likes to wear zipper-closed clothes, which is warmer, and in summer, she likes to wear button-closed clothes, and she hopes that the buttons can be more, but it is colder in winter, her fingers are stiff, and it is not convenient to button. She said that she did not like high-necked clothes. Although it was warm, it was too uncomfortable to wear. There were not many requirements for the pockets. Two were enough. Usually, the clothes she buys are around 40 RMB, and the coats are usually bought by children. She stated that she likes scarlet, does not like high-purity red, and does not like light colors.

Interviewee F, 84 years old. She said that she did not like pullovers, because her hands were painful when it was too cold in winter, which made it difficult to dress. She said that she likes loose style jackets without zippers. Loose styles are more convenient for adding clothes, and clothes with closed zippers can cause wrinkles on the abdomen when sitting down, which is very uncomfortable. She said that she would usually buy clothes that cost between 20–30 RMB and would not choose too expensive. Respondent F said that she did not like light-colored clothes, but she accepted light red. As for the material of the clothes, she said that warm and close-fitting clothes prefer skin-friendly and comfortable materials, and coats prefer thinner and easier-to-clean fabrics.

Interviewee G, 73 years old. She said that she likes loose clothes. She chooses 4X or 5X sizes. The price ranges from 30 to 50 RMB. She likes bright colors, but she does n't like red with high purity, she doesn't like light blue, and she likes scarlet in winter. Summer likes light red and white.

Interviewee H, 65 years old. She said she rarely buys clothes and usually prefers comfortable materials and loose styles. She thinks the zipper is more trendy and tends to buy it. She said that she likes rose red and likes fashion, and hopes that the clothes of the elderly can be a little red, but not high-purity red, which is too bright.

Interviewee I, 80 years old. She said that she likes reddish brown or vermilion, and thinks that the clothing should have a little color because a single color will look too dull. She likes loose vest styles and close-fitting long-sleeved styles. It can accept high collars in cold weather. The price of clothes is around 20 to 100 RMB.

Interviewee J, 69 years old. She said that she prefers zippering to outer jackets rather than buttons. She does not like high-necked pullovers. Although warm but not very comfortable, low-necked winter dresses are a bit cold and prefer lapels. There are no special requirements for colors, as long as they are not too bright. In general, she will choose to buy clothes at 30 yuan or more, and the more expensive coats will be purchased by children.

3   Analysis and Discussion

3.1   Analysis of Measurement Data

The total number of samples for this measurement was 42 (Fig. 8).

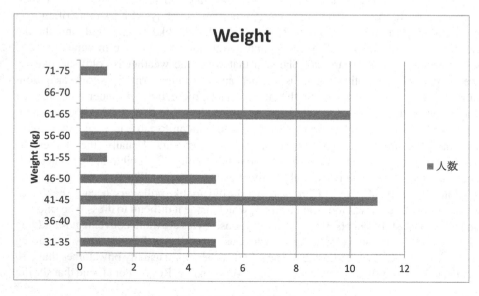

Fig. 1. Weight distribution

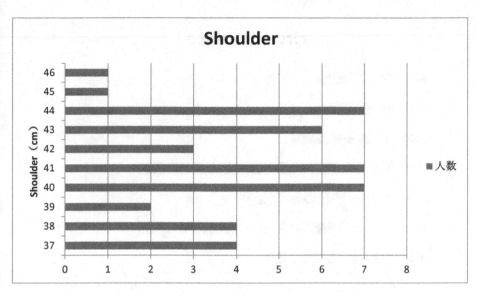

Fig. 2. Shoulder width distribution

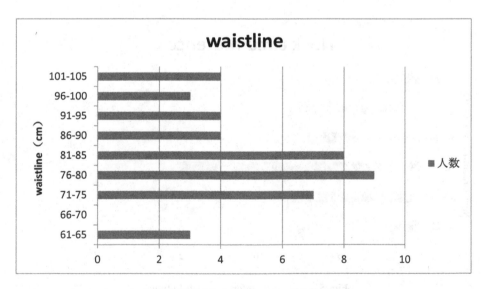

Fig. 3. Waist circumference distribution

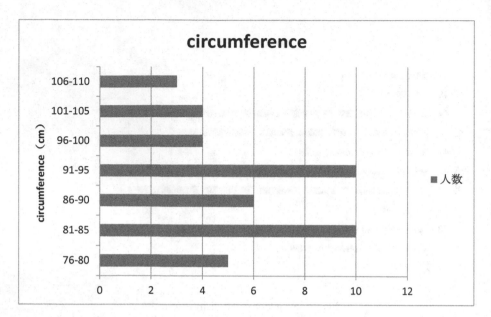

Fig. 4. Hip circumference distribution

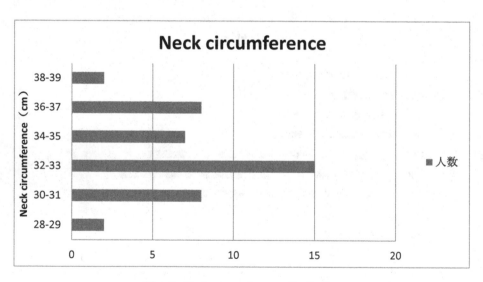

Fig. 5. Neck circumference distribution

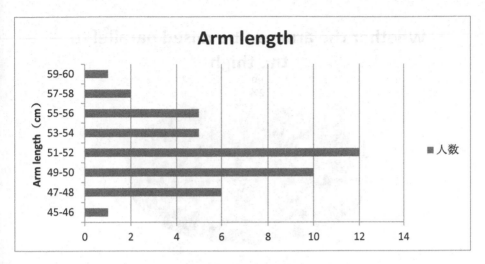

Fig. 6. Arm length distribution

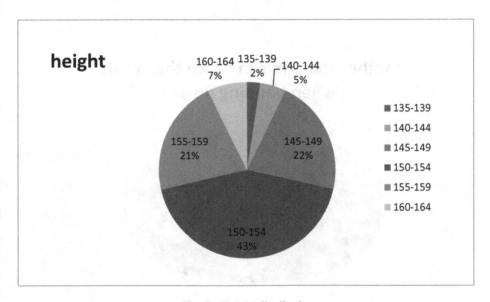

Fig. 7. Height distribution

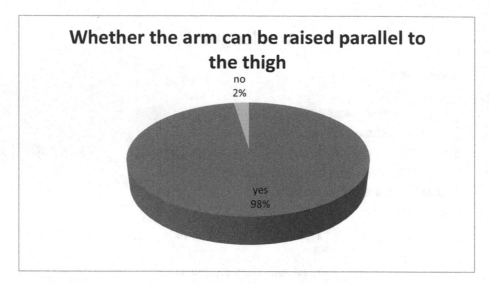

Fig. 8. Arm lift capability

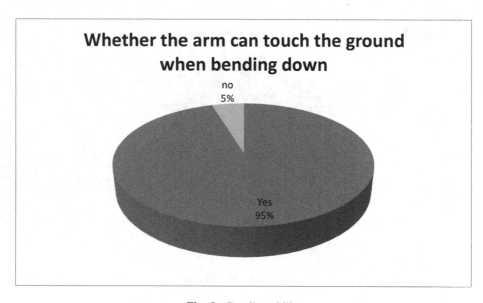

Fig. 9. Bending ability

As can be seen from Fig. 1 and 7, the weight span of the elderly over 65 years old in Panyu District, Guangzhou, Guangdong Province, China is relatively large, distributed between 41–45 kg and 61–65 kg. Height data is more concentrated in the distribution between 145–159 cm, of which 150–154 cm height of the elderly accounted for 43%. Measurements show that the maximum height of people over 65 years of age is not prominent, as human aging is associated with the degradation of bodily functions, and significant degradation of bones, muscles and metabolic systems. The elderly encounter a variety of age-related physical changes from clothes-changing, including a weakened sense of balance, dizziness and joint degeneration [4] (Fig. 9).

According to Figs. 2, 3 and 4, the shoulder width distribution span of the surveyor was average, and the waist circumference data was more between 71–81 cm, which did not show the phenomenon of centralized distribution; the hip sloping is consistent with the waist circumference and the distribution is scattered. Measurements show that older people have more fat in their waists and abdomens.

Figures 5 and 6 show that the neck circumference data of the elderly in Guangzhou is more concentrated in 32–33 cm, with a range of changes within 10 cm, and arm length data is concentrated between 49–52 cm, accounting for about 60%. The difference between the body shape of the elderly in the figure above is larger, so the span of the number of clothing codes is more demanding. A study of the clothing needs of older Chinese people shows that the market is now available for older people to choose fewer sizes [5].

3.2 Conclusion

The rising number of elderly people bodes well for the ageing clothing market. The Chinese Communists argue that building a moderately prosperous society in 2020, which predicts well for rising material standards and people's ability to buy. The results of this interview show that the cost of clothing for women in Guangzhou is not high, the average item is about 50 RMB, most of the elderly are not willing to buy expensive clothes. While the children of the respondents usually buy more expensive clothing for the elderly, the majority of respondents said that their children for their purchase of clothing, often the size of the problem, too loose or too narrow to wear uncomfortable. According to the 2015 1% population survey conducted by the Guangzhou Municipal Bureau of Statistics, as of 2015, 72.806% of the elderly in Guangzhou depended on retirement pensions and pensions [2]. This shows that although the elderly has the capacity to shopping by their own, but the purchasing power is not strong, the elderly daily living clothes are largely purchased by children. According to the interview records, most elderly people are reluctant to buy expensive clothes. Although the elderly interviewed had some different requirements for clothing, their sources of income were not very high, which limited their desire to buy to some extent.

Fifteen of the 18 elderly people interviewed said they didn't like high-purity reds and whites. Interviews show that older women generally prefer a lower purity of red, add a little purple red or yellow red is popular with older people. China's elderly women have a different kind of dedication on red. Red in China is the color of joy, representing enthusiasm and joy, is the symbol of life, and red is particularly prominent, representing the vivid vitality. White is the color of silence in China, representing silence and bereavement, is the symbol of death. The elderly choose low purity red is the rejection of vitality, but the realization of the yearning for a better celebration. The older generation of Chinese women are hard-working and thrifty, dark red relative to light red, more resistant to dirt. Black and grey tones are not the first choice for older women.

For styles, older women don't like to wear high-necked clothing, because neck will be tight, it is not comfortable, but they like its warm performance. Coats prefer lapel style, both warm and comfortable. More than half of the old people don't like the style of the coat that is too long, too drown-out. As the results of the interview can be seen, zipper style jacket is not convenient to sit down, there is a clothing hem will overlap to form a fold problem, you can replace the traditional one-way zipper with two-way zipper to solve this problem. For pockets, the old man agreed that the two pockets are good to use and do not need to be reduced or increased. Close-length long-sleeved warm-up jacket with a down vest, and then put on a fitting style of coat jacket, which is the way old people like to wear in winter.

3.3   Style Designs and Advises

Through the interview analysis, we can clearly summarize the elderly upper clothing design needs to adjust the three problems are:

The bottom of the zipper-style coat is easy to form folds, and the elderly is not comfortable when he/she sits down.

The cuffs of the coat are easy to wear, but not warm.

High-neck style warm clothes are warm, but they strangle neck, which are not comfortable.

Plan A

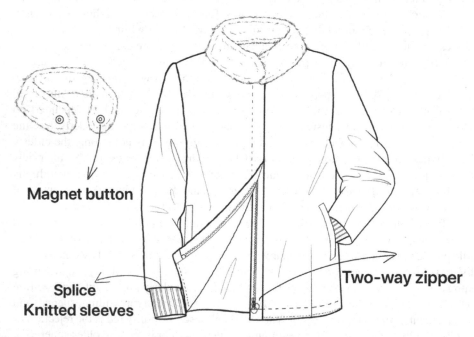

Magnet button

Splice
Knitted sleeves

Two-way zipper

Fig. 10. Coat detail improvements

Common winter coat styles are generally lapel styles, and the neck will feel cold with non-high collar thermal clothing. The design in Fig. 10 abandons the traditional lapel style and uses a detachable fur collar to alleviate the urgency brought about by the high-necked warm clothing holding the neck. The detachable fur collar is highly mobile and can be fastened to clothes with buttons or wrapped around the neck alone. The fur collar is fixed with a magnet button. It is considered that the elderly's fingers are stiff when the weather is cold, and it is inconvenient to button. The cuff stitching knit material has the effect of tightening the cuffs and protecting against wind and warmth, and solves the discomfort caused by too large or too short sleeves. Many clothing designs often only consider the elegance and comfort of the human body when standing. When the human body is in a sitting position, if the zipper is pulled up, the clothes will usually pile up on its belly. The two-way zipper can effectively eliminate the accumulation of wrinkles in the abdomen, which is both warm and comfortable (Fig. 11).

Plan B

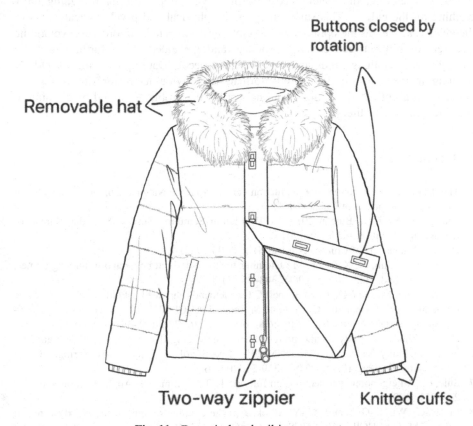

Fig. 11. Down jacket detail improvements

In winter, light and warm materials are the general requirements of seniors for clothing materials. Solution two is designed for down jacket styles. Combining the zipper and the button closed by rotation increases the selectivity and makes it easier to put on and take off. The button is closed with a rotating cross. Unlike traditional buttons, this button only needs to be aligned with the shape. Even in cold weather, the hand can be easily buckled. The two-way zipper design gives the elderly more choices for daily life. Detachable hat design can deal with more weather, economical and practical, knitted stitching cuffs increase warmth performance.

4   Conclusion

There are many elderly people in Guangzhou City, Guangdong Province, and there is a large market for elderly products. The Chinese nation has had the virtue of being thrifty since ancient times. According to interviews and surveys, it is not difficult to find that the interviewed elderly people are unwilling to spend too much money on clothing products. Therefore, the material cost factor is very important for designing daily clothing for the elderly. This study analyzes the physical and psychological needs of the elderly, as well as the optimization of clothing style details, in order to explore the best relationship between clothing products and the elderly, and further meet the elderly's daily clothing needs and psychological needs. Data updates for the elderly clothing market provide the latest information. Provide ideas for optimizing the detailed design of elderly clothing, and help solve the problems caused by clothing to the elderly's normal life.

References

1. The data of the sixth nationwide population census from the National Bureau of Statistics of the People's Republic of China (2011)
2. Guangzhou Statistics Bureau 2015 1% Population Sampling Survey. Statistics Bureau of Guangdong Province. (table1-9) (2015)
3. Human Dimensions of Chinese Adults(GB/T10000-1988)
4. Rosenblad-Wallin, E., Karlsson, M.: Clothing for the elderly at home and in nursing homes. J. Consum. Stud. Home Econ. **10**(4), 343–356 (1986)
5. Hu, X., Feng, X., Men, D., Chen, Robert C.C.: Demands and needs of elderly chinese people for garment. In: Stephanidis, C., Antona, M. (eds.) UAHCI 2013. LNCS, vol. 8010, pp. 88–95. Springer, Heidelberg (2013). https://doi.org/10.1007/978-3-642-39191-0_10
6. Hu, X., Zhao, Y.: Study on the body shape of middle-aged and old women for garment design. In: Duffy, Vincent G. (ed.) DHM 2015. LNCS, vol. 9185, pp. 53–61. Springer, Cham (2015). https://doi.org/10.1007/978-3-319-21070-4_6
7. Sule, C.: An ergonomic garment design for elderly Turkish men. J. Applied Ergonomics **35**, 243–251 (2004)
8. Lu, H.-C., Wu, F.-G., Yang, W.-Y., Book, A.: The clothing design for the elderly care. In: Kurosu, M. (ed.) HCII 2019. LNCS, vol. 11568, pp. 33–46. Springer, Cham (2019). https://doi.org/10.1007/978-3-030-22636-7_3

Comfort Evaluation of the Range of Motion of Human Upper Limb Joints

Zhongqi Liu[1,2], Xiaocong Niu[1,2], and Qianxiang Zhou[1,2(✉)]

[1] Key Laboratory for Biomechanics and Mechanobiology of the Ministry of Education, School of Biological Science and Medical Engineering, Beihang University, Beijing 100191, China
zqxg@buaa.edu.cn
[2] Beijing Advanced Innovation Centre for Biomedical Engineering, Beihang University, Beijing 102402, China

Abstract. To evaluate the discomfort degree of upper limb joint motions, the experiment with external load was carried out based on subjective feeling scale and sEMG signal analysis. Eleven university students participated the experiment. the data of subjective feeling of comfort and the sEMG of the related muscle of shoulder joint (forward extension, rear protraction, adduction, abduction, flex level, stretch level), elbow joint (flexion), wrist joint (palmar flexion, dorsal flexion, and ulnar flexion) and ulnar radial joints (pronation and supination) with 1 kg of loads. Each joint movement was parted into 4 range (25% ROM, 50% ROM, 75% ROM, 100% ROM) to collect the above data. The results showed that the subjective comfort is related to the joint type, joint movement, joint movement angle and other factors. Under the effect of external load, the highest degree of discomfort was horizontal extension of shoulder joint, followed by dorsal flexion of wrist joint; Elbow flexion was the most comfortable, followed by shoulder forward extension and horizontal flexion. The sEmg data could more sensitively reflect the change of human discomfort than subjective sensation, among which IEMG value was a better indicator.

Keywords: Range of Motion (ROM) · Upper limb joint · External load · Comfort · EMG · Ergonomics

1 Introduction

Globally, the number of workers suffering from various types of musculoskeletal diseases caused by work is gradually increasing, resulting in many losses, such as loss of labor, economic compensation to workers, etc. [1]. The design and layout of various seats, operating platforms, and various display and control components in the operation space should not only consider the functionality and accessibility, but also consider the comfort of human operation, so as to avoid or reduce the risk of various musculoskeletal diseases and improve the operation efficiency [2, 3]. In manufacturing, construction, equipment maintenance and other work, workers need to use the upper limbs to complete the work with load [4], so the comfort of the upper limb range of

© Springer Nature Switzerland AG 2020
V. G. Duffy (Ed.): HCII 2020, LNCS 12198, pp. 167–177, 2020.
https://doi.org/10.1007/978-3-030-49904-4_13

motion should be considered above all, that is, the comfort of the motion angle of the upper limb joint presented by a task action.

At present, there are many researches on the comfort Of ROM (Range Of Motion) in foreign countries. Genaidy et al. were earlier researchers who used the 10-point scale to grade the discomfort of people, and made subjective evaluations on the comfort of joint activities of the upper limbs and the whole body [5, 6]. Kee et al. evaluated the joint mobility comfort of the spine, upper limbs and lower limbs in the sitting and standing posture of male and female subjects [7, 8]. The above studies all evaluated the comfort of a human body at a certain angle without a task. In a work environment, where a person has to perform a task operation, so there are additional loads, Kee et al. thought that the comfort of human joint movements should be different under the load. Therefore, Kee [9] and Na et al. [10]. used subjective scales to perform comfort evaluation to the postures on the shoulders and elbows under the load. Chihara et al. evaluated the comfort of shoulders, elbows and wrists with joint torque [11]. There were few domestic researches on the comfort of human ROM, and only two literatures had been reported publicly. The research method was also subjective sensory evaluation method, which evaluate the comfort of the whole body and upper limbs of the human body in static posture without external load [12, 13]. Due to the differences in physiques of different races at home and abroad, foreign data cannot be copied and used, and domestic research has some gaps from the actual task environment. Therefore, further research on task design and evaluation methods is needed.

Joint activity is a complex process involving physiology, behavior, etc. Its evaluation cannot be based on a single index, but should be based on the existing research on joint comfort, from multiple perspectives, through a combination of subjective and objective evaluation methods to make the research of the ROM comfort of human upper limb joints more accurate. The sEMG (surface electromyogram) directly reflects muscle activity, which is considered as one of the most reliable and effective indicators in objective evaluation methods, and is widely used in the study of muscle fatigue or comfort [14]. Wu Xiaoying et al. Studied the correlation between the surface electromyographic signal of the upper arm and the elbow joint, and found that there is a correlation between the related indexes of sEMG and the change of the angle of the elbow joint [15]. Based on this, this study added a certain external load to the subject in the experimental task, and measured its sEMG signals in different joint poses. It was hoped that the subjective evaluation and objective sEMG signal can be combined to evaluate the comfort of human upper limb ROM with external load. The results of the study will provide reference for the design of the working space, the design of the operating platform, and the layout design and evaluation of various display and control elements.

2   Method

2.1   Participants

Eleven male college student volunteers participated this study. Their age was 21.4 ± 0.67 years old, height was 172.4 ± 5.4 cm tall and weight was 63.5 ± 8.4 kg. Their health was well. They had good skeletal and muscular development, and no sports-related diseases. They were in a good mental state when he participated in the experiment. They have no recent severe exercise or sports injuries. They could correctly express the inner feeling scales, and they are all right-handed. All participants voluntarily participated in the trial and filled out written informed consent.

2.2   Apparatus and Materials

The main experimental equipment and materials used in this experiment were as follows.

(1) JE-TB0810 surface myoelectric signal acquisition system。

This system was developed and produced by Anhui Aili Intelligent Technology Co., Ltd. It had 8 channels that could collect the surface EMG signals of 8 muscles at the same time; the sampling rate was 1000 Hz, as shown in Fig. 1.

(2) Electronic joint angle ruler.
(3) An 1 kg weight.
(4) Stopwatch.
(5) Disposable ECG electrodes.
(6) 75% medical alcohol and gauze.

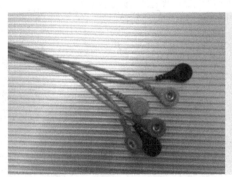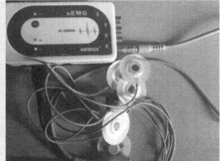

Fig. 1. Surface myoelectric collection box and wires

2.3   Joint Movements to Be Evaluated

The upper limb joints and their movements involved in this experiment included shoulder joint (forward extension, rear protraction, adduction, abduction, flex level, stretch level), elbow joint (flexion), wrist joint (palmar flexion, dorsal flexion, and ulnar flexion) and ulnar radial joints (pronation and supination), a total of 12 joint movements, and their specific definitions were referred to the correlation literature [16]. Comfort was evaluated at 25%, 50%, 75%, and 100% of the maximum range of motion for each joint. Restricted by physiological structures such as musculoskeletal, the difference in ROM of each joint is relatively large. After the measurement of 2 subjects before the experiment, it was found that ROM of some joints is narrow. For example, ROM for shoulder horizontal extension and carpal ulnar flexion was less than 50, and ROM for carpal dorsiflexion was less than 60. Therefore, it was not convenient to evaluate their four active action ranges, and only one or two of them were evaluated. The specific evaluation actions and ranges were shown in Table 1. Therefore, the joint motions that needed to be evaluated in this study included 12 large motions and 30 small motions.

Table 1. Range of motion of joints to be evaluated and muscles attached to electrode

Joint	Movement	Muscle with electrode	ROM%			
			25%	50%	75%	100%
Elbow	Flexion	Flexor ulnar carpal, biceps, brachioradialis	√	√	√	√
Distal radioulnar	Pronation	Flexor ulnar carpal, brachioradialis, triceps		√		√
	Supination			√		√
Wrist	Palmar flexion	Flexor ulnar carpal, biceps		√		√
	Dorsal flexion	Biceps, brachioradialis				√
	Ulnar flexion	Flexor ulnar carpal, triceps humerus				√
Shoulder	Forward extension	Biceps, deltoid, trapezius	√	√	√	√
	Rear protraction			√		√
	Adduction			√		√
	Abduction		√	√	√	√
	Flex level		√	√	√	√
	Stretch level			√		√

2.4   External Load Design

The general principle of load loading mode is to hinder joint movement and make the subject feel the additional load. There Were differences in the loading mode of each joint movement, which are referred to foreign literature [11]. In the formal experiment, weights were connected by a light cord, one end was connected to the subject's hand, and one end was suspended around the table around a pulley on the table.

In this paper, the external load was used to simulate the normal work load. In order to facilitate comparison, the individual differences of the subjects were not considered, and the external loads applied by the subjects were the same. In abroad studies, the load of some documents was 0 kg, 1.5 kg and 3.0 kg, and the load was divided into light, medium and heavy loads [9, 10].

There were no uniform regulations in the published literature, so this paper considered the experimental time and the difference between Chinese and foreign participants' physical fitness. This paper used a medium load of 1 kg as an external load and conducted the pre-tests. During the pre-experiment, the subjects could obviously feel the change from very comfortable to very uncomfortable, so an external load of 1 kg was used.

2.5   Muscle to Collect SEMG Signals

The general principle for selecting muscles is to participate in the movement of the joints. The shallower position facilitates the acquisition of EMG signals, and the larger shape facilitates identification and placement of electrode pads. A subject was randomly selected, healthy, 22 years old, 165 cm/60 kg in height and weight, and first performed joint activities without external load. According to physiological knowledge [17], the electrode pads were affixed to the muscles involved in the above four joint activities. After connecting the computer, the subjects were asked to repeat each joint movement for several times, and at the same time recorded the sEMG signal, observed the strength of the EMG signal, and initially selected the muscle with more obvious changes in the EMG signal as the measurement muscle. Then, based on the no-load experiment, perform joint activities with an additional load of 1 kg to further verify the identified relevant muscles and make modifications. Through comparison, it was found that no relevant muscles with significant changes in EMG signals were found when the Ulnar radial joint was under no-load activity. Due to the need for a hand grip when an additional 1 kg load was applied, the brachioradialis, ulnar carpi flexor, and triceps brachii appeared obvious electromyographic signal change. Therefore, the above three muscles were determined to be muscles that need to collect sEMG signals during formal experiments. Based on this method, the relevant muscles to be collected for the other three joints were determined. Eventually the muscle results of collecting myoelectric signals were shown in Table 1.

2.6   Procedure

The main steps of the experiment in this study were as follows:

(1) Let participants understand the purpose, process, and precautions of this experiment, and be familiar with joint movements and scoring rules.
(2) Participants should warm up first to ensure that their upper limbs are flexible.
(3) Measured the maximum motion angle ROM of the 12 joint movements of each subject.
(4) Polished with an emery cloth and wiped with alcohol on areas of skin that require electromyographic electrodes to remove the oil on the skin surface and the dead cuticle.
(5) Attached electrode pads to the muscle parts that need to collect the EMG signals of the subjects.
(6) Loaded the load and started the formal experiment. Participants completed 30 joint movements in Table 1 in sequence, each of which was held for 60 s. During this

period, the subjects were required to remain stationary and collect EMG signals. After the completion of each joint action, stop the collection of EMG signals, and then asked the subjects to score according to the subjective comfort evaluation scale in Table 2. The higher the score, the worse the comfort. Take a break of at least 3 min after each action before proceeding to the next action.

Table 2. Subjective comfort evaluation scale

Score	Grade	Description
1–2	Very comfortable	Very relaxed, relaxed
3–4	Comfortable	No special sensation
5–6	Not comfortable	Slight discomfort and sore muscles
7–8	Less comfortable	The joints are uncomfortable and demanding
9–10	Very uncomfortable	Joints ache and muscles are stiff

3   Results

3.1   Subjective Comfort Evaluation Results

Because subjective scale of each subject was different, the score results of the same action had certain difference; there might be small or large abnormal data. Therefore, before statistical analysis to subjective comfort score data, the Grubbs criterion was used to preprocess the subjective evaluation data to remove outliers [18]. In order to understand the overall comfort of all joints and compare the comfort of different joints, referred to documents and calculated the relative discomfort index (RDI) of each joint, which indicate The degree of discomfort in the angle of the joint movement unit. The subjective comfort evaluation results and RDI data of all joint movements were shown in Table 3.

Table 3. Comfort statistics of each joint movement with external load

Joint	Movement	Discomfort level				ROM	RDI
		25%	50%	75%	100%		
Wrist	Palmar flexion	\	4.09	\	4.36	67.6°	0.64
	Dorsal flexion	\	\	\	6.27	60.0°	1.08
	Ulnar flexion	\	\	\	5.09	49.6°	1.03
Elbow	Flexion	5.11	4.64	5.00	4.20	140.5°	0.33
Distal & radioulnar	Pronation	\	4.20	\	4.80	88.6°	0.5
	Supination	\	5.09	\	6.60	93.3°	0.63
Shoulder	Forward extension	5	6.91	7.55	6.60	183.6°	0.34
	Rear protraction	\	4.45	\	7.18	63.2°	0.94
	Adduction	\	2.45	\	4.82	56.4°	0.66
	Abduction	4.10	7.55	8.45	7.36	184.1°	0.39
	Flex level	3.73	4.09	4.82	5.64	138.2°	0.33
	Stretch level	\	6.45	\	7.18	38.2°	1.79

As could be seen from Table 3, the comfort of 12 joints changed significantly when the range of motion angle is 75%. For the shoulder joint rear protraction, adduction, flex level, stretch level, ulnar and radial joints, wrist joints, with the increase of ROM, the degree of discomfort increased, and the discomfort was the strongest when ROM is 100%. Among them, the discomfort of the ulnar and radial joints and wrist joints increased slowly, which indicate that as the range of ROM increased, the feeling of discomfort increased but not strongly. For shoulder joint forward extension and abduction, as the range of joint motion increased, the discomfort score increased in fluctuation. At 75%, the feeling of discomfort was the strongest, and then it showed a downward trend, but the elbow joint changed in the opposite direction. As the ROM increased, the discomfort value showed a downward trend.

The RDI is a parameter that evaluate the change in overall comfort of joint activity. A larger RDI value indicates a higher degree of joint discomfort. It could be seen from Table 3 that the highest degree of discomfort was the horizontal extension of the shoulder joint, which indicate that under the effect of external load, the human arm was longer, which make the resistance arm large, with a greater load on the shoulder joint, leading to increased discomfort. Secondly, the discomfort degree of wrist joint was also very high, this was because of its ROM is narrow, the holding time of movement is long, and its discomfort will be more intense with an external load. The most comfortable were flexion of the elbow joint and flex level of the shoulder joint. Flexing made the resistance arm smaller, which mean less discomfort. In general, the comfort value of most joint movements toward the inside of the body was greater than the comfort value toward the outside of the body. For example, the discomfort of the supination of the ulna-radio joint was greater than the pronation, the discomfort of the wrist joint dorsal flexion was greater than the palm flexion, and the discomfort of the stretch level was greater than the flex level.

3.2   sEMG Data

After pre-processing the surface EMG signals collected in the experiment, MATLAB was used to calculate integrate electromyography, root mean square, Mean Power Frequency and Median Frequency of each joint, and then the correlation between the four EMG indicators and the subjective comfort evaluation results was calculated. The results were shown in Table 4.

Table 4. Correlation between sEMG index and subjective scale score

Joint		Muscle	IEMG	RMS	MF	MPF
Elbow	Flexion	Biceps	−.925**	−.906*		
Wrist	Dorsiflex	Flexor ulnar carpal	.752*			
Shoulder	Flex level	Deltoid muscle	.817**	.825**	.754**	.511*
	Abduction		.717**			
	Forward extension		.899*			

**The correlation was significant at the 0.01 level (bilateral)
*There was a significant correlation at the 0.05 level (bilateral)

It could be seen from Table 4 that for elbow joint flexion, the IEMG, RMS, and subjective comfort scores of the biceps brachii are significantly correlated and negatively correlated; The correlation between the electromyographic index IEMG and the subjective comfort score was the highest at the P < 0.01 level, and RMS also had a negative correlation with subjective comfort score at P < 0.05. From the above subjective comfort evaluation results, it could be seen that as the elbow flexion angle increase, the subjective comfort score showed a downward trend. IEMG and RMS were negatively correlated with the subjective comfort score, which means that the IEMG and RMS values increase with the increasing elbow flexion angle (Fig. 2). This result was consistent with the results of the study in literature [15]. Therefore, the comfort of elbow flexion could be evaluated by analyzing IEMG and RMS data collected from the biceps brachii.

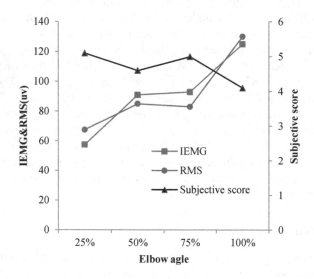

Fig. 2. Relationship between IEMG and RMS values and elbow flexion angle

There was a significant positive correlation between the IEMG value of the ulnar carpi flexor and the subjective comfort score at the level of P < 0.05 when the wrist was dorsiflexed. It showed that as the angle of dorsiflexion of the wrist joint increase, the IEMG value increased and the comfort decreased. This indicated that the comfort of the wrist dorsiflexion can be evaluated by analyzing the IEMG value collected from the ulnar carpi flexor muscle. There was no correlation between other electromyographic parameters and wrist dorsiflexion. As for the shoulder joint, only the three joint movements of horizontal flexion, abduction, and forward extension were positively correlated with the sEMG index value. No correlation was found between other joint movements and sEMG data.

4 Discussion

According to the subjective fatigue evaluation data, the fatigue level was divided, and the corresponding fatigue state of the physiological index was obtained. The Borg scale scores 0–3 for the relaxed state, 4–6 for the mild fatigue state, and 7 points or more for the fatigue state. The sEMG signal was integrated with the ECG signal fatigue evaluation index, and combined with the subjective fatigue evaluation classification label corresponding to the physiological index, 70% of the data was randomly selected as the training data, and the remaining 30% data was used as the test set data for verifying the generalization ability of the model. The polynomial kernel function, the radial basis kernel function and the Sigmoid kernel function were selected to map the training data set. Meanwhile, Three kinds of three-class supporting vector machine models with different kernel functions were trained, and the classification effect was judged by the classification accuracy rate. The results were as follows. As shown in Table 3, the model constructed by the radial basis kernel function had the highest accuracy. Using the pedaling motion testing set data to verify the generalization performance of the model, the classification accuracy rate for pedaling exercise fatigue was 89%.

As a kind of subjective state of self-perception, comfort is affected by many factors, such as the type of joint movement, the direction of joint movement, the size of the joint movement range, and the presence or absence of an external load. On the basis of previous studies, this experiment evaluated the comfort of the range of motion of the 12 joints of the human upper limb by applying a load to the upper limb. Most studies at home and abroad have used the subjective sensory evaluation method to study the comfort of human joint movements under no external load. As for the research on the comfort of human joint movements under an external load, only two studies of Kee [9] and Na [10] can be retrieved

Here we compare this study with the research by Kee [9] and Na [10] to compare the differences in physical fitness at home and abroad and the differences in comfort with changes in the range of joint movement. In Kee's research, because the data is normalized, it was not possible to compare the size of the comfort score, but the change trend of comfort could be seen when the angle of joint movement change. Kee found that for wrist palmar flexion and dorsal flexion, when the angle increased, the degree of discomfort increased, and the discomfort of dorsal flexion was slightly greater than that of the palm flexion; With the increase of the angle of joint motion, the discomfort caused by elbow flexion first increased and then decreased with a small change. The degree of discomfort was the lowest when flexing to the maximum angle. It can be seen that the results of Kee's research were basically consistent with this study in the trend of discomfort. Compared with Na's study, the discomfort of shoulder extension and elbow flexion with the angle of the joint was also consistent with this study, but the discomfort score in this experiment was significantly higher, which may be caused by the differences in physical fitness at home and abroad.

Taking into account the differences in physical conditions at home and abroad, the results of this experiment were compared with the research of Zhang Libo [12] and Xu et al. [13]. The subjective discomfort score of the joint action under external load was significantly higher than that it was without load. In both literatures, the most comfortable joint activities in subjective feeling were flexion of the elbow joint and extension of the shoulder joint, which is completely consistent with this study; the literature [13] showed that the most uncomfortable subjective feeling was shoulder joint forward extension. So it indicated that the elbow joint flexion is the most comfortable joint movement regardless of the load effect, and some of the working movements of the shoulder joint can easily make the operator feel uncomfortable. With external load, the discomfort of the wrist joint became strong. This means that the working position and time of the shoulders and wrists should be shortened as much as possible when working on site to avoid harm to the operator.

Xu's research also used objective sEMG indicators to study the comfort of the wrist movement [13]. He found that the RMS and IEMG index values increased with the increase of ROM range of wrist dorsiflexion and the discomfort score of wrist dorsiflexion also increased with the increase of the range of ROM. The IEMG signal index of ulnar carpi flexor muscle collected during dorsiflexion of the wrist had a certain correlation with the subjective scale score (Table 4). This meant that in addition to use the subjective scale scoring method, collecting surface EMG signals and calculating their index values to evaluate joint comfort were also of reference value.

In general, there are certain differences in the physical fitness of subjects at home and abroad. This study is more suitable for China. This experiment more realistically simulates on-site operations, combining subjective and objective evaluation methods, and the experimental results are more credible. The study can provide reference for the design of the work space, the design of the operating table, and the layout design and evaluation of various display and control elements.

5 Conclusion

In the case of external load, the comfort of 12 joint movements of human upper limbs was evaluated based on subjective scale method and surface sEmg index in this sdudy. Meanwhile, the correlation between subjective comfort score and objective surface emg index was studied. The main conclusions were as follows:

The subjective comfort level is related to the joint types, joint movements, and joint motion angles of the upper limbs; under the load, the highest degree of discomfort is the horizontal extension of the shoulder joint, followed by the wrist dorsiflexion. The most comfortable movement is elbow flexion, followed by shoulder forward extension and horizontal flexion.

For joint movements such as elbow flexion and wrist dorsiflexion, there is a clear correlation between subjective scores and related indicators of sEMG. The sEMG is more sensitive to joint discomfort than subjective scores.

In this study, the comfort of human joints was evaluated with external the load, so the experiment task is closer to the actual task situation, and the research results are more accurate.

References

1. Kee, D., Lee, I.: Relationships between subjective and objective measures in assessing postural stresses. Appl. Ergon. **43**(2), 277–282 (2012)
2. Wang, R., Zhuang, D.: Layout optimization of cockpit based on human comfort. Acta Armamentarii **29**(9), 1149–1152 (2008)
3. Li, P., Chen, G., Zhang, L., et al.: Analysis of influencing factors triggering operator's error in nuclear power plants. China Saf. Sci. J. **27**(7), 42–47 (2017)
4. Chen, X., Chen, W.: Study on construction workers' attitude to safety and its affecting factors. China Saf. Sci. J. **27**(4), 31–36 (2017)
5. Genaidy, A.M., Karwowski, W.: The effects of neutral posture deviations on perceived joint discomfort ratings in sitting and standing postures. Ergonomics **36**(7), 785–792 (1993)
6. Genaidy, A.M., Barkaw, I.H., Christen, D.M.: Ranking of static non-neutral postures around the joints of the upper extremity and the spine. Ergonomics **38**(9), 1851–1858 (1995)
7. Kee, D., Karwowski, W.: The boundaries for joint angles of isocomfort for sitting and standing males based on perceived comfort of static joint postures. Ergonomics **44**(6), 614–648 (2001)
8. Kee, D., Karwowski, W.: Joint angles of isocomfort for female subjects based on the psychophysical scaling of static standing postures. Ergonomics **47**(4), 427–445 (2004)
9. Kee, D.: Investigation on perceived discomfort depending on external load upper limb posture and their duration. J. Korean Inst. Ind. Eng. **30**(2), 76–83 (2004)
10. Na, S., Kim, D., Park, G., Kee, D., Chung, M.K.: Perceived discomfort of shoulder and elbow postures with externalloads. Japan. J. Ergon. **42**, 590–593 (2010)
11. Chihara, T., Izumi, T., Seo, A.: Perceived discomfort functions based on joint moment for various joint motion directions of the upper limb. Appl. Ergon. **45**(2), 308–317 (2014)
12. Zhang, L.B., Yuan, X.G., Wang, L.J., et al.: Evaluation of joint motion based on perceived discomfort. Space Med. Med. Eng. **19**(6), 412–416 (2006)
13. Xu, F.G., Liu, Z.Q., Zhao, Y.Q., et al.: Discomfort evaluation of upper limb joint motion. J. Med. Imag. Health Inf. **4**(3), 370–373 (2014)
14. Pi, X.T., Chen, F., Peng, C.L., et al.: Methods applied to muscle fatigue assessment using surface myoelectric signals. J. Biomed. Eng. **23**(1), 225–229 (2006)
15. Wu, X.Y., Hou, W.S., Zheng, X.L., et al.: Relationship between surface EMG and angle of elbow joint. Space Med. Med. Eng. **20**(4), 259–263 (2007)
16. GJB/Z 131-2002: Human Engineering Design Handbook for Military Equipment and Facilities (2002)
17. Yang, M.Y., Yu, Y.W.: Anatomical Physiology, pp. 41–58. China Press of Traditional Chinese Medicine, Beijing (2012)
18. Sun, H.Y.: Mathematical Statistics, pp. 304–310. Beihang University Press, Beijing (2016)

A Reliable and Inexpensive Integration of Virtual Reality and Digital Human Modelling to Estimate Cervical Spine Function

Nicola Francesco Lopomo[1](✉) ⓘ, Paolo Mosna[1] ⓘ,
Stefano Elio Lenzi[2] ⓘ, Carlo Emilio Standoli[3] ⓘ, Paolo Perego[3] ⓘ,
Stefano Negrini[4] ⓘ, and Giuseppe Andreoni[3] ⓘ

[1] Department of Information Engineering, Università degli Studi di Brescia,
Brescia, BS, Italy
nicola.lopomo@unibs.it
[2] Consiglio Nazionale delle Ricerche, Neuroscience Institute, Parma, PR, Italy
[3] Department of Design, Politecnico di Milano, Milan, MI, Italy
[4] IRCCS Fondazione Don Carlo Gnocchi ONLUS, Spalenza Center, Rovato,
BS, Italy

Abstract. Musculoskeletal disorders present one of the most prominent impact among the work-related diseases. Cervical spine is indeed one of the anatomical regions most affected by these issues; the main impairments concerning the cervical segment inherently limit its ranges of motion (ROMs). In the last years, novel technologies have been developed to support clinicians in assessing and quantifying these limitations, including wearable sensors and Virtual Reality (VR). In this perspective, interest in Digital Human Modeling has been also increasing due to the possibility of using it together with wearable technologies, thus to obtain enhanced information on body dynamics. This study aimed to validate a novel approach, which integrated VR technology and multi-body modelling to reliably estimated the ROMs of the cervical spine during the execution of three specific tasks (i.e. flexion-extension, lateral bending, axial rotation). Comparison with standard optoelectronic system reported strong correlation and good reliability, with an average difference in estimating ROMs of 8.0° and a mean RMSE of 4.7°. Furthermore, a preliminary test in managing different visual cues through VR highlighted interesting trends for future developments. The performed analysis supported the use of the proposed solution for both the clinical settings and telemedicine applications.

Keywords: Cervical spine · Functional test · Virtual Reality · Digital Human Model

1 Introduction

Among all the most widespread work-related diseases, musculoskeletal disorders (MSD) present one of the most prominent impact on the national health systems and the occupational insurance institutes, in terms of both morbidity and prevalence. The work-related MSD (WRMSD) include a wide range of inflammatory and degenerative

© Springer Nature Switzerland AG 2020
V. G. Duffy (Ed.): HCII 2020, LNCS 12198, pp. 178–193, 2020.
https://doi.org/10.1007/978-3-030-49904-4_14

conditions, frequently presenting pain and functional limitations. Furthermore, WRMSD present a multifactorial etiopathogenesis, with significant co-occurrent causes related to both psycho-physical and organizational aspects.

One of the main anatomical districts, which is prevalently interested by WRMSD, is indeed the spine, affecting - above all - the cervical segment [1]. Main impairments of the cervical spine are inherently related to limitations of its ranges of motion (ROMs) [2]. In order to test these limitations, clinicians developed several functional tests [3] which, however, were not able to provide quantitative information, although they were fairly reliable from a clinical point of view [4]. Furthermore, the symptomatic variability associated with WRMSD requires the implementation of specific diagnostic protocols, with the inclusion of objective clinical criteria and instrumental assessment, which need to address not only the kinematics but also the muscular strength and fatigue [5].

In the last years, several technologies and methodologies capable of objectively estimating biomechanical characteristics have been thence introduced to support the clinicians, including wireless wearable inertial sensors (IMUs) [6] and surface electromyography (EMG) [7]. Both these technologies presented indeed significant advantages related to their non-invasiveness and the possibility to perform the assessment in the most ecological way. Furthermore, these solutions allow to acquire general parameters related to the joint function (e.g. range of rotation, muscle activation, muscular strength and fatigue, etc.). Such specific applications addressed also the cervical spine [8].

Furthermore, Digital Human Modelling (DHM) has been reporting a growing interest also for the clinical employment, since it allows to integrate kinematic and muscular parameters thus to obtain enhanced information related to joint dynamics and muscles activation [9–11].

Very recently, the Virtual Reality (VR) has been also introduced and applied to the clinical field. VR is basically a dedicate computer interfaces which aims to mimic the real world by giving an immersive 3D visual experience. Interesting and valuable VR applications are related to the possibility of supporting not only the rehabilitation – providing, for instance, dedicated game-based training – but also the functional assessments [12]. Concerning cervical spine, VR headset can be used indeed both to provide visual cues to the subjects and track head kinematics during the execution of specific tasks. The obtained kinematic data can be used thence to feed multi-body models, thus to obtain reliable information about the functionals status of the neck. Furthermore, VR give us additional capabilities related to the possibility to manage the visual information we provide to the subject. Indeed, we can introduce visual stimuli that are "competing" with respect to the information coming from the vestibular system, thus to push the subject to reach her/his actual physiological limits.

The main goal of this work was therefore to design, develop and validate a novel methodological approach, which integrated VR technology and multi-body modelling to reliably estimated the range of motion of the spinal cervical segment.

2 Materials and Methods

The approach we proposed was based on the integration of several methodologies and technologies, thus focusing on the possibility to use it in both clinical settings and telemedicine applications.

2.1 Virtual Reality System

The system we designed and developed was made of different hardware and software components, used to provide the subject with the functional tests in a VR environment and thus obtain information about the ROMs of the cervical spine.

Hardware

The hardware was composed of a commercial VR headset (HTC Vive, HTC Corporation) connected via USB 3.0 and HDMI port to a PC Workstation. For the validation tests we specifically used a computer embedding an Intel i7 quad core 6770 HQ, 32 GB Ram Memory, a Nvidia GeForce GTX 1050 video card, a 512 GB SSD + a 1 Tb 7200rp HD drive, and running Windows 10 Pro (Microsoft Corporation) as operating system. The used HTC Vive headset reported a refresh rate of 90 Hz and a 110° field of view, ensured by a two OLED panels, each one with a display resolution of 1080 × 1200 pixels. To track the movement of the headset two HTC laser-emitting stations were also powered and placed in front of the subjects, in order to ensure the correct line-of-sight. The SteamVR tracking technology (Valve Corporation) is provided by HTC as part of its VR system and is based on the use of fan-shaped laser beam emitters and small optical detector mounted on the VR display; the position and orientation of the headset can be estimated by measuring the time at which each swept beam crosses each receiver. Furthermore, this headset was embedded with additional sensors, such as inertial and proximity ones, to support the estimation of the orientation of the head in the 3D space. The complete setup is graphically reported in Fig. 1.

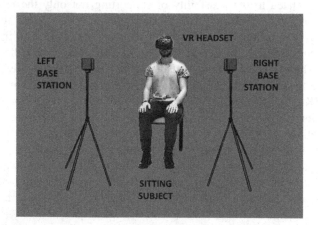

Fig. 1. Graphical representation of the setup used to provide the functional task in a Virtual Reality (VR) environment and track the movements realized by the head.

In order to estimate the cervical spine function, the head movements performed by the subjects during the functional tests were acquired by using the VR headset itself, keeping into account the proper technical reference system with respect to the anatomical one, as hereinafter explained.

Software

A custom-made software was specifically designed to address a single end user (i.e. the physician) who can manage several virtual "scenes" (each one associated to a specific task) and realize the functional assessment on a defined subject.

Through the analysis of several paradigmatic use cases, the end user was identified to interact with the system through a simple Graphical User Interface (GUI), which allowed her/him to quickly perform the procedures required within a single session of assessment, including headset setup and calibration, definition of the scene/test parameters, viewing in real-time what the subject was performing during the execution of the tests themselves, and managing the kinematic data recording. The specific workflow designed to be performed by the end user in each functional assessment session is reported in Fig. 2.

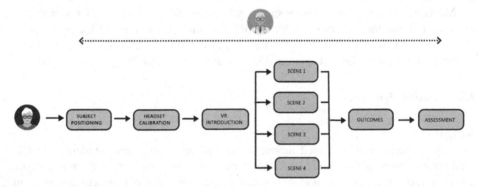

Fig. 2. Workflow of each session designed to realize the functional assessment of the cervical spine. Scene 1, Scene 2, Scene 3 and Scene 4 correspond to the different (prototypical) tasks required to be performed by the subject.

The designed modular approach allowed to remove or add specific scenes/tasks.

The GUI was completely realized by using a cross-platform game engine (Unity 3D, Unity Technologies). The same software platform was used also to design each VR test, since it allowed to easily manage the design of 3D scene keeping into account the interaction with the objects and the type of movement realized by the subject. In order to integrate the functionalities of the VR headset within the development platform, we imported among the Unity assets the SteamVR SDK (Valve Corporation), a library which included, among the others, the "SteamVR" and "CameraRig" prefab components which allowed the rendering of the VR camera and the control of the headset, respectively.

For this study, the designed VR scenes specifically included:

- a vertical "*laser&balloons*" game to test head flexion-extension (**SCENE 1**, Fig. 3-A): the subject was required to pop several vertically-arranged balloons with a laser beam exiting from his eyes;
- a horizontal "*laser&balloons*" game to test head axial rotation (**SCENE 2**, Fig. 3-B): the subject was required to pop several horizontally-arranged balloons with a laser beam exiting from his eyes;
- a "*bar&balls*" game to assess the head lateral bending (**SCENE 3**, Fig. 3-C): the subject was required to crash several frontally-and-circularly-arranged balls by using a wooden bar, which followed the movements of his head.

Furthermore, we introduced a "modified" version of the "bar&balls" games (**SCENE 4**), which exploited the possibility of weighting visual and vestibular stimuli in different "ratios"; in particular we worked on the ratio between the velocity of the moving bar seen by the subject and the real velocity of his/her head while bending laterally. We specifically hypothesized that decreasing the velocity of the virtual object with respect to the velocity of the moving head, would allow to increase the corresponding range of motion achieved by the subject.

Moreover, several features were specifically developed by means of C# scripts and integrated within the core of the software, thus to allow the control of the scenes/tests parameters (e.g. velocity, number of items, etc.), the monitoring of the presence of any involuntary excessive head displacements and the recording of the kinematic data.

2.2   Testing Protocol

Subjects
Healthy subjects were recruited amongst the university staff and students for this preliminary investigative study. All the participants had neither acute nor chronic diseases, did not report any previous spinal surgery and did not present any evident neck disability. All the subjects were volunteers and gave their voluntary consent to participate to this study.

The assessment protocol was explained to each subject before starting the tests; all the participants performed a quick training session to test the required tasks, with the support of the experimenters. The subjects were instructed to interrupt the test, whenever they experienced nausea, dizziness, or any visual problem.

Functional Tests
At the beginning of the session, each participant was invited to sit on a fixed stool and, after training with the required movements, assisted to wear the headset. Thence, after a quick introduction to the VR environment, the subjects were asked to perform three different functional tasks with their head, as reported in Fig. 4, following the defined scene; specifically:

- head flexion-extension;
- head axial rotations;
- head lateral bending.

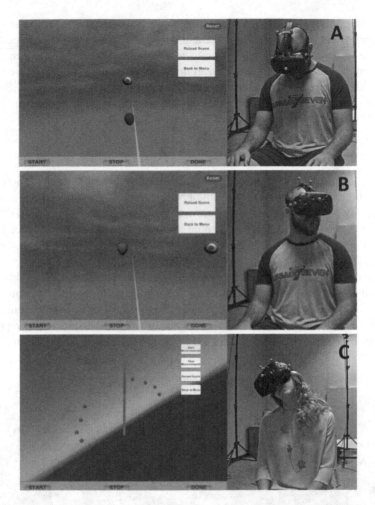

Fig. 3. Example of the three implemented VR scenes and the corresponding realized movements: A) vertical *"laser&balloons"* (**SCENE 1**); B) horizontal *"laser&balloons"* (**SCENE 2**); C) *"bar&balls"* (**SCENE 3** and **SCENE 4**).

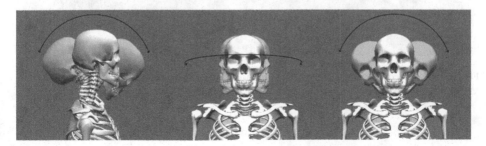

Fig. 4. The three main movements tested during the study: flexion-extension (left), axial rotation (center) and lateral bending (right).

At the beginning of each task, each participant was required to maintain a static position, with trunk in the upright posture and the head aligned in its neutral pose. Each task was performed in a randomized order at a self-defined pace. For each task the subjects were instructed to move their head up to the maximum of its specific range of motion, without forcing the movement. Between each task a pause of 30 s was introduced. During each break, all the subjects were asked for the presence of any discomfort or feelings of dizziness and nausea.

2.3   Experimental Setup

As previously reported, the movement of the head realized during the execution of each task was acquired by using the very same headset used to provide the VR scenes. In particular, only the information coming from the rotation angles was used to define the corresponding head rotation matrix, keeping into account the correspondence between the headset reference system and the anatomical one. Data from VR system were sampled at 20 Hz.

In order to assess the validity of the proposed approach, a marker-based eight-cameras optoelectronic system (Smart DX400, BTS Bioengineering) with a custom-made markerset, was employed. In particular, in order to avoid any infrared interference, all the cameras were placed in a semi-circular arrangement behind the subject. As reported in Fig. 5, three reflective spherical markers were placed on the headset, three more markers

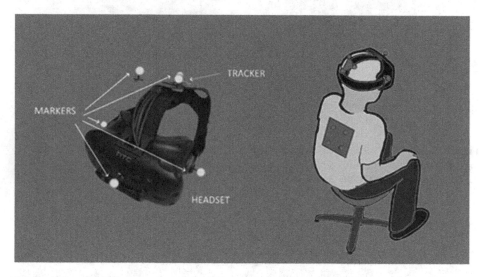

Fig. 5. Setup used to compare the cervical motion estimated by using the data acquired by the VR headset with respect to those registered with the marker-based optoelectronic system.

were fixed on the upper-back of the head by means of a rigid tracker, and further four markers were placed on the back of the trunk by using a squared rigid plate; rigid trackers on the head and on the back were placed in the same position by using specific anatomical references (vertex position, transverse and sagittal plane alignment for the head; C7/T1 position, sagittal and coronal plane alignment for the trunk). The marker trajectories were sampled at 100 Hz and reported with respect to the global reference system. The calibrated volume was about $1.5 \times 1.5 \times 2.0$ m with a reported accuracy of less than 0.3 mm in the identification of the position of each single marker.

2.4 Data Analysis

In order to compare the outcomes obtained by using the headset with respect to the results acquired with the optoelectronic system, a validated digital human multi-body model was used [10]. This model was developed in OpenSim (OpenSim 3.2, Simbios, Stanford, CA, USA), an open source simulating software [9], and presented 35 rigid anatomical segments, 34 joints and 30 kinematic constraints; furthermore the model specifically had 43 degrees of freedom, but for this application, only the degrees of freedom of the head (roll, pitch and yaw) and − just for the analysis of the data coming from the optoelectronic system - the degrees of freedom of the trunk (tilt, list and axial rotation) were unlock, while all the other ones were locked into the neutral sitting posture.

The model was specifically used to solve the inverse kinematic problem by following two different approaches:

1) concerning the data acquired with the optoelectronic systems, inverse kinematics was estimated minimizing the distance between the trajectories of the real markers (down-sampled by a factor 5) and of the virtual ones opportunely placed on the model itself;

2) regarding the data acquired with the VR headset, the calculated rotation matrix was used as it was the information coming from a "virtual" inertial sensor placed on the head of the subject and keeping into account the starting position coming from the static pose acquisition.

In this latter approach, we obviously hypothesized that only the head was moving. These approaches allowed us to compare the data by using the very same reference systems. All the simulations were run in OpenSim 4.1 (Inverse Kinematics and OpenSense modules). The angles corresponding to the main rotation direction was considered for each task (e.g. pitch angle for flexion-extension task). Temporal synchronization of the data coming from the two systems was realized by identified the lag with the maximum value of cross-correlation.

In order to estimate the reliability of the proposed method, both the ROMs and the Root Mean Square Error (RMSE) - evaluated between the two systems - were estimated for each task and each subject, following Eq. 1 and Eq. 2, respectively:

$$ROM_i^S = |\max(\alpha_i^s) - \min(\alpha_i^s)| \tag{1}$$

where i = {FE: flexion-extension; AR: axial rotation; LB: lateral bending; MLB: modified LB}

s = {HS: headset; OE: optoelectronic}

$$RMSE_i = \sqrt{\sum_n [\alpha_i^{HS}(n) - \alpha_i^{OE}(n)]^2 / N} \tag{2}$$

where n = nth time frame

N = overall number of frames contained in the single acquisition

Descriptive statistics were reported for each parameter, individually for each test. Furthermore, correlation (via Pearson correlation coefficient ρ) and Bland-Altman analyses were used to verify the agreement between the two systems.

In order to have a global view of the usability of the system from the subjects' perspective, we asked all the participants to fill a 5-grade ten-items form, which allowed us to estimate the overall System Usability Scale (SUS) [13] for the developed solution; the ten items specifically focused on elicit information about the effectiveness and efficiency of the system and the satisfaction of the involved subjects.

3 Results and Discussion

The main objective of this study was to assess the reliability and the usability of an integrated system which combined the use of VR technology and DHM to estimate the function of the cervical spine, in terms of ROMs, addressing its use in both the clinical settings and the telemedicine applications.

Data from fourteen healthy subjects were available for the analysis; as hereinafter highlighted, all the subjects were able to finish the sessions without reporting any critical issue. In particular, the subjects were twelve males and two females with an age ranging from 21 to 35 years old. The demographic data are reported in Table 1.

Table 1. Summary of the characteristics of the recruited subjects.

Female/male ratio	Weight [kg]	Height [cm]	Body mass index	Age [years old]
2/12	82 ± 16	181 ± 6	24.8 ± 3.2	26 ± 3

Example of the data obtained from the DHM are reported in Fig. 6.

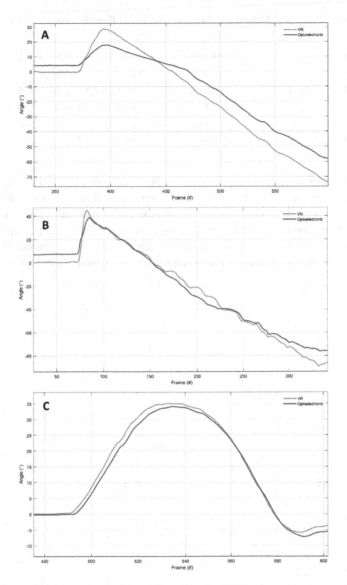

Fig. 6. Example of join angles estimated by using the VR headset data (green line) and the marker-based optoelectronic system (red line). A: pitch angel during flexion-extension test; B: yaw angle during axial rotation task; C: roll angle during lateral bending task. (Color figure online)

Average ROM values for each task and each system are instead reported in Table 2.

Table 2. Average Range of Motion (ROM) and Root Mean Square Error (RMSE) for each test and system.

Test	ROM [°]				RMSE [°]	
	VR		OE		Mean	Max
Flexion-extension	99.5	±22.1	90.1	±22.4	6.6	±9.2
Axial rotation	149.4	±13.3	138.5	±7.7	8.1	±9.9
Lateral bending	86.8	±14.5	82.0	±12.6	2.1	±6.4
"Modified" lateral bending	91.0	±16.1	83.8	±11.2	2.1	±5.3

For all the performed tests, we found an average difference in estimating the ROM of about 8.0° (corresponding to 8.6% percent error), with a maximum difference of 10.9° (i.e. 7.7% percent error) in the axial rotation and a minimum difference of 4.9° (i.e. 6.2% percent error) for the lateral bending test. The maximum percent error was registered in the flexion-extension test (i.e. 12.2% error); this is probably due to a partial motion of the trunk during the execution of this specific movement.

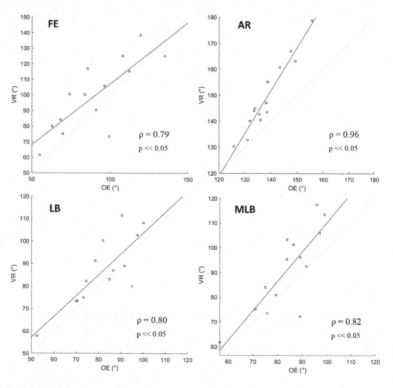

Fig. 7. Correlation plots of the ROMs for each performed test. ρ coefficients and corresponding p values are reported. VR: Virtual Reality headset data; OE: optoelectronic system data. FE: flexion-extension test; AR: axial rotation test; LB: lateral bending test; MLB: "modified" lateral bending test.

Although analysis of average ROMs highlighted a wide range of variability, data provided good consistency between the two used systems, reporting a strong correlation (i.e. ρ values ranged from 0.79, for flexion-extension test, to 0.96 for axial rotation test), with an average value of 0.85. Specific ρ values and graphical representations of these correlations are reported in Fig. 7.

The Bland-Altman analysis (Fig. 8) highlighted that, for all the tests, the VR system overestimated the ROMs, with positive bias that ranged from 4.9° in the lateral bending to 11° in the axial rotation. Furthermore, the analysis of the axial rotation highlighted a linear trend of the bias that increased as the axial rotation grew; similar trends are not evident in the other tests. Even in this analysis is evident that there was a relationship between the type of movement realized by the subject and the errors that were estimated; this is mainly due to the motion of the trunk that, during flexion-extension and axial rotation, strived to follow more the corresponding movement of the head.

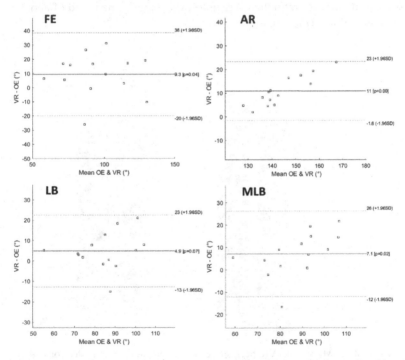

Fig. 8. Bland-Altman plots of the ROMs for each performed test. Corresponding bias (with p value) and 95% confidence intervals are also reported.

Considering all the tests, we obtained an overall average RMSE value of 4.7° with a maximum in the axial rotation test (i.e. 8.1°) and a minimum value in both the lateral bending tests (i.e. 2.2°), when comparing the use of the VR headset with respect to the gold standard. The overall maximum value of RMSE was registered for the axial rotation tests and corresponded to 9.9°. These biases can be mainly ascribed to the reference position, which was estimated for both the systems by using the static pose; however, for the optoelectronic system the initial position of the head was evaluated by using also the information coming from the trunk. Indeed, for the VR headset, the only information coming from the head was used.

Summarizing the findings obtained in the ROM analysis, the VR headset resulted to be reliable in defining the ranges of movement, with values that were in general comparable with those ones estimated by using the optoelectronic system. Main issues are related to the presence of systematic errors that led to an overestimation of the current ROMs. However, the obtained ROMs are fairly in agreement with the results reported by different studies based on the use of similar methodologies [14–24]; main differences can be traced back to the different setup used.

In order to use the system reliably, the end user should pay attention in the definition of the reference position and in maintaining the trunk of the subject as stable as possible during the execution of the tests.

Focusing on the possibility of managing different visual cues, when considering a 0.75 visual/vestibular cues ratio the average ROM averagely increased of about 2° with respect to standard test (Fig. 9).

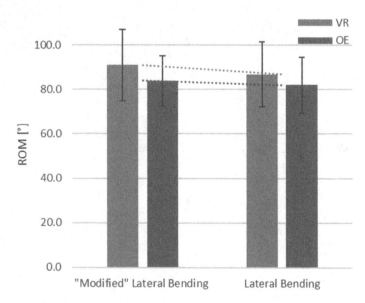

Fig. 9. Values of ROMs for the VR headset (green color) and the optoelectronic system (red color) considering the "modified" lateral bending and the lateral bending. Standard deviation and linear trends are also reported. (Color figure online)

Therefore, this finding is worth to be further analyze by increasing the number of subjects and by designing new scenes that can provide different control in the cues.

Furthermore, literature provides important information on different parameters that can be used to estimate the presence of functional limitations, including peak velocity, number of peaks in velocity, smoothness index, etc. [24, 25].

From the SUS analysis, the system and the protocol were reported to be properly designed and easy to use, with a very simple but effective interface, no necessity of technical support and a quick learning curve. Average values for the SUS are reported in Table 3.

Table 3. System Usability Scale (SUS) report with values averaged for all the subjects.

Questions	Reported values [from 1 (strongly disagree) to 5 (strongly agree)]
I think that I would like to use this system frequently	3.7
I found the system unnecessarily complex	1.6
I thought the system was easy to use	4.3
I think that I would need the support of a technical person to be able to use this system	2.7
I found the various functions in this system were well integrated	4.0
I thought there was too mush inconsistency in this system	1.3
I would imagine that most people would learn to use this system very quickly	3.9
I found the system very cumbersome to use	2.3
I felt very confident using the system	4.1
I needed to learn a lot of things before I could get going with this system	1.7

The main limitation of this study is indeed the small number of subjects recruited and used in the analysis. Future works will necessarily introduce more subjects, both healthy and with specific functional limitation, thus to verify the possibility of using such an approach in the classification of defined WRMSD that affect the cervical spine.

4 Conclusion

By wearing a VR headset, the subjects could be easily projected into a virtual environment, where they were able to perform functional tasks as they were playing (serious) games. The use of VR presented several advantages related to the management of the clinical assessment (i.e. reduced anxiety and more engagement) and of the testing itself (test definition and balancing between visual and vestibular cues). This study well highlighted all these added values in the developing a specific application addressing the functional assessment of the cervical spine. Furthermore, the proposed methodology resulted to be reliable when compared to the gold standard, although particular attentions should be given by the end user to obtain clinically valid outcomes. Future developments should address telemedicine applications by exploiting also mobile technology.

Acknowledgement. This study was supported by the project ID 08/2016 founded by INAIL within the call BRIC 2016. NFL would like to thank Alessandro Bianciardi for his support in the development of this work.

References

1. Nordander, C., et al.: Exposure-response relationships for work-related neck and shoulder musculoskeletal disorders - analyses of pooled uniform data sets. Appl. Ergon. **55**, 70–84 (2016)
2. Ernst, M.J., et al.: Extension and flexion in the upper cervical spine in neck pain patients. Man. Ther. **20**, 547–552 (2015)
3. Childs, J.D., et al.: Neck pain. J. Orthop. Sport. Phys. Ther. **38**, A1–A34 (2008)
4. Audette, I., Dumas, J.-P., Côté, J.N., De Serres, S.J.: Validity and between-day reliability of the Cervical Range of Motion (CROM) device. J. Orthop. Sport. Phys. Ther. **40**, 318–323 (2010)
5. Baillargeon, E., Anderst, W.J.: Sensitivity, reliability and accuracy of the instant center of rotation calculation in the cervical spine during in vivo dynamic flexion-extension. J. Biomech. **46**, 670–676 (2013)
6. Dahlqvist, C., Hansson, G.Å., Forsman, M.: Validity of a small low-cost triaxial accelerometer with integrated logger for uncomplicated measurements of postures and movements of head, upper back and upper arms. Appl. Ergon. **55**, 108–116 (2016)
7. Qin, J., Lin, J.H., Faber, G.S., Buchholz, B., Xu, X.: Upper extremity kinematic and kinetic adaptations during a fatiguing repetitive task. J. Electromyogr. Kinesiol. **24**, 404–411 (2014)
8. Raya, R., et al.: An inexpensive and easy to use cervical range of motion measurement solution using inertial sensors. Sensors **18**, 2582 (2018)
9. Delp, S.L., et al.: OpenSim: open-source software to create and analyze dynamic simulations of movement. IEEE Trans. Biomed. Eng. **54**, 1940–1950 (2007)
10. Cazzola, D., Holsgrove, T.P., Preatoni, E., Gill, H.S., Trewartha, G.: Cervical spine injuries : a whole-body musculoskeletal model for the analysis of spinal loading. PLoS One **12**(1), 1–24 (2017)
11. Mortensen, J.D., Vasavada, A.N., Merryweather, A.S.: The inclusion of hyoid muscles improve moment generating capacity and dynamic simulations in musculoskeletal models of the head and neck. PLoS ONE **13**, e0199912 (2018)
12. di Luzio, F.S., Lauretti, C., Cordella, F., Draicchio, F., Zollo, L.: Visual vs vibrotactile feedback for posture assessment during upper-limb robot-aided rehabilitation. Appl. Ergon. **82**, 102950 (2020)
13. Lewis, J.R.: The system usability scale: past, present, and future. Int. J. Hum. Comput. Interact. **34**, 577–590 (2018)
14. Moghaddas, D., de Zoete, R.M.J., Edwards, S., Snodgrass, S.J.: Differences in the kinematics of the cervical and thoracic spine during functional movement in individuals with or without chronic neck pain: a systematic review. Physiother. **105**, 421–433 (2019). (United Kingdom)
15. Sommer, B.B.: Concurrent validity and reliability of a mobile tracking technology to measure angular and linear movements of the neck. J. Biomech. **96**, 109340 (2019)
16. Bahat, H.S., Sprecher, E., Sela, I., Treleaven, J.: Neck motion kinematics: an inter-tester reliability study using an interactive neck VR assessment in asymptomatic individuals. Eur. Spine J. **25**, 2139–2148 (2016)

17. Sarig Bahat, H., Takasaki, H., Chen, X., Bet-Or, Y., Treleaven, J.: Cervical kinematic training with and without interactive VR training for chronic neck pain - a randomized clinical trial. Man. Ther. **20**, 68–78 (2015)
18. Sarig Bahat, H., Croft, K., Carter, C., Hoddinott, A., Sprecher, E., Treleaven, J.: Remote kinematic training for patients with chronic neck pain: a randomised controlled trial. Eur. Spine J. **27**, 1309–1323 (2018)
19. Sarig Bahat, H., Chen, X., Reznik, D., Kodesh, E., Treleaven, J.: Interactive cervical motion kinematics: sensitivity, specificity and clinically significant values for identifying kinematic impairments in patients with chronic neck pain. Man. Ther. **20**, 295–302 (2015)
20. Williams, G., Sarig-Bahat, H., Williams, K., Tyrrell, R., Treleaven, J.: Cervical kinematics in patients with vestibular pathology vs patients with neck pain: a pilot study. J. Vestib. Res. Equilib. Orientat. **27**, 137–145 (2017)
21. Sarig-Bahat, H., Weiss, P.L., Laufer, Y.: Neck pain assessment in a virtual environment. Spine (Phila. Pa. 1976) **35**, 105–112 (2010)
22. Sarig-Bahat, H., Weiss, P.L., Laufer, Y.: Cervical motion assessment using virtual reality. Spine (Phila. Pa. 1976) **34**, 1018–1024 (2009)
23. Bahat, S.: Neck motion analysis using a virtual environment. Virtual Real. (2010)
24. Mihajlovic, Z., Popovic, S., Brkic, K., Cosic, K.: A system for head-neck rehabilitation exercises based on serious gaming and virtual reality. Multimed. Tools Appl. **77**, 19113–19137 (2018)
25. Kiper, P.: Assessment of the cervical spine mobility by immersive and non-immersive virtual reality. J. Electromyogr. Kinesiol. **51**, 102397 (2020)

Development of a Wearable IMU System for Automatically Assessing Lifting Risk Factors

Ming-Lun Lu[1(✉)], Menekse S. Barim[1], Shuo Feng[2], Grant Hughes[2], Marie Hayden[1], and Dwight Werren[1]

[1] National Institute for Occupational Safety and Health, Cincinnati, OH, USA
uzl5@cdc.gov
[2] FocusMotion, Focus Ventures Inc., Santa Monica, CA, USA

Abstract. The objective of this study was to develop a five inertial measurement unit (IMU) sensor system attached to the human body for automatically identifying the duration of the lifting task (LD) performed symmetrically with two hands at various hand locations relative to the body, and three other lifting risk variables including the trunk flexion angle (T), the vertical distance (V) and horizontal distance (H) of the lifting task defined by the revised National Institute for Occupational Safety and Health lifting equation (RNLE). The algorithm that processed the IMU data consisted of two modules: the synchronization module that extracted the synchronization feature of wrists' motion data to identify the lifting event; and the lifting variable calculations module that employed a body segment length ratio model for calculating the risk variables. The variable calculation module was further modified to include subjects' body segment length information for improved accuracy. The wearable system was validated by motion data collected by a laboratory grade motion capture system on 10 human subjects performing 360 lifting trials. Results showed that the model performed well for determining the LD (~ 1 s error) and T ($\sim 2°$ error). However, the mean errors for V and H were large (33 and 6.5 cm, respectively). Inclusion of subjects' five body segment length measurements improved the mean errors of V and H to 14 and 2.2 cm, respectively.

Keywords: IMU · Lifting · Ergonomic assessment

1 Introduction

1.1 Background

Musculoskeletal disorders (MSDs) are a major workplace health problem and economic burden. Recent data showed that workplace overexertion injuries were estimated to cost $15.1 billion a year, accounting for about 25% of the total workers' compensation cost [1]. Low back disorders (LBDs) are the largest contributor to the total workers' compensation cost. The total health care expenditures incurred by individuals with low back pain alone in the United States reached $90.7 billion a year [2].

V. G. Duffy (Ed.): HCII 2020, LNCS 12198, pp. 194–213, 2020.
https://doi.org/10.1007/978-3-030-49904-4_15

To control and prevent MSDs in the workplace, accurate quantifications of risk factors are imperative. Substantial evidence has shown that work-related physical risk factors are the main source of LBDs [3–5]. These physical risk factors include heavy/repetitive manual lifting, awkward posture, and long work hours. Combinations of these physical risk factors may lead to an increasing risk of developing LBDs [6]. Reductions of work-related physical risk factors have been the main goal of ergonomic interventions. To assess the physical risk factors for LBDs, ergonomic checklists or video task analyses are commonly used by practitioners. However, these observational risk assessment methods with the primary goal of quantifying postural risks are subjective, resource intensive; and cannot effectively quantify a variety of postures used by the worker during an 8-h workday [7, 8].

1.2   Trend in the Use of IMU for Ergonomic Assessments

Direct-reading measurements of postural risk exposures were developed by several researchers in the 90's [9–12]. However, the complex and bulky set ups did not seem to be an attractive option for field applications. With the advent of the small, wearable and light weight features of inertial measurement unit (IMU) sensors, the IMU-based ergonomic assessments are becoming a new method for tracking postural risks [13]. Many recent studies utilizing IMU sensors for ergonomic research have developed useful algorithms for measuring body postural angles, primarily the trunk flexion angle [13–15].

An IMU combines information obtained from multiple electromechanical sensors (e.g., accelerometers, gyroscopes and magnetometers) to estimate the dynamic human body motions [16]. The application of IMUs for tracking human motion as a part of the ergonomic assessment is becoming popular because the collection of the human body motion does not greatly interrupt with workers' job performance [13, 17].

Using IMU sensors for ergonomic assessments is a growing research area. Research over the past 10 years has mainly focused on the accuracy and validation of these sensor technologies. A literature search was performed using the Web of Science and Scopus databases. Records identified through the databases with the search term "ergonomic assessment" showed more than 7000 articles. The number of the articles was reduced to 450 using additional keyword search terms "inertial measurement unit" or "wearable sensor". Of 450 articles, 42 were identified manually by the authors of this study to have a research topic related to estimating joint kinematics. These selected 42 studies include various research topics of estimating joint kinematics of: the upper arm/shoulder [18–29], the cervical spine [30–32], the lower extremity [33–40], the trunk [13–15, 41–49], the whole body [13, 17, 50–53] and hand movement [54]. The majority (60%) of the literature had a focus on estimating the whole body posture and trunk movements.

1.3   Physical Risk Factors for LBDs

Manual repetitive lifting has been identified by many studies as one of the main risk factors for MSDs [3, 4]. NIOSH has identified several task variables for manual lifting that are associated with increased risks of LBDs [55]. These task variables are summarized in the NIOSH Applications Manual for the RNLE [56]. The manual provides detailed information on the definitions of the task variables as well as the measuring methods for them.

Some of the previous studies have developed useful algorithms for measuring body postural angles, such as the trunk flexion angle [57–59]. However, these algorithms for processing data from IMU sensors have not been developed for identifying other lifting risk factors defined by the RNLE [56]. Therefore, the task variables of interest in this study were the duration of a lifting task (LD), the vertical distance between the load and the floor (V) and the horizontal distance (H) between the load and the center of the two ankles. The identification of these lifting task variables and lifting physical risk factors using IMU sensors provides valuable risk information for interventions.

1.4   Purpose of the Study

Generally, the accuracy of the wearable ensemble of sensors in measuring the body posture is a function of the number of sensors used. Detailed whole-body biomechanical models for tracking accurate body motion typically require 13 to 17 IMU sensors mounted on various body segments. For example, a commercially popular IMU-based body tracking system Xsens MVN requires wearing a body suit with 17 IMUs [60]. In our opinion, the high cost, the lengthy setup time and required expertise for using the software programs for analyzing the IMU data present a challenge for adoption in the field. One previous study [61] has shown that a five IMU sensor configuration may adequately reconstruct the whole-body posture to discriminate gross movement activities. The previous study inspired the researchers to examine the feasibility of using such a simpler system to increase the adoption of the wearable technology. In short, the purpose of this study was to assess the feasibility of using a five IMU-based wearable sensor system for automatically measuring multiple physical risk factors associated with two-handed manual lifting.

2   Methods

2.1   Design of the Five-Sensor Wearable System

Five IMU sensors (Kinetic Inc.) were attached to the subject's specific body landmarks, as shown in Fig. 1. These IMU sensors were attached to the wrists, right upper arm, upper back, and right thigh. To process data from the sensors, we used a hybrid model that incorporated machine learning and trigonometric functions for detecting lofting motion and the location of the hands in relation to the body. The input of the model was 6-axial IMU data (accelerometer and gyroscope in 3 axes respectively) sampling at 25 Hz from each of the sensors. The data were fed into two major modules including the lifting detection module and the sensor fusion module that ran in parallel. The lifting detection module detected the occurrence of a lifting event with the timestamps of the beginning (BOL) and the ending (EOL) of the event. The sensor fusion module kept track of the device orientations in real time at 25 Hz and provided the angles of the sensors in three dimensions relative to the ground. The sensor fusion model was primarily used for correcting the gyroscope data for estimating the orientations of the body segments during a dynamic workplace environment.

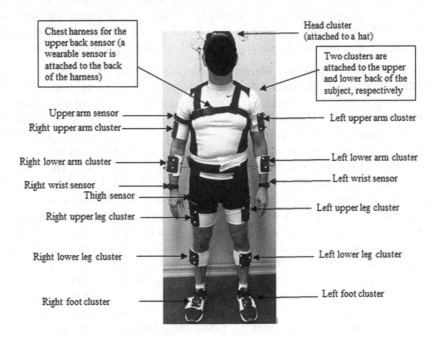

Fig. 1. Locations for five IMU sensors (one sensor located on the T12 region on the upper back is not visible) [Photo credit: CDC/NIOSH].

2.2   Lifting Risk Variables

To determine physical risk factors associated with two-handed manual lifting, the BOL and EOL were required to be identified first. Once the two time instants were determined, lifting risk factors during the lifting duration could be estimated with the lifting detection module. Three main lifting task variables used in this study were trunk flexion angle, V and H. The V and H variables were defined by the RNLE and used by the American Conference of Governmental Industrial Hygienists Threshold Limit Values (TLVs) for lifting.

2.3   Lifting Detection Module

The detection of the BOL and EOL was executed by a two-layer algorithm. The lower layer used data from two wrist sensors as input to check the motion synchronization feature of the two wrists during lifting; and outputted a binary result of the onset of synchronization and no synchronization. The higher layer or representative motion detection was a digital signal processing (DSP) layer that monitored certain events that had high correlations with the features of lifting, such as bending over and reaching out with arms. This layer ran only when the lower layer detected synchronization.

Synchronization Feature of Wrist Sensor Data. The lifting detection module constantly monitored motions (i.e., acceleration and rotation) of the two wrist sensors and determined the level of synchronization of their motions. We assumed that the two wrist sensors had high levels of synchronized motion when an object was held and moved by both hands. This assumption was based on the property of a non-elastic lifting objective that coupled the accelerations and rotations of the wrist sensors.

Machine Learning Algorithm. We used a machine learning approach to build the lifting detection module. Motion data were collected on 6 subjects performing two categories of activities: 1) performing common activities while holding a rigid box and 2) performing common activities without holding a rigid box. More specifically, for the holding-box activities, subjects performed activities of walking, turning around, raising and lowering arms while holding a rigid box for 30 s each. For the arm free activities, subjects repeated the above activities without holding the rigid box. The total data collection times for activities (1) and (2) were about 5 and 15 min, respectively. A typical sliding window approach [62–65] with a window of 2.5 s and a 0.5 s overlap was employed. For each window, IMU data from both wrist sensors were used to extract features which best represented synchronization of the wrist motions. A binary classification model was trained using a random forest classification algorithm [66]. Open source languages R and Python/C++ random forest tools were used for programming the algorithm. The binary training labels were prior-known from one of the two categories of activities. This approach was used to detect whether the two wrists were in synchronization at a 0.5 s step size over a 2.5 s long window. Namely, a decision was made based on previous 2.5 s data and updated every 0.5 s. The ratio of training and validation datasets is 5:1, resulting in a use of 25 min of hands synchronized data for training and 5 min of data for validation. This module achieved a training accuracy of 83%–85% detection rate, and about 32% in false alarm rate [67].

Representative Motion Detection. The motion detection layer or the higher layer was necessary in that the lower layer only provided a binary decision over a 2.5 s window without providing the exact starting and ending moment of a lifting event. This module was aimed to detect certain events that were highly likely to happen during lifting events by tracking the motion data of certain body parts. Sample motions included: extending arms out together, bending over and turning around in whole body motion. Each of these motions are extracted from sensor data of corresponding body parts as a one dimensional signal. The signal had peaks at the moment of these events. These signals were combined together to amplify the signature event. The exact moment of BOL and EOL were then available using the peaks of the combined signal. This higher layer only ran when the lower layer detected the motion synchronization feature of the two wrists. The lower layer remained idle when both wrists were not in synchronization, such as walking.

2.4   Sensor Fusion Module

IMU sensors typically measure three-dimensional data from accelerometer and gyroscope sensors. The accelerometer sensor, measuring three-dimensional linear acceleration, produces a vector sum of the acceleration caused by gravity and the acceleration caused by motion. The gravity acceleration provides the device orientation information if it can be isolated from the sum. The gyroscope measures the three-dimensional angular velocity (i.e., rotation rate) [68, 69], and the track of history indicates the changes of device orientation. However, the track has to be done by an integral from angular rate to angles, which generates a large accumulative drift [70]. An extended Kalman filter algorithm, similar to that used by Rigatos and Tzafestas [71] was used to fuse the accelerometer and gyroscope data of a single device and then output gravity vector information (from accelerometer data) with motion induced acceleration and bias of gyroscope data attenuated. This gravity vector provided information of device orientation in real time for improving the identification of the lifting event.

2.5   Calculations of Trunk Flexion Angle, V and H

This sensor fusion was applied to all the individual sensors prior to the calculations of the lifting risk variables. The trunk flexion angle was directly available from gyroscope data from the upper back sensor placed on the T12 region of the spine. A calibration for the trunk flexion angle was performed to account for the natural lordosis of the spine while standing upright. This means that the trunk flexion angle was calibrated by subtracting the slight angle from the line of gravity using the data collected during quiet upright standing.

As shown in Fig. 2, the angular data of four sensors (Q_{UA}, Q_{FA}, Q_{back}, Q_{thigh}) were input into the equations below for calculating V and H. Because of the redundant information of the synchronized wrist motion, data from the left wrist sensor was ignored in calculating the two variables. Because subjects did not significantly flex the lower legs during the lifting tasks, the Q_{calf} angle during lifts was assumed to have little effect on the calculations of the lifting risk variables. Therefore, the Q_{calf} angle was not input into the equations.

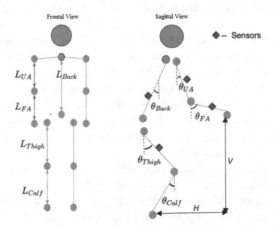

Fig. 2. Body length ratio model and angular data of four sensors used for estimating V and H.

$$V = L_{back} \times \cos(\theta_{Back}) + L_{Thigh} \times \cos(\theta_{Thigh}) + L_{calf} - L_{UA} \times \cos(\theta_{UA}) - L_{FA} \\ \times \cos(\theta_{FA})$$

$$H = L_{UA} \times \sin(\theta_{UA}) + L_{FA} \times \sin(\theta_{FA}) + L_{Back} \times \sin(\theta_{Back}) - L_{thigh} \times \sin(\theta_{Thigh})$$

The variable calculation module was based on a body length ratio model using the right forearm length as the basic unit to estimate the lengths of other body segments. Based on population anthropomorphic data, the length of the upper arm (L_{UA}) approximated the length of the forearm (L_{FA}); the length of the upper leg (L_{Thigh}) or the lower leg (L_{Calf}) approximated 1.2 times L_{FA}; and the length of the spine (L_{back}) was estimated to be 1.4 times L_{FA}. This body length ratio model simplified the data collection process without a need for measuring the lengths of various body segments.

Because the calculations of V and H were based on the actual measurement of the forearm length, the body length ratio model was able to compute V and H as distances. To improve the accuracy of the variable calculations method, it was revised to include input of subjects' specific anthropometric measurements of forearm length, upper arm length, back length, thigh length and calf length. In this paper, we used the terms "ratio" and "ratio + length" as the first and second models, respectively.

2.6   Validation of the Algorithm for Measuring the Lifting Risk Variables

Human Subjects. Ten subjects (five males and five females) in NIOSH, Cincinnati, Ohio, volunteered to participate in the study. The subjects' mean and SD for age, statue and weight were 51.50 ± 9.83 years; 170 ± 7.4 cm and 85.7 ± 20.2 kg, respectively. Prior to data collection, written consents were obtained from the subjects in accordance with NIOSH's Internal Review Board's approved study protocol.

Instrumentation and Data Collection. Subjects' motion data were collected in a laboratory environment with the five wearable IMU sensor system and a motion capture system (OptiTrack, NaturakPoint Inc. and the MotionMonitor® system, Innovative Sports Inc.). During data collection, the IMU data were streamed continuously from 5 sensors to a data logger at a rate of 25 samples per second through Bluetooth connection. Prior to data collection, the internal clock of the sensor data logger was synchronized with the universal time clock (UTC), which was used to synchronize the motion capture data and the videos recorded by a Microsoft web camera at a resolution of 480p. The camera viewing angle was approximately perpendicular to the subjects' sagittal plane.

Subjects were asked to perform symmetrical lifting tasks to produce commonly used body postures for 12 lifting zones defined by the ACGIH TLVs for lifting classification (Fig. 3). The definitions of the V and H originated from the RNLE. Basically, these lifting zones were defined by the combination of H and V for symmetrical lifting on the sagittal plane. The midpoints of the lifting zones were used as the positions for starting the lifting tasks, except for zones 1–3, 4, 7, and 10. The alternative starting locations of the lifting tasks for the exceptional zones were chosen for realistic lifting motion within subjects' reach distances. Each task was repeated three times for a total

36 lifting trials for each subject. The initial lifting positions were adjusted according to each subject's anthropometric information. These trials were assigned to each subject in random order to reduce learning effects.

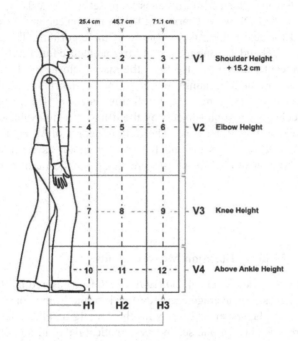

Fig. 3. Initial lifting positions based on the ACGIH TLV for lifting (H1: Near horizontal distance from the basket, H2: Middle distance, H3: Far distance, V1: Vertical height shoulder level, V2: Waist level, V3: Knee level and V4: Floor level)

A wired grid weighing about 0.45 kg and measuring 36 × 12 cm in size with two cutout handles was used to simulate lifting a tote box during the trials. The grid was designed to help subjects create a realistic lifting motion while minimizing obstructions for body motion measurements by the optical motion capture system. A small platform (12 × 12 cm) was used to hold the grid for setting the initial lifting height. A shelf (77.5 cm in height) as the ending position of the lifting trials was set up opposite of the initial lifting location. The distance between the initial and ending positions of the lifting trials was 3.4 m.

Before each trial, three distances of H were marked on the floor to guide the subjects to lift from one of the designated zones classified by H (25.4, 45.7 and 71 cm from the center of the two ankles to the center of the grid). With the pre-determined locations of the feet and hands in the zones, the lifting postures from the 12 zones were assured.

Identification of BOL and EOL. Video recordings from the motion capture system were used to manually identify the beginning and ending of each lifting trial. Two NIOSH researchers reviewed the video recordings to identify the video frame numbers for the BOL and the EOL for each trial. The criteria for determining the frame numbers were based on the moment when the grid started to move for the BOL and the moment when the grid was set down completely by two hands for the EOL.

Data Analysis. Because the 12 lifting zones were set up at the BOL, the V, H, and trunk flexion (T) at the BOL were determined by the motion capture system and used as the gold standard for determining the accuracy of the algorithm. The motion capture system calculated V, H and T using matrix and trigonometric functions applied to body segment and joint center data estimated from the marker clusters in Fig. 1 [8, 72]. The arithmetic difference in the timestamps identified by the algorithm and the observation method was used as the error measure for lifting duration. The mean of this error measure was calculated across all subjects by the lifting zone to evaluate different error levels as a function of the lifting zone. The measurements of V, H and trunk flexion angle between the wearable system and the motion capture system were compared using the Bland-Altman plots. The plots were made for the ratio and ratio + length models respectively.

3   Results

3.1   Accuracy of Lifting Duration Measurements

Table 1 shows the accuracy levels of LD (EOL − BOL) measured by the IMU system for the 12 lifting zones. The average accuracy level for the lifting zones was about one sec (0.939 s), with the largest error 1.079 s for the zone 12 and the smallest 0.622 s for the zone 5. There was about a one-second systematical delay in identifying BOL and EOL for each lifting trial by the algorithm. The input of additional body segment length data did not affect the estimation of the lifting duration.

Table 1. Lifting duration differences between the wearable IMU and motion capture systems (lifting zone number is presented in the parentheses)

Lifting duration differences (sec) Average ± SD		
Total difference within all subjects and zones is 0.939 ± 0.673		
(1) 1.056 ± 0.586	(2) 1.036 ± 0.596	(3) 0.949 ± 0.705
(4) 0.879 ± 0.820	(5) 0.622 ± 0.386	(6) 0.754 ± 0.528
(7) 1.052 ± 1.029	(8) 1.032 ± 0.976	(9) 0.913 ± 0.466
(10) 0.884 ± 0.548	(11) 1.014 ± 0.493	(12) 1.079 ± 0.565

3.2   Accuracy of V Measurements

Figure 4 shows the Bland-Altman plots for comparing the V variable measured by the ratio model of the wearable system and the motion capture system. In the Bland-Altman plot, the Y axis represents the difference in V measured by the two systems

(Vw: wearable system; Vm: motion capture system), whereas the X axis represents the mean value of V measured by the two systems. The mean of the differences in all measurements represents the bias or error of the wearable system. The lower and upper levels of agreement (LOA) represent the 95% confidence interval (± 1.96 SD) of the mean difference. Negative and positive signs of the differences or errors on the Y axis indicate under- and over-estimation of the wearable system. As shown in Fig. 7, the mean error (Vw-Vm) of all the measurements was -33 cm. The mean errors of V for the four vertical zones V_1–V_4 were -43, -30, -28 and -31 cm, respectively. The scattered data points of the wearable system for the vertical zone V_3 crosses 0 difference (i.e., 100% matched with the motion capture data), indicating an increased accuracy level for measuring V between the knuckle and mid-shin heights.

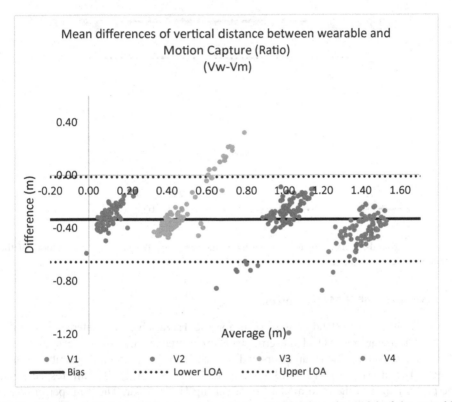

Fig. 4. The Bland-Altman plot for comparing V measured by the ratio model of the wearable system and the motion capture system

Figure 5 shows the Bland-Altman plots for comparing the V variable measured by the ratio + length model of the wearable system and the motion capture system. The mean error (Vw-Vm) of V measured by the wearable system was -14 cm. The mean errors of V for the four vertical zones V_1–V_4 were -14, -4, -12 and -28 cm, respectively. The scattered data points of the measurement errors for all four vertical zones cross 0 (i.e., 100% matched with data measured by the motion capture data), indicating an improved accuracy level for measuring V for all vertical zones.

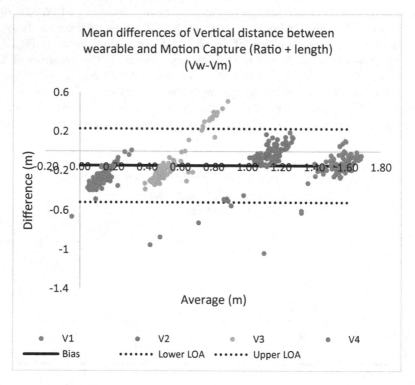

Fig. 5. The Bland-Altman plot for comparing V measured by the ratio + length model of the wearable system and the motion capture system

3.3   Accuracy of H Measurements

Figures 6 shows the Bland-Altman plots for the H variable calculated by the ratio model. The mean and SD of the error in H measured by the wearable system was −6.2 cm and 19 cm. The mean errors and SDs of H measured by the wearable system for H_1, H_2 and H_3 were -12 ± 13.5, -7 ± 13.7 and -23.5 ± 10.9 cm, respectively. The performance of the ratio model for measuring H was poor. The poor performance was significantly affected by the horizontal location of the lift deviated from the middle zones.

Figures 7 shows the Bland-Altman plots for the H variable calculated by the ratio model. The mean and SD of the error in H measured by the wearable system was −2.2 cm and 21.9 cm. The mean errors and SDs of H measured by the wearable system for H_1, H_2 and H_3 were -18 ± 16, -0.9 ± 13.7 and -19 ± 15 cm. With the input of the body segment length data, the performance of the ratio model for measuring H was improved. However, the performance was still significantly affected by the horizontal location of the lift deviated from the middle zones.

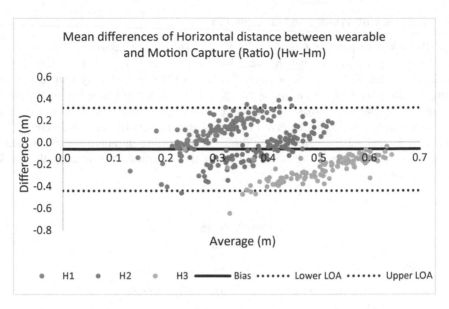

Fig. 6. The Bland-Altman plot for comparing H measured by the ratio model of the wearable system and the motion capture system

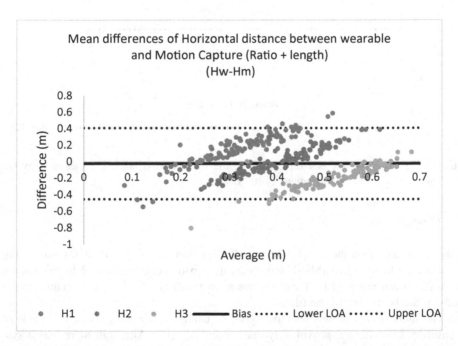

Fig. 7. The Bland-Altman plot for comparing H measured by the ratio + length model of the wearable system and the motion capture system

3.4   Accuracy of Trunk Flexion Angle (T)

The Bland-Altman plot for T is shown in Fig. 8. The mean ($\pm$SD) of T measured by the motion capture system and the wearable system were 37.5° ($\pm$32.8°) and 39.8° ($\pm$32.9), respectively. The mean error (Tw-Tm) of the wearable system across all lifting heights was $-2.4°$. To examine the effect of the different lifting heights on the T measurements, the mean error is presented as a function of the vertical zones (V_1, V_2, V_3 and V_4) in four different colors in Fig. 8. The mean errors for V_1 to V_4 were $-2.3°$, $-1.6°$, $-7.8°$ and $-2.5°$, respectively. Similar to the lifting duration, the use of additional body segment length data did not affect the accuracy of estimating the trunk flexion angle.

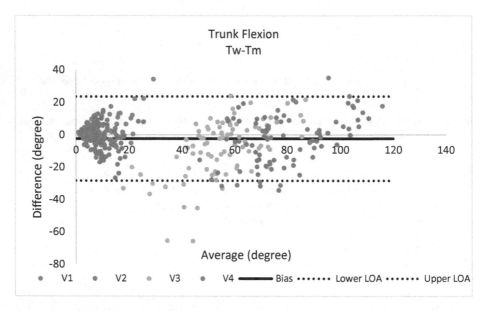

Fig. 8. The Bland-Altman plot for comparing the trunk flexion angle (T) measured by the wearable (Tw) and the motion capture (Tm) systems

4   Discussion

This paper describes the development and validation of an algorithm for processing motion data from a five IMU-based wearable sensor system attached to the human body for measuring the LD, T and various hand locations (V and H) in relation to the body at the beginning of the lift.

The study results showed that the algorithm using two wrist sensors was capable of measuring LD within approximately one second of error. Although there was a systematic delay in timestamping both BOL and EOL, the large differences in LD between the two motion measuring systems were primarily caused by increased differences in the measurements for estimating the timestamps for EOL. The two analysts noticed that during EOL, many subjects may have turned their torso while releasing the grid. This inconsistent lifting behavior may have caused the increased differences in the identification of EOL between the two motion measuring systems.

The body segment length ratio model using the gyroscope data relative to the gravity direction did not perform well in measuring V and H. The poor performance (mean errors of 33 and 6.5 cm for V and H, respectively) of the model was caused by two main factors. First, a small change in the body segment ratio may result in a large measurement in the simplistic body segment ratio model. A precise measurement of the body segments improved the performance of the equations, as shown in the reduced mean errors of (6.2 and 2.2 cm for V and H, respectively) of the ratio + length model. Second, the rotations of the sensors on the arm may have caused inaccurate angular data. The X axis of the gyroscope data relative to the gravity direction was used for calculating V. The pronation of the arms, in particular the lower arms observed during the lifting trials in the V_1 zone, changed the projection of the x axis on the sagittal plane. Consequently, the angular data of the sensors on the pronated arms might have caused inaccurate calculations of V. This finding is substantiated by the increased errors of both V and H variables in the V_1 zone. Because of the increased errors, cautions should be exercised when using both models for measuring H in the lifting zones that deviated from the middle horizontal zone.

Upon a closer review of the motion capture data of the lifting trials, we found that the lifting motion of a small percentage (7%) of the lifting trials was not even (i.e., difference in Vm of both wrists > 3 cm) during BOL. This uneven motion may have produced two effects on the study results. First, it may have caused inconsistent identifications of the frame numbers for BOL and EOL for even and uneven lifts. Second, it may have resulted in increased differences of V and H between the two motion measuring systems. The wearable system, however, could only record the movements of the right arm. Consequently, inaccurate measurements of V and H by the wearable system were anticipated due to the uneven lifting motion of both arms.

There was a small percentage (8%) of missing motion data captured by the motion capture system. Proxy data were used based on the data available within 15 frames of the frame numbers identified for BOL and EOL. We decided to use the proxy data after a careful review of the hand and foot positions that matched the position for the BOL and EOL. This manual identification of the matched body movements may have caused slight bias in the comparisons of the V and H measured by the two systems.

One of the first direct-reading instruments for mearing trunk kinematics for ergonomic assessments was the lumbar motion monitoring (LMM) developed by Marras et al. [11] using multiple three-axial electro-goniometer attached to an exoskeleton system worn by the user. In that study, the accuracy (average 1.7° error) of the LMM was determined by 20 different ranges of lifting motion. In this study, the 2° error in measuring the trunk flexion angle by one wearable IMU was similar to that in Marras et al.'s [11] study and another previous study using an IMU sensor [73].

As compared with other vertical zones, the increased error (7.8°) of this wearable IMU system in measuring the trunk flexion angle for V3 is unclear. It is speculated that the trunk flexion angels for the lifting trials in V3 were varying to a larger degree, which potentially lead to a wider spread of data and the increased average error for this zone.

The H and V variables are very critical factors for using the RNLE or the ACGIH TLV for lifting. Taking measurements for these two variables in the field, the interruption of the worker's task is inevitable. Using the proposed wearable system for measuring the variables may provide a practical solution to the challenge of field data collection. Although results from this study showed large errors in the measurements of V and H for a variety of lifting postures, the identifications of BOL, EOL, LD and T by the system may be useful.

Several limitations of the wearable system are worth mentioning. First, the body length ratio model used in this study simplifies the data collection process at a cost of reduced accuracy. Second, with the additional input of the body segment length information, the improved average accuracy levels of H and V measurements may not be adequate for measuring hand location deviating from the middle horizontal zone, above the shoulder and below mid-shin heights. Third, the algorithm cannot be applied to one-handed or two-handed lifting tasks with uneven lifting movements of the two wrists. Finally, the algorithm was not designed for any lifting tasks involving trunk rotation or lateral movements.

5   Conclusions

A five-IMU sensor system attached to the human body was developed and validated for automatically identifying the duration of the two-handed lifting tasks and three other lifting risk variables including T, V and H defined by the RNLE and the ACGIH TLV for lifting. We used a hybrid approach that incorporated a machine learning algorithm to identify the lifting event first, followed by a body segment length ratio model that computed V and H with an optional input of the body segment length information for improved accuracy. The machine learning algorithm performed well for determining the LD within one second error. The calculation of T using the gyroscope data of one sensor on the upper back was fairly accurate within $2°$ error. However, the body segment length ratio model did not produce robust accuracy levels for V and H, even with additional input of body segment length information. Some of the findings from this study may be used for designing an IMU-based instrument for real-time risk monitoring of two-handed lifting activities in the workplace.

Acknowledgements and Disclaimer.   The study was financially supported by intramural funding from the National Institute for Occupational Safety and Health (NIOSH). No conflict of interest is declared. This project was supported in part by an appointment to the Research Participation Program at the Centers for Disease Control and Prevention administered by the Oak Ridge Institute for Science and Education through an interagency agreement between the U.S. Department of Energy and the Centers for Disease Control and Prevention. Disclaimer: The findings and conclusions in this article are those of the authors and do not necessarily represent the official position of the National Institute for Occupational Safety and Health, Centers for Disease Control and Prevention.

References

1. Liberty Mutual Research Institute for Safety: Liberty Mutual Workplace Safety Index. Liberty Mutual 175 Berkeley St., Boston, MA 02116 (2014)
2. Luo, X., Pietrobon, R., Sun, S.X., Liu, G.G., Hey, L.: Estimates and patterns of direct health care expenditures among individuals with back pain in the United States. Spine **29**(1), 79–86 (2004)
3. Bernard, B.P.: Musculoskeletal Disorders and Workplace Factors: A Critical Review of Epidemiologic Evidence for Work-Related Musculoskeletal Disorders of the Neck, Upper Extremity, and Low Back. U.S. Department of Health and Human Services, Center for Disease Control and Prevention, National Institute for Occupational Health and Safety, Cincinnati OH (1997)
4. National Research Council: Musculoskeletal Disorders and the Workplace: Low Back and Upper Extremities, Washington, DC (2001)
5. da Costa, B.R., Vieira, E.R.: Risk factors for work-related musculoskeletal disorders: a systematic review of recent longitudinal studies. Am. J. Ind. Med. **53**(3), 285–323 (2010)
6. Lu, M.L., Waters, T.R., Krieg, E., Werren, D.: Efficacy of the revised NIOSH lifting equation to predict risk of low-back pain associated with manual lifting: a one-year prospective study. Hum. Factors **56**(1), 73–85 (2014)
7. Callaghan, J.P., Salewytsch, A.J., Andrews, D.M.: An evaluation of predictive methods for estimating cumulative spinal loading. Ergonomics **44**(9), 825–837 (2001)
8. Lu, M.L., Waters, T., Werren, D.: Development of human posture simulation method for assessing posture angles and spinal loads. Hum. Factors Ergon. Manuf. Serv. Ind. **25**(1), 123–136 (2015)
9. Radwin, R.G., Lin, M.L.: An analytical method for characterizing repetitive motion and postural stress using spectral-analysis. Ergonomics **36**(4), 379–389 (1993)
10. Bhattacharya, A., Warren, J., Teuschler, J., Dimov, M., Medvedovic, M., Lemasters, G.: Development and evaluation of a microprocessor-based ergonomic dosimeter for evaluating carpentry tasks. Appl. Ergon. **30**(6), 543–553 (1999)
11. Marras, W.S., Fathallah, F.A., Miller, R.J., Davis, S.W., Mirka, G.A.: Accuracy of a three-dimensional lumbar motion monitor for recording dynamic trunk motion characteristics. Int. J. Ind. Ergon. **9**(1), 75–87 (1992)
12. Freivalds, A., Kong, Y., You, H., Park, S.: A comprehensive risk assessment model for work-related musculoskeletal disorders of the upper extremities. In: Proceedings of Human Factors and Ergonomics Society Annual Meeting, vol. 44, no. 31, pp. 5-728–5-731. SAGE Publications, Los Angeles (2000)
13. Battini, D., Persona, A., Sgarbossa, F.: Innovative real-time system to integrate ergonomic evaluations into warehouse design and management. Comput. Ind. Eng. **77**, 1–10 (2014)
14. He, Z., Jin, L.: Activity recognition from acceleration data based on discrete cosine transform and SVM. In: 2009 IEEE International Conference on Systems, Man and Cybernetics, San Antonio TX, pp. 5041–5044. IEEE (2009)
15. Dahlqvist, C., Hansson, G.Å., Forsman, M.: Validity of a small low-cost triaxial accelerometer with integrated logger for uncomplicated measurements of postures and movements of head, upper back and upper arms. Appl. Ergon. **55**, 108–116 (2016)
16. Schall Jr., M.C., Fethke, N.B., Chen, H., Oyama, S., Douphrate, D.I.: Accuracy and repeatability of an inertial measurement unit system for field-based occupational studies. Ergonomics **59**(4), 591–602 (2015)

17. Brents, C., Hischke, M., Reiser, R., Rosecrance, J.: Low back biomechanics of keg handling using inertial measurement units. In: Bagnara, S., Tartaglia, R., Albolino, S., Alexander, T., Fujita, Y. (eds.) IEA 2018. AISC, vol. 825, pp. 71–81. Springer, Cham (2019). https://doi.org/10.1007/978-3-319-96068-5_8

18. Zhou, H., Hu, H., Tao, Y.: Inertial measurements of upper limb motion. Med. Biol. Eng. Comput. 44(6), 479–487 (2006)

19. Zhou, H., Stone, T., Hu, H., Harris, N.: Use of multiple wearable inertial sensors in upper limb motion tracking. Med. Eng. Phys. 30(1), 123–133 (2008)

20. Zhou, H., Hu, H.: Reducing drifts in the inertial measurements of wrist and elbow positions. IEEE Trans. Instrum. Meas. 59(3), 575–585 (2010)

21. Zhou, H., Hu, H.: Upper limb motion estimation from inertial measurements. Int. J. Inf. Technol. 13(1), 1–14 (2007)

22. Cutti, A.G., Giovanardi, A., Rocchi, L., Davalli, A., Sacchetti, R.: Ambulatory measurement of shoulder and elbow kinematics through inertial and magnetic sensors. Med. Biol. Eng. Comput. 46(2), 169–178 (2008)

23. de Vries, W., Veeger, H., Cutti, A., Baten, C., van der Helm, F.: Functionally interpretable local coordinate systems for the upper extremity using inertial & magnetic measurement systems. J. Biomech. 43(10), 1983–1988 (2010)

24. El-Gohary, M., McNames, J.: Shoulder and elbow joint angle tracking with inertial sensors. IEEE Trans. Biomed. Eng. 59(9), 2635–2641 (2012)

25. Vignais, N., Miezal, M., Bleser, G., Mura, K., Gorecky, D., Marin, F.: Innovative system for real-time ergonomic feedback in industrial manufacturing. Appl. Ergon. 44(4), 566–574 (2013)

26. Caputo, F., D'Amato, E., Spada, S., Sessa, F., Losardo, M.: Upper body motion tracking system with inertial sensors for ergonomic issues in industrial environments. In: Goonetilleke, R., Karwowski, W. (eds.) Advances in Physical Ergonomics and Human Factors. AISC, vol. 489, pp. 801–812. Springer, Cham (2016). https://doi.org/10.1007/978-3-319-41694-6_77

27. Morrow, M.B., Lowndes, B., Fortune, E., Kaufman, K.R., Hallbeck, M.: Validation of inertial measurement units for upper body kinematics. J. Appl. Biomech. 33(3), 227–232 (2017)

28. Chen, H., Schall Jr., M.C., Fethke, N.: Accuracy of angular displacements and velocities from inertial-based inclinometers. Appl. Ergon. 67, 151–161 (2018)

29. Peppoloni, L., Filippeschi, A., Ruffaldi, E., Avizzano, C.A.: A novel 7 degrees of freedom model for upper limb kinematic reconstruction based on wearable sensors. In: 2013 IEEE 11th International Symposium on Intelligent Systems and Informatics, Subotica Serbia, pp. 105–110. IEEE (2013)

30. Jasiewicz, J.M., Treleaven, J., Condie, P., Jull, G.: Wireless orientation sensors: their suitability to measure head movement for neck pain assessment. Manual Ther. 12(4), 380–385 (2007)

31. Theobald, P.S., Jones, M.D., Williams, J.M.: Do inertial sensors represent a viable method to reliably measure cervical spine range of motion? Manual Ther. 17(1), 92–96 (2012)

32. Duc, C., Salvia, P., Lubansu, A., Feipel, V., Aminian, K.: A wearable inertial system to assess the cervical spine mobility: comparison with an optoelectronic-based motion capture evaluation. Med. Eng. Phys. 36(1), 49–56 (2014)

33. Favre, J., Jolles, B.M., Aissaoui, R., Aminian, K.: Ambulatory measurement of 3D knee joint angle. J. Biomech. 41(5), 1029–1035 (2008)

34. Picerno, P., Cereatti, A., Cappozzo, A.: Joint kinematics estimate using wearable inertial and magnetic sensing modules. Gait Posture 28(4), 588–595 (2008)

35. Ferrari, A., et al.: First in vivo assessment of "Outwalk": a novel protocol for clinical gait analysis based on inertial and magnetic sensors. Med. Biol. Eng. Comput. **48**(1), 1–15 (2010)

36. Fong, D.T., Chan, Y.Y.: The use of wearable inertial motion sensors in human lower limb biomechanics studies: a systematic review. Sensors **10**(12), 11556–11565 (2010)

37. Bolink, S.A.A.N., et al.: Validity of an inertial measurement unit to assess pelvic orientation angles during gait, sit-stand transfers and set-up transfers: comparison with an optoelectronic motion capture system. Med. Eng. Phys. **38**(3), 225–231 (2016)

38. Beravs, T., Rebersek, P., Novak, D., Podobnik, J., Munih, M.: Development and validation of a wearable inertial measurement system for use with lower limb exoskeletons. In: 2011 11th IEEE-RAS International Conference on Humanoid Robots, Bled Slovenia, pp. 212–217. IEEE (2011)

39. O'Reilly, M.A., Whelan, D.F., Ward, T.E., Delahunt, E., Caulfield, B.: Classification of lunge biomechanics with multiple and individual inertial measurement units. Sports Biomech. **16**(3), 342–360 (2016)

40. Teufl, W., Miezal, M., Taetz, B., Frohlich, M., Bleser, G.: Validity of inertial sensor-based 3D joint kinematics of static and dynamic sport and physiotherapy specific movements. PLOS One **14**(2), 1–18 (2019)

41. Lee, R.Y.W., Laprade, J., Fung, E.H.K.: A real-time gyroscopic system for three-dimensional measurement of lumbar spine motion. Med. Eng. Phys. **25**(10), 817–824 (2003)

42. Goodvin, C., Park, E.J., Huang, K., Sakaki, K.: Development of a real-time three-dimensional spinal motion measurement system for clinical practice. Med. Biol. Eng. Comput. **44**(12), 1061–1075 (2006)

43. Giansanti, D., Maccioni, G., Benvenuti, F., Macellari, V.: Inertial measurement units furnish accurate trunk trajectory reconstruction of the sit-to-stand manoeuvre in healthy subjects. Med. Biol. Eng. Comput. **45**(10), 969–976 (2007)

44. Plamondon, A., et al.: Evaluation of a hybrid system for three-dimensional measurement of trunk posture in motion. Appl. Ergon. **38**(6), 697–712 (2007)

45. Roetenberg, D., Slycke, P.J., Veltink, P.H.: Ambulatory position and orientation tracking fusing magnetic and inertial sensing. IEEE Trans. Biomed. Eng. **54**(5), 883–890 (2007)

46. Kim, S., Nussbaum, M.A.: Performance evaluation of a wearable inertial motion capture system for capturing physical exposures during manual material handling tasks. Ergonomics **56**(2), 314–326 (2013)

47. Bauer, C.M., et al.: Concurrent validity and reliability of a novel wireless inertial measurement system to assess trunk movement. J. Electromyogr. Kinesiol. **25**(5), 782–790 (2015)

48. Bergamini, E., Guillon, P., Camomilla, V., Pillet, H., Skalli, W., Cappozzo, A.: Trunk inclination estimate during the sprint start using an inertial measurement unit: a validation study. J. Appl. Biomech. **29**(5), 622–627 (2013)

49. Monaco, M.G.L., et al.: Biomechanical overload evaluation in manufacturing: a novel approach with sEMG and inertial motion capture integration. In: Bagnara, S., Tartaglia, R., Albolino, S., Alexander, T., Fujita, Y. (eds.) IEA 2018. AISC, vol. 818, pp. 719–726. Springer, Cham (2019). https://doi.org/10.1007/978-3-319-96098-2_88

50. Brodie, M.A., Walmsley, A., Page, W.: Dynamic accuracy of inertial measurement units during simple pendulum motion. Comput. Methods Biomech. Biomed. Eng. **11**(3), 235–242 (2008)

51. Brodie, M.A., Walmsley, A., Page, W.: Fusion motion capture: a prototype system using inertial measurement units and GPS for the biomechanical analysis of ski racing. Sports Technol. **1**(1), 17–28 (2008)

52. Robert-Lachaine, X., Mecheri, H., Larue, C., Plamondon, A.: Validation of inertial measurement units with an optoelectronic system for whole-body motion analysis. Med. Biol. Eng. Comput. **55**(4), 609–619 (2017)
53. Maurice, P., et al.: Human movement and ergonomics: an industry-oriented dataset for collaborative robotics. Int. J. Robot. Res. **38**(14), 1529–1537 (2019)
54. Nemec, D., Hrubos, M., Pirnik, R., Janota, A., Simak, V.: Ergonomic remote control of the mobile platform by inertial measurement of the hand movement. In: 2016 ELEKTRO, Strbske Pleso Slovakia, pp. 445–449. IEEE (2016)
55. Waters, T.R., Putz-Anderson, V., Garg, A., Fine, L.J.: Revised NIOSH equation for the design and evaluation of manual lifting tasks. Ergonomics **36**(7), 749–776 (1993)
56. Waters, T.R., Putz-Anderson, V., Garg, A.: Applications Manual for the Revised NIOSH Lifting Equation. U. S. Department of Health and Human Services, National Institute for Occupational Safety and Health, Cincinnati OH (1994)
57. Aoki, T., Feng-Shun Lin, J., Kulic, D., Venture, G.: Segmentation of human upper body movement using multiple IMU sensors. In: 2016 38th Annual International Conference of the IEEE Engineering in Medicine and Biology Society (EMBC), Orlando FL, USA, pp. 3163–3166. IEEE (2016)
58. Fang, Z., Yang, Z., Wang, R.-B., Chen, S.-Y.: Inertial sensor-based knee angle estimation for gait analysis using the ant colony algorithm to find the optimal parameters for Kalman filter. In: 2018 3rd International Conference on Automation, Mechanical and Electrical Engineering (AMEE 2018), pp. 249–254 (2018)
59. Seel, T., Raisch, J., Schauer, T.: IMU-Based joint angle measurement for gait analysis. Sensors **14**(4), 6891–6909 (2014)
60. Roetenberg, D., Luinge, H., Slycke, P.: Xsens MVN: full 6 DOF human motion tracking using miniature inertial sensors. Xsens Motion Technologies BV, Enschede, The Netherlands (2009)
61. Wouda, F.J., Giuberti, M., Bellusci, G., Veltink, P.H.: Estimation of full-body poses using only five inertial sensors: an eager or lazy learning approach. Sensors **16**(2), 2138 (2016)
62. Spriggs, E.H., De La Torre, F., Hebert, M.: Temporal segmentation and activity classification from first-person sensing. In: 2009 IEEE Computer Society Conference on Computer Vision and Pattern Recognition Workshops, Miami FL, USA, pp. 17–24. IEEE (2009)
63. Bulling, A., Blanke, U., Schiele, B.: A tutorial on human activity recognition using body-worn inertial sensors. ACM Comput. Surv. (CSUR) **46**(3), 1–33 (2014)
64. Moncada-Torres, A., Leuenberger, K., Gonzenbach, R., Luft, A., Gassert, R.: Activity classification based on inertial and barometric pressure sensors at different anatomical locations. Physiol. Meas. **35**(7), 1245 (2014)
65. Attal, F., Mohammed, S., Dedabrishvili, M., Chamroukhi, F., Oukhellou, L., Amirat, Y.: Physical human activity recognition using wearable sensors. Sensors **15**(12), 31314–31338 (2015)
66. Liaw, A., Wiener, M.: Classification and regression by randomForest. R News **2**(3), 18–22 (2002)
67. Powers, D.M.: Evaluation: from precision, recall and F-measure to ROC, informedness, markedness and correlation (2011)
68. Foxlin, E.: Inertial head-tracker sensor fusion by a complementary separate-bias Kalman filter. In: Proceedings of the IEEE 1996 Virtual Reality Annual International Symposium, Santa Clara, CA, pp. 185–194. IEEE (1996)
69. You, S., Neumann, U.: Fusion of vision and gyro tracking for robust augmented reality registration. In: Proceedings IEEE Virtual Reality 2001, Yokohama, Japan, pp. 71–78. IEEE (2001)

70. Lee, H.J., Jung, S.: Gyro sensor drift compensation by Kalman filter to control a mobile inverted pendulum robot system. In: 2009 IEEE International Conference on Industrial Technology, Gippsland, VIC, Australia, pp. 1–6. IEEE (2009)
71. Rigatos, G., Tzafestas, S.: Extended Kalman filtering for fuzzy modelling and multi-sensor fusion. Math. Comput. Model. Dyn. Syst. **13**(3), 251–266 (2007)
72. Lu, M.-L., Waters, T., Werren, D., Piacitelli, L.: Human posture simulation to assess cumulative spinal load due to manual lifting. Part II: accuracy and precision. Theor. Issues Ergon. Sci. **12**(2), 189–203 (2011)
73. Faber, G.S., Kingma, I., Bruijin, S.M., van Dieen, J.H.: Optimal inertial sensor location for ambulatory measurement of trunk inclination. J. Biomech. **42**(14), 2406–2409 (2009)

Study on Chinese Elderly Women's Clothing Design Based on Ergonomics

Longlin Luo[✉] and Xiaoping Hu

School of Design, South China University of Technology,
Guangzhou 510006, People's Republic of China
Linlongluo@163.com

Abstract. The aging of China's population is on a rise trend. With the continuous growing of the elderly women market group, the variety of clothing demand is proposed, and less clothing is designed on the basis of elderly women's own needs. The group of elderly women receives less attention, which leads to the mismatch between supply and demand. Therefore, the clothing design needs to make corresponding improvements. The subjects in this paper are mainly elderly women. Questionnaire survey and anthropometric survey were used to investigate their preference and comfort for clothes in daily life, which mainly analyzes the psychological needs and physiological needs of clothing in combination with the body shape characteristics of elderly women and compares them with the differences in the mean body shape of adult women. Different from the body shape of adult women, the vertical size of the body shape of elderly women, mainly in height, is decreasing, while the horizontal size, mainly in circumference, is increasing. Clothing design should focus on comfort, health, safety, dirt resistance and lightness from the perspective of elderly women.

Keywords: Elderly women · Demand · Body shape analysis · Clothing design

1 Introduction

With the development of economic society, the clothing consumption demand of the elderly will also expand day by day [1]. However, there is still a shortage of clothing for elderly women in the domestic market, which needs further development in this domain. By the end of 2018, the dependency ratio of the elderly in China is as high as 16.8%, and the population aged 65 and above is 166.58 million [2]. It is predicted that China's elderly population will reach 297 million by 2025 and 438 million by 2050 [3], indicating that China's elderly population will face the trend of aging in the future, and female elderly population will account for a large number. With the growth of age, the body shape and structure of the elderly are changing, which is different from that of adult women.

© Springer Nature Switzerland AG 2020
V. G. Duffy (Ed.): HCII 2020, LNCS 12198, pp. 214–227, 2020.
https://doi.org/10.1007/978-3-030-49904-4_16

The clothing design based on the perspective on ergonomics pays more attention on the elderly women's physical and mental health, which lies on solving the problems, such as clothing size, color, material, style, price that cannot meet the demand of the elderly women, and improving the quality of elderly women's life. Since there are few clothes for elderly women to buy in the market, the precise positioning of this group in clothes is ignored [4].

Since the corresponding changes in posture, the optimization design is carried out from the perspective of user needs, facilitate the elderly to carry out various activities, eliminate difficulties and obstacles in dressing, reduce friction barriers and damage, and realize the combination of aesthetics and practicality. It reflects the care for the vulnerable groups of the elderly. The functions of products tend to be more reasonable, amiable and humanized, which provides relevant theoretical guidance for the development and promotion of clothing.

2 Method

One method is to develop about 103 questionnaires to be distributed to elderly women, which are targeted at elderly women over the age of 58 in China. Due to some elderly people's blurred vision and other problems, the questionnaire was mainly conducted in the form of on-site interviews. The survey sites were parks, activity centers for the elderly, universities for the elderly and other places. The questionnaire mainly collects and analyzes the main problems of the elderly women's clothing needs from two aspects: psychological needs and physiological needs. The second method: About 103 elderly women were selected as samples, and about 11 main parts of them were measured according to the relevant standards of GB/T16160-2017 "Definition and methods of garment anthropometric measurement" and GB/T38131-2019 "Method for obtaining reference points of apparel anthropometric" [5], which are applicable to various clothing sizes of adults in China. The measuring method is manual measurement, and the auxiliary tools are soft leather scales and weight scales. The measurement method is manual measurement, and the auxiliary tools are soft leather ruler and weight scale. The length includes height, cervical point height, sitting cervical point height, arm length and waist circumference height. Girth includes neck, chest, waist and hip. The width is shoulder width, and other measurement parts include weight, etc.

3   Statistical Analysis of Questionnaire Survey on Elderly Women

3.1   The Basic Information Composition Proportion of the Survey Members

■ 58 to 60 years old   ■ 61 to 65 years old   ■ 66 to 70 years old
■ 71 to 79 years old   ■ 80 to 90 years old   ■ Age 90 and above

Fig. 1. Frequency and percentage of age

There are altogether 103 valid questionnaires, which are divided into 6 parts according to age group. As can be seen from Fig. 1, the age groups of the main respondents in this questionnaire are mainly between 60 and 89, while the relatively small ones are between 58 and 60 and 90 and above. As can be seen from Fig. 2, for the occupation composition before retirement, civil servants and workers accounted for the largest proportion respectively, followed by farmers and enterprise managers, less self-employed and other industries. The proportion distribution of the members of the questionnaire is in line with the requirements of the research objectives.

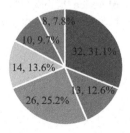

■ Civil servant   ■ Enterprise managers
■ Workers   ■ Farmers
■ Self-employment venture   ■ Others

Fig. 2. The frequency and percentage of occupations

3.2   Analysis of the Psychological Needs of the Elderly Women's Clothing

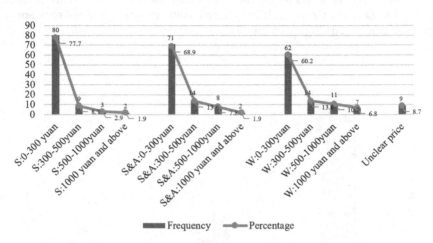

Fig. 3. Price segments for different seasons

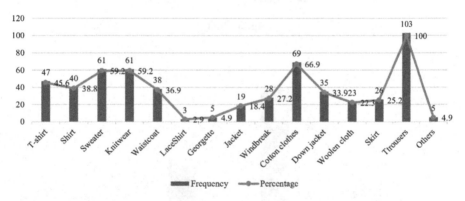

Fig. 4. Clothing items

As shown in Fig. 3, the demand of elderly women for clothing prices is as follows: the proportion of 0–300 yuan is 77.7% in summer, 68.9% in spring and autumn, and 60.2% in winter. Then, the price increases gradually with the cooling of the season, but the price fluctuation does not change much, which is closely related to social and economic development. Since the average living standard in China was relatively low before, many elderly women developed the habit of hard work and frugality, which directly affected their purchasing behaviors now. In addition to their children buying clothes for them, some of the elderly women said they had not bought clothes for many years, which is the reason that some women did not know the price in this inquiry.

As is shown in Fig. 4, the clothing items preferred by elderly women are mainly T-shirts (45.6%), trousers (100%), sweaters (59.2%), knitwear (59.2%) and cotton-padded clothes (66.9%), among which trousers are the must-have items frequently worn in all seasons. In terms of clothing items, comfort, health and softness are generally more considered (Figs. 5, 6 and 7).

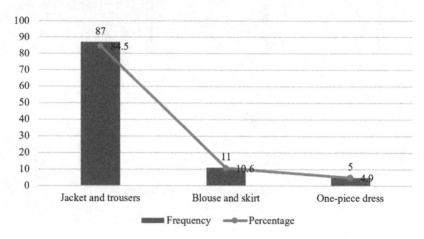

Fig. 5. Suit

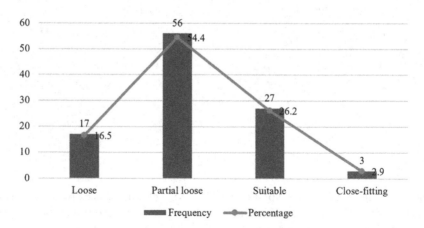

Fig. 6. Fitness

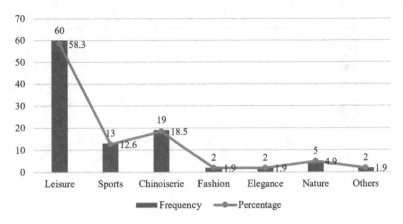

Fig. 7. Style

84.5% of the elderly women prefer to wear a top and trousers, while only a few groups choose to wear a top and skirt or dress. Most said they had worn skirts when they were young but not now. As they get elderly, on the one hand, wearing skirts is inconvenient, on the other hand, wearing skirts is too dazzling, in their eyes, that's the young's business.

In terms of looseness, "looseness" and "fit" dominated, which mainly considered the convenience for the body to carry out various activities and display a decent appearance as the main factor.

Leisure style accounted for 58.3%, followed by Chinese style at 18.5% and sports style at 12.6%. This is mainly because elderly women after retirement have more ways of leisure and entertainment, such as morning exercise, walking, square dancing, cards, etc., which is consistent with the daily leisure activities. The main reason for choosing Chinese style is that some elderly women are keen on the yearning and tracing of traditional culture. Cultural elements should be integrated into clothing design as a new design language to better meet the aesthetic needs of the elderly at the present stage [6] (Figs. 8, 9 and 10).

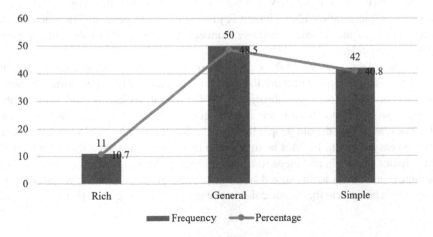

Fig. 8. Degree of decoration

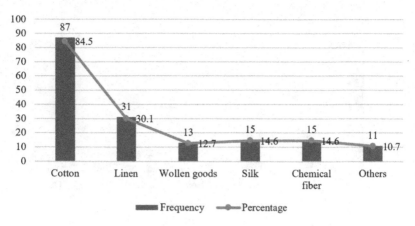

Fig. 9. Fabric

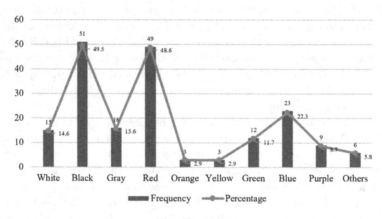

Fig. 10. Color

Many elderly women said they preferred to wear "modest" and "concise" clothing. Clothes as long as a little embellishment is just right, do not need too complicated, this will appear atmospheric, this decorative concept and the needs of the elderly group happens to coincide.

In terms of fabric, 84.5% of the elderly women chose cotton fabric, far higher than other fabrics. This is mainly because the cotton fabric has excellent performance such as softness, permeability and easy absorption, so the overall feeling is more comfortable.

Elderly women who chose black and red accounted for 49.5% and 48.6%, respectively. The reason why the old people like to wear black is that black clothes are resistant to dirt and easy to wash. Besides being easy to take care of, black clothes also have the characteristics of simple and elegant, calm and steady. More importantly, they are versatile and wearable. In addition, red belongs to auspicious color, with a festive atmosphere, which belongs to the classic color in the gorgeous color system (Figs. 11 and 12).

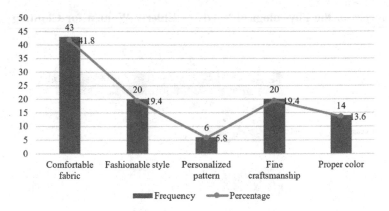

Fig. 11. Priority attention

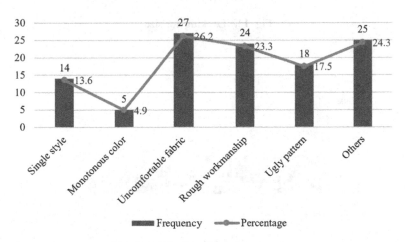

Fig. 12. The shortage of the garment

In terms of "Priority attention", comfortable fabrics account for 41.8%, followed by fashionable styles and fine workmanship. For the "deficiency of existing clothing", it is likely that most elderly women are more concerned about the composition of comfortable fabrics. So pointing out the shortcomings of "comfortable fabric" is the most, followed by rough workmanship, single style and monotonous pattern. It can be seen that the importance of fabric selection, however, the style, pattern and production cannot be ignored.

3.3   Analysis of the Physiological Needs of Elderly Women for Clothing

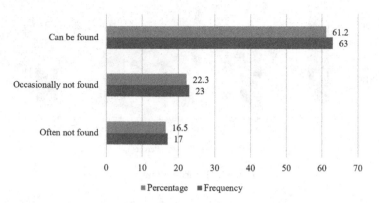

Fig. 13. Looking for size

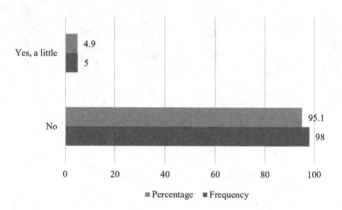

Fig. 14. Obstacle of limb movement

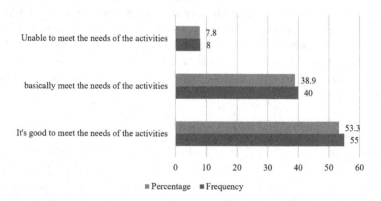

Fig. 15. Whether to meet the needs of the activities

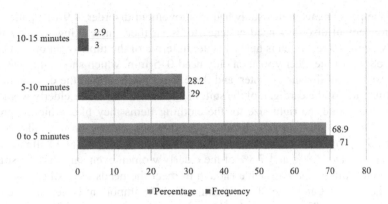

Fig. 16. The time it takes to put on or take off a garment

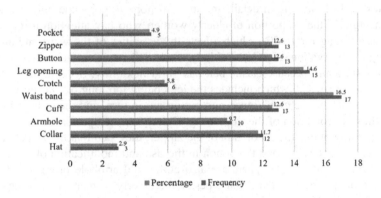

Fig. 17. The shortage of local details

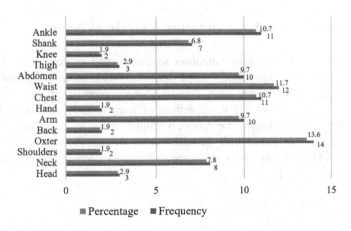

Fig. 18. Hinder parts

Most of the participants in this study had no movement disorder. 4.9% of patients with certain movement disorders need crutches to assist them in walking. Elderly women generally keep active, which is healthy state. In terms of the time to put on and take off the suit, 68.9% of the elderly women only need 0–5 min, which shows that the time to put on and take off the suit is faster, and there is no problem that the dress is hindered by the limitation of the cardigan of the suit. In addition, most of the elderly women said that they could find the right size for the clothing items they like, which is probably largely related to the "looser" clothing type that the elderly women like to wear. However, the proportion of "occasionally unable to find the size" and "often unable to find the size" was 38.8%, and 7.8% of the elderly women even said that the structural design of clothing is not reasonable enough to meet the needs of flexible limbs. It can be seen that comfort and ease of use is still one of the important issues that the elderly pay attention to [7] (Figs. 13, 14, 15, 16 and 18).

Although many women said that they usually pay less attention to the details of clothing, they all have their own opinions, and can explain the quality defects of a particular detail of clothing in detail, and they all hope to get some improvement. As shown in Fig. 17, the proportion of elderly women who pay attention to pants is the highest, accounting for 16.5%, which affects the activities of the waist and abdomen. According to observation see, a lot of elderly woman like to wear the trousers of type of elastic belt, basically because elastic belt has good flexibility. Second, the legs of the trousers come in second, which includes the legs being too long or too short, too wide or too narrow. Then, the cuff, zipper, and button are in turn, and the description of the cuff matches the condition of the trouser leg. Elderly women prefer the button type of opening, but do not like the decoration of the zipper, they said that the zipper is broken repair is very troublesome, and the button in the use and modification of the operation are more convenient, simple. There are also collar and armhole problems. Although different people prefer different collar types, some elderly women say that the collar is too low to wear, while armhole problems are usually caused by too narrow, affecting movement between the chest, armpits and the upper arms.

4 Analysis of Body Shape Data for Elderly Women

Clothing design should pay more attention to the pursuit of comfort and style for people of different body types. Body shape data analysis reflects the special needs of the clothing industry for human body data, and more specialized human body data information is a direction of the development of human body database [8]. In this analysis, the mean value, standard deviation, minimum value and maximum value were calculated, and then compared with the mean value of size [9] of adult women. The body shape of elderly women showed some differences compared with that of adult women (Tables 1 and 2).

Table 1. Numerical statistics of various body parts of elderly women (unit: cm)

	Height	Cervical height	Sitting cervical height	Arm length	Waist height
N	103	103	103	103	103
Mean	153.5	132.1	58.0	48.3	93.5
SD	6.1	5.6	3.4	2.2	4.2
Min	140	118	50	44	85
Max	172	151	67	55	105

Table 2. Numerical statistics of various body parts of elderly women (unit: cm/ weight: kg)

	Neck circumference	Bust	Waist	Hip circumference	Shoulder width	Weight
N	103	103	103	103	103	103
Mean	33.7	93.5	85.0	95.1	40.3	56.2
SD	1.8	7.4	8.0	5.4	1.8	8.4
Min	28	75	67	82	34	35.0
Max	37	110	106	110	44	75.0

The domestic garment size divides the human body shape into Y, A, B and C, which is mainly based on the difference between chest size and waist circumference. Among them, size B indicates that the difference between chest circumference and waist circumference is between 9–13 cm, while size C indicates that the difference between chest circumference and waist circumference is between 4–8 cm. The difference between the measurement of chest circumference and waist circumference of elderly women is 8.5 cm, which should be classified according to the size between size B and size C. In addition, the national size standard classifies the height with 5 cm, and the average height calculated by measuring the body shape of the elderly women is 153.5 cm, which is close to the size of 155 cm described in the national standard document. Figure 19 also shows the comparison of size B and size C between the mean value of elderly women and the mean value of adult women. If size C is taken as an example, it can be found that body size such as the height of the cervical spine, the height of the sitting cervical spine, the full arm length, the waist height and neck circumference are basically within the coverage range of size C, however the chest circumference of 93.5 cm, waist circumference of 85 cm, hip circumference of 95.1 cm and shoulder width of 40.3 cm are beyond the coverage range of size. Because the bodily form of old person follows the decline of physiology function, each articular cartilage atrophies, neck column is bent and compare prime when slightly short, back appears fruity, chest outline is flat, abdomen is enlarged and flabby drop, form adipose accumulation [10]. If the data of the size of adult women's clothing are used, it may not be able to meet the needs of some elderly women's body shape to some extent.

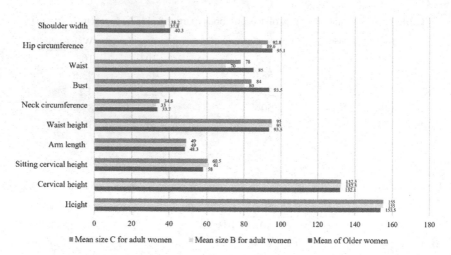

Fig. 19. Differences in mean body size between older and adult women

5   Some Suggestions for Costume Design

Clothing design should pay more attention to the psychological and physiological needs of consumers from the perspective of ergonomics, and take the relationship between people and clothing as the basis, grasp the important factors and cater to the main needs of consumers.

Comfort, health, safety, durability, lightness is always the starting point of the elderly women's clothing design.

Since the size of the old woman is different from that of the adult woman, the size of the garment needs to be adjusted according to the actual situation. Through the comparison, it is found that the 3D data is particularly worthy of attention.

6   Discussion

The analysis of clothing preference and comfort mainly focuses on the elderly women from psychological needs and body structure. Generally speaking, a fixed mode of thinking is usually formed, that is, what kinds of clothing type the elderly group usually like or suitable for. In this survey, it is found that this is somewhat different from our previous assumption. What we think may not be what they like, For example, Adults think that older people prefer rich decorative patterns, but in fact they prefer simple ones, the elderly still have a lot of ideas and demands for clothes, but as they get elderly, they seldom express their true thoughts with others.

In the questionnaire, Although the number of members who proposed that the comfort of clothing is still insufficient is relatively small, However, the description is very specific, such as the relationship between collar and neck, armhole and armpit, trousers and waist and abdomen, etc., which plays a certain role in the local improvement of clothing. The importance of details is the most easily overlooked, but the local details of clothing are often the most critical.

According to the survey, the average height of elderly women was 153.5 cm, which showed a certain decrease compared with the average height of adult women. There were also some changes in other values, and the difference in body shape among the elderly female group was also large. The design of clothing size and structure needs to be adjusted according to the changes of the body shape of elderly women, so as to meet the needs of more elderly women's body shape.

7 Conclusion

In conclusion, in terms of psychological needs, the range of demand for clothing prices for elderly female groups in China is relatively low to medium, and they prefer healthy and comfortable clothing. What wear commonly is in slant loose and fit between jacket bottom trousers outfit, like adornment degree is general or concise, give priority to recreational style with cotton qualitative fabrics. In terms of color, they prefer black and red, and give priority to comfortable fabrics and fine workmanship in their clothing choices. In terms of physical needs, clothing sizes cannot meet the body shape needs of some elderly women, and the structural design is still unreasonable, which leads to restrictions on the activities of corresponding parts of the body. There are still some defects in the design of the local details of the trousers, trousers, cuffs, buttons and zippers. In terms of body shape data, there are certain differences between the body shape of elderly women and that of adult women. The vertical size, mainly height, decreases, while the horizontal size, mainly chest circumference, waist circumference, hip circumference and shoulder width, increases. Clothing size should be made on the basis of the elderly women themselves, and combined with the body data of elderly women as a reference.

References

1. Fangyi, C.: Research on China elderly clothing consumption market. J. China Market **35**, 94–95 (2016)
2. National Bureau of Statistics of China (2019). http://www.stats.gov.cn
3. Mengting, S., Qiuyue, W.: Relevant research on middle-aged and elderly clothing. J. China Market **10**, 121–122 (2019)
4. Twigg, J.: Clothing, age and the body: a critical review. J. Ageing Soc. **27**(2), 285–305 (2007)
5. Xiuyue, Y., Nini, M., Shuangxi, Z.: Study on the definition and method of clothing anthropometric measurement. J. Text. Test. Stand. **10**, P32–P36 (2019)
6. Yugang, C.: The application of humanistic care thinking mode in the elderly clothing design. J. Fashion Colour **01**, 60–62 (2019)
7. Civitci, S.: An ergonomic garment design for elderly Turkish men. J. Appl. Ergon. **35**, 243–251 (2004)
8. Yongmei, L., Xiaoxue, Z., Yunxin, G.: Survey and analysis on domestic and overseas human body database for garments' use. J. Text. Res. **06**, 141–147 (2015)
9. National standards of the People's Republic of China, Standard sizing systems for garments-Women, GB/T 1355, February 2008
10. JianHua, P.: Clothing ergonomics and design. Donghua University Press, 43 (2008). ISBN: 7-81111-306-6

Depth and Colour Perception in Real and Virtual Robot Cells in the Context of Occupational Safety and Health

Peter Nickel[(✉)]

Department of Accident Prevention: Digitalisation – Technologies,
Institute for Occupational Safety and Health of the German Social
Accident Insurance (IFA), Sankt Augustin, Germany
peter.nickel@dguv.de

Abstract. Investigations into comparisons of real and virtual environments serve multiple purposes. Results may improve development, implementation and application of virtual environments, inform about potentials for positive transfer of effects and facilitate decision making about appropriate virtual reality techniques in specific situations on human factors and ergonomics in human-system interaction. Absolute and relative estimations of object sizes, colours and greyscales were differentially investigated in virtual and real robot cells. Analyses revealed differences for environments (e.g. size, colour) and in some cases even for specific characteristics under investigation (e.g. robot cell size, 10% greyscales). Differential results on human task performance in virtual environments with potential technical constraints are crucial for safety and health reasons and because they provide a basis for human behaviour consequences and work system design decisions and requirements for transfer research. Results support informed decision making about virtual reality techniques and media selection in OSH applications on training and work systems design.

Keywords: Size estimation · Colour estimation · Greyscale estimation · Virtual reality · Human-system interaction · OSH · Robot cell · Human factors

1 Introduction

1.1 Virtual Reality in the Context of Occupational Safety and Health

Occupational safety and health (OSH) refers to human activities in the context of work and focuses on primary prevention of hazards. WHO principles [1] characterise health as a state of complete physical, mental and social well-being and not merely the absence of disease or infirmity. However, in OSH, safety and health is an interwoven entity and measures to foster OSH often are more specific and emphasise interventions that pursue prevention of occupational accidents, occupational diseases and work-related health risks [2–4].

The hierarchy of controls is an international and well-recognised concept in primary prevention, as it guides selection of effective measures for OSH promotion in work systems design [3, 5, 6]. The number of levels across hierarchy versions may

© Springer Nature Switzerland AG 2020
V. G. Duffy (Ed.): HCII 2020, LNCS 12198, pp. 228–242, 2020.
https://doi.org/10.1007/978-3-030-49904-4_17

vary, but usually include levels as presented below, and classify measures according to effectiveness for prevention; with all levels being required. Substitution measures (e.g. hazard elimination) are assumed to be most effective in risk reduction; they take top level of hierarchy. Technical measures (e.g. safeguard) are classified next with organisational measures (e.g. exposure time limitation) following at a lower level. Personal measures (e.g. personal protective equipment) range before information measures (e.g. instructional signs) at the lowest level of hierarchy [3–5, 7].

Primary prevention strategies have the potential to improve OSH when they allow transfer of existing knowledge about safety and health to similar and new applications and work environments. They facilitate effects, when considering OSH implications and human factors and ergonomics requirements early in the design stage while anticipating the work system life cycle. Moreover, human-centred applications of procedures and technologies for improving OSH are seen particularly helpful for future work system design and especially in that they may extend the effective range of prevention (e.g. simulating human-system interaction in unknown future) [4, 8, 9].

Modelling and simulation of work systems have a long tradition and play a prominent role in terms of tools and techniques to support OSH across the systems life cycle. Among simulation techniques available, virtual reality (VR) has technically matured into a simulation tool for humans to interact with dynamic, 3D virtual environments (VE) and into a simulation technique for different areas of applications [10]. In industry and services, techniques of VR serve in design reviews, visualisations and demonstrations [8, 11]. In training applications, VR attracts participants and may facilitate intended human-system interactions [12, 13]. In systems design, VR is seen helpful to support systems development and verification, while in human factors and ergonomics disciplines it serves analysis, design and evaluation procedures [14, 15]. VR as a simulation technique is instrumental in OSH research and development. Designed according to human factors concepts [16], it may provoke human responses and behaviour similar to those revealed in real environments (RE) [17].

However, this does not mean that development of VR techniques in OSH contexts simply result in suitable or effective OSH interventions. Transfer research for VE is scarce and evidence for positive transfer has not often been demonstrated; few times not, because hazardous situations in reality should be avoided or due to lack of transfer environments [18]. While in VE development, high fidelity is often assumed important for improving immersion into VE and for increasing the feeling of presence [17], it may not always be required to establish complete realism or high fidelity to establish a sense of presence [19]. Sometimes, discussions about the importance of fidelity in VE miss requirements referring to human recipients, purposes of applications and human factor and ergonomics in general. As a result, fidelity is rather misunderstood and limited to technical or physical fidelity or photorealism. A concept more relevant in the development of suitable simulation environments for human-system interaction is seen in psychological fidelity [20]. Dimensions such as cognitive, functional, construct and physical fidelity are included and differential impacts with regard to objective, task, stakeholder and context of VR applications are taken into account.

1.2   Differential Size and Colour Estimations

Investigations into comparisons between RE and VE serve multiple purposes. Results may improve development, implementation and application of VE, inform about potentials for positive transfer of effects and facilitate decision making about appropriate VR techniques in specific situations. Studies pursue applications of standardised testing procedures [21], ergonomics evaluations of VE [22], examinations of factors influencing human perception [17], and direct comparisons of virtual and real work scenarios and work procedures [23].

Several applications in the context of OSH are necessarily similar to some other application contexts in industry and services (see above) [24]. For basic orientation in 3D environments, depth and colour perception is a relevant feature of information acquisition for human task performance and OSH in applications with human-system interaction [6]. Depth perception in 3D space, size and colour perception are among important mental cues relevant for the design of close to reality VE [25, 26].

Visual depth perception comprises information on size of volumes and relative position of objects in space [27]. In general, humans usually tend to underestimate egocentric (human-object) distances [25] and may rather overestimate exocentric (object-object) distances in VE as compared to RE [28]. However, results especially for exocentric distances are not consistent and depend among others on distances under investigation, VR techniques used and design of the environmental context [26].

Colour perception covers the visible electromagnetic spectrum for humans (380–740 nm) with a specific brightness. In VE colour is limited to mixtures within the triangle of RGB primaries. Achromatic (colour) perception or perception of black, white and greyscales corresponds to perceiving colours without hues. However, white could be any colour with added maximum level of brightness, black could be any colour without any brightness and greyscales reflect points on a scale of brightness (without hue). Few studies differentially investigated colour perception in RE and VE with the latter showing higher impairments in colour perception [26]. In addition, impacts on size perceptions in VE could be demonstrated [29]. Differences, however, may often have been due to vision characteristics and types of VR techniques used in the studies, i.e. underestimations tending to attenuate when using large projections [30].

1.3   Depth and Colour Perception in Occupational Safety and Health

Depth perception and especially size and colour estimations are crucial characteristics for safe and healthy human orientation and performance in 3D space (e.g. navigation at work, anticipation and identification of hazards, perception of warnings [3]). This is due to human information processing requirements for human task performance and OSH and relevant in applications for humans interacting with technical systems (e.g. human-robot interaction in manufacturing). Therefore, differential effects were investigated for size and colour estimates in a real and virtual robot cells.

2 Methods

2.1 Participants

Ten participants (M = 45.9 years, SD = 10.3), familiar with industrial applications, provided informed consent to take part in empirical investigations for two hours each. All participants were right-handed and all passed screenings on (corrected) visual acuity [31], colour vision (extract from [32]), and stereo vision [33].

2.2 Robot Cell in Real and Virtual Environment

A section of the Environmental Laboratory of the Institute for Occupational Safety and Health of the German Social Accident Insurance (IFA) is allocated for investigations into safety devices for robotic applications. A robot cell with an industrial robot system (R 30–16, Reis Robotics, Kuka AG, Germany) has been used and set-up for the present study (see Fig. 1, left) while a copy has been developed to be presented in the Virtual Reality Laboratory (see Fig. 1, right, [34]). Industrial robot movements were restricted by safety-rated soft axis and space limiting [35] and human access into the robot cell was safeguarded by light curtains (miniTwin4, Sick AG, Germany) attached to left and right walls. A black and yellow stripe safety tape attached to the ground informed participants about the safety area of the real and virtual robot cell, not to be crossed by participants during the study.

The VR model of the robot cell scenario was composed in the Vizard Virtual Reality Toolkit (WorldViz LLC, USA) using the lab environment (i.e. walls of robot cell, boxes, wooden slats) and a mesh of the 3D CAD model of the above-mentioned industrial robot suitable for comparisons between real and virtual robot cells.

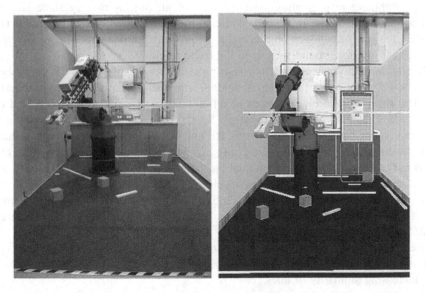

Fig. 1. Robot cell in real (left) and virtual (right) laboratory environment. (Color figure online)

The VR laboratory of the IFA [34] contains a 7 m^2 operating space in front of a curved presentation wall of 24 m^2 (3 m × 8 m). The wall represents a 164° circle segment of 2.8 m arc radius. Physical dimensions allow the workspace and projection area big enough to fully cover the human field of vision for stereoscopic depth perception when facing the projection wall. Dimensioning facilitates interaction of humans with large machinery [e.g. 8, 15, 36]. Interference filter technology (Infitec®, Infitec GmbH, Germany) is applied to 3D rear projection with three pairs of high luminance projectors (F2 series, projectiondesign®, Belgium) as well as applied to participants' 3D glasses to maintain a high level of colour fidelity and to experience depth cues in 3D space. Four infrared cameras for motion capturing (VICON®, Vicon Motion Systems Ltd, UK) mounted on top of the projection wall serve a dynamic match in real-time between participant body and head movements with the adaptation required for visualization of the VE. This way, dynamics in the VE and participant movements adjust optimally and in real time to the vision of an individual participant; while at the same time support participants' experience of presence and immersion in the VE.

2.3   Task Environment

The task environment consisted of the robot cells including all objects for performing different mental tasks with regard to quality and use of design for applied research into OSH. Depth, size and colour perception are relevant for design of close to reality VE [25, 26].

Therefore, in the robot cell (width 3000 mm, height 3000 mm, depth 6000 mm; Fig. 1) of both labs, eight wooden slats different in length (2100, 1900, 1900, 1100, 1100, 400, 300, 300 mm) and six cuboid cardboard boxes different in edge length (400, 400, 200, 150, 150, 150 mm) were placed at different height levels and distances from the front of the robot cells. The robot cell in reality served as a model for the virtual task environment in presenting virtual copies of all objects at very same size and location. In front of the robot cell, participants could move along the safety tape, allowing to recognise hidden objects and to improve depth perception (e.g. movement of objects in the foreground relative to the background).

In addition, greyscale as well as colour patterns were displayed on flip chart sheets in 297 × 420 mm format [37] (Fig. 2) at 4000 mm distance from the front of the robot cell. The sheets served investigations of differential perception of greyscales and colours in OSH relevant work environments. Spatial representation of objects and greyscale and colour patterns was the same in RE and VE. Besides black and white, shades of grey were graded in 10% steps resulting in 11 black/white combinations. Flip chart sheets in both robot cells (Fig. 1) in total presented 11 greyscales and 12 colours, with the colours different in hue. Colours selected in RGB notion and with W3C similar names were as follows: (255, 0, 0) red, (255, 0, 128) bright pink, (255, 128, 0) orange, (255, 0, 255) fuchsia, (255, 255, 0) yellow, (0, 0, 255) blue, (0, 255, 0) electric green, (0, 255, 128) spring green, (0, 128, 255) azure, (0, 255, 255) aqua, (128, 255, 0) chartreuse, and (128, 0, 255) violet. Comparisons between colours each referred to two colours taken from the RBG colour wheel with primary, secondary and tertiary colours; with increasing similarity of hues.

In total, nine flip chart sheets were presented in each environment; among them three with 6 × 4 colour patterns, two with 6 × 4 greyscale patterns, two with 6 × 2 colour combinations for direct comparison and two with 6 × 2 greyscale combinations for direct comparison. At sheets with 6 × 4 colours or greyscales participants were asked to indicate the number of different colours and greyscales and should tell how many times the first, second, third etc. colour and greyscale is presented (similar to Fig. 2, but with either colour or grey). At sheets with 6 × 2 colours or greyscales (similar to Fig. 2, but with two middle columns left blank) participants were asked, whether each of six combinations of two colours or greyscales is same or different.

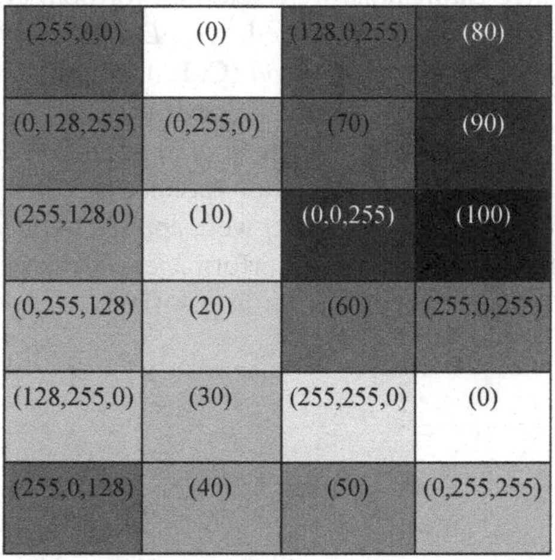

(255,0,0)	(0)	(128,0,255)	(80)
(0,128,255)	(0,255,0)	(70)	(90)
(255,128,0)	(10)	(0,0,255)	(100)
(0,255,128)	(20)	(60)	(255,0,255)
(128,255,0)	(30)	(255,255,0)	(0)
(255,0,128)	(40)	(50)	(0,255,255)

Fig. 2. Presentation sheet with a range of colours and greyscales; the study used sheets with either colours or greyscales patterns (RGB values and greyscale in % not displayed for participants) for estimations in both environments. (Color figure online)

2.4 Experimental Procedure and Study Design

The experiments lasted about 150 min each, subdivided into consecutive sections for preparation, two sessions separated by assessments, and debriefing. At the beginning, participants were asked to provide informed consent and were informed about their rights as participants. They filled in questionnaires on demographics and baseline performance. Before tasking in the virtual robot cell, participants were given 5 min to become familiar with the environment and wearing Infitec® glasses for 3D perception in the SUTAVE laboratory [34]. Between sections of performing in the virtual and/or real robot cell as well as at the end of a session, participants were again asked to provide state self-assessments. Debriefing consisted of interviews about preferences and experiences with both settings and about feedback regarding the investigation. Participants' state assessments referred to ratings of perceived mental workload by using the task load index (NASA-TLX [38]). Participants rated the quality of the VE by questionnaires, i.e. Immersion Tendency Questionnaire (ITQ [19]), Presence Questionnaire (PQ [19, 39]), Presence Self-Assessment Manikins (PSAM [40]) and Simulator Sickness Questionnaire (SSQ [41, 42]).

The investigation aims to inform human factors and ergonomics design requirements by investigation of human differential assessment of absolute and relative size and colour/grey estimations. During sessions, participants answered a set of questions while standing in front of the black and yellow stripe safety tape of the fully equipped robot cell. Required were relative and absolute estimates for height, length and depth of the robot cells as well as number, size of and distance between cuboid boxes, slats and other objects (see Fig. 1, left). For colour and greyscale presented on the flip charts (see Fig. 1, right), only relative estimations were required for both cells.

A mixed $2 \times \# \times 2$ design was employed, with *Environment* (i.e. real and virtual robot cell) by *Characteristic under Estimation* (CuE, i.e. 3 relative and 3 absolute size estimation groups, 4 levels of grey shades, 3 colour groups) as a within-subjects variables and *Sequence* (starting with the RE or VE) being between-subjects variable balanced across both environments. Analysis of variance repeated measures procedures (ANOVA; IBM® SPSS® Statistics 23, USA) were applied to questionnaire results and session parameter estimations during task performance in both environments. For all statistical tests, the significance level was set at $p < 0.05$.

3   Results

3.1   Screenings

Ergonomics Check of Work Environment. An ergonomics checklist for real and virtual work environments [22] indicated no need for action, neither for the real nor for the virtual robot cell. The checklist addressed among others requirements for participant posture, space and reach zones as well as measures for the prevention of hazardous sensors and obstacles.

Luminance Density. Luminance density measurements taken with Optometer P2000 (Gigahertz, Germany) at various locations was slightly lower in the virtual robot cell as compared to the robot cell in reality. Similar results were found for luminance density contrasts, being lower in the virtual robot cell (0.64) than in the real robot cell (0.74).

Spatial Resolution. Visual acuity of the participants was studied by presenting an appropriate Landolt C eye chart on a flipchart in the robot cells at 4 m distance to the participant [31]. All participants passed the screenings in the real robot cell, indicating that (corrected) visual acuity was high.

However, results in the VE were not acceptable due the spatial resolution of the VR projection being much lower than that of the human visual processing system. Consequently, the virtual robot cell seems to be not suitable for detailed information presentation such as for reading tasks or fine-grained pattern recognition.

3.2   Questionnaires

Perceived Mental Workload. The sequence of task processing in the real or virtual robot cell did not reveal any significant influence on the results of this evaluation study. Mental workload during task processing was rated under-average across both labs (M = 34.7; SD = 10.6). Nevertheless, mental load was perceived as significantly higher in the virtual than in the real robotic cell; *Environment* [$F(1.8)$ = 9.88; p < 0.05]; with no further effects significant. Detailed analyses indicated higher dissatisfaction with participants' own performance and higher frustration levels during task processing in the virtual robot cell. This may have possibly reflected sensation of differential results for depth and colour perceptions across both robot cells.

Simulator Sickness. The questionnaire on simulator sickness was rated after task performance in the virtual robot cell and resulted in an acceptable level of simulator sickness (M = 7.30; SD = 2.09); indicating minimal symptoms according to sickness score classifications [43].

Sense of Presence. Although a sense of presence in VE is crucial for human behaviour similar to reality, there is still discussion about relevant factors suitable to improve environmental design quality. Some measures suggest investigating the tendency of participants to experience presence before an assessment of presence should take place [19]. The immersion tendency questionnaire (ITQ) therefore addresses tendencies to become involved in activities, to maintain focus on current activities and to play computer games. Results for the ITQ in the present study suggest a rather high total level of immersion tendency (M = 72.00; SD = 11.46) as well as tendency sub-dimensions ($M_{involve}$ = 25.40; $SD_{involve}$ = 4.72; M_{focus} = 33.90; SD_{focus} = 5.13; M_{games} = 4.40; SD_{games} = 2.46); similar to those reported in the literature [19, 39].

The sense of presence (PQ) in robotic cells yielded an internationally comparable and high level (M = 82.1; SD = 14.7). This could be confirmed by pictorial assessments of presence across robot cells (PSAM) with estimates above average (M = 4.2, SD = 0.94) and, as expected, higher levels in the real robot cell as compared to the virtual one; *Environment* [$F(1.8)$ = 42.67, p < 0.01].

3.3   Parameter Estimations with Regard to Depth Perception

In robot cells, object groups (e.g. cuboid cardboard boxes, wooden slats; Fig. 1) were presented different in number, shape and size. While all participants identified the number of objects correctly in both environments, estimations of absolute and relative size of the robot cells and evenly spread objects differed across environments.

Absolute estimations of robot cell characteristics (e.g. height, length, depth) and characteristics of objects within the cell (e.g. box edge size, slat length) were different for real and virtual environments (M_{real} = 11.5%, SD_{real} = 6.8; $M_{virtual}$ = 14.6%, $SD_{virtual}$ = 7.2), with a total average at 13.1% (SD = 7.0). According to results for *Environment* [$F(1.8)$ = 13.7; p < 0.05], measures were significantly overestimated in virtual robot cells (Fig. 3). In addition, there was a marginally significant difference for *Characteristic under Estimation (CuE)* [$F(2,16)$ = 3.3; p < 0.10], with false absolute estimations being higher for robot cells and cuboid boxes in contrast to those for wooden slats (Fig. 3). An interaction effect of both factors (i.e. *Environment x CuE*) did not reach significance level.

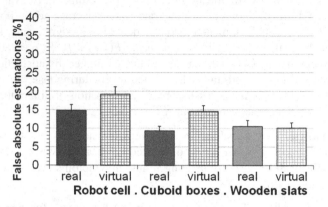

Fig. 3. Deviations for absolute size estimations regarding characteristics of robot cells, cuboid boxes and wooden slats for RE and VE.

Similar, relative estimations of robot cell characteristics (e.g. cell depth longer than cell width) and characteristics of objects within the cell (e.g. relative size differences for boxes and slats) differed for RE and VE (M_{real} = 15.6%, SD_{real} = 14.1; $M_{virtual}$ = 24.9%, $SD_{virtual}$ = 18.2), with a total average at 20.3% (SD = 16.2). According to results for *Environment* [$F(1.8)$ = 43.4; $p < 0.01$], relative estimations were more often misjudged in virtual robot cells (Fig. 4). Although, the result patterns in Fig. 4 resembles Fig. 3, no other factor and factor combination reached significance level.

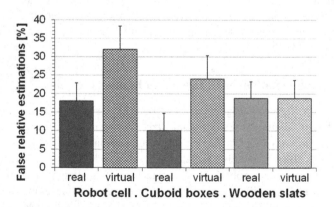

Fig. 4. Deviations for relative size estimations regarding characteristics of robot cells, cuboid boxes and wooden slats for RE and VE.

3.4   Parameter Estimations with Regard to Grey and Colour Perception

Sheets with greyscale patterns (see Fig. 2 for examples) were presented on flip charts in real and virtual robot cells (see Fig. 1, right). Discriminations between shades of grey were in general rather poor in both environments (M_{real} = 14.0%, SD_{real} = 17.1; $M_{virtual}$ = 18.8%, $SD_{virtual}$ = 19.2), with a total average at 16.4% (SD = 18.2). Differences between environments seem to vary across levels of shading (Fig. 5). However, only comparisons for CuE, i.e. between different levels of contrast or shades of grey (e.g. 0%, 10%, 20%, >30%) resulted in statistically significant differences [$F(3,24)$ = 11.5; $p < 0.01$], mainly due to smaller (e.g. 10%) differences between shades in contrast to others (Fig. 5).

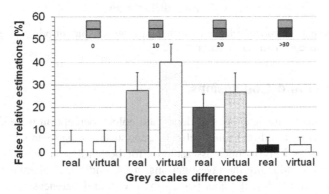

Fig. 5. Deviations from correct relative estimations in RE and VE for two grey shades of 0%, 10%, 20% and >30% difference.

Sheets with colour patterns (different in hues according to RGB colour wheel and limited to primary, secondary and tertiary colours; similar to Fig. 2) were presented on flip charts in real and virtual robot cells (see Fig. 1, right). While discriminations between colours in general were rather poor in both environments (M_{real} = 16.3%, SD_{real} = 16.5; $M_{virtual}$ = 26.8%, $SD_{virtual}$ = 18.9), differences between environments seem to increase with increasing grades of the colour wheel (Fig. 6). Comparisons between both environments resulted in statistically significant differences; *Environment* [$F(1,8)$ = 9.6; $p < 0.05$]. In addition, differences between feature groups of colour ranging from primary, secondary and tertiary hues yielded significant differences for CuE [$F(2,16)$ = 29.7; $p < 0.01$] (Fig. 6). Interactions between factors, however, did not reach level of statistical significance.

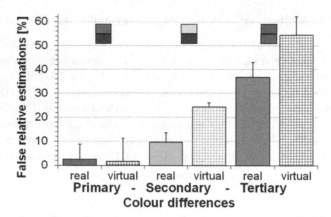

Fig. 6. Deviations from correct relative estimations for two colours of primary, secondary and tertiary hues (RGB colour wheel) in RE and VE.

4 Discussion and Conclusions

In the present study, characteristics of depth and colour perception were differentially investigated in virtual and real robot cells. In general, no impairments were identified according to risk and ergonomics assessments for both robot cells. This provided a suitable basis for conducting the investigations in RE and VE. Nevertheless, analyses of characteristics of depth and colour perception revealed differences between real and virtual robot cells and in some cases even for specific objects under investigation.

False relative estimations across RGB primary, secondary and tertiary colours were at 21.5% (SD = 17.7) on average for both real and virtual robot cell. False estimations increased with increasing similarity between colours and were higher for virtual robot cells. For achromatic (colour) perception or perception of black, white and greyscales, false relative estimations were lower (about 5%) on average. Better results were obtained in real and virtual robot cells for comparisons of two of the very same greyscale or those with differences in shade of 30% and more. For both robot cells, estimations were much worse for shades of 20% or 10%. Differences between shades of 20% and 10% tended to increase and tended to be higher in virtual robot cells, though not being reflected in statistical analysis. This may also lead to the assumption that the smaller existing differences in comparisons of colour or chromatic perception the more likely are error in estimations, especially in VE. In addition, the results may add to other studies suggesting an influence of colour presentation on size perception due to cues relevant in depth perception [26, 29].

While all participants identified the number of objects correctly in both environments, exocentric estimations of absolute and relative size of the robot cells and evenly spread objects differed across environments. In general, false absolute estimations were at 13% on average across both RE and VE. However, false *absolute* estimations were given more often in virtual robot cells and they tended to refer rather to estimations of somewhat bulky dimensions like robot cells and cuboid boxes than estimations of slender wooden slats. False *relative* estimations suggested a similar pattern of results, however, the average of false relative estimations ranged in total at higher level of 20.3% and they were more often misjudged in virtual robot cells; without significant differences between bulky and slender dimensions. Although false estimations of exocentric distances tended to be rather overestimations and seem to be similar to some reports in the literature [26, 28], data revealed no consistent pattern.

Consistent with differences in estimations for RE and VE, perceived mental workload was rated higher for VE due to higher dissatisfaction with participants' own performance and higher frustration levels. This may have well been caused by performance decrements for estimation tasks in the virtual robot cell. On average, however, perceived mental workload was relatively low in both environments.

No relevant symptoms of simulator sickness were detected during the investigations. In addition, the tendency to be immersed in VE was rated high across participants and is comparable to levels in other studies [19]. Similar was true for the feeling of presence during the investigations, with presence ratings even higher for the real as for the virtual robot cell. This may still support the notion, that the feeling of presence may be rated at high level even if the level of fidelity does not represent complete realism [19, 20].

Although, risk and ergonomics assessments of the robot cells did not reveal impairments, luminance density contrasts and resolution of the environment by rear projection were lower in the virtual as compared to the real robot cell. Since other studies reported both mechanical and optical properties of HMDs contributing to distance underestimations in VE [26], it could be assumed that the simulation environment with a projection wall in the present study [34] faced similar constraints.

Consequently, care should be taken in investigations, where depth and colour perceptions are crucial for safety and health in VE and for appropriate human task performance according to applications. While this may be a suitable workaround on an interim basis for some VR techniques already available, future research should address potential limitations for informed decision makings and for VR support in studies on human-system interaction. Some support could be drawn from former discussions on potential equivalence of paper-based or computer-based tasks [44, 45]. Discussions could be disentangled, at least in part, by clarification that total equivalence will not be possible and by research and design strategies improving the quality of media while focusing on human factors and ergonomics analysis of objectives of applications and of human tasks in applications.

Acknowledgements. It is a pleasant duty to acknowledge all participants for taking part in the study and for immersing in the virtual work environment. The author is grateful to the efforts of Mr. Andy Lungfiel for technical development of the VE.

References

1. WHO: Basic documents: forty-ninth edition (including amendments adopted up to 31 May 2019). World Health Organization, Geneva (2020). http://apps.who.int/gb/bd/
2. Radandt, S., Rantanen, J., Renn, O.: Governance of occupational safety and health environmental risks. In: Bischoff, H.-J. (ed.) Risks in Modern Society. TISRRAQ, vol. 13, pp. 127–258. Springer, Dordrecht (2008). https://doi.org/10.1007/978-1-4020-8289-4_4

3. Lehto, M.R., Cook, B.T.: Occupational health and safety management. In: Salvendy, G. (ed.) Handbook of Human Factors and Ergonomics, pp. 701–733. Wiley, Hoboken (2012)
4. Nickel, P.: Extending the effective range of prevention through design by OSH applications in virtual reality. In: Nah, F.F.-H., Tan, C.-H. (eds.) HCIBGO 2016. LNCS, vol. 9752, pp. 325–336. Springer, Cham (2016). https://doi.org/10.1007/978-3-319-39399-5_31
5. EU OSH Framework Directive 89/391/EEC of 12 June 1989 on the introduction of measures to encourage improvements in the safety and health of workers at work (with amendments 2008). Official Journal of the European Union L 183, 29/06/1989, 1–8 (2008)
6. EN ISO 6385: Ergonomic principles in the design of work systems. CEN, Brussels (2016)
7. Nickel, P., et al.: Human-system interaction design requirements to improve machinery and systems safety. In: Arezes, P.M. (ed.) AHFE 2019. AISC, vol. 969, pp. 3–13. Springer, Cham (2020). https://doi.org/10.1007/978-3-030-20497-6_1
8. Nickel, P., Janning, M., Wachholz, T., Pröger, E.: Shaping future work systems by OSH risk assessments early on. In: Bagnara, S., Tartaglia, R., Albolino, S., Alexander, T., Fujita, Y. (eds.) IEA 2018. AISC, vol. 819, pp. 247–256. Springer, Cham (2019). https://doi.org/10.1007/978-3-319-96089-0_27
9. Miller, C., et al.: Human-machine interface. In: Hockey, G.R.J. (ed.) THESEUS Cluster 2: Psychology and Human-Machine Systems – Report, Indigo, Strasbourg, pp. 22–38 (2012)
10. Hale, K.S., Stanney, K.M. (eds.): Handbook of Virtual Environments: Design, Implementation, and Applications. CRC Press, Boca Raton (2015)
11. Zhou, W., Whyte, J., Sacks, R.: Construction safety and digital design: a review. Autom. Constr. 22, 102–111 (2012)
12. Grabowski, A.: Innovative and comprehensive support system for training people working in dangerous conditions. In: Duffy, V.G. (ed.) HCII 2019. LNCS, vol. 11581, pp. 394–405. Springer, Cham (2019). https://doi.org/10.1007/978-3-030-22216-1_29
13. Lawson, G., Shaw, E., Roper, T., Nilsson, T., Bajorunaite, L., Batool, A.: Immersive virtual worlds: multi-sensory virtual environments for health and safety training. IOSH, Leicestershire (2019)
14. Helin, K., Karjalainen, J., Kuula, T., Philippon, N.: Virtual/mixed/augmented reality laboratory research for the study of augmented human and human-machine systems. In: Proceedings of 12th International IEEE Conference on Intelligent Environments, IE 2016, September 2016, London, pp. 14–16 (2016)
15. Kaufeld, M., Nickel, P.: Level of robot autonomy and information aids in human-robot interaction affect human mental workload – an investigation in virtual reality. In: Duffy, V.G. (ed.) HCII 2019. LNCS, vol. 11581, pp. 278–291. Springer, Cham (2019). https://doi.org/10.1007/978-3-030-22216-1_21
16. Eastgate, R.M., Wilson, J.R., D'Cruz, M.: Structured development of virtual environments. In: Hale, K.S., Stanney, K.M. (eds.) Handbook of Virtual Environments: Design, Implementation, and Applications, pp. 353–390. CRC Press, Boca Raton (2015)
17. De Kort, Y.A.W., Ijsselsteijn, W.A., Kooijman, J., Schuurmans, Y.: Virtual laboratories: comparability of real and virtual environments for environmental psychology. Presence 12(4), 360–373 (2003)
18. Champney, R.K., Carroll, M., Surpris, G., Cohn, J.: Conducting training transfer studies in virtual environments. In: Hale, K.S., Stanney, K.M. (eds.) Handbook of Virtual Environments: Design, Implementation, and Applications, pp. 781–795. CRC Press, Boca Raton (2015)
19. Witmer, B.G., Singer, M.J.: Measuring presence in virtual environments: a presence questionnaire. Presence 7(3), 225–240 (1998)

20. Simpson, B.D., Cowgill, J.L., Gilkey, R.H., Weisenberger, J.M.: Technological considerations in the design of multisensory virtual environments: how real does it need to be? In: Hale, K.S., Stanney, K.M. (eds.) Handbook of Virtual Environments: Design, Implementation, and Applications, pp. 313–333. CRC Press, Boca Raton (2015)

21. Lampton, D.R., Knerr, B.W., Goldberg, S.L., Bliss, J.P., Moshell, M.J., Blau, B.S.: The Virtual Environment Performance Assessment Battery: Development and evaluation (TR 1029). US Army Research Institute, Alexandria (1995)

22. McCauley Bell, P.: Ergonomics in virtual environments. In: Stanney, K.M. (ed.) Handbook of Virtual Environments, pp. 807–826. LEA, Mahwah (2002)

23. Marc, J., Belkacem, N., Marsot, J.: Virtual reality: a design tool for enhanced consideration of usability 'validation elements'. Saf. Sci. **45**, 589–601 (2007)

24. Nickel, P., Lungfiel, A.: Improving occupational safety and health (OSH) in human-system interaction (HSI) through applications in virtual environments. In: Duffy, V.G. (ed.) DHM 2018. LNCS, vol. 10917, pp. 85–96. Springer, Cham (2018). https://doi.org/10.1007/978-3-319-91397-1_8

25. Renner, R.S., Velichkovsky, B.M., Helmert, J.R.: The perception of egocentric distances in virtual environments – a review. ACM Comput. Surv. (CSUR) **46**(2), 40, Article 23 (2013). https://doi.org/10.1145/2543581.2543590

26. Badcock, D.R., Palmisano, S., May, J.G.: Vision and virtual environments. In: Hale, K.S., Stanney, K.M. (eds.) Handbook of Virtual Environments: Design, Implementation, and Applications, pp. 39–85. CRC Press, Boca Raton (2015)

27. Goldstein, E.B., Brockmole, J.R.: Sensation and Perception. Cengage Learning, Boston (2017)

28. Maruhn, P., Schneider, S., Bengler, K.: Measuring egocentric distance perception in virtual reality: influence of methodologies, locomotion and translation gains. PLoS ONE **14**(10), e0224651 (2019). https://doi.org/10.1371/journal.pone.0224651

29. Stahre, B., Billger, M.: Physical measurements vs visual perception: comparing colour appearance in reality to virtual reality. In: Proceedings of the Conference on Colour in Graphics, Imaging, and Vision, CGIV 2006, 19–22 June 2006, Leeds, pp. 146-151 (2006)

30. Plumert, J.M., Kearney, J.K., Cremer, J.F., Recker, K.: Distance perception in real and virtual environments. ACM Trans. Appl. Percept. **2**(3), 216–233 (2005). https://doi.org/10.1145/1077399.1077402

31. EN ISO 8596: Ophthalmic optics - Visual acuity testing - Standard and clinical optotypes and their presentation (ISO 8596:2017). Brussels, CEN (2018)

32. Ishihara, S.: Tests for Colour Blindness. Handaya Hongo Harukich, Tokyo (1917)

33. TNO: Test for stereoscopic vision (Netherlands Organization for Applied Scientific Research, Institut for Perception, 17th ed.). Lameris Ootech, Nieuwegein (1972)

34. Nickel, P., Lungfiel, A.: SUTAVE. Safety and usability through applications in virtual environments. Virtual reality in occupational safety and health. An IFA service. DGUV, Berlin (2014). www.dguv.de/ifa/sutave

35. EN ISO 10218: Robots and robotic devices - Safety requirements for industrial robots - Part 1: Robots. Part 2: Robot systems and integration. CEN, Brussels (2012)

36. Nickel, P., Lungfiel, A., Trabold, R.-J.: Reconstruction of near misses and accidents for analyses from virtual reality usability study. In: Barbic, J., D'Cruz, M., Latoschik, M.E., Slater, M., Bourdot, P. (eds.) EuroVR 2017. LNCS, vol. 10700, pp. 182–191. Springer, Cham (2017). https://doi.org/10.1007/978-3-319-72323-5_12

37. EN ISO 216: Writing paper and certain classes of printed matter - Trimmed sizes - A and B series, and indication of machine direction (ISO 216:2007). CEN, Brussels (2007)

38. Hart, S.G., Staveland, L.E.: Development of the NASA task load index (TLX): results of empirical and theoretical research. In: Hancock, P.A., Meshkati, N. (eds.) Human Mental Workload, pp. 139–183. North-Holland, Amsterdam (1988)
39. Witmer, B.G., Jerome, C.J., Singer, M.J.: The factor structure of the presence questionnaire. Presence **14**(3), 298–312 (2005)
40. Weibel, D., Schmutz, J., Pahud, O., Wissmath, B.: Measuring spatial presence: introducing and validating the pictorial presence SAM. Presence Teleoperators Virtual Environ. **24**(1), 44–61 (2015)
41. Kennedy, R.S., Berbaum, K.S., Lilienthal, M.G.: Simulator sickness questionnaire: an enhanced method for quantifying simulator sickness. Int. J. Aviat. Psychol. **3**(3), 203–220 (1993)
42. Pfendler, C., Thun, J.: Der Simulator Sickness Questionnaire von Kennedy et al. (1993) und seine rechnergestützte Version (Technischer Bericht). Forschungsinstitut für Kommunikation, Informationsverarbeitung und Ergonomie (FKIE), Wachtberg (2001)
43. Stanney, K.M., Kennedy, R.S., Drexler, J.M.: Cybersickness is not simulator sickness. In: Proceedings of the 41st Annual Meeting of the Human Factors and Ergonomics Society, HFES 1997, 22–26 September 1997, Albuquerque, pp. 1138–1142. HFES, San Diego (1997)
44. Nickel, P., Nachreiner, F.: Differential usability of paper-based and computer-based work documents for control room operators in the chemical process industry. In: De Waard, D., Brookhuis, K.A., van Egmond, R., Boersema, T. (eds.) Human Factors in Design, Safety, and Management, pp. 299–314. Shaker Publishing, Maastricht (2005)
45. Noyes, J.M., Garland, K.J.: Computer- vs. paper-based tasks: Are they equivalent? Ergonomics **51**(9), 1352–1375 (2008)

A 3-Step Approach for Introducing Computer-Aided Ergonomics Analysis Methodologies

Kirill Sinchuk[1]([⊠]), Abigail L. Hancock[1], Alexandra Hayford[1],
Thorsten Kuebler[2], and Vincent G. Duffy[1]

[1] Purdue University, West Lafayette, IN 47907, USA
kirill.sinchuk@gmail.com,
{hancocl8, ahayford, duffy}@purdue.edu
[2] Human Solutions of North America, Morrisville, NC 27560, USA
Thorsten.Kuebler@human-solutions.com

Abstract. The first step of the methodology focuses on air traffic controllers situated at a workstation within an Air Traffic Control (ATC) room. The 3D CAD software RAMSIS uses manikins to represent subjects under study. Using this software, three air traffic controllers of different heights were added. The three air traffic controllers were modeled sitting at their workstation in different positions while doing typical on-shift duties, including reaching for a phone and looking at each of the three monitors at their workstation. The Joint Capacity analysis tool in RAMSIS was used to study which joints face the most discomfort on each air traffic controller. It was found that the hip joints and the shoulder joints unanimously faced the highest amount of fatigue in this setting. Suggested modifications to the control room include adjustable desks, monitors, and chairs so that different air traffic controllers can be accommodated. Potential discomfort for air traffic controllers facing ergonomic issues on the job can create vulnerabilities that extend to the public. In second step, an analysis tool is introduced for analyzing the obstruction on the window caused by computer monitors in the Air Traffic Control room. Obstruction analysis was done to investigate the need for a reorganized workspace considering the user's need to see out the window to perform their job tasks and to decrease the need for repetitive standing to see out the window. It was found that approximately 40% of the window is obscured by the monitors and therefore the monitor configuration should be changed. The projected change to a three-in-a-row monitor setup decreased the obstruction to the window and therefore improved the ergonomic setup of the workstation. In step 3, a RAMSIS simulation and analysis of the forklift blind spots helps provide improved safety for the forklift operation. A camera system with two different view angles is added to aid the forklift operator. Analysis leads to conclusions that using the camera system eliminates the forklift blind spot and allows for safer forklift operation.

Keywords: Repetitive task · Forklift · Vision blind spots · RAMSIS

© Springer Nature Switzerland AG 2020
V. G. Duffy (Ed.): HCII 2020, LNCS 12198, pp. 243–263, 2020.
https://doi.org/10.1007/978-3-030-49904-4_18

1   Overview of Three Steps in Computer-Aided Ergonomics Analysis

Three steps are outlined in the form of cases that are described to introduce a methodology for ergonomics analysis. RAMSIS software is shown for design using computer-aided ergonomics and digital human modeling. In the first step, a joint capacity analysis is done for air traffic controllers and improved air traffic control room design. The three air traffic controllers were modeled sitting at their workstation in different positions while doing typical on-shift duties, including reaching for a phone and looking at each of the three monitors at their workstation. The Joint Capacity analysis tool in RAMSIS was used to study which joints face the most discomfort on each air traffic controller. In the second step, in similar work setting, an obstruction analysis is conducted for the air traffic controllers. Obstruction analysis was done to investigate the need for a reorganized workspace under the consideration of the user's need to see out the window to perform their job tasks and to decrease the need for repetitive standing to see out the window. Certain properties of the eyes can be simulated (Bubb 2007; Karoui and Kuebler 2019). At that time Bubb showed examples eye tracing research and gave consideration for future industrial applications. In the third step, vision-related simulations are again considered. This time the vision-related simulation is used for simulating the operating circumstance of forklift operator. Vision and blind spots are considered for redesign, awareness and hazard mitigation. A wireless camera system is incorporated with a system perspective on awareness and mitigation of hazards associated with the blindspots that are traditionally present in forklift operator experiences.

1.1   Step 1 Computer-Aided Ergonomic Analysis

Ergonomics is the study of adapting the workplace environment to the worker's needs. Proper ergonomic design increases the efficiency and productivity of the worker, and should be considered early in development process for all workplace settings (van der Muelen and Seidl 2007; Duffy 2007; Demirel and Duffy 2007). The purpose of this first step is to introduce an ergonomic assessment of air traffic controllers' joint analysis in an air traffic control room setting.

The design and analysis for this study was performed using 3D Digital Human Modeling (DHM) tool RAMSIS. This CAD software represents subjects under study as manikins, and allows the user to manipulate their behavior in the environment. For this study, RAMSIS was used to model air traffic controllers sitting at a workstation.

1.2   Step 1 Problem Statement

This first step showed ergonomic risks that are found in air traffic controllers sitting at a workstation in an Air Traffic Control (ATC) room. Three manikins: one tall, one medium, and one short in height, were altered to reach for the phone, while simultaneously looking at three different computer screens at their work station. The discomfort percentage rating for every combination was tabulated. The purpose of this study is to diagnose what joints have the highest ergonomic risk factors in this sitting position.

The motivation to study the design of the ATC room, and of the controllers at the workstation is public safety during air transport. Controllers direct aircraft during flight, and prevent collisions among multiple aircraft at landing/take-off stations. An improperly designed workstation or poor equipment can distract the controller or cause loss of situational awareness. A traffic controller not comfortable at their station can also face long-term consequences such as fatigue, pain and discomfort, which can ultimately lead to musculoskeletal disorders.

The ATC Room is an environment where repercussions of improper ergonomics can extend beyond injuries of the controllers, to the fatalities of many people. Serious accidents have occurred when the environment of the traffic control tower was not factored into design. USAir Flight 1493 in 1991 cited ergonomics within the control tower to be a contributing factor of aircraft collision (USAir Flight 1493 2019). The controller that guided this 1493 flight faced glare from the lights of a nearby building, and had a poor vantage point from the tower she sat in. This ultimately caused two planes to collide with each other.

1.3 Procedure

Loading the Software
To launch the RAMSIS program, the "launchNextGenAutomotive.bat" file is launched from the RAMSIS zip folder. After the RAMSIS program loads, the RAMSIS Air Traffic Control Room session is launched by navigating to *File > Load Session*, selecting the folder "session_AirTrafficControlCenter", then pressing OK. The window will load the air traffic control room environment with the manikins and workstation geometry, as shown in Fig. 1. It is helpful to adjust the render style to "Shaded" through *View > Render Style* on the top menu bar so that the user can easily see and alter the manikins accordingly.

Menu Navigation
As shown in Fig. 1, there are three major sections in the structure tree (sidebar on the left-hand side of the program). These three sections include "TrialSession", "Geometry Scene", and "Named Views". The "Geometry Scene" folder shows all the CAD files that represent the manikins and workstation objects. The "Named Views" folder has pre-set views that the user can click on to change the orientation and view.

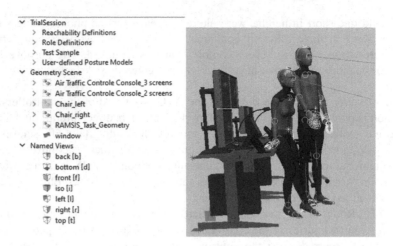

Fig. 1. The general structure tree, and the manikins loaded at the ATC station.

Manikin Characteristics

It is important to know the manikin information and body dimensions to create an optimal working environment for them. As shown in Fig. 2, the "Manikin Information" button and the "Body Dimensions" buttons are used to access this information. Important variables to look for when considering the analysis of these manikins include the sitting height, leg room, and reach.

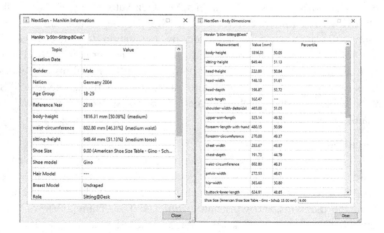

Fig. 2. The manikin information and body dimensions windows.

Moving Manikins to Sitting Position

For the purposes of this study, the manikins were studied in a sitting position. The manikins are made to sit using the posture calculation button, and "Yes to All" is applied to the pop-up that inquires about restarting the calculation without pre-adjustment. At the Status at the bottom of the window, the status "Posture Calculation Successfully Completed for all Manikins" is reported. After the posture calculation is performed, the window will reveal the manikins sitting down.

Altering the Manikin's Joint Positions

Demonstrations of alterations to the manikin's joints are shown in Fig. 3. The *TrialSession* > *"Test Sample"* > *Sitting@Desk* subfolder contains the biometric information, postures, task, and skeleton points of the manikins.

The manikin's joints are adjusted by clicking the joint 🔄 button. In the pop-up window, the joint location is changed by clicking on the manikin's joint, and dragging one axis of the joint coordinate system to the desired position. (Alternatively, the joint position can be altered by manually supplying the manikin's joint name found under the "Skeleton Points" subfolder and entering *[x,y,z]* coordinates, or using the mouse scroll bar to gradually change coordinates.)

One of the most useful tools to rapidly change the position of the manikin's joints is the reverse kinematics 🔄 button. This allows the user have the manikin reach or look at an object simply by clicking and dragging axes of a coordinate system that appears at a joint. (To toggle out of the reverse kinematics section, *Operations* > *Select* is used.)

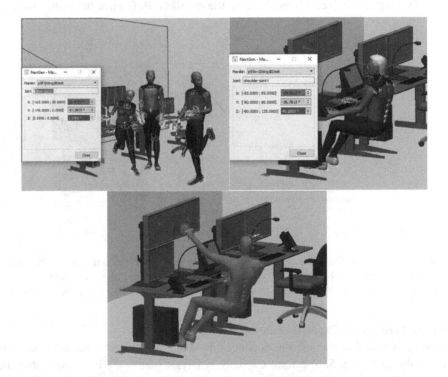

Fig. 3. The left and middle images depict the alteration of the manikin's joints. The right image shows the implementation of the reverse kinematics tool.

Manikin-Object Interaction

A manikin can be modeled to interact with a workstation object ("Env. Object") by utilizing information from the structure tree. The manikin can be changed to interact with an object by altering the Task > Target that corresponds to that specific manikin's name and body part. The name of any Environmental Object can be found by right-clicking it, and selecting "Show Selected Object in Structure Tree".

For example, the user can make a manikin look at the right-hand computer screen by obtaining the name of that screen from the structure tree (e.g. "targetpoint_Screen_1"). To make a manikin look at this screen as its target point, the "Task" folder under the manikin's name in the structure tree is expanded to show the "Target: point-of-vision" task. Reference the left image on Fig. 4. This target is right clicked to select Object properties, and the Env. Object section is changed to "targetpoint_Screen_1" in the resulting pop-up window. When a posture calculation is run, the manikin's view will update to look at the desired screen.

The "Move eye" 🔧 button from the menu can be used to alter if the manikin looks at an object or looks in a certain direction. Their entire head will move to look at the object if "Move Starting With: Neck" is selected. Reference the middle image in Fig. 4.

Lastly, the internal view ⚑ button allows the user to see the objects from the manikin's eyes and is useful in positioning the manikin. Reference the right image in Fig. 4.

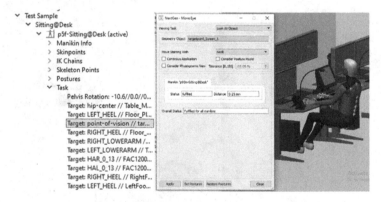

Fig. 4. The left image shows where the point of vision is set in the structure tree. The middle image shows the manikin being altered to look at an object using the Move Eye tool. The right image shows the Internal View feature to view the environment through the manikin's eyes.

Analysis Tool: Joint Capacity Analysis

The analysis tool that was used to conduct this study was the joint capacity analysis tool, as shown in Fig. 5. The Joint Capacity Analysis button 🔲 is found within the analysis tools, and supplies the user with calculations of discomfort, posture, and resistance for any joint on the manikin.

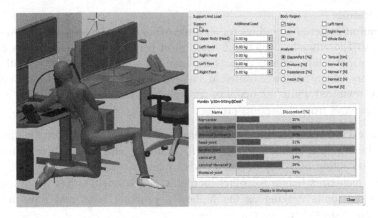

Fig. 5. The left image shows the manikin contorted in an awkward position, and the right image shows the resulting discomfort percent rating for the spinal region.

1.4   Discussion of Step 1 Joint Analysis in Computer-Aided Ergonomics

Analysis Setup

Each of the three manikins supplied in the ATC Room session were modified to reach for the phone to their left, while simultaneously looking at each of the three screens, for a total of 72 runs between all three manikins. The purpose of this analysis was to understand what joints are impacted the most by sitting in this position and what environmental objects may cause most stress on joints. Additionally, the reason that manikins of three different sizes were studied was to see what biometric characteristics could potentially influence discomfort on joints.

The manikins were moved into the desired position by using the Inverse Kinematics tool and the Move Eye functions. The inverse kinematics tool was used to model the manikin reaching for the phone as shown in Fig. 6. The "Move Eye" function was used to model the manikin viewing at the various screens (the Environment Objects with targetpoint_Screen, targetpoint_Screen_1, targetpoint_Screen_2). Then, the joint capacity analysis was performed. Figure 5 in the previous section shows what a joint calculation looks like.

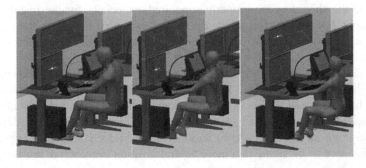

Fig. 6. From left to right: Manikins p95-m, p50m, and p5f reaching for the phone and looking at the screen in front of them

Analysis Results

The discomfort percent (%) ratings for all three manikins under study is shown in a bar chart below. The abscissa depicts the discomfort percentage (from the joint capacity analysis tool), and the ordinate depicts the manikin's joint under study. Within each joint category, there are three different colored bars, representing which computer screen was reviewed while the manikin was reaching for the phone.

The takeaways from the results are:

- The largest and most unanimous ergonomic risk to the manikins are the discomfort found in the right hip, left hip, and left shoulder joint. These three joints had a discomfort rating of 100% no matter what manikin was under study. This means that the manikin's height (or other biometric characteristics) had no influence on these three joints ranking as the highest ergonomic risks and most important ergonomic risks to ameliorate.
- Of the joints with discomfort percentages less than 100%, the tallest user (p95m) was often the least comfortable, or had the highest discomfort percent rating. This manikin is tall and the data suggests that he has to make more adjustments to his environment (such as the desk or chair) than the shorter manikins to feel comfortable.
- Changing the computer screen the manikin looked at while reaching for the phone had negligible impact on the discomfort rating percent for every manikin's joint (varied by one percent at most). This suggests that reaching for the phone had the negative impact on the manikins' joints, and not the computer monitor placement for this combination of movements. (The computer monitor placement could definitely factor into discomfort in combination with other movements!)

Suggested Modifications

From the results of this study, several modifications can be suggested to improve this workstation. When viewing each joint under this particular study, it is evident that the highest discomfort rating is in the hip joints and left shoulder joint.

Environmental changes that can be made to make the workstation more comfortable include changes to the chair, desk, and monitors. To address the discomfort in the lumbar joint and lumbar sacrum joints, the manikins should have a chair with backing that can support lower back curve, and should recline between 100 and 110°. The desk and chair should be adjustable in height so that the arms aren't forced into an awkward position and the shoulders are properly supported, especially for the manikin that is taller in height. For the shoulder joints, the amount of time the manikin has to reach to use the phone should be minimized. If possible, the use of a remote headset can prevent constant reaching.

Some that the manikins should make to their own posture are having their forearms angled slightly downward on the keyboard to ease the stress on the shoulders and elbows. When the baseline aircraft control room session was loaded as-is and a joint capacity analysis was performed on all of the manikins, all of the manikins had a moderate discomfort rating (70–80%) within both shoulder joints. This suggests that the manikins need to be sitting in a more neutral position even before reaching for the phone.

2   Introduction to Step 2 Obstruction Analysis in ATC Room

This analysis will explore the obstruction caused by the monitors in the Air Traffic Control room onto the window. The purpose of the analysis is to investigate if enough of the window is obstructed to the point that operators would have to repeatedly stand to see out the window in order to complete their daily tasks. Repetitive motions cause a large amount of workplace injuries, "the best solution is to ergonomically design workstations to help prevent disorders from occurring in the first place."[1]

2.1   Obstruction Analysis

Below are the steps needed to complete obstruction analysis for the stated problem.

1. Analyze sight limits. Select Analysis -> Vision -> Sightlimits (Fig. 7)
   a. Center C = Manikin (mid eye is suggested)
   b. Object O = Object causing the obstruction to the view, in this case, the computer monitors. Select the monitor that the manikin is looking at (manikin line of sight is depicted as a pink line) by clicking on it. Once selected, the monitor should be shaded pink.
   c. Visual Field V = the view being blocked, in this case, the window. Click anywhere on the window to select the window.
   d. Select "Surfaces" and "Surface rearward object" boxes.
   e. Change the base name as needed.
   f. The length box determines how far the program projects the obstruction view. This can be edited as needed.
   g. Click "Compute", once the gold cone appears, click "close".
2. Move the manikin's target point to another screen.
   a. In the sidebar, use the arrows to extend the view for "Geometry Scene" then "Ramsis_Task_Geometry".
   b. Click "targetpoint_screen" then Operations -> Translate. A compass/crosshairs should appear at the target point on the screen (Fig. 8).
   c. Using the pointer, click and drag on the specific axis's to move it to the center of the screen above.
   d. Select Operations -> Posture Calculation to change the manikin's view. Click the calculate button as before in step 3.
   e. Select Operations -> Select to stop translating objects.
3. Repeat steps 1 and 2 for both monitors. Make sure to select the correct monitor for each vision analysis.
4. Create an intersection between the wall and the cone of obstruction. This will allow us to approximate the area of the window obscured by the monitors.
   a. Select Geometry -> Intersect Objects.
   b. Select object 1 from clicking on the 3D rendering of the sight limit or select the sight limit from the expanded menu on the sidebar. Each sight limit will have it's own intersection with the window.

5. Hide the sight limits. Left click on the rendering or the object name in the side bar -> select hide. For this portion of the analysis, the "back view" is used to make things easier to view. Hide all three sight limits.
6. Calculate approximate distances.
   a. Geometry -> Point then change "Point Type" to "Create on Object", select the object as one of the intersections. Using the cursor, click on the rendering where you want the point to be, then click "Create". Place points in the upper left corner of the top left intersection, lower left corner of the bottom left intersection, and upper right corner of the right intersection. Points will appear as small red *.
   b. Once the points are created, they will turn from red to teal. To make the points easier to see when not selected, find the points in the sidebar, right click, and select "Object Properties". In that box, there is an option to change the color of the object in question (Fig. 9).
      i. Distance across the top: change the distance type to "Y", then select the two highest points. Click "Create" (Fig. 10).
      ii. Height: change the distance type to "Z", then select the two points down the side of the intersection boxes. Click "Create" (Fig. 11).
   c. Select Analysis -> Distance.
7. Calculate the approximate area of obstruction by multiplying the two distances together. This is an approximation, although there is no lower right monitor, it can be assumed that the phone placed on the desk to the right will have a significant obstruction of the lower right hand zone and therefore a rectangle can be calculated for an estimation of area.

Perform these steps on tall, short, and medium manikins of each gender and calculate the average area obscured for each gender.

2.2   Results in Step 2 Obstruction Analysis

The calculations for approximate area are found in the table below. The equation for calculating the area is

$$(Y\ Distance) * (X\ Distance) = Area \tag{1}$$

The equation for calculating the average area is

$$\frac{(Short + Medium + Tall)}{3} = Average\ Area\ Obstructed \tag{2}$$

Table 1. Obstruction analysis results.

Manikin size	Y distance (mm)	Z distance (mm)	Area (mm^2)
Male			
Short	3902.22	2393.27	9,339,066.06
Medium	3845.16	2333.52	8,972,757.76
Tall	3798.75	2310.31	8,776,290.11
Average area obstructed (mm^2)			9,029,371.31
Female			
Short	4090.94	2499.17	10,223,954.52
Medium	4028.72	2445.96	9,854,087.97
Tall	3977.31	2456.57	9,770,540.43
Average area obstructed (mm^2)			9,949,527.64

The dimensions of the window are 7084.86 mm (width, Y Dimension) by 3396.86 mm (height, Z Dimension), giving it an area of 24,066,277.54 mm^2. First, the percentage of the window obstructed by each gender should be calculated using Eq. 3 (Table 2).

$$\frac{Average\ Area\ Obstructed}{Area\ of\ the\ Window} * 100 = \%\ of\ the\ window\ obstructed \qquad (3)$$

Table 2. Percent obstructed

Gender	% obstructed
Male	37.52%
Female	41.34%

The height of one monitor at the approximate correct ergonomic height is 1658.85 mm. From Table 1, the largest contribution to high percentage of obstruction to window is caused by height of monitors. This height is the largest factor in causing the operator to stand in order to see out the window. In this case, due to the large amount of space obscured by the monitors, the suggestion is to move the monitors to a "three-in-a-row" model. With one monitor, the height of the obstruction would be greatly reduced and therefor decrease the need for the operator to stand repetitively. However, this would extend the width of the obstruction on the window, but not any more than the current desk configuration already does. By decreasing the height of the obstruction to the window, the need for the operator to repetitively stand is decreased, therefore protecting the operator from any possible injuries that could be sustained from that movement.

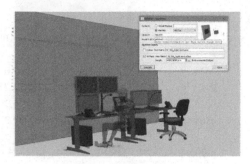

Fig. 7. Selecting objects to compute Sightlimits. (Color figure online)

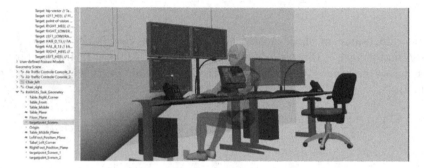

Fig. 8. Select targetpoint_screen from sidebar and Translate function to change location of targetpoint_screen. Change test_manikin's line of sight using Posture Calculation. Workspace view can show all Sightlimit calculations. A view of the intersections can also be shown.

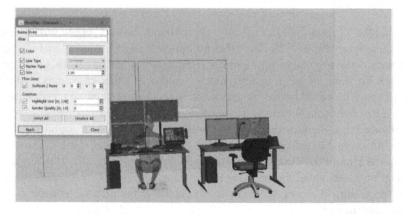

Fig. 9. Creating points and Altering visual characteristics of objects.

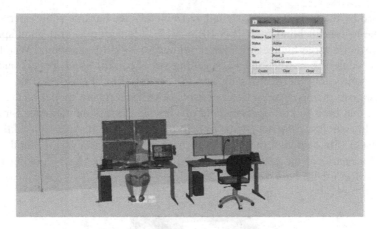

Fig. 10. Finding the Y distance between points.

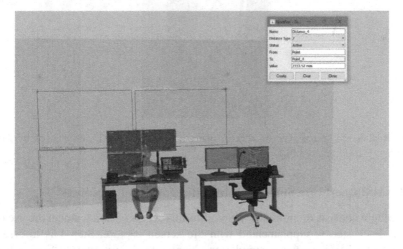

Fig. 11. Finding the Z distance between points.

3 Step 3 Forklift Introduction and Problem Statement

3.1 Introduction and Problem Statement

Forklifts are a very popular tool to have when it comes to moving large objects fast and within a short distance. Today, forklifts are used in the warehouses, lumber and grocery stores, loading docks, production factories, construction sites, and any other places where a large amount or large size objects need to be moved on a regular basis. Being such a popular tool forklift poses a great safety threat to the work environments in which it operates in. Per the United States Bureau of Labor Statistics, in the United States, 614 workers, ages 18 to 65, died from traumatic injuries suffered in forklift-related incidents from 2011 to 2017 (US BLS 2017). Nearly 64% of those fatalities were caused by the forklift operator's failure to clearly see hazards while operating the forklift due to forklift blind spots (US BLS 2017). Managing forklift blind spots can help to prevent a large number of injuries related to forklift operation. "Warehouses, distribution centers, construction sites – getting rid of forklift blind spots is one of the most important safety mechanisms for any lift driver" (FLC Forklift 2018).

The purpose of this analysis is to create RAMSIS software model of the forklift blind spots that limit forklift operator field of view and assess the rationale for the use of the forklift wireless camera systems to help the driver see the area beyond the blind spot to ensure safe operation of the forklift machinery. The analysis is simulating the real-world scenario of the operator obstructed the view as he/she is looking forward through the forklift lift bars (see Fig. 12).

Fig. 12. Real world scenario where forklift operator has obstructed view caused by forward forklift bars (D2000 Safety 2014).

3.2 RAMSIS Software Simulation Introduction and Procedures

The procedure consists of multiple steps within this section that document the use of the software. Each step is supplemented with the screen capture. Step 1 is to create an appropriate RAMSIS software simulation. Next one would launch "*launchNetGen Automotive.bat*" file and loading the Forklift session developed by Thorsten (see Fig. 13).

> launchNextGenAircraft.bat
> launchNextGenAutomotive.bat
> launchNextGenBelt.bat

Fig. 13. *launchNetGenAutomotive.bat* file.

The "forklift" session has a software model for the forklift simulation with the forklift, a forklift pallet, and loader, who is loading the pallet (see Fig. 14).

Fig. 14. Forklift session in RAMSIS.

Step 2 (within Sect. 3.2), Next one could create a manikin with an age group of 18–70, USA nationality and add it to the Forklift session. This is accomplished by clicking the "*Create Manikin*" button within the session tab in the toolbar menu. This opens the Manikin parameter window.

Step 3 (within Sect. 3.2), is to apply manikin settings to the manikin by clicking the "*Apply*" button. As a result, manikin appears within "forklift" session (see Fig. 15).

Fig. 15. Manikin appeared next to forklift.

Step 4 (within Sect. 3.2) is to move manikin behind the forklift steering wheel. One could open project tabs on the left-hand side of the RAMSIS window: *project -> Assessment Postures -> position -> forklift_truck_driving* and select manikin's name "medium_male-driver" to assign it to the driver seat of the forklift (see Fig. 16 and 17).

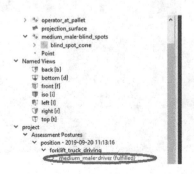

Fig. 16. Folder tree on the left-hand side.

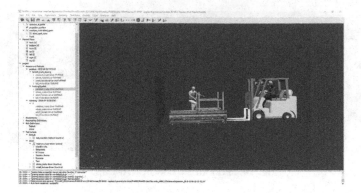

Fig. 17. Manikin is moved behind the forklift steering wheel.

Step 4 occurs after moving the manikin behind the forklift steering wheel, One needs to identify and analyze the forklift operator's blind spots. In order to do so, enable blind spot cone by double-clicking *"blind_spot_cone"* simulation on the right-hand side model panel (see Fig. 18).

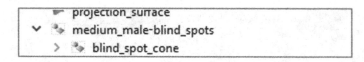

Fig. 18. Blind-spot-cone model location.

The blind spot cone will appear on the forklift scene, clearly defining the blind spots. Analyzing the scene, it is evident that the loader appears to be within the blind spot (see Fig. 19).

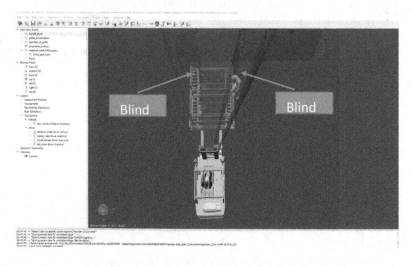

Fig. 19. Blind spot cone created by the forklift bars.

Step 5, is to simulate forklift operator eye perspective and analyze his/her obstructed view. To do so, select the *Analysis tab -> Vision -> Internal View* (see Fig. 20). This will prompt a window that represents the manikin field of view.

Fig. 20. Operator's view analysis.

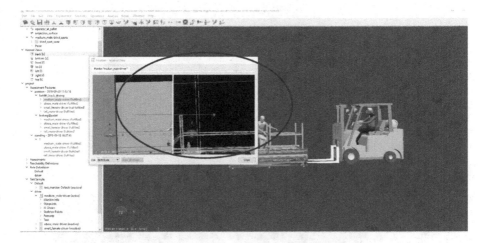

Fig. 21. Operator's view in the window.

Looking at Fig. 21, it is obvious that both eyes of the operator cannot see the loader, who is working within the blind spot area. The view is obstructed by forklift bars. Consequently, this software simulation adequately represents a real-world scenario shown in Fig. 12.

At this point, one is ready to analyze what changes needed for the forklift to eliminate the vision area that goes undetected (blind spot). There several solutions in accordance with Thorsten's presentation. One is to use the mirror and the second is to mount a wireless camera. In this analysis, an analysis is conducted for use of a camera mounted on the forklift to see if it will improve blind spot visibility for the forklift operator.

Step 6 (in Sect. 3.2) is to create a camera in the RAMSIS forklift session. One can click on the menu tab and select *Ergonomics -> Camera Definition* (see Fig. 22). A Camera definition window will pop-up allowing the user to define the camera parameters (see Fig. 22). Initially, one would want to try default camera parameters: the horizontal opening is set at 60° and a vertical opening at 45° (see Fig. 23). The camera is placed on the overhead guard of the forklift (see Fig. 24).

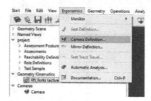

Fig. 22. Creating a camera.

Fig. 23. Camera parameters.

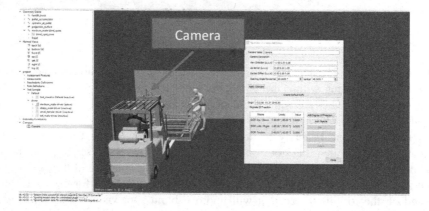

Fig. 24. Camera location and camera parameters window location.

Step 7, having a camera in place, Analyzing its' field of view. This will help one to determine whether the manikin can see beyond the blind spot. To do that, select *Analysis tab* -> *Vision* -> *Camera* to create a camera view (see Fig. 25). This function will open a window with a camera view (see Fig. 26).

Fig. 25. Selection of the camera field of view.

The analysis of the camera's field of view shows that the camera can see beyond the forklift undetected areas and can detect loader next to the pallet (see Fig. 26).

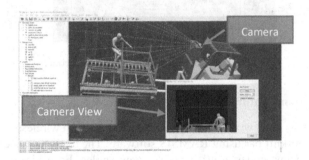

Fig. 26. Camera field of view and visual cone.

Analyzing the picture that is seeing by the camera, one can conclude that the loader can be only seen up to his/her waist and pallet is not visible all the way. As a result, one would like to analyze the effects of the wider camera viewing angles on blind spot management. Step 9 (within Sect. 3.2), double click on camera to activate the Camera definition window. Change both opening horizontal and vertical angle parameters to 70°. As a result, the camera view field allows the operator to see the whole pallet and loader next to it providing better management for the blind spot (see Fig. 27).

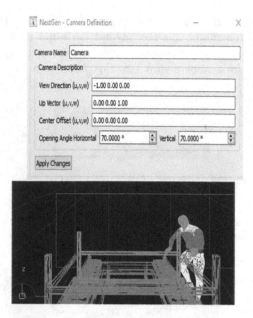

Fig. 27. Camera field of view and visual cone.

3.3   Discussion and Future Work

Forklift driver blind spots were modeled to mitigate them with wireless cameras located on the overhead forklift bar using RAMSIS software. The analysis has considered two different camera view angles at 40° and 70° view angles. Both views were analyzed and compared. It was concluded, that upgrading forklift with the wireless 70° view angle camera is the most optimal way to allow forklift drivers to have greater visibility of areas they typically cannot see. The wireless camera can be mounted on the overhead guard so the driver can see where the forks are lining up with the pallet and loaders who are loading the pallet. The analysis makes obvious that the camera makes it easier for the forklift operator to get a clear and unobstructed view of the forks and rack. The most useful aspects of the forklift video cameras are that they can be attached to any type of forklift. The analysis showed that cameras with wider than 70° view angle had encountered obstruction by the forklift vertical rails.

RAMSIS can overcome limitations of two dimensional human templates, as well as provide methods for predicting driver postures and comfort (Kuebler et al. 2019; EDS Technologies 2019). However, there are certain limitations that cannot be solved using CAD software at this time but it will be very useful to consider them in the future. For instance, calculation and simulation of expected noise levels from machinery in the workplace is something that currently cannot be modeled in using CAD/CAE software and require the use of the noise databases to predict noise effects (Wasserman 2014; Federal Highway Administration 2017; Aviation workers hearing 2019).

References

Are aviation workers losing their hearing?. Accessed 21 Oct 2019. https://au.widex.pro/en-au/care-counselling/people-hearing/aviation-workers-losing-hearing

Bubb, H.: Future applications of DHM in ergonomic design. In: Duffy, V.G. (ed.) ICDHM 2007. LNCS, vol. 4561, pp. 779–793. Springer, Heidelberg (2007). https://doi.org/10.1007/978-3-540-73321-8_89

D2000 Safety. Forklift Blind Spot – Forklift Safety Newsletter, April 2014. https://www.d2000safety.com/forklift-blind-spot/. Accessed 07 Oct 2019

Demirel, H.O., Duffy, V.G.: Applications of digital human modeling in industry. In: Duffy, V.G. (ed.) ICDHM 2007. LNCS, vol. 4561, pp. 824–832. Springer, Heidelberg (2007). https://doi.org/10.1007/978-3-540-73321-8_93

Duffy, V.G.: Modified virtual build methodology for computer-aided ergonomics and safety. Hum. Factors Ergon. Manuf. Serv. Ind. **17**(5), 413–422 (2007)

EDS Technologies: RAMSIS (2019). Accessed 07 Oct 2019. https://edstechnologies.com/solutions/plm-value-solutions/ramsis/

Federal Highway Administration: Noise 28 June 2017. Accessed 08 Oct 2019. https://www.fhwa.dot.gov/Environment/noise/construction_noise/handbook/handbook06.cfm

FLC Forklift Certification: Blind Spot Safety – What You Need to Know (2018). Accessed 07 Oct 2019. https://www.forkliftcertification.com/blind-spot-safety-need-know/

Karoui, M.F., Kuebler, T.: Homologous mesh extraction via monocular systems. In: Duffy, V.G. (ed.) HCII 2019. LNCS, vol. 11581, pp. 182–197. Springer, Cham (2019). https://doi.org/10.1007/978-3-030-22216-1_14

Kuebler, T., Luebke, A., Campbell, J., Guenzel, T.: Size North America – the New North American anthropometric survey. In: Duffy, V.G. (ed.) HCII 2019. LNCS, vol. 11581, pp. 88–98. Springer, Cham (2019). https://doi.org/10.1007/978-3-030-22216-1_7

USAir Flight 1493: Aviation Knowledge. Accessed 20 Oct 2019. http://aviationknowledge.wikidot.com/aviation:managing-aviation-human-factors-lessons-from-usair

United States Bureau of Labor Statistics: Injuries, Illnesses, and Fatalities (2017). Accessed 07 Oct 2019. https://www.bls.gov/iif/oshcfoi1.htm

van der Meulen, P., Seidl, A.: Ramsis – the leading cad tool for ergonomic analysis of vehicles. In: Duffy, V.G. (ed.) ICDHM 2007. LNCS, vol. 4561, pp. 1008–1017. Springer, Heidelberg (2007). https://doi.org/10.1007/978-3-540-73321-8_113

Wasserman, S.: Using Simulation and Aeroacoustics to Make for Quieter Flights. Engineering.com. 4 Mar 2014. https://www.engineering.com/DesignSoftware/DesignSoftwareArticles/ArticleID/7255/Using-Simulation-and-Aeroacoustics-to-make-for-quieter-flights.aspx

Individual Differences in Office Comfort: What Affects Comfort Varies by Person

Masashi Sugimoto[1] , Fan Zhang[1], Noriko Nagata[1(✉)] ,
Kota Kurihara[2], Seiro Yuge[2], Makoto Takata[2], Koji Ota[2],
and Seiji Furukawa[2]

[1] Kwansei Gakuin University, Sanda, Hyogo, Japan
{sugimoto.masashi,nagata}@kwansei.ac.jp
[2] Mitsubishi Electric Corporation, Amagasaki, Hyogo, Japan

Abstract. In the present research, we investigated the factors that affect comfort in the office and individual differences therein. Aside from meta-analysis research, factors that affect comfort were investigated individually (such as thermal factors, lighting, air pollutants, and so on), and the relative importance or relationship between them has not been investigated directly. We conducted a two-week survey in a corporate office and gathered 2075 responses from occupants. For data collection, we applied a method that combined experience sampling method with the evaluation grid method, which allowed us to gather a lot of data in daily situations. The results revealed that subjective comfort was evoked by various factors such as thermal factors, light, sound, inside, and so on. Subjective comfort did not show a significant correlation with the objective thermal comfort index (predicted mean vote; PMV), and subjective productivity was correlated with subjective comfort but not with objective comfort. These results indicate the importance of subjective factors in addition to objective factors. In addition, the 147 occupants were divided into three clusters (inside cluster, balanced cluster, and thermal cluster), each of which had different characteristics indicating the individual differences in components of comfort. In the present research, we succeeded in the reproduction of our previous research, which was conducted in a different season, emphasizing the validity of the present results.

Keywords: Office environment · Comfort · Wellness · Productivity · Individual differences

1 Introduction

In artificial environments, such as offices, houses, and classrooms, people interact with the environment by various means to make it comfortable, such as by turning the air conditioner up/down, wearing other clothes, or opening windows in the room. These activities are induced by the environment and in turn change some aspects of the environment. For example, on a cold morning, office workers will turn on the heater as soon as they arrive at the office. Maybe in the afternoon, the heated up air will make them open the window to ventilate.

© Springer Nature Switzerland AG 2020
V. G. Duffy (Ed.): HCII 2020, LNCS 12198, pp. 264–275, 2020.
https://doi.org/10.1007/978-3-030-49904-4_19

Even when some people feel comfortable in an environment, others may feel uncomfortable for some reason, which results in different reactions across people. Some people might feel that a place is cold, whereas others feel it to be neutral. Some may prefer environments with more noise than others. These individual differences make it difficult to realize a comfortable environment for all people and indicate that different components of comfort exist for each person.

Especially in the office environment, where occupants spend a large part of the day, comfort is an important factor. The importance of office comfort can be seen in WELL certificate [1], which was founded to facilitate comfortable buildings. In addition, comfort is closely related to the productivity of the occupants. Otherwise (or at least if the companies do not recognize it), they will not spend a lot of money to satisfy their employees.

To realize a comfortable environment for each person, it is important (1) to investigate the components of the comfort and (2) to reveal the individual differences in this. In the present study, we investigated the components of comfort in an office and examined individual differences by combining the experience sampling method [2] with the evaluation grid method [3]. We also discuss the relationship between comfort and office productivity. This study is a reproduction of our previous study conducted in November 2018 with 23 participants [4]. The purposes of the reproduction were (1) to test the seasonal effects on comfort and make the results more valid and (2) to investigate the characteristics of individual differences with a larger sample size.

2 Related Studies

2.1 The Effect of Environment on Its Occupants

Many studies about the relationship between an environment and its occupants were conducted according to models in which the physical factors of the environment (independent variable) affected the mental states of the people within it (dependent variable). Among the various environmental factors that affect indoor comfort, the most significant one is the thermal factor (e.g., [5]). Thermal factors affect not only comfort but also motivation and productivity [6]. Another study focused on the physiological aspects of thermal comfort. Low- and high-frequency ratios of heart rate variability may be used to predict thermal comfort [7]. This kind of approach is especially useful with wearable devices [8].

An objective index that measures thermal comfort is predicted mean vote (PMV) [9]. PMV is a scale that predicts the psychological evaluation of the thermal state in an environment, and it is used worldwide [10]. The PMV is calculated using thermal parameters (air temperature, mean radiant temperature, relative air velocity, and vapor pressure in the ambient air) and human parameters (activity level and thermal resistance of clothing), and it is represented on a scale from −3 (cold) to 3 (hot) via 0 (neutral). The PMV corresponds to the predicted percentage of dissatisfied (PPD) [11]. When the PMV is 0, 5% of the people in the environment are dissatisfied with it. When the PMV is 0.5 or −0.5, and 3 or −3, 10% and 80% people are dissatisfied with the environment, respectively.

As well as the thermal factors, various factors affect comfort. These factors include visual factors, sound factors, and indoor air quality. Visual factors usually refer to light. Lighting affects not only psychological health and productivity [12] but also other environmental factors such as perceived temperature and air quality [13]. In addition to the lighting, environmental features perceived through vision affect occupants. For example, ceiling height and wall color change occupants' way of thinking [14] and mood [15].

The environment's effect on occupants varies among people. Sex is one factor that causes individual differences [16, 17]. The "neutral" temperature for a Japanese male is 24.3 °C, whereas the neutral temperature for a Japanese female is 25.2 °C [17]. This difference between males and females in thermal preference was also found in another study [18]. Race can also cause individual differences. A previous study found that the neutral temperature for a non-Japanese male was 22.1 °C. Psychological characteristics can cause individual differences in task performance. A positive mood induced by wall color improved task performance more in participants whose performances were better than average [15].

Even if an environment is consistent, the environmental effects on the people there may change chronically. Being in the same environment for a certain period of time can change how one perceives the environment. One study revealed that taking a rest after bathing decreased the arousal score of participants over time [19]. Another study revealed that although indoor air quality affected the people inside, those who stayed in the environment longer became insensitive to it [20].

3 Components in the Office and Individual Differences in Them: Examination Using the Combination of Experience Sampling Method and Evaluation Grid Method

3.1 Method

Participants. We asked 208 office workers to participate in the study. Among them, 178 (155 males and 23 females) agreed to participate. Their average age was 40.9 (ranging from 24 to 66). All office workers had been working in a common room (2,704 m^2) and participated in the study there. They each had their own desks in the room.

Tasks. In this study, we asked the participants to provide their sequential staying time at their desk, their subjective comfort and the factors that affected it, and their subjective productivity.

The participants reported their sequential staying time by choosing one of the following options: 1: shorter than 5 min, 2: from 5 to 10 min, 3: from 10 to 30 min, or 4: longer than 30 min.

They then responded about their subjective comfort. First, they rated how comfortable their indoor environment was on a scale from 1 (very uncomfortable) to 7 (very comfortable) (subjective comfort). Afterward, they reported up to three factors that affected their subjective comfort (comfort-evoking factors). They also rated how pleasant/unpleasant and how activated/deactivated the factors were in general; this question was asked based on Russell's core affect model [21]. In addition, they rated what kind of factors affected their subjective comfort. These questions were asked with the idea of the evaluation grid method [3]. In the original evaluation grid method, the data are collected through interviews. First, the interviewer asks the interviewee (the participant) to compare items and select which one is better. Then, the interviewer asks the interviewee, "Why is this one better?" and extracts an abstract value judgement. The interviewer also asks the interviewee, "What is needed for the item to be xxx?" and extracts objective understandings for the items. These responses are summarized and represented as a construct system. In the present study, we simplified these procedures to implement it on the Web and gather multiple responses.

The participants also rated their subjective productivity. They were asked to respond to the question, "How would you rate your present work efficiency if your maximum work efficiency in the most proper environment corresponds to 100?"

Procedure. The experiment was conducted during the ten weekdays from April 10, 2019, to April 23, 2019. Over these days, we sent e-mails to the participants five times a day (at 10:00, 11:45, 13:30, 15:15, and 17:00) and asked for a response to the questionnaire in Google Forms. Specifically, we asked participants to respond to the questionnaire at least three times each time. All e-mails were received in the office by the participants, and participants responded to the questionnaire there. During the study, we measured the PMV in the office using HD32.3 (Delta OHM). The present study was conducted according to Kwansei Gakuin University regulations for behavioral research with human participants.

3.2   Results

Basic Data
Response Rate. The number of valid responses gathered in the present study was 2075. The number of responses on each day and at each time is provided in Tables 1 and 2. Many of the responses were given in the earlier part of the study. Regarding response time, many of the responses were given just after the e-mail that asked for the response.

PMV, Comfort and Productivity. Tables 1 and 2 show the participants' PMV, comfort, and productivity changes in this study. PMV was relatively stable, between 0 and 0.5, indicating a stable and comfortable temperature in the office. Comfort and productivity were also stable throughout the study. Although there is a V-shaped decrease and increase from 8:00 to 10:00, the responses were quite few (less than 0.5% of all responses).

Table 1. Daily changes in the indices (numbers in the round bracket indicate *SE*s)

Day	Number of responses	Average comfort	Average productivity	Average PMV
April 10th	400	4.25 (0.06)	71.46 (0.79)	0.40 (0.01)
April 11th	370	4.44 (0.07)	71.39 (0.87)	0.40 (0.01)
April 12th	290	4.35 (0.07)	72.75 (0.93)	0.41 (0.01)
April 15th	269	4.22 (0.07)	68.38 (0.99)	0.45 (0.01)
April 16th	221	4.50 (0.08)	70.71 (1.02)	0.29 (0.02)
April 17th	150	4.45 (0.10)	71.89 (1.28)	0.38 (0.02)
April 18th	127	4.49 (0.10)	71.78 (1.44)	0.38 (0.02)
April 19th	59	4.61 (0.18)	71.07 (2.39)	0.43 (0.03)
April 22nd	114	4.36 (0.13)	70.79 (1.66)	0.33 (0.02)
April 23rd	75	4.44 (0.13)	70.33 (1.84)	0.39 (0.02)

Table 2. Hourly changes in the indices (numbers in the round bracket indicate *SE*s)

Time	Number of responses	Average comfort	Average productivity	Average PMV
08:00	1	5.00 (0.00)	80.00 (0.00)	0.49 (0.00)
09:00	9	3.56 (0.59)	54.22 (11.52)	0.46 (0.05)
10:00	390	4.43 (0.06)	72.03 (0.84)	0.39 (0.01)
11:00	302	4.50 (0.07)	73.91 (0.87)	0.41 (0.01)
12:00	224	4.54 (0.08)	71.42 (1.05)	0.42 (0.01)
13:00	254	4.29 (0.08)	69.11 (1.16)	0.43 (0.01)
14:00	144	4.24 (0.10)	69.80 (1.29)	0.38 (0.02)
15:00	320	4.15 (0.07)	70.28 (0.84)	0.37 (0.01)
16:00	74	4.41 (0.15)	70.78 (1.82)	0.33 (0.03)
17:00	357	4.41 (0.06)	70.72 (0.81)	0.35 (0.01)

Subjective Comfort and Factors That Affect it. Figure 1 represents the evaluation structure of the 11 participants who were selected from the beginning of participants' ID numbers. We used only part of the data because all data are beyond the limitations of the processing capability of the software that we used in the analysis [22]. As in the previous study that we conducted in November 2018, factors that relate to thermal aspects, sound, light, and indoor environment were extracted. Factors that were not extracted in the previous study include wet clothing, work, and pollen. These factors might have been extracted as a result of weather and seasonal changes.

Figure 2 represents the characteristics of the factors that affect comfort. The factors in Fig. 2 are the ones that were listed by the participants more than 20 times (words that seem to represent close meaning were not categorized into one item, and similar words appear in Fig. 2, e.g., silent, tranquility, and silent around). The most frequent factor that affects comfort is "moderate temperature," followed by "silent," "brightness," "noise," "fatigue," and "sleepiness." These factors include not only physical factors (thermal, sound, and light) but also mental factors of the occupants. In addition, the

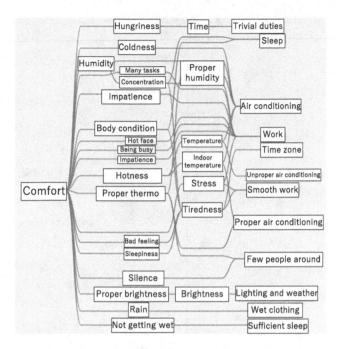

Fig. 1. Evaluation structure on office comfort

valence (pleasant/unpleasant) and arousal (activated/deactivated) varied across factors, indicating the complex effects of the occupants' comfort.

Classification of the Participants. Then, to consider the individual differences among occupants, we conducted cluster analysis based on their responses.

Classification Method. First, we classified the participants' comfort-evoking factors into six categories: thermal factors (52.4% of all responses, e.g., hot, moderate temperature...), sound factors (15.8%, e.g., noisy, silent...), light factors (4.0%, dazzling, dim), inside factors (19.6%, e.g., hungry, sleepy, concentration, body condition, emotion...), work factors (1.8%, e.g., deadline, progress of work...), and other factors (6.4%, e.g., few people around, someone is coughing...). These categories were derived from our previous data and the present data. The classification was conducted by two dependent raters, who were unaware of the purpose of the study. The kappa coefficient was 0.85, indicating almost perfect agreement [23]. When the evaluations by the two raters were different, a third rater evaluated the response.

We conducted clustering analysis based on the relative frequency of the comfort-evoking factors with Ward method. We analyzed data from 147 participants, who had responded to the questionnaire more than four times. We applied three factors, based on the number of each cluster and cluster stability. The demographic features of each

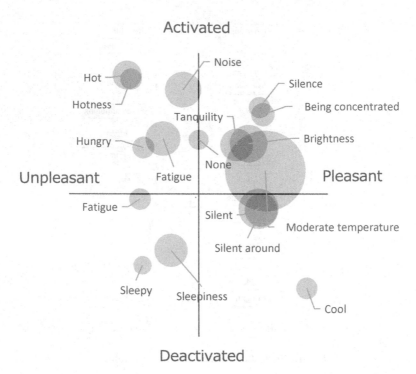

Fig. 2. Circumplex of the factors that affect office comfort (The size of the circle indicates the times of the response of the item)

cluster are represented in Table 3, and the average relative frequency is represented in Fig. 3. A one-way ANOVA of occupants' comfort, productivity, and PMV was conducted. Cluster 1 showed lower comfort and productivity than clusters 2 and 3 (Fs $(2,144) = 9.53, 8.07, \eta_{p}^{2}$s $= .12, .10, t$s$(144) = 3.67, 3.90, 3.26, 3.67$), whereas there was no significant difference in PMV between clusters.

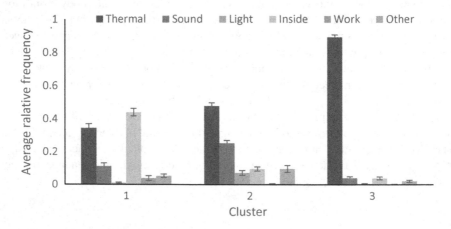

Fig. 3. Average relative frequency of each factor

Table 3. Correlations between comfort, productivity, and PMV in each cluster

Cluster	n	Correlation		
		Comfort and productivity	Productivity and PMV	PMV and comfort
Overall	2075	0.54^{***}	0.05	0.04
1	626	0.59^{***}	-0.10^{*}	-0.05
2	824	0.41^{***}	0.17^{**}	0.05
3	564	0.52^{***}	0.06	0.07

Note: $^{*}p < .05,$ $^{**}p < .01,$ $^{***}p < .001$

Table 4. Demographic data of each cluster

Cluster	Age	n	Sex		
			Male	Female	Unknown
1	37.3	47	40	5	2
2	42.6	61	49	11	1
3	42.9	39	34	3	2

Characteristics of the Clusters. Cluster 1 is distinguished from other clusters by the high relative frequency of the inside factor. Therefore, we named cluster 1 the "inside cluster." Cluster 2 was distinguished by the fact that those in cluster 2 provided relatively different comfort-evoking factors. Therefore, we named cluster 2 the "balanced cluster." Cluster 3 was distinguished by the high relative frequency of thermal factors (nearly 90%). Therefore, we named cluster 3 the "thermal cluster."

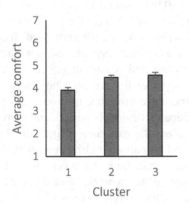

Fig. 4. Average comfort in each cluster (bars indicate *SEs*)

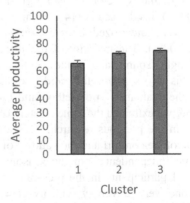

Fig. 5. Average productivity in each cluster (bars indicate *SEs*)

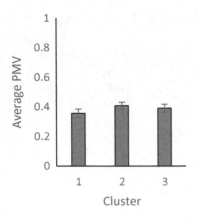

Fig. 6. Average PMV in each cluster (bars indicate *SE*s)

The clusters also differed in the evaluation of the environment. The inside cluster showed lower subjective comfort and subjective productivity, whereas the average PMV did not show significant differences between clusters (Fig. 4, 5 and 6).

To investigate the relationships between objective thermal comfort (PMV), subjective comfort, and subjective productivity, we conducted correlation analysis between these variables. In all clusters, PMV showed no significant correlation with subjective comfort and subjective productivity, whereas subjective comfort showed a strong positive correlation with subjective productivity (Table 4).

4   Conclusions

4.1   Summary of the Results

In the present study, we succeeded in reproducing the previous study we conducted in November 2018 [4].

First, we extracted almost the same comfort-evoking factors. In the present study, we extracted thermal factors, sound factors, light factors, inside factors, work factors, and other factors. In the previous study, we extracted thermal factors (71.4% of all responses), humidity factors (4.5%), light factors (0.9%), sound factors (7.6%), smell factors (0.6%), inside factors (14.4%), and other factors (2.0%) (in the previous study, responses were categorized, allowing duplex classification, and the sum of all factors exceeded 100%). The majority of the responses were classified as common factors (thermal, light, sound, and inside), indicating strong and persistent effects of these factors. This also supports the validity of the method of the present study, a combination of the evaluation grid method and the experience sampling method.

Second, we extracted the same clusters of occupants (inside, balanced, and thermal) as we did in the previous research. This emphasizes the existence of individual differences in office comfort and the validity of our classification. It also suggests that the clusters are independent from the seasonal effect, indicating the robustness of the clusters. All participants in the present study were office workers, and those of the previous one were university students ($n = 9$) and office workers ($n = 14$). This also indicates the relative independence of the clusters from their jobs.

In addition to that, participants in each cluster differed in their levels of subjective comfort and subjective productivity in spite of the common thermal environment suggested by the similar level of PMV (Fig. 4, 5, 6). People in the inside cluster showed lower subjective comfort and subjective productivity under similar physical conditions. This might be due to the differences in the characteristics of the people in each cluster.

Throughout the present research, we relied on the subjective responses of the occupants. As a previous study revealed [24], at least in some aspects, subjective responses are better indicators than objective ones. This was true in the present research. The subjective comfort correlated with the subjective productivity, whereas there was no significant correlation between objective index (PMV) and subjective comfort and subjective productivity. This might be due to the fact that the present research was conducted in a daily setting, in which various kinds of factors affect comfort. This was advantageous in the present research, the aim of which was to reveal the components of office comfort.

4.2   Novelty of the Present Research

The novelty of the present research is revealing the inside factors and their effect, as well as the development of the indoor comfort investigation method, which combines the evaluation grid method and experience sampling method.

The existence and effect of inside factors has been overlooked in previous research. For example, a literature review divided comfort into four subtypes: thermal, visual, acoustic, and respiratory [25], all of which focused on the physical aspects of the environment. In addition to these factors, inside factors were extracted. The inside factors were the second largest type that affect comfort and have a significant effect on office comfort, and they are important for inside and balanced clusters.

One might think that inside factors are not environment ones but to occupants' ones. However, as we stated in the introduction, indoor comfort is realized through the interaction between the outer environment and occupants. Therefore, inside factors should be focused to realize a comfortable environment. The more important thing is that occupants recognize that inside factors affect office comfort, indicating that variation of the levels of inside factors would change the levels of comfort in the environment.

The other novelty of the present research is the development of the comfort measurement method combining the evaluation grid method with the experience sampling method. This method allowed us to conduct a detailed investigation of the comfort in the office, not in the experiment room. The experiment room, which is quite different from daily life environments in multiple aspects, is where a detailed investigation of comfort was conducted. Although this let us examine the causal relationship between an environment and people there, the experiment room and manipulation themselves could have changed how people experienced comfort there, thus hindering expanding the findings to daily situations. This method also allowed us to extract factors that vary in category (Fig. 3) and characteristics (Fig. 2). Using the present method, we could infer what and how environmental factors affect comfort. This was also due to the feature of the present method that let us gather multiple data in a daily environment.

4.3   Future Direction

Future researches have to tackle two things: applying objective indices and providing various occupants with the proper environment.

The present methods rely on subjective responses: how much they feel comfort and productivity, and what kind of factors they attribute to the comfort. In a future study, more objective indices are needed (e.g., physiological variables). These indices would let us shed light on aspects that subjective responses cannot reveal (e.g., minimal comfort changes under sensory threshold and high-resolution sequential changes).

Providing a proper environment for each occupant is another task to tackle. As previous studies point out, the proper thermal conditions differ across people. In addition to the quantitative individual differences, qualitative differences, which the present research revealed, need to be focused on. To realize a proper environment for every person, it will be necessary to manipulate proper variables with personalized environmental controls.

References

1. International WELL Building Institute. https://www.wellcertified.com/about-iwbi/
2. Csikszentmihalyi, M., Larson, R.: Validity and reliability of the experience-sampling method. J. Nerv. Ment. Dis. **175**, 526–536 (1987)
3. Sanui, J.: Visualization of users' requirements: introduction of the evaluation grid method. In: Proceedings of the 3rd Design Decision Support Systems in Architecture Urban Planning Conference, vol. 1, pp. 365–374 (1996)
4. Sugimoto, M., et al.: Components of comfort in the office and its individual differences. In: Proceedings of the 14th International Symposium on Medicine in Information and Communication Technology (2020)
5. Wargocki, P., Frontczak, M., Stefano, S., Goins, J., Arens, E., Zhang, H.: Satisfaction and self-estimated performance in relation to indoor environmental parameters and building features. In: 10th International Conference on Healthy Buildings. International Society of Indoor Air Quality and Climate (2012)
6. Cui, W., Cao, G., Park, J.H., Ouyang, Q., Zhu, Y.: Influence of indoor air temperature on human thermal comfort, motivation and performance. Build. Environ. **68**, 114–122 (2013). https://doi.org/10.1016/j.buildenv.2013.06.012
7. Liu, W., Lian, Z., Liu, Y.: Heart rate variability at different thermal comfort levels. Eur. J. Appl. Physiol. **103**, 361–366 (2008). https://doi.org/10.1007/s00421-008-0718-6
8. Rafaie, M., Tesfay, M., Alsaleem, F.: Utilizing wearable devices to design personal thermal comfort model. In: International High Performance Buildings Conference, vol. 246 (2018)
9. Fanger, PO.: Calculation of thermal comfort-introduction of a basic comfort equation. ASHRAE Trans. **73** (1967)
10. Van Hoof, J.: Forty years of Fanger's model of thermal comfort: comfort for all? Indoor Air **18**, 182–201 (2008). https://doi.org/10.1111/j.1600-0668.2007.00516.x
11. Fanger, P.: Assessment of thermal comfort in practice. Br. J. Ind. Med. **30**(4), 313–324 (1973)
12. Hwang, T., Jeong, T.K.: Effects of indoor lighting on occupants' visual comfort and eye health in a green building. Indoor Built Environ. **20**, 75–90 (2011). https://doi.org/10.1177/1420326X10392017

13. Winzen, J., Albers, F., Marggraf-Micheel, C.: The influence of coloured light in the aircraft cabin on passenger thermal comfort. Light. Res. Technol. **46**, 465–475 (2014). https://doi.org/10.1177/1477153513484028
14. Meyers-Levy, J., Zhu, R.: The Influence of ceiling height: the effect of priming on the type of processing that people use. J. Consum. Res. **34**, 174–186 (2007). https://doi.org/10.1086/519146
15. Terazawa, A., Inomata, K., Nagata, N., Koyama, T., Okushi, A.: Individual differences in influence of mood on creativity task performance. In: Proceedings of HCG symposium 2018, B-7-2 (2018). (Japanese article with English abstract)
16. Indraganti, M., Rao, K.D.: Effect of age, gender, economic group and tenure on thermal comfort: a field study in residential buildings in hot and dry climate with seasonal variations. Energy Build. **42**, 273–281 (2010). https://doi.org/10.1016/j.enbuild.2009.09.003
17. Nakano, J., Tanabe, S., Kimura, K.: Differences in perception of indoor environment between Japanese and non-Japanese workers. Energy Build. **34**, 615–621 (2002). https://doi.org/10.1016/S0378-7788(02)00012-9
18. Laurentin, C., Bermtto, V., Fontoynont, M.: Light source type on visual appraisal. Light Res. Technol. **32**, 223–233 (2000)
19. Katahira, K.: Investigation of effects of micro-bubble bathing using psychological scale. Ergonomics **50**, 29–34 (2014). https://doi.org/10.1007/bf02904077. (Japanese article with English abstract)
20. Wyon, D.P.: The effects of indoor air quality on performance and productivity. Indoor Air Suppl. **14(Suppl 7)**, 92–101 (2004). https://doi.org/10.1111/j.1600-0668.2004.00278.x
21. Russell, J.A.: A circumplex model of affect. J. Pers. Soc. Psychol. **9**(39), 1161–1178 (1980). https://doi.org/10.1037/h0077714
22. Onoue, Y., Kukimoto, N., Sakamoto, N., Koyamada, K.: E-Grid: a visual analytics system for evaluation structures. J. Vis. **19**(4), 753–768 (2016). https://doi.org/10.1007/s12650-015-0342-6
23. Landis, J.R., Koch, G.G.: The measurement of observer agreement for categorical data. Biometrics **33**, 159–174 (1977). https://doi.org/10.2307/2529310
24. Fransson, N., Västfjäll, D., Skoog, J.: In search of the comfortable indoor environment: a comparison of the utility of objective and subjective indicators of indoor comfort. Build. Environ. **42**, 1886–1890 (2007)
25. Song, Y., Mao, F., Liu, Q.: Human comfort in indoor environment: a review on assessment criteria, data collection and data analysis methods. IEEE Access **7**, 119774–119786 (2019). https://doi.org/10.1109/access.2019.2937320

Contributions of Training Programs Supported by VR Techniques to the Prevention of STF Accidents

Anika Weber[1,2,3(✉)], Peter Nickel[3], Ulrich Hartmann[1],
Daniel Friemert[1], and Kiros Karamanidis[2]

[1] Department of Mathematics and Technology,
Koblenz University of Applied Sciences, Remagen, Germany
weber4@hs-koblenz.de
[2] School of Applied Sciences, Sport and Exercise Science Research Centre,
London Southbank University, London, UK
[3] Department of Accident Prevention: Digitalisation – Technologies, Institute for
Occupational Safety and Health of the German Social Accident Insurance (IFA),
Sankt Augustin, Germany

Abstract. Occupational safety and health (OSH) is active at all levels of the hierarchy of controls to prevent accidents associated with slips, trips and falls (STF). Training programs related to STF prevention are increasingly supported by virtual reality (VR) techniques. A review revealed a wide range of applications in practical and scientific areas. Trainings for operational practice vary regarding objectives, target groups, application contexts, media, and effectiveness, if available. Trainings in scientific studies are well designed for specific purposes at hand, but not suitable for direct application in operational practice. Research is required to bridge the gap. An investigation on gait stability and control in a VR-based obstacle avoidance training scenario has been conducted to contribute to developments in STF prevention. Initial results indicated a high level of presence and no evidence for detrimental effects on body and gait stability through application of VR techniques. This provides a sound basis for analysis of other data still required and for guiding similar and subsequent studies along knowledge gained by training programs available.

Keywords: Behavioral training · Gait perturbation · Virtual reality · Slip, trip, and fall hazards · Occupational safety and health

1 Introduction

The prevention of accidents involving slips, trips and falls (STF), accounting for about 20% of all accidents across national studies, is at high priority in occupational safety and health (OSH) [1]. The selection of prevention measures should preferably follow the internationally established hierarchy of controls (STOP model) [2, 3]. By means of substitution measures (e.g. using alternative walking routes without obstacles) or technical measures (e.g. designing work areas without steps, laying anti-slip floors), STF hazards are eliminated in principle and for many employees at the same time. In addition,

© Springer Nature Switzerland AG 2020
V. G. Duffy (Ed.): HCII 2020, LNCS 12198, pp. 276–290, 2020.
https://doi.org/10.1007/978-3-030-49904-4_20

organizational (e.g. tidying up work areas, walking on official paths) and personal measures (e.g. wearing work shoes as personal protective equipment, attending behavioral training programs to reduce the consequences of accidents) can also contribute to protection of employees and improvements in OSH.

Behavioral prevention measures such as training in STF prevention have been discovered for virtual reality (VR) applications and are increasingly popular [4]. It seems rather easy to draw employees' attention to, to sensitize employees to STF hazards, to teach them how to behave safely and healthy and to inform them about strategies and skills for STF prevention or reducing accident severity. In addition, it is assumed that implementation and use of VR in training applications will reduce the amount of physical training equipment required, increases flexibility in terms of training location and time, offers high fidelity training scenarios with hazardous situations at stake, and allows for new interventions for implementing training content. Some of the studies on development and implementation of VR in training environments demonstrate, however, that it might not always be that easy [5, 6].

However, research on the relationship between gait stability as well as coordination and STF give rise to the assumption that motor trainings have the potential to improve stability and coordination even in STF situations (see Sect. 2.3 and e.g. [7]). In addition, studies on walking on treadmills show significantly more natural human behavior when immersed in virtual scenarios as compared to without virtual environments (VE) [8]. Some adult education is rather open-minded towards new methods and media. Development of concepts such as assisted learning [9] offer a framework for integrating new methods or media into training procedures so that technical support for educational methods match didactics to improve learning.

Several training programs have already been developed in the context of STF prevention and the number of trainings that integrate VR technique increases. A review of training programs in the context of STF hazards that integrated VR techniques resulted in a collection with differences in objectives, content, structure and information on the effectiveness in the area of STF prevention. Results will be discussed and a strategy for setting up a new training program will be developed based on advantages and limitations of trainings available.

2 Review of Training Programs

2.1 Procedure for Research and Classification

A review of existing training programs was conducted to collect information about their objectives, target groups, application context, media representation, interventions and statements on effectiveness. The review focused on training programs that referred to potential STF hazards and involvement of VR techniques by means of an internet search with different search engines and combinations of terms (e.g. "training", "tripping", "virtual", "STF") in German and English language.

Two fundamentally different groups of results were identified. On the one hand, several training applications supported by VR techniques and offered for operational practice were found that addressed organizations on OSH, VR service providers, training providers and consulting firms were found. On the other hand, there were references to scientifically oriented studies that analyzed behavioral parameters for body stability and coordination in virtual scenarios or examined effects of variations in training on human gait parameters.

The findings provided a broad range of information with variations across training programs. However, based on information given, it was not always clear whether the training program was focused on training, on application with VE, on OSH or something different. Not all training programs presented information about a rationale or intended use. With the aim to structure the contents, an attempt was made to present information on objectives, target user groups, application context, media and VR techniques required, possible interventions and statements on effectiveness.

2.2 Trainings Supported by VR, Related to STF Prevention and Operational Practice

Work Safe, Texas - Safety in a Box for Construction and Production Safety [10]. The Work Safe training program allows employees to virtually experience deadly and serious accident hazards on construction sites: Falls from height; Struck by an Object; Electrocution; and Caught In or Between. The training program for building safety is similar to production safety. Users virtually experience three safety relevant scenarios that are common in a production environment: Lockout/Tagout When Working with Machinery; Slips, Trips and Falls; and Forklift Awareness. The program requires employees to watch 360° videos on construction and production safety in a Cardboard VR. With several scenarios available, each concludes with a multiple-choice quiz. Employees get feedback, they are informed about potential consequences and are presented appropriate solutions or behaviors.

Plonsker Media/BG Bau - Fall Protection on the Construction Site [11, 12]. An occupational safety training, developed for the German Social Accident Insurance Institution for the building trade, intends to train and instruct employees on a range of topics relevant in OSH in the building trade. In this training program, VR serves as a medium for integrating more naturalistic environmental conditions in training scenarios. The application demonstrates a range of personal protective equipment (PPE) (e.g. helmet, belt) for fall protection. The selection of suitable measures for fall protection (e.g. closing flaps of scaffoldings, attaching cross braces to scaffoldings, putting on PPE, attaching spring safety hooks to a safety rope) is rewarded with tokens to be collected by the user. The user wears a commercially available VR headset, can move freely in space and interact with objects in the virtual environment using controllers.

Safety-and-Health-at-Work - Working Height Safety [13]. The training program intends to train employees on safely working at height. For virtual work on an inspection hood of an air conditioning system on a high roof, equipment (e.g. personal fall distance limiter), colleagues (e.g. full-body harness) and the employee itself (e.g. safety rope attached) are virtually checked. He/She is asked to climb up a ladder to a sloping roof. A scenario is available in which the force applied by the worker to the hood is too great and the user falls backwards over the edge of the roof being restrained by the personal fall distance limiter. The simulation in the VE used in the training program allows different views: first person, observer from near range and from ground level. Navigation in virtual scenarios is carried out with the aid of a commercially available VR headset and two controllers.

American Society of Safety Professionals - Fall Protection Training Tool [14]. The training program intends to train good operational practice through an application in a fall prevention training that is supported by VR techniques. Employees use an app to train in realistic work scenarios without endangering themselves. In the VR application, hazards should be identified and fall protection systems should be selected. A roof scenario is presented with several fall hazards, such as tripping hazards due to devices close to the edge of the roof and open roof windows. Employees are required to assemble a safety system for colleagues. Anchorage points, harnesses and ropes should be selected suitable to serve as protective safety system in the situation. The fall scenario varies with the choice of the assembled safety system.

Energy.Gov - Slips Trips and Falls [15]. This training program is designed to teach workers how to move in work scenarios with various hazards before facing hazardous situations in facilities in reality. Employees walk through a virtual scenario and avoid safety risks (e.g. tripping hazards, piping above floor level, low hanging infrastructure). They identify dangerous objects in their way and remove them, so they have a walking and working area without hazards. While walking in the scenario, trackers are used to record body movements of the employees. Employees are given points for eliminating hazards or hazardous situations. This adds an entertaining video game element to the training program.

BGHW Mobile "More Safety Through Personal Experience" - Warehouse Simulator [16, 17]. A showtruck of the German Social Accident Insurance Institution for the trade and logistics industry includes several areas for OSH related activities. At one activity station, employees walk through various virtual rooms of a logistics center in search of tripping and slipping hazards, wearing a commercially available VR headset. The aim of this simulation application supported by VR techniques is to find as many hazards as possible, to select suitable measures to prevent them and to receive feedback about chosen activities. Among others, the application should be used to get into conversations with employees and to make them realize that each employee can always do something for their own safety and the safety of colleagues in the company (e.g. from picking up objects lying around to informing the supervisor about hazards).

VR Health and Safety Training - Slips, Trips and Falls [18]. This training program advertises that the training of critical safety standards should leave a lasting impression. The VR-based training program intends to improve training effectiveness and training transfer. In a playful way, the employees are challenged to identify typical hazards in a simulated workplace environment. Employees will get feedback about their activities including information about what should have been done. Health and safety training topics include topics like fire alarm or slips, trips and falls. A video also shows the use of PPE (e.g. helmet, safety goggles and gloves).

IBEW - Slips, Trips & Falls [19]. This training program among others, concerns with slip, trip and fall hazards and allows prospective trainees to explore a construction site virtually via a 360° application with a smartphone or a commercially available VR headset. Five one-hour modules show different typical dangers (e.g. module slips, trips and falls). Danger points in the virtual environment are marked with symbols. When the trainee selects a danger point by clicks, the application presents detailed information about relevant hazards. The program was tested in a training center with 20 trainees. Young trainees accepted the VR learning technology better compared to teaching in traditional training and demonstration style.

EdgVR© Health & Safety - Slips, Trips and Falls [20]. The training program includes 360° photos, videos and an interactive platform and among others, presents OSH topics such as slips, trips and falls. This training program is designed to be used with commercially available VR headsets that allows up to 35 users to act independently of each other at the same time. The system intends to detect participants' potentially relevant needs for further training in OSH or required professional knowledge on safety and health issues for a range of task.

2.3   Trainings Supported by VR, Related to STF Prevention and Scientific Research

In addition to practical or commercial offers for training programs with VR support, scientific studies also reported in the context of STF prevention, are often associated with biomechanical motor training programs. Almost all of the training programs have an interest in slipping behavior, i.e. with virtual slipping imposed by tilting the image of the VE presented in VR glasses [21–29].

Results of the studies showed that participants walk more carefully in VE compared to walking outside VE; as indicated by reduced gait speed, shorter strides, longer double support, and higher step width [23–25, 28]. Therefore, it could be assumed that just walking while present in a VE and without virtual perturbations, challenges gait stability and coordination. Virtual perturbation (e.g. by tilting of the image) added to walking in VE, sometimes led to improvements in gait and coordination parameters [25, 28]. In addition, VR support in trainings where participants went shopping in VE under different conditions (e.g. icy, virtual tilt of the environment, stepping over virtual obstacles, multitasking) led to lower fear of falling [21].

In training programs, it could be demonstrated that participants showed reactive and proactive adjustments to tilting VE. Moreover, when transferred to real slipping situations, participants improved interception strategies even without training in real situations [22, 23]. If this training program would indicate long-term effects and were to be transferred into real life scenarios with participants of the general public (e.g. rehabilitation or prevention centers), it may have the potential to reduce the risk of high accident severity in some fall situations.

Since medio-lateral oscillations of the visual field cause greater perturbations of gait than anterior-posterior oscillations [26], alternative procedures have been investigated to simulate slipping experiences in VE. One study showed that perturbations by tilting in the roll plane of a treadmill in the virtual environment with or without physically moving the roll plane of the real treadmill (standing on a 6 DOF motion base) resulted in no significant differences in gait stability and coordination [24]. Although researchers concluded that perturbations initiated by VR systems could generate a cost-effective approach for gait rehabilitation in patients, it seems to be long way for development of an effective and valid training program in this setting. Another study concluded that VE could produce results in fall interventions comparable to training programs with a moveable platform [27]. Besides similar effects in reductions of fall frequencies for both environments, differences occurred for body motions. While virtual slips initiated by tilts in the pitch plane of the VE led to an initial response in the upper body and a secondary response in the lower extremities, slips initiated by the moveable platform led first to a response in the lower extremity and then to a response using hip and trunk. Consequently and although some final effects seemed to be comparable using the moveable platform and the VE [27], differences in motor behavior rather suggested requirements for different compensatory strategies and therefore different behavioral control for fall prevention.

Recently, VE have also been used to train obstacle negotiation [30]. Therefore, participants walked through a virtual corridor and occasionally crossed virtual obstacles. After crossing obstacles, they got feedback about the distance between foot and obstacle by pleasant and unpleasant sounds, depending on close range crossing and out of range crossing of the obstacle. Thus, participant learning to cross the obstacle as close as possible was reinforced. As a result, they found that participants successfully reduced foot clearance as instructed during practice trials, transferred the reduced foot clearance to over-ground obstacle negotiation, and retained the reduced foot clearance after 24 h [30].

2.4 Evaluation of Both Groups of Training Programs

In principle, objectives of the above-mentioned training programs for the research sector (see Sect. 2.3) are relatively easy to understand compared to those for operational practice (see Sect. 2.2). However, illustrations and explanations for practical training programs more closely connect to practical situations at work and more obviously are interested in prevention of STF hazards and accidents.

Each of the above-mentioned training programs related to workplace practice (see Sect. 2.2) aims to contribute to the prevention of STF accidents or at least to reducing their severity. However, due to a lack of information, it is not possible to determine how and to what extend this is feasible and whether the content of the training program contributes to the objective. Potential contributions or results for employees are, among others, informing about hazards, identifying danger points, showing possible courses of action and experiencing dangerous situations without putting oneself in danger.

It is assumed, however, that (1) contributions actually take place, i.e. relevant training participants recognize, understand and take on information given and actions can become effective in the population and therefore, (2) training participants back in real life situations, actively influence STF situations so that near misses and accidents are prevented. An evaluation for both requirements is necessary, before a training program could be assumed to be relevant and significant in the field of STF prevention. Two statements from descriptions of the training program in Sect. 2.2 provide hints at potential evaluation results. One the one hand, it is mentioned, that interest in VR techniques or related media was more interesting compared to classical teaching. Unfortunately, this does not necessarily result in improved effectiveness of training programs. On the other hand, it was pointed out, that studies have shown increases in retention of training content with increasing fidelity of the training environment. Unfortunately, due to lack of reference to an evaluation study and direct referencing to the training program itself, this statement cannot be generalized for all training programs. Nevertheless, practical training programs may have in common that they intend to train participants in identification and elimination of STF hazards.

None of the training programs mentioned in relation to research (see Sect. 2.3) pursues the goal of conclusively developing an effective measure for preventing STF accidents. Rather, the aim is to investigate individual or several behavioral-preventive cause-effect relationships on the path between gait stability and coordination parameters and a potential contribution to reductions in the severity or prevention of STF accidents. Aim of investigations therefore should be the effectiveness of training programs with and without VR support for intended variations in relevant gait parameters including information about the generalizability of results. In addition, transfer of training effects to real life situations should become available and be maintained in the long term. Finally, it should be possible to show that in situations with STF hazards, accidents can be prevented, or their severity reduced.

From the overview of research activities as documented in Sect. 2.3, however, it is obvious that evidence suitable for training programs in STF prevention is rather limited. The same is true for information available about cause-effect relationships between gait stability and coordination and STF. At the same time, it is also evident that development and implementation of effective training programs for STF prevention seem to require more than just VR techniques and appear to be much more complex than offers available for operational practice would suggest.

2.5   Discussion

An increasing number of training programs is available with close links to a rather broad topic like rehabilitation and prevention of STF and OSH. Even if training programs supported by VR techniques range at lower level in the hierarchy of controls for improving working conditions according to OSH [2], they have the potential to support prevention and actively involve employees in activities for prevention of STF accidents. However, research activities should continue to focus on cause-effect relationships between gait stability and coordination parameters and potential contributions to reductions in the severity or prevention of STF accidents. Operational practice should continue to involve in development and implementation of training programs and support the transfer of evidence available to the shop floor level. While high fidelity usually does not result in impairing effects for training programs supported by VR techniques, it is a rather unreliable predictor for immersion and the feeling of presence in VE [5]. In addition, simply developing a VE does not imply that it is good enough to achieve training gains [6].

Unfortunately, the review of already existing training programs was not systematic, so that not all existing training programs could be included. Nevertheless, the programs identified indicated significant differences in objectives, content, structure and information on effectiveness in this area of accident prevention. Training programs related to operational practice have not yet been able to demonstrate and inform about their contribution to prevention of STF accidents. They are nevertheless valuable because they attempt to depict working conditions in relevant scenarios at work and provide visual support for virtual identification and elimination of STF hazards.

Research-based training programs have not yet been able to develop solutions for operational practice although some investigations suggest or believe that the results may significantly contribute to training relevant in practice. Based on training programs presented, it is clear that there are currently more open questions than satisfactory answers. However, results of the review are encouraging and initial achievements increase confidence that ongoing research activities may contribute to prevention of STF accidents.

The review already provides some indications for strategies for further research. A good starting point is provided by a preliminary study that aims to examine learning effects of a virtual obstacle avoidance training on gait stability in young adults (see Sect. 3). Further studies should follow, with investigations into transfer of results to trip hazards in reality and into short as well as long-term effects for gait stability and coordination trainings supported by VR techniques relevant for different age groups and scenarios related to operational practice.

3 Study on Obstacle Avoidance Supported by Virtual Reality Techniques

The prospective study is part of a research agenda with the aim to investigate training procedures with long-lasting effects on gait stability and coordination. The training should be suitable to a broad range of working population and should apply VR techniques to support training procedures. The review of already existing VR training programs for STF prevention shows that VR techniques could be helpful to support training programs. Results also provide some indications for strategies for further research. An initial study will investigate whether gait stability of young adults can be improved by training of obstacle avoidance in VE. Furthermore, it was investigated whether potential adaptation to repeated disturbances of one leg can promote better performance of crossing obstacles with the untrained leg.

Future studies should follow, with investigations into transfer of results to trip hazards in reality and into short as well as long-term effects for gait stability and coordination trainings supported by VR techniques relevant for different age groups and scenarios related to operational practice. The whole research project tries to investigate cause-effect relationship between gait stability and coordination and STF.

3.1 Methods

Participants. Twenty-four young and healthy participants ($M = 22.3$ years, $SD = 2.4$) provided informed consent to take part in empirical investigations. All participants reported high (corrected) visual acuity and no impairments with regard to walking and body movements.

Task Environment. The investigations were conducted in the Laboratory for Biomechanical Studies, RAC facilities of Koblenz University of Applied Sciences. A treadmill (Pluto, h/p/cosmos, Germany) with mechanical fall arrester was placed in the center of the laboratory. While three cameras for motion capturing (Opus, 120 Hz; Qualisys AB, Sweden) were set up at ground level close to the treadmill, five cameras were installed on rails attached to all sides of the ceiling. In addition, of the four lighthouses for head-tracking of a VR headset (Vive Pro, HTC, Taiwan) three were mounted to the rails and one was placed on a tripod close to the treadmill.

On the treadmill, participants walked in a virtual environment along a corridor and were occasionally required to cross obstacles presented in the scenario. For orientation in the scenario, a 3D model of the treadmill was integrated and the participants' body was virtually visualized by an avatar (Fig. 1). Unity (Unity Technologies ApS, USA) served as a software system for VR programming and was used to develop the virtual environment. This system and the motion capturing system were synchronized and used the same coordinate system. The motion capturing system tracked dynamic body, leg and foot postures from markers attached to the participants to feed analyses of parameters for body and gait stability. In addition, participants' foot positions in gait cycle were analyzed to deliver a signal to the VR system that triggered stimulus presentations in VR (virtual obstacle).

Experimental Procedure and Study Design. The experiments lasted about 120 min each, subdivided into consecutive sections for briefing and preparation including initial questionnaires, one session either in the control group or in the intervention group, and debriefing including another assessment with questionnaires. At the beginning, participants were asked to provide informed consent and were informed about their rights as participants. They filled in questionnaires on demographics and baseline performance. Before start of session, both groups were able to familiarize with the equipment by walking on the treadmill without and with wearing a VR headset.

Next, the intervention group started their training session while walking on the treadmill and crossing 51 virtual obstacles (width 500, height 100, depth 100 mm) with one leg only. Obstacles appeared unexpectedly in the virtual scenario in front of the participants. The control group walked on the treadmill for 10 min without obstacles and was then required to cross 16 virtual obstacles. Total time of both groups on the treadmill with VR was the same. The ability to successfully cross obstacles required integration of visual information about the virtual environment and self-assessments of participants own body posture (see Fig. 1).

In the briefing phase, all participants completed questionnaires on simulator sickness (SSQ) [31, 32] and immersion tendency (ITQ) [33]. During the sessions, measures of participants body and gait stability were acquired based on 48 markers attached to foot, leg, body, head and VR headset that were tracked by the tracking system. In the

Fig. 1. Experimenters view of VE from behind at participant (blue avatar) on treadmill (overlay included) while walking along a suburban area. Participants' point of view is the avatars' view. (Color figure online)

debriefing phase, all participants completed questionnaires, such as SSQ, Presence Questionnaire (PQ) [33, 34] and on perceived mental workload by using the task load index (NASA-TLX) [35]. All questionnaires were presented on a Laboratory computer using LimeSurvey (LimeSurvey GmbH, Germany) as an online survey tool.

Since analysis of biomechanical measures to body and gait parameter is not yet available, analysis refers to questionnaire data only. Therefore, data from sessions do not require repeated measures analysis. With the number of participants balanced for the control ($N = 12$) and intervention ($N = 12$) group, a non-randomised controlled trial design is applied (t-Test; IBM® SPSS® Statistics 23, USA) to questionnaire results. For all statistical tests, the significance level was set at $p < 0.05$.

3.2   Results

Simulator Sickness. The questionnaire on simulator sickness was rated before and after the session of both control and intervention group. The analysis of difference measures resulted in minimal symptoms for the control group ($M = 8.74$; $SD = 12.82$) and negligible symptoms for the intervention group ($M = 2.19$; $SD = 3.38$) (Fig. 2) according to sickness score classifications [36]. Statistical analyses revealed no differences between groups.

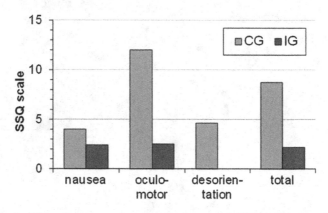

Fig. 2. Results for SSQ sub-scales and total scales for control (CG) and intervention group (IG).

Sense of Presence. It is recommended to investigate the tendency of participants to experience presence before an assessment of presence should take place [32]. Analyses of the ITQ revealed no differences for the control and the intervention group, neither for the total level of immersion tendency ($M = 85.17$; $SD = 10.33$), nor for sub-scales such as tendencies to become involved in activities ($M = 29.96$; $SD = 7.77$), to maintain focus on current activities ($M = 38.17$; $SD = 3.77$) and to play computer games ($M = 8.17$; $SD = 3.36$). Results of the present study are very similar to average values across other studies [33].

The sense of presence (PQ) in the control and in the intervention group yielded no differences between groups, however, an internationally comparable and high level for the total value ($M = 125.88$; $SD = 22.69$) as well as for the sub-scales involvement ($M = 56.04$; $SD = 12.19$), sensory fidelity ($M = 20.63$; $SD = 8.33$), adaptation/immersion ($M = 43.17$; $SD = 6.13$), and interface quality ($M = 6.04$; $SD = 2.18$).

Perceived Mental Workload. The sequence of task processing did not reveal any significant influence on the results of this evaluation study. Mental workload during the sessions was rated under-average in the control group ($M = 24.64$; $SD = 8.08$) and in the intervention group ($M = 29.58$; $SD = 9.96$). Statistical analysis yielded no significant differences between groups.

3.3   Discussion

The study presented intends to investigate learning effects of virtual obstacle avoidance training on gait stability in young adults. Unfortunately, analysis of biomechanical data was not undertaken yet. Procedures for data analysis have already been presented [37] and results for the present study are in preparation [38]. However, positive results could be obtained from the pre and post examinations with questionnaires on relevant dimensions in training studies in virtual environments.

Across all these measures, results suggested no detrimental effects by participating in the study and demonstrated that no differences could be identified between control and intervention group according to statistical analysis of simulator sickness, immersion tendency, feeling of presence and mental workload. In addition, perceived mental workload was rated rather low in general and the feeling of presence was at high level; similar to those reported in the literature [33].

This provides a sound basis for analyses of biomechanical data and for guiding more elaborated training studies along the lessons learned and experiences gained in initial studies. Occupational health and safety should therefore proceed in follow its long tradition in simulation research to use its specific advantages.

4   Conclusions

Regarding the number of accidents related to STF hazards, application as well as development of suitable measures are very welcome. Although the hierarchy of controls is in favour of the strategy to prefer measures at upper levels, all hierarchy levels are required to contribute effectively. Regarding training programs available more information and exhaustive evidence would be required to be able to choose a program that covers demands in operational practice and demonstrates compliance with OSH requirements. This calls for evaluation studies on information quality and on potential contributions for the prevention of STF accidents at shop floor level. Trainings supported by VR techniques and related to STF prevention and scientific research are very helpful as they contribute to an understanding about cause-effect relationships between gait stability and coordination and STF. Most of the training programs available, however, are closely related to the investigations at hand and cannot be applied to training situations in the operational practice for the prevention of STF accidents. An emphasis seems to be rather given to prevention areas related to slipping and falling while obstacle avoidance or tripping prevention could be assumed to be an unknown quantity, if there were not some research groups addressing relevant issues. However, more research is required to provide evidence for effective interventions.

Preliminary information about ongoing investigations allowed to inform about initial results. It could be demonstrated that the study on learning effects of gait stability in young adults in a virtual obstacle avoidance training was well received by the participants. Although, results on biomechanical data is not yet available, the positive assessments of VR techniques in action in the training program provides a sound basis for guiding similar and subsequent studies along lessons learned and experiences gained in the present study and training programs available.

References

1. DGUV: Statistik. Arbeitsunfallgeschehen 2018. Deutsche Gesetzliche Unfallversicherung (DGUV), Berlin (2019). https://publikationen.dguv.de/widgets/pdf/download/article/3680
2. Lehto, M.R., Cook, B.T.: Occupational health and safety management. In: Salvendy, G. (ed.) Handbook of Human Factors and Ergonomics, pp. 701–733. Wiley, Hoboken (2012)
3. EU OSH Framework Directive 89/391/EEC of 12 June 1989 on the introduction of measures to encourage improvements in the safety and health of workers at work (with amendments 2008). Official Journal of the European Union L 183, 29/06/1989, pp. 1–8 (2008)
4. Simeonov, P.: Fall risk associated with restricted and elevated support surfaces. In: Hsiao, H. (ed.) Fall Prevention and Protection: Principles, Guidelines, and Practices, pp. 119–140. CRC Press, Boca Raton (2017)
5. Simpson, B.D., Cowgill, J.L., Gilkey, R.H., Weisenberger, J.M.: Technological considerations in the design of multisensory virtual environments: How real does it need to be? In: Hale, K.S., Stanney, K.M. (eds.) Handbook of Virtual Environments: Design, Implementation, and Applications, pp. 313–333. CRC Press, Boca Raton (2015)
6. Champney, R.K., Carroll, M., Surpris, G., Cohn, J.: Conducting training transfer studies in virtual environments. In: Hale, K.S., Stanney, K.M. (eds.) Handbook of Virtual Environments: Design, Implementation, and Applications, pp. 781–795. CRC Press, Boca Raton (2015)
7. Gordon, D., Robertson, E., Caldwell, G.E., Hamill, J., Kamen, G., Whittlesey, S.N. (eds.): Research Methods in Biomechanics. Human Kinetics, Champaign (2014)
8. Sheik-Nainar, M.A., Kaber, D.B.: The utility of a virtual reality locomotion interface for studying gait behavior. Hum. Factors 49(4), 696–709 (2007)
9. Arnold, R.: Assisted Learning. A Workbook. Bildungstransfer Verlag, Landau (2010)
10. Safety in a Box. www.worksafetexas.com/videos/safety-in-a-box.aspx. Accessed 30 Jan 2020
11. Plonsker, T.: Lernen in und mit virtuellen Welten. DGUV Forum 4, 36–37 (2019)
12. DGUV Forum. https://www.dguv-forum.de/files/594/19-50-035_DGUV_Forum_4_2019_screen.pdf. Accessed 30 Jan 2020
13. Safety and health at work. www.healthandsafetyatwork.com/feature/working-height-safety-london-office-block. Accessed 15 Dec 2019
14. American Society of Safety Professionals. www.assp.org/news-and-articles/2018/07/10/using-virtual-reality-as-a-fall-protection-training-tool. Accessed 30 Jan 2020
15. Savannah River Site. www.energy.gov/em/articles/srs-liquid-waste-contractor-uses-virtual-reality-slips-trips-and-falls-training. Accessed 30 Jan 2020
16. BGHW: In diesem Lkw steckt was drin. BGHW aktuell, vol. 3, pp. 18–21 (2019)
17. BGHW. https://www.bghw.de/medien/bghw-aktuell-die-zeitschrift-fuer-mitgliedsbetriebe/bghw-aktuell-03-19/bghw-aktuell-3-19. Accessed 30 Jan 2020
18. VR Health and Safety Training. www.virtualrealityexps.com/vr-health-and-safety/. Accessed 30 Jan 2020
19. IBEW. www.bitspacedevelopment.com/ibew-slips-trips-falls/. Accessed 15 Jan 2020
20. EdgVR. www.edg-vr.com/. Accessed 15 Jan 2020
21. Giotakos, O., Tsirgogianni, K., Tarnanas, I.: A virtual reality exposure therapy (VRET) scenario for the reduction of fear of falling and balance rehabilitation training of elder adults with hip fracture history. Virtual Rehabil., 155–158 (2007). https://doi.org/10.1109/icvr.2007.4362157

22. Parijat, P., Lockhart, T.E., Liu, J.: Effects of perturbation-based slip training using a virtual reality environment on slip-induced falls. Ann. Biomed. Eng. **43**(4), 958–967 (2014). https://doi.org/10.1007/s10439-014-1128-z

23. Parijat, P., Lockhart, T.E., Liu, J.: EMG and kinematic responses to unexpected slips after slip training in virtual reality. IEEE Trans. Biomed. Eng. **62**(2), 593–599 (2015). https://doi.org/10.1109/tbme.2014.2361324

24. Riem, L., Van Dehy, J., Onushko, T., Beardsley, S.: Inducing compensatory changes in gait similar to external perturbations using an immersive head mounted display. In: Proceedings of the 2018 IEEE Conference on Virtual Reality and 3D User Interfaces (VR), pp. 128–135 (2018). https://doi.org/10.1109/vr.2018.8446432

25. Menegoni, F., et al.: Walking in an immersive virtual reality. In: Annual Review of Cybertherapy and Telemedicine. Studies in Health Technology and Informatics, vol. 144, pp. 72–76 (2009). https://doi.org/10.3233/978-1-60750-017-9-72

26. Martelli, D., Xia, B., Prado, A., Agrawal, S.K.: Gait adaptations during overground walking and multidirectional oscillations of the visual field in a virtual reality headset. Gait Posture **67**, 251–256 (2019). https://doi.org/10.1016/j.gaitpost.2018.10.029

27. Liu, J., Lockhart, T., Parijat, P., McIntosh, J.D., Chiu, Y.P.: Comparison of slip training in VR environment and on moveable platform. In: 52nd Annual Rocky Mountain Bioengineering Symposium and 52nd International ISA Biomedical Sciences Instrumentation Symposium 2015, pp. 192–200. International Society of Automation (ISA) (2015)

28. Peterson, S.M., Rios, E., Ferris, D.P.: Transient visual perturbations boost short-term balance learning in virtual reality by modulating electrocortical activity. J. Neurophysiol. **120**(4), 1998–2010 (2018). https://doi.org/10.1152/jn.00292.2018

29. Nyberg, L., et al.: Using a virtual reality system to study balance and walking in a virtual outdoor environment: a pilot study. Cyberpsychol. Behav. **9**(4), 388–395 (2006). https://doi.org/10.1089/cpb.2006.9.388

30. Kim, A., Schweighofer, N., Finley, J.M.: Locomotor skill acquisition in virtual reality shows sustained transfer to the real world. J. Neuroeng. Rehabil. **16**(1), 113–123 (2019). https://doi.org/10.1186/s12984-019-0584-y

31. Kennedy, R.S., Berbaum, K.S., Lilienthal, M.G.: Simulator sickness questionnaire: an enhanced method for quantifying simulator sickness. Int. J. Aviat. Psychol. **3**(3), 203–220 (1993)

32. Pfendler, C., Thun, J.: Der Simulator Sickness Questionnaire von Kennedy et al. (1993) und seine rechnergestützte Version (Technischer Bericht). Forschungsinstitut für Kommunikation, Informationsverarbeitung und Ergonomie (FKIE), Wachtberg (2001)

33. Witmer, B.G., Singer, M.J.: Measuring presence in virtual environments: a presence questionnaire. Presence **7**(3), 225–240 (1998)

34. Witmer, B.G., Jerome, C.J., Singer, M.J.: The factor structure of the presence questionnaire. Presence **14**(3), 298–312 (2005)

35. Hart, S.G., Staveland, L.E.: Development of the NASA task load index (TLX): results of empirical and theoretical research. In: Hancock, P.A., Meshkati, N. (eds.) Human Mental Workload, pp. 139–183. North-Holland, Amsterdam (1988)

36. Stanney, K.M., Kennedy, R.S., Drexler, J.M.: Cybersickness is not simulator sickness. In: Proceedings of the 41st Annual Meeting of the Human Factors and Ergonomics Society (HFES 1997), Albuquerque, San Diego, 22–26 September 1997, pp. 1138–1142 (1997)

37. Weber, A., Nickel, P., Hartmann, U., Friemert, D., Karamanidis, K.: Capture of stability and coordination indicators in virtual training scenarios for the prevention of slip, trip, and fall (STF) accidents. In: Duffy, V.G. (ed.) HCII 2019. LNCS, vol. 11581, pp. 210–219. Springer, Cham (2019). https://doi.org/10.1007/978-3-030-22216-1_16
38. Weber, A., et al.: A virtual reality obstacle avoidance task leads to limb-specific locomotor adaptations but not interlimb transfer. Manuscript under preparation

Analysis of Effects on Postural Stability by Wearable Tactile Expression Mechanism

Hirotake Yamazoe[1]([⊠]) [iD] and Tomoko Yonezawa[2] [iD]

[1] Ritsumeikan University, Kusatsu, Shiga 525-8577, Japan
yamazoe@fc.ritsumei.ac.jp
[2] Kansai University, Takatsuki, Osaka 569-1095, Japan
yone@kansai-u.ac.jp

Abstract. In this paper, we examine a method for stabilizing walking by using a wearable tactile expression mechanism based on a pneumatic actuator array. So far, we have researched wearable stuffed toy robots and their tactile expression mechanism for supporting elderly people's going out, especially from a cognitive perspective. In addition to the cognitive support, we aim to achieve a physical support by using our device, and we consider walking stabilization using our device. Toward this goal, in this paper, we examine the effects of the tactile stimuli of our device on directions in which the participants felt pulled by the haptic stimuli and the center of gravity (CoG) movements. In the experiment, we evaluated the effects both subjectively and quantitatively.

Keywords: Tactile expression · Postural and walking stability · Wearable robot

1 Introduction

The world's aging societies continue to face a variety of serious problems related to lifestyle changes, such as an increase in nuclear families. In these societies, the elderly and the disabled who are living alone sometimes need the support of caregivers to overcome their anxiety, even when they simply want to leave their homes for a walk or to go shopping. However, due to a shortage of caregivers and volunteers, as well as the emotional burden of seeking help, such people often withdraw from society. Such withdrawal from society causes even greater problems, including advanced dementia.

During outings, the elderly and the disabled face two main problems: *physical problems*, especially for seniors, caused by impaired body functions, and *cognitive problems*, which can exacerbate memory loss and attention deficit issues. Such problems can result in serious accidents.

To solve such problems by using information technology (IT) and robotics technologies, various support systems for walking situations have been proposed [4,7]. These systems can reduce such problems by providing various

---

H. Yamazoe—Currently with University of Hyogo, yamazoe@eng.u-hyogo.ac.jp.

© Springer Nature Switzerland AG 2020
V. G. Duffy (Ed.): HCII 2020, LNCS 12198, pp. 291–300, 2020.
https://doi.org/10.1007/978-3-030-49904-4_21

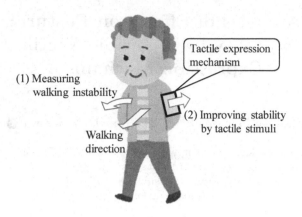

Fig. 1. Final goal of our research

information based on a user's context. We are also researching wearable message robots that can care for and support elderly and disabled people during their outings [8,10]. Because our robots are wearable, they can provide support to users anytime and anywhere. However, these systems focused only on cognitive problems, and did not consider physical problems (Fig. 1).

In this research study, we focus on posture stability during walking as a physical problem. In general, due to their muscle weakness, the older the elderly, the higher the risk of falls. Falls may make the elderly people bedridden. There are several approaches to preventing falls or other physical problems by using robot technologies. One approach is a power suit [6] that can support physical abilities directly. However, such an approach requires large actuators and mechanisms to support the wearer's posture and movements.

Other approaches include the improvement of stability by tactile stimuli: virtually generating the light touch [5] and transmitting vibrations to the feet or neck [2,3]. Light touch [1] is a phenomenon in which stability is improved by lightly touching a wall or other object. Shima et al. proposed a method for generating virtual light touch contact, which can reduce human postural sway in standing and walking states [5]. In their method, the user wears vibration motors on his or her fingertips that present vibrations corresponding to the user's motion, which is captured by a motion capture system. These vibration stimuli can achieve virtual light touch and improve walking stability in standing. Ivanenko et al. reported that neck proprioceptive inputs can affect gait, and neck muscle vibration induces a deviation in head direction when stepping in place [2,3].

In this research, we aimed for the latter, stability improvements by tactile stimuli. Toward this goal, we previously examined a method for stabilizing walking by using a wearable tactile expression mechanism based on a pneumatic actuator array [9]. In this paper, we analyze the effects on postural stability by our method.

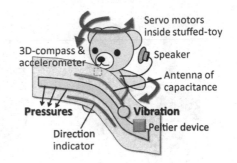

Fig. 2. Wearable stuffed-toy robot [10] (left: appearance, right: system configuration)

2   Wearable Stuffed-Toy Robot and Its Tactile Expression Mechanism

This section describes our proposed wearable robots [10] and their tactile expression mechanisms [8].

Figure 2 shows the appearance and the system configuration of our wearable robot [10]. The system consists of a stuffed-toy robot that includes sensors, actuators, and a fixing textile. The robot has two degrees of freedom (DoFs) in its head and one in its left hand. An IMU sensor detects the activities of both the user and the robot, and there is a speaker inside the robot. In the fixing textile, a vibration motor is attached for tactile stimuli.

We also proposed a tactile expression mechanism based on the pneumatic actuator array for our wearable robot [8]. Figure 3 (left) shows the device's appearance with the proposed mechanism, and Fig. 3 (right) is the proposed mechanism's configuration for tactile expressions. The proposed mechanism is used as a fixed part of the robot. Four actuators are arranged around the user's arm. Through the shortening of a portion of the actuators, various directions can be indicated. We employ pneumatic actuators (SQUSE PM-10RF) that are shortened by increasing their internal pressure. The pneumatic actuators require a compressor (SQUSE ACP-100) and a pressure control unit (PCM-200).

So far, we have researched various tactile expressions, including directional indications, using the proposed mechanism, and confirmed that some of the wearers can feel pulling sensations from the device through the preliminary experiment. Considering these results, we consider that the pulling sensations from our device can improve the wearer's postural stabilization. Toward this goal, in this paper, we evaluate the effects on the stabilization of the wearer's walking by using the proposed tactile expression mechanism.

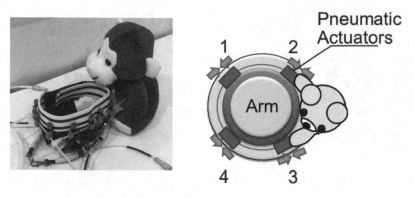

Fig. 3. Tactile expression mechanism [8] (left: appearance, right: system configuration)

3   Walking Stabilization by Tactile Stimuli

As described above, several methods have been proposed for stabilizing walking via tactile stimuli. In our method, we aim to improve walking stability by presenting tactile stimuli, especially pulling sensations.

To evaluate the effects of tactile presentation to the user's upper arm on stability improvement, we first constructed an experimental system in the standing position as shown in Fig. 4. The experimental system consists of our tactile expression mechanism and a Nintendo Wii balance board to measure the movements of the participant's center of gravity (CoG) for stability evaluation. Here, we prepared four patterns of tactile stimuli as shown in Fig. 5. Each stimuli pattern was designed so that the stimuli made the user feel pulling toward the user's front, back, left, and right directions.

4   Experiment

To evaluate the effects of tactile stimuli on stability, we conducted the following experiment.

Environment. Figures 6 and 7 show the experimental environment and setup. The Wii balance board was placed where the distance between the participant standing on the board and the wall was about 70 cm. The gazing point was placed on the wall, and the participant was instructed to gaze at the point during the experiment. The X and Y directions of the obtained data of the Wii balance board are the right and front directions, respectively, as shown in Fig. 7. The participant wore the tactile expression device on his/her left upper arm. Here, the stuffed-toy robot was not attached for evaluating the effects of only the tactile stimuli. One camera was placed behind the participant to record his or her pose during the experiment.

Participant. The number of the participants is 10 (six female and four male, 20–26 years old).

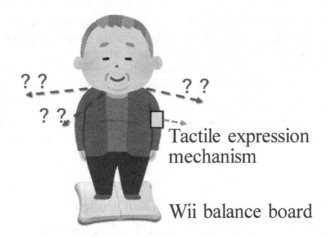

Fig. 4. Overview of experiment

Fig. 5. Tactile stimuli

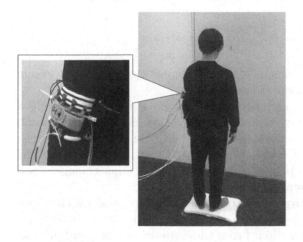

Fig. 6. Experimental environment

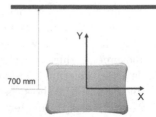

Fig. 7. Experimental setup

Procedure. In each trial, the participant was presented with one tactile stimulus. The movements of the participant's CoG during the experiment were measured by using the Nintendo Wii balance board. After each trial, the participant answered the direction in which he/she felt pulled by the stimuli. The direction was indicated by using a clock position (answered with 0–59 min).

Condition. All participants were presented all four directions three times. The total number of the trial is 12. The order of the stimuli was counter-balanced.

5 Result

5.1 Direction in Which Participants Felt Pulled

First, we evaluated the effects on the direction in which the participants felt pulled by the haptic stimuli.

The front direction of each participant's directional answer did not always match the front direction of the tactile expression device depending on the way in which the participant wore the tactile presentation device. To compensate these differences, we calculated the average direction of the answers when the participant was presented with the stimuli of the front direction, and we subtracted the average direction from the participant's answers.

Table 1 shows the correct answer rate of all of the participants. Here, when the differences between the direction of the presented stimuli and the participant's answer are less than 50 degrees, these answers were determined as the correct answers. As can be seen, the number of participants whose correct answer rates were more than 50% was only four.

Figures 8 (a) and (b) show the examples of the participants' answers and the correct answers of participant nos. 4 and 8, the highest and lowest correct answer rates.

5.2 CoG Movements

Next, we measured the CoG movements of the participants to evaluate the effects on the CoG positions by the haptic stimuli.

We first calculated the average positions of the CoG movements during a period from two seconds before the stimuli presentation timing to the stimuli presentation timing, and we normalized the measured CoG movements using the average position. Then, we calculated the average and standard deviation of the CoG movements during a period from the stimuli presentation timing to two seconds after the stimuli presentation timing.

Table 2 and Fig. 9 show the average of the CoG movements under each stimulus presentation pattern. Here, participant no. 7 was excluded from the analysis due to an error in the data acquisition. From these results, we can confirm that the CoG movements of the Y direction are larger than the ones of X direction. However, we cannot confirm the tendencies of the CoG movements that correspond with the directions of the tactile stimuli.

Table 1. Correct answer rate

No	Correct answer rate
1	0.33
2	0.25
3	0.58
4	0.67
5	0.33
6	0.58
7	0.50
8	0.17
9	0.25
10	0.17
Ave	0.38

Table 2. CoG movements

No	Front ave.X	ave.Y	Back ave.X	ave.Y	Right ave.X	ave.Y	Left ave.X	ave.Y
1	−0.5	3.3	−0.5	−3.0	−0.1	4.5	−0.1	−2.1
2	0.1	0.3	0.1	1.9	0.1	0.4	−0.2	0.2
3	4.5	−4.8	−0.5	−0.0	1.5	−8.0	0.7	−5.6
4	−0.2	−0.1	1.3	1.0	0.5	−2.0	0.4	2.0
5	−0.6	2.4	2.3	1.5	0.7	−3.0	0.6	−2.6
6	1.3	9.1	3.0	−6.3	−0.4	−4.2	−0.1	0.3
7	—	—	—	—	—	—	—	—
8	−0.9	−3.9	0.1	−1.0	0.6	0.3	−0.5	1.7
9	0.5	0.4	1.2	−0.5	0.4	−2.7	1.1	0.7
10	−2.7	−5.7	−3.0	−5.8	3.1	1.1	0.8	2.0
Ave	0.17	0.11	0.44	−1.36	0.71	−1.51	0.30	−0.38
S.D	1.96	4.61	1.77	3.04	1.05	3.59	0.54	2.57

5.3 Discussion

From the subjective analysis in Sect. 5.1, we confirmed that the four participants could answer the correct directions with more than 50% accuracy when the participants were presented with the haptic stimuli by our device. In the preliminary experiment in [8], we already confirmed that some of the users could feel a pulling sensation. From these results, all users could not understand the present pulling sensation by our device, but some of the users could recognize the sensation. We need to examine which factors can affect the effectiveness of our device.

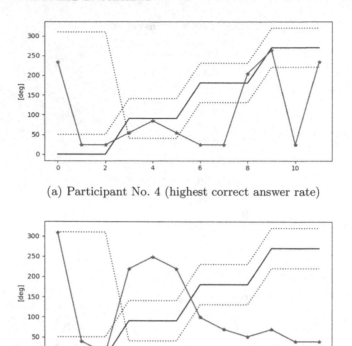

(a) Participant No. 4 (highest correct answer rate)

(b) Participant No. 8 (lowest correct answer rate)

Fig. 8. Participant's answers and stimuli directions. The red line denotes the participant's answers. The blue solid line denotes the direction of the haptic stimuli, the dotted lines show the range of the correct answers. (Color figure online)

From the quantitative analysis in Sect. 5.2, we cannot confirm the tendencies of the CoG movements that correspond to the directions of the tactile stimuli. Even when we focus on the participants who could recognize the pulling sensation, we cannot observe such tendencies of the CoG movements. This means that even if the participants could recognize the pulling sensation, the CoG positions could not be affected by the haptic stimuli.

Here, considering Shima's method [5], the haptic stimuli were presented to the participants corresponding to the postural changes of the participants, and the postural stability could be achieved. Thus, we will investigate a scheme in which haptic stimuli are presented corresponding to the participant's postural changes.

We are now investigating a device that combines the pneumatic actuator arrays (the device used in this paper) and the vibration motors. Through these investigations, we will pursue a more effective method for postural/walking stabilization.

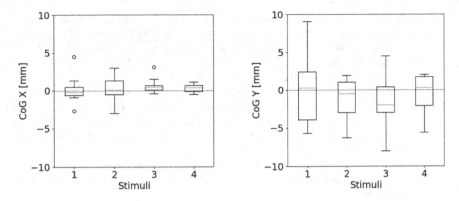

Fig. 9. CoG movements (left: X direction, right: Y direction)

6 Conclusion

In this paper, we proposed and examined a method for improving walking stability by using a wearable tactile expression mechanism based on a pneumatic actuator array.

In the current experiment, only standing situations were considered, and the evaluations were conducted both subjectively and quantitatively. The movements of the participant's CoG during the haptic stimuli presentation were measured by using a Nintendo Wii balance board. In addition, we obtained the participants' answers about the directions in which the participant felt pulled by the stimuli. Unfortunately, we were not able to obtain the CoG movement results showing the effectiveness of the proposed method. However, we confirmed that the four participants could answer the correct directions with more than 50% accuracy.

Future works will include further investigation of the experimental results and the effects of tactile stimuli on standing/walking stability in detail. In addition, we will investigate a scheme in which haptic stimuli are presented corresponding to the participant's postural changes.

Acknowledgments. This research was supported by JSPS KAKENHI Grant Numbers JP15H01698 and JP18K11383.

References

1. Baldan, A., Alouche, S., Araujo, I., Freitas, S.: Effect of light touch on postural sway in individuals with balance problems: a systematic review. Gait Posture **40**(1), 1–10 (2014)
2. Ivanenko, Y.P., Grasso, R., Lacquaniti, F.: Effect of gaze on postural responses to neck proprioceptive and vestibular stimulation in humans. J. Physiol. **519**(1), 301–314 (1999)

3. Ivanenko, Y.P., Grasso, R., Lacquaniti, F.: Neck muscle vibration makes walking humans accelerate in the direction of gaze. J. Physiol. **525**(3), 803–814 (2000)
4. Kaminoyama, H., Matsuo, T., Hattori, F., Susami, K., Kuwahara, N., Abe, S.: Walk navigation system using photographs for people with dementia. In: Smith, M.J., Salvendy, G. (eds.) Human Interface 2007. LNCS, vol. 4558, pp. 1039–1049. Springer, Heidelberg (2007). https://doi.org/10.1007/978-3-540-73354-6_113
5. Shima, K., Shimatani, K., Sugie, A., Kurita, Y., Kohno, R., Tsuji, T.: Virtual light touch contact: a novel concept for mitigation of body sway. In: 2013 7th International Symposium on Medical Information and Communication Technology (ISMICT), pp. 108–111. IEEE (2013)
6. Suzuki, K., Mito, G., Kawamoto, H., Hasegawa, Y., Sankai, Y.: Intention-based walking support for paraplegia patients with Robot Suit HAL. Adv. Robot. **21**(12), 1441–1469 (2007)
7. Tsuji, A., Yonezawa, T., Hiroshima, S.A., Kuwahara, N., Morimoto, K.: Proposal and evaluation of toilet timing suggestion methods for the elderly. Int. J. Adv. Comput. Sci. Appl. **5**(10), 140–145 (2014)
8. Yamazoe, H., Yonezawa, T.: A tactile expression mechanism using pneumatic actuator array for notification from wearable robots. In: Duffy, V.G. (ed.) DHM 2017. LNCS, vol. 10286, pp. 466–475. Springer, Cham (2017). https://doi.org/10.1007/978-3-319-58463-8_39
9. Yamazoe, H., Yonezawa, T.: Preliminary examination of walking stability improvement by wearable tactile expression mechanism. In: Proceedings of the 6th International Conference on Human-Agent Interaction, pp. 350–352 (2018)
10. Yonezawa, T., Yamazoe, H.: Wearable partner agent with anthropomorphic physical contact with awareness of user's clothing and posture. In: Proceedings of the 2013 International Symposium on Wearable Computers, pp. 77–80 (2013)

Applications for Exercising, Physical Therapy and Rehabilitation

Computer-Interfacing with Noninvasive Muscle Activity Diagnostic

Lawrence K. Lam[1](✉) and Wayne D. Kimura[2](✉)

[1] University of Washington – Bothell,
18115 Campus Way NE, Bothell, WA 98011, USA
llam@uw.edu
[2] STI Optronics, Inc, 2647 – 151st Place NE, Redmond, WA 98052, USA
wkimura@stioptronics.com

Abstract. Muscle rehabilitation is vitally important for patients suffering from muscle disorders, stroke, sports injuries, or atrophy due to serious illness. Physical therapy and other methods are typically used for the rehabilitation, but these methods lack a quantitative means for assessing the muscle performance as it responds to the therapy, which makes it difficult to optimize the procedures. To address this need, a noninvasive muscle activity (NMA) diagnostic is proposed in which laser light is sent through the skin into the muscle. Changes in the characteristics of the light passing through the muscle caused by physiologic tetanus are detected, thereby providing a direct, real-time measurement of the onset and degree of muscle contraction. Besides providing valuable data on the muscle performance during therapy, this diagnostic could provide feedback to a computer, which could use this to electrically stimulate the muscle tetanus in a controlled manner. This opens up the possibility of using this system to control muscle movement in paralyzed individuals. Using artificial intelligence, it is conceivable that the computer can learn the proper sequence for contracting multiple muscles in, say, the leg to enable walking. Other applications include using the diagnostic as part of a bio-feedback system where, for example, it can assist in muscle relaxation therapy, or for athletes it can help ensure balanced muscle strength to avoid injuries. By applying microelectronics and micro-photonics techniques, the NMA diagnostic could be designed as a compact, portable, and disposable adhesive unit attached to the skin.

Keywords: Muscle activity · Biomedical diagnostic · Computer-controlled muscles · Artificial intelligence

1 Introduction

Muscle rehabilitation is important for patients with muscle disorders. Muscle atrophy can be a serious and debilitating side-effect for seriously ill and stroke survival patients, which can complicate the recovery process and have lingering effects long after recovery from the illness [1]. Having the patient exercise their muscles may not be feasible if they are unconscious or sedated, or it may require assistance, which can be labor intensive and expensive. Thus, various mechanical schemes have been developed to assist in the rehabilitation process [2–4]. All these methods lack a quantitative means

This is a U.S. government work and not under copyright protection in the U.S.;
foreign copyright protection may apply 2020
V. G. Duffy (Ed.): HCII 2020, LNCS 12198, pp. 303–312, 2020.
https://doi.org/10.1007/978-3-030-49904-4_22

for assessing the muscle performance as it responds to the therapy, which makes it difficult to optimize the procedures. For example, spinal cord injury patients using locomat need to know how well they are maxing out muscle usage.

The conventional way for monitoring muscle activity is via electromyography (EMG), which uses probes inserted into the muscle tissue to measure the electrical activity of contracting muscles. This is an invasive technique that has many drawbacks, including pain, possible infection, and the inability to strenuously exercise the monitored muscle. Electrical impedance myography (EIM) is a noninvasive method for detecting tetanus activity that measures changes in the electrical resistance and reactance of the muscle tissue by applying surface electrodes to the skin, typically in directions parallel and orthogonal to the muscle filaments. As such, it tends to provide wide-area measurements and can be problematic when monitoring multiple muscles where the many electrodes are in close proximity to each other leading to possible inaccurate impedance measurements. The reliability and reproducibility of EIM is also highly dependent on how well the electrodes are attached to the skin, which can be further degraded by perspiration when the muscle is being exercised.

What is needed is a noninvasive muscle activity (NMA) diagnostic able to directly measure the degree of physiologic tetanus in real-time within multiple, well-defined localized regions that is not affected by effects, such as perspiration. The availability of such a diagnostic would enable monitoring the performance of muscles during the rehabilitation treatment, thereby providing valuable feedback information. It may also help improve the effectiveness of electrical stimulation as a method for muscle rehabilitation [5].

The availability of the NMA diagnostic also opens the door to possible new "smart" muscle therapies, whereby the diagnostic sends muscle activity data to a computer. This would permit a feedback system to be established in which the computer utilizes the data to control the muscles by applying traditional electro-motor stimulation (EMS) techniques [6]. One possible application of this marriage between the NMA diagnostic and computer is using the system to control muscle movement in paralyzed individuals. EMS is a common practice in these individuals to help combat muscle atrophy; however, there lacks a way to monitor the degree and duration of the tetanus. The NMA diagnostic would enable the ability to monitor the muscle activity and with it the possibility for a computer to actively control the muscle contractions. Using artificial intelligence (AI), it is conceivable that the computer can learn the proper sequence for contracting multiple muscles in, say, the leg to enable walking.

Another potential application of the NMA diagnostic is as part of a bio-feedback system where, for example, it can assist in muscle relaxation therapy, or for athletes it can help during the recovery from injuries or to ensure balanced muscle strength to avoid injuries.

The global physiotherapy equipment market size was $18.6 billion in 2018 with the lion's share of this to treat musculoskeletal ailments [7]. The NMA diagnostic could be eventually designed as a compact, portable, and disposable system with multiple sensing heads that can be strapped around, say, arms or legs, and the output from the sensing heads sent via fiber optics to a central microprocessor. Thus, this configuration for the NMA diagnostic would make it usable by hospitals, health clinics, doctor's offices, and sports clinics.

2 Noninvasive Muscle Activity Diagnostic

The NMA diagnostic probes the muscle tissue through the skin using laser light where the muscle tetanus changes the characteristics of the light passing through the muscle. Hence, detecting these changes can be directly correlated with the muscle contraction. This basic technique has already been demonstrated by Belau, *et al.* [8] where they used near-infrared (NIR) diffusing-wave spectroscopy (DWS). They used a diode laser (single longitudinal mode) emitting light at 802 nm that is coupled into a multimode fiber (MMF). This sends NIR light through the skin and into the muscle tissue where some of the light backscatters from the muscle tissue and reemerges through the skin. A bundle of 32 single-mode fibers (SMF) collects the scattered light from the muscle tissue. Belau, *et al.* used 32 individual avalanche photodiodes (APDs) to detect the output from the fibers, performed an autocorrelation of the signals, and analyzed the results with a PC.

While DWS is certainly a viable technique for noninvasive detection of muscle activity, it requires a significant amount of computational analysis to convert the raw autocorrelation data into useful information about the muscle activity, for example, converting the time-dependent shear motions into the corresponding muscle strain. Our scheme greatly simplifies the detection/analysis process by not relying on DWS and instead it relies on one of two other optical phenomena that occur within muscle tissue. The first phenomenon is polarization changes associated with birefringence of the muscle filaments during tetanus and the second is refractive index changes caused by the influx of Ca^{2+} ions during tetanus. Note this is entirely different from using fluorescent dyes to detect Ca^{2+} ions [9].

2.1 Birefringence Changes Caused by Tetanus

It is well-known that muscle tissue displays birefringence effects during tetanus where the index of refraction varies depending on whether the light is polarized parallel or perpendicular to the muscle filament axis [10, 11]. This is caused by axial rotation of the head domain of the myosin cross-bridge. During tetanus, the heads bind to actin with their long axis more perpendicular to the filament axis. Irving [10] performed extensive birefringence measurements during tetanic contractions of frog leg muscle fibers.

For our NMA diagnostic, polarized light would be sent through the skin and into the muscle tissue in a similar arrangement as used for DWS. A polarizer will filter the diffusely transmitted light. The birefringence will cause the amount of light detected through the polarizer to change depending on whether the muscle is relaxed or contracted. This has the advantage of being simple to implement compared to the auto-correlation and complex analysis associated with the DWS method. This basic idea was demonstrated on a mite [12].

A key question is whether the diffuse scattering of the laser light through the muscle tissue and skin will significantly disrupt the polarization of the light. The well-developed field of laser polarity of biological tissues [13] routinely deals with this issue. Sankaran, *et al.* [14] performed measurements on muscle tissue and phantoms to determine how well polarized light propagates through these materials and preserves its polarization. They found that linearly polarized light will travel through 1.5 cm of muscle while preserving ≈90% of its polarization. To quote from their paper, "the polarized portion of the light exiting the sample remained in its initial polarization state" [14]. Thus, this indicates it should be possible to detect birefringence changes after the light travels through the muscle and skin.

2.2   Refractive Index Changes Caused by Tetanus

During muscle tetanus, the concentration of Ca^{2+} ions within the muscle sarcomeres changes from ~ 250 nM to up to ~ 20 μM [15]. This represents a ~ 80 times change in the Ca^{2+} ions concentration. If we can assume the Ca^{2+} ions are analogous to free carrier holes in semiconductors, then we can apply Drude-Zener theory to estimate the change in the index of refraction Δn caused by the presence of free carriers. In semiconductors, this is given by [16]

$$\Delta n = -\frac{q^2 \lambda^2}{2\pi^2 c^2 \varepsilon_0 n} \left(\frac{\Delta P}{m_{ch}^*} \right), \tag{1}$$

where q is the electronic charge, λ is the wavelength, ΔP is the density of injected/depleted holes, c is the speed of light, ε_0 is free space permittivity, n is the refractive index of the material, and m_{ch}^* is the effective conductivity mass of the holes. The "holes" in our case are the Ca^{2+} ions and their double charge has already been accounted for in Eq. 1. Note the index change scales as λ^2 ; hence, it strongly favors using long wavelengths.

All the parameters on the right side of Eq. 1 are either known or can be chosen, except for m_{ch}^*, the effective conductivity mass of the Ca^{2+} ions, which we believe is not known. It represents the equivalent mass of the Ca^{2+} ions as they move through the tissue and undergo various biochemical interactions, such as binding to other molecules. Nonetheless, if we assume for the sake of this discussions that m_{ch}^* is roughly the atomic mass of calcium, i.e., 40.078 amu (i.e., 6.7×10^{-26} kg), and we assume $\Delta P = 20$ μM for the Ca^{2+} ion concentration, then for $\lambda = 0.3$ mm (1 THz light), which transmits well through tissue, we find Eq. 1 yields $\Delta n = 8 \times 10^{-5}$. When $\Delta P = 250$ nM, this refractive index change will be 80 times smaller.

Hence, this relative change in the refractive index should manifest itself as a detectable change in the character of the light transmitted through the muscle. For example, a change in the refractive index will cause the light to refract differently during tetanus as the light passes through the muscle. A photodetector sensing the transmitted light will measure a relative change in the transmitted light. Note, unlike the birefringence method, this scheme does not require using or detecting polarized light. The phototransceiver can be packaged in a pair along with flexible electronics into a very compact adhesive unit on the skin to make a portable and disposable device.

We should emphasize that it is not uncommon for m_{ch}^* to be significantly less than the mass of the particle since it reflects the effective net result of the particles interacting with the medium. This will tend to increase the value of Δn.

3   Possible Proof-of-Principle Experiment

As mentioned, it has already been shown that birefringence during muscle tetanus alters the polarization of the laser light and that diffuse scattering by the muscle tissue does not drastically alter the polarization of the transmitted light. However, there is a need to demonstrate that this is still true when these two effects are integrated into a system for noninvasively detecting muscle activity, i.e., directing laser light through the skin into the muscle tissue, and detecting the change in polarization of the light that reemerges from the skin during tetanus. For the change in refractive index method, there is the more difficult challenge of detecting whether any significant change of refractive index occurs during tetanus, which is equivalent to determining, indirectly, the effective conductivity mass of the Ca^{2+} ions.

As Irving demonstrated [10], experiments can be performed on frog legs to exa-mine the aforementioned issues. Using frogs will enable initiating and detecting muscle tetanus, which is not possible with phantoms. Figure 1 illustrates the basic setup for the experiment. The polarized output from a pulsed Nd:YAG laser is focused into an optical fiber (delivery fiber) with the distal end of the fiber secured to the frog leg using an elastic band. This laser emits light at 1.06 μm, which will penetrate well through the tissue. A half-wave ($\lambda/2$) plate will be used to rotate the polarization so that the polarization direction of the light entering the frog leg can be adjusted to be either parallel or perpendicular to the muscle fibers.

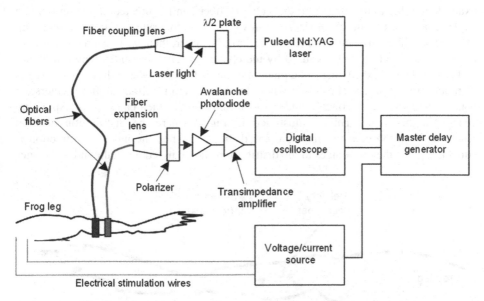

Fig. 1. Schematic layout of proposed frog leg tetanus experiment.

Attached on the frog leg close to the fiber delivering the laser light will be another optical fiber (sensing fiber) for collecting the diffuse scattered light passing through the muscle. The output from this fiber is sent through a polarization analyzer, which permits determining the change of the polarization of the light traveling through the muscle. This light is detected using an avalanche photodiode (APD) connected to a transimpedance amplifier, which is capable of sensing very low levels of laser light. The output from the amplifier can then be captured using a digital oscilloscope or, if needed, a lock-in amplifier can be used. A master delay generator will control the triggering of the laser and oscilloscope relative to the tetanus-inducing voltage applied to the leg.

Tetanus will be controlled using electrodes connected to the sciatic nerve and outer leg. The output level from the voltage/current source will be adjusted to achieve maximal stimulus of the gastrocnemius muscle. Having the optical fibers secured to the leg using the elastic bands will ensure the alignment of the fibers on the leg remains constant when the leg abruptly contracts during tetanus.

For the birefringence tests, the amount of light detected by the photodiode should change when the muscle is relaxed versus contracted, and the relative amount of this change should depend on whether the incoming light is polarized along or orthogonal to the muscle fibers and on the rotation angle of the analyzer polarizer. Thus, these parameters will be varied in order to maximize the observed change. Once this has been done, the next step is to vary the distance between the delivery and sensing fibers on the leg in order to provide data on how this distance impacts the received signal strength. The amount of laser energy being sent through the delivery fiber can also be varied.

The same apparatus shown in Fig. 1 can also be used to investigate changes in the index of refraction caused by the release of Ca^{2+} ions into the muscle sarcomeres. For example, the light emerging from the delivery fiber can be directed at a semi-oblique angle relative to the muscle as depicted in Fig. 2. Due to scattering, the light entering the muscle will diverge into a cone-like pattern; however, there will be a mean angle of this cone relative to the fiber caused by the change in refractive index between the air and tissue. This is exactly the same phenomenon that occurs when a laser beam passes from air into, say, a vessel of water where the laser beam is refracted after it enters the water. Changes in the refractive index of the muscle will then cause a corresponding change in this angle. This is illustrated in Fig. 2 where the distribution of light emerging from the delivery fiber is colored in green when the index of refraction is equal to n_1, and then it changes to the distribution shown in red when the index changes

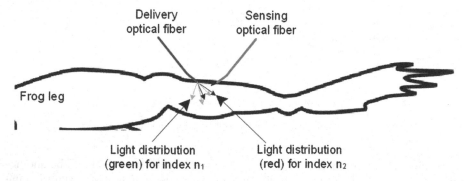

Fig. 2. Close-up detail illustrating changes in mean propagation angle of light being refracted while travelling the through muscle due to changes in the refractive index. (Color figure online)

to n_2. The sensing fiber will tend to detect more light from the red distribution than the green one. It is also possible to position the sensing fiber on the opposite of the leg to observe changes in the transmitted light.

As shown in Eq. 1, the change in refractive index scales as the square of the laser wavelength; hence, it strongly favors using long wavelengths. For example, a THz source could be used, which emits mm-wavelength light that penetrates well through biological tissue [17]. Since optical fibers are not available for delivering the THz light, a THz lens system could be used to focus the THz light into the tissue. Various options are available for detecting the THz light, including video cameras sensitive to far-infrared radiation [18, 19].

For both experiments, changes in the optical signal with the strength of the tetanus would be determined, since it is important to not only detect the onset of tetanus, but also its relative strength. The strength of the frog leg tetanus can be varied by adjusting the amount of voltage applied to the leg.

Once the viability of either the birefringence method, change in refractive index method, or both methods have been demonstrated, the next step would be to build a prototype diagnostic system that could be tested on animals (e.g., mice) or human subjects. It is likely we would switch to using a near-infrared (NIR) laser diode for the laser source, similar to the one used by Belau, *et al.* because of its compact size and low cost. There are various options for automating the conversion of the photodiode output signal into a form that indicates muscle tetanus strength.

4   Computer Control of Muscle Tetanus

Functional electrical stimulation (FES) is commonly used to provide people who are paralyzed with postural support and the ability to exercise their muscles to counter atrophy. Computers can be programmed to control the FES in order to more optimally achieve the desired results. For example, muscle fatigue can be undesirable, which means the computer needs to adjust the frequency and duration of the FES in order to avoid muscle fatigue [20]. But, without a means for quantifying the degree of muscle tetanus during each contraction, the frequency and duration can only be prepro-grammed into the computer control software using best-guess values. Obviously, this makes it difficult to accurately customize the FES for each individual patient and their particular muscular condition. It is also dependent on the experience and opinion of the therapist entering the values into the computer program.

The NMA diagnostic would be able to provide quantitative, real-time data on the degree of muscle tetanus, which can be used as input to the computer program. For example, the NMA diagnostic will detect that the muscle is beginning to show signs of fatigue. The computer program can then gradually decrease the frequency and duration of the FES, analogous to the cool-down routine followed by athletes. Conversely, the NMA diagnostic might indicate that the muscle is not being contracted sufficiently, which will cause the computer program to increase the frequency and duration of the FES. Thus, this will enable highly optimized therapy customized to each individual patient and how well they are responding to the treatment during the FES session.

Going to the next logical step, FES along with the NMA diagnostic can be applied to whole groups of muscles, for example, all the major muscles in the upper and lower parts of the leg. Using the NMA diagnostic as a feedback guide, the computer using artificial intelligence (AI) will trigger the FES in each muscle in order to achieve smooth retraction and extension of the entire leg. This is what is ideally needed to maintain muscle tone and strength of the entire leg.

This potential of combining NMA diagnostic technology with neuroprosthesis opens up exciting, new opportunities related to brain-computer interfaces (BCI) [21]. As described thus far, the computer receives feedback from the NMA diagnostic, but the computer is acting essentially independent of the patient's control. Using BCI, it is possible for the paralyzed patient to now control the computer, which then controls the muscle contractions using AI and feedback from the NMA diagnostic. For example, the patient, using various existing BCI interfaces to their brain [21], would instruct the computer to, say, grab an object with the patient's hand. This is illustrated in Fig. 3.

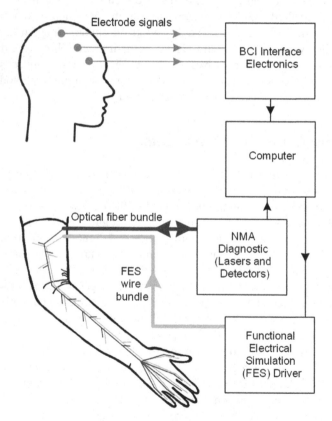

Fig. 3. Schematic layout for possible usage of brain-computer interfacing (BCI) to control muscle tetanus using functional electrical simulation (FES) coupled with feedback from the NMA diagnostic.

In this simplistic example, electrodes attached to the patient's head would be used to detect commands from the brain similar to what is already done to permit patients to create audio messages or control movement of the powered wheelchair [21]. The computer would be programmed to interpret these signals as commands to move, in this case, the arm and hand muscles. It sends the appropriate commands to the FES driver to contract muscles in the arm and hand in the proper sequence and intensity to cause coordinated arm and hand movement. The NMA diagnostic provides the feedback to the computer that is necessary to ensure this coordinated movement. Note, this basic scheme is analogous to that utilized in robotic arms used in manufacturing where appropriate feedback is critical to ensure the arm is moving correctly. Until now, this extensive feedback from an array of multiple muscles has not been possible in a noninvasive manner for biological systems. Our NMA diagnostic now makes this possible, which is why a system as depicted in Fig. 3 is now feasible.

As depicted in Fig. 3, an arm-length glove can cover the arm and hand. Embedded in the glove are the wires from the FES driver for simulating specific muscle groups along the arm and on the hand. Also embedded inside the glove are optical fibers for delivering the laser light to the skin and sensing the light backscattered from the muscle. These optical fibers are connected to the NMA diagnostic, which sends data on the state of the muscle tetanus to the computer. This real-time feedback allows the computer to make appropriate adjustments to the FES driver.

5   Conclusion

The NMA diagnostic coupled with computer-control and AI offers a radical change in the paradigm for muscle rehabilitation and regaining body movement for paralyzed patients. By providing critical feedback information, the NMA diagnostic is the last link needed for a complete automated system for musculoskeletal activation and control. It is hoped that a means to support the development of the NMA diagnostic will emerge in the near future.

Acknowledgments. The authors would like to thank University of Washington - Bothell STEM division for the travel grant that allowed L. K. Lam to attend and present this paper at the HCII2020 conference.

References

1. Puthucheary, Z., Harridge, S., Hart, N.: Skeletal muscle dysfunction in critical care: wasting, weakness, and rehabilitation strategies. Crit. Care Med. **38**, S676–S682 (2010)
2. Needham, D.M., Truong, A., Fan, E.: Technology to enhance physical rehabilitation of critically ill patients. Crit. Care Med. **37**, S436–S441 (2009)
3. Sugar, T.G., et al.: Design and control of RUPERT: A device for robotic upper extremity repetitive therapy. IEEE Trans. Neural Sys. Rehab. Eng. **15**, 336–346 (2007)
4. Burgar, C.G., Lum, P.S., Shor, P.C., Machiel Van der Loos, H.F.: Development of robots for rehabilitation therapy: the Palo Alto VA/Stanford experience. J. Rehab. Res. Dev. **37**, 663–673 (2000)

5. Hummelsheim, H., Maier-Loth, M.L., Eickhof, C.: The functional value of electrical muscle stimulation for the rehabilitation of the hand in stroke patients. Scand. J. Rehab. Med. **29**, 3–10 (1997)
6. Lloyd, T., De Domenico, G., Strauss, G.R., Singer, K.: A Review of the use of electro-motor stimulation in human muscle. Aust. J. Physiotherapy **32**, 18–30 (1986)
7. Physiotherapy Equipment Market Size, Share & Trends Analysis Report by Application (Musculoskeletal), by Type (CPM, Electric Stimulation, Ultrasound), by End Use (Clinic, Hospital), by Demographic, and Segment Forecasts, 2019–2026. Grand View Research, May 2019
8. M. Belau, M. Ninck, G. Hering, L. Spinelli, D. Contini, A. Torricelli, and T. Gisler., "Noninvasive observation of skeletal muscle contraction using near-infrared time-resolved reflectance and diffusing-wave spectroscopy," J. Biomedical Optics **15**, 057007 (2010)
9. Cheng, H., Lederer, W.J.: Calcium sparks. Physiol. Rev. **88**, 1491–1545 (2008)
10. Irving, M.: Birefringence changes associated with isometric contraction and rapid shortening steps in frog skeletal muscle fibres. J. Physiol. **472**, 127–156 (1993)
11. Haskell, R.C., Carlson, F.D., Blank, P.S.: Form birefringence of muscle. Biophys. J. **56**, 401–413 (1989)
12. Aronson, J.F.: Polarized light observations on striated muscle contraction in a mite. J. Cell Bio. **32**, 169–179 (1967)
13. Ushenko, Alexander G., Pishak, Vasilii P.: Laser polarimetry of biological tissues: principles and applications. In: Tuchin, Valery V. (ed.) Handbook of Coherent Domain Optical Methods, pp. 93–138. Springer, New York (2004). https://doi.org/10.1007/0-387-29989-0_3
14. Sankaran, V., Everett, M.J., Maitland, D.J., Walsh Jr., J.T.: Comparison of polarized-light propagation in biological tissue and phantoms. Opt. Lett. **24**, 1044–1046 (1999)
15. Gehlert, S., Block, W., Suhr, F.: Ca^{2+} -dependent regulations and signaling in skeletal muscle: from electro-mechanical coupling to adaptation. Int. J. Mol. Sci. **16**, 1066–1095 (2015)
16. Seeger, K.: Semiconductor Physics. Springer-Verlag, NY (1985)
17. Handley, J.W., Fitzgerald, A.J., Loeffler, T., Seibert, K., Berry, E., Boyle, R.D.: Potential medical applications of THz imaging. In: Claridge, E., Bamber, J., Marlow, K (eds.) Proceedings Medical Image Understanding and Analysis, pp. 17–20 (2001)
18. Butler, N.R., Blackwell, R.J., Murphy, R., Silva, R.J., Marshall, C.A.: Low-cost uncooled microbolometer imaging system for dual use. SPIE Proc. **2552**, 583–591 (1995)
19. Lee, A.W.M., Hu, Q.: Real-time, continous-wave terahertz imaging by use of a microbolometer focal-point array. Opt. Lett. **30**, 2563 (2005)
20. Wise, A.K., Morgan, D.L., Gregory, J.E., Proske, U.: Fatigue in mammalian skeletal muscle stimulated under computer control. J. Appl. Physiol. **90**, 189–197 (2001)
21. Wolpaw, J.R., Birbaumer, N., McFarland, D.J., Pfurtscheller, G., Vaughan, T.M.: Brain–computer interfaces for communication and control. Clin. Neurophy. **113**, 767–791 (2002)

Wireless Aerobic Exercise Monitoring System Based on Multimodal Sensors

Xiang-yu Liu[1], Xing-wei Wang[2], Hai-qiang Duan[2], Guang-hao Li[2], and Mei-yu Zhou[1(✉)]

[1] School of Art Design and Media, East China University of Science and Technology, Shanghai, China
Yl2170017@mail.ecust.edu.cn, zhoutc_2003@163.com
[2] School of Information Science and Technology, Fudan University, Shanghai, China

Abstract. Wearable human-interactive devices have used in many application scenarios, such as medical, security, and fitness. With the emerging use of wearable sensors, they make it possible that people can monitor their physical data with accurate and reliable information in exercise, thereby ensuring exercise intensity within risk-free and moderate physical pressure. Heart rate was acquired by the photoplethysmography (PPG) module to evaluate Heart-rate recovery (HRR); this index regarded as the effectiveness of the aerobic exercise. Respiration could also be proposed as a marker of training intensity; the authors attempted using the non-invasive method to acquire the respiration rate in order to evaluate the strength of aerobic exercise. Global Position System (GPS) module was used to offer location information during and after sports, so as to provide and to match route information in intensity evaluation. In this study, the authors integrate three main signals (heart rate, respiration, and location information) into a fanny bag based on multimodal sensors and wireless transmission module. Moreover, we construct an online monitoring system for showing the signals during and after the aerobic exercise in order to help the athlete and the amateur to evaluate the intensity of aerobic exercise and the effectiveness of sports, and to improve their sports performance.

Keywords: Multimodal-sensors · Wearable device · Aerobic exercise · Human-computer interaction

1 Introduction

Wearable human-interactive devices are a new application trend in human activity monitoring; they can improve human comfort, convenience and security, and have a wide range of applications for human in daily activities monitoring [1]. The basic human activity monitoring system can be described by a diagram; (a simple one is shown in Fig. 1). With the wireless module developing, various human activity monitoring devices have the wireless data transmitting capability; the physical signal can be sent to a central processing unit through a transceiver (a simple diagram is shown in Fig. 2). According to different monitoring tasks, different types of sensors are used in specific application scenarios [2]. The physical data from different sensors are

© Springer Nature Switzerland AG 2020
V. G. Duffy (Ed.): HCII 2020, LNCS 12198, pp. 313–324, 2020.
https://doi.org/10.1007/978-3-030-49904-4_23

collected by a processor and displayed on personal computers and cellphones (the human activity monitoring system is shown in Fig. 3). These simple wearable devices are used by people in many practical scenarios, such as running, swimming, and cycling, where people need to know the physical value and intensity evaluation.

Fig. 1. The simple diagram of wearable sensing devices

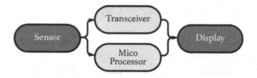

Fig. 2. The simple diagram of wireless wearable sensing devices

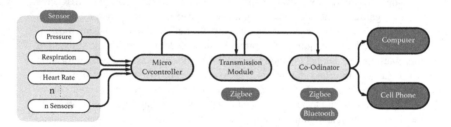

Fig. 3. The diagram representation of the human activity monitoring system.

1.1 The System of Human Activity Monitoring and Public Health Recommendations

The system of human monitoring activity is an active research field, and numerous works has been researching for many years. For the best we know, there are many principles should take into consideration before starting the research: 1) type of sensors to be used in study and experiment; 2) type of wireless module to be employed in the transmission section; 3) kind of activity monitoring to be selected; 4) activity feature extraction 5) light, inexpensive and smart sensors application; 6) multimodal integration 7) ability to be used with mobile devices; 8) user-friendly. According to these principles and considering the demands of sports trainers [1–3].

Public health recommendations suggests a moderate aerobic exercise for at least 30 min during a day, which can be regarded as a way to protect health [4, 5]. However, these suggestions have stirred divergence among exercise experts, based on the current studies, the meaning of "moderate exercise" is still doubtful [6–8]. Recent researches have shown that various factors could influence the persistence of regular exercises, such as pleasure and intensity, and relative behaviors, such as desire. One of the essential experiences is that the average people prefer lower aerobic exercise activity (i.e., less intensity and shorter duration) to high-intensity exercise, thus to induce higher involvement and participation rates [9, 10]. Despite the fact that most health recommendations mentioned above were based on a theoretical perspective instead of the practical one. Actually, exercise suggestions should depend on personal physical fitness, so as to avoid the risk of exercise, and to improve athletic performance.

1.2 Aerobic Exercise and Sports Intensity Based on Personal Physical Signal

Aerobic exercise has been regarding as a significant factor in the renovation and prevention of long-term healthcare [11]. Furthermore, previous research has shown the physical benefits of habitual aerobic exercise, such as enhanced psychological performance and self-confidence, greater sleep efficiency and quality [12], and a reduction of anger, psychological feeling of time urgency, and pressure [9, 13]. Clearly, the physiological and psychological benefits associated with regular aerobic exercise.

Physical signals as an evaluation index of exercise have been used in various aerobic training in recent years. Many athletes and athletic amateurs have pay attention to their individual physical data during sports training; the data could reflect the performance during aerobic exercise and recovery. These promoted the practical application of wearable equipment in aerobic exercise scenarios.

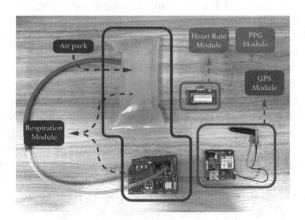

Fig. 4. Multimodal sensors module in this study.

Personal physical data is regarded as an index of kinematic basement [14]. In the area of aerobic exercise training, it is important to understand the reasons behind injuries and fatigue [15]. Therefore, to acquire the physical data, wearable sensors have become popular in many application scenarios and provided accurate and reliable data on kinematic activities [1]. In the meantime, the use of wearable sensors has made it possible to offer the kinematic parameters of human activities and behaviors in aerobic exercises, such as heart rate, respiration, and sports circuit [16]. The multimodal sensors used in this study are shown in Fig. 4.

1.3   Wearable Devices and Industrial Design

The wearable device, as a new trending of application, has used in daily physical sign monitoring field and trained people to continuously monitor their individual health management [17]. In spite of this fast-developing of wearable devices, there are some limitations in the practical application. In the data collection part, each specific physical sign can be simply acquired by a limited device; this leads to the low convenience in application scenarios. From a view of user experience (UX), the low using convenience leads to low user experience, and people have to use different kinds of devices to survey their physical signs during or after sports. Therefore, these limitations have prompted a new trending of multi-sensors applications in data fusion, especially in the fitness and health care. Moreover, systematic and long-term monitoring of individual physiological data is considered as one of the ways to improve exercise performance.

From one view of design, systematic and long-term monitoring of individual physiological data base on the development of multimodal-sensors and wireless transmission. Multimodal detection of individual physical data has always been a critical demand among the amateur. On the one hand, people want to monitor their exercise status and to improve their sports performance through the physical signals and to monitor some important physiological data while aerobic exercise will reduce the risk of sports injuries. On the other hand, people have certain requirements for device about sensor integration and signal multimodality, so convenience may be an essential consideration for people during aerobic exercise, carrying too much equipment is a great risk to their sports safety.

From another view of design, storage may be a common demand during the aerobic exercise for the athlete and amateur, especially in the long-distance training, such as marathon and cycling, or urban low-intensity sports. The storage was used to store personal items and sports supplies during the training; in some way, storage space could also provide a few physical supports for the people. In this study, we attempted combing individual physical signal and the functional storage in a wearable device.

After an investigation of commercial sports equipment, a fanny bag was chosen as the ideal product for the research. Firstly, some sensors used in this research need cling to the skin, so comfort and stability were chosen as high priorities during the investigation. Secondly, as mentioned above, people who involved in exercise training need a space to store their items and sports supplies. Thirdly, the multimodal sensor will be held in some space, and the pack could provide the functional storage to contain the sensor.

2   Method

In this study, we attempted combing three main signals (heart rate, respiration, and GPS) into a wearable device (fanny pack) for evaluating the intensity of exercise and tried structuring an aerobic monitoring system in order to analyze the physical status and exercise state. The technical route is shown in Fig. 5.

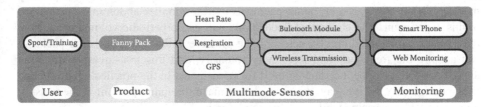

Fig. 5. Technical route of multimodal-sensors aerobic exercise monitoring application.

2.1   The Measuring System of Heart Rate During Aerobic Exercise

Measuring heart rate is probably the most conventional method used in the sports field, especially in aerobic exercise [12]. Relative heart rates are seen as a useful index of the effectiveness of aerobic exercise training and regarded as the decisive factor of endurance, mostly, in sports, the performance of aerobic exercise depends on the development of patience [13]. Under the maximal intensity of sports, training can be estimated by heart rate during and after the aerobic exercise with various wearable sensors. For now, using user-friendly methods to obtain an individual's heart rate during aerobic exercise is deemed as a method of endurance evaluations [14]. In this study, the heart rate is adopted as the index of exercise intensity.

Heart rate can be measured by biotelemetry directly, such as the Radiotelemetry, Photoplethysmography (PPG), Continuous Electrocardiogram (ECG) Recording, and Microcomputer [18]. The photoplethysmography (PPG) was selected to acquire the heart rate. PPG is widely used for evaluation of physical intensity during the aerobic exercise, because most continuous PPG devices are easy to set-up and it support person use freely during the outdoor training, especially for the long-distance runner and cycling sports.

2.2   Contact Based Respiration Monitoring Methods and Wearable Devices

As mentioned above, the heart rate primarily provides information about the intensity of aerobic exercise. However, certain exercise intensity also derived from changes in blood lactate concentration or respiratory. Respiration rate is a critical vital index for human due to its importance for human oxygen circulation [19], especially during exercise, without the particular oxygen-carbon distribution, an athlete will at the risk of hypoxic injury, and affected the exercise performance.

The contact respiration rate is based on one of the measurements as following: respiratory sound, airflow, chest and abdominal movements, CO2 and SpO2, and ECG [20]. For the best we know, chest and abdominal movements are used widely in aerobic training. Based on the chest and abdominal movement, chest straps were seen as a good way to acquire a respiration rate [20].

In this study, we use the pressure-sensing technology base on the abdominal movement to collect the respiration rate, in order to evaluate the intensity of aerobic exercise and establish the multi-sensors ambulatory monitoring system (respiratory module Fig. 6). For purposes, an air pack was used to monitor abdominal fluctuations in this experiment. The abdominal fluctuations will cause periodic volume changes in the air pack while breathing. By detecting the pressure at the outlet of the air pack, we can acquire the frequency and respiratory intensity, and this non-invasive detection technology will provide a certain comfort for participants in the practical environment. In the design part, by the way, the air pack can make the fanny pack fit at the waist, it also can provide certain stability during the exercise.

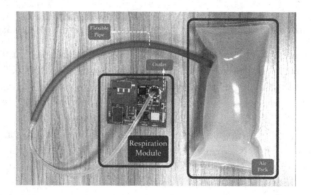

Fig. 6. The respiratory module used in this study.

2.3 Wireless Wearable Health Devices (WHDs) Using in the Aerobic Exercise Monitoring

Wearable health devices (WHDs) are the emerging technology using in daily life, and they make it possible that people can monitor their vital index and health status over the long term (weeks/months). Furthermore, WHDs are able to provide information about the state of movement during the exercise [21]. As a part of personal fitness, WHDs play an important role in long-term exercise intensity and fatigue monitoring. With the use of WHDs, they make it possible that people put their interest in health status monitoring, improving their performance of the exercise and reducing the risk of long-time sports [17].

Traditional physical signal collection of wearable health devices has serval limitations in practical scenarios. Firstly, in the practical aerobic exercise scene, the convenience of multimodal-signals acquisition is still doubtful. In previous attempts, the convenience of wearable sensors and devices was affected by the transmission line.

The participant who involved in the experiment reported a low amenity of acquisition devices. Secondly, the independence of multimodal-signal collection and transmission between different modules induce several perplexities in signal processing after the test. Thirdly, the integration of multimodal sensors in commercial devices is not ideal. Different methods acquire this leads to different vital signs, but it is few to integrate these signs into comprehensive analysis and monitoring.

In this study, we attempt integrating multimodal-sensors modules into the fanny pack for monitoring the vital signs during the aerobic exercise base on three main physical data (System diagram is shown in Fig. 7). In the view of physical data application. Heart rate (HR) was used for evaluating sports intensity and recovery. Respiration information was devoted to offering a dataset to assess the performance during and after the aerobic exercise. In the design part, the fanny pack offered the essential storage for the athlete and amateur to store their phones and supplies in the long-distance aerobic exercise, such as marathon and cycling.

Briefly, heart rate module (Supply voltage: 2.8 v; ADC output voltage: $0 \sim 2.8$ v; Power Consumption: Maximum Dissipation Current ≤ 20 mA;), Bluetooth 4.0 heart rate BLE module (Supply voltage: 2.0–3.6 v; Power Consumption: Maximum Dissipation Current ≤ 35 mA;) and abdominal respiration detection module (temperature: 5 °C $\sim$ 40 °C relative humidity: $18\% \sim 80\%$; atmospheric pressure: 80 kPa $\sim$ 150 kPa; voltage: DC 3.3 v $\sim$ 5 v; Stress/breathing effort dpi: 0.1 kPa; Sensor accuracy: ± 0.4 kPa/3 mmHg; Respiration rate and error: $\leq \pm 3$ times/min; Maximum Dissipation Current: ≤ 10 mA) are fixed inside on the pack belt.

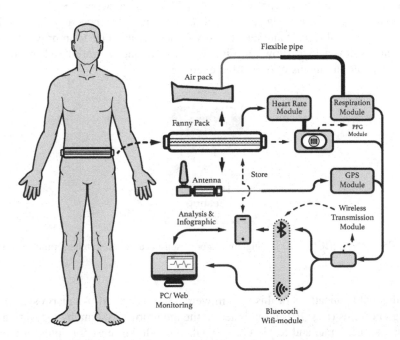

Fig. 7. Cycle diagram of multimodal-sensors system.

In our attempt, three healthy men (BMI < 25) were selected as subjects, and they wore the fanny bag (multimodal-sensor system, Fig. 8) while they were doing aerobic exercise. The multi-physical data was achieved under low intensity for 10 min.

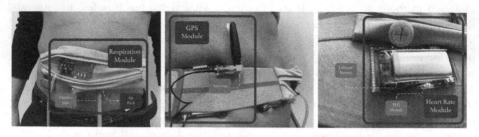

Fig. 8. Fanny pack (beta version) with multimodal-sensors modules

The experimental results were used the Kalman filter to remove motion interference noising and to obtain the respiratory rate and heart frequency. The wireless portable monitoring system for physical efficiency prediction will present in mobile application interaction.

3   Results and Conclusion

The fanny pack integrated a heart rate module (PPG), a respiratory module (pressure), a GPS module and wireless signal transmission module (Zigbee and Bluetooth) to monitor the physical signals and the intensity of aerobic exercise to improve the sports performance (project logo shown in Fig. 9). All components were fixed in the fanny pack to evaluate the intensity of aerobic exercise.

HCII 2020
Testing
Multimodal-sensors
aerobic exercise monitoring system

Fig. 9. Project logo (HCII 2020 Testing: multimodal-sensors aerobic exercise monitoring system)

Additional applications of this system were also considered. An alarm system, two warning interfaces (Fig. 10) are designed in the monitoring system, by measuring two-dimensional (heart rate and respiration) signals through the sensors (represent intensity of aerobic exercise), if heart rate exceeds 80% of maximum heart rate (set before) and respiratory rate exceeds 25 beats per minute, and 'warning' (Fig. 10.Left) alarm will be triggered. If the heart rate exceeds 90% of maximum heart rate (set before) and respiratory rate exceeds 30 beats per minute, and 'Danger' (Fig. 10.Right) alarm will be triggered.

Fig. 10. The warning interfaces on the cellphone (screenshot)

In this study, we proposed and demonstrated a wireless aerobic exercise monitoring system (cellphone Fig. 11 and PC Fig. 12) to evaluate the intensity of aerobic exercise. This system can help people to improve the performance of aerobic exercise and shown on the display Although cost-effective smart wearable devices were used in our daily life (such as smartwatch and smart bracelet), this system was attempted to integrate with the similar performance compared to other sensors fabricated by conventional multimodal sensors.

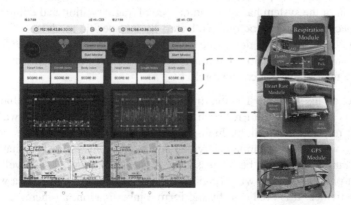

Fig. 11. The interface of monitoring system on the cellphone (screenshot)

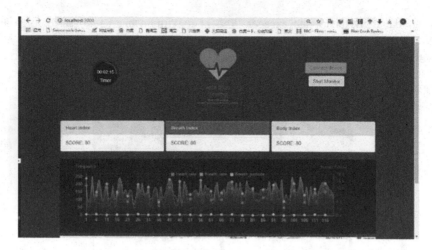

Fig. 12. The interface of monitoring system on the personal computer (screenshot)

Besides, the system should realize a new function for aerobic exercise monitoring. Although this study did not integrate other physical sensors such as gyroscope, gait stability, and electromyography, this attempt should play a constructive role in the future and contribute to human health care.

4 Limitation and Prospect

In this work, we proposed and designed a wearable monitoring system in a fanny pack to supervise the intensity of aerobic exercise to improve the performance of sports. We successfully acquired the physical date from 3 adult subjects, including their heart rate, respiratory information, and location signals, and presented these data on the system. Nevertheless, our work still has some limitations:

- The limitation of integration; we improved mature commercial modules for our study. Although their performance is stabilized during the signal acquisition, the integration of the system has a certain degree of fragmentation and complexity, due to the specific signal can be only collected by the specific module.
- The limitation of comfort; due to the fragmentation and complexity, the fanny pack was decreased some certain comfortable to wear during the experiment, which has great potential in subsequent research.

The prospect of this research: The multimodal sensors human fitness (aerobic exercise) monitoring is a vibrant field of research, and many inspire development was reported by previous research. More light, high-performance, and smart wearable devices for monitoring a wide range of human activities is needed in this field. The challenges we met by the current limit will be addressed in future technology. The development of light-weight physical sensors will bring a comfortable method to monitor a wide range of human activities. It is predicted by the formal investigation, an increase of interest and usages of wearable devices (including systems) in the future, and the cost of these devices and systems is also expected to fall due to wide application in the application.

References

1. Mukhopadhyay, S.C.: Wearable sensors for human activity monitoring: a review. IEEE Sensors J. **15**, 1321–1330 (2015). https://doi.org/10.1109/JSEN.2014.2370945
2. Honda, W., Harada, S., Arie, T., Akita, S., Takei, K.: Wearable, human-interactive, health-monitoring, wireless devices fabricated by macroscale printing techniques. Adv. Funct. Mater. **24**, 3299–3304 (2014). https://doi.org/10.1002/adfm.201303874
3. Dias, D., Paulo, J.: Wearable health devices—vital sign monitoring, systems and technologies. Sensors. **18**, 2414 (2018). https://doi.org/10.3390/s18082414
4. Blair, S.N., Connelly, J.C.: How much physical activity should we do? The case for moderate amounts and intensities of physical activity. Res. Q. Exerc. Sport **67**, 193–205 (1996). https://doi.org/10.1080/02701367.1996.10607943
5. Physical Activity and Public Health: A Recommendation From the Centers for Disease Control and Prevention and the American College of Sports Medicine, 6
6. Morris, J.N.: Exercise versus heart attack: questioning the consensus? Res. Q. Exerc. Sport **67**, 216–220 (1996). https://doi.org/10.1080/02701367.1996.10607947
7. Morris, J.N., Clayton, D.G., Everitt, M.G., Semmence, A.M., Burgess, E.H.: Exercise in leisure time: coronary attack and death rates. Heart **63**, 325–334 (1990). https://doi.org/10.1136/hrt.63.6.325
8. Lee, I.M.: Exercise intensity and longevity in men. The harvard alumni health study. JAMA, J. Am. Med. Assoc. **273**, 1179–1184 (1995). https://doi.org/10.1001/jama.273.15.1179
9. Ekkekakis, P., Petruzzello, S.J.: Acute aerobic exercise and affect: current status, problems and prospects regarding dose-response. Sports Med. **28**, 337–374 (1999). https://doi.org/10.2165/00007256-199928050-00005
10. Yeung, R.R.: The acute effects of exercise on mood state. J. Psychosom. Res. **40**, 123–141 (1996). https://doi.org/10.1016/0022-3999(95)00554-4
11. DiLorenzo, T.M., Bargman, E.P., Stucky-Ropp, R., Brassington, G.S., Frensch, P.A., LaFontaine, T.: Long-term effects of aerobic exercise on psychological outcomes. Prev. Med. **28**, 75–85 (1999). https://doi.org/10.1006/pmed.1998.0385
12. Brassington, G.S.: Relationship between aerobic exercise and sleep quality in elderly individuals (1993). https://scholarworks.sjsu.edu/etd_theses/672. https://doi.org/10.31979/etd.d6dp-tmmc
13. DiLorenzo, T.M., Bargman, E.P., Stucky-Ropp, R., Brassington, G.S., Frensch, P.A., LaFontaine, T.: Long-term effects of aerobic exercise on psychological outcomes. Prev. Med. **28**, 75–85 (1999). https://doi.org/10.1006/pmed.1998.0385
14. Mizrahi, J., Verbitsky, O., Isakov, E., Daily, D.: Effect of fatigue on leg kinematics and impact acceleration in long distance running. Hum. Mov. Sci. **19**(2), 13–151 (2000)
15. Assumpção, C. de O., Lima, L.C.R., Oliveira, F.B.D., Greco, C.C., Denadai, B.S.: Exercise-induced muscle damage and running economy in humans. Sci. World J. **2013**, 1–11 (2013). https://doi.org/10.1155/2013/189149
16. Harms, H., Amft, O., Winkler, R., Schumm, J., Kusserow, M., Troester, G.: ETHOS: miniature orientation sensor for wearable human motion analysis. In: 2010 IEEE Sensors. pp. 1037–1042. IEEE, Kona, HI (2010). https://doi.org/10.1109/ICSENS.2010.5690738

17. Paradiso, R., Loriga, G., Taccini, N.: A wearable health care system based on knitted integrated sensors. IEEE Trans. Inform. Technol. Biomed. **9**, 337–344 (2005). https://doi.org/10.1109/TITB.2005.854512

18. Karvonen, J., Vuorimaa, T.: Heart rate and exercise intensity during sports activities practical application. Sports Med. **5**, 303–311 (1988). https://doi.org/10.2165/00007256-198805050-00002

19. Khan, Y., Ostfeld, A.E., Lochner, C.M., Pierre, A., Arias, A.C.: Monitoring of vital signs with flexible and wearable medical devices. Adv. Mater. **28**, 4373–4395 (2016). https://doi.org/10.1002/adma.201504366

20. AL-Khalidi, F.Q., Saatchi, R., Burke, D., Elphick, H., Tan, S.: Respiration rate monitoring methods: a review. Pediatr. Pulmonol. **46**, 523–529 (2011). https://doi.org/10.1002/ppul.21416

21. Di Rienzo, M., Rizzo, F., Parati, G., Brambilla, G., Ferratini, M., Castiglioni, P.: MagIC system: a new textile-based wearable device for biological signal monitoring. applicability in daily life and clinical setting. In: 2005 IEEE Engineering in Medicine and Biology 27th Annual Conference, Shanghai, China, pp. 7167–7169. IEEE (2005). https://doi.org/10.1109/IEMBS.2005.1616161

An Ergonomic Solution for Hand Rehabilitation Product Design for Stroke Patients

Jing Luo, Yan Luximon[⊠], Wen Zhan, and Xiaoyang Chen

School of Design, The Hong Kong Polytechnic University,
Kowloon, Hong Kong SAR
yan.luximon@polyu.edu.hk

Abstract. Rehabilitation training is a crucial part that helps stroke patients to train their muscles and rebuild the connection between muscle, nervous system and brain. This study conducts an ergonomic redesign of hand rehabilitation products based on the interview investigation to the user behavior and psychology during the training rehabilitation. The driving part of the device was relocated from the palm to the back of the hand to enhance the experience of stroke subjects to grab objects. Moreover, the device can drive the user to have a positive attitude towards their rehabilitation by visualizing the training improvement. Body scan and 3D printing technologies were utilized to ensure the accuracy of the position of the electric stimulation pads on the hands. The design also enhanced the voluntary motor functions at the palm and the fingers. The research results will contribute in formulating the design criteria of hand rehabilitation training products for stroke subjects.

Keywords: Hand rehabilitation · Ergonomics · 3D scanning · Product design

1 Introduction

Stroke is a common disease that occurs among the ageing population, especially for people who are older than 64 years [1]. As an ageing society, Hong Kong is expected to have an increased number of stroke patients in the future [2, 3]. Stroke is a disease that causes disability after the incidence [1]. The high proportion of stroke patients experience serious suffering due to the impact of an instant drop in intellectual and physical capability, which is also very likely to affect their families [4]. A systematic solution is urgently needed to enable patients to go back to healthy, efficient and comfortable living without affecting their self-esteem [5].

The medical treatment procedure for stroke patients contains three stages: diagnosis, treatment, and rehabilitation [1]. Recovery is a crucial part that helps patients to train their muscles and rebuild the associations among muscle, nervous system and brain [6]. The rehabilitation training, in most cases, takes place in the hospital or clinic under the supervision of a doctor. Continuous repetition after the first six months are beneficial for recovery [6]. However, there is a shortage of public medical resources in Hong Kong, which may lead to insufficient training for patients [4, 5].

© Springer Nature Switzerland AG 2020
V. G. Duffy (Ed.): HCII 2020, LNCS 12198, pp. 325–334, 2020.
https://doi.org/10.1007/978-3-030-49904-4_24

Traditional rehabilitation training methods are mainly carried out manually or through simple instruments to move or manipulate the affected body. This training method generally requires the assistance of multiple medical personnel [1]. Therefore, it is difficult to ensure the intensity and durability of rehabilitation training. At the same time, artificial rehabilitation training methods are easily affected by the subjective factors of therapists. The lack of the objectivity of training limits further optimization of rehabilitation training methods and the monitoring and evaluation of rehabilitation effects.

Electronic rehabilitation products are produced and developed to deal with the shortcomings of traditional rehabilitation training methods. It is a kind of automatic rehabilitation training equipment which combines advanced mechanical technology and clinical rehabilitation medicine. It provides advantages of mechanical equipment that is good at performing repetitive heavy work [9]. Rehabilitation robot, as an example, can realize accurate, automatic and intelligent rehabilitation training. Furthermore, improvement in approaches to rehabilitation medicine, increase the chances of patients receiving rehabilitation treatment, and improve the quality of life of patients.

Research related to rehabilitation technology rose in the 1990s. Professor Hogan's team at the Massachusetts Institute of Technology has carried out related research earlier [10]. The MIT-MANUS developed by this research team is a typical representative of the end-type upper limb rehabilitation robot. MIT-MANUS provides patients with shoulder and elbow joint exercise training [10]. A large number of clinical experiments on MIT-Manus showed that the rehabilitation robot has a positive effect on improving the upper limb function of patients [11]. At the same time, related research teams have also developed other upper limb rehabilitation products, such as the GENTLE/s developed by the University of Reading in the United Kingdom [12], and the MIME system developed by the Rehabilitation Research and Development Center in Palo Alto, California [13]. Besides, in order to make up for the shortage of the end type upper limb rehabilitation robot, which is difficult to control the human upper limb joints accurately, the relevant scholars have proposed the exoskeleton type upper limb rehabilitation robot. At present, the most typical exoskeleton upper limb rehabilitation robot is the ARMin upper limb rehabilitation robot developed by Professor Riener of the Federal Institute of Technology in Zurich, Switzerland [14]. After more than 20 years of development, many achievements have been made in the technical research of upper limb rehabilitation products. These achievements include active training, compliance control, prescription design, rehabilitation evaluation and many other technologies, which have been applied in clinical practice [15]. However, the existing upper limb rehabilitation products still have problems such as high production cost, limited application and limited rehabilitation effects.

In order to solve the above problems, researchers at the Department of Biomedical Engineering (BME) of The Hong Kong Polytechnic University have developed a new kind of robotic arm that provides self-service and upper limb mobility rehabilitation service for stroke patients [7]. The robotic arm is beneficial for muscle recovery. It guides the patient to gain the ability to grab back through a series of training towards the muscles in the arm and fingers. It helps patients to gain control of their muscles. Their prototype provides rehabilitation training solutions mainly based on two technologies, electric stimulation and air chamber [8]. Compared with other products, the robotic arm has the merits of low production cost, small size and portability. Therefore, the new kind of rehabilitation product has wide potential applications and broad research spaces.

Based on the previous research, we have designed an ergonomic solution of hand rehabilitation product with the objective of improving user experience and training efficiency by providing a more convenient and comfortable way of donning it with improvement in positioning of the electric stimulation pads. At first, observation and interview were used as design methods for user research. It was aimed to investigate the user behaviour and psychology during training rehabilitation. These methods can also find ergonomic issues related to the rehabilitation training process. Accordingly, the design criteria were formulated, design solutions were proposed, and product prototypes were developed. This paper presents in detail the application of ergonomic principles in the design process for hand rehabilitation product for stroke patients.

2 User Research

The user research comprised two parts: (a) an observation to find design insights which based on the realistic difficulties and problems by patients in training process, and (b) an interview with user and therapist to prove design insights from part (a) and collect more information to develop the design concept.

2.1 Observation

Two rehabilitation sessions were observed that included two therapists and two patients. Patient A is a female. She is left paralyzed and lives alone with help of a domestic helper. Patient B is a male. He is left paralyzed and lives with his wife. An existing prototype was used as a basis for further improvement [8].

The first rehabilitation session was the wearing process. Two issues were identified based on the observation study. User needed to involve other persons' help (not necessarily professional) to secure the placement of the air chamber and the securing ring. Previous product requires medical profession when positioning the electrical stimulation pads. Positioning is also based on experience. The electrical stimulation pads need to be repositioned during the wearing session by a medical professional.

The second rehabilitation session was the training process. Several problems were identified based on this part. During the training, the loops holding the fingers and the airbag came off several times. The patient and the professional had to constantly reposition the securing ring in order to make sure it is at the right place, especially the position of the airbag of the thumb. The other issue was that the professional has to manually stretch the patient's hands open since the air chamber cannot efficiently open up the patient's hands entirely. In addition, the patient's wrists were often obviously compressed by the edges and corners of the desktop edge. Patients needed to alternate between two different arm positions to train arm muscles. Patients often miss training opportunities due to distraction, but the equipment are not be adjusted due to changes in the patient's state.

2.2   Interview

Interviews were conducted for both the patient and the therapist to understand how they use and feel about the previous hand rehabilitation product [8]. Questions were asked about their usage experience and problems for the current product. These are some common issues collected.

First of all, they hope that the design can be improved to facilitate wearing because the patients want to do it independently. Secondly, during training, patients are required to hold firmly to locate the extensors and flexor muscle which is rather challenging for stroke patients as they have little muscle strength compared to other people. Finally, they believe that the setting of feedback will effectively assist training and increase patient training confidence.

3   Design Process and Prototype Development

Results of the user research provided valid data for design concept and prototype development. It was found that the issues of wearing style, positioning and driving mode were the most pronounced problem for users with previous products. Accordingly, the design criteria were identified to design a new rehabilitation robot arm. The rehabilitation robot arm design was firstly aimed to provide users experience for patients through better wearing style and positioning system. In addition, it aimed to enhance the training confidence by providing better feedback. The whole concept design is shown in Fig. 1.

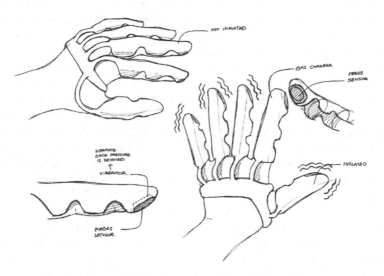

Fig. 1. Concept design demonstrating the new wearing way

3.1   3D Hand Data

Based on the concept design, an experimental prototype of the rehabilitation robot arm was developed. 3D scanning the hand and analyzed the surface of the side to gain data supporting from ergonomic. According to the 3D scanning data, the shape and surface of the prototype are tested and modified repeatedly to fit the hand structure. Figure 2 showed the ergonomic data from 3D scanning.

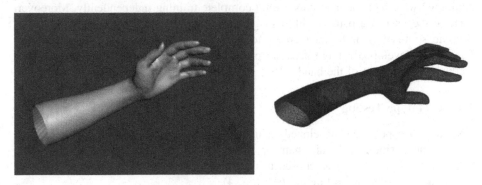

Fig. 2. The human hand data from 3D scan

3.2   Prototype Developing

According to the previous user research, this research was carried on the prototype design from the following three aspects.

Firstly, the previous rehabilitation robot arm by BME is unable to provide users with enough feedback, such as grabbing and putting down objects. Taking the training of grasping and dropping objects as an example, the users need to see that they can complete and the corresponding actions. Thus they can have a sense of achievement in rehabilitation training. However, the air chamber of the rehabilitation robotic arm is inside the palm, which makes it difficult for users to train grasping objects. Therefore, in this design, the traction device is changed to the back of the hand, so that the palm can be used to practice grasping objects (see Fig. 3).

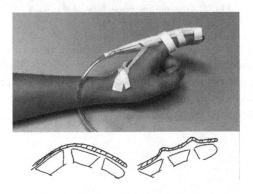

Fig. 3. The air chamber at the back

Secondly, the previous fixing method makes the airbag of the thumb part easy to rotate, which makes it difficult for the thumb to be fully exercised. At the same time, the remaining four fingers did not reach the desired extension so that the therapist needed to spread the thumb manually. 3D ergonomic data was used in this prototype design, and the product shape was designed to better fit the structure of the finger itself and have a better fixing effect.

Third, the patient needs the help of another person to wear the product in the traditional wearing style, and thus cannot complete training independently. Moreover, because the user is a patient with a long-term stroke, the muscles will be relatively strophic, so it is difficult for the therapist to identify the muscles for electric stimulation. This study developed a more accurate positioning method by considering the ergonomic structural data of the hand.

3.3   Prototype Testing

Several prototypes were developed to improve the experience of grabbing objects, emulate the position of the air chamber, as well as enlarge the stretching angle. The final designed prototype was chosen to use the mechanical rope traction method for hand muscle rehabilitation training (see Fig. 4).

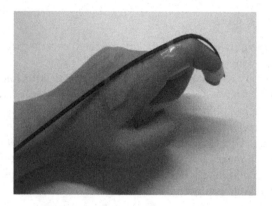

Fig. 4. The pulling rope type at the back

Since the patient use the existing product with the help of others, this situation increases costs and discourages the self-confidence of patients. The design concept was to experiment on the form of the rehabilitation device so that the patients can wear the hand part by themselves as well as facilitate the user to wear the electric stimulation pads without the supervision of professionals (see Fig. 5).

Fig. 5. Wearing testing

4 Evaluation of Design

Several 3D prototypes were designed then 3D printed by using 3D printing technology. 3D designed prototype (Fig. 6) including rendering can show clear structures for the new rehabilitation robot arm. Simpler design were first evaluated using test based on realistic difficulties and problems encountered by hand rehabilitation products. The results indicated that, by creating a new ergonomic dressing method that allows patients to complete rehabilitation training independently, can greatly improve the user experience, increase their enthusiasm and self-confidence in rehabilitation training, and enhance the rehabilitation effect.

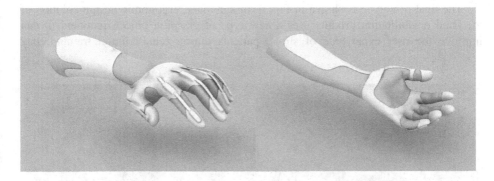

Fig. 6. Rendering of the final design

As shown in Fig. 7, the functional prototype shows the rehabilitation training driven by the electric motor and the pulling rope, the energy training process, and the intuitive feedback of the rehabilitation training effect. This result makes patients more willing to participate in treatment actively.

Fig. 7. Mechanism process

The wearing processes are shown in Fig. 8. Patients can independently complete the entire process of wearing this hand rehabilitation device. This design can greatly save labor costs.

Fig. 8. Wearing process

The final prototype is shown in Fig. 9. In summary, ergonomic design solution of the hand rehabilitation product uses a new type of grasping object treatment. It can improve the user experience of stroke patients during rehabilitation training, pay

Fig. 9. Final prototype

attention to the psychological feelings of stroke patients, and visualize the treatment process. This design solution can promote patients to change from passive treatment to active treatment, which greatly improves the patient's self-confidence and dignity.

5 Conclusion

This study mainly focuses on an ergonomic redesign of hand rehabilitation products with the objective of improving the user experience of hand rehabilitation training for stroke patients. The design relocated the driving part from the palm to the back of the hand to enhance the experience of stroke subjects to grab objects. According to the interview, patients mentioned that the improvement highly motivated them. By visualizing training improvement of patients, the device can drive the user to have a positive attitude towards their rehabilitation. The project also utilized 3D scanning and 3D printing technology to ensure the accuracy of the position of the electric stimulation pads on hands. The voluntary motor functions at the palm and the fingers could be enhanced by the rehabilitation training. These results will help in formulating the design criteria of hand rehabilitation training products for stroke patients.

References

1. Feigin, V.L., Lawes, C.M., Bennett, D.A., Anderson, C.S.: Stroke epidemiology: a review of population-based studies of incidence, prevalence, and case-fatality in the late 20th century. Lancet Neurol. 2(1), 43–53 (2003)
2. Cheng, S.T., Lum, T., Lam, L.C., Fung, H.H.: Hong Kong: embracing a fast aging society with limited welfare. Gerontologist 53(4), 527–533 (2013)
3. Hui, E.C.M., Yu, K.H.: Residential mobility and aging population in Hong Kong. Habitat Int. 33(1), 10–14 (2009)
4. Sim, T.C., Lum, C.M., Sze, F.K., Or, K.H., Woo, J.: Outcome after stroke rehabilitation in Hong Kong. Clin. Rehabil. 11(3), 236–242 (1997)
5. Lam, S.C., Lee, L.Y.K., To, K.W.: Depressive symptoms among community-dwelling, post-stroke elders in Hong Kong. Int. Nurs. Rev. 57(2), 269–273 (2010)
6. Langhorne, P., Bernhardt, J., Kwakkel, G.: Stroke rehabilitation. Lancet 377(9778), 1693–1702 (2011)
7. Rong, W., et al.: A Neuromuscular Electrical Stimulation (NMES) and robot hybrid system for multi-joint coordinated upper limb rehabilitation after stroke. J. Neuroeng. Rehabil. 14(1), 34 (2017)
8. Qian, Q., Hu, X., Lai, Q., Ng, S.C., Zheng, Y., Poon, W.: Early stroke rehabilitation of the upper limb assisted with an electromyography-driven neuromuscular electrical stimulation-robotic arm. Front. Neurol. 8, 447 (2017)
9. Yang, Y., Wang, L., Tong, J., Zhang, L.: Arm rehabilitation robot impedance control and experimentation. In: 2006 IEEE International Conference on Robotics and Biomimetics. IEEE Computer Society (2006)
10. Krebs, H.I., et al.: Robot-aided neurorehabilitation: a robot for wrist rehabilitation. IEEE Trans. Neural Syst. Rehabil. Eng. 15(3), 327–335 (2007). https://doi.org/10.1109/tnsre.2007.903899

11. Krebs, H.I., Hogan, N., Volpe, B.T., Aisen, M.L., Edelstein, L., Diels, C.: Overview of clinical trials with MIT-MANUS: a robot-aided neuro-rehabilitation facility. Technol. Health Care **7**(6), 419–423 (1999)
12. Loureiro, R., Amirabdollahian, F., Topping, M., Driessen, B., Harwin, W.: Upper limb robot mediated stroke therapy-GENTLE/s approach. Auton. Robots **15**(1), 35–51 (2003). https://doi.org/10.1023/a:1024436732030
13. Burgar, C.G., Lum, P.S., Shor, P.C., Van der Loos, H.F.M.: Development of robots for rehabilitation therapy: the Palo Alto VA/Stanford experience. J. Rehabil. Res. Dev. **37**(6), 663–667 (2000)
14. Nef, T., Guidalic, M., Riener, R.: ARMin III-arm therapy exoskeleton with an ergonomic shoulder actuation. Appl. Bion. Biomech. **6**(2), 127–142 (2009). https://doi.org/10.1155/2009/962956
15. Maciejasz, P., Eschweiler, J., Gerlach-Hahn, K., Jansen-Troy, A., Leonhardt, S.: A survey on robotic devices for upper limb rehabilitation. J. Neuro Eng. Rehabil. **11**(1), Article no. 3 (2014)

End-User Programming Architecture for Physical Movement Assessment: An Interactive Machine Learning Approach

Jessica M. Palomares-Pecho[1]([✉]) [iD], Greis Francy M. Silva-Calpa[2]([✉]) [iD],
César A. Sierra-Franco[2]([✉]) [iD], and Alberto Barbosa Raposo[1,2]([✉]) [iD]

[1] Department of Informatics, Pontifical Catholic University of Rio de
Janeiro (PUC-Rio), Gávea, Rio de Janeiro 22451-900, Brazil
jessika.palomares@gmail.com
[2] Tecgraf Institute, Pontifical Catholic University of Rio de Janeiro (PUC-Rio),
Gávea, Rio de Janeiro 22451-900, Brazil
{greis,casfranco,abraposo}@tecgraf.puc-rio.br

Abstract. In this article, we propose an end-user adaptive architecture
for movement assessment from RGB videos. Our method allows physiotherapists to add customized exercises for patients from only a few video
training examples. The main idea is to take leverage of Deep learning-
based pose estimation frameworks to track in real-time the key-body joints
from the image data. Our system mimics the traditional physical rehabilitation process, where the therapist guides patients through demonstrative
examples, and the patients repeat these examples while the physiotherapist monitors their movements. We evaluate our proposed method on four
physiotherapeutic exercises for shoulder strengthening. Results indicate
that our approach contributes both to reduce physiotherapist time needed
to train the system, and to automatically assess the patients' movements
without direct monitoring from the physiotherapist.

Keywords: Interactive Machine learning · OpenPose · Programming
by example · Rehabilitation · Human activity recognition

1 Introduction

Physiotherapy aims to improve physical functionality, seeking to attenuate dis-
abilities caused by some injury, disorder, or disease [2]. Physiotherapy supports the rehabilitation process that involves the definition, implementation,
and evaluation of activities and exercises [38], when physiotherapists take care
of restoring the loss of functionality, as well as preventing or delaying their
deterioration [39].

Several computational technologies have arisen to contribute to the physiotherapists in the rehabilitation process, such as end-user adaptable technologies
[1,11,13,33]. These technologies allow physiotherapists to tailor applications and

© Springer Nature Switzerland AG 2020
V. G. Duffy (Ed.): HCII 2020, LNCS 12198, pp. 335–348, 2020.
https://doi.org/10.1007/978-3-030-49904-4_25

create activities with personalized characteristics according to the preferences and needs of each patient.

In the literature, several studies have been using end-user approaches to support physical rehabilitation, reporting benefits to patients and physiotherapists [1,11,33]. Regarding the benefits for patients, studies report the improvements in motor movement, autonomy to perform the exercises, increasing motivation during therapy sessions, and thus, the effectiveness of the training program. The benefits for the physiotherapists include the contribution to access to the reports quickly, the feasibility to reuse of already available exercises, and the possibility to customize tasks according to the patients' performance [13,33]. However, the authors mentioned that physiotherapists faced some difficulties in using technology, especially for the limited time they have to learn and customize activities [5,11,16,33]. In some cases, physiotherapists report little interest in learning [11,33] or knowing even simple programming aspects to adapt the system.

In this sense, other approaches have arisen to mitigate these difficulties, such as robot-based systems, showing positive results by making it easier for the physiotherapists to specify exercises through demonstrations [31,35]. However, robots are usually very expensive and only available to rehabilitation in hospitals or clinics.

These aspects motivate this study, which proposes an end-user architecture that aims to support physiotherapists to create programs in an natural way and without requiring software coding. Our study focuses on empowering physiotherapists (end users) to train a physical rehabilitation system using programming by demonstration (PbD). PbD is an End-User Programming (EUP) technique that consists of enabling end-users to create programs through instructions or examples [10,20]. The system records these examples and infers a generalized program to be used on new examples [4].

In this work, we develop an interactive machine learning (IML) [3] method for movement evaluation from RGB videos. IML introduces the human-in-the-loop concept for Machine Learning techniques. Our method allows the physiotherapist to add customized exercises for patients from only a few video training examples (less than ten samples). Our method also avoids the need for additional capture hardware like a Kinect device, relying only on RGB video sequences.

The main idea is to take advantage of Deep learning-based pose estimation frameworks (e.g., openPose [6]) to track in real-time the key-body joints from the images. Then, we process the resulting key-body points as a temporal series through the Dynamic Time Warping algorithm to feed an Anomaly detection procedure. This entire process allows us to develop an end-user adaptive architecture for movement assessment. Our system mimics the traditional physical rehabilitation process: the therapist guides patients through demonstrative examples, the patients repeat these examples while the physiotherapist monitors their movements. We envision our system's architecture completes the process in two phases/modules. In the first phase, the physiotherapist configures and trains the system to recognize custom movements for further patient's assessment, while at the same time save those videos as visual instructions. Then the system processes these videos and creates an assessment model. In the second phase, this model serves as a movement evaluator for the patient's module.

We evaluate our proposed architecture on four upper physiotherapeutic exercises performed by seven participants. Results indicate that our approach contributes to automatically assess the patients' movements without direct monitoring from the physiotherapist, reducing the physiotherapist time needed to train an adaptable system.

The rest of this paper is organized as follows. In Sect. 2, we describe existing approaches to address the development of end-user adaptable technologies for physical rehabilitation. In Sect. 3, we present our proposed architecture for physical movement assessment. The evaluation process of our architecture is described in Sect. 4. Finally, in Sect. 5 we present the conclusion and future work direction.

2 Related Work

Studies in the Human-Robot Interaction field proposes the use of coaching robots, capable of demonstrating rehabilitation exercises to patients [12,15,31]. According to [25], a coaching robot must be capable of, in the absence of the therapist, leading a user through a rehabilitation program, particularly in the home settings. Therefore, the therapist adapts the behavior of a robotic couch to the individual user needs through movement demonstration. Previous works using a robotic coach for rehabilitation suggested that the system identifies incorrectly performed exercises and gives corrective feedback on user errors [12,31]. However, the cost of these robotic approaches is the main barrier for the general adoption of robotic coach in-home, restricting their use, only in clinics or hospitals.

In this work, we propose a highly flexible and low-cost architecture that offers support to the patient in a similar way as robot coaching but without using complex hardware. Our proposal uses the technique of Human Motion Recognition through an RGB camera, device present in any smartphone, or laptop. Human motion recognition (HMR) consists of the automatic identification of human behaviors from images or video sequences. Over the last years, this field has been extensively studied the use of machine learning-based motion recognition, for rehabilitation purposes [7,27,29,36,40]. Usually, these studies focus on the extraction of skeleton data (e.g., using the Kinect sensor) to then be processed by ML algorithms and model unique characteristics of a gesture or an activity. Vox and Wallhoff [36] reached a motion recognition accuracy of 81%, and concluded that autonomous systems for the recognition of motion exercises are a promising tool for rehabilitative purposes.

In [7,27,36], the authors proposed machine learning algorithms to monitor and evaluate the patient exercises. Results from these studies suggest that Machine learning-based motion recognition showed up accuracy and efficiency. However, training of machine learning (ML) algorithms usually requires a large dataset to recognize human body motion patterns. For this reason, a flexible and adaptable technology for physical rehabilitation requires the acquisition of a large dataset containing specific/customized patient interactions, which is impractical in most cases. Therefore, our approach relies on only a few video training examples (less than ten samples). Here, we take leverage of pose estimation algorithms to track the key-body joints and analyze them through k-nearest neighbors (k-NN) and DTW algorithms. Through this process, we were able to perform movement recognition and assessment using small training datasets.

OpenPose [6] is an open-source library released in 2017, which has achieved significant interest among researches due to its computational performance for the extraction of the body joints. Several works focus on the recognition and the automatic validation of movements in the context of rehabilitation [9,14,19,37]. Kojima et al. [19] implemented a system for cognitive rehabilitation based on daily routines. The authors reached an average estimation accuracy 95.2% of cleaning behavior on a laboratory-controlled ambient and 33,8% in a real clinical rehabilitation environment. In [14,37], the authors used a geometric/heuristic method for patient gesture recognition using the key points extracted by Open-Pose library. The objective is to measure the degree of agreement between the patient's motion data and the standard defined by the therapist. It consists of comparing a range of angles predefined by a therapist to the joint angles obtained from the patient's motion. Chen and Yang [9] developed Pose Trainer, an application that uses two methods: geometric/heuristic and machine learning. The geometric algorithm provides personalized feedback on specific exercise improvements, and ML algorithm to determine posture correctness. The authors obtained a classification accuracy between 73%–100%. The effectiveness of the mentioned studies in human gesture recognition on RGB images motivated us to adopt a similar methodology.

To overcome data limitations, we create synthetic data from the therapist's motion examples for the training phase [17]. Are mentioned, in the rehabilitation context, usually a few examples available for training ML algorithms. In [32] the author used synthetic time series data generation methods to synthesize new samples from those already available. The authors suggested that for custom gestures, even when many samples were provided, synthetic data generation is useful.

In the literature, studies that use DTW to classify a gesture/action define a 'threshold' value to assess motion [9,28]. Usually, this value is compared to a 'warping distance' measure between the user motion and the selected motion by k-NN. We use an anomaly detection procedure to evaluate motion. The anomaly detection procedure is the identification of rare items, events, or observations differing significantly from the majority of the data [30]. Several studies addressing anomaly event detection in surveillance videos such as violence detector [24] and traffic accident detector [18] show motivating results to be efficient in automatic detect abnormal events. These studies motivate us to adopt an anomaly detection model for the patient's movement assessment.

3 Proposed End-User Programming Architecture for Physical Movement Assessment

Our proposed architecture intends to facilitate physiotherapists to create customized exercises in a software tool for rehabilitation motion assessment. For this, our system architecture mimics the traditional physical rehabilitation process. First, the therapist guides patients through demonstrative examples. Only then, the patients repeat these examples while the physiotherapist (in our case, the patient assessment module) monitors their movements. Figure 1 shows the system architecture details. Here, we envision the entire process in two phases: physiotherapist and patient ones. In the first phase, the physiotherapist configures and trains the system to recognize custom movements for further patient assessment, while at the same time save those videos as visual instructions. The system processes the videos, and as a result, the module returns an assessment model. Afterward, in a second phase, the model generated by the physiotherapist module serves as a motion evaluator for the patient module.

In our architecture, both the physiotherapist and the patient modules share the same functionalities for video capture, image processing and key-body point extraction. In the next subsections, we present the details for video processing, the physiotherapist module (motion assessment learning phase), and the patient module (motion evaluation phase)

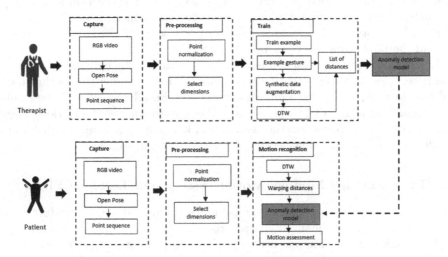

Fig. 1. End-User Programming Architecture for Physical Movement Assessment: physiotherapist programming exercises module (top), and patient movement assessment module (bottom).

3.1 Video Processing and Key-Body Point Extraction

As we mention earlier, we take leverage of the Deep learning-based pose estimation architecture called OpenPose. This architecture allows us to track in real-time the key-body joints from a video camera, avoiding the need for additional movement capture hardware like a Kinect device. The benefit of this approach is double. First, the overall solution could rely only on RGB video cameras, reducing implementation costs, and second, it gives us low dimensional data to apply machine learning algorithms when compared with pixel-based image processing. This second benefit was crucial for our purpose of interactively training a movement assessment model from a small number of examples.

Figure 2a shows an example of the output generated by the OpenPose model. This model process in real-time image content, returning the 18 predicted 2D-key-points coordinates (x,y) from the human skeleton. In order to asses the physiotherapeutic movement, we retrieve the key-points from each video frame processed by the OpenPose model. Then, we concatenate each frame's results obtaining the full movement per-key-point data. Afterward, we perform two processing steps to allow the patient's invariance and dimensional data reduction. First, in order to allow invariance to the patient's size and position, we normalize the point coordinates as in ([8,28]). Here, we reposition the neck-key-point at the origin and translate all the surrounding points in correspondence. Then all key points are scaled such that the distance between the left shoulder and right shoulder key point be one. Second, in order to reduce the data dimensionality, we analyze only the relevant points for motion assessment according to each exercise. For instance, in a double shoulder exercise, only the key points of the left and the right arms are relevant.

In contrast, the others lack of information useful for the corresponding exercise. Here, select the point IDs whose variance on time is higher than a threshold, and therefore discarding the uninformative points. Finally, we smooth the resulting information using a Gaussian filter and a zero-mean transformation. These preprocessing steps transform the sequence of key-point per frame (Fig. 2a) in a low-dimensional motion time-series data, as depicted in Fig. 2b.

3.2 Physiotherapy Module: Motion Assessment Learning Phase

The physiotherapist module is responsible for facilitating the introduction of new exercises with personalized characteristics according to the preferences and needs of each patient. The main idea is that the physiotherapist creates these exercises in a natural way and without requiring software coding. Here we implemented the programming by demonstration technique through an interactive ML approach. The training process initiate when the physiotherapist performs a custom rehabilitation exercise (motions) in front of the camera, providing correct examples. The module saves the videos for future patients visual reference, and also process them to extract the necessary information for performing ML (as explained in Subsect. 3.1). Then, the training sub-module takes the processed examples as time-series data to obtain a motion assessment model.

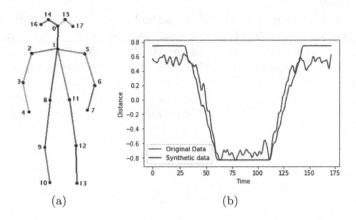

(a)   (b)

Fig. 2. (a) Human Pose Key points format (b) Synthetic times data from the original

We based our motion assessment model in anomaly detection techniques since we only have the "correct" examples for training purposes. Anomaly detection techniques learn the distribution (rules) that captures the normal behavior of specific data. Then, in a test instance, new data is analyzed, pointing out the samples that are not covered by the learned distribution as anomalies. Here, we process each motion time-series data through the Dynamic Time Warping algorithm and the One-Nearest-Neighbor (1NN) classifier to feed an Anomaly detection algorithm. Initially, we find a "motion sample" between all the motion examples provided by the physiotherapist using the 1NN classifier. Then we increase the motion samples synthetically through the python TimeSynth package [23], adding white noise with a standard deviation of 0.1 (Fig. 2b). Subsequently, all the motion time-series are compared with the selected "motion sample" through the DTW algorithm, resulting in a list of "warping distances," which will serve as input for training the anomaly detection model.

We selected an outlier detection technique on a univariate data set to validate the patient's movement. Univariate data (UI) consists of observations on only a "single characteristic" or "attribute" independent from the others concerning time and parameter setting [34]. Outlier detection techniques measure and select anomalies samples from a data set. These techniques select the outlier samples on the numerical data value, which usually are smaller or larger that the majority of the observations. As we mentioned earlier, we selected the list of "warping distances" as data information for outlier detection. We used two outlier detection methods for motion assessment: the Isolation Forest (IF) algorithm [21], and Interquartile Range (IQR) method [34]. We chose these methods because they do not make any distributional assumption and not depend on a median or standard deviation of the data set. Isolation Forest (IF) is an algorithm based on decision trees. It detects anomalies by isolating samples without relying on any density or distance measure. The idea behind IF is that isolating anomalous observations in a random forest is easier since few conditions are required to separate those observations from the normal cases.

On the other hand, IQR is a statistic method measure of variability in a data set, dividing it into quartiles. Figure 3, illustrate the interquartile range, which is the range between the first (Q1) and the third quartiles (Q3). Then, any data point that falls outside of either 1.5 times the IQR below the first quartile or 1.5 times the IQR above the third quartile is considered an outlier.

For a detailed review on IF and IQR techniques for anomaly detection, the reader is referred to [21,22,34], and [26] for a more technical and thorough discussion.

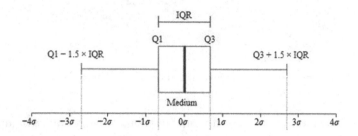

Fig. 3. Inter quartile range.

3.3   Patient Module: Motion Assesment Phase

The patient module is responsible for providing visual guides to the patients to realize customized physiotherapeutic exercises. This module also gives feedback to the patient, indicating if the executed motion is correct or incorrect. For the motion assessment step, the module uses the motion assessment pre-trained model by the physiotherapist. In more detail, we align the motion sequence of the patient to the example "motion sample" using the DTW algorithm, obtaining a warping distance. Then, the patient module uses the pre-trained outlier detection model to assess the patient's movement. As a result, if the warping distance is detected as an outlier, the motion is considered incorrect; otherwise, it is considered correct.

4   Evaluation of the Proposed Architecture

We evaluated our method using four upper rehabilitation exercises. In the first exercise, the patient raises both arms to the side of the body above shoulder height (Fig. 4a). In the second exercise, the patient raises both arms to the sides and slightly forward above his body and lower them back down in the same pathway they were raised at shoulder level (Fig. 4b). In the third exercise, the patient raises only the right arm and letting it rest on the head (Fig. 4c). In the four exercise, the patient raises the left arm to the side of the body to shoulder height (Fig. 4d).

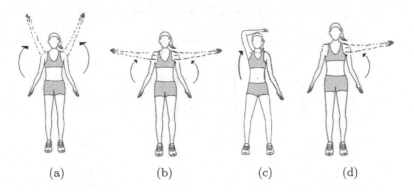

(a)   (b)   (c)   (d)

Fig. 4. Four upper limb exercises performed by the participants.

We tested our proposed architecture on healthy subjects, evaluating precision and usability. Eight subjects were recruited and received an information booklet describing the system and the protocol. All subjects read and signed a consent term. From them, seven participants (ages between 20 and 38 years old) took part in the tests in the role of patients and one participant in the role of a physiotherapist. We requested the participants to perform eight times each shoulder exercise (following the video instructions), resulting in 224 evaluated movements (7 subjects * 4 motions * 8 repetitions). From now, we will use the term *expert demonstration* to refer to the human motion sequences.

Two participants of the remaining seven participants performed incorrect exercises to simulate errors for the four motions (64 test motion sequences with error have been captured). Therefore, we tested each exercise with correct and incorrect motion sequences.

4.1 Experimental Results

Initially, we carry out a visual inspection to categorize the correctness of each movement. Then, we compare these manual results with the automatic model assessment. From the 160 movements manually validated as correct, the patient module assesses as correctly 152 of them (95% of accuracy). On the other side, from the 64 movements visually validated as incorrect, the trained models' cath them all of them as wrong movements.

Figure 5 shows the range between the lower and upper range of whiskers of the warping distances values for the four exercises using the IQR method. Figure 6 shows the range of values of warping distances and the respective anomaly score for each motion, using IF algorithm. The range of values of no anomalies warping distances for the IQR method is higher compared to the range of IF algorithm. For example, the max value of warping distance to the motion sample accepted by IQR method is 41. However, the value 41 is considered such outlier by the Isolation Forest algorithm.

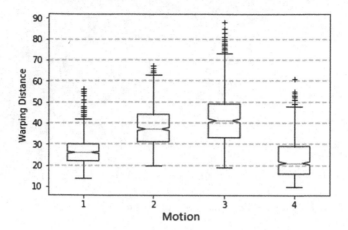

Fig. 5. Boxplot of motion assessment. The central line represents the median, the edges of the box are the 25th and 75th percentiles, and the whiskers extend to $(+,-)1.5$ of the interquartile range. Outliers upper this range are labeled as '+.'

Table 1. Evaluation result for all motion with the two anomaly models tested.

	IQR		Isolation forest	
	Motion recognized	Motion not recognized	Motion recognized	Motion not recognized
G1 correct	39	1	37	3
G1 error	0	16	0	16
G2 correct	40	0	39	1
G2 error	0	16	0	16
G3 correct	36	4	21	19
G3 error	0	16	0	16
G4 correct	37	3	31	9
G4 error	0	16	0	16
Total	**152**	**72**	**128**	**96**

The results of the patients' motions are reported in Table 1. The obtained scores for correct exercises by the IQR method (152) are higher than those obtained by the Isolation Forest algorithm (128). Both methods (IQR and IF) detected all error exercises as incorrect (64). Results show that our method can detect when an exercise is not correctly performed. Further, results obtained evidence that our method is appropriate regardless of the size or age of the subject. Also, exercise 3 obtained lower scores than the other exercises in both anomaly detection methods. This can be explained by the fact that exercise 3 lasts longer than the other motions. Thus, we can deduce that the error tendency is higher when the motion lasts longer. Results show that our architecture is

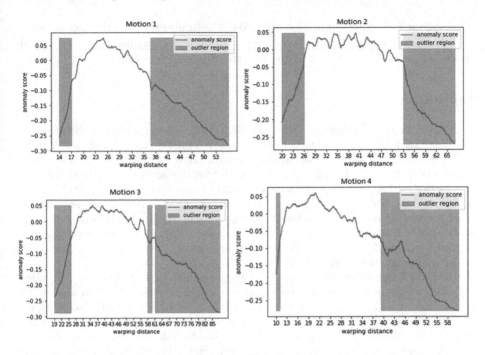

Fig. 6. Assessment of each motion using Isolation Forest for anomaly detection.

accurate to detect and evaluate if an exercise is correct or incorrect. However, when an exercise involves longer-lasting movements, there is a higher probability that the patient will not perform it as proposed by the physiotherapist. This will be part of our future work to improve our architecture.

5   Conclusion

In this study, we propose an end-user programming architecture for Physical Movement Assessment. Using an interactive machine learning approach, we enable physiotherapists to add customized exercises without requiring software coding. Our architecture also avoids the need for expensive capture data for motion assessment, relying only on RGB video cameras. For this, we combined a Deep Learning-based pose estimation framework with anomaly detection techniques. As a result, the architecture allows training motion assessment models from a small number of examples. These models provide feedback to the patient, indicating if the executed motion is correct or incorrect. The experiments results showed the effectiveness of our approach to: 1) allow physiotherapists to train a system in the same way as they would be taught to their patients. 2) Reduce physiotherapist time needed to program/train the system, and 3) automatically assess the patients' movements without direct monitoring from the physiotherapist. As the next steps, we intend to include different kinds of physiotherapist exercises, including lower limb motions. We also intend to asses the motion exercise by several steps, providing more insightful information and detailed feedback for the patients about the correctness of the motion execution.

References

1. Afyouni, I., et al.: A therapy-driven gamification framework for hand rehabilitation. User Model. User-Adap. Interact. **27**(2), 215–265 (2017). https://doi.org/10.1007/s11257-017-9191-4. http://link.springer.com/10.1007/s11257-017-9191-4
2. American Physical Therapy Association: Interactive guide to physical therapist practice (2019). http://guidetoptpractice.apta.org/. Accessed 08 Oct 2019
3. Amershi, S., Cakmak, M., Knox, W.B., Kulesza, T.: Power to the people: the role of humans in interactive machine learning. AI Mag. **35**(4), 105–120 (2014)
4. Barricelli, B.R., Cassano, F., Fogli, D., Piccinno, A.: End-user development, end-user programming and end-user software engineering: a systematic mapping study. J. Syst. Softw. **149**, 101–137 (2019)
5. Braz, P., Felipe David, V., Raposo, A., Barbosa, S.D.J., de Souza, C.S.: An alternative design perspective for technology supporting youngsters with autism. In: Schmorrow, D.D., Fidopiastis, C.M. (eds.) AC 2014. LNCS (LNAI), vol. 8534, pp. 279–287. Springer, Cham (2014). https://doi.org/10.1007/978-3-319-07527-3_26
6. Cao, Z., Hidalgo, G., Simon, T., Wei, S.E., Sheikh, Y.: Openpose: realtime multi-person 2d pose estimation using part affinity fields (2018). arXiv preprint arXiv:1812.08008
7. Capecci, M., et al.: Physical rehabilitation exercises assessment based on hidden semi-markov model by kinect v2. In: 2016 IEEE-EMBS International Conference on Biomedical and Health Informatics (BHI). pp. 256–259. IEEE (2016)
8. Celebi, S., Aydin, A.S., Temiz, T.T., Arici, T.: Gesture recognition using skeleton data with weighted dynamic time warping. In: VISAPP no. 1, pp. 620–625 (2013)
9. Chen, S., Yang, R.: Pose trainer: correcting exercise posture using pose estimation (2018)
10. Cypher, A., Halbert, D.C.: Watch What I Do: Programming by Demonstration. MIT press, Cambridge (1993)
11. Da Silva, M.L., Gonçalves, D., Silva, H.: User-tuned content customization for children with Autism Spectrum Disorders. In: Procedia Computer Science (2013). https://doi.org/10.1016/j.procs.2014.02.048
12. Devanne, M., Remy-Neris, O., Le Gals-Garnett, B., Kermarrec, G., Thepaut, A., et al.: A co-design approach for a rehabilitation robot coach for physical rehabilitation based on the error classification of motion errors. In: 2018 Second IEEE International Conference on Robotic Computing (IRC), pp. 352–357. IEEE (2018)
13. Garzotto, F., Gonella, R.: An open-ended tangible environment for disabled children's learning. In: Proceedings of the 10th International Conference on Interaction Design and Children, pp. 52–61. ACM (2011)
14. Godse, S.P., Singh, S., Khule, S., Yadav, V., Wakhare, S.: Musculoskeletal physiotherapy using artificial intelligence and machine learning. Int. J. Innov. Sci. Res. Technol. **4**(11), 592–598 (2019)
15. Görer, B., Salah, A.A., Akın, H.L.: A robotic fitness coach for the elderly. In: Augusto, J.C., Wichert, R., Collier, R., Keyson, D., Salah, A.A., Tan, A.-H. (eds.) AmI 2013. LNCS, vol. 8309, pp. 124–139. Springer, Cham (2013). https://doi.org/10.1007/978-3-319-03647-2_9

16. Hamzabegovic, J., Kalpić, D.: A proposal for development of software to support specific learning difficulties. In: Proceedings of the 12th International Conference on Telecommunications, pp. 207–214. IEEE (2013)
17. Houmanfar, R., Karg, M., Kulić, D.: Movement analysis of rehabilitation exercises: Distance metrics for measuring patient progress. IEEE Syst. J. **10**(3), 1014–1025 (2014)
18. Jain, N.K., Saini, R.K., Mittal, P.: A review on traffic monitoring system techniques. In: Ray, K., Sharma, T.K., Rawat, S., Saini, R.K., Bandyopadhyay, A. (eds.) Soft Computing: Theories and Applications. AISC, vol. 742, pp. 569–577. Springer, Singapore (2019). https://doi.org/10.1007/978-981-13-0589-4_53
19. Kojima, H., Kitano, M., Yokota, K., Ooi, S., Sano, M.: Cleaning behavior estimation for self-supported cognitive rehabilitation system. In: 2018 IEEE International Conference on Artificial Intelligence in Engineering and Technology (IICAIET), pp. 1–6. IEEE (2018)
20. Lieberman, H.: Your Wish is My Command: Programming by Example. Morgan Kaufmann, Burlington (2001)
21. Liu, F.T., Ting, K.M., Zhou, Z.H.: Isolation forest. In: 2008 Eighth IEEE International Conference on Data Mining, pp. 413–422. IEEE (2008)
22. Liu, Z., Liu, X., Ma, J., Gao, H.: An optimized computational framework for isolation forest. Math. Prob. Eng. **2018** (2018)
23. Maat, R. and Malali, A.: A Multipurpose Library for Synthetic Time Series in Python (2019). https://github.com/TimeSynth/TimeSynth. Accessed 09 Oct 2019
24. Mohammadi, S., Perina, A., Kiani, H., Murino, V.: Angry crowds: detecting violent events in videos. In: Leibe, B., Matas, J., Sebe, N., Welling, M. (eds.) ECCV 2016. LNCS, vol. 9911, pp. 3–18. Springer, Cham (2016). https://doi.org/10.1007/978-3-319-46478-7_1
25. Ross, M.K., Broz, F., Baillie, L.: Towards an adaptive robot for sports and rehabilitation coaching (2019). arXiv preprint arXiv:1909.08052
26. Rousseeuw, P.J., Hubert, M.: Anomaly detection by robust statistics. Wiley Interdisc. Rev. Data Min. Knowl. Disc. **8**(2), e1236 (2018)
27. Saha, S., Pal, M., Konar, A., Janarthanan, R.: Neural network based gesture recognition for elderly health care using kinect sensor. In: Panigrahi, B.K., Suganthan, P.N., Das, S., Dash, S.S. (eds.) SEMCCO 2013. LNCS, vol. 8298, pp. 376–386. Springer, Cham (2013). https://doi.org/10.1007/978-3-319-03756-1_34
28. Schneider, P., Memmesheimer, R., Kramer, I., Paulus, D.: Gesture recognition in RGB videos usinghuman body keypoints and dynamic time warping (2019). arXiv preprint arXiv:1906.12171
29. Su, C.J., Chiang, C.Y., Huang, J.Y.: Kinect-enabled home-based rehabilitation system using dynamic time warping and fuzzy logic. Appl. Soft Comput. **22**, 652–666 (2014)
30. Sultani, W., Chen, C., Shah, M.: Real-world anomaly detection in surveillance videos. In: Proceedings of the IEEE Conference on Computer Vision and Pattern Recognition, pp. 6479–6488 (2018)
31. Tanguy, P., Rémy-Néris, O., et al.: Computational architecture of a robot coach for physical exercises in kinaesthetic rehabilitation. In: 2016 25th IEEE International Symposium on Robot and Human Interactive Communication (RO-MAN), pp. 1138–1143. IEEE (2016)
32. Taranta II, E.M., Maghoumi, M., Pittman, C.R., LaViola Jr, J.J.: A rapid prototyping approach to synthetic data generation for improved 2d gesture recognition. In: Proceedings of the 29th Annual Symposium on User Interface Software and Technology, pp. 873–885. ACM (2016)

33. Tetteroo, D., et al.: Lessons learnt from deploying an end-user development platform for physical rehabilitation. In: Proceedings of the 33rd Annual ACM Conference on Human Factors in Computing Systems - CHI 2015, pp. 4133–4142. ACM Press, New York (2015). https://doi.org/10.1145/2702123.2702504, http://dl.acm.org/citation.cfm?doid=2702123.2702504
34. Tukey, J.W.: Exploratory Data Analysis, vol. 2. Reading, Mass (1977)
35. Velloso, E., Bulling, A., Gellersen, H.: Motionma: motion modelling and analysis by demonstration. In: Proceedings of the SIGCHI Conference on Human Factors in Computing Systems, pp. 1309–1318. ACM (2013)
36. Vox, J.P., Wallhoff, F.: Recognition of human motion exercises using skeleton data and SVM for rehabilitative purposes. In: 2017 IEEE Life Sciences Conference (LSC), pp. 266–269. IEEE (2017)
37. Wang, Z., Ding, Z.: Rehabilitation system for children with cerebral palsy based on body vector analysis and gmfm-66 standard. J. Phys. Conf. Ser. **1325**(1), 012088 (2019)
38. World Health Organization: Rehabilitation. In: World Report on Disability, chap. 4, p. 350. World Health Organization (2011). https://www.who.int/disabilities/world_report/2011/chapter4.pdf
39. World Health Organization: WHO — Rehabilitation in health systems. In: WHO, World Health Organization (2019). http://www.who.int/disabilities/rehabilitation_health_systems/en/
40. Zhao, W., Reinthal, M.A., Espy, D.D., Luo, X.: Rule-based human motion tracking for rehabilitation exercises: realtime assessment, feedback, and guidance. IEEE Access **5**, 21382–21394 (2017)

Deep Learning Based Gesture Classification for Hand Physical Therapy Interactive Program

Maleewan Rungruanganukul and Thitirat Siriborvornratanakul[✉]

Graduate School of Applied Statistics, National Institute of Development Administration (NIDA), 118 SeriThai Road, Bangkapi, Bangkok 10240, Thailand
yimyamii.ii@gmail.com, thitirat@as.nida.ac.th

Abstract. In this paper, we propose using the Google Colab deep learning framework to create and train convolutional neural networks from scratch. The trained network is part of a core artificial intelligent feature of our interactive software game, aiming to encourage white-collar workers to exercise hands and wrists frequently through playing the game. At this moment, the network is trained with our self-collected dataset of 12,000 bare-hand gesture images shot against a static dark background. The network focuses on classifying a still image into one of the six predefined classes of gestures and it seems to cope well with slight variation in size, skin tone, position and orientation of hand. This network is designed to be light in computation with real-time running time even on CPU. The network yields 99.68% accuracy on the validation set and 78% average accuracy when being tested with 50 different users. Our experiment on actual users reveals useful insight about problems using a deep learning based classifier in a real-time interactive system.

Keywords: Gesture recognition · Gesture classification · Deep learning · Convolutional neural network · Carpal Tunnel Syndrome · Hand physical therapy

1 Background

Recently Carpal Tunnel Syndrome (CTS) has become common symptoms for white-collar workers in Thailand. According to the information provided by National Institute of Neurological Disorders and Stroke [6], CTS is a medical disease that involves pressed or squeezed median nerve, resulting in numbness, weakness, or pain in hand, wrist and/or forearm; it is said to be three times more likely in women than men. Like other symptoms involving abnormality of nerves, proper physical therapy is a key to sustainable treatment of CTS. Hence, the simplest and cheapest therapy for an individual white-collar worker is to exercise hands and wrists regularly by themselves. Inspiring by this, we want to develop an interactive software game that encourages white-collar workers to do hand physical therapy more frequently in a more convenient and enjoyable manner.

© Springer Nature Switzerland AG 2020
V. G. Duffy (Ed.): HCII 2020, LNCS 12198, pp. 349–358, 2020.
https://doi.org/10.1007/978-3-030-49904-4_26

By using the software to show postures of effective hand physical therapy, a user can simply mimic the postures shown by the software in order to proceed to next game stages. This software helps not only eliminate the need for remembering many postures but also allow new postures to be easily added in the future. The rest of this paper explains our development of a core artificial intelligent feature of this software whose main responsibility is to verify whether a user is doing a right hand posture or not.

Speaking of gesture recognition techniques, there is a long history of researches and developments in both software and hardware aspects. Because our software focuses on being a simple and healthy game for white-collar workers, gesture recognition techniques requiring special hardware devices are not preferable—for example, Myo armband (production ended in October 2018), usb-connected Leap Motion sensor (https://www.leapmotion.com/) and other depth-camera based solutions as in [8], Google Soli with an internal miniature radar [5], Gest glove (https://gest.co/) and other special gloves as proposed in [2]. From our point of view, a vision-based technique using one monocular camera (operating in the visible light spectrum) is the most attractive solution. This is because of three main reasons—(1) these techniques are not intrusive and require neither a prior setup nor fiducial markers, (2) cameras are common hardware found in most recent smartphones, (3) majority of white-collar workers in Thailand have at least one smartphone in possession and are quite familiar with using smartphone's camera(s).

Before the disruption of deep learning based artificial intelligence, it is non-trivial to detect or recognize dynamic bare-hand gestures using a single monocular camera operating in pure visible light spectrum. This is because bare-hand gestures involve a large number of degrees of freedom and many unpredictable visual artifacts during actual uses. For example, Chen et al. [1] assume a static background so that a hand can be simply extracted using a background subtraction technique. To cope with bare-hand gestures in a dynamic background, the work of [4] proposes a set of carefully handcrafted visual features that combines 3D hand model, edge likelihood, Bayesian classifier and distance transformation. Instead of solely relying on handcrafted features, Guo et al. [3] improve their way of detecting hands in a complicated background with a multi-stage HOG-SVM classifier; the classifier helps classify image patches into five predefined categories (i.e., face, arm, simple background, complex background and fist), resulting in a more accurate hand detector that is robust to complex backgrounds. In short, it can be said that vision-based bare-hand gesture detection and recognition are difficult because they require us to carefully engineer visual models or algorithms that can tolerate high degree of visual unpredictability regarding not only the hand gestures themselves but also the background.

Dealing with visual information of extremely high uncertainty is what recent deep learning models excel at. This is in particular for Convolutional Neural Network (CNN or ConvNet) that changes the most difficult and time-consuming process of visual feature extraction into an automatic process of example-based supervised training. In Sect. 2, we explain two CNN models that are specifically designed for bare-hand gesture classification in the context of hand physical therapy software program. Instead of using transfer learning techniques or some pre-trained models for gesture classification, our CNN models are trained from scratch using a set of bare-hand gesture images collected by ourselves. This is in order to achieve a resultant model that consumes as less computational resources as possible, enabling the model to run in real time in common smartphones.

2 Proposed Methods

According to the pamphlet [7] distributed by one of the most prestigious hospital and medical school in Thailand, we notice that the suggested postures for hand physical therapy are similar to those of counting 0–5 digits. Starting from this assumption, the goal of this paper is to develop at least one CNN model that is able to correctly classify an input image into one of the six predefined counting gestures as shown in Fig. 1.

As mentioned earlier in Sect. 1 that we create the image dataset by ourselves. The data collection is done by using an OKER A229 webcam to capture bare-hand gesture images from five volunteer persons (two males and three females). Each collected image is an RGB image of 640×480 resolution, containing one hand shot against a static dark background in a normal lighting environment. The purpose of using a static background here is to focus on gesture classification capability of the CNN model first, rather than the background-foreground subtraction or lighting robustness capabilities. The final dataset consists of 12,000 image samples equally distributed into six predefined classes. All 12,000 image samples are later split into 11,400 training samples (=95%) and 600 validation samples (=5%). Figure 1 shows some images from our dataset. According to the figure, although our samples are all shot upright on a static dark background, there is a lot of variation in bare-hand gestures. For example, the gestures involve different sizes, positions and rotations of hands (relative to the image) and include images shot from both left and right hands.

After finished preparing the dataset, we move to the next step of building our first CNN model for bare-hand gesture classification. The first model is a simple and small CNN model with three main trainable layers as concluded in Table 1. Before being fed to the model, all RGB image samples of 640×480 resolution in our dataset are converted to single-channel greyscale images and resized to 28×28 resolution using a bilinear interpolation; this is done to keep the model's size as well as computational time as small as possible and to make the model invariant to slightly different skin tones. After that, the model is trained with Adam optimizer on categorical cross-entropy loss using default parameter values. In this paper, our development is based on Google Colab's Tesla K80 GPU (Keras with TensorFlow backend). Hence, it limits us to 12 GB of GPU RAM, the maximum of 12 continuous training hours, and training time per one epoch may be varied significantly according to traffic loads of Google Colab at a moment. With these limitations in mind, we train the first CNN model with batch's size of 128 for 300 epochs. Because the simplicity of this model,

count 0   count 1   count 2   count 3   count 4   count 5

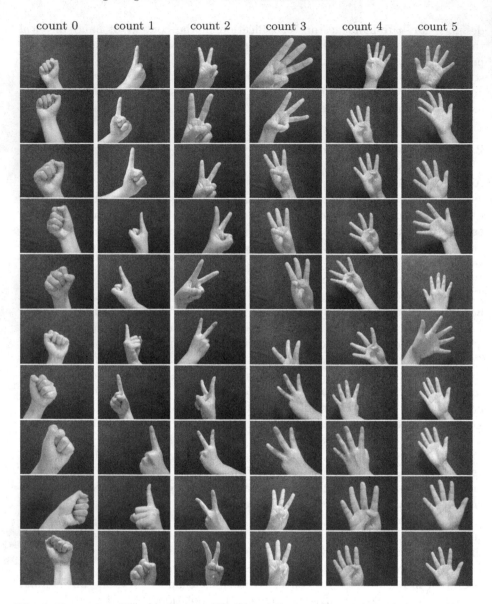

Fig. 1. Examples of images in our self-collected dataset. Six predefined classes of bare-hand gestures (regarding counting 0 to 5) are represented as six columns of images.

it takes about 2–5 min for training one epoch and the total training time is 10 h approximately. Nevertheless, the resultant model with 78.86% validation accuracy is not enough and the model performs poorly when being tested with our testing program (more details about the testing program in Sect. 3).

Table 1. The architecture of our first CNN model following the example codes of [9].

No.	Description	Output	Param
	Input layer	$28 \times 28 \times 1$	0
1	Conv2D (32 3×3 kernels, stride = 1, Relu)	$26 \times 26 \times 32$	320
2	Conv2D (64 3×3 kernels, stride = 1, Relu)	$24 \times 24 \times 64$	18,496
	MaxPooling2D (pool size = 2, stride = 2)	$12 \times 12 \times 64$	0
	Dropout (drop 25% of inputs)	$12 \times 12 \times 64$	0
	Flatten	9,216	0
3	Dense (128 nodes, Relu)	128	1,179,776
	Dropout (drop 50% of inputs)	128	0
	Output layer (6 nodes, Softmax)	6	774

Total parameters = 1,199,366 (all trainable)

To improve accuracy of the model, we move to the second design of CNN with more complicated architecture as concluded in Table 2. Comparing to the first model, in the second model, the size of input image is increased from $28 \times 28 \times 1$ to $160 \times 120 \times 1$, more convolution and dense layers are added, and a batch normalization layer is inserted after each convolution and dense layer. Because this second model is larger, it is not possible to finish training within the 12-h limitation of Google Colab. Hence, the total 300-epoch (batch size = 128) training is divided into six consecutive sub-training steps (50 epochs per one sub-training step). After 48 h of training, the resultant model yields a very high validation accuracy of 99.68%.

3   Experimental Results

Despite of the high validation accuracy of 99.68%, we still want to validate our second CNN model with actual white-collar Thai workers in the context of an interactive software for hand physical therapy. For this purpose, we develop a separated testing software program and setup an experiment as shown in Fig. 2. This experiment involves 50 different participants whose ages range from 25 to 35; there are 20 males and 30 females included with no duplication with the five volunteers during the dataset creation in Sect. 2.

During one experiment for one participant, the participant sits in front of our experimental laptop in a position that their hand is clearly seen by the camera. Once the testing program is started, the participant is asked to perform the 0, 1, 2, 3, 4 and 5 counting gestures respectively. For each counting gesture, the participant is asked to show the same gesture repeatedly for three times (each for about 3 s) but with slightly different positions and orientations of hand relative to the camera. This means that for one participant, our testing program collects 6 * 3 = 18 experimental data as shown in Fig. 3. Hence, for 50 participants, there are 50 * (6 * 3) = 900 experimental data collected. Running this testing

Table 2. The architecture of our second experimented CNN model.

No.	Description	Output	Param
	Input layer	$160 \times 120 \times 1$	0
1	Conv2D (64 3 × 3 kernels, stride = 1, Relu)	$158 \times 118 \times 64$	640
	BatchNorm	$158 \times 118 \times 64$	256
2	Conv2D (64 3 × 3 kernels, stride = 1, Relu)	$156 \times 116 \times 64$	36,928
	MaxPooling2D (pool size = 2, stride = 2)	$78 \times 58 \times 64$	–
	BatchNorm	$78 \times 58 \times 64$	256
	Dropout (drop 25% of inputs)	$78 \times 58 \times 64$	0
3	Conv2D (128 3 × 3 kernels, stride = 1, Relu)	$76 \times 56 \times 128$	73,856
	BatchNorm	$76 \times 56 \times 128$	512
4	Conv2D (128 3 × 3 kernels, stride = 1, Relu)	$74 \times 54 \times 128$	147,584
	MaxPooling2D (pool size = 2, stride = 2)	$37 \times 27 \times 128$	0
	BatchNorm	$37 \times 27 \times 128$	512
	Dropout (drop 25% of inputs)	$37 \times 27 \times 128$	0
5	Conv2D (256 3 × 3 kernels, stride = 1, Relu)	$35 \times 25 \times 256$	295,168
	BatchNorm	$35 \times 25 \times 256$	1,024
6	Conv2D (256 3 × 3 kernels, stride = 1, Relu)	$33 \times 23 \times 256$	590,080
	MaxPooling2D (pool size = 2, stride = 2)	$16 \times 11 \times 256$	0
	BatchNorm	$16 \times 11 \times 256$	1,024
	Dropout (drop 25% of inputs)	$16 \times 11 \times 256$	0
	Flatten	45,056	0
7	Dense (256 nodes, Relu)	256	11,534,592
	BatchNorm	256	1,024
	Dropout (drop 50% of inputs)	256	0
8	Dense (60 nodes, Relu)	60	15,420
	BatchNorm	60	240
	Dropout (drop 50% of inputs)	60	0
	Output layer (6 nodes, Softmax)	6	366

Total parameters = 12,699,482 (trainable = 12,697,058)

software program on Lenovo Ideapad 320S notebook (Intel Core i5-8250U CPU, 8GB RAM), the speed of prediction is good even in the CPU-only computational mode. Some gestures (i.e., two-finger and five-finger gestures) use only one second for a single prediction. Hence, it can implied that, in term of speed, our second CNN model is suitable for being used as part of an interactive software program.

Figure 4 shows accuracies regarding each gesture from the total 900 experimental data. The average testing accuracy of 78% is not so bad. In detail, testing accuracies of the six counting gestures are: 111/150 = 74% for no-finger gesture, 130/150 = 86.67% for one-finger gesture, 121/150 = 80.67% for two-finger

Fig. 2. Validating the trained CNN model with actual users. Left image is our experimental setup. Right image is a screenshot of our testing software program.

gesture, $106/150 = 70.67\%$ for three-finger gesture, $100/150 = 66.67$ for four-finger gesture, and $134/150 = 89.33\%$ for five-finger gesture. From these results, it can be seen that gesture with the highest testing accuracy is the five-finger gesture of 89.33% whereas gesture with the least testing accuracy is the four-finger gesture of 66.67%. Investigating the four-finger gesture closely, we discover that our current CNN model often misclassifies four-finger gestures as five-finger gestures. This issue of misclassification needs to be considered carefully in our future work.

Next, we investigate the experimental results in order to find differences (if any) among the three continuous attempts of a participant performing one gesture. According to Fig. 5, results from all six gestures agree that testing accuracies are always lowest in the first attempt and highest in the third attempt. Average testing accuracies regarding all six gestures in this experiment are 57% for the first attempt, 83.33% for the second attempt and 93% for the third attempt. Our conclusion regarding this is that the first attempt suffers the most from ambiguous or unknown shapes of hand during the short period of time when a participant is changing from one gesture to another.

Apart from problems of misclassifying the four-finger gesture and unreliable prediction during the changing period between two gestures, we also discover a problem of moving gestures from this experiment. When a participant moves their hand, sometimes it causes motion blur in captured images, resulting in incorrect prediction.

4 Conclusion and Future Works

This paper proposes a prototype system of an interactive software program whose goal is to encourage white-collar workers in Thailand to exercise their hands and wrists regularly. Focusing on the core artificial intelligent feature of the program, we develop and train two convolutional neural networks from scratch using our self-collected dataset of 12,000 bare-hand gesture images shot against a static

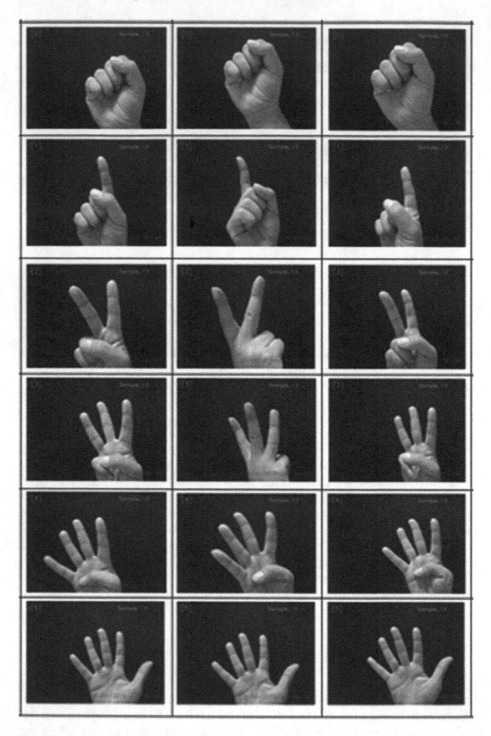

Fig. 3. An example of 18 experimental data (3 data per one gesture) collected from one participant.

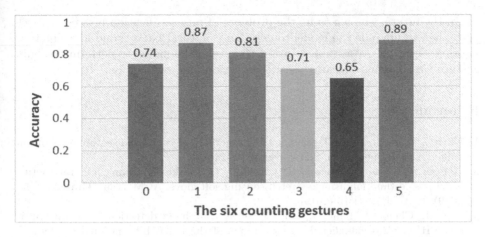

Fig. 4. Evaluating the trained CNN model with actual human. This graph shows testing accuracies (vertical axis, 0.0–1.0 scale) regarding the six predefined 0–5 counting gestures (horizontal axis). The number of all experimental data is 900; for each gesture, there are 3 data per one participant, equaling the total of 150 data per one gesture.

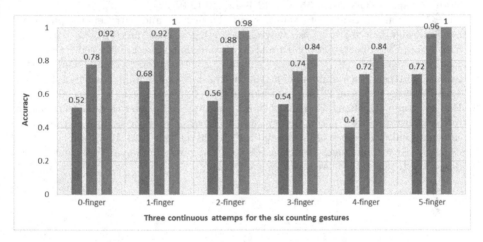

Fig. 5. Evaluating the trained CNN model with actual human. Vertical axis shows testing accuracies ranging from 0.0 to 1.0. The horizontal axis illustrates six predefined 0–5 counting gestures where each gesture consists of three values of accuracies from the first, second and third attempts respectively from left to right. The number of all experimental data is 900; for each gesture, there are 50 data per one attempt, equaling the total of 150 data per one gesture.

dark background. The networks are trained to classify an image into one of six predefined gestures. Our second network with more complicated architecture yields a very high validation accuracy of 99.68% in the validation set. However, when being tested with 50 different users, the average testing accuracy drops to 78%.

In the future, we plan to fix the problem of misclassification between classes first, then to upgrade the model to cope with natural background and different lighting variation. After that, we want to extend the model to perform not only gesture classification but also gesture detection and localization.

References

1. Chen, Z., Kim, J., Liang, J., Zhang, J., Yuan, Y.: Real-time hand gesture recognition using finger segmentation. Sci. World J. (2014)
2. Glauser, O., Wu, S., Panozzo, D., Hilliges, O., Sorkine-Hornung, O.: Interactive hand pose estimation using a stretch-sensing soft glove. ACM Trans. Graph. (TOG 2019) **38**(4), 41:1–41:15 (2019)
3. Guo, J., Cheng, J., Pang, J., Guo, Y.: Real-time hand detection based on multi-stage HOG-SVM classifier. In: Proceedings of the IEEE International Conference on Image Processing (ICIP 2013) (2013)
4. Kerdvibulvech, C.: Hand tracking by extending distance transform and hand model in real-time. Pattern Recogn. Image Anal. (PRIA 2015) **25**(3), 437–441 (2015)
5. Lien, J., et al.: Soli: ubiquitous gesture sensing with millimeter wave radar. ACM Trans. Graph. (TOG 2016) **35**(4), 142:1–142:19 (2016)
6. The National Institute of Neurological Disorders and Stroke: Carpal tunnel syndrome fact sheet. https://www.ninds.nih.gov/Disorders/Patient-Caregiver-Education/Fact-Sheets/Carpal-Tunnel-Syndrome-Fact-Sheet. Accessed 1 Dec 2019
7. Phoojaroenchachai, R.: Physical therapy for everyone: Hand and finger exercise. https://www.si.mahidol.ac.th/th/division/hph/admin/news_files/627_49_1.pdf. Accessed 28 Aug 2019. (Thai language)
8. Ren, Z., Yuan, J., Zhang, Z.: Robust hand gesture recognition based on finger-earth mover's distance with a commodity depth camera. In: Proceedings of the ACM International Conference on Multimedia (MM 2011), pp. 1093–1096 (2011)
9. Tan, C.: Real-time finger detection. https://becominghuman.ai/real-time-finger-detection-1e18fea0d1d4. Accessed 28 Aug 2019

Study on the Effect of Cervical Spine Somatosensory Games of Virtual Reality and Augmented Reality on Relieving Neck Muscle Fatigue

Zishan Song, Ting Han[⊠], Dian Zhu, Yufei Xie, Hanyue Xiao,
Tianjia Shen, and Jingran He

School of Design, Shanghai Jiao Tong University, Shanghai, China
songzishan1996@163.com, hanting@sjtu.edu.cn

Abstract. The purpose of this study was to explore whether virtual reality (VR) and augmented reality (AR) cervical somatosensory games can effectively alleviate neck discomfort caused by mobile phones. If validation was effective, the effect of VR and AR games on neck muscle fatigue alleviation was compared. Twenty-four healthy adults between ages 19 and 25 participated in the study. Experiment 1 was to verify the fatigue of neck and shoulder muscles caused by long-term use of mobile phones. Experiment 2 explored whether the VR game and the AR game have an impact on neck muscle fatigue and compared the degree of influence. The integrated electromyography (IEMG) and median frequency (MF) of the upper trapezius, splenius cervical muscles, and sternocleidomastoid muscles were collected. Experiment 1 showed that the MF of some muscles of the participants of both the VR group and the AR group decreased with time, while the IEMG of some muscles increased with time. Experiment 2 showed that the MF of some muscles of the participants of both the VR group and the AR group showed an upward trend, while the IEMG of some muscles showed a downward trend. There were significant differences between experiment 1 and experiment 2 ($P < 0.05$). The results of the subjective evaluation scale of neck muscle fatigue filled in by the participants were consistent with the experimental results, which showed that both the VR group and the AR group could feel the cervical relief, and the VR game could better alleviate the neck and shoulder muscle fatigue.

Keywords: Virtual reality games · Augmented reality games · Neck muscle fatigue

1 Introduction

The touch screen smartphone has become an indispensable handheld communication device in people's daily life and work. Because of the rapidly-developing technology and various useful features of mobile phones, more people use them for more extended periods daily [1, 2]. Despite the benefits of mobile phones, their use can increase risks of musculoskeletal pain and injuries, especially in the neck and upper extremities [3–5]. The cervical vertebra is the crucial part connecting the trunk and head of the human body. Once

© Springer Nature Switzerland AG 2020
V. G. Duffy (Ed.): HCII 2020, LNCS 12198, pp. 359–375, 2020.
https://doi.org/10.1007/978-3-030-49904-4_27

cervical vertebra has pathological changes, patients may have many symptoms. Cervical muscle fatigue is one of the essential causes of cervical spondylosis. Timely relieving and eliminating neck fatigue can effectively prevent the occurrence of cervical spondylosis. The incidence of cervical spondylosis in long-term ambulatory workers is 4-6 times that of non-long-term ambulatory workers, and the overall incidence has reached 15%. The etiology of cervical spondylosis is various, and the pathological mechanism is complicated. However, the cervical pain of various causes is closely related to chronic neck muscle fatigue and reduction of contractility to varying degrees [6]. The stability of the cervical spine is maintained by the ligament system of bone and joint 20% and the rest 80% by the surrounding muscles, which play a vital role in maintaining the stability of the cervical spine [7, 8]. Most modern people suffer from neck and shoulder muscle fatigue-related diseases due to improper use of mobile phones, which significantly affects their physical, and mental health. In the process of using the mobile phone in a sitting position, long-term neck bending is a factor that causes neck pain and changes in neck muscle activity. When the smartphone is used in a static state and the arm is not supported, it will cause abnormal alignment of the neck and shoulder. Due to the small screen of the smartphone, the head must be bent to see the screen, which increases the activity of neck extensor, the overload of neck and shoulder and muscle fatigue, and reduces the working ability and affects the musculoskeletal system [9, 10].

The application of virtual reality (VR) games and augmented reality (AR) games in the field of medical rehabilitation training has gradually attracted the attention of researchers. Researchers have developed a virtual reality (VR) device for evaluating neck kinematics, and the device has been proved to be a useful and reliable evaluation tool for neck pain [11, 12]. It may also be used as a training tool. Experiments have proved that VR can effectively reduce pain and anxiety [13, 14], stimulate people's physical activity, and improve exercise compliance and effectiveness [15–18]. Cervical kinematic training can improve chronic neck pain with and without interactive VR training. However, VR training is considered to be better to improve these factors because VR can interact and potentially disperse pain and anxiety [19]. Home VR exercise may contribute to neck pain intensity and selected kinematics, but may not be sufficient to treat chronic neck pain [20]. Researchers used a new customized VR system to evaluate neck kinematics and compare neck pain with neck kinematics characteristics of patients in the control group in the process of interactive movement. Because VR can shift participants' attention from their body movement (internal focus of attention) to their external focus of attention (external focus of attention) [21], which can enhance the operation Compared with traditional balance training, VR balance training has better effect [22]. Oculus Rift, a virtual reality (VR) head-mounted display embedded in inertial sensors, monitors head movement, and measures cervical kinematics through rift and reference motion tracking system [23]. Similarly, researchers have developed a little-known AR game (Neck Pet) for relieving neck fatigue. However, there is a lack of experimental research to prove the effectiveness of non-medical VR and AR cervical somatosensory games in daily life for relieving neck fatigue.

Muscle fatigue is a state in which muscle fibers are active for a long time, resulting in muscle strength decrease, and the functional level of muscle fibers cannot load the energy needed by current exercise. It is essential to measure the fatigue of neck muscles. The traditional method of muscle evaluation is based on the determination of lactate content in blood, but it is not easy to accept because of its damage. Surface electromyography (sEMG) signal analysis and detection have the advantages of non-invasive, practical and multi-target, and become an effective tool to evaluate local muscle fatigue [24, 25]. It has been widely used in clinical medicine, sports medicine, rehabilitation medicine, ergonomics, and sports biology. Seong yeol Kim [26] studied the effect of smartphone use time on neck and shoulder muscle fatigue and pain by surface electromyography, and combined with vas visual simulation scoring method. It was found that with the extension of smartphone use time, the pain and fatigue of spine muscle and trapezius muscle upper fiber increased, and the median frequency (MF) decreased with the gradual increase of fatigue. Kraemer [27] and Gustafsson E [3] found that when muscles keep the same static state, fatigue will occur with the increase of time. In the study of the influence of smartphones on the upper limb muscles when they are used and whether there is a difference between the use of smartphones and computers, the spectrum variables obtained from the frequency area of sEMG are used as an objective measurement of muscle fatigue [28]. The research of the above scholars has proved that the surface electromyography signal (sEMG) shows the characteristics of regular changes in the process of neck-shoulder muscle fatigue, and it is believed that sEMG can be used to study neck-shoulder muscle fatigue. However, up to now, there is no system to determine the degree of muscle fatigue.

The purpose of this study is to explore whether the cervical somatosensory game of VR and AR can effectively alleviate the discomfort of the neck caused by the use of mobile phones through experiments. If the intervention is verified to be effective, the degree and effect of VR and AR games on the alleviation of cervical fatigue will be compared. The results of this experiment can be used to guide the development and improvement of VR and AR cervical somatosensory games, and help people who use mobile phones for a long time to choose a more suitable and effective way to relieve neck fatigue.

2   Methods

2.1   Participants

The voluntary participants in the current study were 24 healthy adults (average age: 22 ± 3 years old) with an equal sex distribution (12 males and 12 females), they were recruited through e-mail Solicitation in a university community. All participants were experienced mobile phone users (average mobile phone use experience: 10 ± 2.2 hours per day). Currently (past six months), there was no history of musculoskeletal pain and neck and upper limb musculoskeletal diseases, and they did not participate in strenuous exercise within 48 h before participating in the experiment. The University's Institutional Review Committee approved the experimental protocol for the study, and all participants agreed in writing before participating in the study.

2.2 Apparatus

Muscle can be divided into smooth muscle, cardiac muscle, and skeletal muscle according to their functions. The skeletal muscle in this experimental study is distributed in the head, neck, trunk, and limbs, usually attached to the bone. The skeletal muscle contracts rapidly, powerfully, and easily fatigue. Electromyography (EMG) signal is the action potential change of one-dimensional time series produced by the contraction of muscle fiber caused by the excitation of skeletal muscle in the process of the activity. The EMG signal generated by muscle activity is guided, amplified, and recorded by the EMG signal measurement system. The EMG signal is divided into needle electromyography signal (nEMG) and surface electromyography signal (sEMG) [29].

The mean power frequency (MPF) and median frequency (MF) analysis of muscle activity have reasonable specificity and sensitivity. Generally, when MF and MPF values decrease, muscle fatigue begins [30, 31]. In the aspect of time-domain analysis, the results show that: with the increase of hand-held load, the integrated electromyography (IEMG) increases, and with the increase of time, the IEMG first increases and then decreases. At the end of the experiment, the IEMG decreases to the lowest value, and at this time, the participants feel fatigued gradually increases. Therefore, when the IEMG value is lower than the initial value, muscle fatigue occurs, and the EMG power spectrum shifts to the left.

In this experiment, the Ultium-EMG signal acquisition system produced by Noraxon in the United States was used to measure and analyze the sEMG in combination with myoMUSCLE software (Fig. 1). The Ultium EMG sensor system is a multi-mode wireless device, which can provide accurate data analysis and evaluation functions. It mainly includes the wireless sensors, amplifiers, data lines, sensor power supply, and other system components. In the process of collecting the original EMG, it is easy to be interfered with by other electrical signals with the magnetic field. Therefore, in order to keep the environment of collecting the EMG signal in the laboratory as ideal and straightforward as possible, a series of artificial processing should be carried out for the collected original EMG signal to eliminate the influence of other factors as much as possible [32].

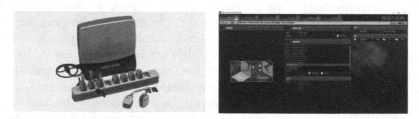

Fig. 1. The EMG acquisition equipment (left) and software interface (right)

Surface electromyography (sEMG) was used to measure muscular activation levels of three sampled muscles: upper trapezius, cervical muscles, and sternocleidomastoid.

This study analyzed the time-domain and frequency-domain indexes of the above three sampled muscle sEMG, and the IEMG and MF were selected for statistical analysis. Combined with the biomechanical analysis method, this study explored the characteristic parameters that could not be affected by random circumstances and adequately represented the fatigue degree of the participants.

2.3   Experimental Design

The experimental design of the influencing factors of muscle fatigue was designed according to the type of games. In Experiment 1, the change of neck and shoulder muscle fatigue caused by using the mobile phone for a long time was verified through the surface electromyography experimental instrument. In Experiment 2, whether the VR game and the AR game had an impact on neck fatigue through the control experiment was explored, and the influence degree was compared. Three questionnaires were designed for each time node. The subjective evaluation scale measured the fatigue degree of neck and shoulder muscles.

The muscles mainly involved in the mobile phone use were selected (Fig. 2): the upper trapezius, the cervical muscles, and the sternocleidomastoid muscles: 1) Superior trapezius muscle: it starts from the external occipital protrusion, the upper nuchal line, the nuchal ligament, the 7th cervical vertebra and all the spinous processes of the thoracic vertebra. It connects the upper part of the occipital bone, which plays a significant supporting role for the shoulders and arms. When the scapula is fixed, the right trapezius muscle can bend the neck to the right when contracting; when both muscles contract at the same time, the head can move backward. 2) Cervical musculus: it starts from the spinous process of the third to the sixth thoracic vertebrae and ends at the posterior transverse process node of the upper two or three cervical vertebraes. When the right muscle contracts, the head bends to the right; when the two muscles contract at the same time, the head tilts back. 3) Sternocleidomastoid muscle: it starts from the front of the sternal stalk and the sternal end of the clavicle and extends obliquely to the mastoid process of the temporal bone. When the right sternocleidomastoid muscle contracts, the head inclines to the right; when the two muscles contract at the same time, the head inclines forward. The primary function of the sternocleidomastoid muscle is to keep the head in a normal upright position and maintain the head in a horizontal direction.

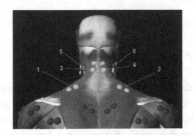

Fig. 2.   Three sampled muscles in the study:1) Upper left trapezius, 2) Upper right trapezius, 3) Left cervical muscle, 4) Right cervical muscle, 5) Left sternocleidomastoid muscle, 6) Right sternocleidomastoid muscle

Experimental stimuli included: 1) Mobile VR game - Froggy VR (Fig. 3). It was a casual VR adventure scenario game. In Froggy VR, the player played a frog on the way to rescue the princess. In the game, the player needed to move his/her head and upper body to relieve neck muscle fatigue. 2) Mobile AR game - Neck Pet (Fig. 4). It was a more intense and exciting leisure game, which was equivalent to the AR version of Pac-Man. This game advocated game-based fitness, and paid attention to people's cervical spine health, and guided people to release the pressure of the cervical spine and lumbar spine through the way of the game.

Fig. 3. Froggy VR

Fig. 4. Neck Pet

2.4 Questionnaires Design

The neck fatigue scale was used to send out a questionnaire to the subjects. The participants filled in the questionnaire to evaluate the muscle fatigue, to collect and count the subjective fatigue feelings of the subjects at three experimental nodes. Three questionnaires were needed in the experiment.

Questionnaire 1: According to the relevant research and literature at home and abroad, combined with the interview survey of young mobile phone users and the experimental design, three questionnaires were finally designed for the participants. Questionnaire 1 was composed of three fundamental dimensions: basic information/dependence on mobile phone/fatigue of using the mobile phone. The participants who met the experimental requirements were selected through questionnaire 1: there was no strenuous exercise within 48 h before the experiment, and no neck and shoulder disease within the past six months. The filling time of the questionnaire was within one day before the experiment. The questionnaire included: participants' basic information (name/gender/age/occupation), filter criteria (whether there was strenuous exercise within 48 h before the experiment, whether there was neck and shoulder disease within the past six months), dependence (whether there has been continuous use of mobile phones for more than 40 min: 0-never, 1-occasionally, 2-often, 3-always), whether long-term use of mobile phones would feel tired (0-no fatigue, 1-slight fatigue, 2-moderate fatigue, 3-severe fatigue).

Questionnaire 2: The self-assessment questionnaire of the cervical fatigue status of the participants, which aimed to obtain the subjective cervical shoulder fatigue status of the subjects through the main complaint mode. It could supplement and support the following experimental data and explored the relationship between the participants' feelings and physiological indicators. The questionnaire was divided into two parts: the current overall fatigue level of the neck and the respective fatigue level of the tested muscle position. (In order to make the participants clearly and intuitively know the position of each muscle, it was presented in the form of pictures.) According to the existing literature and the existing fatigue scale, the questionnaire adopted the eleven-level scale. The time required for filling in the questionnaire was 1 min before the 30-min mobile task and 1 min after the 30-min mobile task. The content of the questionnaire included: the current level of neck fatigue (0–10: very non-fatigue - very fatigue), the level of fatigue of each of the six muscles in the neck (0–10: very non-fatigue - very fatigue). The schematic diagram shown in Fig. 2 was attached to the questionnaire to help the fillers distinguish the position and name of the muscles.

Questionnaire 3: The self-assessment questionnaire of neck fatigue degree and the game relief fatigue degree of the participants. The subjective state of the neck and shoulder fatigue and the degree of relief of neck fatigue after VR or AR games were obtained through the main complaint, and also explored the relationship between the participants' feelings and physiological indicators. The questionnaire was divided into three parts: the current overall fatigue level of the neck, the fatigue level of the tested muscle position, and the relief level of the tested muscle position after the game. The filling time of the questionnaire was required to be one minute after the VR/AR game. The questionnaire included: the current level of neck fatigue (0–10: very non-fatigue - very fatigue), the level of fatigue of six muscles in the neck (0–10: very non-fatigue - very fatigue), the level of relief of six muscles in the neck after the experiment (0–10: no relief - very relief). The questionnaire was also attached to the schematic diagram, as shown in Fig. 2 to help the fillers distinguish the position and name of the muscles.

2.5 Tasks and Procedure

The control experiment was used in the study. Twenty-four healthy participants were randomly divided into the VR group and the AR group. Twelve participants in each group, and six males and six females were included in both groups. The participants in the VR group and the AR group needed to keep their heads down and used the mobile phone for 30 min. Then, the VR group needed to play the mobile phone VR neck somatosensory game-Froggy VR for 10 min, and the AR group needed to play the mobile phone AR neck somatosensory game-Neck Pet for 10 min. During the experiment, the EMG data of the neck and shoulder were collected (Fig. 5), and the subjective fatigue evaluation scale was filled before and after the experiment.

Fig. 5. Equipped with electrode patch and EMG sensors

Before the experiment, each participant was explained the whole process of the experiment, and to be familiar with the requirements and precautions of the experiment. After filling in the necessary information, the participants needed to relax for 5 min, and formally enter the experimental state after the physical condition was stable. The experiment was divided into two small experiments. 1) Experiment 1: the participants used the mobile phone in the sitting position under the laboratory conditions and made the neck a certain bending angle. The time was 30 min. When using the mobile phone, there was no special requirement for the content. 2) Experiment 2: at the end of Experiment 1, the participants randomly played VR/AR neck somatosensory games for 10 min (Fig. 6). The EMG of neck and shoulder was measured during both the two experiments. Before the beginning of Experiment 1 and at the end of the two experiments, the subjective fatigue assessment scale was filled in. In the process of the experiment, the muscles mainly involved in the mobile phone's behavior activities were selected: the upper trapezius, the cervical muscles, and the sternocleidomastoid muscles, and measured the IEMG and MF. The experimental data were analyzed by Excel and SPSS 22.0.

Fig. 6. VR game activity (left) and AR game activity (right)

2.6   Data Processing

The qualified participants were selected through questionnaire 1. A total of 25 questionnaires were sent out. According to the requirements of the ratio of males and females and the condition of neck and shoulder disease, 24 qualified participants were finally selected. There were 12 males and 12 females, who were aged between 19-25 years old (SD = 1.0198), and their occupation range was college students, designers, and programmers.

Questionnaire 1 showed that nearly all the participants had the experience of continuous use of mobile phones for more than 40 min, and more than 75% of them often used mobile phones for more than 40 min. Almost all of the participants felt tired after using the mobile phone for a long time, and nearly 40% of them had moderate fatigue.

The measurement of sEMG was divided into three-time nodes: 1) recorded the average value of IEMG and MF of the muscles when the participants were in the relaxed sitting state before using the mobile phone. 2) recorded the average value of IEMG and MF when the participants were in the sitting position and using the mobile phone for 30 min with their heads down. 3) recorded the IEMG and MF after the participants played the VR/AR game for 10 min in the sitting position. Data measure of sEMG in two states: 1) state I: kept the head down and held for two seconds at most; 2) state II: turned the head right and held for two seconds at most.

The sEMG measured was processed and analyzed in myoMUSCLE software. Firstly, the original EMG was filtered and rectified, and the noise was filtered out to the maximum extent, then the IEMG value and MF were calculated. IEMG was the total discharge of the action potential of all the motor units participating in the activity in a certain period of time. MF is the result of the fast Fourier transform of the electromyographic signal of all the neck and shoulder muscles involved in the activity power spectral density (PSD), the frequency value corresponding to half of the power spectral area, which represents the power spectral density function of the electric signal of the neck and shoulder muscles at a certain time point. After data processing, IEMG and MF were calculated directly in the software. After exporting the processed data, SPSS 22.0 and Excel were used to calculate the average value of all participants in each period of time, as the corresponding muscle value of each part in this period. The processed and analyzed data in myoMUSCLE software (Fig. 7).

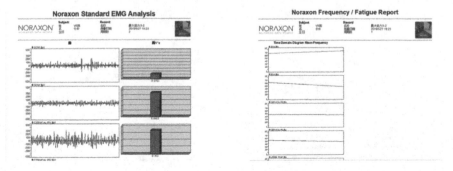

Fig. 7.   IEMG report (left) and MF report (right)

3 Results

3.1 Experimental Data Analysis

The data comparison between the VR group and the AR group is shown in Fig. 8, Fig. 9, Fig. 10, and Fig. 11. Generally speaking, most of the data turned at time node 2, and the slope of the line graph changed obviously. The results of Experiment 1 showed that the MF of some muscles in the VR group and the AR group decreased with the increase of time, while the IEMG of some muscles increased with the increase of time, which indicated that the fatigue degree of some muscles increased with the increase of time. The results of Experiment 2 showed that the MF of some muscles in VR group and AR group was on the rise, while the IEMG of some muscles was on the decline, which showed that playing 10 min VR/AR game in sitting posture could alleviate the fatigue of some muscles in varying degrees. By comparing the data of the VR group and the AR group, it could be concluded that the slope of the broken line graph of the MF of some muscles in the VR group was more significant, and the upward trend was more obvious. Similarly, the slope of the broken line graph of IEMG was more significant, and the downward trend was more evident. The expected result before the experiment was measurement state II: the trend of data change in the maximum right turn state was more obvious because the peak value of sEMG recorded during the experiment was evident. However, it was found that the trend of data change in measurement state I: the maximum low turn state was more visible, which conformed to the experimental hypothesis results.

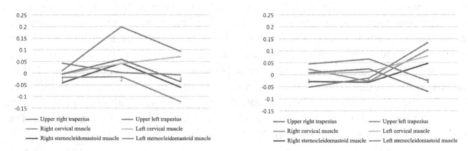

Fig. 8. IEMG (uV) with maximum head-down: VR group (left) and AR group (right)

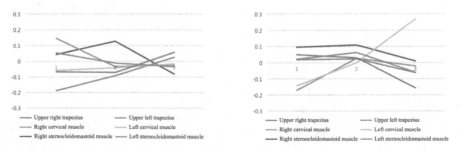

Fig. 9. IEMG (uV) with maximum right-turn: VR group (left) and AR group (right)

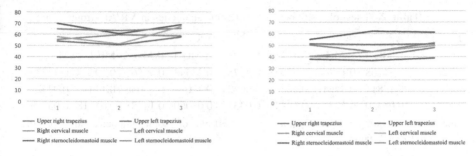

Fig. 10. MF (Hz) with maximum head-down: VR group (left) and AR group (right)

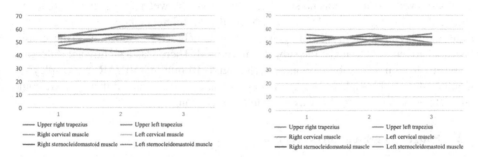

Fig. 11. MF (Hz) with maximum right-turn: VR group (left) and AR group (right)

According to the T-test of the EMG value of the VR group and the AR group, there was no significant difference between the VR group and the AR group in relaxed sitting state and 30 min after playing the mobile phone. After playing VR/AR game for 10 min, a T-test was conducted between the VR group and the AR group, which proved that there was a significant difference between experiment 1 and experiment 2 ($P < 0.05$), as shown in Table 1.

Table 1. T-test of EMG: Maximum head-down (up) and maximum right-turn (down)

Time node	MF (VR&AR)	IEMG (VR&AR)
1	0.53245756	0.46021979
2	0.352073792	0.445729001
3	0.015078285	0.129537497
Time node	MF (VR&AR)	IEMG (VR&AR)
1	0.245757404	0.498391796
2	0.375243633	0.438725332
3	0.01382726	0.06974133

Time nodes: 1) sitting relaxed; 2) after playing 30 min of mobile phone; 3) after playing 10 min of VR/AR game.

Table 2. T-test of EMG between different time nodes in VR/AR group

Time node	AR				VR			
	IEMG 1	IEMG 2	MF 1	MF 2	IEMG 1	IEMG 2	MF 1	MF 2
1&2	0.41268	0.15464	0.38951	0.32753	0.23548	0.49662	0.19208	0.32779
1&3	0.13811	0.39647	0.06801	0.06621	0.42097	0.45056	0.17443	0.02521
2&3	0.05410	0.22783	0.10445	0.03310	0.08060	0.14488	0.04118	0.03619

Time nodes: 1) sitting relaxed; 2) after playing 30 min of mobile phone; 3) after playing 10 min of VR/AR game.

Table 2 showed the T-test between different time nodes in VR and AR groups. The results showed that there was no significant difference between sitting relaxed state and sitting after playing 30 min. There was no significant difference between sitting relaxed state and playing 10 min VR/AR game. It was concluded that 30 min of the mobile task was not enough to make the subjects more tired. There was a significant difference between 30 min of mobile phone playing and 10 min of VR/AR game playing. Combined with the analysis of experimental data, it was concluded that VR/AR could alleviate neck fatigue, which was a reliable conclusion.

3.2   Fatigue Questionnaires Analysis

The questionnaire results of 12 participants in the VR group showed that all users felt neck fatigue after performing mobile tasks, two-thirds of them felt neck fatigue relief after VR games, two of them thought that VR games increased neck fatigue. Two of them showed no relief effect.

According to the result of whether there was relief to the neck after VR and AR games in questionnaire 3 (0–10: very unrelieved-very relieved), both the VR group and the AR group felt the relief of the neck, among which the VR game could better relieve the feeling of neck and shoulder fatigue (Table 3 and Fig. 12).

Table 3. Whether the neck was relieved after VR and AR games (0–10: very unrelieved - very relieved)

	Upper trap. Left	Upper trap. Right	Cervical PS. Left	Cervical PS. Right	SCM Left	SCM Right
VR	6.16666667	6.23719473	7.08333333	6.93184726	6.50	6.5833333
AR	5.15384615	4.84615385	5.46153846	5.38461538	5.3076923	4.7692308

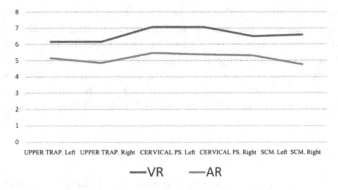

Fig. 12. Whether the neck was relieved after VR and AR games

According to the self-assessment of the total fatigue level of the neck and shoulder in the questionnaire, the two experimental groups felt a high level of neck fatigue after performing mobile tasks. After the VR/AR game, the fatigue level of the neck and shoulder returned to the initial level of neck and shoulder fatigue. According to the comparison between the second self-assessment of neck and shoulder fatigue (after mobile phone task) and the third self-assessment of neck and shoulder fatigue (after the VR/AR game), it could be seen that the neck and shoulder fatigue in the VR group decreased more, and the VR game was more effective in relieving neck fatigue (Table 4 and Fig. 13).

Table 4. Total fatigue of neck and shoulder in VR and AR groups

Time node	AR	VR
1	7.07692308	6.000
2	8.38461538	8.416666667
3	7.07692308	6.416666667

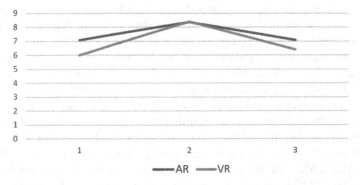

Fig. 13. Total fatigue of neck and shoulder in VR and AR groups

There was a significant difference between experiment 1 and experiment 2 (P < 0.05). Combined with the analysis of experimental data, it could be concluded that VR or AR cervical somatosensory games played a specific role in relieving neck fatigue. The conclusion of the subjective evaluation scale of neck muscle fatigue filled in by the participants was consistent with the experimental results, which showed that the VR group and the AR group felt the relief of neck. At the same time, the VR game could give the participants more sense of relief of neck and shoulder fatigue.

4 Discussion

Both VR and AR games could alleviate some neck muscle fatigue, but their effects on different muscles were different. For example, VR had a weak relieving effect on the cervical muscles, while AR had a weak relieving effect on the superior trapezius muscles. It may be due to the different ways of performing VR and AR tasks: VR was headwear while AR was handheld, which may cause a particular impact on the cervical muscles in VR group due to the weight-bearing of VR glasses. In contrast, the handheld operation of AR would increase the burden on the upper trapezius muscles. For example, during the experiment, some participants lifted VR glasses with their hands, which was also the defect of VR games and AR games. In future research, how to balance the mitigation effect of VR games and the weight-bearing pressure and vertigo of VR glasses, as well as the relationship between AR games to alleviate neck fatigue and inability to complete long-term handheld games, is one of the issues to consider. In future research, how to balance the mitigation effect of VR games and the weight-bearing pressure and vertigo of VR glasses, as well as the relationship between AR games to alleviate neck fatigue and inability to complete long-term handheld games, is one of the issues to consider.

The results of the self-assessment of the state of neck fatigue in a small part of the questionnaire data were inconsistent with the sEMG in the experiment. For example, the participants thought that cervical fatigue was much relieved, while the objective data showed that the relieving effect was weak. It proved that there were differences between subjective self-assessment and objective data. The differences in the results may be affected by the VR/AR game design itself. The annoying behavior of head-turning to relieve neck fatigue was gamified, which could increase the interest degree of participants and distract their attention, increase their pleasure degree, and then generate positive feedback on the perception of neck fatigue. Therefore, in the process of relieving neck fatigue VR/AR games, game design itself is also essential, and it needs to design games that users are willing to use and generate pleasure. It further showed that the effect of VR and AR games on neck fatigue varied from person to person.

There was a significant difference between the expected results of the T-test and the actual test results. There was a significant difference between the expected downward/rightward turn in sit down and the downward/rightward turn after 30 min of mobile phone task. However, the actual results showed no significant difference. Combined with IEMG and MF curves, it was found that the slope of the broken line increases obviously after time node 2, and the slope between node 2 and node 1 was relatively gentle. It may be caused by two reasons: the participants had reached neck fatigue before the experiment, and the 30-min task of the mobile phone could not make them reach the fatigue state of the neck and shoulder. However, there was a significant difference between 30 min mobile task and 10 min VR/AR game. According to the experimental IEMG and MF values, the game task alleviated the neck, so that the participants may have a certain degree of fatigue in the initial state. At the beginning of the experiment, the participants should be guided to turn their heads to relax and increase the relaxation time, and increase the task duration of the mobile phone or use fixed posture to make the fast neck fatigue.

Some of the participants used the mobile phone for 30 min without reaching significant muscle fatigue. Therefore, in further study, longer cell phone time can be defined. Alternatively, from a time-saving perspective, explore the most likely sitting posture that causes fatigue, and let the participant maintain the position to use the mobile phone. The time of the experiment was distributed in the morning, afternoon, and evening. The initial muscle state of the participants was different at the beginning of the experiment, which may have some influence on the experimental results. Further study can unify the experimental period, such as in the evening, because some data showed that the initial fatigue of the muscles in the evening is slightly more apparent than in other periods.

5 Conclusion

According to the experimental results, both VR and AR could relieve neck fatigue, especially VR. The conclusion of subjective filling in the neck fatigue state scale was consistent with the experimental results and supported the conclusion that the VR game tasks could alleviate neck fatigue more. It could be seen from the questionnaire data that after the VR/AR game task, most of the participants' neck and shoulder fatigue returned to the state before 30 min of mobile phone task. The effects of VR and AR on neck fatigue were different from person to person. Most of the participants' neck fatigue was relieved, but some of them aggravated neck fatigue after VR/AR game task. The maximal head down was more evident to reflect the fatigue degree of neck and shoulder. Although the peak value of surface electromyography of the maximal head right was more obvious, compared with the maximal head right, the variation of IEMG and MF which could reflect the fatigue degree was more evident. The experimental results showed that the IEMG of the time domain index increased gradually, while the MF of the frequency-domain index decreased gradually. In the process of carrying out mobile tasks, the fatigue degree of some muscles gradually increased with the increase of time.

Acknowledgement. The research is supported by National Social Science Fund (Grant No. 18BRK009).

References

1. Ko, P.-H., Hwang, Y.-H., Liang, H.-W.: Influence of smartphone use styles on typing performance and biomechanical exposure. Ergonomics **59**, 821–828 (2016). https://doi.org/10.1080/00140139.2015.1088075
2. Shan, Z., Deng, G., Li, J., Li, Y., Zhang, Y., Zhao, Q.: Correlational analysis of neck/shoulder pain and low back pain with the use of digital products, physical activity, and psychological status among adolescents in Shanghai. PLoS ONE **8**, e78109 (2013). https://doi.org/10.1371/journal.pone.0078109
3. Gustafsson, E., Johnson, P.W., Hagberg, M.: Thumb postures and physical loads during mobile phone use–a comparison of young adults with and without musculoskeletal symptoms. J. Electromyogr. Kinesiol. **20**, 127–135 (2010)
4. Kim, M.-S.: Influence of neck pain on cervical movement in the sagittal plane during smartphone use. J. Phys. Ther. Sci. **27**, 15–17 (2015)
5. Xie, Y., Szeto, G.P., Dai, J., Madeleine, P.: A comparison of muscle activity in using touchscreen smartphone among young people with and without chronic neck-shoulder pain. Ergonomics **59**, 61–72 (2016)
6. Bonfort, G., Evans, R., Nelson, B., et al.: A randomized controlled trial of exercise and spinal manipulation for patients with chronic neck pain. Spine **26**, 196–205 (2001)
7. Panjabi, M.M., Cholewicki, J., Nibu, K., et al.: Critical load of the human cervical spine: an invitro experimental study. Clin. Biomech. **13**, 11–17 (1998)
8. Harms-Ringdahl, K., Ekholm, J., Schuldt, K., et al.: Load moments and myoelectric activity when the cervical spine is held in full flexion and extension. Ergonomics **29**(12), 1539–1952 (1986)
9. Shin, G., Zhu, X.: User discomfort, work posture, and muscle activity while using a touchscreen in a desktop PC setting. Ergonomics **54**, 733–744 (2011)
10. Greig, A.M., Straker, L.M., Briggs, A.M.: Cervical erector spinea and upper trapezius muscle activity in children using different information technologies. Physiotherapy **91**, 119–126 (2005)
11. Sarig Bahat, H., Weiss, P.L., Laufer, Y.: Cervical motion assessment using virtual reality. Spine **34**, 1018–1024 (2009)
12. Sarig Bahat, H., Weiss, P.L., Laufer, Y.: The effect of neck pain on cervical kinematics, as assessed in a virtual environment. Arch. Phys. Med. Rehabil. **91**, 1884–1890 (2010)
13. Hoffman, H.G., et al.: The analgesic effects of opioids and immersive virtual reality distraction: evidence from subjective and functional brain imaging assessments. Anesth. Analg. **105**, 1776–1783 (2007)
14. Sharar, S.R., et al.: Applications of virtual reality for pain management in burn-injured patients. Expert Rev. Neurother. **8**, 1667–1674 (2008)
15. Holden, M., Todorov, E., Callahan, J., Bizzi, E.: Virtual environment, training improves motor performance in two patients with stroke: case report. Neurol. Rep. **23**, 57–67 (1999)
16. Rizzo, A., Kim, G.J.: A SWOT analysis of the field of virtual reality rehabilitation and therapy. Presence-Teleoperators Virtual Environ. **14**, 119–146 (2005)
17. Bryanton, C., Bosse, J., Brien, M., McLean, J., McCormick, A., Sveistrup, H.: Feasibility, motivation, and selective motor control: virtual reality compared to conventional home exercise in children with cerebral palsy. Cyberpsychol. Behav. **9**, 123–128 (2006)
18. Mirelman, A., Bonato, P., Deutsch, J.E.: Effects of training with a robot-virtual reality system compared with a robot alone on the gait of individuals after stroke. Stroke **40**, 169–174 (2009)

19. Sarig Bahat, H., Takasaki, H., Chen, X., et al.: Cervical kinematic training with and without interactive VR training for chronic neck pain – a randomized clinical trial. Manual Ther. **20** (1), 68–78 (2015)
20. Bahat, H.S., Croft, K., Hoddinott, A., et al.: Remote kinematic e-training for patients with chronic neck pain, a randomized controlled trial. Manual Ther **25**, 35 (2016)
21. Sarig Bahat, H., Chen, X., Reznik, D., et al.: Interactive cervical motion kinematics: sensitivity, specificity, and clinically significant values for identifying kinematic impairments in patients with chronic neck pain. Manual Ther. **20**(2), 295–302 (2015)
22. Vogt, S., Skjæret-Maroni, N., et al.: Virtual reality interventions for balance prevention and rehabilitation after musculoskeletal lower limb impairments in young up to middle-aged adults: a comprehensive review on used technology, balance outcome measures and observed effects. Int. J. Med. Informatics **126**, 46–58 (2019)
23. Xu, X., Chen, K.B., Lin, J.H., et al.: The accuracy of the Oculus Rift virtual reality head-mounted display during cervical spine mobility measurement. J. Biomech. **48**(4), 721–724 (2015)
24. Pi, X., Chen, F., Peng, C.: A method of evaluating muscle fatigue by sEMG. J. Biomed. Eng. **23**(1), 225–229 (2006)
25. Zhang, Y., Ma, G.: Study on the surface electromyographic characteristics of exercise-induced muscle fatigue. Hubei Sports Sci. Technol. **30**(1), 42–44 (2011)
26. Kim, S.-Y., Koo, S.-J., et al.: Effect of duration of mobile phone use on muscle fatigue and pain caused by forward head posture in adults. J. Phys. Ther. Sci. **28**, 1669–1672 (2016)
27. Kraemer, W.J., Volek, J.S., Bush, J.A., et al.: Influence of compression hosiery on physiological responses to standing fatigue in women. Med. Sci. Sports Exerc. **32**, 1849–1858 (2000)
28. Kim, G.Y., Ahn, C.S., Jeon, H.W., et al.: Effects of the use of mobile phone on pain and muscle fatigue in the upper extremity. J. Phys. Ther. Sci. **24**, 1255–1258 (2012)
29. Huang, N.: Research and implementation of muscle fatigue analysis and muscle strength prediction based on sEMG. University of Science and Technology of China (2014)
30. Li, Y.: Evaluation method and experimental study of muscular atrophy based on electromyography. Tianjin University, Tianjin (2002)
31. Farina, D., Fosci, M., Melletti, R.: Motor unit recruitment strategies invesmentigated by surface EMG variables. Appl. Phys. **92**(1), 235–247 (2002)
32. Fan, J.: Analysis of the surface electromyographic characteristics of the main muscle groups in the lumbar abdomen during static exercises in different stable states. Sichuan Normal University (2018)

Research and Design of Relieving Neck Muscle Fatigue Based on Serious Game

Dian Zhu, Zishan Song$^{(\boxtimes)}$, Jingran He$^{(\boxtimes)}$, Chufan Jin$^{(\boxtimes)}$, and Xi Chen$^{(\boxtimes)}$

Shanghai Jiao Tong University, Shanghai, China
songzishan1996@163.com, 467166057@qq.com

Abstract. The contemporary "mobile phone family" has become an increasingly common label, and the neck muscle fatigue caused by it has gradually become common. There are many ways to prevent neck muscle fatigue on the Internet. Among them, the most common methods are aerobics teaching, serious games to move the neck, and hot packs have been massaged. Among them, users generally think that they cannot adhere to health exercises, hot packs and massage You need to use the instrument and you need to know the right way, otherwise, it will be counterproductive. Therefore, serious games that can move the neck have become a popular way to prevent neck muscle fatigue. Previous studies have mostly explored whether certain games are effective in alleviating neck muscle fatigue, and there are no specific numerical studies. The innovative point of this research is to explore relatively specific values and combine them with game design to help users with potential muscle fatigue to relax while entertaining. The range is the most important in serious games, and it will affect the parameters of multiple serious games. Therefore, it is necessary to carry out experimental best numerical research on the operating parameters of these two control methods. Stretching and isometric contraction, observing its characteristic changes in electromyography and changes in subjective fatigue, the results of the study better combine serious games with alleviating muscle damage, so that users can prevent cervical muscle damage during the entertainment.

Keywords: Neck relaxation · Serious games · Neck muscle fatigue · Game design

1 Introduction

Neck pain is a common musculoskeletal disease that affects daily life, often causes disability and increases medical costs. [1] A survey of 2,000 patients with cervical spondylosis in 2018 showed that neck muscle fatigue is no longer the patent of middle-aged and elderly patients, and the proportion of adolescents and office workers has increased rapidly. 12% of patients aged 1–20 years; 25% of patients aged 21–30 years; 15% of patients aged 30–50 years; 48% of patients over 50 years old. Cervical spondylosis can be complicated by myelopathy or radiculopathy [2]. Existing programs to relieve neck muscle fatigue include the use of endurance exercise programs, or coordinated exercises, routine treatments (analgesics, non-steroidal anti-inflammatory

V. G. Duffy (Ed.): HCII 2020, LNCS 12198, pp. 376–388, 2020.
https://doi.org/10.1007/978-3-030-49904-4_28

drugs, or muscle relaxants) [2] and heat packs. Injections and medications are considered first-line treatments for neck pain, including cervical spondylosis. However, although nonsteroidal anti-inflammatory drugs (NSAIDs) are generally effective in treating the pain of spinal origin [3], they often cause adverse events (AE) such as gastritis, gastric ulcers, internal bleeding, and myocardial infarction [4]. Exercise therapy and massage are more effective for chronic neck pain than less aggressive treatments (medicine, education, counseling). However, manual manipulation is occasionally accompanied by severe neurological complications (approximately 5–10 per 10 million manual manipulations) [5]. When bending the cervical spine, there is also a risk of dislocation if you do not pay attention to the slow and correct movement. Another very important issue in the stretching process is that the muscles must be stretched within the allowable range, and the position should be maintained for a specific length of time [6]. Serious Educational Games (SEG) refers to an alternative learning method that applies game technology to primarily promote player learning and gain positive cognition and experience in such learning processes [7]. The elements of challenge and learning in this game constitute motivation and entertainment [8].

Serious games, as a tool for education, learning, and communication, have been steadily growing in health products since the 2000s [9]. Appropriate rather than excessively increasing player anxiety and brainpower can enhance the effectiveness of learning. Serious games provide users with effective learning opportunities because serious games cause slight player anxiety and mental stress, while a simple serious game system can only provide users with a smooth experience, which is not conducive to user adherence [10]. In past studies, there was no quantitative study of game speed and amplitude for serious games that relieved neck muscle fatigue. And because of the popularity of mobile phones and other electronic products, interactive serious games have become a new option for adjuvant therapy [11].

2 Method

2.1 Experiment Preparation

Electromyography. Electromyographic analysis has been proposed as a method for assessing this type of fatigue [12]. This experiment uses a surface muscle instrument of the UltiumTMEMG model produced by NORAXON, USA. The software version is MyoMuscle3 3.12.70, and the measurement method is the online real-time measurement.

Sampling and Determination of Surface EMG Signals

(1) Paste the electrode: Use a 75% volume medical ethanol cotton sheet to repeatedly wipe the skin of the pasted part before pasting, so that the skin impedance is less than 5Ω, and paste the disposable electrode sheet at the corresponding position.
(2) Measurement of maximum voluntary contraction force (MVC): The test subject is required to exert his maximum muscle strength, the test subject is required to be

seated, the upper body is straight, the head is vertical, and the tape is placed on the position of the occipital bone behind the head. The person manually pulls the tension meter forward, the subject's neck is pulled backward, and the test is performed before the test subject begins to work. Each movement lasts for 5 s, without using explosive power, repeat 3 times, each time 5 min rest, take 3 the maximum of the two measurements is the result.

(3) Measurement of 60% MVC: Knowing the 60% value of MVC, instruct the test subject to press (2) the measurement action (same as the MVC measurement action), and maintain it for 5 s after reaching the 60% MVC value, and record the muscle at this time electric signal. The 60% MVC of 4 muscles needs to be measured 3 times before and after the test subjects play and relax.

(4) Monitoring time of myoelectric signal during work: set the measurement before each game; lower the mobile phone game time 8 min, measure after the game; neck movement relax game time 2 min, measure after the game.

(5) To obtain the best sEMG signal acquisition effect, the following factors should be considered during electrode application: avoid the interference of adjacent muscles; in the experiment, select muscles that are relatively far away as the sEMG signal acquisition object, so that the scanning direction of each group of electrodes is the same. The electrode should be placed as far as possible on the muscled abdomen to maintain the consistency of the muscle temperature as much as possible; [13]. This experiment was in June, using an air conditioner to maintain the laboratory temperature at about 25–26 °C (Fig. 1).

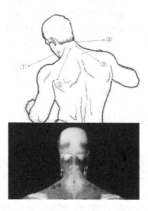

Fig. 1. The position of electrode.

Neck Exercise Relaxation Game (Based on Python). Based on python, a simple game prototype was made for experimental analysis. The black triangle is the area where the nose is in the initial state; the amplitude (cross-movement amplitude) is set to the up and down angle: −20° −20°, left and right angle: −30° −30°, up and down angle: −30° −30° Angle: −45° −45°, which are medium and high. The speed (cross speed) is set to 30°/s, 20°/s, and 10°/s for high speed, medium speed, and low speed, respectively. After starting the game, the participant should point the tip of his nose at the cross sign and follow the amplitude and frequency of the cross-movement for neck movement. The movement track of the cross symbol is a circle.

Experimental amplitude-frequency setting: medium-speed with medium-amplitude, medium-speed with high-amplitude, high-speed with medium-amplitude, low-speed with medium-amplitude (Fig. 2).

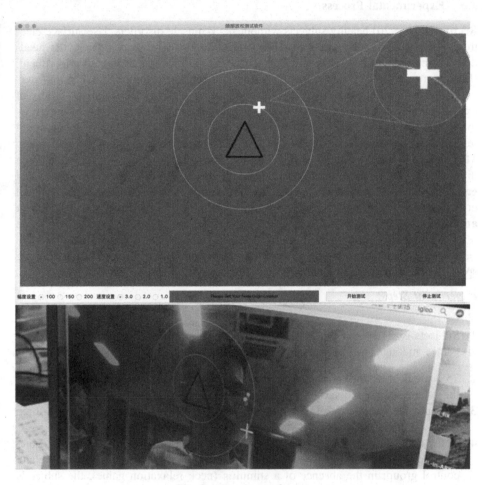

Fig. 2. The demo of game

2.2 Subjects

Recruiting 20 (n = 20) healthy subjects without neck muscle disorders, 20 students from Shanghai Jiao Tong University, aged 21−24 years, body mass index (BMI) (21.5 ± 3.6), chair height 45 cm, table height 80 cm. All subjects had no smoking and drinking habits, no history of neck muscle or upper limb musculoskeletal disease, and no history of trauma. There was no severe neck exercise one week before the experiment.

The questionnaire is used to obtain the user's subjective neck muscle fatigue evaluation. Before the measurement, explain the main points and precautions of the experiment with the participants, and make predictions, find out the problems in the experiment and correct them in time. A sign informed consent before the experiment.

2.3 Experimental Process

Recruit 20 (n = 20) healthy subjects without neck muscle disorders. Use surface electromyography to measure and record the self-made relaxation game demos after head-down games (8 min per game period) and after head-down games in each experiment. (Each game period of 2 min) After the bilateral cervical erector spine (CES) and sternocleidomastoid muscle (SCM) electromyographic signals. Before each group of experimental tests, the maximum voluntary contraction (MVC) and 60% of the maximum voluntary contraction of the tester's bilateral CES and SCM were measured respectively. After each test, 60% of the CES and SCM were measured again. MVC EMG signal. The obtained EMG signals were analyzed by t-test and significant differences. Among them, the frequency combinations of 4 different game speeds and game amplitudes are: **medium-speed high-amplitude** (movement speed 20°/s, up and down angle −30° −30° left and right angle −45° −45°), **medium speed Medium amplitude** (moving speed 20°/s, up and down −20 angle −20° −20° left and right angle −30° −30°), **high speed medium amplitude** (moving speed 30°/s, up and down angle −30° −30° Left and right angle −45° −45°) and **low speed medium amplitude** (moving speed 10°/s, up and down angle −20° −20° left and right angle −30° −30°).

Experiment Steps:

1. Subjects experimental procedures and precautions, explain the use of neck sports games and sign the experimentally informed consent.

2. 75% medical alcohol cotton swab wipe the subject's sticking electrode pad, wipe the electrode pad and sensor.

3. Measure the maximum muscle strength MVC of the neck muscle, measure three times, and take the maximum value to calculate 60% MVC.

4. Blank control group test: 60% MVC EMG signal was measured in the initial state, head down for 8 min, and two minutes of sitting. The purpose of setting a blank control group: in the absence of a stimulus (neck relaxation game), the subject's fatigue and muscle relaxation.

5. The first experiment: measuring 60% MVC EMG signal after 8 min of head-down mobile phone games and two minutes of neck relaxation (medium-speed and medium-amplitude).

6. The second experiment: 8 min of head-down mobile phone games and neck relaxation Measurement of 60% MVC EMG signal after two minutes of play (medium-speed and high-amplitude).

7. Third experiment: 60% MVC EMG measurement after head-down mobile phone game for 8 min and neck relaxation for two minutes (high-speed and medium-amplitude) Signal.

8. The third experiment: 60% MVC EMG signal was measured after 8 min of head-down mobile game and two minutes of neck relaxation (low-speed and medium-amplitude) (Fig. 3).

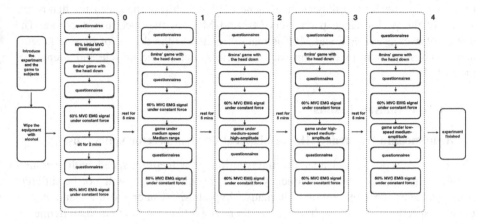

Fig. 3. Experiment steps

3   Results

The main purpose of this report is to track and analyze fatigue-related changes in neuromuscular recruitment. Changes in frequency and amplitude parameters (zero-crossing and mean absolute) can be used to determine local fatigue. From the beginning to the end of the selected analysis cycle, these time-domain calculations are performed in 1-second steps.

3.1   General Rules of Several Changes During Muscle Movement

When the muscles start to move, the first increase in the discharge frequency of the unit potential of the exercise, which appears as a high shift in the spectrum. With the gradual increase of strength, the number of gathered motor units is further increased, which manifests as the EMG spectrum continues to move higher. At the same time, the volatility increases. If you increase the force further, there will be an overlap in the unit potential of the motor, and the amplitude will further increase, but the frequency increase will slow down or stop at this time. When exercise to muscle fatigue occurs, the conduction velocity of muscle fiber excitement decreases, but the amplitude of the wave does not change much [14].

3.2   Research Indicators of Surface EMG and Their Changes

Surface electromyography is commonly used in clinical studies to study muscle fatigue, and the most commonly used are frequency spectrum analysis and amplitude analysis. The indicators of spectrum analysis are the median frequency (MF) and average power frequency (MPF) and their changes MF slope and MPF slope. The indicator of volatility is mean square. At the same time, the surface EMG can also analyze power, muscle movement sequence and so on [15].

Regardless of static or dynamic movement, with the occurrence and development of muscle fatigue, there will be a phenomenon of a left shift of the spectrum, that is, the values of the performance parameters MF and MPF of the spectrum decrease. The degree of decrease in MF and MPF is mainly related to the degree of muscle fatigue, and also has a certain relationship with the factors such as the muscle and strength of the test [16].

3.3   t-Test Analysis Results

1 Mean median frequency (Hz) of bilateral cervical erector spine muscles

The original hypothesis: Under the intervention of a medium-speed with medium-amplitude game, the median frequency before the intervention will not be different from that after the intervention. Alternative hypothesis: Under the intervention of a medium-speed with mid- amplitude game, there is a difference in the median frequency before and after the intervention.

By performing T-test, we get t-value = -0.85, $p > 0.05$ ($p = 0.935$). In the case of 5 degrees of freedom and significance greater than 0.05, the null hypothesis is supported. That is to say, the median frequency before the intervention will not be different from that after the intervention, and the specific performance is that under the intervention of the medium-speed with medium-amplitude game, the median frequency of the participants will not change significantly, and the intervention will not be effective.

2 Mean median frequency of bilateral rectus spinal muscles (Hz)

Initial hypothesis: Under the intervention of a medium-speed with high-amplitude game, the median frequency before the intervention is the same as the median frequency after the intervention. Alternative hypothesis: Under the intervention of medium-speed with high-amplitude game, there are differences in the median frequency before and after the intervention.

By performing a T test, we get a t-value = -7.311, $p < 0.05$ ($p = 0.001$). With 5 degrees of freedom and significance less than 0.05, we oppose the null hypothesis. That is, there is a difference between the median frequency before and after the intervention, which is specifically manifested by a significant change in the median frequency of the subject under the intervention of the high-speed with high-amplitude game, and the intervention is effective.

3 Comparison of the median frequency (Hz) of the bilateral cervical erector spinal muscles before and after high-speed mid-range game intervention

The original hypothesis: Under the intervention of a high-speed with mid-range game, the median frequency before the intervention will not be different from that after the intervention. Alternative hypothesis: Under the intervention of a high-speed with mid-range game, there is a difference in the median frequency before and after the intervention.

By performing T-test, we get t-value = -3.487, p < 0.05 (p = 0.10). In the case of the degree of freedom 7 and significance less than 0.05, we oppose the null hypothesis. That is, there is a difference between the median frequency before and after the intervention, which is specifically manifested by the significant change in the median frequency of the subjects under the intervention of a high-speed with mid-amplitude game, and the intervention is effective.

4 Mean median frequency (Hz) of bilateral cervical erector spinal muscles comparison before and after a low-speed and medium-range game intervention

The original hypothesis: Under the intervention of a low-speed with mid-range game, the median frequency before the intervention will not be different from that after the intervention. Alternative hypothesis: Under the intervention of a low-speed with mid-amplitude game, there is a difference in the median frequency before and after the intervention.

By performing the T-test, we get t = 1.126, p > 0.05 (p = 0.311), and support the null hypothesis when the degree of freedom is 5 and the significance is greater than 0.05. That is to say, the median frequency before the intervention will not be different from that after the intervention. Specifically, under the intervention of the low-speed with mid- amplitude game, the participants' median frequency will not change significantly and the intervention will not be effective.

5 Mean median frequency (Hz) of bilateral sternocleidomastoid muscles

The original hypothesis: Under the intervention of a medium-speed with medium-range game, the median frequency before the intervention will not be different from that after the intervention. Alternative hypothesis: Under the intervention of a medium-speed with mid- amplitude game, there is a difference in the median frequency before and after the intervention.

By performing the T-test, we get t-value = -0.888, p > 0.05 (p = 0.425), and support the null hypothesis when the degree of freedom is 4 and the significance is greater than 0.05. That is to say, the median frequency before the intervention will not be different from that after the intervention, and the specific performance is that under the intervention of the medium-speed with medium-amplitude game, the median frequency of the participants will not change significantly, and the intervention will not be effective.

6 Comparison of the median frequency (Hz) of bilateral sternocleidomastoid muscles before and after a moderate and high-speed game intervention.

The original hypothesis: Under the intervention of the medium-speed with high-amplitude game, the median frequency before the intervention will not be different from that after the intervention. Alternative hypothesis: Under the intervention of medium-speed and high- amplitude games, there is a difference in the median frequency before and after the intervention.

By performing T-test, we get t-value = -3.028, p < 0.05 (p = 0.029). In the case of 5 degrees of freedom and significance less than 0.05, we oppose the null hypothesis. That is, there is a difference between the median frequency before the intervention and the post-intervention. Specifically, under the intervention of the medium-speed with high- amplitude game, the median frequency of the subjects changed significantly and the intervention was effective.

7 Comparison of the median frequency (Hz) of bilateral sternocleidomastoid muscles before and after a high-speed and mid-range game intervention

The original hypothesis: Under the intervention of a high-speed with mid- amplitude game, the median frequency before the intervention will not be different from that after the intervention. Alternative hypothesis: Under the intervention of a high-speed with mid- amplitude game, there is a difference in the median frequency before and after the intervention.

By performing the T-test, we get t-value = -5.585, $p < 0.05$ ($p = 0.003$). In the case of 5 degrees of freedom and significance less than 0.05, we oppose the null hypothesis. That is, there is a difference between the median frequency before the intervention and the post-intervention. The specific performance is that under the intervention of the high-speed with mid- amplitude game, the median frequency of the subjects changed significantly, and the intervention was effective.

8 Mean median frequency (Hz) of bilateral sternocleidomastoid muscle comparison before and after vulgar mid-range game intervention

The original hypothesis: Under the intervention of a low-speed mid-range game, the median frequency before the intervention will not be different from that after the intervention. Alternative hypothesis: Under the intervention of a low-speed mid-range game, there is a difference in the median frequency before and after the intervention.

By performing the T-test, we get t-value = -1.075, $p > 0.05$ ($p = 0.318$), and support the null hypothesis when the degree of freedom is 7 and the significance is greater than 0.05. That is to say, the median frequency before the intervention will not be different from that after the intervention. Specifically, under the intervention of the low-speed mid-range game, the participants' median frequency will not change significantly and the intervention will not be effective.

3.4 Experimental Conclusions

Neck muscle fatigue is represented by the median frequency and integrated myo-electricity. The experiment passed four-game intervention experiments with different combinations of speed and amplitude. After data analysis and subjective scale analysis, it was concluded that the medium-speed and high-amplitude neck relaxation games and the high-speed and medium- amplitude neck relaxation games were effective on both sides of the neck. The relaxation of the spinal muscle has a more obvious effect (t value = -3.487, $p < 0.05$ ($p = 0.01$), in the case of 7 degrees of freedom, significance less than 0.05). Among them, medium and high-speed games have the most significant effects. According to the interview, the results of the four frequencies of serious games to alleviate the fatigue of the neck muscles are: the high amplitude exercise has a significant effect on the relaxation of the cervical spine muscles behind the neck. For bilateral sternocleidomastoid muscles, mid-speed high- amplitude games and high-speed mid-range games have a relaxing effect, and the effect of high-speed mid-amplitude games is more obvious. Because the bilateral sternocleidomastoid muscles are not exhausted, simple activities can relax. At other speeds and frequencies, game relaxation interventions have no significant effect on neck relaxation.

When playing at low-speed (moving speed 10°/s), subjects will feel delayed and lag, which is not suitable for relaxation. Moderate and high-speed games are more effective for neck relaxation. Therefore, the production of the game should be based on high-speed mid- amplitude (upper and lower angle −30° −30°, left and right angle −45° −45°, movement speed 20°/s). Based on this data, a more advanced game design is carried out.

4 Design

4.1 Concept

Dodge games are a branch of action games. Dodge games have become a popular game type on mobile phones because of the simple operation of the game and easy-to-use game modes. Although the operation is simple, the requirements for response are high. Dodge games are mostly based on parkour, shooting, flying, etc. The game styles are different, suitable for giving players a certain amount of stimulation, which is conducive to attracting players' attention (Fig. 4).

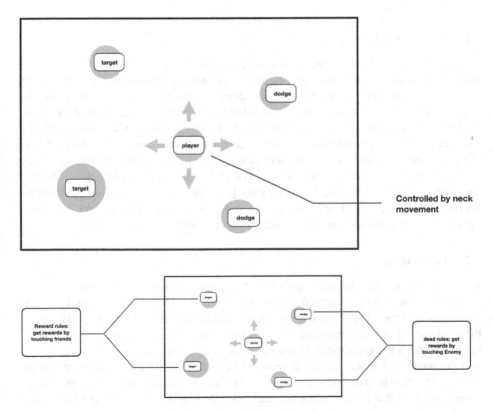

Fig. 4. Game mechanism

4.2 Game Framework

The theme of the jungle adventure is selected on the visual elements. As a jungle explorer, the player must avoid the scary jungle creatures such as leopards, pythons, and crocodiles while touching the cute creatures. Recognize the goals and dodges of the game, quickly understand the rules of the game, and the visual elements of animals and plants enhance the immersion of the game to enhance the game experience (Fig. 5).

Fig. 5. Experiment-driven game design

5 Discussions

5.1 Research Advantages

According to the results of the experiment, serious games can relieve neck muscle fatigue. According to the interview, it can be known that evasion games are serious games with a design core, which is more conducive to the player's focus and allows the player to gain more game motivation and reduces the treatment effect caused by giving up halfway. Also, the study found that not all speeds and amplitudes are suitable for alleviating neck muscle fatigue. In some incorrect speed and amplitude games, it may even increase the player's neck muscle fatigue. Therefore, games appearing on the market to relieve neck muscle fatigue may not always have positive benefits. Research also shows that when players feel neck muscle fatigue, they will give up to continue playing, so the appropriate speed range can not only allow players to stick to serious games for longer but also effectively relieve neck muscle fatigue.

5.2 Limitations

But at the same time, the study also found certain limitations. The serious game is designed to incorporate the activity trajectory that is beneficial for neck muscle relaxation into the code of the serious game monster appearance trajectory. However, the relaxation of the neck muscles is fixed and the movements are relatively single. If the player plays the game multiple times, it is easy to master the rules of serious games and the interest in serious games is reduced [17]. In the future serious game design, more other muscle movement trajectories that can relax the neck muscles will be incorporated, so that players retain the freshness while also increasing the relaxation of other muscles. According to the interview, players tend to have more combinations of game scenes. A single game scene will make players feel repetitive and predictable, lacking the tension, excitement, and freshness brought by the game and certain visual feedback [18]. In the future design, the design of more scenes will be incorporated. After the player clears each level, a new map mode is opened to provide players with more fun.

The study also found that older players are not comfortable with serious neck muscle relaxation training, and young college students are more than happy to play such serious games [19].

6 Conclusion

This article explores the appropriate game speed and amplitude for serious games where users relieve neck muscle fatigue. More specifically, the game under study pays close attention to the user's ability to correctly correct the user's muscle contraction while playing the game. The exercise program in the study provided safety because it was generated based on the trajectory of the neck relaxation exercise and was professional [20]. Besides, it also stimulated the interest of users and reduced the rate of abandonment.

The game can be used in multiple places, for example, at work, at home, in a hospital, etc. It only needs to be installed on an iPad or a mobile phone and tracked by Aikit facial recognition, which can meet the needs of exercise and relaxation.

Not only is the quality of the game highly rated in terms of relevance, ease of use, the effectiveness of relaxation exercises and overall satisfaction, but more importantly, participants have shown positive experiences in relaxing neck muscle movements. It also shows that serious gaming solutions can greatly enable people to independently participate in neck muscle relaxation exercises and posture exercises. The solution can remind individuals to understand their posture deviations and improve their posture and health.

References

1. Punnett, L., Bergqvist, U.J.S.: Visual display unit work and upper extremity musculoskeletal disorders: a review of epidemiological findings (Ergonomic Expert Committee Document No. 1). National Institute of Working Life, Sweden (1997)
2. Ylinen, J., Takala, E.-P., Nykänen, M., et al.: Active neck muscle training in the treatment of chronic neck pain in women. A randomized controlled trial. JAMA **289**(19), 2509–2516 (2003)
3. White, A.P., Arnold, P.M., Norvell, D.C., et al.: Pharmacologic management of chronic low back pain: synthesis of the evidence. Spine **36**, S131–S143 (2011)
4. Fine, M.: Quantifying the impact of NSAID-associated adverse events. Am. J. Manag. Care **19**(14 Suppl), s267–s272 (2013)
5. Lee, S., Shin, J.-S., Lee, J., et al.: Effectiveness of pharmacopuncture for cervical spondylosis: a systematic review and meta-analysis. Eur. J. Integr. Med. **20**, 154–164 (2018)

6. Rodrigues, M.A.F., Serpa, Y.R., Macedo, D.V., et al.: A serious game to practice stretches and exercises for a correct and healthy posture. Entertain. Comput. **28**, 78–88 (2018)
7. Michael, D.R., Chen, S.L.: Serious Games: Games that Educate, Train, and Inform. Muska & Lipman/Premier-Trade, New York (2005)
8. Gee, J.P.: Good Video Games and Good Learning: Collected Essays on Video Games, Learning and Literacy (New Literacies and Digital Epistemologies). Peter Lang Publishing, Bern (2007)
9. Jacquier, A., Briot, M., Barillot, G., et al.: «Discovering Pathology», un serious game dédié à la découverte de l'anatomopathologie pour les étudiants en médecine. Annales de Pathologie **39**(2), 151–157 (2019)
10. Hsu, T.-C.: Learning English with Augmented Reality: Do learning styles matter? Comput. Educ. **106**, 137–149 (2017)
11. Zmily, A., Mowafi, Y., Mashal, E., et al.: Study of the usability of spaced retrieval exercise using mobile devices for Alzheimer's disease rehabilitation. JMIR mHealth uHealth **2**(3), e31 (2014)
12. Basmajian, J.V., De Luca, C.J.: Muscles Alive: Their Functions Revealed by Electromyography. Williams & Wilkins, Baltimore (1985)
13. Cram, J.R.: The history of surface electromyography. Appl. Psychophysiol. Biofeedback **28**(2), 81–91 (2003). https://doi.org/10.1023/A:1023802407132
14. Feldner, H.A., Howell, D., Kelly, V.E., et al.: "Look, your muscles are firing!": A qualitative study of clinician perspectives on the use of surface electromyography in neurorehabilitation. Arch. Phys. Med. Rehabil. **100**(4), 663–675 (2019)
15. Preston, D.C., Shapiro, B.E.: Electromyography and Neuromuscular Disorders E-Book: Clinical-Electrophysiologic Correlations (Expert Consult-Online and Print). Elsevier Health Sciences, Amsterdam (2012)
16. Huijuan, P.: The basic principle and research progress of surface electromyography. In: The 17th China Endoscopic Doctor Conference, Beijing, China (2007)
17. Lee, J., Lee, M., Lim, T., et al.: Effectiveness of an application-based neck exercise as a pain management tool for office workers with chronic neck pain and functional disability: a pilot randomized trial. Eur. J. Integr. Med. **12**, 87–92 (2017)
18. van den Heuvel, M.R., Kwakkel, G., Beek, P.J., et al.: Effects of augmented visual feedback during balance training in Parkinson's disease: a pilot randomized clinical trial **20**(12), 1352–1358 (2014)
19. Bauer, R., Conell, J., Glenn, T., et al.: Internet use by patients with bipolar disorder: results from an international multisite survey. Psychiatry Res. **242**, 388–394 (2016)
20. O'Riordan, C., Clifford, A., Van De Ven, P., et al.: Chronic neck pain and exercise interventions: frequency, intensity, time, and type principle. Arch. Phys. Med. Rehabil. **95**(4), 770–783 (2014)

Health Services

Excessive Smartphone Use and Associated Physiological Disorders – A Survey on Research Status in India

D. Bhanu Priya[1], Murali Subramaniyam[1(✉)], and Seung Nam Min[2(✉)]

[1] Department of Mechanical Engineering, SRM Institute of Science and Technology, Kattankulathur, Chennai, Tamil Nadu, India
murali.subramaniyam@gmail.com
[2] Department of Drone and Industrial Safety, Shinsung University, Dangjin, Republic of Korea
msnijnl2@hanmail.net

Abstract. BACKGROUND: In our current generation, smartphone is considered a basic handheld device utilized for many tasks. Almost a billion people spend 50% of their time on any digital media like smartphone, tablet, laptop computer or television. Excessive use of the smartphone can cause physiological problems, mental disorders and so on.

OBJECTIVE: The key objective of the research is to identify factors and effects of smartphone addiction and how it is correlated with mental disorders. Furthermore, to examine the measuring techniques available to evaluate the addiction levels of smartphone.

METHODS: Bibliographic search was conducted through IEEE, science direct, PUBMED, PMC with the keywords' physiological disorders, mental activity, usage duration, smartphone addiction and were limited to recent 10 years from 2010–2019 for literature.

RESULTS: Due to the rising trend of addiction to smartphones, physiological disorders and mental activities are becoming a negative concept and researchers have mostly focused on its harmful applications. Relatively, no studies were found in India even though the utilization is extremely high.

CONCLUSION: It is observed that most of the studies are from other nations, the research on this domain in India is considerably less and needs to be done, also the correlation between the smartphone addiction and physiological disorders are to be analyzed.

Keywords: Physiological disorders · Mental activity · Usage duration · Smartphone addiction

1 Introduction

In our current generation, the easy accessibility of the internet has led to excessive usage of smartphone in our daily lives for various tasks. Approximately a billion people spend 50% of their time on any digital media like smartphone, tablet, laptop computer

© Springer Nature Switzerland AG 2020
V. G. Duffy (Ed.): HCII 2020, LNCS 12198, pp. 391–401, 2020.
https://doi.org/10.1007/978-3-030-49904-4_29

or television [9]. Globally, many surveys were conducted and stated that smartphone is circulated over 92.5% in 2019 [41]. The survey also confirms that Indians are amongst the second-highest smartphone users in all Nations. It was reported that most of the Indian teenagers spend an average of 4 h daily on their mobile phone [41]. The dissemination of smartphones in India started in the year 2008 with devastating results. Excessive usage of smartphone can cause physiological problems, including eye pain, decreased visual acuity, blurred vision, dry eyes, headache, neck stiffness, wrist pain, back pain, etc. If the visual fatigue continues in everyday life, it will significantly affect the attention, focus, and also create functional impairment to the individuals. The excessive usage of internet and smartphone also causes negative effect on individuals and their mental health. Recent studies confirmed that addiction to social media and the internet lead to compulsive behaviour and cognitive emotions. It is identified that empathy, severity and life satisfaction are also affected by social media and internet addiction. Various psychological aspects including anxiety and depression are positively correlated with addiction to social media and the internet [9, 18, 30, 38].

Considering that smartphones share many common aspects with the Internet, the physical and psychosocial problems are caused by the smartphone addiction that are similar to those caused by the Internet. Physical problems are posture and neck issues caused by utilizing smart phones or tablets for longer duration, also known as "text neck", pain and discomfort of eyes, eye burning, itching and headache caused by digital eye strain [42]. Psychosocial effects of addiction are depression, obsessive compulsive disorder, relationship problems, anxiety, sleep disturbances like the chances of insomnia increases by utilizing any digital medium for longer duration before bed, thereby reducing sleep quality and could increment the measure of time taken to fall asleep [42]. In particular, the addiction of the Internet and smartphone utilization over socio-graphic groups have become a current research domain. Significantly, several studies have focused on adolescents who are especially susceptible to excessive mobile phone and Internet use. Studies noted that excessive smartphone use could affect the mental health of an adolescent as much as Internet and computer use. The study also states that addiction of smartphone increases due to the larger distribution of smartphone. Furthermore, various convenient functions and applications of smartphones may be the primary factors that contribute to excessive usage [31].

Among researchers, adolescents have received considerable attention as the most vulnerable group of having addictive behavior than other demographic user groups. However, no studies have presented the characteristics of adolescents' addictive behavior and how it is distinctive from other demographic user groups. Considering the high circulation of smartphones, the instant messaging, number of times checking their smartphones of adolescents helps to reveal the different levels of smartphone addiction [16]. Also, studies have examined by conducting a set of questionnaires with score from 15–60 range based on the amount of smartphone utilization and the smartphone activities type and revealed that a score above 42 are considered as addicts and below are non-addicts or mild level of addiction and also stated internet is not only the core symptoms of excessive use but the user's time reliance on online activities. Addicts tend to use the Internet differently than non-addicts. For example, addicted users utilize smartphone for applications such as gaming, fun and entertainment compared to non-addicts. The finding shows that the mild level of Internet users are utilizing the Internet for communication and messaging. Entertainment and gaming are the major activities that addicts are frequently exposed to [27].

Any kind of addiction to digital media like addiction of smartphone, social media, internet, gaming are considered as the problematic smartphone usage which causes anxiety, loneliness, depression, low self-esteem and so on. These behavioral addicts lead to mental disorders and reducing in the level of psychological well-being. Psychological well-being refers to the mental health of an individual, it is about how the choices are made, behave, feel, think, engage with others and so on. It is identified by 6 important components, which are (i) the condition of a feeling of purpose and meaning in life, (ii) competence, (iii) personal growth and development, (iv) autonomy, (v) personal mastery and (vi) having positive relation with others [40]. Psychological well-being is a state of balance achieved by attaining both rewarding and challenging life events. As the addiction of smartphone increases, the level of psychological well-being will be reduced which causes mental disorders.

This paper discusses about the studies in developed countries to India and explains what are the factors and prevalence for addiction of smartphone, internet, social media and gaming. Also, it illustrates what are the effects caused by the increase in addiction level and report on different types of scales available to measure and rate the addiction levels.

2 Methods

A bibliographic search was conducted through IEEE, science direct, PUBMED, PMC with the keywords' physiological disorders, mental activity, usage duration, smartphone addiction and were limited to recent 10 years from 2010–2019. The search results were analyzed critically to select the appropriate papers. A total of forty papers are selected from fifty papers by reading the full paper for the review on mental or physiological disorders caused by excessive usage of smartphone.

3 Result and Discussions

In this paper, forty papers are reviewed, which are concerned about the mental fatigue or physiological disorders caused by smartphone addiction or digital medium addiction. In this study, the factors and prevalence for addiction of smartphone, internet, social media and gaming are examined. Also, what are the effects caused by the increase in addiction level and scales available to measure and rate the addiction levels are analyzed. The main focus of this paper is to study about mental or physiological disorders in India.

3.1 Reasons for Smartphone Addiction

Here, the reasons and prevalence for addiction of smartphone, social media, internet and games are discussed. Namsu Park [39] studied on correlation of smartphone use and physiological well-being. They Identified that caring for others, trend, communication, information, accessibility and time pass are the reasons for incremental smartphone usage or smartphone addiction, which also leads to low self-esteem, loneliness, depression. Suliman S. Aljomaa [33] also examined that there exists a difference in addiction of smartphones based on independent factors like age, gender, social status, educational level, marital status, monthly income, hours of utilization. They also forwarded a set of questionnaires to subjects for measuring smartphone addiction, which comprises of basic details and five specific categories: health, overuse of smartphone, technological advancement, the psychological-social advancements and preoccupation with smartphones. Concluded that gender differences, marital status plays a vital role in the addiction of smartphone. It states that, unmarried subjects were ascertained in a higher degree of addiction levels, as unmarried males were more addicted to internet gaming or gambling, besides females are addicted to social networking sites (SNS). Yusong Gao [32] examined the association between smartphone usage, loneliness and social anxiety. They collected the subject's app-usage duration, frequency, text messages and call log data through MobileSens Application which directly collects and stores data in the server. After analyzing the data, they drew the inference that a high level of loneliness and social anxiety leads to frequent usage of text messages, calls, camera apps, and other SNS. Ahmet Rıfat Kayis [30] proposed five different factors of internet addiction and performed a meta-analysis. The five factors are neuroticism, extraversion, openness, agreeableness, and conscientiousness, moreover, the study determined that internet addiction is positively related to neuroticism and other factors are negatively related. Hatice Kumcagiz [29] investigated the correlation between levels of psychological well-being with addiction to digital medium for university scholars. By utilizing smartphone addiction scale and psychological well-being scale, obtained perception, gender, parental attitudes, grade and family's economic status as the factors that affect the range of psychologically well-being and digital medium addiction. Yongsuk Hwang [27] distinguished the users of smartphone-based on addiction levels and smartphone usage pattern by questionnaire data and categorized into 3 groups like addicts, potential addicts, and non-addicts' group. Furthermore, the study stated that adolescents are more prone to smartphone addiction by utilizing mobile games and SNS, whereas adults use smartphone for gambling, videos, SNS, mobile games and SNS. Zaheer Hussain [25] studied on anxiety, personality factors and narcissism, and how it is related to problematic smartphone usage. Developed a web-based questionnaire and obtained a significant relationship among time spent on smartphones, anxiety, age, openness, conscientiousness, emotional stability. Also, concluded that all these factors also lead to internet gaming disorder. Cheng Kuang-Tsan [24] analyzed the interrelation between life satisfaction and smartphone addiction among university students by multiple regression analysis, correlation analysis of product-moment and descriptive statistics. Also suggested that stress due to academics, family-stress, career issues and love-affair would cause addiction and reduces life-satisfaction. Jon D. Elhai [23] reviewed on causes of problematic smartphone usage and examined the connection between low self-esteem, chronic stress, anxiety, depression, and smartphone addiction. The study ranked the causes for smartphone addiction and usage in the order of high to low impact from depression, stress, lack of confidence and impatience. JoseÂ de-Sola [22] predicted the problematic smartphone usage by daily use, level of education, gender and age, also classified the user's as problematic, at risk, regular and casual usage with obtained results. In total at-risk users are 15.4% and problematic users are 5.1%. Factors for problematic smartphone usage are Social environment dependence, loss of control, craving, abuse, and dependence. Eunhyang Kim [20] investigated the connection between attachment and addiction of smartphones through self-esteem, anxiety within the age of adolescents by generating structural equation modelling (SEM). They recommended that, attachment of smartphone increases the level of anxiety and lowers the level of self-esteem, and in turn may prompt to addiction of smartphone. Aljohara A. Alhassan [19] studied on the interrelation between depression and smartphone addiction, factors and their similarity associated with depression. They came to an inference that there is a high level of depression and addiction between high school students than college students or university students. Among depression and addiction there is a positive and linear relationship. Here Hye-Jin Kim [17] inspected the connection between addiction of smartphone in adolescents, and, their status and surroundings (parental addiction o digital media, domestic violence, quality of friendship and self-control). Finally stated that family dysfunction leads to an increase in the addiction of phone, and, friendship and self-control reduces the level of addiction. Mi Jung Rho [13] identified the psychiatric symptoms and problematic usage types of smartphone for adults by utilizing the decision tree method and Korean smartphone addiction proneness scale. They classified the subjects by utilizing the scale: 26% as smartphone independent and 74% as smartphone-dependent group. Also, observed that dependent smartphone users of about 74% are prone to psychiatric signs (dysfunctional impulsivities, depression, anxiety and self-control). Qiufeng Gao [9] predicted the bond between parent-child, and, its effect on education level, quality of life (QOL), physiological perspective and smartphone usage disorder (SUD). The results suggested that subjects with the good-parent-child association have a negative relation with SUD and positive relation with QOL. Also, as the education level increases the SUD and parent-child association gradually reduces. Marc Nahas [8] determined the problematic smartphone usage and the extent among subjects with age of 18–65, by generating a questionnaire data based on types of smartphone usage, positions and other demographic data to observe the symptoms of obsessive-compulsive disorder and depression. They obtained results showing that subjects of 18–34 years with internet subscription and unmarried are more addicted and chatting was the most utilized function. Sharon Horwood [7] analyzed the correlation between psychological well-being and problematic smartphone usage with the measure of life scale and psychological well-being scales. Subjects with problematic smartphone usage have low psychological well-being scores which reflect to lower well-being. Psychological well-being is linked with compulsive behavior, autonomy, maladaptive coping, lack of control, negative emotions and anxiety which is negatively associated. As a reduction in psychological well-being score leads to problematic smartphone usage.

3.2   Effects of Smartphone Addiction

Here, the effects caused by the addiction of smartphone, social media, internet and games are discussed. Joshua Harwood [37] examined the link between mental health and smartphone usage by considering call, text, email and application usage data by subjective evaluation. They assumed that increased usage of smart-device causes weaker mental health. Stress levels, anxiety and depression are evaluated and based on those scores' subjects were divided into 3 categories like more addicted (score > 80), moderate addiction (score 50–79) and no addiction (score 0–49). Yu-Kang Lee [36] studied the interconnection between compulsive behaviors and behavioral characteristics of smartphone users and determine the strain due to compulsive behavior. They analyzed different behavioral characteristics are needed for touch, materialism, social anxiety and locus of control by subjective analysis utilizing SEM with competing models. They validated that smartphones provoke various social ills; also, psychological traits are positively related to technostress and compulsive utilization of smartphone. Jian Li [35] inspected the locus of control over the mobile phone and its negative outcomes associated due to excessive usage of smartphone i.e., more often to use while studying, in class and at bed-time. A subjective assessment was conducted that determines how smartphone addiction effects for different parameters like phone usage duration, academic performance and quality of sleep. A path model was generated to monitor mobile phone usage and locus of control, which obtained results showing that mobile phone usage prompts negative effect on psychological behavior. Maya Samaha [34] identified how risk of smartphone addiction is associated with life satisfaction by academic performance and stress. By conducting a web-based subjective assessment, they concluded that life satisfaction reduces and stress increases with an addiction of smartphone which also affects the academic performance through addiction scale measure. Jacob E. Barkley [31] monitored the cell-phone usage position and examined how cell-phone usage interrupts with physical activities or exercising behavior. They concluded that any digital medium like smartphone or television leads to sedentary leisure behavior which leads to reduced physical activities and exercise, also, frequent users of the digital medium are more prone to health issues and have fewer fitness levels. Jocelyne Matar Boumosleh [26] studied on smartphone addiction symptoms and its prevalence by developing a web-based assessment on various smartphone-related variables, personality trait, lifestyle, academic, sociodemographic. They observed that anxiety and depression are positively related to addiction of smartphone and lifestyle habits, work duration, work type and gender are not associated with addiction levels, but decreased sleep quality, duration and tiredness as effects of addiction. Yeon-Jin Kim [18] examined on addiction of smartphone and internet on anxiety and depression for sociodemographic factors. They classified the subjects into 3 classes: normal users, internet adductors, smartphone adductors based on the web-based survey and concluded internet adductors have less range of anxiety and depression when compared with smartphone adductors. Andr«e O Werneck [16] inspected the correlation between television watching, time spent sitting, levels of physical activity and insomnia among Brazilian subjects. They analyzed based on the above parameters by subjective assessment and, concluded that there will be a higher risk of insomnia when sitting time exceeds 4 h, which also leads to difficulties in sleep irrespective of their age and physical activities. Jessica Peterka-Bonetta [7] validated internet usage disorder (IUD) and SUD with specific personality traits. They procured that impulsivity, social anxiety as effects of IUD and SUD with positive correlation. Thiago Paulo Frascareli Bento [6] determined the mental issues and prevalence of lower back pain associated with electronic devices, habitual practice of physical activity and sociodemographic variables. Multivariate, bivariate logistic regression and descriptive analysis are conducted on data collected and confirmed that daily smartphone or tablet or television or laptop computer usage for more than 3 h or watching in inappropriate position leads to mental health problems and lower back pain. Leonardo S. Fortes [1] analyzed decision-making performance in professional soccer athletes and how it is affected by smartphone usage. They conducted a set of experiments with soccer athletes under 4 different conditions like watching television, using a smartphone for 15 min, 30 min and 45 min before the game. Each subject has gone through subjective assessment and objective assessment of perceived recovery before game, urine, heart rate variability and decision-making index (DMI). Decision making relies on memory, anticipation, attention, perception and DMI is based on the number of appropriate actions to the total number of actions. They concluded there is not much effect with 15 min smartphone usage but 30 min and 45 min usage before the game reduces the DMI.

3.3 Assessment Scales

Here the scales available to evaluate addiction levels are explained. Yu-Hsuan Lin [38] proposed Smartphone Addiction Inventory (SPAI) in which tolerance, withdrawal, functional impairment, compulsive behavior was analyzed, based on Chinese internet addiction. Maya Samaha [34] utilized satisfaction with life scale, perceived stress scale and smartphone addiction scale in which smartphone addiction rates are computed by considering various parameters. Yusong Gao [32] analyzed loneliness and anxiety through University of California Los Angeles Loneliness Scale (UCLA-LS) and Interaction Anxiousness Scale (IAS) which depends on subject's smartphone application usage like health apps, text messages, calls. Julia Machado Khoury [28] adapted, validated and translated SPAI for Brazilian citizens and named it as SPAI-BR. They collect the data through SPAI-BR and determine addiction levels. For ranging addiction, Jocelyne Matar Boumosleh [26] updated the SPAI scale with 26-item questionnaires. Yeon-Jin Kim [18] developed scale of symptom checklist with 90-items, addiction proneness scale and scale for internet addiction based on sociodemographic variables. Halley M. Pontes [8] measured gaming disorder by developing gaming disorder test (GST) and validated with internet gaming disorder scale (IGDS) through concurrent validity, convergent and discriminant validity, nomological validity and factorial validity. I-Hua Chen [2] determined smartphone addiction by Internet Gaming Disorder Scale (IGDS), Bergen Social Media Addiction Scale (BSMAS) and Smartphone Application-Based Addiction Scale (SABAS) in which IGDS evaluates amount of time spent daily on gaming, BSMAS evaluates amount of time spent daily on social media and SABAS evaluates total time spent daily on applications of smartphone.

3.4 Other Methods Available to Measure Mental Fatigue

Here other two methods available for evaluating mental fatigue are given. Mei-Lien Chen [21] studied on air traffic controllers and the correlation between physiological stress symptoms and fatigue. They concluded 50% of subjects felt weary and tired after work and results suggested that ATC job is a stressful job with excess work stress and mental disorders. Yasunori Yamada [15] proposed two models to identify mental fatigue while watching videos for adults and younger people. In the first model, they developed a novel method to measure mental fatigue from the picture of the eye captured and in the second model they adapted the feature selection method. They gathered the data of eye-tracking from older and younger subjects before and after cognitive tasks while watching videos, and, eye-tracking data comprises of gaze allocation, saliency-based metrics, eye-movement direction, oculomotor-based metrics, blink behavior, pupil measures. Shitong Huang [14] studied on smart electrocardiogram (ECG) to measure mental fatigue state by subjective assessment which is interconnected to smartphone and transferred the data through Bluetooth transmission. They utilized KNN to classify the variables which have 8 heart rate variability indicators, collecting data at 5 min interval.

3.5 Study on Physiological Disorders in India

Anjali Sharma [10] examined how mobile phone radiations affects the human nervous system and leads to illness. They conducted experiments on animals by dividing them into two categories: one under normal conditions and other they exposed to microwave radiations, and understand that microwave radiations have toxic effects which affects central nervous system and leads to illness. Yatan Pal Singh Balhara [11] studied on digital medium which acts as the main source of behavioral addicts and suggested that there is a need in developing measuring equipment for behavioral addicts. Yatan Pal Singh Balhara [12] also examined how problematic internet usage is correlated with students of college and university in 8 different countries including India and obtained results stating that 5 Asian countries have higher score among participants for generalized problematic internet usage scale than 3 European countries. Yatan Pal Singh Balhara [13] studied on school students' pattern and extent of problematic internet usage in Delhi from Cyber awareness program. Concluded that problematic internet usage was recorded for 19% and for mood regulations utilized internet was almost 37%.

4 Summary

Finally, as an inference of this study, it is observed that most of the study is from other nations, the research on this domain in India is less and it is needed to be done. In this research, the factors, effects and prevalence for addiction of smartphone, internet, social media, gaming and, what are the scales available to measure the addiction levels are discussed. There are five major factors which leads to increase in addiction level of digital medium are parent-child relationship, self-esteem, depression, loneliness and anxiety which affects the life satisfaction, academic performance, sleep quality and also interrupts the physical activities or exercising behavior, in turn, all these leads to weaker mental health. Also, the addiction levels are different for different age groups, gender, socio-status, education level and work-type. These addiction levels can be reduced by engaging themselves in other physical activities like outdoor games, by interacting with people and by locus of control. The smartphone addiction can be reduced up to some extent by locus of control, which is to reduce smartphone usage at unwanted times by the individual ability to control or avoid usage of smartphone. Also, different techniques like an electroencephalogram (EEG), electrocardiogram (ECG) can be utilized to monitor the mental behavior of the subject other than the subjective assessment for more appropriate results.

Acknowledgement. The work was supported by the National Research Council of Science & Technology (NST) grant by the Korea government (MSIP) (No. CRC-15-05-ETRI).

References

1. Fortes, L.S., Lima-Junior, D., Nascimento-Júnior, J.R.A., Costa, E.C., Matta, M.O., Ferreira, M.E.C.: Effect of exposure time to smartphone apps on passing decision-making in male soccer athletes. Psychol. Sport Exerc. **44**, 35–41 (2019)
2. Chen, I.-H., et al.: Time invariance of three ultra-brief internet-related instruments: Smartphone Application-Based Addiction Scale (SABAS), Bergen Social Media Addiction Scale (BSMAS), and the nine-item Internet Gaming Disorder Scale- Short Form (IGDS-SF9) (Study Part B). Addict. Behav. **101**, 105960 (2019)
3. Horwood, S., Anglim, J.: Problematic smartphone usage and subjective and psychological well-being. Comput. Hum. Behav. **97**, 44–50 (2019)
4. Nahas, M., Hlais, S., Saberian, C., Antoun, J.: Problematic smartphone use among Lebanese adults aged 18–65 years using MPPUS-10. Comput. Hum. Behav. **87**, 348–353 (2018)
5. Gao, Q., Sun, R., Fu, E., Jia, G., Xiang, Y.: Parent–child relationship and smartphone use disorder among Chinese adolescents: the mediating role of quality of life and the moderating role of educational level. Addict. Behav. **101**, 106605 (2019)
6. Bento, T.P.F., Cornelio, G., de O Perrucini, P., Simeão, S.F.A.P., de Conti, M.H.S., de Vitta, A.: Low back pain in adolescents and association with sociodemographic factors, electronic devices, physical activity and mental health. Jornal de Pediatria **19** (2019)
7. Peterka-Bonetta, J., Sindermann, C., Elhai, J.D., Montag, C.: Personality associations with smartphone and internet use disorder: a comparison study including links to impulsivity and social anxiety. Front. Public Health **7**, 1–12 (2019)
8. Pontes, H.M., Schivinski, B., Sindermann, C., et al.: Measurement and conceptualization of gaming disorder according to the world health organization framework: the development of the gaming disorder test. Int. J. Mental Health Addict. **19**, 31242 (2019)
9. Rho, M.J., Park, J., Na, E., et al.: Types of problematic smartphone use based on psychiatric symptoms. Psychiatry Res. **275**, 46–52 (2019)
10. Sharma, A., Sharma, S., et al.: Mobile phone induced cognitive and neurochemical consequences. J. Chem. Neuroanat. **102**, 1–10 (2019)
11. Balhara, Y.P., Anwar, N.: Behavior: a digital platform for prevention and management of behavioural addictions. WHO South-East Asia J Public Health **8**, 101–103 (2019)
12. Balhara, Y.P., et al.: Correlates of problematic internet use among college and university students in eight countries: an international cross-sectional study. Asian J. Psychiatry **45**, 113–120 (2019)
13. Balhara, Y.P., et al.: Extent and pattern of problematic internet use among school students from Delhi: findings from the cyber awareness programme. Asian J. Psychiatry **34**, 38–42 (2018)
14. Huang, S., Li, J., Zhang, P., Zhang, W.: Detection of mental fatigue state with wearable ECG devices. Int. J. Med. Informatics **119**, 39–46 (2018)

15. Yamada, Y., Kobayashi, M.: Detecting mental fatigue from eye-tracking data gathered while watching video: evaluation in younger and older adults. Artif. Intell. Med. **91**, 39–48 (2018)
16. Werneck, A.O., Vancampfort, D., Oyeyemi, A.L., Stubbs, B., Silva, D.R.: Associations between TV viewing, sitting time, physical activity and insomnia among 100,839 Brazilian adolescents. Psychiatry Res. **269**, 700–706 (2018)
17. Kim, H.J., Min, J.Y., Min, K.B., Lee, T.J., Yoo, S.: Relationship among family environment, self-control, friendship quality, and adolescents' smartphone addiction in South Korea: findings from nationwide data. PLoS ONE **13**, 1–13 (2018)
18. Kim, Y.J., Jang, H.M., Lee, Y., Lee, D., Kim, D.J.: Effects of internet and Smartphone addictions on depression and anxiety based on propensity score matching analysis. Int. J. Environ. Res. Public Health **15**, 1–10 (2018)
19. Alhassan, A.A., Alqadhib, E.M., Taha, N.W., Alahmari, R.A., Salam, M., Almutairi, A.F.: The relationship between addiction to smartphone usage and depression among adults: a cross sectional study. BMC Psychiatry **18**, 4–11 (2018)
20. Kim, E., Koh, E.: Avoidant attachment and smartphone addiction in college students: the mediating effects of anxiety and self-esteem. Comput. Hum. Behav. **84**, 264–271 (2018)
21. Chen, M.L., Lu, S.Y., Mao, I.F.: Subjective symptoms and physiological measures of fatigue in air traffic controllers. Int. J. Ind. Ergon. **70**, 1–8 (2019)
22. De-Sola, J., Talledo, H., Rodríguez de Fonseca, F., Rubio, G.: Prevalence of problematic cell phone use in an adult population in Spain as assessed by the Mobile Phone Problem Use Scale (MPPUS). PLoS One **12**, 1–17 (2017)
23. Elhai, J.D., Dvorak, R.D., Levine, J.C., Hall, B.J.: Problematic smartphone use: a conceptual overview and systematic review of relations with anxiety and depression psychopathology. J. Affect. Disord. **207**, 251–259 (2017)
24. Kuang-Tsan, C., Fu-Yuan, H.: Study on relationship among university students' life stress, smart mobile phone addiction, and life satisfaction. J. Adult Dev. **24**, 109–118 (2017). https://doi.org/10.1007/s10804-016-9250-9
25. Hussain, Z., Griffiths, M.D., Sheffield, D.: An investigation into problematic smartphone use: the role of narcissism, anxiety, and personality factors. J. Behav. Addict. **6**, 378–386 (2017)
26. Chłoń-Domińczak, A., Sienkiewicz, Ł., Trawińska-Konador, K.: The development of the polish qualifications framework as an application of knowledge management in public policy. In: Proceedings of the European Conference on Knowledge Management, ECKM, vol. 1, pp. 214–222 (2014)
27. Hwang, Y., Park, N.: Is smartphone addiction comparable between adolescents and adults? examination of the degree of smartphone use, type of smartphone activities, and addiction levels among adolescents and adults. Int. Telecommun. Policy Rev. **24**, 59–75 (2017)
28. Khoury, J.M., de Freitas, A.A.C., Roque, M.A.V., Albuquerque, M.R., das Neves, M.D.C. L., Garcia, F.D.: Assessment of the accuracy of a new tool for the screening of smartphone addiction. PLoS One **12**, 1–13 (2017)
29. Kumcagiz, H., Gunduz, Y.: Relationship between psychological well-being and smartphone addiction of university students. Int. J. High. Educ. **5**, 144–156 (2016)
30. Kayiş, A.R., Satici, S.A., Yilmaz, M.F., Şimşek, D., Ceyhan, E., Bakioğlu, F.: Big five-personality trait and internet addiction: a meta-analytic review. Comput. Hum. Behav. **63**, 35–40 (2016)
31. Barkley, J.E., Lepp, A.: Mobile phone use among college students is a sedentary leisure behavior which may interfere with exercise. Comput. Hum. Behav. **56**, 29–33 (2016)
32. Gao, Y., Li, A., Zhu, T., Liu, X., Liu, X.: How smartphone usage correlates with social anxiety and loneliness. PeerJ **16**, 1–12 (2016)

33. Aljomaa, S.S., Mohammad, M.F., Albursan, I.S., Bakhiet, S.F., Abduljabbar, A.S.: Smartphone addiction among university students in the light of some variables. Comput. Hum. Behav. **61**, 155–164 (2016)
34. Samaha, M., Hawi, N.S.: Relationships among smartphone addiction, stress, academic performance, and satisfaction with life. Comput. Hum. Behav. **57**, 321–325 (2016)
35. Li, J., Lepp, A., Barkley, J.E.: Locus of control and cell phone use: Implications for sleep quality, academic performance, and subjective well-being. Comput. Hum. Behav. **52**, 450–457 (2015)
36. Lee, Y.K., Chang, C.T., Lin, Y., Cheng, Z.H.: The dark side of smartphone usage: psychological traits, compulsive behavior and technostress. Comput. Hum. Behav. **31**, 373–383 (2014)
37. Harwood, J., Dooley, J.J., Scott, A.J., Joiner, R.: Constantly connected - the effects of smart-devices on mental health. Comput. Hum. Behav. **34**, 267–272 (2014)
38. Lin, Y.H., Chang, L.R., Lee, Y.H., Tseng, H.W., Kuo, T.B.J., Chen, S.H.: Development and validation of the Smartphone Addiction Inventory (SPAI). PLoS One **9**, 2014
39. Park, N., Lee, H.: Social implications of smartphone use: Korean college students' smartphone use and psychological well-being. Cyberpsychol. Behav. Soc. Network. **15**, 491–497 (2012)
40. Helen, R.W., Tiffany, K.G., Anne, W.T., Rhiannon, M.P.: Psychological well-being and psychological distress: is it necessary to measure both? Psychol. Well-Being **2**, 1–14 (2012)
41. https://www.statista.com/statistics/274774/forecast-of-mobile-phone-users-worldwide/
42. https://www.psychguides.com/behavioral-disorders/cell-phone-addiction/signs-and-symptoms/

Semi-autonomous Collaborative Mobile Platform with Pre-diagnostics for Hospitals

Vishal Reddy Gade, Ashish Soni, Bharghava Rajaram, and Deep Seth[✉]

Mahindra Ecole Centrale, 1A, Survey No: 62, Bahadurpally,
Hyderabad 500043, Telangana, India
{vishal160210,ashish160204,bharghava.rajaram,deep.seth}@mechyd.ac.in

Abstract. There is a need to improve the working conditions of medical professionals and health care providers in hospitals, especially in developing and under-developed countries. While completely autonomous bots are not preferable in medical field semi-autonomous robots can help people to work more efficient for a longer time. This paper discusses one such mechanism, a semi-autonomous mobile platform which helps in measuring vital health parameters of a patient on a route to the doctor. Measurements of the body's most basic functions are routinely monitored by health care providers before a doctor's appointment. This paper discusses how such a health monitoring system can be integrated into a semi-autonomous mobile platform and its features. In this system, different vital signs of the body are measured to generate an initial database of the report, which will save time to carry out tests for all these processes. The mobile platform traverses to all inpatients in order of arrival. The user interface will ask few important medical questions digitally as well as vocally. The information generated is used to assign the patient to a doctor. It will guide the patient and perform all the measurements, collect the data and upload it to the cloud for further analysis. This will reduce the waiting time and treatment can be performed on time, especially for certain emergency case.

Keywords: Hospital robots · Collaborative robot · Autonomous system · Health monitoring system · ROS · Mobile robot

1 Introduction

Time management plays a crucial part in the health care industries. It is proved that autonomous delivering improves the efficiency of hospital transportation. Items that can be transported within the hospitals are medical supplies, Linens, Hospital wastes, patient meals, Sterile equipment, Lab samples, Reports etc. Özkil [1] made a deep study on things that are transported within the hospitals every day. Use of mobile robots reduce the time of the diagnostic process as well as cut on expenses of the hospital and patient and make it cost effective [2].

Supported by Mahindra Ecole Centrale.

Also, these items are transported by professionally trained nurses. This not only squanders the expertise of nurses but also increases their exposure to contagious germs and viruses. compared to Automated Guided Vehicle's, a mobile robot does not move along a fixed track and thus is more suitable for a hospital like environments where humans are heavily involved. Different perspectives that robot technology can be perceived as; an alien, a machine, a worker and a colleague. These may mutually coexist and are related to time and familiarity with the robot [3]. The need for continuous health monitoring is increasing day by day. The health care systems are highly complex which increases the challenges faced by medical staff [4]. In hospitals, nurses assist the doctors. Each nurse has her responsibility for the delivery duties in the hospital. In general, nurses bring several medical documents/reports, instruments to patients using a cart. The conventional cart is required some external force to push and pull the cart to the patient bed and bring it back many times in a day. This can be tiresome for the nurse because she needs to service several patients in the hospital. While doing this, it is hard for the nurse to focus on his/her daily routine. Many studies have revealed the complexity of workflows at hospitals where many different artefacts take part [5], and how tasks that are physically distributed are a challenge for the staff [6]. To generate initial database report of a patient, different vital signs like pulse rate, body temperature, emotions like stress level, oxygen content, blood pressure are reported with the help of Galvanic Skin response sensor, Oximeter Sensor, Barometric sensor respectively [7,8]. Different features and applications of the mobile platform in the hospital are shown. This paper mainly discusses one such feature **Diagnostics**.

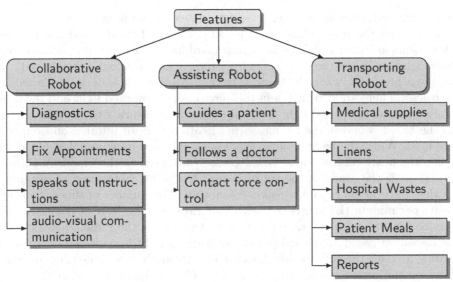

2   Literature Survey

2.1   Galvanic Skin Response Sensor

GSR Sensor stands for galvanic skin response and it is a method of measuring the electrical conductance of the skin. It can be used to reflect the human emotional activity. When we are emotionally stressed or have strong expressions on the face, sympathetic activity increases and promotes the secretion of sweat glands, which increases the skin's electrical conductivity. GSR allows you to spot such strong emotions by simply attaching two electrodes to two fingers on one hand. The method to measure a GSR signal for emotional research purposes is based on a constant voltage system (exosomatic method). The GSR sensor applies a constant voltage—usually 0.5 V—to the two electrodes that are in contact with the skin. The circuit also contains a very small resistance compared to the skin resistance that is in series with the voltage supplier and the electrodes. The purpose of this circuit is to measure the skin conductance and its variation by applying Ohm's law (Voltage = Intensity × Resistance = Intensity/Conductance). As the voltage (V) is kept constant, skin conductance (C) can be calculated by measuring the current (I) flow through the electrodes. With this setup, any fluctuation in the current flow is due to a change in the electrical properties of the skin, and therefore in the sweat gland activity. This sensor is specifically used to measure the stress levels [9, 10].

2.2   Oximeter Sensor(MAX030100)

The pulse oximeter is the device used to measure the amount of oxygen that is carried by the haemoglobin in a blood sample. The red blood cell contains this chemical called haemoglobin which combines with oxygen and forms oxy-haemoglobin. When the blood is rich with oxygen, its colour is bright red, and on the other hand, when the blood is oxygen-depleted, it is dark purple reddish in colour. There are two LED's in this device, one emits red light and the other emits infrared light. Red light is mainly used for measuring the oxygen content in the blood, whereas the for measuring heart rate both infrared and red light are used. When the heart pumps, there is an increase in oxygenated blood and when the heart relaxes, there is a decrease in oxygen in the blood. A person's heartbeat is the sound of the valves in his/ her heart contracting or expanding as they force blood from one region to another. The number of times the heartbeats per minute (BPM), is the heartbeat rate and the beat of the heart that can be felt in any artery that lies close to the skin is the pulse. Heartbeat can be measured based on optical power variation as light is scattered or absorbed during its path through the blood as the heartbeat changes. The time difference between the increase and decrease of oxygen in the blood is used to determine the pulse rate (in beats per minute). Since oxygenated blood is bright red in colour, it absorbs more IR light and passes red light. The absorption levels of both lights are stored in a buffer, which is read via I2C protocol [11].

2.3   Barometric Pressure Sensor(BMP180)

Your heart is a continuous pump. It works life long, and it safely pumps blood – one of the trickiest liquids around. In the same way, your blood vessels are pipes. They take the output from the pump and distribute it throughout the body. A blood pressure gauge is simply a way to measure the performance of the pump and the pipes. The BMP180 consists of a piezo-resistive sensor, an analog to digital converter and a control unit with E2PROM and a serial I2C interface. The BMP180 delivers the uncompensated value of pressure and temperature. A finger is used to press the sensor to measure blood pressure. The microcontroller sends a start sequence to start a pressure or temperature measurement. After converting time, the result value (pressure or temperature respectively) can be read via the I2C interface. For calculating temperature in °C and pressure in hPa, the calibration data has to be used. These constants can be read out from the BMP180 E2PROM via the I2C interface at software initialization. The sampling rate can be increased up to 128 samples per second (standard mode) for dynamic measurement. In this case, it is sufficient to measure the temperature only once per second and to use this value for all pressure measurements during the same period [12].

2.4   Roboclaw

Roboclaw has a software that allows for pre-configuration of Controller values of closed-loop control or debugs any specific problem in general called BasicMicro Motion Studio. The Roboclaw has supported drivers for Robot Operating System, Arduino, Python in RaspberryPi and LabView. The Roboclaw requires a sensor for closed-loop control and in the case of terrestrial robots with wheels encoders are the best choice. The Roboclaw works well with 2-Phase Rotary encoders. This brings a whole level of functionality to the motor controller and enables it to perform accurate manoeuvres. With the encoders, the Roboclaw can Autotune itself when commanded to [13] (Fig. 1).

2.5   Robot Operating System (ROS)

The Robot Operating System (ROS) is an open source framework for robotics software development with its roots at Willow Garage and Stanford University. The philosophy is to make a piece of software that could work in other robots by making little changes in the code without much effort so that we do not have to reinvent the wheel. It consists of modular tools divided into libraries and supports different languages such as C++, Python and LISP. The sensors and actuators used in robotics have also been adapted to be used with ROS.

ROS provides standard operating system facilities such as hardware abstraction, low-level device control, implementation of commonly used functionalities, message passing between processes, and package management. It is based on graph architecture with a centralized topology where processing takes place in nodes that may receive or post data in the form of standard message formats,

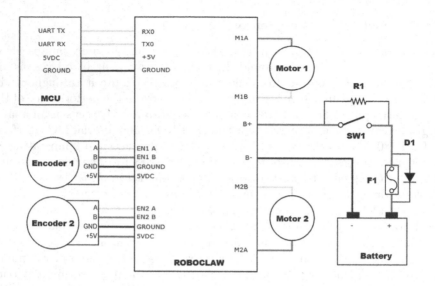

Fig. 1. Roboclaw connections

such as multiplex sensor, control, state, planning, actuator, and so on. Many of the capabilities frequently associated with ROS are the libraries which gives a powerful set of tools to work with ROS easily. Of these, navigation library, gmapping package, rviz visualizer, simulators, and debugging tools are the most important ones [14].

2.6 Gmapping

Maps in ROS are basically a bitmap image representing an occupancy grid, where white pixels represent free space, black pixels represents obstacles, and grey pixels indicate "unknown". Therefore the map is build using graphical program, or use the map that has been created earlier. Since the mobile platform is equipped with lidars, we can create our own map by using Gmapping. In our case, we used SLAM gmapping that combines the data from the lidar(for depth) and odometry into occupancy map.

Gmapping is one of the more popular SLAM algorithms used in robotics. Pairing with the Rao-Blackwellized Particle Filter, it uses the filter to sort out laser data. It then takes into account the altered movements and the recent observations of the robot. PFs utilize a system where each particle is a sample containing both its own map of the environment and a robot pose. Every time the robot moves, the particles are updated with a new map and pose corrected to the movement. Each individual particle in the system is associated with a weight. By doing this the algorithm decreases the chances of uncertainty in the robots pose

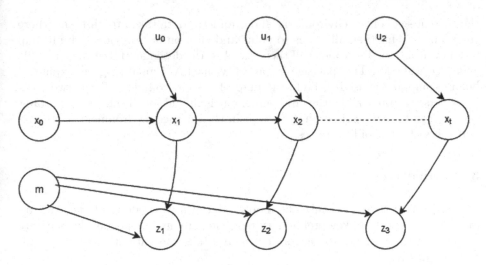

Fig. 2. Graphic representation

for the prediction step of filtering. This weight is utilized by the algorithm to filter out the weakest samples converge toward the strongest representation [15] (Fig. 2).

$$x_{1:t} = x_1, x_2, ...x_t : \quad represents \quad the \quad trajectory \quad of \quad the \quad robot$$

$$m : \quad map \quad of \quad the \quad environment$$

$$z_{1:t} = z_1, z_2, ...z_t : data \quad received \quad from \quad thelaser \quad scanner$$

$$u_{1:t-1} = u_1, u_2, ...u_t - 1 : odometry \quad data \quad of \quad the \quad robot$$

2.7 Adaptive Monte Carlo Localization (AMCL)

Monte Carlo Localization (MCL) is a package commonly used in robotics. There is several different types of this package, it is usually used with different algorithms and filters to help robots complete different tasks and goals. The AMCL is one of the ROS packages used on the turtlebot, what is particularly special about this package is that it helps the turtlebot self-localize itself when it is navigating through different environments. Adaptive Monte Carlo Localization is one of the many ROS packages used in robotics. This package stands out as stated before it lets the robot self-localize itself. This is accomplished by using the current scan of the environment and odometry data taken to pinpoint where the robot is. This then allows us to point and click on our previously built map to a new location. The robot will then travel to the designated destination while avoiding obstacles. This package is paired with SLAM gmapping, as explained before gmapping is used to build the map of the environment. These two combined lets the robot know the environment it is in and localize itself. The robot can then go to any destination it is given in the mapped environment it is given and successfully avoid obstacles [16].

3   Objective

The main objective is to make the mobile platform work alongside health care providers and perform key preliminary tests on patients independently, generate a report of the patient, appoint a doctor and take the patient to doctor semi-autonomously.

4   Methodology

The mobile platform that we are using operates on ROS (Robot Operating System) architecture with RPLidar A2 used as a laser sensor for Simultaneous Localization and Mapping, wheel encoders for odometry, Intel NUC as the main processing unit which runs ROS. It has a payload capacity of 100 kg with a two-wheel differential drive mechanism (refer Fig. 3). Since ROS is used to combine these hardware, initially different sensor nodes publish into topics which are then processed and are subscribed by other nodes. Different publishers and subscribers are mentioned below.

Publishers. The Laser sensor LIDAR continuously publishes point cloud data into a topic called /**scan**(refer (Figs. 4, 5). The micro-controller unit publishes wheel encoder data into /lwheel_ticks and rwheel_ticks which are processed and published into /**odom** topic (refer Fig. 6).

Subscribers. Environmental mapping is done with the help of Gmapping algorithm which subscribes from /**scan** and /**odom** topics and the generated map is published into /**map** topic (refer Fig. 7). Localization is done with the help of amcl package which subscribes to /**scan**, /**odom** and /**map** topics. Micro-controller node i.e., rosserial subscribes from /cmd_vel topic to give commands to the motor driver Roboclaw.

4.1   Architecture

The hardware architecture of this project consists of Intel NUC, RPlidar, Robo-claw, Arduino Mega, Pulse oximeter sensor, Barometric Pressure Sensor and Galvanic Skin Response Sensor. Each component must be calibrated individually beforehand to avoid errors (refer Fig. 8).

Fig. 3. Mobile platform - 650 mm × 450 mm × 180 mm

The data thus obtained is filtered and processed by NUC and can also be uploaded into the cloud as the system is connected to Wi-Fi. A touch screen is added for User Interface to interact with the user like giving instructions, directions, or a questionnaire about the medical conditioning of the patient

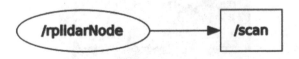

Fig. 4. Lidar node publishing into scan topic

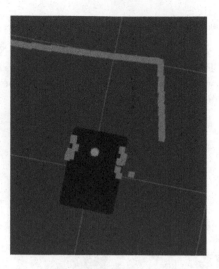

Fig. 5. Visualizing scan topic

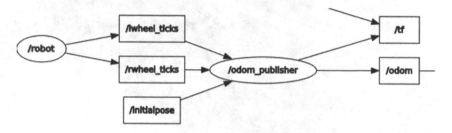

Fig. 6. Processing of encoder data

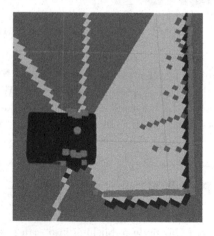

Fig. 7. Gmapping

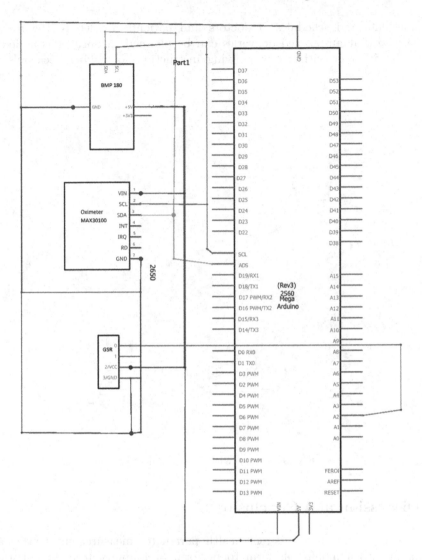

Fig. 8. Sensors Circuit Schematics

like previous doctor appointment, past accidents or diseases or allergies, Blood Group etc. Once the doctor. Doctor appointments can also be made with the User Interface. Java and TKinter in python are used for creating a graphic user interface to interact with the user. For a Human-Robot Interaction feature, current sensors are added directly to the motors to take the physical contact force feedback applied by a human to make it move in that direction, so that a small force applied by a user is enough to move the bot around the work-space.

Appointments and schedules of doctors and patients are fed to the robot's database so that automated deliveries can be planned. A speaker is added to the bot to interact with user for giving instructions or asking decision's etc (Fig. 9).

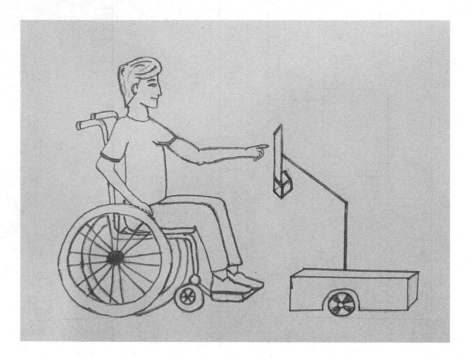

Fig. 9. System with Pre-Diagnostics

5   Discussion and Conclusion

This paper presents how different health parameter measurement sensors are integrated into a mobile platform to perform preliminary tests to a patient and appoint an appropriate doctor by analyzing the obtained data. The data is uploaded to the cloud, to perform efficient data analysis and process the reports further. The database can be monitored by the support staff to fix appointments of the patients. The System is made semi-autonomous which makes it better to work along-side humans collaboratively than to work independently in a hospital-like environment. So that it can collaborate with nurses to transport things, update medical status of patient, thus giving nurse more time for patient care or with doctor to go on rounds. It also enables the flexibility to ride elevators without changing the hospital infrastructure by simply asking the human to select the floor number. Audio visual patient-doctor communication is also made possible without installing additional display or conferencing systems.

In terms of assisting features it can act as a guide to a patient following a treatment protocol or follows a doctor during his rounds. It can easily be moved around the room by slightly pushing the bot in the desired direction.

6 Perspective/Future Scope

To make the transporting system more flexible for different situations, replaceable tops are to be designed, like a chair to carry a person, a rack with shelves to carry medical supplies, Linens, Hospital wastes, patient meals, an organ box and a mobile refrigerator, etc. Further, sensors like Respiratory Rate Sensor, more advanced Blood Pressure Sensor, Ultrasound Sensor can be added to the current health monitoring system.

Acknowledgement. The Mobile Platform was built in collaboration with Indian Institute of Technology, Delhi. We would like to extend our sincere gratitude to Prof. S.K. Saha and his team for their support in building the mobile platform.

References

1. Fan Ozkil, Z., Dawids, S., Srensen, T.: Design of a robotic automation system for transportation of goods in hospitals. In: Proceedings of the 2007 IEEE International Symposium on Computational Intelligence in Robotics and Automation (2007)
2. Ahn, H.S., Xie, J., Rouse, P., Broadbent, E., Orejana, J.R., Bruce, A.: The cost-effectiveness of a robot measuring vital signs in a rural medical practice. In: 24th IEEE International Symposium on Robot and Human Interactive Communication, Korea, Japan. IEEE (2015)
3. Ljungblad, S., Kotrbova, J., Jacobsson, M., Cramer, H., Niechwiadowicz, K.: Hospital robot at work: something alien or an intelligent colleague? pp. 177–186, 02 2012
4. National institute of biomedical imaging and bioengineering. http://www.nibib.nih.gov/science-education/science-topics/sensors (2020). Accessed 31 Jan 2020
5. Bardram, J.E.: Activity-based computing for medical work in hospitals. ACM Trans. Comput Hum. Interact. **16**(2), 1–36 (2009)
6. Bardram, J.E., Bossen, C.: Mobility work: the spatial dimension of collaboration at a hospital. Comput Supported Coop Work **14**, 131–160 (2005). https://doi.org/10.1007/s10606-005-0989-y
7. Khatri, S.K., Warsi, G.G., Hans, K.: IOT based remote patient health monitoring system. In: 2019 International Conference on Machine Learning, Big Data, Cloud and Parallel Computing (Com-IT-Con), India (2019)
8. Hoque, S.I., Rahman, M.N., Baqee, I.A., Hamim, M., Paul, S.: Iot based remote health monitoring system for patients and elderly people. In: 2019 International Conference on Robotics, Electrical and Signal Processing Techniques (ICREST) (2019)
9. Villarejo, M.V., Zapirain, B.G., Zorrilla, A.M.: A stress sensor based on galvanic skin response (GSR) controlled by zigbee. Sensors **12**, 6075–6101 (2012)
10. Kurniawan, H., Maslov, A.V., Pechenizkiy, M.: Stress detection from speech and galvanic skin response signals, pp. 209–214, 06 2013

11. MaximIntegrated. Usage of max30100. https://www.maximintegrated.com/en/products/sensors/MAX30100.html (2020). Accessed 31 Jan 2020

12. Barometric pressure sensor bmp180. https://learn.sparkfun.com/tutorials/bmp180-barometric-pressure-sensor-hookup-/all (2020). Accessed 31 Jan 2020

13. Ionmc. Use of roboclaw. http://downloads.ionmc.com/docs/roboclaw_user_manual.pdf (2020). Accessed 31 Jan 2020

14. Conley K.: ROS: an open-source robot operating system. In: ICRA Workshop on Open Source Software (2009)

15. Gonçalves, J., Lima, J., Costa, P.: Real-time localization of an omnidirectional mobile robot resorting to odometry and global vision data fusion: an EKF approach, pp. 1275–1280, 08 2008

16. Liu, S., Li, S., Pang, L., Hu, J., Chen, H., Zhang, X.: Autonomous exploration and map construction of a mobile robot based on the TGHM algorithm. Sensors **20**, 490 (2020)

A Personal Health-Tracking System Focused on Social Communication for Motivation

Pengyuan Li$^{(\boxtimes)}$ ⓘ and Jiro Tanaka ⓘ

Graduate School of IPS, Waseda University, Tokyo, Japan
lipengyuan@fuji.waseda.jp, jiro@aoni.waseda.jp

Abstract. Personal health-tracking technology which is to record and improve health is becoming popular. The personal health-tracking tools collect user's living data and analyze it, planning for user to change his unhealthy behavior. However, there is was a lack of motivation in the current personal health-tracking system because it mainly focused on individuals. The importance of others in health behaviors and in personal health-tracking was well-established but designer still focused on the individual. How to design a part which allows other users to take part in personal health-tracking technologies system is a new challenge. Our research aims to help people to reach the right audiences and guidance when they share health information to get the motivation to change their behavior to maintain health. We designed a system to help people to finish the process: record data, find friends and coach, change behavior, help others. We use Augmented Reality technology to make the communication and interaction smooth. Also, an Augmented Reality game part is designed in our system to offer people more motivation to change their behavior. Preliminary experiment was carried out to verify the system is effective in terms of providing people with motivation.

Keywords: Augmented reality · Motivation · Personal health-tracking

1 Introduction

Using personal health-tracking tools to keep health is getting popular. In personal health-tracking system, user inputs his food and exercise data which will be analyzed by the system. After that, a plan is made for the user. User needs to follow the plan to change his behavior.

Previous food tracking systems have often been designed to help people improve their behaviors. Researchers have also made more research and design focusing on positive interactions and experiences with food [1]. In the traditional personal health-tracking system, people focus on how to collect the data and how to analyze the data. The models still mainly focus on the individual. Recently, some research shows that focusing on the individual will have some problems [2].

Due to the focus of individual, people will struggle with how to present themselves to other people, and people will lack of motivation to change their behavior. So, some people turn to the social software to share their food photo and get motivation. But the

© Springer Nature Switzerland AG 2020
V. G. Duffy (Ed.): HCII 2020, LNCS 12198, pp. 415–427, 2020.
https://doi.org/10.1007/978-3-030-49904-4_31

problem is that the social software is not designed for personal health-tracking, people need lots of efforts to use it for managing the health.

Our system is designed to solve this problem. The idea is switching the point from individual to social. Using Augmented Reality to support the environment (photo of food) to create a platform for people to communicate with each other and get motivation.

2   Related Work

2.1   Social Health-Tracking System

The importance of others in health behaviors and in personal health- tracking has been well-established. But the models the HCI community uses to understand and design for health-tracking tools still focus on the individual [3]. Andrea Grimes and Richard Harper observed that food could bring people together and have discussed the role of technology in human-food interaction [4].

Within our knowledge, there are some social health-tracking systems we could find about the social health-tracking system.

The paper [5] presents a social health-tracking system which focus on aging populations by creating a social net by fridge. They propose FridgeNet as a way of promoting social activities for these people—this social technology assists older people in re-establishing communication with their families, old acquaintances, and new friends. By automating and encouraging the sharing of dietary information, FridgeNet helps members of this population to establish mutual support in a virtual community. FridgeNet records personal food intake information and promotes communication and social activity among senior citizens. The system uses sensor-equipped processing units (tablets mounted on standard refrigerators) and a cloud service to store and propagate food information. The system automatically stores users' dietary histories and down-loads the corresponding nutritional information. Similar to existing social networking websites, the system lets users post comments, pictures, and voice messages.

2.2   Gamification

There are some basic gamification elements in the gamification applications. Among these typical game design elements [6], are points, badges, leader-boards, performance graphs, meaningful stories, avatars, and teammates. We mainly use three of them: points, badges, leaderboards in the system.

Points are basic elements of a multitude of games and gamified applications. They are typically rewarded for the successful accomplishment of specified activities within the gamified environment and they serve to numerically represent a player's progress [7]. Various kinds of points can be differentiated between, e.g. experience points, redeemable points, or reputation points, as can the different purposes that points serve. One of the most important purposes of points is to provide feedback. Points allow the players' in-game behavior to be measured, and they serve as continuous and immediate feedback and as a reward [8].

Badges are defined as visual representations of achievements and can be earned and collected within the gamification environment. They confirm the players' achievements, symbolize their merits, and visibly show their accomplishment of levels or goals. Earning a badge can be dependent on a specific amount of points or on activities within the game. Badges have many functions, serving as goals, if the prerequisites for winning them are known to the player, or as virtual status symbols. In the same way as points, badges also provide feedback, in that they indicate how the players have performed [9]. Badges can influence players' behavior, leading them to select certain routes and challenges in order to earn badges that are associated with them. Additionally, as badges symbolize one's membership in a group of those who own this badge, they also can exert social influences on players and co-players, particularly if they are rare or hard to earn.

Leaderboards rank players according to their relative success, measuring them against a certain success criterion [10]. As such, leaderboards can help determine who performs best in a certain activity and are thus competitive indicators of progress that relate the player's own performance to the performance of others. However, the motivational potential of leaderboards is mixed. Werbach and Hunter [7] regard them as effective motivators if there are only a few points left to the next level or position, but as demotivators, if players find themselves at the bottom end of the leaderboard. Competition caused by leaderboards can create social pressure to increase the player's level of engagement and can consequently have a constructive effect on participation and learning. However, these positive effects of competition are more likely if the respective competitors are approximately at the same performance level [9].

3   Goal and Approach

3.1   Goal and Problem

In the traditional personal health-tracking system, designers usually focus on the data-collection and data-analyze. How to motivate user to change his behavior is not seriously considered. Some research shows that now the motivation in traditional personal health-tracking system is not enough [11]. Let's take MyFitnessPal's motivation ways for example [12]. MyFitnessPal is a popular personal health-tracking tool which has more than 100 million users. It uses two ways to motivate its user:

1. It will recommend user some victory stories. Some users read the victory story and get some motivation.
2. It offers user a forum. Users can talk about things about eating or body exercising.

Many health personal tracking tools are hard to inspire long-term adoption because of the lack of motivation. The lack of motivation also causes less behavior change of user [3].

So, the lack of motivation is a serious problem in the personal health-tracking system.

3.2   Approach

To motivate the user to change his behavior, the system must use something to motivate user. The input of user in personal health-tracking system is eating data and exercise data. According to the Characteristics of them, eating data is decided to use for social communication. And exercise data is for gamification part.

To design an augmented reality communication part, we must decide some framework. In terms of content used for communication, we have decided that the communication would be based on photo. Because photo-based data makes tracking easier and more engaging [13]. Using photos to record is appropriate than the traditional way where people share text or blog information.

Augmented Reality technology is used in this part. To use our system, user needs to take picture for the food. And when user uses camera to focus on the food, AR system can start to work for user. AR makes the interaction smoother.

In terms of designing the game part, we must find some ideas to guide us how to design this part. The first idea is to not to make the gamification part alone. An alone game part in the personal tracking system is strange and unnatural. Combine the gamification with the social communication.

Personal tracking includes two kinds of data: food and exercise. Food data is photo-based, which is designed to use in social communication part. Then the exercise data will be used in gamification.

Make use of past and future selves in the game. Provide user with a representation of her past and future selves along her present self, in order to trigger behavior, change processes. Past can favor user reflection about the choices she made, the objectives she achieved and the transformations she produced on her own identity in time. Future can trigger behavior change strategies by presenting ideal states that the user can tend to. It aims at suggesting behavior change strategies based on the presentation of user's representations that embody her past and future states [14].

The Fig. 1 shows how the game motivates user to change his behavior in generally. Motivational affordances are provided for users. For example, points, levels, progress, feedback and rewards. These affordances can cause users' psychological outcomes which includes motivation, attitude, fun, enjoyment. Then it can make behavioral outcomes. We followed this model to design the gamification part in our system.

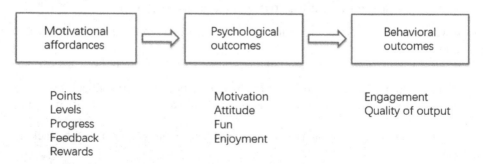

Fig. 1. The model of how game motivates player

Provide meaningful rewards that incorporate some kinds of values for users. While aesthetic values can leverage the users' desire for appearing, and instrumental values can exploit their need of power and achievement, social values can trigger engagement based on the need of being recognized by others. Offering users valuable rewards to recognize their skills and contribution. Rewards, like points and badges, are not meaningful per se. They show that the user has done something in the system. And we need to tell user that something is meaningful, and the rewards are useful. How to find values that can give meanings to these representations should be one of the main aims of gamification strategies and how designing a reward system based on competence could enhance users' intrinsic motivation [14].

Group and cooperation encourage users to become part of a group and promote their identification in it, by fostering cooperation among members. People can communicate with others and get the feeling of the group. Feeling of attachment to a community can arise through common identity, whereby members feel connected to a group's purpose (Tajfel and Turner [15]), or from interpersonal bonds, when individuals develop relationships, such as friendships, with other members (Prentice, Miller, Light dale [16]).

4 Personal Health-Tracking System Focused on Social Communication for Motivation

4.1 Scenarios

There is Augmented Reality Communication part's user scene:

1. User uses this part for the first time. The system helps him to find new friends.
2. User invites one of the friends to be his coach.
3. User changes lots of unhealthy behaviors with the motivation from his friends and coach.
4. User becomes a coach of his friend.

In terms of game part, the scene is:

1. The system sets some Augmented Reality missions in random place.
2. User can get the information about the location of the AR mission in the application and can go to receive the mission.
3. After finishing the mission, user can get points. If user thinks the mission is not appropriate for himself, he can send the mission to his friends.

These are the things which link the two parts together:

1. The friend list is shared between the two parts.
2. The achievement point is shared between the two parts. More points make a higher rank in leaderboard of game part. More points give user a higher priority to show comment and share content in Augmented Reality communication part.

4.2   System Design

The system consists of two main parts: Augmented Reality communication part and game part. Augmented reality communication part is based on food data which input by user to motivate. And the game part is based on food data. The aim of game part is to support the Augmented reality social communication part. The Fig. 2 shows how the system works. Photo-based data and exercise data will be input by the mobile phone and take part in social communication and game. The server will store the data and control these two parts.

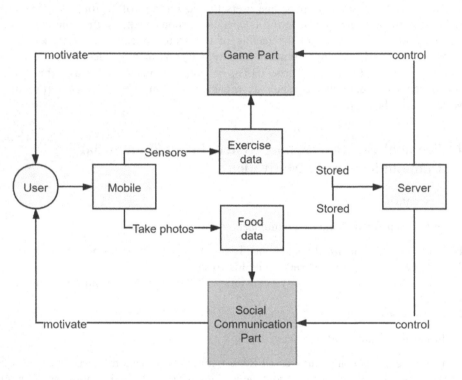

Fig. 2. System overview

Augmented reality social communication part is designed to motivate user to change his unhealthy eating behavior. User can take a photo of food at the start interface as shown in Fig. 3(a).

Then the Augmented Reality system will start to work. When user enters the main interface, as shown in Fig. 3(b). There are some Augmented Reality comments which are given by other users. The left part shows some Augmented Reality avatars. Each avatar presents one other user. The right part shows user's assistant. User can get guidance and information from her.

(a) Start interface

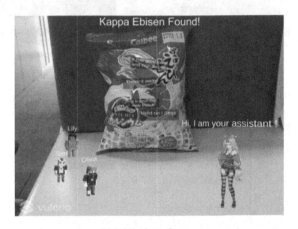

(b) Main interface

Fig. 3. Start and main interface in the system

User can click the Augmented Reality avatars to interact with other users. Figure 4(a) shows the examples of the interface with stranger. User can chat with her and get some information. Figure 4(b) shows the examples of the interface with friends. User can see the last picture which his friend took and give comment.

In the game part, the system will set some Augmented Reality missions randomly. As the Fig. 5 shows, the user can look over the map and find the mission card which is near the user. User can go around the specific place to find it.

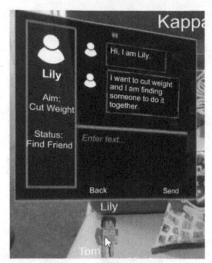

(a)Interact with strangers

(b)Interact with friends

Fig. 4. Interface with other users

Fig. 5. Get the mission location

The mission is attached in the Augmented Reality avatar (see in Fig. 6). User can get the detailed information about the mission in the application (see in Fig. 7). After the user get the mission, he will try to complete it. He can get some achievement points as rewards.

Fig. 6. Find the Augmented Reality mission

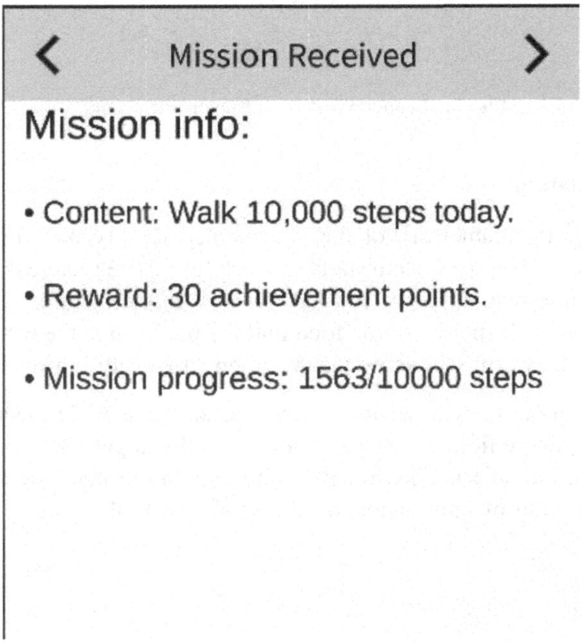

Mission Received

Mission info:

• Content: Walk 10,000 steps today.

• Reward: 30 achievement points.

• Mission progress: 1563/10000 steps

Fig. 7. The mission contents

Each area has its own leaderboard of achievement points every week (see in Fig. 8). User can know his rank among all the users in the specific area. Then he will know he should exercise more or exercise less next week.

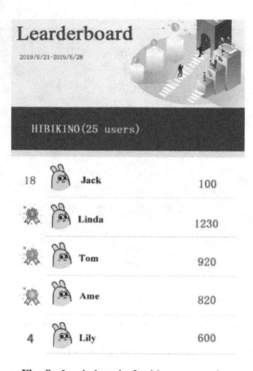

Fig. 8. Leaderboard of achievement points

4.3   Implementation

The Fig. 9 shows the framework of the Augmented Reality part. First, user take a picture for the food. Then the system starts to work for it. The picture is uploaded to the API URL to get information about the food which is in the picture. At the same time, the system will detect the border of the food and the platform in the picture. After these works are finished, system will show the Augmented Reality information to the user.

Object Service. In our system, we use google cloud vision API to identify the object. After getting the picture from the user, we send it to the target URL to get the detailed information about the object. Then we infer the data in our database about the object and decide which kind of information would be shown to the user.

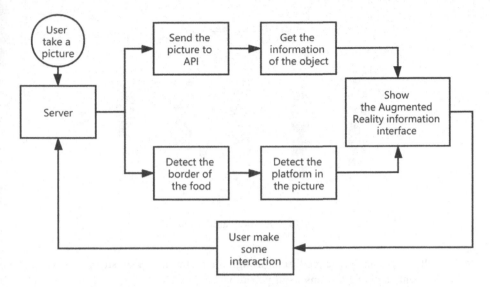

Fig. 9. Framework of the Augmented Reality communication part

Augmented Reality SDK. We use ARCore as the Augmented Reality SDK in our system. It helps us to do understand the environmental. ARCore looks for clusters of feature points that appear to lie on common horizontal or vertical surfaces, like tables or walls, and makes these surfaces available to our app as planes. We can use this information to place virtual objects resting on flat surfaces.

5 Preliminary Evaluation

We invited 10 participants to use our system, ranging in age from 20 to 25 and including 2 female and 8 males. All participants are given a brief introduction of the system. Each participant needs to use our system to record their eating and. During the process, they also will communicate with other users in the system. After that, the participant will be asked to fill in a questionnaire. The questionnaire has following 5 questions and these questions use the 5-point Likert scale. We plan to investigate the basic information of each participant and get their feedback. All the participants are asked to rate on a Likert Scale ranging from 1 to 5. The results are shown in Table 1 and Fig. 10.

Table 1. Answers statistics of investigative questions

Question	1	2	3	4	5
Q1: The system is easy to operate			2	6	2
Q2: The way of interaction is useful or interesting				3	7
Q3: The system is easy to make new friends		1	1	7	1
Q4: The rewards in the game part is enough?			3	7	
Q5: The system can motivate you to change behavior				9	1

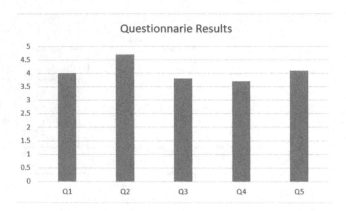

Fig. 10. Questionnaire results

Overall, we got a positive feedback through the preliminary user study. We also get some comments and suggestions from participants:

1. "You can find more beautiful 3D figures as the Augmented Reality avatars in the system. It will look better!"
2. "Maybe more factors should be added in the game part."
3. "The interaction of the system is a little bit complex, sometimes I don't know where to look at my current state."

6   Conclusion and Future Work

In this paper, we described a health-tracking system which focuses on motivating the user to change their unhealthy behaviors.

We took use of user's eating data and exercise data to create a social communication system. And we designed a game part to support it. Augmented Reality technology also is used to make the interaction more smoothly and attractive. We provided a user scene to show how the system worked. The scene contained four stages, where the user changed from the beginner to a coach. User in the system could make friends with the help of system quickly. Then user could interface with other users in the Augmented Reality environment when he took record of his eating data. Also, user could invite his friend to be a coach to give him more suggestions. The coach would get rewards as achievement points for motivation. Last step, the user became a coach to give his friends suggestions. During this process, the user changed his role: from beginner to the people who were coached, then became a coach for others. The game part also was designed to offer people more motivation to change their behavior. User could set the Augmented Reality mission in the place to communicate with other users. It was a chance for user to make more friends. The game part also provided achievement points to user as the motivation. Last, several experiments were performed to verify the system is effective in terms of providing people with motivation.

Our system is a new attempt about how to design a social health-tracking system. So, the system focused on how to create the platform for users to communicate with each other. And the guidance from the system is a little poor. Using the new technology like deep learning or big data to analyze the data which the user recorded and generate some specific suggestion is one kind of possible idea.

References

1. Grimes, A., Harper, R.: Celebratory technology: new directions for food research in HCI. In: CHI (2008)
2. Chung, C.F., Agapie, E., Schroeder, J., Mishra, S., Fogarty, J., Munson, S.A.: When personal tracking becomes social: examining the use of instagram for healthy eating. In: 2017 CHI Conference on Human Factors in Computing Systems, pp. 1674–1687 (2017)
3. Asimakopoulos, S., Asimakopoulos, G., SpillerStavros, F.: Motivation and user engagement in fitness tracking: heuristics for mobile healthcare wearables. Informatics 4(1), 5 (2017)
4. Grimes, A., Harper, R.: Celebratory technology: new directions for food research in HCI. In: Proceedings of the SIGCHI Conference on Human Factors in Computing Systems, CHI 2008, New York, NY, USA, pp. 467–476 (2008)
5. Lee, Y., Huang, M.C., Zhang, X., Xu, W.: Fridgenet: a nutrition and social activity promotion platform for aging populations. IEEE Intell. Syst. 30, 23–30 (2015)
6. Sailer, M., Hense, J., Mayr, S.K., Mandl, H.: How gamification motivates: an experimental study of the effects of specific game design elements on psychological need satisfaction. Comput. Hum. Behav. 69, 371–380 (2017)
7. Werbach, K., Hunter, D.: For the Win: How Game Thinking Can Revolutionize Your Business. Wharton Digital Press, Philadelphia (2012)
8. Sailer, M., Hense, J., Mandl, H., Klevers, M.: Psychological per- spectives on motivation through gamification. Interact. Des. Arch. J. 19, 18–37 (2013)
9. Rigby, S., Ryan, R.M.: Glued to Games: How Video Games Draw us in and Hold us Spellbound. Praeger, Santa Barbara (2011)
10. Costa, J.P., Wehbe, R.R., Robb, J., Nacke, L.E.: Time's up: studying leaderboards for engaging punctual behaviour. In Proceedings of the First International Conference on Gameful Design, Research, and Applications, Gamification 2013, pp. 26–33. ACM (2013)
11. Clawson, J., Pater, J.A., Miller, A.D., Mynatt, E.D., Mamykina, L.: No longer wearing: investigating the abandonment of personal health-tracking technologies. In: 2015 ACM International Joint Conference on Pervasive and Ubiquitous Computing, pp. 647–656 (2015)
12. MyFitnessPal reference. https://community.myfitnesspal.com/en/categories. Accessed 20 Dec 2019
13. Cordeiro, F., Bales, E., Cherry, E., Fogarty, J.: Rethinking the mobile food journal: exploring opportunities for lightweight photo-based capture. In: SIGCHI Conference on Human Factors in Computing Systems, pp. 3207–3216 (2015)
14. Rapp, A.: Designing interactive systems through a game lens: an ethnographic approach. Comput. Hum. Behav. 71, 455–468 (2017)
15. Tajfel, H., Turner, J.C.: Psychology of Intergroup Relations, pp. 7–24 (1986)
16. Prentice, D.A., Miller, D.T., Lightdale, J.R.: Asymmetries in attachments to groups and to their members: distinguishing between common-identity and common-bond groups. Pers. Soc. Psychol. Bull. 20(5), 484–493 (1994)

A Technology-Driven Approach
for Child-Friendly Diabetes Management

Martin Lurz[(⊠)], Maren Billmann, Markus Böhm, and Helmut Krcmar

Technical University of Munich, Boltzmannstr. 3, 85748 Garching, Germany
martin.lurz@tum.de

Abstract. As one of the most common chronic diseases, diabetes negatively affects the lives of many people. Owing to the recent technological developments, blood sugar monitoring applications have become an important assistant means to support people with diabetes. Although, the existing blood sugar monitoring applications can demonstrate the real-time data collected from sensors for the self-monitoring purpose, they mostly are not intended for children with diabetes, even though the rate of the cases of newly diagnosed childhood type 1 diabetes increases by 3%–4% in Europe each year. Considering a child-friendly approach,

We propose an application that enables parents to monitor their child's glucose level remotely. To implement such application, we developed a plush toy that can register sensor values, synchronize with the parents' phones and thereby help the children to cope with diabetes. The aim of the present paper is to outline the two iterations of the system development. We share the results of the expert interviews, which have been conducted in the first evaluation round and have provided important insights in terms of further development and psychological aspects. Furthermore, we highlight the positive feedback from the second evaluation round involving parents and experts, which has led us to the conclusion that the proposed system can serve as a helpful and novel approach to support children with diabetes and their parents.

Keywords: Diabetes · Management · Monitoring · Support · Child-Friendly · Children · Mobile · Smartphone · App · Toy

1 Introduction

Diabetes is one of the most common chronic diseases in the world. According to the data provided by the World Health Organization (WHO) in 2016, there are 422 million diabetics in the world [1]. The WHO further estimated that 1.6 million deaths in 2016 were directly related to diabetes, and another 2.2 million in 2012 were related to the critical levels of high blood sugar [2].

As high glucose levels can damage the body, untreated diabetes can cause different diseases, such as hypertension, depression, blindness, kidney failure, stroke, and heart attacks. These diseases together with diabetes adversely affect the life quality of patients and complicate their daily life [3]. If the treatment if provided timely and effectively, including precise blood sugar control, diabetes patients can live a long life,

© Springer Nature Switzerland AG 2020
V. G. Duffy (Ed.): HCII 2020, LNCS 12198, pp. 428–441, 2020.
https://doi.org/10.1007/978-3-030-49904-4_32

especially, when receiving appropriate treatment from the early stages of the disease. However, treatments need to be tailored to the individual patient groups and be initiated immediately after diagnosis.

In Europe, 286.000 children were diagnosed with diabetes in 2017 with 28.200 new diagnosed children registered every year [4]. All over the world, there are 1.1 million children and adolescents under the age of 20 with diabetes [5], and the numbers are continuously increasing by approximately 3%–4% corresponding to the cases of newly diagnosed children with diabetes in Europe each year [6]. Currently, the recovery treatment for diabetes does allow curing the disease completely but helps to slow its progression down [7].

With regard to children, treatment can specifically be challenging, as blood sugar needs to be monitored on a regular basis, and respective actions need to be undertaken. Often the parents need to take over responsibility of performing appropriate monitoring and treatment, particularly, if the children are diagnosed at a young age [8]. Therefore, the need to perform continuous monitoring of blood sugar is highly valued by the parents as a means to prevent hypoglycemia as well as hypoglycemia-related anxiety [9]. In accordance with these facts, technology advances should be employed to develop and improve an approach aiming to support children with diabetes and their families in their daily life.

Therefore, in the present study, we developed the prototype of a smartphone application connected to a smart toy used to support the children with diabetes and their families. In the present paper we describe the development process and share the results of the two iterations of evaluation involving experts and parents of children with diabetes.

2 Related Work

Various studies evaluated the usage of technologies for diabetes mellitus. Investigations were mainly dedicated to continuous monitoring systems, however, tailoring health games for adults and children was also studied.

The advantages of digital approaches in comparison to the traditional paper-based diaries have been outlined by Palermo et al. [10]. They showed that children had a higher acceptance rate toward such digital solutions and perceived them as easy to use. Furthermore, they identified out that the digital version contained less errors compared to the entries of a paper-based control group, and that the compliance rate was significantly higher for male participants.

The research conducted by Franklin et al. in 2008 revealed a novel approach for early notification systems for the diabetics [11]. In this study, a messaging system was proposed to encourage and support young people with diabetes. It was found that young people accepted this system and used it to send positive responses to the central message provider. Therefore, notifications and alerts are deemed as significant components of smartphone applications, as they are widely accepted by users.

Mougiakakou et al. introduced a complex technology-driven method to support diabetics in 2009 [12]. According to this research, the intervention included a combination of physical activity monitoring, food intake counter, blood sugar measuring, and a pressure measurement device. The application they developed combined all features and measurements within a single platform. Moreover, it included a physician platform to monitor the patient health situation. Therefore, the physicians could access the data from their phones or computers. To facilitate the connection between the patients and physicians, they employed a mobile or Wi-Fi network. As a result, they proposed a two-sided complex system for supporting diabetes patients. However, the proposed system implied having an assistant partner to perform monitoring and intervention.

Van der Drift et al. discussed the advantages of using a robot to motivate children for keeping a diary [8]. They demonstrated that the robot allowed increasing the motivation of children to write more details into their diaries with the average number of characters written augmented from 37 to 83, indicating a highly efficient interaction between child and a toy.

Further, Al-Taee et al. in 2017 illustrated how a robot assistant could help children to manage their diabetes [13]. The robot interacted with the child and talked to the child to understand how the situation of the child was. Moreover, the robot provided advises, and thereby educated the child how to cope with diabetes. After recording interactions with the child, it sent the dialog data to a health care partner, so that it was possible to monitor the health situation of the child through a web application. As a result, they reported positive outcomes indicating high acceptance rates of over 80%.

In turn, Toscos et al. in 2012 evaluated the impact of technologies on the parent-child relationships [14]. They conducted interviews involving children and parents. As a result, they demonstrated the potential of the positive influence of pervasive technologies on the parent-child relationship and highlighted the possibilities to design an application, which could be used to support the users in changing their behavior by focusing on their emotional reaction to the corresponding health data.

3 The System

The aim of the present study was to provide the parents with a tool to assist them to nudge the children to measure their blood glucose level regularly and thereby to maintain a healthier lifestyle [15].

3.1 Development Methodology

Seeking to develop a user-friendly and scientifically solid application, we followed the design science research approach [16].

To obtain insights into the existing methods of developing applications for diabetics, as well as to investigate functional requirements corresponding to child-friendly applications in this area, we conducted a structured literature review based on the approach of Webster and Watson [17]. This helped us to obtain first insights into important features of the planned application as well as to evaluate the possibilities of motivating and teaching children through the technologies, as shown in Sect. 2 of this paper.

Thereafter. we proceeded with the definition of requirements. With this purpose, we analyzed the findings obtained from the literature review to derive essential functionality of the planned application.

After the first iteration, the system design was evaluated involving experts to ensure inclusion of important features in terms of medical treatment from the viewpoint of a doctor. The obtained feedback was incorporated during the next development session. After completing the second development iteration, the prototype was evaluated involving several experts of the first evaluation session as well as parents of children with diabetes.

3.2 The Prototype

The main purpose of the proposed system is to provide the patients with a child-friendly solution, while supporting parents in monitoring their child's health.

As shown in Fig. 1 the proposed system is composed of the four following components: a blood glucose measuring sensor placed on the skin of the child (1), a plush toy, which functions as a data receiver connected to the sensor (2), a parent application to process and represent currently measured blood glucose values (4), and a cloud database to exchange the data between the toy and the parent application (3).

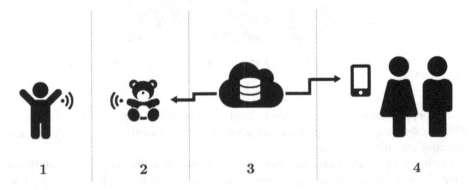

Fig. 1. The four different components of the proposed system.

The Blood Glucose Sensor. A Freestyle Libre NFC-sensor [18] was employed as an example of a state-of-the-art technology for continuous measurement of the blood glucose level. Furthermore, its high prevalence among diabetes patients made it a suitable example to present to the target group. The sensor is placed on the skin to measure the glucose level of diabetics constantly. For this purpose, a small, sterile needle is placed under the skin and fixed by a plaster. To send the data to the receiver, the sensor uses near-field communication (NFC). Therefore, the data are only transmitted when the receiver is placed at a maximum distance of 4–5 cm in front of the sensor.

The Sensor-Value Receiving Toy. A teddy bear was chosen as the children's companion, as shown in Fig. 2. We decided to use a widely popular plush toy due to multiple reasons. First, the children can easily get attached to it and build up an emotional relationship. We hoped that this could not only increase the probability that the children would take it with them everywhere, but also that such form would encourage them to follow the nudges. Second, it is a simple and portable toy, which provides the sufficient space for the hardware, and its material does not severely restrict the wireless connection. Finally, it is made of soft materials and thereby provides certain protection to the hardware inside.

Fig. 2. During the prototyping process, a smartphone was used as hardware within the teddy bear.

The application implemented into the teddy bear is able to register the data from the NFC sensor. After receiving the information, the most recent data are sent out and uploaded into the online database.

Furthermore, we attempted to provide the experimental teddy bear with the ability to speak. This would allow parents to enter phrases in the parent's app which would be send to the bear and there synthesized to an audio output via TextToSpeech (TTS) technology. The idea behind this feature was to provide the supervisors with an option to encourage the child to measure their current blood glucose (through pushing the "Hug me" button, so that the child would attach the bear near to the sensor) or to give instructions if the child would be in a state close to hypoglycemia or hyperglycemia.

The Database. We used the open-source database MongoDB as a back-end program and Amazon Web Services as a cloud platform for the storage area. To integrate the back-end with the toy and the parent app, a REST API running on a Flask9 microframework was implemented. This architecture enabled the back-end to send and retrieve the data to and from two applications in the JavaScript Object Notation (JSON) format.

Furthermore, as the application is intended to gather personal information of users such as name and age as well as highly sensitive health data, such as measurement values, data security is an important issue to address. In the proposed system, the data are secured via state-of-the-art hashing, access management, and encrypted transmission.

The Parent App. To enable parents to monitor the current glucose level of their child through a convenient user interface, we specifically developed the parent app. Furthermore, to use the TTS feature of the plush toy, parents could transmit directives to the child, as shown in Fig. 3. This feature was implemented to encourage the parent to support their children, even if they were far away from each other.

However, the main purpose of the user app, was to present the measured data and valuable insights to the parents. The home page was implemented in such way to provide an overview of the daily data including the latest measured blood sugar level and an overview of the measurements during the last twelve hours. In addition, the home page included a battery level indicator, as well as the "Hug Me" button, which was intended to trigger the plush toy to ask the child for taking a new measurement.

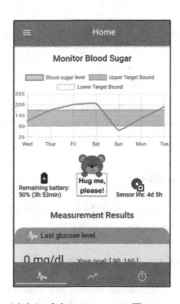

Fig. 3. Directives input (left) and the home page (right) of the parent app. The measuring unit was mg/dl; demonstration target ranges of the blood glucose level were based on [19].

Next to the daily overview of the child's blood sugar level, the app was able to retrieve reports over a flexible period of time, which allowed deriving further insights such as average levels or notable patterns, as shown in Fig. 4.

Additionally, the user app allowed the parents to save important telephone numbers, such as the number of the kindergartner. When the glucose level of the child appeared to be critical, the parents would receive a push notification from the app, which would redirect them either to the home page or to the emergency phone numbers. Using the list of emergency phone numbers into which new numbers could be added flexibly from the list of contacts, they could directly contact the person watching over the child and inform them about the critical blood glucose level.

Fig. 4. Report page (left) and emergency number management (right) of the parent app. The measuring unit was mg/dl; demonstration target ranges of the blood glucose level were based on [19].

4 Evaluation

To develop a user-friendly and a scientifically sound end product, we conducted two rounds of evaluation.

4.1 First Iteration Evaluation

In the first evaluation round, we conducted structured interviews involving experts from the medical and psychological fields to obtain professional feedback and inputs. We focused on collecting feedback on the current prototype and thereby obtained insights with regard to additional features of the application, as well as required changes in the design.

Methodology. We conducted structured interviews to collect qualitative data with regard to the first prototype of the system. Therefore, we aimed to recruit experts from the area of diabetic treatment for children, as well as psychologists to provide feedback on the proposed system and help to improve the design.

We were able to recruit eight experts from two different universities for the interview sessions: six child endocrinology doctors (E1–E6), and two child and family psychologists (E7–E8). To conduct each interview, we visited the experts at their working places. We followed the same structure and asked the same questions in every interview. To facilitate retrospective evaluation, all interviews were recorded.

In the beginning, we explained the functionality and interface of the initial parent application prototype and the matching interactive toy. Additionally, we showed a demo video to help the experts to get an impression of how the prototype was supposed to work. After that, we asked about existing problems faced by children and their parents regarding during the management of diabetes. Then, we asked to describe expectations and requirements for such application from the professional viewpoint and evaluated, which psychological aspects were important to address during the application development.

After finishing all fourteen interviews, we evaluated the individual responses to identify and prioritize change requests to be considered in the next development phase.

Results. According to the experts, one important feature corresponding to the parent app would be the option to register results of a glucometer (in addition to the values tracked automatically through the sensor), as the results obtained via different tools might have discrepancies. E6 stated that the possibility to observe differences in measurements would provide important information about child's metabolism, as the sensor results corresponded to delayed values, while the glucometer results were much more precise with regard to the current state. Therefore, glucometer results would be helpful to determine the amount of insulin to be taken by the child to regulate the blood sugar level.

E4 also emphasized the need in multiple visualization options including hourly, daily, weekly and monthly graphs. This was deemed important to assist parents and doctors in identifying the glucose trends and to provide them with better insights into the child's health situation.

Regarding the interactive toy, E2 and the interviewed psychology experts outlined that the children should not know that their parents are able to control the teddy bear. Additionally, it was suggested to limit the direct control of the toy to a single parent device. The use of all other connected devices was suggested to be limited only to monitoring functionality and displaying the current values.

E7 advised to make it as interesting as possible (e.g., by varying the possible instructions the teddy bear can give to the child) as otherwise, the children might quickly lose the motivation to play with it.

Furthermore, E2 suggested to limit the number of information messages sent to parents/supervisors. This idea was also supported by E7 who stated, that the parent app could result in making the parents overprotective and advised to limit the interaction options between parents and the interactive toy (especially in regard to the TTS feature).

Finally, three of the experts also stated, that supporting would be a very helpful characteristic to implement in the final product, as it would not only allow enabling the toy to track the current glucose levels without the need in direct contact between the child and the toy, but also facilitating measurements during sleeping hours, as E3 suggested.

Overall, the experts appreciated the idea behind the project and agreed that it would be a suitable product for the children aged between 4–10 years.

System Changes. After finishing the expert interview sessions, we analyzed the collected feedback to define and prioritize required changes to be incorporated in the system. We decided to focus on the following changes.

First, we focused on expanding the available data graphs to include hourly, weekly, and monthly bases. The expanded visualization feature was requested by E1, E2, E4 and E6, as these tables were very crucial for treatment purposes considering that doctors used them as the knowledge base to adjust the insulin amount prescribed to the patients.

Second, we enabled to entering the manual measurement data to compare the glucometer results with the sensor results.

Third, we limited the TTS functionality to predefined directives to prevent the possibility of parents getting overprotective or entering aggressive directives. The new predefined directives were selected in cooperation with experts.

Finally, we refined the alert/notification functionality. We added three different levels (yellow, orange, and red zones), as shown in Fig. 5, with different alarm settings.

The yellow zone was intended for the low glucose level deviations (up to 10 mg/dl) from the target range. The plush toy would autonomously provide the child with the directives corresponding to this zone. If the child followed advises and the blood glucose level normalized accordingly, the teddy bear would not send any notification to the parents.

However, if the child did not follow the directives, and the glucose level reached the orange zone (between 10 and 20 mg/dl from the target range), parents would get notified as well as emergency contacts.

Once the blood glucose level reached the red zone (more than 20 mg/dl deviation), the toy would notify the emergency contacts. Moreover, it would initiate the alarm to notify people around the child.

Implementing these zones, we hoped to ease the burden on the parents, so that they would only need to get involved if situations became critical. Moreover, we hoped that this approach could encourage the children to learn how to cope with diabetes with the help of their toy and support the children to build new healthy habits.

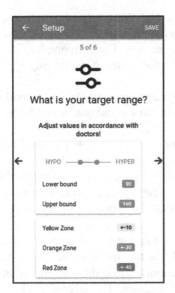 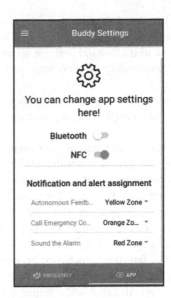

Fig. 5. The added zones and setting options in the parent app. The measuring unit was mg/dl; demonstration zone ranges were based on [19]. (Color figure online)

4.2   Second Iteration Evaluation

To ensure the usability and detect possible usage barriers we performed the second evaluation round to obtain feedback from the experts, as well as from the intended target group of the application users. Therefore, the aim was to interview the parents and experts to obtain opinions from the both sided about the final app.

Methodology. We contacted the experts who participated in the first evaluation round again to request them to analyze the progress and provide feedback about the new version. Two of them, E6 and E7, were willing to participate in the second evaluation round. Recruiting parents to be interviewed was more challenging than expected, as most of families were not willing to share their experience and opinions. We could only find the two parents (P1, P2) having a child in the aimed age range from 4 to 10-year-old, who agreed to participate in the review interviews.

During the parent interview, we first introduced them to the project and provided them with information about the system architecture and the application. We suggested them to consider the two main criteria to evaluate the app. These criteria were defined as perceived usefulness (PU) and perceived ease-of-use (PEOU) and were derived according to the technology acceptance model [20]. Then, we demonstrated the screenshots of the final app prototype. Afterwards, we asked for their opinions about how useful and how easy to use the app was.

During the expert interviews, we introduced them to the final app functionality and explained the new features and modifications. Then, we demonstrated the screenshots of the app and asked for feedback regarding PU and PEOU.

Results. P1 stated that he considered the toy and the app to be very useful and innovative. Moreover, he outlined that he perceived the app as very clear and simple. He was able to understand and use all available features. Furthermore, he was familiar with the functionality of such apps, as he used other glucose monitoring applications for his child.

P2 confirmed the positive feedback from P1 and outlined that she found the app very useful and simple. The app was deemed to be easy to use and would be helpful for families and doctors.

E7 found the application very functional and stated that it was a novel method to use the toy as a data receiver that children could carry with them. Moreover, she found the app very simple and its user interface very clear. However, she noted that the colors of the app were too light, and they tired her eyes. She suggested us to use stronger color tones to prevent this issue. Her overall opinion on the proposed system was positive, and she assumed the parents would be willing to use this app.

E6 found the app very useful and stated that this kind of intervention was highly demanded in families. Moreover, he expressed that the app was very easy to use and noted that the user interface was too simple. He emphasized that the graphs and tables could be more detailed and include more information. His overall evaluation was positive and he approved the usefulness and functionality of the app.

5 Discussion

While the overall feedback is positive, and the proposed system is deemed to be a suitable approach to support families with children with diabetes, several ethical concerns remain unclear.

So, we do not yet have any insights into the system's possible impacts on the family, and therefore, it is not clear how the proposed system may affect its dynamics and single members. During the interviews, one of the psychologists, E7, mentioned the danger that parents may become overprotective. Although we attempt to mitigate such impacts by introducing the zone-based system with the automatic directives feature, parents might still feel responsible to regularly check the blood glucose levels of their child to ensure that they are within the acceptable range. This can be even increased in the case when other persons, such as supervisors in day-care centers or primary schools, have access to the system. The social pressure concerned with being constantly informed about the child health state may therefore increase. Additionally, the proposed system might also affect the child. Although the experts suggest that parents should not tell the child that they can control the toy, children still might feel constantly monitored and therefore pressured. Furthermore, if, by chance, they discover this, they may feel betrayed by their parents.

Another concern is the acceptance by the children. Currently, the design of the teddy bear does not provide a possibility to actually communicate with the child, as communication is one-sided from the toy to the child. Children might perceive this as either boring after a particular period of time, or they may perceive the toy as a supervisor, which may affect the emotional connection and possibly lead to the resistance against bringing the toy everywhere. Furthermore, small children might be confused by the fact that their plush toy talks to them but does not respond to their questions.

Finally, as the system synchronizes the measured data with the phone of the parents, the measured values are sent to an online server. Therefore, the highly sensitive medical data are supposed to be stored in the cloud. Although security measurement was performed to protect the information in the best way possible, the residual risk remains. All data accessible on the Internet are potentially at risk of being stolen in the case of a hacker attack. This has been demonstrated by successful attacks against large and established technology companies, such as Apple and Sony. Due to this reason, we need to investigate whether there are alternative ways to process the data, or whether the medical data in general should not be stored online.

6   Conclusion, Limitations, and Future Work

In the present study we demonstrate that the concept of a supportive toy for children with diabetes is deemed to be appropriate for younger children of the age between four and ten years. We have obtained qualitative feedback to improve the application in two rounds and have developed a system which not only helps parents to monitor the blood glucose level of their child, but moreover, is developed considering the self-caring approach by using automated directives by the plush toy. This might be used not only to help in increasing the child's self-confidence but also in building new healthy habits.

Overall, the general feedback provided by the parents and experts during the conducted interviews was positive. Their interests and reactions were affirmative and they were willing to use the proposed system. The evaluation outcome indicated that people were interested in using this novel approach to monitor their child's diabetes. Moreover, all interviewees agreed that the app was easy to use. Therefore, based on the obtained feedbacks, we assume that the users can get adapted to the app.

However, there are several limitations to be considered with the regard to the present study. Although we collected feedback from the experts and parents, we currently do not have any insights yet on how the children might react to the plush toy. Therefore, at present, we cannot make any assumption on how well the children might adopt the proposed toy and how carefully they would follow the predefined directives. Moreover, it is not clear how successfully they might establish a connection and thereby considering the toy their companion and bringing it with them wherever they go.

Therefore, in the future, we plan to conduct an intervention study in which the children will actually use the proposed system for several weeks. This would help to clarify the knowledge gap regarding the potential of the toy acceptance, as well to provide insights on how the proposed tool would influence the behavior of parents.

Furthermore, the system can be expanded by adding various auxiliary features. First, sensors with Bluetooth connection should be integrated to increase the ease of use on the children side. Using Bluetooth sensors can facilitate the plush toy to update the current blood glucose value even when it is several meters away from the child and thereby enabling constant measurement during the night when the child is sleeping.

Moreover, adding a speech recognition unit into to the toy may increase interactivity and thereby help establishing a long-lasting interest of the children.

Finally, machine learning-based approaches which can analyze the data on the cloud server, might be applied to extract meaningful patterns from the measured data und therefore, support parents, doctors and children to improve the diabetes treatment.

References

1. World Health Organization: 10 facts on Diabetes (2016). https://www.who.int/features/factfiles/diabetes/en/
2. World Health Organization: Diabetes (2018). https://www.who.int/news-room/fact-sheets/detail/diabetes
3. Deutsche Diabetes Stiftung: Diabetes-was IST das eigentlich (2020). https://www.diabetesstiftung.de/diabetes-was-ist-das-eigentlich
4. International Diabetes Federation. IDF Diabetes Atlas, 8th edition 2017. https://www.worlddiabetesfoundation.org/sites/default/files/Atlas-8e-regional-fact-sheet-18-99-EUR.pdf
5. International Diabetes Federation: IDF Diabetes Atlas, 9th edition (2019). https://www.diabetesatlas.org/en/
6. Patterson, C.C., et al.: Trends in childhood type 1 diabetes incidence in Europe during 1989–2008: evidence of non-uniformity over time in rates of increase. Diabetologia **55**(8), 2142–2147 (2012)
7. Devendra, D., Liu, E., Eisenbarth, G.S.: Type 1 diabetes: recent developments. BMJ **328** (7442), 750–754 (2004)
8. van der Drift Esther, J., Beun, R.-J., Looije, R., Henkemans, O.A.B., Neerincx, M.A. (eds.) A remote social robot to motivate and support diabetic children in keeping a diary. In: 2014 9th ACM/IEEE International Conference on Human-Robot Interaction (HRI). IEEE (2014)
9. Cemeroglu, A.P., Stone, R., Kleis, L., Racine, M.S., Postellon, D.C., Wood, M.A.: Use of a real-time continuous glucose monitoring system in children and young adults on insulin pump therapy: patients' and caregivers' perception of benefit. Pediatric Diab. **11**(3), 182–187 (2010)
10. Palermo, T.M., Valenzuela, D., Stork, P.P.: A randomized trial of electronic versus paper pain diaries in children: impact on compliance, accuracy, and acceptability. Pain **107**(3), 213–219 (2004)
11. Franklin, V., Greene, A., Waller, A., Greene, S., Pagliari, C.: Patients' engagement with "Sweet Talk"–a text messaging support system for young people with diabetes. J. Med. Internet Res. **10**(2), e20 (2008)
12. Mougiakakou, S.G., Kouris, I., Iliopoulou, D., Vazeou, A., Koutsouris, D. (eds.) Mobile technology to empower people with diabetes mellitus: design and development of a mobile application. In: 2009 9th International Conference on Information Technology and Applications in Biomedicine. IEEE (2009)
13. Al-Taee, M.A., Al-Nuaimy, W., Muhsin, Z.J., Al-Ataby, A.: Robot assistant in management of diabetes in children based on the Internet of things. IEEE Internet Things J. **4**(2), 437–445 (2016)
14. Toscos, T., Connelly, K., Rogers, Y. (eds.): Best intentions: health monitoring technology and children. In: Proceedings of the SIGCHI Conference on Human Factors in Computing Systems. ACM (2012)
15. Thaler, R.H., Sunstein, C.R.: Nudge: Improving Decisions About Health, Wealth, and Happiness. Penguin Books (2009)

16. Hevner, A., Chatterjee, S.: Design science research in information systems. In: Design Research in Information Systems: Theory and Practice, pp. 9–22. Springer, Boston (2010). https://doi.org/10.1007/978-1-4419-5653-8_2
17. Webster, J., Watson, R.T.: Analyzing the past to prepare for the future: writing a literature review. MIS Q., xiii–xxiii (2002)
18. Abbott Laboratories. FreeStyle Libre, 22 January 2020. https://www.freestylelibre.us
19. Hinneburg, I.: Diabetes bei Kindern: Tagtägliche Herausforderung. Pharmazeutische Zeitung 2016, 15 August 2016
20. Davis, F.D.: Perceived usefulness, perceived ease of use, and user acceptance of information technology. MIS Q., 319–340 (1989)

TrackSugAR

David A. Plecher[(✉)] [iD], Christian Eichhorn[iD], Conrad Steinmetz[iD],
and Gudrun Klinker[iD]

Chair for Computer Aided Medical Procedures and Augmented Reality,
The Technical University of Munich (TUM), Munich, Germany
{plecher,klinker}@in.tum.de,
{christian.eichhorn,conrad.steinmetz}@tum.de

Abstract. *Motivation* - According to WHO about 41 million people per
year die from the consequences of Noncommunicable Diseases like cancer, diabetes and cardiovascular diseases. Physical inactivity and poor
dietary behavior like expressive sugar consumption have been observed
to promote the emergence of such a disease significantly. *Objective* - As
part of this paper, a native iOS application called "TrackSugAR" shall
be developed, which is capable of visualizing sugar amounts in foods with
Augmented Reality (AR) to support users in continuously diminishing
their daily sugar consumption. *Methods* - For this purpose the Design
Science Research Methodology by Peffers et al. [31] is used. This method
provides guidance through the entire process of developing a functional
software prototype. To evaluate the usability of the application, approved
questionnaires such as SUS and HARUS are applied in a first evaluation
stage with 14 participants. *Results* - Based on the data from these questionnaires, the TrackSugAR app scored 89 ± 8 in the SUS and 91 ± 7 in
the HARUS. Likewise, the results from the first evaluation phase admit
the conclusion that AR increases the ability of users to quantify the sugar
amounts present in food products.

Keywords: Health · Augmented Reality · Mobile application ·
Consumer behavior · Sugar · Diabetes

1 Introduction

Sugar is present in a variety of foods and is even contained in baby meals. The
body is thus already accustomed to sugar-sweetened foods during the growth
phase. Small amounts of sugar are not harmful. However, the worldwide increase
in per capita sugar consumption in recent decades is a cause for concern. Particularly in countries such as India, China, Brazil and also in Africa there has
been a significant increase in recent years.

Most of sugar-sweetened beverages consist of at least 10% added sugar, which
means that the recommended daily limit is already exceeded after consuming
500 mL of it. The WHO has been warning for years about the metabolic risks of
excessive sugar consumption. These risks include overweight, obesity and various

© Springer Nature Switzerland AG 2020
V. G. Duffy (Ed.): HCII 2020, LNCS 12198, pp. 442–459, 2020.
https://doi.org/10.1007/978-3-030-49904-4_33

severe incurable diseases. To counteract this trend, the WHO proposes the pursuit of various objectives on global and national level, e.g. to promote healthier diets. However, the implementation of these goals is not mandatory and does not take place in every country, or at least not sufficiently, as the WHO Country Profiles [52] show.

As a result, the obesity rate and the number of new diabetes diagnoses are rising steadily both worldwide. To tackle this problem, the technology of an iOS smartphone app is to be used. A new approach is to combine a nutrition tracking app with Augmented Reality (AR) features in order to offer more than just tracking the added sugars in foods, but also visualizing them clearly. The visualization of the sugar content in the form of three-dimensional sugar cubes in AR is intended to simplify the user's understanding of the quantity of sugar described on the packaging of consumed food products. In addition, this visualization mechanism should help users to memorize the amount of sugar contained in each of their consumed foods, whereby a simple traffic light system with three categories red, yellow and green provides support. In order to retrieve information about the sugar contained in the users' food products various concepts like Optical Character Recognition (OCR) of nutritional information, barcode scans and a manual input option are featured. Combined with the ability to monitor the individual sugar consumption using diagrams, this system is designed to help users in reducing their daily sugar consumption and improving their dietary habits in the long term.

This paper is logically divided according to the steps of the Design Science Research Methodology proposed by Peffers et al. [31]. Analogously, we motivate the process of designing an appropriate app solution by identifying the issues of unhealthy dietary behavior and excessive sugar consumption. In Sect. 4 we define the objectives and research questions that guide our software development process. Section 5 continues this process by giving a detailed functional description and reasoning for certain design decisions. Subsequently, the methodical approach and the materials used to evaluate the usability and functionality of "TrackSugAR"[1] shall be specified in Sect. 6.

2   Theoretical Background

Diseases that are encouraged by unhealthy diets mostly are chronic diseases or also called Noncommunicable Diseases (NCDs). The clinical picture of these diseases is characterized by a long duration. NCDs include cardiovascular diseases (like heart attacks and strokes), diverse forms of cancer (polyps, adenoma, tumor), chronic respiratory diseases (diseases of the airways and the lung) as well as diabetes. According to the WHO, globally 41 million people[2] die from NCDs, causing 71% of all deaths worldwide. Among NCDs, cardiovascular diseases account for most deaths, followed by cancers, respiratory diseases and diabetes [51,52]. The issue of NCDs is also acute in Germany. According to WHO's

---

[1] https://apps.apple.com/de/app/tracksugar/id1494886708.
[2] This number refers to 2016 (published by the WHO in 2018).

"Noncommunicable Diseases Country Profiles 2018" [52], in 2016, 839,500 people died of NCDs in Germany alone, which is equivalent to 91% of all deaths in Germany 2016. In 2016, the risk of dying of NCDs a premature death in Germany at the age of 30–70 years was 12% averaged among women and men.

The WHO divides two categories of risk factors that encourage the emergence of NCDs. One is metabolic risk factors like overweight/obesity, raised blood pressure, hyperglycemia (high blood glucose levels) and hyperlipidemia (high levels of fat in the blood). Second is modifiable behavioral risk factors including unhealthy diets, physical inactivity, tobacco use and excessive consumption of alcohol [51]. Risks belonging to the second category are largely preventable. Thus overweight and obesity are for the most part preventable as well. In a NHANES (National Health and Nutrition Examination Survey) data analysis, Yang et al. [56] investigated the relationship between sugar consumption and increased mortality risk from cardiovascular diseases and derived a significant positive relationship. They compared participants consuming 10% calories from sugars with those consuming 25% or even more of the total daily energy intake from sugars. For the 10% group they specified an adjusted hazard ratio[3] of 1.3 and for the 25% group an adjusted hazard ratio[4] of 2.75 [56].

Conversely, some do not consider the relationship between sugar and cardiovascular diseases to be final. Rippe et al. [38] argue that the NHANES data acquisition is based on the memory of the participants through questionnaires and that this may lead to falsified results. They come to the conclusion that there is a risk, if any, only for the 10% of the population who consume the largest amount of sugar. In the context of sugar consumption, some studies also directly assess the link of sugar-sweetened beverages with the development of diabetes type 2. In their meta-analysis of several studies, Malik et al. [26] confirm that a higher consumption of soft drinks is significantly associated with the development of type 2 diabetes. The participants in the selected studies were divided into several categories, with some participants consuming no or less than 1 unit (serving of sugar-sweetened beverages) per month in the lowest category and up to 2 units per day in the highest category. The standard size of one unit of sugar-sweetened beverages was 12 oz or about 355 mL. Malik et al. [26] describe that the participants in the highest category had a 26% higher probability of developing type 2 diabetes compared to those in the lowest. The issue of reducing excessive sugar consumption is part of various campaigns carried out on national and international levels. One approach by the UK government [20] is to mark up the prices of sugar-sweetened beverages (SSBs) by applying a tax called "Soft Drinks Industry Levy".

Afshin et al. [1] state reasons for such tax measures in their article about "the prospective impact of food pricing on improving dietary consumption" from

---

[3] The term **Hazardratio** is a measure that quantifies the difference of survival times in different groups of patients. It indicates by how much the mortality rate in one group is higher compared to the mortality rate in the other group [57].

[4] If the hazard ratio, as in the present data analysis, is 2.75 for one group, the mortality rate in this group is 2.75 times as high as in the reference group (or 175% higher).

2017. In analyses of 23 studies, they conclude that a 10% decrease in prices of healthful foods (by subsidizing) results in a 12% increased consumption of healthful foods, whereas a 10% increased price (by applying taxes) resulted in 6% decreased intake of unhealthful foods. By food group, they state that subsidies on healthful foods would increase the respective intake of fruits and vegetables by 14% without significant effects on more healthful beverages. According to their findings, each 10% price increase of unhealthful foods would reduce sugar-sweetened beverage intake by 7% and fast foods by 3% [1]. Besides the UK, similar tax measures on sugar-sweetened beverages are also applied in a few other EU Member States, including Norway, Finland, Denmark and France [54].

Apart from this rather theoretical approach, there also have been practical ones, which aim to tackle health in general, unhealthy diets as well as an excessive sugar consumption.

3   Related Work

Health and healthy nutrition is a very important topic in recent years in Serious Games and apps for people of all ages. E.g. for adolescents the Serious Game "Fit, Food, Fun" [42] was developed. It is running on smartphones and teaches the player very useful information about healthy nutrition in a playful manner. As a logical consequence of the aging society these technologies are also used for the elderly adapted to their needs. Apps and games for this generation have to be designed according to certain guidelines [15]. For example reduced fluid intake is a big problem with age. There are many reasons why elderly people are not drinking enough, e.g. they are simply forgetting about that. So games for motivating and reminding them were developed and gadgets for the measurement of drinking income were designed. The collected data can be analyzed by the nursing personnel and has also an impact on the games [14, 16, 36].

Reducing the amount of sugar is an age-independent problem especially for people suffering from diabetes. Today's apps can help to make living with this chronic disease easier. For example, the management of diabetes will be important and can be improved by using mobile devices for personal health record management [18]. Scheibe et al. [43] are seeing a high usability of mobile devices in the area of diabetes by offering relevant features such as the ability to add personal remarks for the glucose diary in combination of an intuitive design. Increasing compliance when facing the challenges of diabetes, self-care advise in the form of reminders is recommended [43]. Furthermore, making health data management more accessible for physicians and patients can greatly improve care outcomes and efficiency for every patient group. Therefore, development of easy distributable mobile applications is needed to make the concept of mHealth (Mobile Health) available for everyone [50]. The reason behind such a design is the One fits all Approach, which has limitations for certain user groups [22, 49]. Seaborn et al. [44] are describing this approach as the narrow focus on the "ideal" average user, which can exclude a substantial percentage of the actual target group from the beginning.

Lopes et al. [24] have tried to combine mobile web services (database access) with a motivation approach of social connection (e.g. Twitter, Facebook) in their application development process to achieve greater success. This behavior-image model approach tries to inspire the user to self-comparison with others and to rethink their current lifestyle, also called self-reevaluation in the Transtheoretical Model [19,37]. The focus is here on healthy role models to motivate the user to change their behavior. Connecting to people is a reinforcing factor which can have a great impact on situations where intrinsic elements alone may not be sufficient. Future Work?: A combination of intrinsic, e.g. first monitoring the own progress, and extrinsic elements, then reporting and comparing it in a social network, are a strategy targeting the challenge of motivating people [7]. Besides social networks, simple images in the application are also often used, which are showcasing sport activities, healthy people or healthy nutrition [19]. To further enhance the motivation for a user to reach a healthier lifestyle, goal setting is an important topic for Carter et al. [11]. In their application My Meal Mate they give the user the possibility to make own goals and help to reach them by converting the goals into daily energy targets, which are saved in a daily diary. Besides setting a goal, self-monitoring to see improvements or detect problems helps to enhance further development. Self-monitoring therefore is deeply connected with the goal setting approach, "[...] generates a daily calorie target so that the user is monitoring towards a daily proximal calorie goal, a distal overall weight loss goal" [11, p. 82] and also helps to communicate the progress in small steps to further motivate the user. In previous studies, which were not only focusing on diet apps, self-monitoring could already achieve a positive relationship with weight management, frequent monitoring of the nutrition intake was associated with twice the weight loss [5,48]. The improved results of mobile apps compared to non-app users on the calorie intake and weight loss process in total could be mirrored in other evaluations [48]. On top of that, Burke et al. [9] discovered ample evidence for a consistent and significant positive impact on weight loss. Self-monitoring enables a more realistic feeling for the weight loss process and therefore increases the chance for the user to stay with the diet. Therefore, a passive participant can be more easily transformed into an active participant. Direct feedback from the application is shown in parts with graphical representation about the total weight loss and calorie intake. Messages were included because of the positive response of adolescents to receiving motivating feedback messages [7,55]. Providing diverse feedback should enable the user to better understand the progress and reminds about the usage of the application. Together goal setting, self-monitoring and giving feedback [49] is forming the Self-Regulation Theory to create a better focus on a user's independent motivation with intrinsic elements. By not only targeting the monitoring of the diet, but also motivating physical activity, My Meal Mate tries to achieve behavior change with a diverse approach to reach more users [11,48].

As part of the public health program "Change4Life" [32] in England, which was initiated as a national social marketing campaign by Public Health England in 2009, a mobile application called "Sugar Smart app" [45,53] was launched in 2016. Targeting to tackle childhood obesity in the UK, this app features visualization of nutrition facts by virtually showing the respective amount of sugar cubes as well as suggesting alternative food options in a simplified manner appropriate for children.

As shown there are already apps for tracking the daily consumed sugar, so our goal was to add AR to additionally visualize the amount of sugar with plain sugar cubes. If we are looking at Mixed Reality VR is already used in different serious applications - often called VR training - that support the user to understand or to learn many different topics like public speech [29], assembly tasks [30] or also leadership development [12].

The same applies to AR therefore it is used for a plethora of various subjects like games [46] or superhuman sports [13] and also in serious contexts for learning languages [41], experiencing cultural heritage [33] or art [10] and also for health related topics. In this case AR triggered behavioural changes [25,39] or was utilized to support stroke rehabilitation [21]. Like in our app AR was already combined with gamification [23] or furthermore with Serious Games for learning Japanese Kanji [34] or getting to know Celtic history [35].

4   Objectives

The application "TrackSugAR" shall serve mainly two purposes. The first objective is to encourage users to reduce their sugar consumption by promoting a behavioral change. The second objective is to manifest this change by conveying knowledge to the users.

Given these objectives, several research questions arise about how to design such an application, including how best to visualize the sugar contained in foods in an application aiming towards achieving the above mentioned goals. For this purpose, our main approach is to make use of AR, which is relatively new for the use in smartphones. By means of AR functionality sugar amounts shall be represented in the form of three dimensional sugar cubes. It shall be assessed to what extent gamification can be combined with the AR environment without distracting from the subject. In addition, different visualization options and technologies such as mere numbers and 2D charts shall be integrated to extend the user experience.

5   Artifact Design and Implementation

We have designed "TrackSugAR" in accordance with User Experience heuristics proposed by Nielsen [27] and the Apple Human Interface guidelines [4] prescribing the overall constraints for developing iOS apps. Aiming towards intuitive usability and navigation options, the application is based on the concept of a single view application with simple forward backward navigation. Internally, the software architecture is based on the Cocoa variant of the Model-View-Controller design pattern proposed by Apple [3] introducing a strict separation of data handling, UI views and controls.

The application is structured in a way that combines the idea of a tracking app with AR features highlighting the sheer amount of sugars contained in food products. For that to work out properly, several features are integrated that extract sugar information from food products, display sugar amounts using multiple approaches and track the data by persisting on the device's memory. These features shall be described in more detail in the Subsects. 5.1–5.3.

5.1 Extraction of Sugar Information

In order to track the daily sugar consumption of users, the "TrackSugAR" app needs to retrieve detailed information about their meals (e.g., the portion consumed, the sugar content contained in one portion of the product and other). Since iOS devices as of today (2019) do not monitor the food products consumed by users themselves, instead, the users need to communicate consumed meals to the app in order to track them. Nevertheless, in favor of usability, the addition of consumed products should be simplified as much as possible for the user, since entering the same information several times will bore the user and prevent him from using the app in the long run. However, it seems reasonable to provide a manual input option as a fallback solution if all other options do not lead to the desired result. A first remedy for the repeated input problem might be to provide a quick select list of products, that had been consumed and stored previously in the app.

5.2 Augmented Reality (AR)

For the visualization of sugar with AR two different approaches are pursued. The first approach is to determine the sugar content in foods using the scan measures as described above and subsequently extract the corresponding amount of sugar cubes visually in AR to demonstrate the pile "hidden" in the product. The virtual information is environmental mounted [47] on a flat surface. The animated virtual sugar cubes are "flying" out of the product and are building the pile (see Fig. 1).

The second approach seeks to achieve the same result with a reverse course of action. In a gamified manner the user is asked to throw as much sugar cubes as possible into a cup of coffee to make him feel like he'd never put so much sugar in the cup himself. The wake-up effect and the understanding is to be achieved only in the next view. This summary view highlights all of the user's favorite products that contain even more free sugars at same quantity than he had tossed into the coffee cup. The game mode of the sugar toss feature is inspired by the well known mobile game "Paper Toss" by "Backflip Studios" that was published in 2009 but in the meantime already removed from the app stores. By differentiating between two different approaches for displaying sugar amounts the level of included gamification elements can be varied. This enables us to assess the effect of gamification combined with AR on dietary behavior.

As Noreikis et al. describe, a positive effect of Gamification and AR on the learning ability as well as the perceived enjoyment of users during the use of a

Fig. 1. Augmented Reality feature concept art of TrackSugAR (The iPhone device frames or images of Apple products that are used in this figure or might be included in later figures in this paper are artworks provided by Apple in https://developer.apple. com/app-store/marketing/guidelines/ and are used solely for the purpose of visualizing the features in the TrackSugAR app, which has been designed for those devices.)

smartphone application can be observed [28]. In the sugar toss feature exactly this positive effect should be leveraged, using gamified elements such as the increasing sugar score and a splash effect to clearly illustrate how the amount of sugar in a drink increases with each sugar cube put in. The basic idea is as follows. As the game begins, the player has a virtual account with sugar cubes that can be spent. By clever throwing these sugar cubes the player is incentivized to hit as many sugar cubes into a virtual coffee cup as possible. The player should perceive two elementary facts. First, each sugar cube corresponds to three grams of additional sugar in the coffee cup and second, that he'd never thrown that amount of sugar cubes into a real coffee cup himself. In order to demonstrate the respective three grams upon hitting a sugar cube into the cup, each time an animated label moves up in the view to be added to the counting label in the upper right corner (as depicted in Fig. 2).

5.3   Tracking and Charts

TrackSugAR saves the meals consumed by an user internally in the device's memory. This enables the users to track their behavior with regard to sugar consumption over a longer period of time by means of the two-dimensional charts depicted in Fig. 3. For the chart visualization we have integrated the common framework "Charts"[5] by Daniel Gindi via Cocoa Pods. Some charts are based on a daily sugar recommendation, which can be individually adjusted by the user

---

[5] More information on the Charts framework under https://github.com/danielgindi/ Charts.

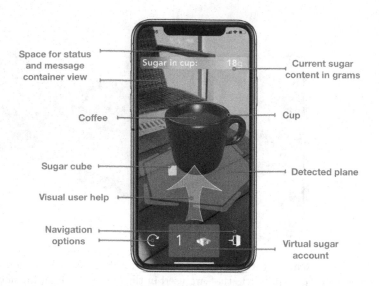

Fig. 2. Screenshot of AR view in sugar toss feature.

in the menu settings. In the formulation of discrete recommendations regarding sugar intake limits, the various national and international institutions represent different views. Analogously, the individual daily sugar limit is variable and initially preset at 50 g/day, which was the consensus of most institutions. This value can be increased up to a maximum of 90 g/day, which is the reference value used on product labels in the EU [17, p. 62, Part B of Annex XIII].

The pie chart "Track your daily sugar intake" is based on that individually defined daily sugar limit and visualizes the user's sugar consumption on the current calendar day. It is divided into the three segments (sugar from solid meals, sugar from drinks and remaining), where each value corresponds to the respective gram weight and not to the percentage. The percentages with respect to the maximum daily limit are indicated by the proportions that the segments represent in this diagram. In the second chart "Track your highest sugar intake", tracking is extended to a longer period of time. The user can choose between 3 time periods (Last week, Last month, Entire period) by means of a Segmented Control. The bar chart then visualizes the daily intakes on each day in the selected time period. This enables the user to quickly identify peak and valley values for that period. For the chart visualization we have integrated the framework via Cocoa Pods.

The third chart is a combined chart consisting of a line and a bar chart. The horizontal line shows the current daily sugar limit, which can be set by the user as described above. The bars visualize for each of the last up to six months the highest daily consumption in this month (left bar in a group), as well as the average daily sugar consumption over the month (right bar in a group), where this right bar consists of two bars indicating which portion comes from drinks and which from solid meals.

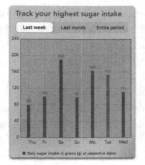

Fig. 3. Charts in the detailed chart view.

6 Evaluation

In this section, we describe the methodical approach and the materials used to evaluate the usability and functionality of "TrackSugAR". For this purpose, we made use of common measures like the System Usability Scale (SUS) [8] and the Handheld AR Usability Scale (HARUS) [40] to determine a score comparable to other apps. We specify how we applied these measures and prepared functionality to gather additional behavioral app usage data by means of analytic tools in Sect. 6.2. We outline the results obtained through these methods in Sect. 6.3.

6.1 Setting and Participants

The evaluation is planned to be performed in two stages. Within the scope of this paper, we performed the first stage to test the app before publishing it to the app store. The second stage is planned to be conducted after releasing the app in the app store and is described in Sect. 8.

Throughout the entire period of the evaluation phase 14 people were testing the app on our testing device. All participants received a link to an online questionnaire in order to evaluate the app after using it. The participants were instructed to try out all app features in a time period of 20 min and to take part in the questionnaire afterwards. If a participant was not familiar with the device or had issues with operating the device, we provided guidance. The results of the online questionnaire were statistically analyzed.

6.2 Methods and Materials

The intention of the first evaluation stage is to capture the views and feelings about the app usability and the AR technology before actually publishing the application to the app store. Therefore, we designed an online questionnaire to be answered by participants after using the application. This questionnaire includes the ten question items of the SUS [8] and the 16 items of the HARUS [40]. The statistical evaluation of the SUS and the HARUS scale returns a score between

0 and 100 each. They both consist of negatively and positively worded items that need to be weighted differently for calculating the final score. According to Bangor et al. [6] an acceptable SUS value is 70 and above. Likewise, an acceptable HARUS score is 70 and above due to the strong relationship between HARUS and SUS as Santos et al. [40] point out.

In addition, demographic questions, behavioral questions regarding sugar intake, knowledge-based questions and a few items regarding the prior experience of AR were integrated. The participants were instructed to take part in the questionnaire after testing out the application. Afterwards, we have determined the values of the SUS and the HARUS by means and analyzed the results of the remaining question items.

6.3   Results

In the first evaluation phase, a total of 14 people tested "TrackSugAR" on our testing device and participated in the online questionnaire afterwards. Out of these 14 participants, 9 were male and 5 were female. Considering the age segments, 7 participants were between 18 and 25 years old, 4 were between 26 and 40 years old and 3 were at the ages between 41 and 60. We did not have participants at ages older than 60 years.

By means of statistical analysis, we determined the average SUS value of 89 ± 8 and a median SUS value of 90 considering all participants (n = 14). The HARUS value on average was even slightly better at 91 ± 7 with n = 14 participants and a median HARUS value of 93. As already mentioned, an acceptable SUS value is 70 and above according to Bangor et al. [6]. Following Santos et al. [40], an acceptable HARUS score is also at 70 and above due to the strong relationship between HARUS and SUS (Table 1).

Table 1. Results of TrackSugAR in SUS and HARUS.

Score	Mean $\pm$ SD	Median
SUS	89 ± 8	90
HARUS	91 ± 7	93

Comparing the results of the SUS evaluation from male and female participants, we observed that the averaged SUS score was slightly higher in the evaluation results retrieved from female participants (87 ± 9 for male and 93 ± 4 for female). The SUS values of males and females are listed in Table 2 on page 12.

Due to that we tested the null hypothesis H_0 assuming that male and female results do not differ using the unpaired two-tailed t-test and taking into account that both samples have different standard deviation and variance. For a significance-level $\alpha = 0.05$ we calculated the t-statistics 1,7 and $-1,7$ for both sides, which are closer to zero than the critical t-value of 2.2. Following that, the null hypothesis is not rejected and there is no significant difference in the results of male and female participants.

When comparing the results of the SUS with respect to the age segments, there is no significant difference either. Furthermore, the number of participants was simply too small to deduce meaningful differences in the evaluation results across age groups.

Table 2. Comparison of male and female SUS evaluation.

Number	SUS from male	SUS from female
1	95	90
2	85	95
3	100	87,5
4	70	95
5	87,5	97,5
6	92,5	
7	90	
8	85	
9	77,5	

7   Discussion

Considering the results and the feedback given by participants throughout the first evaluation stage, the use of AR technology was appropriate for the task of visualizing sugar. It simplified the process of conveying both knowledge and understanding about hidden sugars in food products to the users. We observed that the animated charts and counting labels that were integrated to summarize the content of the AR views worked greatly to complete the user experience. In contrast, the charts that were linked in the main menu were less often viewed and didn't raise the same level of excitement. But as we didn't capture any data about the long term use yet, it would be necessary in the future to validate these observations. In direct comparison of both AR views in terms of gamification, the sugar toss AR view including more elements of gamification raised higher levels of perceived enjoyment. We could make this observation by watching the participants when using both AR features and directly asking them after the session. From this it can be concluded that the combination of AR and gamification is reasonable in serious contexts as long as the usefulness is given. Again, this observation needs to be verified by tracking the respective data in a second evaluation stage. In our research, there was no nutrition-based application found which was evaluated using SUS or HARUS during the software development process. The only comparable action was driven by Ahn et al. [2] who investigated the usability of existing cardiopulmonary resuscitation training smartphone applications. For this study, Ahn et al. selected the most promising apps based on different criteria, where the best app achieved a SUS value of 81 with a quite high standard deviation of 19 (n = 30) [2]. In comparison, "Track-SugAR" scored pretty well in the SUS evaluation. Although the lower number of participants in our case is a limiting factor, the SUS value of 89 ± 8 marks an excellent result and confirms good usability of "TrackSugAR".

8 Limitations and Future Work

Throughout the first evaluation stage as described in Sect. 6.3, the participants have responded positively with respect to TrackSugAR's usability and the AR technology that was integrated. In particular, the visualization using sugar cubes has found unanimous approval. All participants in our first evaluation phase indicated they could more easily imagine the amount of sugar after having seen the corresponding sugar cubes in AR. We can derive for future projects that the utilization of the AR technology offers a real added value in terms of visualization. That's why also with regard to developing nutrition apps AR is a strong feature to be considered. Unfortunately, we couldn't make any statements about long term effects of the "TrackSugAR" app by only taking into account the results of the first evaluation stage.

Thus, the second evaluation stage is strongly required to ascertain the extent to which a change in the users' behavior emerges. In addition, it remains to be determined to what extent the application itself drives the users to improve their dietary behavior regarding sugar intake.

Considering the feedback participants gave us during the first evaluation phase, one highly requested feature is image recognition of food products or meals without labels or barcodes. We had decided not to include an image classifier due to the high risk of ambiguous results and uncertainty. Indeed, as users would highly appreciate such functionality it may be one important area to focus on when extending the app in the future.

In addition, one participant suggested to extend the sugar toss functionality by including a quiz. In this quiz, the users should initially be presented different products. Afterwards, they should try to remember the correct amount of sugar cubes included in these products by having to toss the corresponding number of sugar cubes into a glass in AR. In a subsequent quiz resolution, the users could then be informed about the correct amounts in a gamified manner.

9 Conclusion

We have developed a native iOS application capable of visualizing the sugar contents present in foods by using different approaches. The main research interest was to apply and validate the AR technology as one visualization option. But we also implemented alternative visualization techniques like animated charts, counting numbered labels and mere numbers. The procedure for creating this application was based on the Design Science Research Methodology proposed by Peffers et al. [31].

Analogously, we identified severe, life threatening diseases like cancer and diabetes to be strongly correlated with bad dietary habits like excessive sugar consumption and physical inactivity. From this we have derived the necessity and motivation for developing an application that aims towards behavioral change and sustained knowledge about proper nutrition.

We designed "TrackSugAR" according to Nielsen's UX heuristics [27] targeting intuitive and simple usability. We integrated three options for users to input their food product information by either scanning the barcode, scanning the nutritional information or manually typing in the values. Users are featured to visualize the sugar content by means of AR and different charts highlighting the respective proportion of their daily sugar aim. In particular, we have implemented two different AR views. One AR view attracting users by gamification elements and the other by confronting users with the sheer amount of sugar. By suggesting substitutes with less sugar, the users shall continuously learn to reduce their sugar intake. In addition, charts support users to track their sugar consumption on a daily, weekly and monthly base.

We evaluated the usability and functionality of "TrackSugAR" by using the common measures SUS and HARUS in a first evaluation phase. TrackSugAR attained an excellent SUS value of 89 ± 8 and an even better HARUS value of 91 ± 7 showing that the participants had liked the usability of the application as a whole and in particular, the realization of AR functionality. The participants requested even more AR functionality, which led us to the conclusion that implementing AR functionality was a success. We observed that the AR technology raised the users' ability to quantify sugar amounts. Especially converting the AR experience into a game environment by including gamified elements increased the perceived enjoyment and the level of immersion that participants experienced when testing the application. Our results underline the great potential of AR in nutrition based applications.

Acknowledgments. The preparation of this paper was supported by the enable cluster and is catalogued by the enable steering committee as enable **55** (http://enable-cluster.de). This work was funded by a grant of the German Ministry for Education and Research (BMBF) **FK 01EA1807A**.

References

1. Afshin, A., et al.: The prospective impact of food pricing on improving dietary consumption: a systematic review and meta-analysis. PLoS ONE **12**(3), e0172277 (2017). https://doi.org/10.1371/journal.pone.0172277
2. Ahn, C., et al.: Evaluation of smartphone applications for cardiopulmonary resuscitation training in South Korea. BioMed Res. Int. **2016**, 6418710 (2016). https://doi.org/10.1155/2016/6418710
3. Apple: Concepts in objective-c programming (2012). https://developer.apple.com/library/archive/documentation/General/Conceptual/CocoaEncyclopedia/Model-View-Controller/Model-View-Controller.html. Accessed 28 Oct 2019

4. Apple: Human interface guidelines (2019). https://developer.apple.com/design/human-interface-guidelines/ios/system-capabilities/ratings-and-reviews/. Accessed 03 Nov 2019
5. Azar, K.M., et al.: Mobile applications for weight management: theory-based content analysis. Am. J. Prev. Med. **45**(5), 583–589 (2013)
6. Bangor, A., Kortum, P.T., Miller, J.T.: An empirical evaluation of the system usability scale. Int. J. Hum.-Comput. Interact. **24**(6), 574–594 (2008). https://doi.org/10.1080/10447310802205776
7. Blake, H.: Innovation in practice: mobile phone technology in patient care. Br. J. Commun. Nurs. **13**(4), 160–165 (2008)
8. Brooke, J.: SUS - a quick and dirty usability scale. In: Jordan, P., Thomas, B., Weerdmeester, B. (eds.) Usability Evaluation in Industry, pp. 189–194. Taylor & Francis, London (1996). https://hell.meiert.org/core/pdf/sus.pdf. Accessed 8 Nov 2019
9. Burke, L.E., Wang, J., Sevick, M.A.: Self-monitoring in weight loss: a systematic review of the literature. J. Am. Diet. Assoc. **111**(1), 92–102 (2011)
10. Bäck, R., Plecher, D.A., Wenrich, R., Dorner, B., Klinker, G.: Mixed reality in art education. In: 2019 IEEE Conference on Virtual Reality and 3D User Interfaces (VR), pp. 1583–1587, March 2019. https://doi.org/10.1109/VR.2019.8798101
11. Carter, M., Burley, V., Cade, J.: Development of 'my meal mate'-a smartphone intervention for weight loss. Nutr. Bull. **38**(1), 80–84 (2013)
12. Cichor, J.E., Egorov, M., Plecher, D.A., Schmid, E., Peus, C.: Everything starts with a handshake: effects of character design and character interactions on leadership development in virtual reality. In: 5th International Augmented Reality & Virtual Reality Conference (IAVR), June 2019
13. Eichhorn, C., Plecher, D.A., Inami, M., Klinker, G.: Physical objects in AR games - offering a tangible experience. In: 2019 IEEE Conference on Virtual Reality and 3D User Interfaces (VR), pp. 1801–1806, March 2019. https://doi.org/10.1109/VR.2019.8798056
14. Eichhorn, C., et al.: Innovative game concepts for Alzheimer patients. In: Zhou, J., Salvendy, G. (eds.) ITAP 2018. LNCS, vol. 10927, pp. 526–545. Springer, Cham (2018). https://doi.org/10.1007/978-3-319-92037-5_37
15. Eichhorn, C., et al.: Combining motivating strategies with design concepts for mobile apps to increase usability for the elderly and Alzheimer patients (2020)
16. Eichhorn, C., et al.: The innovative reminder in senior-focused technology (THIRST)—evaluation of serious games and gadgets for Alzheimer patients. In: Zhou, J., Salvendy, G. (eds.) HCII 2019. LNCS, vol. 11593, pp. 135–154. Springer, Cham (2019). https://doi.org/10.1007/978-3-030-22015-0_11
17. European Parliament: Regulation (EU) no 1169/2011 of the European parliament and of the council of 25 October 2011: No 1169/2011 (2011). https://eur-lex.europa.eu/legal-content/EN/ALL/?uri=CELEX:32011R1169. Accessed 28 Oct 2019
18. Eysenbach, G.: CONSORT-EHEALTH Group: CONSORT-EHEALTH: improving and standardizing evaluation reports of Web-based and mobile health interventions. J. Med. Internet Res. (2011). https://doi.org/10.2196/jmir.1923
19. Hebden, L., Cook, A., van der Ploeg, H.P., Allman-Farinelli, M.: Development of smartphone applications for nutrition and physical activity behavior change. JMIR Res. Protoc. **1**(2), e9 (2012)
20. HM Treasury: Soft drinks industry levy comes into effect (2018). https://www.gov.uk/government/news/soft-drinks-industry-levy-comes-into-effect. Accessed 19 Dec 2019

21. Hoermann, S., Hale, L., Winser, S.J., Regenbrecht, H.: Augmented reflection technology for stroke rehabilitation-a clinical feasibility study. In: Proceedings 9th International Conference on Disability, Virtual Reality & Associated Technologies, pp. 317–322 (2012)

22. Kuerbis, A., Mulliken, A., Muench, F., Moore, A.A., Gardner, D.: Older adults and mobile technology: factors that enhance and inhibit utilization in the context of behavioral health (2017)

23. Langbein, A., Plecher, D.A., Pankratz, F., Eghtebas, C., Palmas, F., Klinker, G.: Gamifying stereo camera calibration for augmented reality. In: Adjunct Proceedings of the IEEE International Symposium for Mixed and Augmented Reality (ISMAR), pp. 125–126 (2018)

24. Lopes, I.M., Silva, B.M., Rodrigues, J.J., Lloret, J., Proença, M.L.: A mobile health monitoring solution for weight control. In: 2011 International Conference on Wireless Communications and Signal Processing (WCSP), pp. 1–5. IEEE (2011)

25. Ma, M., Jain, L.C., Anderson, P. (eds.): Virtual, Augmented Reality and Serious Games for Healthcare 1. ISRL, vol. 68. Springer, Heidelberg (2014). https://doi.org/10.1007/978-3-642-54816-1

26. Malik, V.S., Popkin, B.M., Bray, G.A., Després, J.P., Willett, W.C., Hu, F.B.: Sugar-sweetened beverages and risk of metabolic syndrome and type 2 diabetes: a meta-analysis. Diab. Care 33(11), 2477–2483 (2010). https://doi.org/10.2337/dc10-1079. https://www.ncbi.nlm.nih.gov/pmc/articles/PMC2963518/. Accessed 28 Oct 2019

27. Nielsen, J.: Enhancing the explanatory power of usability heuristics. In: Adelson, B. (ed.) Human Factors in Computing Systems, pp. 152–158. Addison-Wesley, Reading (1994). https://doi.org/10.1145/191666.191729

28. Noreikis, M., Savela, N., Kaakinen, M., Xiao, Y., Oksanen, A.: Effects of gamified augmented reality in public spaces. IEEE Access 7, 148108–148118 (2019). https://doi.org/10.1109/ACCESS.2019.2945819

29. Palmas, F., Cichor, J.E., Plecher, D.A., Klinker, G.: Acceptance and effectiveness of a virtual reality public speaking training. In: 2019 IEEE International Symposium on Mixed and Augmented Reality (ISMAR). IEEE, October 2019

30. Palmas, F., Labode, D., Plecher, D.A., Klinker, G.: Comparison of a gamified and non-gamified virtual reality training assembly task. In: 2019 11th International Conference on Virtual Worlds and Games for Serious Applications (VS-Games), pp. 1–8, September 2019. https://doi.org/10.1109/VS-Games.2019.8864583

31. Peffers, K., Tuunanen, T., Rothenberger, M.A., Chatterjee, S.: A design science research methodology for information systems research. J. Manag. Inf. Syst. 45–77 (2008). http://citeseerx.ist.psu.edu/viewdoc/download?doi=10.1.1.535.7773&rep=rep1&type=pdf. Accessed 28 Oct 2019

32. PHE (Public Health England): Reducing sugar — cutting out sugar - change4life (2016). https://www.nhs.uk/change4life/food-facts/sugar. Accessed 28 Oct 2019

33. Plecher, D.A., Wandinger, M., Klinker, G.: Mixed reality for cultural heritage. In: 2019 IEEE Conference on Virtual Reality and 3D User Interfaces (VR), pp. 1618–1622, March 2019. https://doi.org/10.1109/VR.2019.8797846

34. Plecher, D.A., Eichhorn, C., Kindl, J., Kreisig, S., Wintergerst, M., Klinker, G.: Dragon tale-a serious game for learning Japanese kanji. In: Proceedings of the 2018 Annual Symposium on Computer-Human Interaction in Play Companion Extended Abstracts, pp. 577–583. ACM (2018)

35. Plecher, D.A., Eichhorn, C., Köhler, A., Klinker, G.: Oppidum - a serious-AR-game about celtic life and history. In: Liapis, A., Yannakakis, G.N., Gentile, M., Ninaus, M. (eds.) GALA 2019. LNCS, vol. 11899, pp. 550–559. Springer, Cham (2019). https://doi.org/10.1007/978-3-030-34350-7_53
36. Plecher, D.A., et al.: Interactive drinking gadget for the elderly and Alzheimer patients. In: Zhou, J., Salvendy, G. (eds.) HCII 2019. LNCS, vol. 11593, pp. 444–463. Springer, Cham (2019). https://doi.org/10.1007/978-3-030-22015-0_35
37. Prochaska, J.O., Norcross, J.C., Fowler, J.L., Follick, M.J., Abrams, D.B.: Attendance and outcome in a work site weight control program: processes and stages of change as process and predictor variables. Addict. Behav. 17(1), 35–45 (1992)
38. Rippe, J.M., Angelopoulos, T.J.: Relationship between added sugars consumption and chronic disease risk factors: current understanding. Nutrients 8(11) (2016). https://doi.org/10.3390/nu8110697. https://www.ncbi.nlm.nih.gov/pmc/articles/PMC5133084/. Accessed 28 Oct 2019
39. Riva, G., Baños, R.M., Botella, C., Mantovani, F., Gaggioli, A.: Transforming experience: the potential of augmented reality and virtual reality for enhancing personal and clinical change. Front. Psychiatry 7, 164 (2016)
40. Santos, M.E.C., Taketomi, T., Sandor, C., Polvi, J., Yamamoto, G., Kato, H.: A usability scale for handheld augmented reality. In: Spencer, S.N., et al. (eds.) Proceedings, VRST 2014, pp. 167–176. ACM, New York (2014). https://doi.org/10.1145/2671015.2671019
41. Santos, M.E.C., et al.: Augmented reality as multimedia: the case for situated vocabulary learning. Res. Pract. Technol. Enhanced Learn. 11(1), 4 (2016)
42. Schäfer, H., et al.: NUDGE-nutritional, digital games in enable (2017)
43. Scheibe, M., Reichelt, J., Bellmann, M., Kirch, W.: Acceptance factors of mobile apps for diabetes by patients aged 50 or older: a qualitative study. Med. 2.0 4(1), e1 (2015)
44. Seaborn, K., et al.: Accessible play in everyday spaces: mixed reality gaming for adult powered chair users. ACM Trans. Comput.-Hum. Interact. (TOCHI) 23(2), 12 (2016)
45. Swift, J., Strathearn, L., Morris, A., Chi, Y., Townsend, T., Pearce, J.: Public health strategies to reduce sugar intake in the UK: an exploration of public perceptions using digital spaces. Nutr. Bull. 43(3), 238–247 (2018)
46. Tan, C.T., Soh, D.: Augmented reality games: a review. In: Proceedings of Gameon-Arabia, Eurosis (2010)
47. Tönnis, M., Plecher, D.A., Klinker, G.: Representing information-classifying the augmented reality presentation space. Comput. Graph. 37(8), 997–1011 (2013)
48. Turner-McGrievy, G.M., Beets, M.W., Moore, J.B., Kaczynski, A.T., Barr-Anderson, D.J., Tate, D.F.: Comparison of traditional versus mobile app self-monitoring of physical activity and dietary intake among overweight adults participating in an mhealth weight loss program. J. Am. Med. Inform. Assoc. 20(3), 513–518 (2013)
49. Vasconcelos, A., Silva, P.A., Caseiro, J., Nunes, F., Teixeira, L.F.: Designing tablet-based games for seniors: the example of cogniplay, a cognitive gaming platform. In: Proceedings of the 4th International Conference on Fun and Games, pp. 1–10. ACM (2012)
50. Ventola, C.L.: Mobile devices and apps for health care professionals: uses and benefits. Pharm. Ther. 39(5), 356 (2014)
51. WHO (World Health Organisation): Noncommunicable diseases (2018). https://www.who.int/news-room/fact-sheets/detail/noncommunicable-diseases. Accessed 28 Oct 2019

52. WHO (World Health Organisation): Noncommunicable Diseases: Country Profiles 2018. WHO (2018). https://www.who.int/nmh/publications/ncd-profiles-2018/en/. Accessed 28 Oct 2019

53. Wise, J.: Bar code app aims to cut sugar intake (2017)

54. Wissenschaftliche Dienste - Deutscher Bundestag: Steigender zuckerkonsum zahlen, positionen und steuerungsmaßnahmen (2016). https://www.bundestag.de/resource/blob/480534/.../wd-9-053-16-pdf-data.pdf. Accessed 28 Oct 2019

55. Woolford, S.J., et al.: Omg do not say lol: obese adolescents' perspectives on the content of text messages to enhance weight loss efforts. Obesity **19**(12), 2382–2387 (2011)

56. Yang, Q., Zhang, Z., Gregg, E.W., Flanders, W.D., Merritt, R., Hu, F.B.: Added sugar intake and cardiovascular diseases mortality among us adults. JAMA Intern. Med. **174**(4), 516–524 (2014). https://doi.org/10.1001/jamainternmed.2013.13563. https://jamanetwork.com/journals/jamainternalmedicine/fullarticle/1819573. Accessed 28 Oct 2019

57. Zwiener, I., Blettner, M., Hommel, G.: Survival analysis. Deutsches Ärzteblatt (2011). https://doi.org/10.3238/arztebl.2011.0163. https://www.aerzteblatt.de/archiv/81171/Ueberlebenszeitanalyse. Accessed 28 Oct 2019

EVIDENT: Extraction and Visualization Interface of Drawing Execution in Neuropsychological Tests

Ryukichi Sekimoto[1]([✉]), Sachio Saiki[1], Masahide Nakamura[1,2],
Naoki Kodama[3], and Atsushi Sato[4]

[1] Kobe University, Rokkodai-cho 1-1, Nada-ku, Kobe, Hyogo, Japan
sekimoto@ws.cs.kobe-u.ac.jp, sachio@carp.kobe-u.ac.jp,
masa-n@cs.kobe-u.ac.jp
[2] 1-4-1 Nihon-bashi, Chuo-ku, Tokyo, Japan
[3] Niigata University of Health and Welfare, 1398 Shimami-cho, Kita-ku,
Niigata, Japan
kodama@nuhw.ac.jp
[4] Niigata University of Rehabilitation, 2-16 Kaminoyama,
Murakami-shi, Niigata, Japan
a.satou@nur.ac.jp

Abstract. In order to support health professionals and clinical psychologists to understand the execution process of neuropsychological drawing tests without expert knowledge of data analysis, we develop a Web application **EVIDENT** (Extraction and Visualization Interface of Drawing Execution in Neuropsychological Tests). The service provides users with visualization result of dynamic features such as stroke speed, stroke order, time between strokes, in the neuropsychological drawing tests. Also, EVIDENT calculates drawing statistics, such as the stroke average speed, the number of strokes and average time between strokes, and display them on the screen with additional data of subject. Therefore, EVIDENT helps them to get some knowledge by dynamic features of drawing. In this paper, as an experiment which measures practicability of this service, we visualized dynamic features of drawing of dementia patients, and analyzed dynamic features with clinicians. As a result, we got two knowledges that some patients with Alzheimer's dementia draw in a strange order in drawing test and there is a significantly difference in dispersion of time between strokes, between health control (HC) and mild cognitive impairment (MCI).

Keywords: Neuropsychological Test · Drawing test · Clock Drawing Test · Cube Drawing Test

1 Introduction

Today, in the field of medical and psychological assessment, various simple and useful drawing tests are used. For example, Clock Drawing Test (CDT) [3],

© Springer Nature Switzerland AG 2020
V. G. Duffy (Ed.): HCII 2020, LNCS 12198, pp. 460–472, 2020.
https://doi.org/10.1007/978-3-030-49904-4_34

Cube Copying Test (CCT) [6], Rey-Osterrieth complex figure (ROCF) [7] and BaumTest [8]. A drawing test is a test in which a clinical psychologist or health professional hands a piece of paper to the subject and has them write or copy the specified object freely on paper [2]. They grasp the subject's personality characteristics and nervous and psychological states through the drawn pictures and figures. These drawing tests are also used in screening tests for dementia, which has become a social issue in Japan.

In the past, many of these drawing inspections were scored by experts looking at the "final shape of the drawn figure". As a assessment criteria, various things are taken into account, such as the accuracy of the drawn figure and the overall balance [4, 10]. Since these drawing inspections have traditionally been performed on a paper basis, It was difficult to use the "drawing process" of how the drawing proceeded for evaluation. The reason is that in paper-based inspection, Fine and dynamic data such as stroke order, stroke speed, and stroke pressure of the object could not be obtained. In recent years, by using ICT devices such as liquid crystal pen tablets and smart pads, it is possible to acquire fine-grained and dynamic data in drawing. Therefore, the drawing process itself can be analyzed. As a result, more reliable assessment criteria can be established and it may be possible to obtain knowledge on neuropsychology involved in the drawing process, which was unknown until now.

As such an approach, data-driven research of drawing test using ICT device [9] has been accelerated in recent years. For example, there are studies on automatic scoring of drawing tests [5] by machine learning and automatic discrimination of dementia. However, automated scoring with machine learning has not been implemented widely yet because there are various problems, for example, interpreting the results and improvement of accuracy are related to the transactions, or interpretation of the relationship between the drawing process and the diagnosis may be difficult.

Therefore, as a method that does not rely on machine learning, it is important to develop new evaluation methods and diagnostic methods that use features of the drawing process that have not been used until now. For that purpose, it is necessary to present it to clinical psychologist or health professional (analysts) who are trying to analyze fine-grained and dynamic data in an easy-to-understand manner. However, since various features are mixed in the time series data of the drawing process, it is necessary to consider an appropriate and intuitive visualization method suitable for each feature. Therefore, in this research, we propose a web application **EVIDENT** (Extraction and Visualization Interface of Drawing Execution in Neuropsychological Tests) that supports the analysis of the drawing process by humans.

EVIDENT reproduces the drawing process by plotting the point data (x, y), pen pressure, time, etc. obtained by the drawing device on the screen in real time. In addition, from point data, it calculates the dynamic features such as change in pen pressure, stroke speed, stoke acceleration, stroke order, stroke direction, and average time between stroke, and, from these dynamic features, it can calculates the statistics such as average pen pressure, dispersion of pen pressure, stroke average speed, dispersion of stroke speed, total number of strokes, total time taken for drawing (time from the beginning to the end of drawing), the time the pen was off the paper, the time the pen was touching the paper, the average time between strokes, and the dispersion of the time between strokes. It highlights them on the screen in a way that depends on the features. For example, if the speed of drawing strokes is low, it increase the thickness of the line, or it apply color according to the time between strokes. In addition to these features, Displays additional information such as the presence or absence of a disease related to the cognitive function of the subject and the scores of other screening tests, along with the visualization results.

In this paper, we focus on a method of presenting fine-grained dynamic data to analysts in an easy-to-understand manner, and we examined various visualization methods for dynamic features, and visualized actually by implementing a prototype of EVIDENT. Using the implemented prototype, we visualized the CDT and CCT drawing data acquired at the actual clinical site, and conducted an experiment on the possibility of using it for analysis in collaboration with health professional. As a result of the experiment, it was confirmed that the analyst could grasp various dynamic features of the drawing process without requiring specialized data analysis. Also, we discovered two knowledges, incorrect order of drawing that was overlooked in conventional inspection and significant difference in dispersion in time in stroke between HC and MCI.

This research is part of a joint study with Niigata University of Health and Welfare and Niigata University of Rehabilitation, and ethical considerations have been approved by the Ethics Committee of Niigata University of Health and Welfare.

2   Preliminary

2.1   Neuropsychological Drawing Test

Neuropsychology is a study that clarifies the central nervous system such as language, cognition, action, memory, and frontal lobe function, and deals with various symptoms based on the disorder. The neuropsychological drawing test (hereinafter called drawing test) is a test that is often used in neuropsychology to measure the state of cognitive function. This is done by a health professional handing a piece of paper to the test subject, who draws or writes the indicated picture or character on the paper. As a drawing test, Clock Drawing Test (CDT) [3], which measures cognitive decline by drawing a clock as shown in the Fig. 1, and Cube Copying Test (CCT) [6], which measures cognitive decline by drawing a cube as shown in the Fig. 3, are famous.

In recent years, attempts have been made to save and accumulate drawing test data by performing drawing inspection using ICT device such as pen tablets.

2.2   Dementia Test and Drawing Test

With the recent aging society, dementia has become a major social problem in Japan. Early detection and early treatment of dementia are essential, and

Fig. 1. A sample of CDT

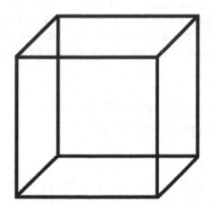

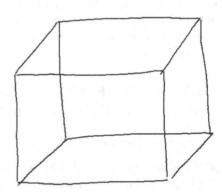

Fig. 2. A copy of CCT   **Fig. 3.** A sample of CCT

various dementia tests have been performed. Dementia can be roughly divided into four categories: Alzheimer's disease (AD), vascular dementia (VaD), dementia with Lewy bodies (DLB), and frontotemporal lobar degeneration (FTLD). In addition, this study discriminates cognitive dysfunction in combination with mild cognitive impairment (MCI), which is one step before becoming AD, and cognitively healthy control (HC) without abnormal cognitive function (Fig. 2).

Drawing tests such as CDT and CCT are simple screening tests that classify only the presence or absence of cognitive problems. If abnormalities are found, a test of the question form by a doctor and brain imaging are used to identify the type of dementia.

2.3   Scope of Research

Research on drawing inspection using ICT device and regression and classification by machine learning has become widespread, especially in the field of CDT.

However, automated scoring with machine learning hasn't been implemented widely yet because there are various problems, for example, interpreting the results and improvement of accuracy are related to the transactions, or interpretation of the relationship between the drawing process and the diagnosis may be difficult, and we think it will take some time to put it to practical use. The scope of this research is to obtain new knowledge in the drawing process by a method that does not use machine learning. The scope of this research is, by a method that does not use machine learning, to obtain new knowledge in the drawing process or develop new evaluation and diagnostic methods that use features of the drawing process that have not been used before. n order to realize this, it is necessary to present it to clinical psychologist or health professional (analysts) who are trying to analyze fine-grained and dynamic data in an easy-to-understand manner. However, since various features are mixed in the time series data of the drawing process, it is necessary to consider an appropriate and intuitive visualization method suitable for each feature. In this study, we propose and implement a Web application **EVIDENT** (Extraction and Visualization Interface of Drawing Execution in Neuropsychological Tests) that supports the analysis of the drawing process by humans, which will be described in the following chapters.

3   EVIDENT (Extraction and Visualization Interface of Drawing Execution in Neuropsychological Tests)

3.1   System Requirement

Various information is needed for analysis through the drawing process. First, in order to grasp the drawing process itself, it is necessary to be able to reproduce how the subject performed drawing in time series. In addition, in order to analyze multiple drawing processes, a mechanism that can quantitatively evaluate not only time-series features but also features of the drawing process is required. Furthermore, what kind of cognitive function-related disease the subject himself has been diagnosed can be important information in analyzing the drawing process. It is necessary for an analysis tool to set various conditions and present these pieces of information in parallel. Also, the ability to constantly update and modify information is essential for developing applications for continuous use.

Based on the above assumptions, we conclude that EVIDENT needs the following five functions as a drawing process analysis support Web service.

R1:Visualization of Drawing Process
EVIDENT reproduces the drawing process, and can extract dynamic features such as stroke, stroke order, stroke direction, stroke speed, stroke acceleration, time between strokes, pen pressure and change in pen pressure in the drawing process and visualize it as two-dimensional data.

R2:Calculation and Display of Statistics
EVIDENT calculates and display statistics such as time spent drawing, total time pen touched paper, total time pen had been away from paper, number

of strokes, average time between strokes, dispersion of time between strokes, the stroke average speed, median of stroke speed, average of stroke speed, dispersion of stroke speed, median of pen pressure and average of pen pressure which is calculated from dynamic features.

R3:Display of Additional Data

EVIDENT simultaneously displays the visualization result of each subject and various addition data such as age, sex, condition, other test scores and years of education of that subject.

R4:Analysis Support

EVIDENT extracts and sorts visualization results based on calculated statistics and additional data.

R5:Data Maintenance

EVIDENT allows medical and psychological specialists to add, refer to, update, and delete subjects' drawing data and additional data without requiring specialized knowledge of ICT.

3.2   System Architecture

Figure 4 shows the architecture of EVIDENT. The user prepares and pass to EVIDENT drawing data including the (x, y) coordinates, pen pressure, and time information, and converts the drawing data to the plot data format handled by EVIDENT. However, it is assumed that the pen pressure of the drawing data handled by EVIDENT is expressed as a percentage with the maximum measurable pen pressure of the ICT device used to acquire the drawing data being 100%. Each data passed to EVIDENT is automatically stored in the database. The transfer of the databases on the EVIDENT-service side and the EVIDENT-UI side is all performed through the EVIDENT-API, and an external application can cooperate with the EVIDENT-service to provide another service. R5 is realized by "data maintenance" at EVIDENT-UI, R1 is realized by "playback" and "image creation", R2 is rasterized by "display statistics", R3 is realized by "display additional information" and R4 is realized by "sort and extraction".

3.3   Visualization of Dynamic Features

Visualization is achieved by reproducing the original final shape with white or black plots, and then performing highlighting based on the dynamic features using the color and line thickness.

I visualize in 15 different ways such as "a method of highlighting by lowering the opacity of the plot as the pen pressure is lower and the opacity is higher as the pen pressure is lower", "a method that reproduces the final shape of the drawing with a black plot, and highlights it by overlaying a thin cyan plot whose radius increases with increasing pen pressure in plot", "a method that changes the color of the stroke from cold to warm as you follow the stroke order", in addition this method, "the method of writing the stroke number near the stroke in the same color as the corresponding stroke", "A method in which the final shape of the drawing is reproduced in black and emphasized by overlaying a purple plot whose

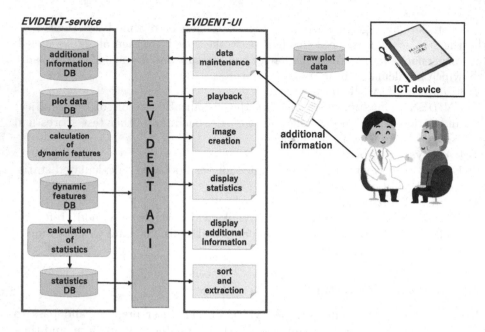

Fig. 4. System architecture

radius decreases as the stroke speed increases", "A method of emphasizing by plotting with the color changed from cool to warm in the order of blue, green, and red as the stroke speed increases", "A method in which the radius decreases as the stroke speed increases, and is emphasized by plotting so that the color approaches a warm color", "a method for expressing the direction of a stroke with an arrow", "a method that draws a red plot for a part where a constant positive change is seen in the pen pressure change and stroke acceleration, and draws a blue plot if a negative change is seen", "At the time between strokes, the corresponding strokes are connected by arrows, and the color of the arrows changes from cool to warm according to the time", in addition it, "a method that draws the order next to the arrow" and "a method that draws the time next to the arrow" as concrete methods.

3.4 Visualization Interface

Figure 5 shows the screen design of the EVIDENT visualization interface. Select the type of drawing inspection to be visualized in "Select test", and select which feature is to be visualized by which visualization method in "visualization method" next to it. To select and visualize a single test (called a session in this paper) for one subject, check the "a session" checkbox, select the subject by "subject ID", and select the date and time of the session to draw by "date time". Also, you can check the "multiple sessions" checkbox and use the "classification" select tab to select, for example, only sessions for subjects with a specific disease.

By specifying the sort order on the "sort" tab, the corresponding sessions can be displayed in a specific order.

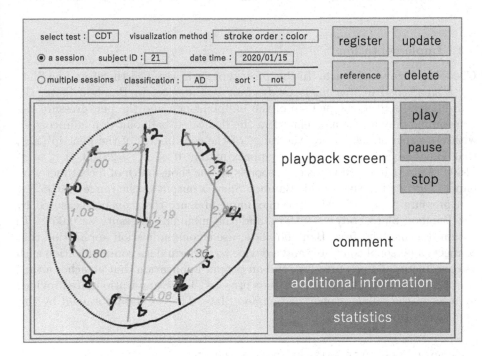

Fig. 5. Screen design of EVIDENT-UI (Color figure online)

4   Prototype Implementation

In the previous chapter, we defined the requirements for the drawing process analysis support Web service EVIDENT, and proposed the required mechanisms and various visualization methods. In this chapter, in order to verify the effectiveness of EVIDENT, we first focus on realizing the functions required for use in verification, and develop a prototype system.

4.1   Prototype System Overview

The prototype realizes data visualization and additional information display functions in EVIDENT-UI, data shaping and feature value calculation of EVIDENT-service, and match with additional information. In this prototype, drawing data is obtained by directly reading data output from the smart pad via a browser. Calculation of dynamic features from drawing data is performed on the client side at the time of data loading, and can be visualized by all visualization methods. At the same time, statistics can be calculated from the dynamic features, and by passing the subject's supplementary information to the EVIDENT prototype in advance, the statistics in the drawing data and the additional information of the drawn subject are output with the visualization result.

4.2   Implementation

Creating Drawing Data. In this prototype, it is assumed that Bamboo Slate [1], a smart pad of wacom, is used as an ICT device. In Bamboo Slate, the coordinates (x, y) of the pen tip of the ballpoint pen and the pen pressure can be acquired only at the moment when the dedicated ballpoint pen is in contact with the paper surface. Here, the range of the coordinates of the pen tip (x, y) that Bamboo Slate can obtain is approximately $0 \leq x \leq 29700$, $0 \leq y \leq 21600$. A size 1 in coordinates corresponds to one thousandth of a centimeter on paper. The pen pressure of this Bamboo Slate is output in the range of $0.05\% \leq$ pen pressure $\leq 99.95\%$, with the maximum pressure that can be measured by the Bamboo Slate body as 99.95% and the minimum pressure as 0.05%. To obtain drawing data from Bamboo Slate, use a communication application that connects a personal computer and a device to perform data communication such as coordinates and pen pressure, and an output application that attaches a time stamp to the obtained data and outputs it as csv. These applications are provided by wacom, the selling agency of Bamboo Slate. The csv data obtained by this application is as follows.

```
pres:21.04%, x:14955, y:17839, time:22:43:44.769
pres:22.61%, x:14937, y:17841, time:22:43:44.777
pres:26.03%, x:14883, y:17849, time:22:43:44.784
```

The csv data consists of the pen pressure, x-coordinate, y-coordinate, and time stamp of a point.

Loading and Shaping of Drawing Data. In the prototype, the visualization interface is implemented using HTML5, CSS, and JavaScript, and the csv obtained from the output application is read on the browser. In this prototype, instead of using EVIDENT-API, the read drawing data is replaced with an array in the plot data format using JavaScript.

The prototype uses this array instead of the plot database, and calculates dynamic features and statistics from this array using JavaScript. The dynamic features and statistics calculated here are not stored in the database but are stored in an array using JavaScript.

Creating a Visualization Interface. Visualization presented in 3.3 is performed using HTML5 and JavaScript. Visualization is performed by drawing points on Canvas, which is a specification for drawing figures on JavaScript and

HTML5 browsers. Also, arrows necessary for visualizing some dynamic features are drawn using canvas-arrow.js, a library for drawing arrows on Canvas.

In addition, HTML5, css, and JavaScript were used to directly write the additional information of the subjects in a JavaScript file instead of the additional information database, and to output the statistics and the additional information to the screen simultaneously with the visualization results.

5   Experimental Evaluation

Various visualization of drawing test can be realized by using EVIDENT prototype. In this section, we verify how the visualization method implemented using the EVIDENT prototype can be used in drawing test analysis, using actual test results.

5.1   Experimental Purpose and Method

EVIDENT's main function is to realize various analyses by presenting dynamic features of results of drawing test to clinicians and medical professionals who do not have specialized knowledge of data analysis. It is difficult to directly evaluate the visualization method itself. However, considering the original purpose of EVIDENT, if health professional can visualize dynamic features using EVIDENT, and if they can confirm any trends from these results, at least, it is possible to evaluate the effectiveness as a support tool for analyzing dynamic features without knowledge of data analysis.

Therefore, in this experiment, using the EVIDENT prototype created in the previous section, we analyze the visualization results of CDT and CCT drawing data for a total of 60 people, including about 50 people with abnormal cognitive function and about 10 suspected HC.

In order to focus on the analysis of the visualization result itself, all operation were performed by the authors, and the analysis of the visualization result was performed in the presence of health professional.

The drawing data used in the experiment uses the results of drawing tests performed by healthcare workers at medical institutions as part of dementia tests, and results of tests performed to HC under similar conditions for this experiment.

5.2   What EVIDENT Prototype Revealed

Case1: Abnormality of Drawing Strategy in CCT. Figure 6 shows the results of CCT for a patient with a definitive diagnosis of AD, and Fig. 7 shows the visualization of the drawing order in the same drawing data. This is a method that changes the color of the stroke from cold to warm as you follow the stroke order and write the stroke number near the stroke in the same color. When the CCT of this patient was scored using only the conventional final form, there was no tendency for AD. However, if you look at Fig. 7, you can see that the line connecting the lower left back vertex to the lower right back vertex is drawn in two strokes instead of one.

Normally, when copying a cube, it is rare that HC describes a straight line connecting vertices into two lines, which is considered to be a lack of planning in cube copying. In this way, EVIDENT was able to express abnormalities that could not be determined only by the final shape of the drawing.

Case2: Dispersion of Time Between Strokes. The time between strokes was visualized with arrows and their colors for each case and compared. As a result, the visualization results of HC showed mostly blue arrows, and the visualization results of MCI tended to have many arrows of various colors from blue to red. In addition, as for the visualization results of AD, similar to the visualization results of MCI, there were some that had various colors from blue to red, and some visualization results were only blue arrows. From these facts, we thought that there was something to do with the vividness of the colors and the cases.

Therefore, in this experiment, it is assumed that the chromaticity of the arrow and the dispersion of the time between strokes are equivalent (the dispersion is large if the color is vivid, and the dispersion is small if the color is not vivid), and The average of the dispersion of the time between strokes for each painter's case (HC, MCI, AD) was 2.726106 for AD, 4.384947 for MCI, and 1.687476 for HC. However, in calculating this average, two data with a dispersion of $Q3 + (Q3 - Q1) * 1.5$ ($Q1$:first quartile, $Q3$:third quartile) or more were excluded as outliers.

Therefore, when the difference of the mean of the obtained variances was subjected to t-test, no significant difference was found between HC and AD, but there was a significant difference between HC and MC as $t(21) = 2.209$ and $p = 0.0192$. The reason is that HC can draw numbers and hands with a constant rhythm at a good tempo because the complete drawing of the clock is in the head from the beginning, while many MCI think about what to draw next immediately after drawing a stroke. The reason why the difference between AD and HC was smaller than HC and MCI is probably because there were a certain number of subjects who roughly and quickly draw clocks in AD to deceive facts that cannot be drawn accurately. Figure 8 and 9 show the results of CDT drawn by such AD and the time between strokes visualized by arrows and their colors.

5.3   Problem

In this study, the following two issues are raised. One is about a method to add arrows and visualize them.

As you can see in Fig. 9, it is very difficult to grasp the features where the arrows are displayed overlapping. In the future, we plan to consider some other methods, such as adding a function in which EVIDENT users display arrows one by one on the screen by clicking on them one after another, and plan to improve them.

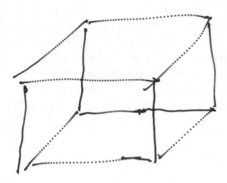

Fig. 6. Drawing result in CCT of an AD

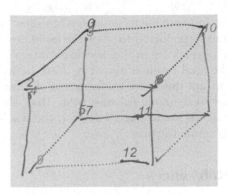

Fig. 7. Stroke order in CCT of an AD (Color figure online)

Fig. 8. Drawing result in CDT of an AD

Fig. 9. Time in air in CDT of an AD (Color figure online)

The other is about dynamic features to be visualized. In this experiment, we visualized various dynamic features with the advice of two health professionals. However, besides the dynamic features visualized this time, there may be dynamic features that are useful for discovering new knowledge. In the future, EVIDENT will be also used by health professionals and clinical psychologists other than these two, and we will continue to develop new systems while receiving feedback on new dynamic features and feedback on visualization results.

6   Conclusion

In this paper, we proposed EVIDENT, a support tool to analyze dynamic features in drawing test for health professionals and clinical psychologists who do not have specialized knowledge such as data mining.

In experiments conducted to show the usefulness of this service, In an experiment conducted to show the usefulness of this service, it was possible to express abnormalities in the drawing strategy of AD, which were difficult to grasp from the final result of drawing, Also, between HC and MCI, we could find the significant difference in dispersion of time between strokes. However, there may be useful dynamic features other than the dynamic features visualized this time, and we would like to develop the whole proposed system while exploring such dynamic features.

References

1. Bamboo slate—wacom. https://www.wacom.com/ja-jp/products/smartpads/bamboo-slate?utm_campaign=wcl-jpn-sm-316700-ongoing-social-se-smartfolio&utm_source=youtube.com&utm_medium=social&utm_content=slate. Accessed on 03 Feb 2020
2. How the clock-drawing test screens for dementia. https://www.verywellhealth.com/the-clock-drawing-test-98619. Accessed on 15 Nov 2019
3. Agrell, B., Dehlin, O.: The clock-drawing test. Age Ageing 27(3), 399–403 (1998)
4. Manos, P.J., Wu, R.: The ten point clock test: a quick screen and grading method for cognitive impairment in medical and surgical patients. Int. J. Psychiatry Med. 24(3), 229–244 (1994)
5. Müller, S., Preische, O., Heymann, P., Elbing, U., Laske, C.: Increased diagnostic accuracy of digital vs. conventional clock drawing test for discrimination of patients in the early course of alzheimer's disease from cognitively healthy individuals. Front. Aging Neurosci. 9, 101 (2017)
6. Mori, S., et al.: Clinical examination of reliability/validity of scoring methods for cube-copying test (CCT). Japan. J. Compr. Rehabil. Sci. 5, 102–108 (2014)
7. Shin, M.S., Park, S.Y., Park, S.R., Seol, S.H., Kwon, J.S.: Clinical and empirical applications of the rey-osterrieth complex figure test. Nat. Protoc. 1(2), 892 (2006)
8. Small, A.C.: The contribution of psychodiagnostic test results toward understanding anorexia nervosa. Int. J. Eat. Disord. 3(2), 47–59 (1984)
9. Souillard-Mandar, W., Davis, R., Rudin, C., Au, R., Penney, D.: Interpretable machine learning models for the digital clock drawing test (2016)
10. Sunderland, T., et al.: Clock drawing in alzheimer's disease: a novel measure of dementia severity. J. Am. Geriatr. Soc. 37(8), 725–729 (1989)

Developing Parameters for a Technology to Predict Patient Satisfaction in Naturalistic Clinical Encounters

Tianyi Tan[✉], Enid Montague, Jacob Furst, and Daniela Raicu

College of Computing and Digital Media, DePaul University,
Chicago, IL 60604, USA
ttan6@mail.depaul.edu,
{emontag1, jfurst, draicu}@cdm.depaul.edu

Abstract. Patient-centered communication is crucial in the clinical encounter. Previous studies on patient satisfaction have focused on nonverbal cues and demographics of the patient separately; the integrated influence of both aspects is yet to be explored. This study aims to build a model to learn the quantitative relationship among nonverbal behaviors such as mutual gaze and social touch, demographics of the patients such as age, education and income, and patient perceptions of clinicians. Using 110 videotaped clinical encounters of patients from a study of assessing placebo, Echinacea, and doctor-patient interaction in the acute upper respiratory infection and a decision tree machine learning approach, duration per mutual gaze, percentage of mutual gaze, age, and social touch were identified as the top four important features in predicting how much patients liked their clinicians. Patients of older age, with higher percentage of mutual gaze, longer social touch duration and moderate duration per mutual gaze tended to report greater rating on likeness towards their clinicians. Findings from this study will be used to inform the design of a real-time automatic feedback system for physicians. By using the decision tree machine learning approach, the findings help determine the parameters required for the design of a real-time monitoring and feedback system of the quality of care and doctor-patient interaction in natural environments.

Keywords: Healthcare IT & Automation · Quality and safety in healthcare · Machine learning · Patient satisfaction · Decision tree · Automatic feedback system

1 Introduction

Effective patient-centered communication is integral to the patient-provider relationship and has been identified as a dimension of physician competency. The quality of clinician communication is associated with patient outcomes, such as understanding recommendations for treatment, adherence to therapy, and health outcomes [1]. Patient satisfaction, the key identifier of the quality of the communication [2], is defined as patients' reactions to salient aspects of the clinical experience including cognitive evaluations and emotional reactions [3]. However, accurate measurement of the quality

© Springer Nature Switzerland AG 2020
V. G. Duffy (Ed.): HCII 2020, LNCS 12198, pp. 473–490, 2020.
https://doi.org/10.1007/978-3-030-49904-4_35

of the patient-provider relationship can be challenging. Standardized questionnaires are commonly used as a quantitative method to assess patient satisfaction while unobtrusive observation, video recording, and shadowing are common approaches of qualitative methods [2]. The survey results might be affected by false memory and recall, internal (e.g., emotions) and external factors (e.g. measurement effects). Qualitative data may be difficult to collect, summarize and interpret [3]. The timing of measurement might also affect the ratings due to recall inaccuracies [4]. Mixed methods that incorporate both methods with real-time feedbacks may provide more accurate evaluations. Previous studies have examined correlations between patient satisfaction and eye contact, touch with specific social meaning such as handshaking (social touch) [5], demographics such as gender [6], age, and literacy [7]. Few studies focus on the integration effects of both aspects on patient satisfaction. Effective guidelines and reliable evaluation of physician-patient interactions are needed for practical innovations such as a dynamic feedback system, which can help physicians emphasize positive interactions and build better relationships for longer periods of time.

The purpose of this study was to determine how to develop parameters for a system to provide real-time feedback about the quality of patient-physician interactions in naturalistic settings. In this study, behavioral data from videotaped clinical visits and self-reported surveys were analyzed using a decision tree machine learning approach. The findings can inform the future design of clinical settings and computational health tools focused on patient care. They also provide guidance for personnel recommendation as well as procedures and the care system.

1.1 Assessment of Communication

The effectiveness of communication can be accessed by patient satisfaction which is dependent on good communication skills demonstrated by care providers [4, 5]. Patient satisfaction can be the key identifier of the communication and reliable judgment of the quality of clinical experience [2]. The empathy which provides supportive interpersonal communication is an essential aspect to the patient-clinician relationship and has been linked to greater patient satisfaction [10]. The effectiveness of empathy is related to patient satisfaction, adherence, anxious and stressful emotions, patient enablement, diagnostics and clinical outcomes [11]. Empathy has been studied in healthcare services [12, 13] and linked with satisfaction and nonverbal behavior to health encounter outcomes [5]. There is a general lack of research on the role of empathy regarding clinical outcomes in primary care [12]. This study will further explore the relationship between empathy and patient satisfaction by predicting the level of satisfaction based on nonverbal interaction.

1.2 Nonverbal Interaction in Clinician-Patient Communication

Both verbal and non-verbal communication have been studied by significant research on clinician-patient communication. Most tools available to analyze physician-patient interactions are found based on verbal cues such as the process analysis system, the verbal response mode, or the Roter Interaction Analysis System (RIAS) but the role of nonverbal interaction has comparatively less focused in the literature [14]. Nonverbal behavior, however, plays an important role in physician-patient communication and interpersonal judgment mainly depends on nonverbal cues [14]. For example, research found that distancing behaviors of physical therapists such as the absence of smiling and lack of eye contact were associated with a decrease in physical and cognitive functioning of the patients [15]. Another research has shown that patient satisfaction was related to physician expressiveness: less time for medical chart reading, more gazing, more forward lean, more nodding, more gestures and closer interpersonal distance [14, 16]. Montague et al. [5] revealed that there was a positive correlation between the length of the visit and eye contact and the patient's assessment of clinician empathy. In their study [5], apart from eye gaze, touch was found to be also important for patient satisfaction. Social touch such as handshake and hug (defined as a touch with specific social meaning as opposed to task touch defined as a touch with clinical purpose) were also linked to the perception of clinician empathy. In our proposed study, we will not only quantify the importance of different nonverbal cues but also learn how to make predictions of patient satisfactions based on interaction data annotated from videos.

1.3 Patient Demographics and Communication

Interpreting the meaning of specific nonverbal cues can be also affected by patient demographics. A study shows that many factors affect whether and how a specific nonverbal interaction is associated with patient satisfaction [14] such as gender [6], age, race, literacy, and optimism [7]. For example, older, non-White, optimistic, and literacy deficient patients had greater satisfaction among the low-income populations [7]. Although there is much research about the effects of demographics on patient satisfaction, less research has studied both demographic and nonverbal effects. This study will incorporate the demographics of the patients and explore the interaction effects between the demographics and nonverbal cues.

1.4 Machine Learning Techniques Related to Patient Satisfaction and Healthcare Industry

Several machine learning techniques have been used to understand patient satisfaction in the context of the health industry. Li et al. [17] identified clinical risk factors such as self-evaluation of health, education level, race, treatment and new medication pre-scription associated with patient satisfaction with the Least Absolute Shrinkage and Selection Operator (LASSO) algorithm, which analyzed binary variables and identified risk factors for various aspects of a hospital through correlations. Galatas et al. [18] applied forward selection and Naïve Bayes to predict patient satisfaction.

2 Methods

The study was motivated by the findings of Montague et al. [5, 19] and served to give direction for the development of the design of an interactive feedback system based on user needs and guidelines for information as well as communication technologies in clinical practice. The study aims to identify the important factors and quantify the relationships among nonverbal interactions, demographics of the patient and patient satisfaction using decision tree algorithm by answering the following questions:

1. Which factors in the demographic features and nonverbal interaction features have more deterministic contributions to patient satisfaction?
2. What are the quantitative relationships between important features and patient satisfaction?

Our methodology is illustrated in Fig. 1.

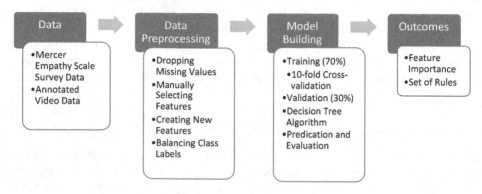

Fig. 1. Methodology diagram

2.1   Data Sources

The data set was a subset of the data collected for a study of assessing placebo, Echinacea, and doctor-patient interaction in the acute upper respiratory infection (common cold). It contained the annotated data from videotaped clinical encounters of patients with the common cold. The methodology of the study design was published in the research of Barrett et al. [20] previously. The clinical encounters took place in two different locations in Dane County, Wisconsin between April 2004 and February 2006. The protocols were approved by the University of Wisconsin School of Medicine and Public Health and clinical review boards. Patient rights and privacy were protected by following the Health Insurance Portability and Accountability Act (HIPPA) strictly.

There were 719 patients and 6 clinicians involved in this dataset. Participants were randomly assigned to three groups of different interaction mode: standard interaction, enhanced interaction and no clinical encounter [19, 20]. Data from 110 of the videotaped encounters were included in the study. The videos were of high quality and reliability of nonverbal interaction evaluation.

The detailed procedure of the annotation was published in the research of Montague et al. [5]. The non-verbal behaviors was classified using a coding scheme developed by Montague et al. [21]. The start and the stop time for each behavior were coded with Noldus Observer XT 9.0. The duration of each behavior over the course of the encounter was recorded. A coding procedure was developed by researchers [5] to ensure the reliability of the coders. The coders coded the behaviors of patients and clinicians separately with video reduced to half-normal speed. Each coder had training videos to practice and to be evaluated on. During the final coding, the same video was assigned to all the coders each week to check the agreements by reliability tests using Cohen's Kappa coefficient. The average reliability among high-quality videos was 0.76 which was considered excellent reliability based on the study by Bakeman [5, 22].

The survey data was obtained by the survey instruments completed by participants immediately after the consultation. Questionnaires measured the perception of the patients on the clinician empathy using the Consultation and Relational Empathy (CARE) Measure (Table 1) which was a patient-rated measure of the clinician's the communication skills, the reliability of which has been validated [5, 10].

Table 1. Survey questions in Mercer Empathy Scale (The CARE Measure)

"How was the clinician at...?"
with Options (Poor; Fair; Good; Very Good; Excellent)

1.Making you feel at ease......
(being friendly and warm towards you, treating you with respect; not cold or abrupt)
2. Letting you tell your "story" ......
(giving you time to fully describe your illness in your own words; not interrupting or diverting you)
3. Really listening......
(paying close attention to what you were saying; not looking at the notes or computer as you were talking)
4. Being interested in you as a whole person......
(asking/knowing relevant details about your life, your situation; not treating you as "just a number")
5. Fully understanding your concerns......
(communicating that he/she had accurately understood your concerns; not overlooking or dismissing anything)
6. Showing care and compassion......
(seeming genuinely concerned, connecting with you on a human level; not being indifferent or "detached")
7. Being positive......
(having a positive approach and a positive attitude; being honest but not negative about your problems)
8. Explaining things clearly......
(fully answering your questions, explaining clearly, giving you adequate information; not being vague)
9. Helping you to take control......
(exploring with you what you can do to improve your health yourself; encouraging rather than "lecturing" you)
10. Making a plan of action with you......
(discussing the options, involving you in decisions as much as you want to be involved; not ignoring your views)

Satisfaction
with Options (Very Little; Not Very Much; Somewhat; Quite A Lot; Very Much)

11. How much did you like this doctor?
12. How connected did you feel to him/her?

The questionnaire had two sections. The first section was the CARE Measure with ten questions, each with options from 1 to 5 (Poor; Fair; Good; Very Good; Excellent). The second section measured patient satisfaction containing the likeness and connectedness towards the clinician options from 1 to 5 (Very Little; Not Very Much; Somewhat; Quite A Lot; Very Much). In this study, Likeness ("How much did you like this doctor?") was chosen as the class label and an indicator of patient satisfaction, which has strong correlations with all variables in the CARE survey.

2.2   Data Preprocessing

The original dataset contained 110 records and 98 features. There were 41 features annotated from videos including the duration, frequency and proportion of the duration of the visit of the non-verbal interactions. There were 13 features containing information of patients including age, gender, race, education, income and smoking history. 15 Features extracted or calculated from the Mercer Empathy Scale survey indicated the patients' perception of empathy. 29 features obtained from other surveys aimed to access placebo. 59 features were manually selected from the data set as variables of interests due to their high relevance to the research questions and fewer missing records for each feature.

The records with 59 features containing 11 missing values in education, 8 missing value in household income and 1 missing values in features extracted from survey. After dropping all the records with missing values, the cleaned dataset had 93 records with 59 features. The features included all the video data with total time, frequency and percentage, the demographic data with age, gender, education and household income, patient satisfaction data with mercer scores and all the sections in the Mercer Empathy Scale Survey. From the non-verbal interaction features, 3 features that were directly related to the research goal were manually selected for simplicity and popularity in literature: Total duration of social touch (*Social touch (total time)*), percentage of visit in mutual gaze (*% of visit in mutual gaze*), percentage of visit in gazing chart together (*% gaze chart together*). There were 2 new calculated interaction features added to test if the length of each interaction might relate to patient satisfaction: Time per Mutual Gaze calculated by dividing the total time of mutual gaze by the frequency and Time per Social Touch. Both features were not analyzed by previous literature which provided a new angle of understanding the non-verbal interaction in the clinical encounters. To incorporate demographics of the patients, Age, Gender(*1 = Male; 2 = Female*), Education (*1: High School or High School Grad/GED; 2: Some college/tech school; 3: College Grad (bachelor's)*), Household Income (*1 =< $15 K; 2 = $15–25 K; 3 = $25–50 K; 4 = $50–75 K; 5 = $75–100 K; 6 = Over $100 K*) were selected as relevant features mentioned in the literatures from the data set. The original levels of Education were re-categorized for balanced distributions for different levels. There were in total 9 features related to nonverbal interactions and patient demographics analyzed by the model.

The possible values to the Likeness class variable ("How much did you like this doctor?") had a scale from 1 to 5 indicating different level of likeness to the clinician shown in Fig. 2.

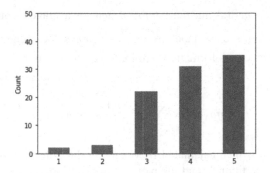

Fig. 2. Bar chart of likeness before discretization

The class distribution of Likeness was very imbalanced for level 1 ("Very little") and level 2 ("Not very much"). An empirical study has shown that classifier tended to have worse performance on the minority class and balanced class distribution provided better results with fixed amount of the data in the training set [23]. Due to the fact that the size of the data set was limited, the first three levels were binned together as a group, which provided a more balanced class distribution.

2.3 Decision Tree Algorithm

To build the classification model, decision trees approach was used considering its simplicity of result understanding, interpreting and validating. It also has no assumptions on the distribution of the data. More importantly, it helps identify the most significant attributes with the highest differential influence for prediction. The important features in the model provide insights for clinicians and inspirations for the future design of interactive technology between clinicians and patients. A decision tree has a flowchart structure, where each non-terminal node serves as a test for an attribute, each branch denotes test results, and each terminal node represents a class label [24]. Decision trees are constructed in a top-down recursive manner. It starts with the topmost node which is the root node and ends with the terminal nodes which hold the class prediction [25].

There are two commonly used impurity measures used to optimize the model performance: Information Gain and Gini Index.

ID3 decision tree algorithm uses information gain. Assume node N represents the instances of partition D. The attribute with the least entropy is chosen as the splitting attribute for node N. The information needed to classify an instance in D is calculated by the formula (1) *where* p_i = nonzero probability that tuple in D in class C_i, m = m classes:

$$Info(D) = -\sum_{i=1}^{m} p_i log_2(p_i) \tag{1}$$

Suppose the tuples are tested to be partitioned by attribute A with v distinct values $\{a_1, a_2, \ldots, a_v\}$. D is split into v partitions, $\{D_1, D_2, \ldots, D_v\}$, where D_j contains tuples in D with the value of a_j of A attribute. *Info*(D) denotes average amount of information needed to identify tuple class label in D, $\frac{|D_j|}{|D|}$ denotes the weight of jth partition, *Info*$_A(D)$ denotes expected information required to classify a tuple from D based on the partitioning by A.

$$Info_A(D) = \sum_{i=1}^{v} \frac{|D_j|}{|D|} \times Info(D_i) \tag{2}$$

Information gain is then calculated by obtaining the difference between the information required for partition D and the new requirement obtained after partitioning on certain attribute [24].

$$Gain(A) = Info(D) - Info_A(D) \tag{3}$$

The Gini index is used in CART. It measures the impurity of partition D *wherep*$_i$ = nonzero probability that tuple in D in class C_i, m = m classes:

$$Gini(D) = 1 - \sum_{i=1}^{m} p_i^2 \tag{4}$$

With the notation previously described, the Gini index determines the best binary split on attribute A with v distinct values. All the possible subsets $(2^v - 2)$ can be formed and considered using values of A. For example, if for one binary split, D is partitioned into D_1 and D_2, the Gini index of D:

$$Gini_A(D) = \frac{|D_1|}{|D|} Gini(D_1) + \frac{|D_2|}{|D|} Gini(D_2) \tag{5}$$

The decrease in impurity by a binary split:

$$\Delta Gini(A) = Gini(D) - Gini_A(D) \tag{6}$$

The splitting attribute which maximizes the reduction in impurity will be selected [24].

Pre-pruning approach prunes the tree by halting the growing process early. The growth of the tree can be halted by choosing a maximum depth and setting values of minimum number of nodes to split and minimum number of nodes in the leaf after splitting. With all the parameters, the tree will not further split at a given node [24].

The feature importance is calculated as the normalized total reduction of the node impurity brought by that feature, known as Gini importance. Assuming only two child nodes, the importance of node j is calculated by formula (7) where ni_j = the importance of node j, w_j = weighted number of samples reaching node j, C_j = the impurity value of node j, $w_{left(j)}$ = weighted number of samples of child node from left split on node j, $w_{right(j)}$ = weighted number of samples of child node from right split on node j,

$C_{left(j)}$ = the impurity value of child node from left split on node j, $C_{right(j)}$ = the impurity value of child node from right split on node j:

$$ni_j = w_j C_j - w_{left(j)} C_{left(j)} - w_{right(j)} C_{right(j)} \tag{7}$$

The importance for each feature on decision tree is then calculated as the formula where fi_i = the importance of feature I, ni_j = the importance of node j:

$$fi_i = \frac{\sum_{j: node \, j \, splits \, on \, feature \, i} ni_j}{\sum_{k \in K (all \, nodes)} ni_j} \tag{8}$$

2.4 Parameter Tuning and Model Validation

The classifier model built in the experiment and trials was evaluated based on the accuracy performance of the validation set. To obtain reliable results, a stratified sampling validation was used with 70% training and 30% validation for all experiments. The validation set was selected using stratified sampling regarding the distribution of the class variable. The best parameters were determined by grid search techniques. The validation set would be held out for final evaluation. The training set was split into 10 smaller sets. The model was trained using 9 of the folds as training data. The resulting model is validated on the remaining data. The performance metrics reported by 10-fold cross-validation were the average of the accuracy computed on each fold. The best parameters chosen will then build the model tested by the validation set. The accuracy of the training and the validation set will be compared to avoid overfitting. The hyperparameters of the Decision Tree model were tuned by trying all the combination of the parameters in a given range. Parameter tuning using grid search provided the best performance by searching for the best combinations of parameters. The score function was leveraged to determine model performance. Accuracy was used for measuring classification performance.

3 Results

3.1 Sample Characteristics

There were 93 records in the dataset. The total visit time of the patients was 189.14 s on average and ranged from 26.29 s to 642.45 s. The duration of the encounter was rather short. During such a short period of time, the physicians might not be able to provide sufficient nonverbal interactions. As shown in Table 2, both distributions of the total time of social touch and time per social touch in the dataset were right-skewed. % of visit in mutual gaze was on average around 25% of the visit length and approximately 20% of the visit time were spent for gazing chart together. The duration of a mutual gaze was 3.32 s but can range from 0.54 s to 21.64 s. As shown in Table 3, patients were from different age groups with the minimum age of 14.21 to maximum age of 71.76. There were more female patients (60) than male patients (33) in the dataset. 64 of the 93 patients graduated from college. A majority of the patient had household income larger than 25 K.

Table 2. Descriptive statistics for numeric data

Feature	Social touch (total time) (s)	Time per social touch (s)	% of mutual gaze	% gaze chart together	Time per mutual gaze (s)	Age
mean	1.12	0.57	25.34	20.03	3.32	35.63
std	1.65	0.81	17.27	16.53	3.13	14.65
min	0	0.00	1.59	0.00	0.54	14.21
25%	0	0.00	10.61	1.62	1.38	23.27
50%	0	0.00	25.07	21.84	2.40	33.60
75%	1.74	1.09	40.15	30.85	3.92	46.66
max	7.55	5.34	73.04	61.08	21.64	71.76

Table 3. Descriptive statistics for nominal/ordinal data

Feature	Gender		Education			Household income						Likeness		
Levels	M	F	1	2	3	1	2	3	4	5	6	1	2	3
Counts	33	60	17	22	64	6	10	21	19	22	15	27	31	35

As the correlation between the features in the CARE questionnaires were all moderate to strong and significant at 0.01 level (2-tailed test) evaluated by Spearman correlation for ordinal data shown in Table 4, the study chose Likeness ("How much did you like this doctor?") as the class label as an indicator of patient satisfaction which has strong correlation (0.854, $p <= 0.01$) with Connectedness ("How connected did you feel to this doctor?") and also moderate to strong correlation (0.60–0.86) with other 10 features measuring patient satisfaction.

Table 4. Correlation matrix for Mercer empathy scale variables (each feature indicated by question numbers in the survey; results of Likeness (11) is in bold type; F. means features)

F.	1	2	3	4	5	6	7	8	9	10	11	12
1	1.00	0.71	0.79	0.76	0.67	0.87	0.73	0.73	0.69	0.70	**0.78**	0.65
2	0.71	1.00	0.81	0.66	0.72	0.74	0.67	0.71	0.66	0.58	**0.60**	0.53
3	0.79	0.81	1.00	0.78	0.73	0.82	0.75	0.75	0.71	0.72	**0.71**	0.64
4	0.76	0.66	0.78	1.00	0.78	0.86	0.81	0.71	0.81	0.77	**0.86**	0.79
5	0.67	0.72	0.73	0.78	1.00	0.84	0.76	0.79	0.73	0.75	**0.73**	0.69
6	0.87	0.74	0.82	0.86	0.84	1.00	0.86	0.85	0.83	0.78	**0.85**	0.72
7	0.73	0.67	0.75	0.81	0.76	0.86	1.00	0.84	0.79	0.73	**0.76**	0.70
8	0.73	0.71	0.75	0.71	0.79	0.85	0.84	1.00	0.73	0.75	**0.71**	0.61
9	0.69	0.66	0.71	0.81	0.73	0.83	0.79	0.73	1.00	0.81	**0.76**	0.69
10	0.70	0.58	0.72	0.77	0.75	0.78	0.73	0.75	0.81	1.00	**0.76**	0.72
11	**0.78**	**0.60**	**0.71**	**0.86**	**0.73**	**0.85**	**0.76**	**0.71**	**0.76**	**0.76**	**1.00**	**0.85**
12	0.65	0.53	0.64	0.79	0.69	0.72	0.70	0.61	0.69	0.72	**0.85**	1.00

3.2   Decision Tree Model Building

The dataset was divided into training and validation subsets using stratified sampling. 30 random repeated independent trials were conducted to obtain the mean accuracy and confidence interval for decision tree models with different hyperparameters. The hyperparameters consisted of different splitting criteria (Gini index or Entropy), minimum number of samples needed in a parent node (ranging from 4 to 20), minimum number of samples needed in a child node (ranging from 2 to 10), and maximum depth (ranging from 3 to 9). The model with validation accuracy closest to the average was chosen to provide stable results. The model with chosen parameters was tested and evaluated in training and validation set with 30 trials. After building the models, the importance of each feature was recorded and compared. The top four features were then chosen based on the rank of feature importance to build simpler models with high performance.

As shown in Table 5, the average accuracy of the classifier with the corresponding width of 95% confidence interval, generated by 30 trials, was $59.74\% \pm 1.78\%$. The mean accuracy gained from validation set was $52.74\% \pm 3.24\%$.

Table 5. Summary table for decision tree results for with different features and hyperparameters (mean accuracy and 95% confidence interval constructed by 30 trials)

Mean accuracy	All features	Four most important features
Training (10-Fold Cross-validation)	$59.74\% \pm 1.78\%$	$61.29\% \pm 2.27\%$
Validation	$52.74\% \pm 3.24\%$	$54.29\% \pm 4.69\%$
Final model	Splitting criteria: Entropy; Maximum tree depth:3; Minimum number of samples needed in a child node: 5; Minimum number of samples needed in a parent node:13	Splitting criteria: Gini Index; Maximum tree depth: 4; Minimum number of samples needed in a child node: 3; Minimum number of samples needed in a parent node:13
Training	$53.03\% \pm 2.28\%$	$52.30\% \pm 2.12\%$
Validation	$52.02\% \pm 3.01\%$	$51.67\% \pm 2.77\%$

The performance of the final model with all features and chosen parameters shown in the row of final model and the second column in Table 5 was $53.03\% \pm 2.28\%$ in training and $52.02\% \pm 3.01\%$ in validation set. The difference between the mean accuracies of training and validation was 1.01% which did not indicate an overfitting problem.

The average feature importance was calculated among the 30 trials from decision trees with the chosen parameters. There were three features had the average importance much higher than other features: Time per Mutual Gaze, % of Visit in Mutual Gaze and Age. Social Touch (Total Time) ranked the fourth most importance features (Fig. 3).

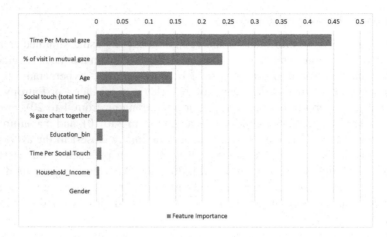

Fig. 3. Bar chart of the average feature importance

The rank was learned by the models and was consistent across random training and validation sets. To have a more efficient prediction, the top four features were selected to construct simpler trees with a similar process.

To build a simpler model with only 4 features, the dataset was divided into training and testing subsets using stratified sampling and 30 random repeated independent trials were conducted to obtain the mean and confidence interval for the performance metrics. The average accuracy of the classifiers with the corresponding width of 95% confidence intervals across the 30 trials was $61.29\% \pm 2.27\%$. The accuracy gained from the validation set was $54.29\% \pm 4.69\%$. The parameters with its validation accuracy closest to the mean testing accuracy was chosen for final model shown in the third column and the row of final model. The mean accuracy generated by the cross-validation among all different sampling of given optimal parameters was $52.30\% \pm 2.12\%$. The accuracy gained from validation set was $51.67\% \pm 2.77\%$. The difference between the accuracies of training and validation was 0.63% which did not indicate the overfitting problem. The results above have shown that the performance of four features was comparable to the performance of all features. The model with only four features helped learn simple and interpretable rules.

3.3   Rule Extraction

While the above analysis provided feature importance, further analysis also was conducted with the intent to understand how these features were combined to produce classification rules. To accomplish the rule extraction, a sample tree was chosen with validation accuracy close to the mean validation accuracy of the 30 trials, without overfitting issues and contained all four features. The training accuracy for this sample tree was 58.75% and the validation accuracy was 57.14%.

Table 6 concluded other important performance metrics for the model on the validation set. Precision indicated the percentage of correct predictions of the level of likeness among all positive predictions. Recall indicated the percentage of correct predictions of the level of likeness among all actual positive cases. F1-score was calculated and indicated the weighted average of Precision and Recall, which took both false positives and false negatives into account. The model performed better in classifying the lower and upper level of the class variable. The model performed better for the class label 'Excellent' with highest precision, recall, and F1-score, which might due to the fact that there were more cases for the 'Excellent' label.

Table 6. Other performance metrics for sample tree

Likeness metrics	Precision	Recall	F1-score
1: Very Little to Somewhat	0.40	0.25	0.31
2: Quite A Lot	0.50	0.67	0.57
3: Very Much	0.73	0.73	0.73

Rules extracted by the model shown in Fig. 4 from the training set were summarized in Table 7. All class labels had rules with the class probability larger than 80%. Both class label "Quite A Lot" and "Very Much" had rules which correctly predicted all the cases at the terminal nodes.

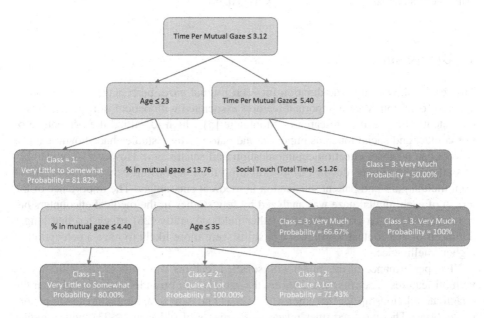

Fig. 4. Sample decision tree graph (different colors for different class levels, left arrow: yes, right arrow: no) (Color figure online)

Table 7. Rules extracted by pruned sample tree

Rules	Class: "How much did you like this doctor?"	Class probability
Time Per Mutual Gaze <= 3.12 Age <= 23	**1: Very Little to Somewhat**	81.82%
Time Per Mutual Gaze <= 3.12 Age > 23% of Mutual Gaze <= 4.40	**1: Very Little to Somewhat**	80.00%
Time Per Mutual Gaze <= 3.12 23 < Age <= 35% of Mutual Gaze > 13.76	**2: Quite A Lot**	100%
Time Per Mutual Gaze <= 3.12 Age > 35% of Mutual Gaze > 13.76	**2: Quite A Lot**	71.43%
3.12 < Time Per Mutual Gaze <= 5.40 Social Touch (Total Time) > 1.26	**3: Very Much**	100%
3.12 < Time Per Mutual Gaze <= 5.40 Social Touch (Total Time) <= 1.26	**3: Very Much**	66.67%
Time Per Mutual Gaze >= 5.40	**3: Very Much**	50%

4 Discussion

The results showed that the duration for each mutual gaze, percentage of eye contact, age and social touch were important features associated with patient satisfaction. It was consistent with previous research of Montague [5] which identified the percentage of eye contact and social touch as important indicators. Many studies had shown that eye contact had a robust effect on communication and satisfaction. However, considerably less attention had been devoted to investigating the relationship between the length of each mutual gaze and patient satisfaction in medical encounters. The importance of the length of each mutual gaze was analyzed by few studies in the medical encounters but was considered as a crucial factor in other fields. A study [26] suggested that longer durations of eye contact with fewer eye shifts were more likely to have a perception of higher intelligence.

The performance of the model with selected features was comparable with models with all features. The rules extracted by the sample tree provided some insights on the quantitate relationship for those non-verbal cues and demographic features with patient perceptions. The extracted rules reveal that patients of older age (>23), with a higher percentage of mutual gaze (>13.76%), longer social touch duration (>1.26 s) and moderate duration per mutual gaze (larger than 3.12 s but smaller than 5.40 s) tended to report greater rating on likeness towards their clinicians. To suggest simple and reliable rules, the rule for each class label providing the highest purity was analyzed in detail. When time per mutual gaze was smaller than 3.12 and age was smaller than 23, the patient tended to have a low rating for their likeness towards the clinician. When time per mutual gaze was smaller than 3.12, age was larger than 23 and smaller than 35 and percentage of mutual gaze was larger than 13.76 the patient would rate "Quite a Lot". When time per mutual gaze was larger than 3.12 but smaller than 5.40 with time for social touch larger than 1.26, the patient would rate "Very much" as the answer to the likeness. Thus, patients of older age tended to report greater likeness which was consistent with the findings of research on demographic influence on patient-provider communication and satisfaction [7]. A higher percentage of mutual gaze would lead to higher satisfaction towards clinician which was demonstrated in the study of Montague which identified positive beta for eye contact on empathy scores (beta = 0.43, $R^2 = 0.18$) [5]. Longer social touch duration tended to result in higher likeness ratings. It confirmed the results of a study on touch in primary care consultations that patients were sensitive to the nonverbal communications and social touch improved the interactions, especially in situations of severe distress [27]. The rules also revealed that insufficient duration per mutual gaze resulted in low rating in the likeness and moderate duration led to a higher rating. The result of a study on preferred mutual gaze duration was consistent with this rule that longer gazes were preferred to frequent and short eye contact, but gazing for too long or overly short glance can be discomforting [28].

The survey data was self-reported and the video data to extract the non-verbal interaction was annotated by watch videos. Both might provide noisy and inconsistent data. Also, video-recording might influence the behavior of patients and clinicians. The external validity of the research might also be limited due to the fact that the sample was collected from a certain community associated with a certain symptom (common cold), which might result different conclusions for different locations and contexts. There were many exogenous effects might affect patient satisfaction. The study mainly focused on the demographics of the patients and did not have the features for clinicians. However, the gender of the physician can also affect the interpretation of the nonverbal communication of the patients [29].

5 Conclusion

This study identified four most important features in the dataset for patient perceptions of their clinicians: the duration for each mutual gaze, percentage of eye contact, age and social touch. Decision trees approach provided simple and interpretable results. Patients of older age, with a higher percentage of mutual gaze, longer social touch duration and moderate duration per mutual gaze were more likely to report greater likeness towards their clinicians. Although the decision tree algorithm provides great performance with only four most relevant characteristics in the physician-patient interaction, further study with more features and analysis of more data can help increase the performance and support decision making in health settings with more accurate results learning from the entire process.

With the quantitative rules extracted by a sample decision tree model, this study provided insights for the future design of the clinical environment and health information technology. These findings suggest that sufficient training of non-verbal communication skills for physicians can help improve patient satisfaction and outcome.

To help busy primary care clinicians in a highly interruptive and time-pressured environment [30], the future design of the clinical environment and health information technology should facilitate and remind clinicians of satisfactory non-verbal interactions. An automatic feedback system can be built to provide feedback on clinical visits based on real-time analysis of the important features identified by the model. The feedback system customized for primary care visits and with defined functionality of improving the non-verbal communication will provide high effectivity and efficiency [31]. Dynamic feedbacks will not only serve as a reminder but also reinforce important factors in decision making [32].

Acknowledgments. This research was supported by NSF Division of Information & Intelligent Systems Award - "CHS: Small: Extracting affect and interaction information from primary care visits to support patient-provider interactions" (Grant No: 1816010).

References

1. King, A., Hoppe, R.B.: "Best practice" for patient-centered communication: a narrative review. J. Grad. Med. Educ. **5**, 385–393 (2013). https://doi.org/10.4300/JGME-D-13-00072.1
2. Al-Abri, R., Al-Balushi, A.: Patient satisfaction survey as a tool towards quality improvement. Oman Med. J. **29**, 3–7 (2014). https://doi.org/10.5001/omj.2014.02
3. Cleary, P.D., McNeil, B.J.: Patient satisfaction as an indicator of quality care. Inquiry **25**, 25–36 (1988)
4. LaVela, S.L., Gallan, A.S.: Evaluation and measurement of patient experience. Patient Exp. J. **1**(1), 28–36 (2014)
5. Montague, E., Chen, P., Xu, J., Chewning, B., Barrett, B.: Nonverbal interpersonal interactions in clinical encounters and patient perceptions of empathy. J. Participat. Med. **5**, e33 (2013)
6. Hall, J.A., Irish, J.T., Roter, D.L., Ehrlich, C.M., Miller, L.H.: Gender in medical encounters: an analysis of physician and patient communication in a primary care setting. Health Psychol. **13**, 384–392 (1994)
7. Jensen, J.D., King, A.J., Guntzviller, L.M., Davis, L.A.: Patient-provider communication and low-income adults: age, race, literacy, and optimism predict communication satisfaction. Patient Educ. Couns. **79**, 30–35 (2010). https://doi.org/10.1016/j.pec.2009.09.041
8. Berman, A.C., Chutka, D.S.: Assessing effective physician-patient communication skills: "Are you listening to me, doc?". Korean J. Med. Educ. **28**, 243–249 (2016). https://doi.org/10.3946/kjme.2016.21
9. Collins, L.G., Schrimmer, A., Diamond, J., Burke, J.: Evaluating verbal and non-verbal communication skills, in an ethnogeriatric OSCE. Patient Educ. Couns. **83**, 158–162 (2011). https://doi.org/10.1016/j.pec.2010.05.012
10. Bikker, A.P., Fitzpatrick, B., Murphy, D., Forster, L., Mercer, S.W.: Assessing the Consultation and Relational Empathy (CARE) Measure in sexual health nurses' consultations. BMC Nurs. **16**, 71 (2017). https://doi.org/10.1186/s12912-017-0265-8
11. Derksen, F., Bensing, J., Lagro-Janssen, A.: Effectiveness of empathy in general practice: a systematic review. Br. J. Gen. Pract. **63**, e76–e84 (2013). https://doi.org/10.3399/bjgp13X660814
12. Mercer, S.W., Reynolds, W.J.: Empathy and quality of care. Br. J. Gen. Pract. **52**(Suppl), S9–12 (2002)

13. Jolliffe, D., Farrington, D.P.: Development and validation of the Basic Empathy Scale. J Adolesc. **29**, 589–611 (2006). https://doi.org/10.1016/j.adolescence.2005.08.010

14. Mast, M.S.: On the importance of nonverbal communication in the physician–patient interaction. Patient Educ. Couns. **67**, 315–318 (2007). https://doi.org/10.1016/j.pec.2007.03.005

15. Ambady, N., Koo, J., Rosenthal, R., Winograd, C.H.: Physical therapists' nonverbal communication predicts geriatric patients' health outcomes. Psychol. Aging **17**, 443–452 (2002). https://doi.org/10.1037/0882-7974.17.3.443

16. Hall, J.A., Harrigan, J.A., Rosenthal, R.: Nonverbal behavior in clinician—patient interaction. Appl. Prev. Psychol. **4**, 21–37 (1995). https://doi.org/10.1016/S0962-1849(05)80049-6

17. Li, L., Lee, N.J., Glicksberg, B.S., Radbill, B.D., Dudley, J.T.: Data-driven identification of risk factors of patient satisfaction at a large urban academic medical center. PLoS ONE **11**, e0156076 (2016). https://doi.org/10.1371/journal.pone.0156076

18. Galatas, G., Zikos, D., Makedon, F.: Application of data mining techniques to determine patient satisfaction. In: Proceedings of the 6th International Conference on PErvasive Technologies Related to Assistive Environments - PETRA 2013, pp. 1–4. ACM Press, Rhodes (2013)

19. Montague, E.: An intervention study of clinician-patient nonverbal interactions and patient perceptions of visits. J. Healthc. Commun. **3** (2018). https://doi.org/10.4172/2472-1654.100120

20. Barrett, B., et al.: Rationale and methods for a trial assessing placebo, echinacea, and doctor-patient interaction in the common cold. Explore (NY). **3**, 561–572 (2007). https://doi.org/10.1016/j.explore.2007.08.001

21. Montague, E., Xu, J., Chen, P.-Y., Asan, O., Barrett, B.P., Chewning, B.: Modeling eye gaze patterns in clinician-patient interaction with lag sequential analysis. Hum. Factors **53**, 502–516 (2011). https://doi.org/10.1177/0018720811405986

22. Bakeman, R.: Behavioral observation and coding. In: Handbook of Research Methods in Social and Personality Psychology, pp. 138–159. Cambridge University Press, New York (2000)

23. López, V., Fernández, A., García, S., Palade, V., Herrera, F.: An insight into classification with imbalanced data: Empirical results and current trends on using data intrinsic characteristics. Inf. Sci. **250**, 113–141 (2013). https://doi.org/10.1016/j.ins.2013.07.007

24. Han, J., Kamber, M., Pei, J.: 9 - Classification: advanced methods. In: Han, J., Kamber, M., Pei, J. (eds.) Data Mining (Third Edition), pp. 393–442. Morgan Kaufmann, Boston (2012)

25. Patel, B.N., Prajapati, S.G., Lakhtaria, K.I.: Efficient Classification of Data Using Decision Tree. Presented at the (2012)

26. Wheeler, R.W., Baron, J.C., Michell, S., Ginsburg, H.J.: Eye contact and the perception of intelligence. Bull. Psychon. Soc. **13**, 101–102 (1979). https://doi.org/10.3758/BF03335025

27. Cocksedge, S., George, B., Renwick, S., Chew-Graham, C.A.: Touch in primary care consultations: qualitative investigation of doctors' and patients' perceptions. Br. J. Gen. Pract. **63**, e283–e290 (2013). https://doi.org/10.3399/bjgp13X665251

28. Nicola, B., Charlotte, H., Antoine, C., Alan, J., Isabelle, M.: Pupil dilation as an index of preferred mutual gaze duration. Roy. Soc. Open Sci. **3**, 160086 (2016). https://doi.org/10.1098/rsos.160086

29. Mast, M.S., Hall, J.A., Köckner, C., Choi, E.: Physician gender affects how physician nonverbal behavior is related to patient satisfaction. Med. Care **46**, 1212–1218 (2008). https://doi.org/10.1097/MLR.0b013e31817e1877

30. Kim, M.S., Clarke, M.A., Belden, J.L., Hinton, E.: Usability challenges and barriers in EHR training of primary care resident physicians. In: Duffy, V.G. (ed.) DHM 2014. LNCS, vol. 8529, pp. 385–391. Springer, Cham (2014). https://doi.org/10.1007/978-3-319-07725-3_39
31. Bundschuh, B.B., et al.: Quality of human-computer interaction - results of a national usability survey of hospital-IT in Germany. BMC Med. Inf. Decis. Mak. **11**, 69 (2011). https://doi.org/10.1186/1472-6947-11-69
32. Hartwig, M., Windel, A.: Safety and health at work through persuasive assistance systems. In: Duffy, V.G. (ed.) DHM 2013. LNCS, vol. 8026, pp. 40–49. Springer, Heidelberg (2013). https://doi.org/10.1007/978-3-642-39182-8_5

Heart Sound Recognition Technology Based on Deep Learning

Ximing Huai, Siriaraya Panote[(⊠)], Dongeun Choi[(⊠)],
and Noriaki Kuwahara[(⊠)]

Kyoto Institute of Technology, Matsugasaki bashi cho, Sakyo-ku, Kyoto, Japan
joey_huaiximing@126.com, spanote@gmail.com,
g0024004@yahoo.co.jp, nkuwahar@kit.ac.jp

Abstract. With the development of medical technology, many diseases can be cured. However, the mortality rate of cardiovascular disease is still high and showing an upward trend. Reducing the mortality of such diseases is one of the difficulties that modern medicine needs to overcome. Heart sound auscultation is one of the most basic detection methods for cardiovascular disease, but it is more difficult for inexperienced medical staff. Therefore, it's urgent to develop assistive technology to assist heart sound auscultation.

According to previous works [1–4], it was concluded that deep learning has a notable effect on heart disease detection. The aim of this study is to develop a detection system to assist heart sound auscultation. Firstly, in the pre-experiment by debugging the batch size of CNN model, we determined that the accuracy of the model is the highest with the batch size of 256, which is 93.07%. Then, we used, a combined CNN and Long Short-Term Memory (LSTM) neural network model for heart sound detection, and obtained an accuracy of 91.06%.

Keywords: Heart disease · Heart sound · Convolutional neural network · Long Short-Term Memory

1 Introduction

1.1 Background

According to WHO statistics, except for Africa, cardiovascular disease is the leading cause of death in all countries and regions in the world [5]. Data show that the number of deaths from cardiovascular disease increased from 12.3 million in 1990 (25.8% of the total deaths) to 17.9 million (32.1%) in 2015 [6, 7]. It can be seen that even with the development of medical technology, the mortality of cardiovascular disease has not decreased, but has increased. According to research, there are many factors that cause cardiovascular disease, such as unhealthy diet, lack of physical activity, tobacco use and harmful use of alcohol. However, it is estimated that 90% of cardiovascular diseases are preventable [8]. Therefore, as an early diagnosis method for cardiovascular disease, auscultation of heart sounds plays a pivotal role. Improving the accuracy of auscultation of heart sounds is of great help in the early detection of cardiovascular diseases.

© Springer Nature Switzerland AG 2020
V. G. Duffy (Ed.): HCII 2020, LNCS 12198, pp. 491–500, 2020.
https://doi.org/10.1007/978-3-030-49904-4_36

1.2   Cardiovascular and Heart Sound Auscultation

Cardiovascular disease (CVD) is a class of diseases that involve the heart or blood vessels [5]. CVD includes coronary artery diseases (CAD) such as angina and myocardial infarction (commonly known as a heart attack) [5]. Other CVDs include stroke, heart failure, hypertensive heart disease, rheumatic heart disease, cardiomyopathy, abnormal heart rhythms, congenital heart disease, valvular heart disease, carditis, aortic aneurysms, peripheral artery disease, thromboembolic disease, and venous thrombosis [5, 6].

In physiology, a heart sound is a shock wave that is generated when blood flows through the heart while the heart is operating. Specifically, it is a vibration wave caused by turbulence generated when the valve opens and closes, or vibration caused by contraction of the heart muscle, closing of the heart valve, and blood hitting the walls of the ventricle and aorta. Generally speaking, this kind of vibration wave has low energy and is not easy to be transmitted to the air to form sound waves. However, a stethoscope can still be used to convert the wave into sound at a certain part of the chest wall. Because the sound can reflect the operation of the heart valve, doctors can use a stethoscope to hear these unique and distinctive sounds which provides important information about the heart condition. Because some abnormal activities of the heart can produce murmurs or other abnormal heart sounds, auscultation of heart sounds has important clinical significance for the diagnosis of certain heart diseases [9].

1.3   Deep Learning

Deep learning is one of the most important breakthroughs in the field of artificial intelligence in the past decade. It has achieved great success in many areas such as speech recognition, natural language processing, computer vision, image and video analysis, and multimedia.

At the same time, deep learning is also applied to the field of heart sound detection. Tien-En Chen et al. [10] proposed a deep neural network (DNN) method for identifying S1 and S2 heart sounds. Experiments were performed using actual heart sound signals recorded by an electronic stethoscope. Accuracy, recall, F-measurement and accuracy were used as evaluation indicators. The final accuracy rate is over 91%. Chen, Lili et al. [11] developed a deep neural network based on stacked autoencoders and softmax layers for predicting heart sound signals. Eight features are obtained from each heart sound signal through three feature extraction algorithms. They then used stacked autoencoders to learn the advanced features of heart sound signal representation. Finally, a softmax layer was added as a classification layer on top of the stacked autoencoders, thereby generating a deep neural network. The results show that the sensitivity, specificity, accuracy, and accuracy of the deep neural network are 98%, 88%, 89.1%, and 93%, respectively. Varghees, V. et al. [12] propose a novel unified PCG signal description and noise classification method. The main component of this method is PCG signal decomposition based on empirical wavelet transform, which is used to distinguish heart sounds in heart murmurs and suppress background noise., Boundary determination based on instantaneous phase, extraction of heart sound and murmur parameters, systolic/diastolic pressure discrimination and murmur classification based on decision rules. The results show that the average sensitivity (Se) of the method to heart sound segmentation is 94.38%, the positive predictiveness (Pp) is 97.25%, the total accuracy (OA) is 91.92%, the Se is 97.58%, the Pp is 96.46% and OA At 94.21%.

From the above research, we can see that the application of deep learning in heart sound detection is very effective. Therefore, in this paper, we examine the use of CNN and LSTM models for heart sound detection in order to obtain a higher recognition rate.

2 Method

2.1 Data Set

The data used in this paper is from Classification of Heart Sound Recordings - The PhysioNet Computing in Cardiology Challenge 2016 [13], which includes a total of 3,153 heart sound recordings from 764 subjects/patients.

The data was obtained from multiple research groups across the world, recorded in different real-world clinical and nonclinical environments. The data include not only clean heart sounds but also very noisy recordings. The data were also recorded from different locations, depending on the individual protocols used for each data set [13].

All heart sound recordings were divided into two types based on expert labelling from the original data contributors: normal and abnormal. This left us with 2576 normal heart sound recordings and 664 abnormal heart sound recordings.

2.2 CNN

Convolutional neural network (CNN) is a feed-forward neural network. Its artificial neurons can respond to a part of the surrounding cells in the coverage area, and it has excellent performance for large-scale image processing [14].

A convolutional neural network consists of one or more convolutional layers and a fully connected layer at the top (corresponding to a classic neural network). It also includes association weights and a pooling layer. This structure enables the convolutional neural network to take advantage of the two-dimensional structure of the input data. Compared with other deep learning structures, convolutional neural networks can give better results in terms of image and speech recognition. This model can also be trained using a back-propagation algorithm. Compared with other deep and feedforward neural networks, convolutional neural networks need to consider fewer parameters, making it an attractive deep learning structure [15].

Such network have applications in image and video recognition, recommender systems [16], image classification, medical image analysis, and natural language processing [17]. Therefore, CNN is helpful for creating a heart sound detection system.

Data Production. In the pre-experiment, firstly, the heart sound data was divided into 5-s intervals and used as sample heart sounds. This is because the shortest heart sound length in the database is 5 s, and we consulted a doctor who agreed with this assumption. Secondly, the sample heart sound is then converted to spectrogram using an automated program by Python (Fig. 1, Fig. 2). This program uses python's audio conversion toolkit such as wave, numpy, os, etc. And finally convert the wav file into a grayscale image with 864 by 504 pixels. This is done to improve the speed of processing. Overall, we obtained 12,378 heart sound spectrograms, then the data set is divided into three groups: training group, validation group, and test group with the corresponding ratio being 8:1:1.

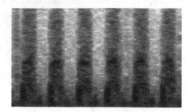

Fig. 1. Spectrogram of abnormal heart sounds

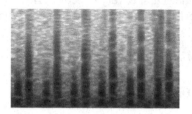

Fig. 2. Spectrogram of normal heart sounds

Configuration of CNN Model. As for the learning method, the CNN machine learning model was used to train the heart sound data. In this model, three convolutional layers and three pooling layers are used to extract features from the samples. The filters of the convolution layer are 32, 64, 128, and the kernel size is 3 × 3, and the pool size of the pooling layer is 2 × 2. ReLU is used as the activation function. Dropout [19] is used after each pooling layer to prevent overfitting. Adam [18] for the optimizer and Binary cross-entropy is used as the objective function.

2.3   CNN + LSTM

Long short-term memory (LSTM) is an artificial recurrent neural network (RNN) architecture used in the field of deep learning [20]. Unlike standard feedforward neural networks, LSTMs have feedback connections. It can handle not only a single data point (such as an image) but also an entire data sequence.

LSTM networks are very suitable for classifying, processing, and making predictions based on time series data. Therefore, we combine LSTM with CNN for the detection of heart sound spectrograms, hoping to reduce the omission of information in simple cutting, as there may be a lag of unknown duration between important events in time series data.

Data Production. In the pre-experiment, the heart sound data was divided into 5-s intervals and converted to spectrogram. After that, a sliding window was used to intercept the heart sound like samples (Fig. 3). The length of the sliding window is 2 s and coverage is 50%. Then, each 5-s heart sound image is cut into 4 of 2-s heart sound spectrograms and used as a sample input CNN + LSTM model. Also, the data set is divided into three groups: training group, validation group, and test group, the corresponding ratio is 8:1:1.

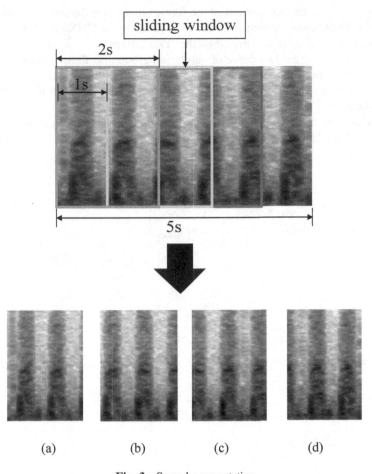

Fig. 3. Sound segmentation

Configuration of CNN + LSTM Model. In the experiment, the neural network model that combined with CNN and LSTM is used for heart sound detection. The CNN part is similar to the CNN model used before, but only one layer is used for the convolution layer and the pooling layer, the filter of the convolution layer is 32. In the LSTM part, a layer of LSTM is used, and a dropout layer is also used to prevent overfitting.

3 Result

3.1 Comparison of the Result of Different Batch Size for CNN

The established CNN model was used to test the existing data set. Due to the importance of batch size, the batch size was first examined in this experiment. Three batch sizes of 128, 256, and 512 were used. The obtained results are shown in Figs. 4, 5, 6, 7, 8 and 9, and the specific test accuracy and test loss are shown in Table 1. It can be clearly seen from the comparison of the figures that when the batch size is 256, the accuracy curve of training group and validation group in the CNN model are closer and the shapes are more consistent than the other two groups.

At the same time, the loss curve of validation group also flattens with the increase of epoch. When the batch size is 128 and 256, although the loss curve of validation group also decreases along with the loss curve of training group at the beginning, it rises gradually and the magnitude was large.

In addition, through 10 groups of specific values of test accuracy and test loss, it can be seen that when the batch size is 256, the test accuracy is even higher. Therefore, 256 was selected as the batch size.

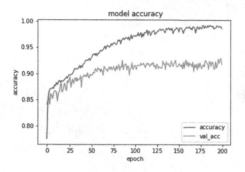

Fig. 4. Identification result of batch size 128

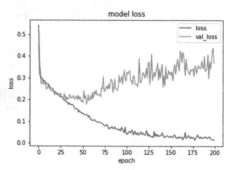

Fig. 5. Loss of batch size 128

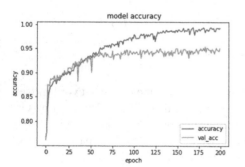

Fig. 6. Identification result of batch size 256

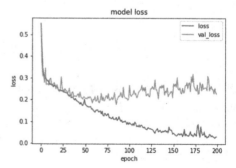

Fig. 7. Loss of batch size 256

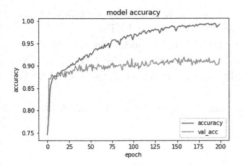

Fig. 8. Identification result of batch size 512

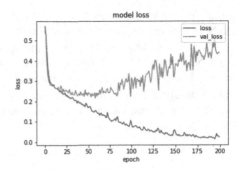

Fig. 9. Loss of batch size 512

Table 1. Test_accuarcy and Test_loss of CNN model with batch size 128/256/512

Round	Batch size = 128		Batch size = 256		Batch size = 512	
	Test accuracy (%)	Test loss	Test accuarcy (%)	Test loss	Test accuarcy (%)	Test loss
1	93.21	0.3578	93.45	0.4003	92.25	0.2547
2	90.55	0.4239	93.30	0.4009	92.57	0.3959
3	93.86	0.2517	92.48	0.2688	93.21	0.3534
4	93.62	0.3266	93.05	0.3483	92.41	0.3388
5	93.62	0.2475	92.25	0.4100	92.00	0.3255
6	91.38	0.3563	92.41	0.3765	92.08	0.3665
7	94.10	0.3235	93.46	0.3092	93.38	0.2831
8	93.05	0.4078	94.43	0.2840	93.94	0.3011
9	91.68	0.4739	93.62	0.2801	92.73	0.3339
10	92.97	0.3955	92.25	0.3883	91.92	0.4531
Average	92.80	0.3565	93.07	0.3466	92.65	0.3406

3.2   Comparison of the Result of CNN and CNN + LSTM

According to the previous results, selecting 256 as the batch size resulted in the best performance. Therefore, in the CNN + LSTM model, 256 is still used as the batch size. The results obtained are shown in Fig. 10, 11, 12 and 13. The specific test accuracy and test loss are shown in Table 2. From the comparison between Fig. 10 and Fig. 12, it can clearly be seen that the accuracy curve of training group and validation group of the CNN model are closer, and the trends are consistent. However, the accuracy curve of validation group of the CNN + LSTM model tends to be parallel after epoch = 50, and the accuracy curve of the training group increases with the increase of epoch, which eventually leads to an increasing distance between the two curves, indicating that the sample was better trained in training group, but the effect was worse in validation group. It can also be seen from the specific data in Table 2 that the accuracy of the CNN model in the test group is 2% higher than that of CNN + LSTM.

At the same time, it can be seen in Figs. 11 and 13 that although the loss curve of the CNN model has a larger oscillation amplitude than that of the CNN + LSTM model, but the curve eventually flattens, while the loss curve of the CNN + LSTM model finally shows an upward trend.

Therefore, from the results obtained so far, samples have obtained better results in the CNN model.

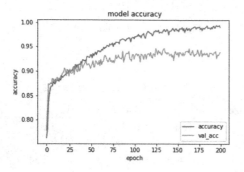

Fig. 10. Identification result of CNN model

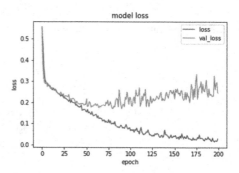

Fig. 11. Loss of CNN model

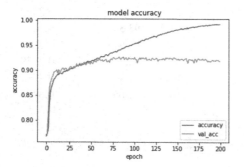

Fig. 12. Identification result of CNN + LSTM model

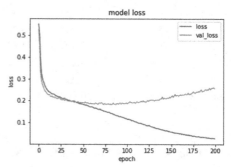

Fig. 13. Loss of CNN + LSTM model

Table 2. Test_accuarcy and Test_loss of CNN and CNN + LSTM

Round number	CNN		CNN + LSTM	
	Test accuarcy (%)	Test loss	Test accuarcy (%)	Test loss
1	93.45	0.4003	91.64	0.2702
2	93.30	0.4009	91.64	0.2433
3	92.48	0.2688	90.93	0.2987
4	93.05	0.3483	90.67	0.2875
5	92.25	0.4100	91.46	0.2601
6	92.41	0.3765	91.01	0.2745
7	93.46	0.3092	90.99	0.2655
8	94.43	0.2840	90.83	0.2849
9	93.62	0.2801	90.73	0.2926
10	92.25	0.3883	90.65	0.3142
Average	93.07	0.3466	91.06	0.2792

4   Discussion

In this study, we used data from Classification of Heart Sound Recordings-The PhysioNet Computing in Cardiology Challenge 2016 [13] as the data set. A CNN model and CNN + LSTM model were created to analyze these data, which finally obtained an accuracy of 93.07% and 91.06%, respectively. But from the accuracy and loss curves of the CNN + LSTM model, there is still room for improvement in this model. Higher accuracy can be achieved by trying to adjust several parameters such as class weights, etc., or trying to increase the coverage rate between spectrograms.

References

1. Rubin, J., Abreu, R., Ganguli, A., et al.: Recognizing abnormal heart sounds using deep learning. arXiv preprint arXiv:1707.04642 (2017)
2. Potes, C., Parvaneh, S., Rahman, A., et al.: Ensemble of feature-based and deep learning-based classifiers for detection of abnormal heart sounds. In: 2016 Computing in Cardiology Conference (CinC), pp. 621–624. IEEE (2016)
3. Nirschl, J.J., Janowczyk, A., Peyster, E.G., et al.: A deep-learning classifier identifies patients with clinical heart failure using whole-slide images of H&E tissue. PLoS ONE 13(4), e0192726 (2018)
4. Ryu, H., Park, J., Shin, H.: Classification of heart sound recordings using convolution neural network. In: 2016 Computing in Cardiology Conference (CinC), pp. 1153–1156. IEEE (2016)
5. Mendis, S., Puska, P., Norrving, B.: Global Atlas on Cardiovascular Disease Prevention and Control. World Health Organization in collaboration with the World Heart Federation and the World Stroke Organization, pp. 3–18 (2011)

6. Naghavi, M., et al.: Global, regional, and national age-sex specific all-cause and cause-specific mortality for 240 causes of death, 1990-2013: a systematic analysis for the Global Burden of Disease Study 2013. Lancet **385**(9963), 117–171 (2015)

7. Wang, H., et al.: Global, regional, and national life expectancy, all-cause mortality, and cause-specific mortality for 249 causes of death, 1980-2015: a systematic analysis for the Global Burden of Disease Study 2015. Lancet **388**(10053), 1459–1544 (2016)

8. McGill, H.C., McMahan, C.A., Gidding, S.S.: Preventing heart disease in the 21st century: implications of the Pathobiological Determinants of Atherosclerosis in Youth (PDAY) study. Circulation **117**(9), 1216–1227 (2008)

9. Luisada, A.A., Liu, C.K., Aravanis, C., Testelli, M., Morris, J.: On the mechanism of production of the heart sounds. Am. Heart J. **55**, 383–399 (1958)

10. Chen, T.-E., et al.: S1 and S2 heart sound recognition using deep neural networks. IEEE Trans. Biomed. Eng. **64**(2), 372–380 (2016)

11. Chen, L., et al.: The diagnosis for the extrasystole heart sound signals based on the deep learning. J. Med. Imaging Health Inform. **8**(5), 959–968 (2018)

12. Varghees, V.N., Ramachandran, K.I.: Effective heart sound segmentation and murmur classification using empirical wavelet transform and instantaneous phase for electronic stethoscope. IEEE Sens. J. **17**(12), 3861–3872 (2017)

13. Liu, C., et al.: An open access database for the evaluation of heart sound algorithms. Physiol. Meas. **37**(9), 2181 (2016)

14. Convolutional Neural Networks (LeNet) - DeepLearning 0.1 documentation. DeepLearning 0.1. LISA Lab, 31 August 2013

15. Convolutional Neural Network, 16 September 2014

16. van den Oord, A., Dieleman, S., Schrauwen, B.: Deep content-based music recommendation (PDF). Burges, C.J.C., Bottou, L., Welling, M., Ghahramani, Z., Weinberger, K.Q. (eds.) Curran Associates, Inc. pp. 2643–2651, 01 January 2013

17. Collobert, R., Weston, J.: A unified architecture for natural language processing: deep neural networks with multitask learning. In: Proceedings of the 25th International Conference on Machine Learning. ICML 2008, pp. 160–167. ACM, New York, 01 January 2008. https://doi.org/10.1145/1390156.1390177. ISBN 978-1-60558-205-4

18. Kingma, D., Ba, J.: Adam: a method for stochastic optimization. arXiv preprint arXiv: 14126980 (2014)

19. Srivastava, N., Hinton, G.E., Krizhevsky, A., Sutskever, I., Salakhutdinov, R.: Dropout: a simple way to prevent neural networks from overfitting. J. Mach. Learn. Res. **15**(1), 1929–1958 (2014)

20. Hochreiter, S., Schmidhuber, J.: Long short-term memory. Neural Comput. **9**(8), 1735–1780 (1997). https://doi.org/10.1162/neco.1997.9.8.1735. PMID 9377276

DHM for Aging Support

Advancing a 'Human Factors & Ethics Canvas' for New Driver Assistance Technologies Targeted at Older Adults

Joan Cahill[1]([⊠]) [iD], Katie Crowley[1], Sam Cromie[1], Ciaran Doyle[2],
Eamonn Kenny[1], Alison Kay[1], Michael Gormley[1], Sonja Hermann[1],
Ann Hever[1], and Robert Ross[3]

[1] Trinity College Dublin, Dublin, Ireland
cahilljo@tcd.ie
[2] University of Limerick, Limerick, Ireland
[3] Dublin Institute of Technology, Dublin, Ireland

Abstract. Automated driving solutions represent a potential solution to promoting driver persistence and the management of fitness to drive issues in older adults. This paper reports on the application of a 'Human Factors & Ethics Canvas' and associated methodologies, to support the preliminary specification of an ethically responsible solution for a new driver assistance system. The proposed driving assistance solution has emerged from an analysis of certain ethical principles in relation to the goals and needs of specific older adult drivers (i.e. personae) in different situations (i.e. scenarios). The driving solution is designed to optimize the abilities and participation of older adults.

Keywords: Automated driving · Human factors · Ethics · Successful ageing · Wellbeing · Research & innovation · Fitness to drive

1 Introduction

Mobility in the form of driving is very important for older adults. There is a relationship between driving, mobility, independence and quality of life/living a fulfilled life. Age-related declines in the abilities of older adults provide certain obstacles to safe driving. Automated driving solutions represent a potential solution to promoting driver persistence and the management of fitness to drive issues in older adults. However, such solutions need to be carefully thought out in relation to promoting successful ageing, wellbeing and self-efficacy for older adults. New driving solutions should not have negative consequences on an older adult's identity, autonomy, mental health and their ability to achieve their goals.

The responsibilities of designers and questions concerning the moral quality of technology belong to the field of Applied Ethics. However, such questions also pertain to the field of Human Factors. Design/technology teams must carefully consider the human and ethical dimensions of automated driving systems. Specifically, they must question the purpose and intended use, implications in relation to human identity and rights, psychosocial implications and broader societal impacts.

© Springer Nature Switzerland AG 2020
V. G. Duffy (Ed.): HCII 2020, LNCS 12198, pp. 503–520, 2020.
https://doi.org/10.1007/978-3-030-49904-4_37

This paper reports on the use of a 'Human Factors and Ethics Canvas' (HFEC) along with other human factors (HF) methodologies, to support the preliminary specification of an ethically responsible driver assistance system. Primarily, the focus is on reporting the vision and system logic for the proposed system, as defined using the HFEC. Further, the paper reports on certain other elements recorded in the HFEC, namely, underlying ethical principles, ethical issues, impact assessment and key performance indicators (KPI).

2 Introduction

2.1 Older Adults and Older Adult Drivers

Older adults are a highly heterogeneous group. Often, older adults are segmented based on factors such as aging phases, levels of fitness, severity of physical limitations, mobility patterns and social activities. Successful aging is multidimensional, encompassing the avoidance of disease and disability, the maintenance of high physical and cognitive function, and sustained engagement in social and productive activities [1]. Factors that contribute to maintaining a license include vision, physical health and cognitive health [2]. Several medical conditions and associated impairments are more prevalent in the older adult population. These medical conditions can potentially impact the crash risk of older road users [3]. A systematic review of the literature by Marshall (2008) identified specific conditions including: alcohol abuse and dependence, cardiovascular disease, cerebrovascular disease, depression, dementia, diabetes mellitus, epilepsy, use of certain medications, musculoskeletal disorders, schizophrenia, obstructive sleep apnea, and vision disorders [4].

2.2 Automated Driving Solutions

Automated driving systems are defined as 'systems that control longitudinal and lateral motions of the vehicle at the same time' [5]. Largely, the proposed solutions follow established automation models such as the six levels of automation as defined by the National Highway Transportation Safety Administration [6]. The 'IEEE Global Initiative on Ethics of Autonomous and Intelligent Systems' have defined a set of core ethical principles for autonomous and intelligent systems (A/IS) (2018) [7]. Overall, the goal is to 'create technology that improves the human condition and prioritizes wellbeing' [7].

2.3 Vehicle Automation and Ethical Issues

The public opinion on automation and driverless cars will determine the extent to which these new systems will be purchased and accepted [8]. Four clusters of issues have been identified [9]. These are (1) legal issues, (2) functional safety issues, (3) societal issues (including issues of user acceptability) and (4) human machine interaction (HMI) design issues [9]. Largely, the literature around ethics and driverless cars addresses issues pertaining to ethical issues related to transferring the responsibility of driving to vehicles, managing conflict dilemmas on the road, protecting privacy, and minimizing technology misuse. However, other ethical issues are worth addressing. This includes issues pertaining to the intended use and purpose of this technology, the role of the person/driver and the potential negative consequences of this technology. In relation to the latter, this includes the social consequences of this technology and the potential impact on older adult identity and wellbeing.

2.4   Human Factors and Ethics Canvas

According to Cahill (2019), methodologies are required to enable the active translation of ethical issues pertaining to the human and social dimensions of new technologies [10]. Critically, developers/designer's human factors and ethical issues must be explored in an integrated way. The 'Human Factors & Ethics Canvas' introduced by Cahill (2019) reflects an integration of ethics and HF methods, particularly around the collection of evidence using stakeholder evaluation methods [11, 12], personae-based design [13] and scenario-based design approaches [14]. Further, it makes use of ethical theories/perspectives that are used in relation to the analysis of technology innovation (i.e. analysis of benefit versus harm) including Consequentialism, Deontology & Principlism [15].

The HFEC can be used at any stage in the HCI design/evaluation process and spans the classification of ethical assessment methods as proposed by Reijers et al. (2017) [16]. Overall, it blends anticipatory/foresight approaches and participatory/ deliberative ethics approaches [17]. The specific canvas is divided into seven stages or sections [10]. Stage 1 is all about framing the problem. Stage 2 involves understanding how the technology fits to the problem, defining stakeholder goals and needs and the specification of expected benefits for different stakeholders. This is followed by several more detailed examinations of core themes. These are: benefits, outcomes and impact (stage 3), personae and scenario (stage 4), data ethics (stage 5) and implementation (stage 6). The final stage (stage 7) presents the outcomes of the preceding analysis.

3   Method and Overview of Human Factors and Ethics Canvas

3.1   Research Objective

The project objective is to advance a driving assistance system which enables older adult mobility, independence and quality of life. The technology should support a driving experience which promotes driver satisfaction through increased control (and therefore confidence and enablement).

3.2   Overview of Research Methods and Status

Overall, this research has involved the application of human factors (HF) methodologies to the specification of a proposed driving assistance system. As indicated in Table 1, this research is structured in terms of two parts – the first of which is complete.

The first part of this research has been theoretical (i.e. does not involve field research with participants). As indicated in Table 1 below, this has comprised seven stages of research.

To date, a preliminary workflow and multimodal communications concept have been specified in relation to several demonstration scenarios. In Part 2 of this research, the proposed multimodal solution will be further validated using a combination of co-design techniques and simulator evaluation, involving the participation of older adults reflective of the specified older adult driver profiles.

Table 1. Summary of research

Part	#	Description	Status
1	1	Multidisciplinary Literature Review – including (a) older adults and positive ageing, (b) driving task, (c) segmentation of older adult drivers, (d) medical and age-related conditions that impact on driving ability and safety, (e) the detection/interpretation of driver states (i.e. physical, cognitive and emotional states) using a combination of sensor-based technology and machine learning techniques, (f) innovative human machine interaction (HMI) communication methods, (i) new driver monitoring, task support and feedback systems and (j) the analysis of legal, ethical and acceptability issues	Complete
	2	Secondary analysis of data from the Longitudinal Study on Ageing in Ireland (cite)	
	3	Advancement of preliminary driver profiles	
	4	Specification of driver personae and demonstration scenarios	
	5	Application of 'Human Factors & Ethics Canvas' to support specification of system concept	
	6	Detailed specification of system concept	
	7	Detailed specification of multimodal solution using personae/scenarios and outcome of HFEC analysis	
2	8	Participatory co-design and evaluation	To do
	9	Simulator evaluation	

3.3   Driver Profiles

Driver profiles were created following an analysis of the overall literature review and Tilda data (i.e. Part 1, phase 1 & 2). Specifically, drivers were segmented based on health and ability attributes (fitness to drive characteristics) and the goals of the project (i.e. safety, driver persistence and driver experience/enjoyment).

3.4   Specification of Personae and Scenario

In line with a HF approach, these user profiles were further decomposed into a series of personae. Each persona included information about the older adult's goals, their ability and health, medications, typical driving routines, typical driving behavior's and driver pain-points. For more information, please see Fig. 1 – Example Personae.

In parallel, several scenarios were defined. These scenarios followed from (1) the project goals (i.e. top down approach) and, (2) specific driving challenges and older adult driver behaviors, as identified in the literature review (i.e. Part 1, phase 1). These include:

1. Driver is enjoying drive – everything going well
2. Driver is distracted by their mobile phone ringing
3. Driver feels stressed given traffic delays
4. Driver has taken pain medications and is drowsy
5. Driver is fatigued after long day minding grandchildren
6. Driver is having difficulty parking (visual judgement)
7. Sudden advent of acute medical event
8. Driver is having difficulty remembering the correct route
9. Driver has taken alcohol and is over the legal limit

The different scenarios were then classified in terms of several interpretation challenges. This includes, Task support/feedback, Activation/"Flow", Distraction & Concurrent Task Management, Fatigue & drowsiness, Intoxication (alcohol/drugs) & Heart Attack/Stroke. Following this, the scenarios were associated with specific user profiles and personae. Figure 1 below provides an example of a personae.

James, 79 years

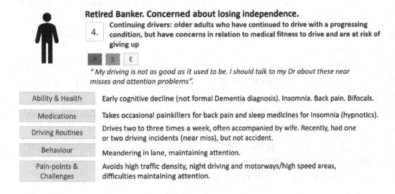

Retired Banker. Concerned about losing independence.

4. Continuing drivers: older adults who have continued to drive with a progressing condition, but have concerns in relation to medical fitness to drive and are at risk of giving up

" *My driving is not as good as it used to be. I should talk to my Dr about these near misses and attention problems".*

Ability & Health	Early cognitive decline (not formal Dementia diagnosis). Insomnia. Back pain. Bifocals.
Medications	Takes occasional painkillers for back pain and sleep medicines for Insomnia (hypnotics).
Driving Routines	Drives two to three times a week, often accompanied by wife. Recently, had one or two driving incidents (near miss), but not accident.
Behaviour	Meandering in lane, maintaining attention.
Pain-points & Challenges	Avoids high traffic density, night driving and motorways/high speed areas, difficulties maintaining attention.

Fig. 1. Example Personae

3.5 Application of 'Human Factors & Ethics Canvas'

As the first part of this study did not involve field research, the ethics canvas has made use of evidence obtained in the literature review, and the outcomes of team problem solving activities – in particular, the specification of user profiles, personae and scenarios. Thus-far, 6 stages of the HFEC have been completed. This includes Stages 1 to 5 and Stage 7. As noted previously, stage 1 is about formulating the problem. The initial literature review outputs (Part 1, phase 1) were analyzed to understand the multidimensional nature of the problem, contributory factors to the problem, the impact of the problem and ethical issues embedded in the problem statement. Stage 2 concerns stakeholder needs and expected benefits. This was analyzed using the outputs of the initial literature view (Part 1, phase 1) and the outcomes of the TILDA analysis (Part 1, phase 2). Benefits, impacts and outcomes were then documented – linking to problem solving undertaken in a series of group workshops with project researchers. The existing user profiles, personae and scenarios (Part 1, phases 3 & 4) were then further decomposed in relation to specific impacts and consequences. Critically, the system logic is advanced in relation to addressing the needs and requirements of these specific personae. Currently, it is anticipated that the solution will be developed for profiles 1 to 7, and potentially profile 9. A deep dive was then undertaken in relation to data ethics (phase 5 of HFEC). As implementation has not occurred, phase 6 was skipped. The overall analysis was then summarized (phase 7 of HFEC).

4   Understanding Human and Ethical Issues, Framing Human Factors and Ethics Problem and Specifying Design Challenge

4.1   Driver Profiles

Older adult drivers can be segmented into nine profiles. The profiles are as follows:

1. Older adults in optimal health and driving as normal
2. Older adults who regulate their driving in relation to managing specific driving challenges and/or stressful (difficult) driving situations
3. Older adults who are currently driving but have a medical condition that impacts on their ability to drive
4. Continuing drivers - older adults who have continued to drive with a progressing condition - but have concerns in relation to medical fitness to drive and are at risk of giving up
5. Older adults who are currently driving and at risk of sudden disabling/medical event
6. Older adults who have stopped driving on a temporary basis
7. Older adults who have stopped driving (ex-drivers) before it is necessary
8. Older adults who have stopped when it is necessary
9. Older adults who have never driven a car (never drivers)

4.2   Ethical Issues

In principle, ethical issues and issues concerning societal/user acceptability pertain to all driver profiles. Table 2 provides a summary of key ethical issues and questions.

Table 2. Key ethical issues & questions

#	Issue/Question
1	Should the purpose of these systems go beyond safety? Is it ethical to promote driver persistence?
2	How is the human role and wellbeing being considered in relation to the development of these systems?
3	Should the system determine the level of automation/assistance, or the older adult?
4	What is the role of older adult and what level of choice do they have in relation to mode of operation?
5	What level of impairment is acceptable for an older driver to keep driving?
6	Should the driver be able to take control of the car at any point?
7	Overreliance on technology and impact on driver competency & identity
8	Is full automation an appropriate solution to effectively managing the apparent conflict between two goals – (1) promoting driver persistence and (2) ensuring road safety?
9	Ethics in terms of how the system/algorithms treats older adults with different conditions (i.e. bias re MH or other conditions)
10	Ethics of personalization and nudging older adult towards specific automation modes. Appropriateness of mode options – for example, consideration of safety for persons with sensory or functional limitations?
11	How is information about the health status of the driver, their driving challenges, driving routines and any driving events being stored?
12	Who has access to driver profiles, health information and incident information?
13	Who is to blame if there in accident – the driver or the co-pilot? What are the legal obligations of the driver, if the driver is taken out of the loop (i.e. full automation)? Should the human back-up driver of intervened?
14	Addressing conflict dilemmas on the road?
15	Software hack and misuse
16	Should the system provide the driver with feedback about their health?
17	Environmental implications of pursing driver persistence

4.3 Ethical Principles Underpinning System Concept

Specific principles underpinning the system concept include:

1. The system should benefit all road users including older adults
2. The system should support road safety (benefits all road users)
3. The system should protect the rights of other road users and pedestrians who may be negatively impacted by older adult driving challenges and specifically, health events such as strokes and heart attacks.
4. The system should enable continued and safe driving for all adults, including those adults at risk of limiting their driving and/or giving up
5. The system should enable driver persistence – thereby supporting mobility and social participation for older adults

6. The system should be premised on concepts of successful/positive ageing and self-efficacy (i.e. avoid ageist stereotypes)
7. The system should promote driver engagement and provide alternatives to full automation
8. The proposed technology should maintain the autonomy of older adults (i.e. the starting point is the engaged driver).
9. The system should support all three pillars of older adult wellbeing (i.e. biological, psychological & social)
10. The system should enable social inclusion and participation of older adults - this benefits society as a whole
11. The system should protect human rights – including right to autonomy/choice, privacy (information access and protecting health and driver profile information)
12. The system should be usable, accessible, and understood by people of all ages with different abilities and health conditions.
13. Solution needs to comprehensively address real needs of people (diversity) and potential adoption barriers
14. Human activity should not compromise the long-term balance between the economic, environmental, and social pillars (triple bottom line)
15. The proposed mobility solution should consider environmental issues

Technologies can be narrowly conceived from an ethical standpoint. Such technologies might be designed to be legal, profitable and safe in their usage. However, they may not positively contribute to human well-being. Human benefit, wellbeing and respect for human rights and identity are key goals/principles for new assisted driving technologies. From a design perspective, this includes promoting driver persistence and self-efficacy and protecting driver data (i.e. privacy and rights). The driver assistance system must also be verifiably safe and secure. In this way, the solution needs to carefully balance potentially conflicting goals around driver persistence and safety.

4.4   Design Challenge and Framing the Problem

The design challenge (i.e. prolonging safe driving for older adults) is framed in relation to a philosophy of (1) driver persistence and 'enablement' and positive models of ageing – and (2) benefit for all – specifically in relation to safety and driver experience. This philosophy is further refined in relation to specific driver profiles and personae. To this end, a traffic light coding is assigned to specific personae. For more information, please see Fig. 1 – Example Personae. The traffic light coding is in relation to risk of not obtaining the predefined goals (i.e. goals in relation to persistence, safety and experience). In principle, all older adults should be green for persistence, safety and experience. If the older adult is having health issues, and taking some medications, or struggling with driving task, they might be at risk in relation to persistence (i.e. red on persistence mean close to giving up). If prone to anger, or have penalty points for speeding, then this gives you different colors for safety (i.e. yellow or amber depending on severity). Older adults who find driving difficult, and often drive with passenger and get easily stressed have amber or yellow on experience, meaning it is less fun for them. The co-pilot system should put all older adults 'back in the green' for relevant project goals.

5 Addressing Human Factors and Ethical Issues: Specification of Driving Assistance System Concept

5.1 Vision and Underlying Concept of the Older Adult/Person

The vision for this system is to promote the active participation of older adults in society (i.e. social inclusion and positive ageing). The proposed co-pilot system is premised on concepts of successful/positive ageing and self-efficacy. Ageing (and the associated changes in functional, sensory and cognitive function) is a normal part of life. To this end, the system seeks to normalize ageing, and not treat ageing as a 'problem' or 'disease'. To this end, the proposed driving assistance system is premised on a conceptualization of the driver/older adult as a person (and not a set of symptoms/conditions/holistic approach).

The driving solution (i.e. car, sensor system, co-pilot and HMI) is designed to opt mise the abilities and participation of older adults. Specifically, biopsychosocial concepts of health and wellness inform the logic of the proposed driving assistance system. The system is concerned with all aspects of the driver's wellness, including the driver's physical, social, cognitive and emotional health.

Further, the driving assistance system logic is premised on the idea that all older adult drivers are not the same. Older adult drivers vary in many ways including body size and shape, strength, mobility, sensory acuity, cognition, emotions, driving experience, driving ability (and challenges) and confidence.

5.2 Goals and Intended Purpose

Three high level goals for the system have been defined. These are enabling safe driving for older adults, driver persistence a positive driver experience. Overall, the purpose is to prolong safe driving for older adults with different ability levels, and in doing so help maintain cognitive and physical abilities. In so doing, the system should detect the health and psychological/emotional condition of the driver, so that the vehicle responds as appropriate. This can be achieved by promoting engagement/alertness, providing task supports and taking over the driving task if the driver is impaired and/or calling an ambulance. As indicated in Table 3, these goals can be further refined in relation to specific user profiles.

Table 3. System goals & user profiles

#	User profiles	Goals/role of new technology
1	Older adults in optimal health and driving as normal	Driving enabling life-long mobility Monitor driver's task and driver's capability Monitor driver states that impact on driver capability and provide task assistance to ensure safety Promote confidence for older driver Promote comfortable, enjoyable and safe driver experience
2	Older adults who regulate their driving in relation to addressing specific driving challenges	As (1) and…Technology directly addresses causes of self-regulation
3	Older adults who are currently driving but have a medical condition that impacts on their ability to drive	As (1) and…New car directly addresses challenges associated with condition. Monitor driver state in relation to specific medical condition, and provide task assistance to ensure safety
4	Continuing drivers - older adults who have continued to drive with a progressing condition - but have concerns in relation to medical fitness to drive and are at risk of giving up	As (1) and…New tech might monitor conditions and provide feedback – continue with licence/evidence, keep safe
5	Older adults who are currently driving and at risk of sudden disabling/medical event	As (1) and…New tech might monitor conditions and provide feedback New tech might take relevant action based on detection of onset of medical event
6	Older adults who have stopped driving on a temporary basis	As (1) and…Monitor driver state and health condition and provide task assistance to optimise safety
7	Older adults who have stopped driving (ex-drivers) before it is necessary	As (1), (2), (3), (4) and (5)
8	Older adults who have stopped when it is necessary	N/A
9	Older adults who have never driven a car (never drivers)	As (1) and…Motivate to buy car/learn to drive, given protections provided by new car and associated driver experience

5.3   System Concept and Logic

The system logic is underpinned by concepts of ability, adaption and assistance as opposed to full vehicle automation. The ability of the driver to perform the driving task depends the driver's ability (i.e. physical, sensory and cognitive), their driving experience, and the 'real time' state of the driver (i.e. health, level of fatigue, emotional state etc.) and the operational context (i.e. cabin context, road context, weather and traffic). Thus, to provide targeted task support to the driver, the system combines (1) an understanding of the driver's profile (i.e. ability and driving experience) and (2) an interpretation of the real time context (i.e. the state of the driver and the operational context).

We are proposing a collaborative system underpinned by the 'co-pilot' concept. The co-pilot is conceptualized a supportive and vigilant friend, who works in partnership with the driver to ensure a safe and enjoyable drive. The driving assistance system logic is predicated on the idea that driving is accomplished as a team task. Accordingly, it is conceived as a collaboration between the vehicle and the driver interacting with the driving environment/road context. The team includes driver and the vehicle (including car/hardware, sensing system, co-pilot and multimodal HMI). It is this team (and not simply the driver), that enables the different goals of safe driving, driver persistence and positive driving experience.

The driving assistance system is predicated on three levels of co-pilot intervention in response to driver factors (no response, driving assistance and safety critical intervention). The system recommends different levels of assistance based on the driver's profile (level of ability), and real time context (i.e. driver state and driver behavior). In principle, the driver selects the level of assistance required. However, if the system detects that (1) the driver is in a seriously impaired state (i.e. alcohol or medications), (2) there is a potential for a safety critical event, or (3) the driver is incapacitated, then authority moves to the 'co-pilot'.

The critical objective for the system is not to precisely diagnose the drivers' condition/state but to interpret the implications for the driving task and the driver. In this way, the system logic addresses 'interpretation challenges' rather than the driver condition or state. As indicated in Table 4, this is achieved in relation to six high level interpretation challenges.

Table 4. Interpretation challenges

#	Interpretation challenge	Explanation of the interpretation challenge
IC1	Task support/feedback	Addresses driving challenges and typical supports required (i.e. parking support, navigational assistance and assistance changing lanes)
IC2	Activation/"Flow"	Incorporates Multiple Psychological States: Stress/Anger/Excitement/Workload/Engagement including driver difficulties & driver behaviours
IC3	Fatigue & drowsiness	Many medical conditions & drugs also manifest this way
IC4	Distraction & concurrent task management	Addresses age-related cognitive & perceptual challenges including driver difficulties & driver behaviours
IC5	Intoxication – alcohol/drugs/related medical conditions	Other drugs & some medical conditions manifest similarly
IC6	Heart attack/stroke	Addresses fear factor – "What if … ?" which may discourage older drivers from driving

5.4   Goals, Objectives and Key Performance Indicators

As specified in Part 1 & Part 7 of the HFEC, it is possible to define key performance indicators (KPIs) relevant to the potential success of this technology once it is introduced and used by the public. As indicated in Table 5, system goals can be reformulated in terms of objectives concerning human benefit and wellbeing and associated measures/KPI's.

Table 5. Key Performance Indicators (KPI)

#	System goal	Human benefit & wellbeing objectives/targets (design outcomes)	Metric (outcome indicators)
1	Safe driving for older adults	Driver feels safe Driver feels in control The car is in a safe state	Subjective perception of safety/security Objective measure of car safety (position on road/lane, speed)
2	Driver persistence	Car as an enabler of active ageing/positive ageing – and allied health benefits Car contributing to eudaemonia (living well) Car contributing to a sense of having a purpose Car as an enabler of mobility Supporting social connection and participation Supporting citizenship etc.	Health status Mobility status Positive human functioning and flourishing Social capitol Personal growth
3	Driver experience	Driver feeling happy/enjoying driving activity Emotional state/psychological wellbeing (avoidance of stress) Driver in control Focus on ability (available capacity) Promote adaptation and bricolage	Subjective enjoyment of driving Subjective feeling of human agency/independence Subjective wellbeing

5.5   Defining and Managing Impacts: Design Considerations

Stage 3 and Stage 4 of the HFEC requires the specification of potential impacts and unknowns. These are grouped as follows: positive impacts, negative impacts, specific psychosocial impacts, specific environmental impacts, unintended consequences and unknown impacts. Table 6 provides an overview of those identified.

Positive impacts (for example, promoting driving persistence and the participation of older adults in society) must be supported by the system concept. Potential negative impacts must be carefully managed in relation to the design concept and execution. To this end, we are recommending:

Table 6. Defining impacts

#	Impact type	Description
1	Positive impacts	Simplify driving task for all
		Promote driver persistence for all
		Enable older adults with health issues, impairments and/or disability to continue driving
		Promote older adult wellbeing
		Promote older adult enablement
		Increase older adult mobility
		Enable social participation
		Enable older adults to undertake instrumental activities of daily living
		Increase older adult cognitive functioning
		Augment driver ability
		Mitigate the crash risk of specific medical conditions on driver
		Reduce risk of safety events for all
		Reduce no of road accidents
		Reduce crash risk of older road users
		Reduce/mitigate ageism
		Reduce anxiety for family members/concerns about fitness to drive
		Reduce passenger anxiety
		Increase medical attention response time for older adults experiencing health events while driving
2	Negative impacts	Unnecessary monitoring of older adult drivers
		Impact in terms of older adult drivers' identity – reduction to a set of symptoms to be monitored by technology – and not a person (holistic sense)
		Impact on perception of older adult driver by other drivers – need protections
		Impact on perception of older adult driver by other car occupants
		Impact in terms of privacy and changing norms for this
		Potential negative environmental impact – more cars on road (older adults driving themselves and not taking public transport or ride-shares)
		Potential data hacking and malicious intent (safety issues)
		Potential data hacking and data sharing breeches - sharing of sensitive/private information about a person's health condition and potential driving risk
		Overreliance on technology and impact on driver competency

(continued)

Table 6. (*continued*)

#	Impact type	Description
3	Specific Psychosocial impacts	Contributing to a culture of over-intrusive assessments/monitoring of persons including older adults, impacting on morale and dignity Loss of individual privacy – feedback about real time driving available to other occupants in car Increase anxiety of passengers
4	Specific environmental impacts	Older adults using cars/e-cars and not public transport or ride shares – impact on transport behavior and sustainability (carbon emissions)
5	Unintended consequences	Unnecessary nudging towards automation Over reliance and automation and loss of ability (driving task and competency) Changing norms about individual freedoms/rights Unnecessary monitoring of drivers – including older adult drivers Contribute to a reduction in freedom for older adults Contribute to lack of trust in older adult drivers Contributing to a culture of over-intrusive assessments/monitoring impacting on morale and dignity Older adults using cars/e-cars and not public transport or ride shares – impact on transport behavior and sustainability (carbon emissions)
6	Unknowns	Contribute to a reduction in freedom for older adults Contribute to lack of trust in older adult drivers Contributing to a culture of over-intrusive assessments/monitoring impacting on morale and dignity

- Stepped level automation (not full automation)
- Sensors capture data about physical and emotional/psychological state
- Smart sensors to monitor vital signs
- Include functionality to call emergency services if serious health event detected

5.6   Data Ethics

This proposed system must uphold an older adult's rights in relation to the protection of personal information (i.e. data protection and data sovereignty). The driver is in control of their own data and any decisions about how it is stored and shared with others. Information captured about the person's current health and wellness and driving challenges/events is private and not accessible to other parties. Models and algorithms must avoid bias in terms of model of older adults and specific medical conditions impacting on driving performance.

6 Discussion

Typically, the human factors discipline is concerned with issues around intended use, user interface design and technology acceptability. Arguably, human factors and human machine interaction design research must extend its remit and 'go beyond the user interface'. Specifically, it should address issues pertaining to the psycho-social impact of technology, and how wellbeing, rights and human value/benefit are considered in terms of the design solution.

The specification of benefits is not straightforward. People benefit differently. Also, benefits are not always equal for all people. As driving system that benefits older adults must also benefit other road users and pedestrians. The analysis of relevant health literature and TILDA data has identified specific conditions that impact on older adult driving ability (2019). As such, it has provided an empirical basis for addressing ethical dilemmas around whether full automation is an appropriate solution to effectively managing the conflict between two goals – namely, (1) promoting driver persistence and (2) ensuring road safety.

It is argued that the three levels of driver assistance represent an ethically aligned solution to enabling older drivers to continue driving, even if there is a risk of a serious accident given their medical background. Evidently, some medical conditions do not negatively impact on safe driving. However, there are other conditions that pose challenges to safe driving, and others still that make it unsafe to drive. The proposed solution is designed to directly address this fact– to promote driver persistence and enablement in these different circumstances, albeit while simultaneously maintaining safety.

The proposed system maintains the autonomy of the individual. In principle, the driver can choose (and/or switch off) task support and advanced levels of automation, if they so choose. As such, the starting point for the system concept is an engaged older adult driver (i.e. older adult who has capacity and ability). In this way, the system supports a vision of the older adult driver as 'in control'. The role of the driver is to work in partnership with the 'co-pilot', to achieve a safe and enjoyable drive. Critically, the system treats the driver as 'capable' and 'in charge' unless it detects that the driver is incapacitated and/or there is a potential for a safety critical event (i.e. level 3 assistance/safety critical intervention). If the system detects that the driver is in a seriously impaired state and/or incapacitated, or that a safety critical event is imminent, then the principle of 'driver autonomy' is outweighed by that of safety. In such cases, authority moves to 'automation'. As such, our vision of 'technology progress' is closely intertwined with concepts of progress from a societal values perspective (i.e. how we think about ageing and how we value the participation of older adults in society – including enabling older adult mobility).

The initial concept requires further elaboration and specification. In line with a human factors approach, a series of co-design and evaluation sessions will be undertaken with end users. In addition, the proposed solution will be evaluated in using a driving simulator. A health event cannot be induced as part of a driving simulation exercise. However, we can evaluate the overall concept, driver responses and the usability of specific driver input/output communication mechanisms.

The HFEC requires further development and iteration. Participatory evaluation of ethical issues and principles to consider will be undertaken with stakeholders (Steps 3 & 4). Moreover, the HFEC requires further consideration of ethical issues as part of implementation and evaluation research. This step will require completion and will generate a further iteration of step 7 of the HFEC.

Assisted driving solutions are evidently very positive in relation to promoting positive ageing and older adult mobility and social participation. However, potential negative impacts such as the impact on travel models and transport decisions must be considered. Further research is required in relation to understanding how environmental impacts might be considered. Potentially, these concepts could be extended in relation to a consideration of car-pools and ride shares.

7 Conclusions

Design/technology teams exercise choice in relation to what is valued and advancing technology that improves the human condition (and not worsens it). Technologies need to positively contribute to human wellbeing and our lived experience.

Overall, it is argued that the specification of an ethics canvas as part of a broader human factors design approach ensures that ethical issues are considered. Although valuable, the existing ethics canvases require further emphasis on framing the problem, specifying the psychosocial dimensions and impacts of new technologies and addressing specific stakeholder/end user requirements and impacts. The HFEC supports the production and documentation of evidence in relation to addressing the human and ethical dimensions of future technologies and their potential impacts (including both positive and negative impacts). The HFEC is employed as one strand of HF method. This is not a stand-alone method and requires integration with other HF methodologies.

Arguably, existing high automation approaches do not support positive ageing. Intelligent assisted driving solutions must put the human at the center and consider benefits in relation to the three pillars of human wellbeing.

The proposed driving assistance solution has emerged from an analysis of certain ethical principles in relation to the goals and needs of specific older adult drivers (i.e. personae) in different situations (i.e. scenarios). The driving solution (i.e. car, sensor system, co-pilot and HMI) is designed to optimize the abilities and participation of older adults. That is, it recognizes what older adults can do as opposed to focusing on declining capacities. The proposed technology supports continued and safe driving for all adults, including those adults at risk of limiting their driving and/or giving up when there is no medical/physical reason for doing so.

Appendix 1: Scenarios and Personae

See Table 7.

Table 7. Scenarios & personae

#	Interpretation challenge	Scenario	Profile	Personae
IC1	Task support/feedback	Driver needs assistance with parking	2. Older adults who regulate their driving in relation to managing specific driving challenges and/or stressful (difficult) driving situations (perceived safety risk or complexity)	Mary
IC2	Activation/"Flow"	Flow	4: Continuing drivers: older adults who have continued to drive with a progressing condition, but have concerns in relation to medical fitness to drive and are at risk of giving up	Sarah/James
		Stress	5. Older adults who are currently driving and at risk of sudden disabling/medical event	Louise
		Intelligent driving	2. Older adults who regulate their driving in relation to managing specific driving challenges and/or stressful (difficult) driving situations (perceived safety risk or complexity)	Mary
IC3	Fatigue & drowsiness	Fatigue	1. Older adults in optimal health and driving as normal	Elizabeth/Sam
IC4	Distraction & concurrent task management	Distraction	2: Older adults who regulate their driving in relation to managing specific driving challenges and/or stressful (difficult) driving situations (perceived safety risk or complexity)	Tom
		Concurrent task management	3: Older adults who are currently driving but have a medical condition that impacts on their ability to drive	Richard
IC5	Intoxication – alcohol/drugs/related medical conditions	Alcohol	1. Older adults in optimal health and driving as normal	James
		Prescription drugs	5. Older adults who are currently driving and at risk of sudden disabling/medical event	Rory
IC6	Heart attack/stroke	Heart attack	5. Older adults who are currently driving and at risk of sudden disabling/medical event	Brian
		Stroke	5. Older adults who are currently driving and at risk of sudden disabling/medical event	Louise

References

1. Rowe, J.W., Kahn, R.L.: Successful Aging. Pantheon Books, New York (1988)
2. Road Safety Authority. Medical Fitness to drive Guidelines. http://www.rsa.ie/Documents/Licensed%20Drivers/Medical_Issues/Sláinte_agus_Tiomáint_Medical_Fitness_to_Drive_Guidelines.pdf. Accessed 22 Jan 2020
3. Charlton, J., et al.: Influence of chronic illness on crash involvement of motor vehicle drivers: 2nd edition (No. 300). MUARC (Monash University Accident Research Centre), Victoria, Australia (2010)
4. Marshall, S.C.: The role of reduced fitness to drive due to medical impairments in explaining crashes involving older drivers. Traffic Inj. Prev. **9**(4), 291–298 (2008). https://doi.org/10.1080/15389580801895244
5. Thrun, S.: Toward robotic cars. Commun. ACM **53**(4), 99–106 (2010). https://doi.org/10.1145/1721654.1721679
6. National Highway Traffic Safety Administration. Preliminary statement of policy concerning automated vehicles. http://www.nhtsa.gov/staticfiles/rulemaking/pdf/Automated_Vehicles_Policy.pdf. Accessed 22 Jan 2020
7. IEEE: Ethically Aligned Design, A Vision for Prioritizing Human Well-being with Autonomous and Intelligent Systems. First Edition (EAD1e). https://ethicsinaction.ieee.org/. Accessed 22 Jan 2020
8. Kyriakidis, M., Happee, R., De Winter, J.C.F.: Public opinion on automated driving: results of an international questionnaire among 5,000 respondents. Transp. Res. Part F Traffic Psychol. Behav. **32**, 127–140 (2015)
9. Gasser, Westhoff: BASt-study: definitions of automation and legal issues in Germany (2012)
10. Cahill, J.: Human Factors & Ethics Canvas: A White Paper. https://www.tcd.ie/cihs/projects/hfaecanvas.php. Accessed 22 Jan 2020
11. Cousins, J.B., Whitmore, E., Shulha, L.: Arguments for a common set of principles for collaborative inquiry in evaluation. Am. J. Eval. **34**, 7–22 (2013)
12. Wenger, E.: Communities of Practice: Learning, Meaning, and Identity. Cambridge University Press, Cambridge (1998)
13. Pruitt, J., Grudin, J.: Personas: practice and theory. In: Proceedings of the 2003 Conference on Designing for User Experiences (DUX 2003), pp. 1–15. ACM, New York (2003). http://dx.doi.org/10.1145/997078.997089
14. Carroll, J.M.: Scenario-Based Design: Envisioning Work and Technology in System Development. Wiley, New York (1995)
15. Beever, J., Brightman, A.O.: Reflexive principlism as an effective approach for developing ethical reasoning in engineering. Sci. Eng. Ethics (2015). https://doi.org/10.1007/s11948-015-9633-5
16. Reijers, W., et al.: Methods for practising ethics in research and innovation: a literature review, critical analysis and recommendations. Sci. Eng. Ethics **24**(5), 1437–1481 (2017). https://doi.org/10.1007/s11948-017-9961-8
17. Brey, P.: Ethics of emerging technologies. In: Hansson, S.O. (ed.) Methods for the Ethics of Technology. Rowman and Littlefield International (2017)

Investigations on Monitoring Sensor Usage and Decision-Making: A Case Study in an Elderly Care Facility

Isamu Kajitani[✉] ⓘ, Keiko Homma, and Yoshio Matsumoto

National Institute of Advanced Industrial Science and Technology,
Kashiwa, Chiba 2770882, Japan
isamu.kajitani@aist.go.jp

Abstract. This paper discusses the usage of a robotic monitoring device and decision-making by staffers at a care facility. The target monitoring device is a commercial product (Silhouette Monitoring Sensor, King Tsushin Kogyo Co., Ltd.) that monitors a person on a bed through silhouette images. We conducted research at a care facility before and after it started using the monitoring device, and recorded device operations and alert outputs over a three-month period. We conducted interviews in meetings to understand the decision-making processes of the staff. Through these interviews and by studying data logs on the device we detected changes in the usage of the device and leaned the reason for the changes.

Keywords: Monitoring device usage · Decision-making · Elderly care

1 Introduction

Demographic data [1] show that the ratio of people over 65 years old in Japan has already exceeded 28.1% of the total population (i.e., 1 in every 4 persons). On the other hand, the child population (0–14 years old) decreased to 12.2% of the total population. This means that the productive-age population (15–64 years old) accounted for just 59.7% of the entire population. Japan is facing a severe shortage in the productive-age population, which could lead to a reduction in the quality of nursing and care services for older adults; therefore, robot technologies are expected to be utilized increasingly in such services.

To deal with the issue, the Ministry of Economy, Trade and Industry (METI) and the Ministry of Health, Labour and Welfare (MHLW) worked together to formulate six priority areas [2, 3] in an aging society in which robots are expected to be utilized. They are: (1) transferring support (wearable/non-wearable), (2) mobility support (outdoor/indoor/wearable), (3) toileting support, (4) bathing support, (5) monitoring (care facility/private home) and communication, and (6) care service support. For these priority areas, there are many research and development projects [4, 5] looking to utilize such robot technologies in the elderly care field.

In these research and development activities, attempts have been made to ascertain the effects of the developed devices, and we can find the results in several reports [6, 7]

© Springer Nature Switzerland AG 2020
V. G. Duffy (Ed.): HCII 2020, LNCS 12198, pp. 521–530, 2020.
https://doi.org/10.1007/978-3-030-49904-4_38

on these projects; however, there is little academic research output. Even in the project reports, there are no detailed explanations as to how the devices were used. It is, therefore, difficult for the target users to understand the validity of the confirmed effects.

Most of these developed devices are new category products, so there is no widely accepted usage of the devices. This can be compared to medicine with unclear dosage and administration. Under such conditions, we consider that it is too early to discuss the effect of the devices; and instead appropriate usage should be discussed at this stage.

To deal with the appropriate usage of the device, the following two points need to be discussed. Firstly, current usage of the device; and secondly, how the users made their decisions, before and after they started to use the device. No research has been conducted to investigate both the usage and related decision-making, so it is worthwhile to investigate these points.

When the current usage of a device is investigated by human observers, it places a heavy mental burden on the device users. In addition to this, it might be possible for the users to use the device to a greater extent or differently than usual, which will affect the result of the research. This relates to the well-known phenomenon of the Hawthorne Effect. We, therefore, decided to use commercial products, which have a logging function to record users' operations or alert outputs, so as to avoid direct observation in this work. The primary purpose of this work is to discuss the possibility of estimating device usage from their recorded logger data sets.

The target robot care device is a robotic monitoring device (Silhouette Monitoring Sensor, King Tsushin Kogyo Co., Ltd.), which was developed during a five-year national project [4, 5] launched in 2013 for the development of assistive robots in priority areas. This product monitors a person on a bed through silhouette images, and operation logs and alert outputs are recorded in an installed memory card [8].

The usage of the device is dependent on decision-making on the part of the user. An understanding of the device function, target users and safety of the device ought to play a central role in making such decisions; however, there were no previous studies conducted to investigate the level of understanding of the users when they made decisions. In this study, we also explore the levels of user understanding with respect to device function, target users and safety (residual risk); in addition to investigating how users made their decisions.

We conducted interviews in monthly meetings at the target care facility. The first interview was conducted prior to the start of use of the monitoring device. In this meeting, the possibility of using the new monitoring device was discussed. After use of the monitoring device started, we conducted interviews three times during the monthly meetings over a three-month period.

Even if we were to just use the logger data, we could detect any changes in device usage pattern, but it would be difficult to know the reason for the change. But if we combine the logger data with the results from the interviews conducted in the monthly meetings, we can determine the reason for the change. For example, we found a clear reduction in the number of operations during the three months. This type of reduction in operation might be regarded as users simply refusing to use the device; however, from the interview results, we determined the cause of the reduction was due to a better understanding of the characteristics of appropriate target usage of the system, and users thus deciding to limit the usage of the monitoring device.

In the rest of the paper, as the background to this work, we summarize previous studies on the monitoring of the elderly, and show the importance of the purpose of the monitoring. Appropriate selection of technology candidates is also an important factor, but we do not have many commercial products. Next, the method of our investigations and the results of the work are presented, before concluding this paper.

2 Background

This paper focuses on a monitoring system for elderly people; therefore, with respect to the background of this paper, we discuss the monitoring of elderly people in terms of necessity and resent research activities.

Monitoring literally means "to observe someone carefully for a period of time under a clear purpose," which determines target behavior or the situation of the observation. Observation frequency depends on the purpose, as well. Response actions to monitored behavior or the situation ought to be decided beforehand.

The main purpose of monitoring elderly people is not to restrict their freedom, but to keep them safe while they go about their daily activities. If they are in an unsafe situation, we cannot give them permission to act freely as they want. This means that maintaining a safe situation is important in maintaining the target person's independence and dignity in living, therefore, we stress the safety of elderly people.

The most fundamental way to monitor target elderly people is direct visual observation, which means that someone stays in the same space with the target people and observes directly on the spot. If it is possible, it is surely the most reliable monitoring method; however, this requires almost the same number of observers as the number of target elderly people.

The alternative is to use an indirect or a remote monitoring system, which enables one to observe someone from a distant place or a different room. A basic remote monitoring system consists of: (1) data acquisition system, (2) data processing system, (3) end terminal, and (4) communication network [9]. Some recent system have a function to (5) store data sets of monitored behavior or situation (See Fig. 1).

(1) Recently, there are a large number of acquisition system candidates. Some systems include a function to sense essential vital signs such as an electrocardiogram or heart rates, as well as video images of the target persons. The sensor technology varies from sensors attached to the body (with-contact) to ambient sensors attached to the environment (contactless). The with-contact system has advantages in that it enables stable sensing; however, it has disadvantages in that it can be uncomfortable, or that it places restrictions on target users daily activities. For its part, the contactless system does not require direct contact with the body, which might cause discomfort; but the downside is that the system might be affected by external circumstances, such as sunlight for the video system. The technology used in such data acquisition systems has been summarized in several review articles. For example, in [10], inertial sensors, footswitches, pressure sensors,

physiological sensors, and GPS sensors; and in [11], with respect to contactless sensors, passive infrared (PIR) sensors, video sensors, sound sensors, floor sensors, and radar sensors are listed. Combinations of contactless sensors and with-contact (wearable) sensors are also explained in [11]. Each technology has its merits and demerits, so the users of the monitoring system are required to select an appropriate technology or combination of technologies for the purpose of monitoring.

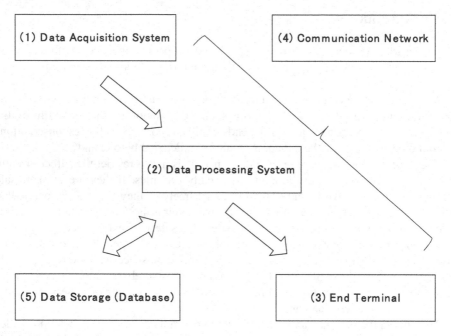

Fig. 1. Schematic of basic monitoring system, which consists of: (1) data acquisition system, (2) data processing system, (3) end terminal, (4) communication network, and (5) data storage (database).

(2) The data processing system receives output data from the data acquisition system, and processes the acquired data to recognize the target behaviors or situations by the use of algorithms appropriate for the purpose. To process the acquired data, the user is required to set some parameters to fit the monitoring purpose. Such parameters might be required for the data acquisition system as well. Examples of these parameters include thresholds to the output of the sensing device and the frequency of monitoring. After being processed, outputs of this system are transmitted to the end terminal.

(3) The end terminal is a personal computer or a smartphone at the place of the observer, who receives the processed data and makes decisions with respect to the next actions to keep the target elderly person safe.

(4) The communication network connects these components. The wireless communication network is relatively convenient; but it has the possibility of being affected by connection problems, which reduces the reliability of the system.

(5) The data storage stores the monitoring, such as monitored behaviors or situations, and the times of the behaviors or when the situations happened.

As mentioned before, the user needs to select an appropriate combination of these elements; however, we have limited candidates of commercial products. We, therefore, have to try those products that are on the market to find the appropriate product and the appropriate usage of the product to fit the monitoring purpose.

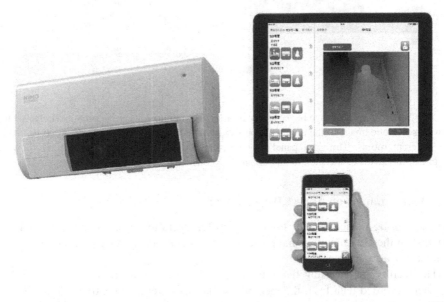

Fig. 2. Photograph of the monitoring sensor product (Silhouette Monitoring Sensor, King Tsushin Kogyo Co., Ltd.). Left is the sensor unit, and the right images show the applications on a smartphone and a tablet. (Photos courtesy of the company)

3 Methods

The target robot care device is a robotic monitoring device (Silhouette Monitoring Sensor, King Tsushin Kogyo Co., Ltd.) (See Fig. 2, Fig. 3).

This study was approved by the Institutional Review Board on Ergonomic Research of the National Institute of Advanced Industrial Science and Technology. The investigation was carried out in a long-term care facility in Tokyo with the approval of the facility manager. Necessary information regarding the investigation was given and informed consent was obtained from each participant before starting the investigations.

The monitoring sensor device has a logger function to record user operations or alert outputs. The device itself has a function to record video images of the target elderly person on a bed, when the alert occurred and predetermined timing. However, we could not use video images in this work, because the Institutional Review Board did not approve video usage.

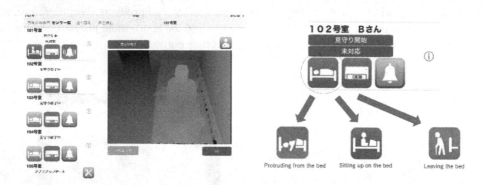

Fig. 3. Captured screen image of the application of the monitoring sensor product (Left), which shows a silhouette image of the monitored person on a bed, along with listed monitored results of four different rooms. The right panel explains that the leftmost of the three icons shows a recognized behavior of the monitored person. (Screen images courtesy of the company)

3.1   Investigations on Target Device Usage

The monitoring device records each user staffer operation, such as the start and termination of the alert function, and power switch operation. Alert outputs and responses to the alerts also are recorded.

The facility started using five sets of monitoring systems on August 4, 2019. We collected recorded data from the memory cards on November 8, 2019.

3.2   Investigations on Device Users' Decision-Making

We conducted interviews in monthly meetings at the target long-term care facility, as mentioned in the previous section. The first interview was conducted prior to the start of use of the monitoring device on July 9, 2019. In this meeting, seven lead staffers and the facility manager discussed the possibility of using the new monitoring device. At the end of the meeting, we asked them about the following:

(1) Levels of understanding (1: worst – 5: best)

  - Monitoring device functions
  - Expected characteristics of the target elderly people
  - Residual risk of the monitoring device

(2) Presence of appropriate target elderly people in the facility (present/absent)
(3) The criteria for selecting the target elderly people

(4) Expectations to use the monitoring device on the target elderly people
(5) Decision-making (Use the device/do not use the device/others).

Use of the device started on August 4, 2019. After the facility started using the device, we conducted interviews three times during the monthly meetings over a three-month period (September 4, October 8, November 8, 2019). In these meeting, the users mostly talked about their findings regarding usage of the monitoring device. At the end of the meeting, we asked about the following:

(1) Levels of understanding (1: worst − 5: best)

- Monitoring device functions
- Expected characteristics of the target elderly people
- Residual risk of the monitoring device

(2) Changes in their work procedures, and the reason for the change.
(3) Change in their ideas with respect to the properties of appropriate target elderly people, and the reason for the changes.
(4) If a user or the facility decided to completely stop or temporarily suspend the usage of the device, the reason for stopping or suspending usage of the device.

4   Results

4.1   Investigations on Target Device Usage

The left image in Fig. 4 shows the distribution of the times (hours) when the facility staffers started and ended operations of the alert function over a three-month period. This graph shows that a large percentage of start-end operations were conducted late at night or early morning. Figure 5 shows the distribution of duration times (minutes) for each period in which the alert function was activated. We can see that short durations of monitoring occurred a lot of the time. These results indicate that short monitoring periods frequently occurred, and it is possible that these short monitoring troubled the staffers. We cannot determine the reason for these short monitoring periods solely from the logger data sets.

Figure 5 shows the distribution of the number of alert start events in one day. At the beginning of the investigation in August, the number of alert activations was high, but the number decreased in the following months. Note that they did not turn off the power of the system, which means that they can watch the video image from the end terminal device.

4.2   Investigations into Device Users' Decision-Making

Table 1 shows the averaged levels of understanding to each question. The number of participants in the four meetings was 7, 7, 5 and 7, respectively. At the first meeting, which was before using the monitoring device, the number of answers was relatively low; however, they decided to use the monitoring sensor.

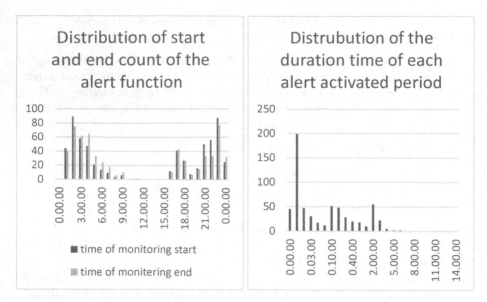

Fig. 4. The graph on the left shows the time (hours) distribution of start and end count of the alert function, and the graph on the right shows the count of duration period (minutes) for each alert-activated monitoring period.

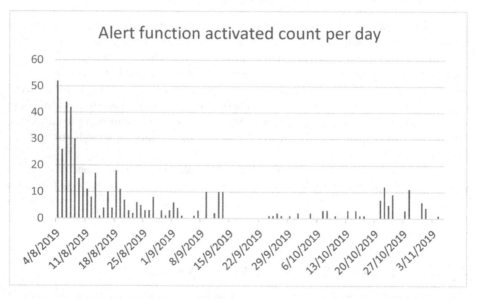

Fig. 5. Distribution in number of alert-activated monitorings per day.

In the subsequent meetings, which were held after the start of use of the monitoring device, their levels of understandings improved. This indicates that the facility staff had learned about the monitoring device through actually using the device.

Table 1. Averaged levels of understanding of the staffers obtained in the meetings.

	Levels of understanding		
	Monitoring device functions	Expected characteristics of target elderly people	Residual risk of monitoring device
2019/07/09	3.571428571	3.5	2.857142857
2019/09/04	3.285714286	3.857142857	4.142857143
2019/10/08	4.2	4.2	4.0
2019/11/08	4.333333333	4.0	4.0

At the second meeting, which was the first meeting after the introduction of the device, the facility staff said they had the impression that the device issued alerts too frequently. At this point, by asking about the details of the alerts, we found that they had not changed the parameters to fit the target elderly persons. We, therefore, advised them to consult the company about providing lessons on appropriate parameter settings. At the next meeting, they mentioned that the frequency of alerts had been reduced.

Figure 5 shows that the number of monitoring device usages decreased; therefore we asked the reason for the change in usage. The answer we received was that the facility staff mostly used the monitoring device only for remote cameras, which enabled them to monitor the target elderly persons from a different room. The staff said that they had found the best advantage of using the device in their case was that they could assign a priority to a situation by watching a remote monitored video image, and so they did not use the alert function of the system.

In the final meeting; however, the facility staff said that their usage of the device, which was to use the device for a remote camera, created some confusions with respect to the privacy of the monitored elderly persons. There have already been some discussions on the ethics of monitoring in elderly care facilities, and in the United States, some states have regulation governing the use of camera devices in care facilities [12]. We need more discussions on the ethics of such monitoring products.

5 Conclusions

Both the monitoring of elderly people and support by caregivers are important in the coming days in our country. Remote monitoring robots, which have the ability to recognize a target person's behavior are one of the key expected solutions to this issue. This work is limited to an investigation conducted in one elderly care facility, but we could see that the usage of such devices is not limited to the way the maker company expected. Our findings suggest that determining the appropriate usage of newly developed products is a key factor in the success of the effective usage of the device. As a matter of fact, some previous works have stressed the importance of "re-invention," which has the potential to accelerate the acceptance speed of newly developed products [13].

References

1. Bureau, S.: The Statistical Handbook of Japan 2019. Ministry of Internal Affairs and Communications (2019)
2. METI Joint Press Release with the Ministry of Health, Labour and Welfare, Revision of the Four Priority Areas to Which Robot Technology is to be Introduced in Nursing Care of the Elderly. https://www.meti.go.jp/english/press/2014/0203_02.html. Accessed 27 Dec 2019
3. METI Press Release: Revision of the Priority Areas to Which Robot Technology is to be Introduced in Nursing Care. https://www.meti.go.jp/english/press/2017/1012_002.html. Accessed 27 Dec 2019
4. Hirohisa, H.: Overview of robotic devices for nursing care project. Stud. Health Technol. Inform. **2017**(242), 449–456 (2017)
5. Hirohisa, H.: Robotic devices for nursing care project. J. Robot. Soc. Jpn. **34**, 228–231 (2016). https://doi.org/10.7210/jrsj.34.228
6. MHLW Homepage for Care Robot Promotion Projects. https://www.mhlw.go.jp/stf/seisakunitsuite/bunya/0000209634.html. Accessed 27 Dec 2019
7. Tokyo Bureau of Social Welfare and Public Health Homepage for Care Robot Promotion Projects. http://www.fukushihoken.metro.tokyo.jp/smph/kourei/shisaku/jisedaikaigo/robot model.html. Accessed 27 Dec 2019
8. Silhouette Monitoring Sensor (King Tsushin Kogyo Co., Ltd.) in Robotic Care Devices Portal. http://robotcare.jp/en/development/06_19.php. Accessed 27 Dec 2019
9. Malasinghe, L.P., Ramzan, N., Dahal, K.: Remote patient monitoring: a comprehensive study. J. Ambient Intell. Hum. Comput. **10**, 57–76 (2019). https://doi.org/10.1007/s12652-017-0598-x
10. Lowe, S.A., ÓLaighin, G.: Monitoring human health behaviour in one's living environment: A technological review. Med. Eng. Phy. **36**(2), 147–168 (2014)
11. Uddin, M.Z., Khaksar, W., Torresen, J.: Ambient sensors for elderly care and independent living: A survey. Sensors **18**(7), 2027 (2018). https://doi.org/10.3390/s18072027
12. Berridge, C., Halpern, J., Levy, K.: Cameras on beds: The ethics of surveillance in nursing home rooms. AJOB Empirical Bioeth. **10**(1), 55–62 (2019)
13. Rice, R.E., Rogers, E.M.: Reinvention in the innovation process. Knowledge **1**(4), 499–514 (1980)

Verifying the Usefulness of Monitoring Sensors Used by Caregivers in Nursing Homes

Yasuko Kitajima[1(✉)] [iD], Isamu Kajitani[2] [iD], Mitsuhiro Nakamura[2],
Keiko Homma[2], Yoshio Matsumoto[2], and Jukai Maeda[1]

[1] Faculty of Nursing, Tokyo Ariake University of Medical and Health Sciences,
2-9-1 Ariake, Koto-ku, Tokyo 135-0063, Japan
{kitajima, jukai}@tau.ac.jp
[2] National Institute of Advanced Industrial Science and Technology,
Kashiwa, Chiba 277-0882, Japan
{isamu.kajitani, keiko.homma,
yoshio.matsumoto}@aist.go.jp, m-nakamura@tau.ac.jp

Abstract. Japan has become a rapidly aging country with a 21% rate of aging as of 2007. Everyone would like to have a situation where the elderly can live their daily lives without trouble. However, the elderly are more apt to develop health problems, and there are more than a few elderly who need care. As the elderly increase as a percentage of the total population, the issue of their care continues to arise. Furthermore, as the number of elderly who need care increases, the lack of caregivers able to deliver that care becomes an issue. Under these conditions, we need to relieve the burden on caregivers who are always short-handed at care facilities, and to make sure that the facilities the care receivers are using are safe. We will report on monitoring sensors that allow caregivers to watch out for the elderly living in care facilities. The purpose of this research is to verify the usefulness of the existing monitoring sensor aids. As the Watch Over Sensor (WOS-114N) by King Tsushin Kogyo Co., Ltd. monitored people living in a care facility, we gathered data and analyzed that data both quantitatively and qualitatively. The monitoring sensors are installed in the rooms of people living in the care facility who need monitoring, so that the movements of the person can be viewed. Data can be sent to the caregiver's cellphone, so that while they are tending to another person, the caregiver can check on the image of the other care receiver. As a result, by using the monitoring sensors, it is suggested that the burden on the caregiver is lessened while contributing to enhanced safety of the person living in the facility. However, a large amount of noise has been detected through the data. By checking the appearance of noise at the same time as the accumulated video data, it became clear that there was a problem with the environment in which the monitoring sensors were installed. Also, because the caregivers were not familiar with how to use the sensors, it was suggested that the original monitoring system may not have been used properly. The results show that even if existing nursing-care equipment is commercially available, the maximization of its abilities depends on the people closest to it at the nursing care facility continually checking on the efficacy of the product. Only showing the proper way to use it to the caregivers at the facility, there are possibilities of wrong usage or barriers for the proper usage that developers won't be able to find. Also, even if you explain the system

© Springer Nature Switzerland AG 2020
V. G. Duffy (Ed.): HCII 2020, LNCS 12198, pp. 531–546, 2020.
https://doi.org/10.1007/978-3-030-49904-4_39

to the caregivers, it should be assumed that these people who are busy day after day may not have time to deeply read the manual. It is necessary to think of a different and easy-to-understand way of explaining the method for using the equipment. abstract should summarize the contents of the paper in short terms, i.e. 150–250 words.

Keywords: Monitoring sensors · Elderly care facility · Lighten the burden on the caregivers

1   Introduction

A society is considered to be aging when the percentage of its population who are 65 or older passes 7%. And when that percentage exceeds 14%, the society is considered to be rapidly aging. When it passes 21%, it is considered a super-aging society. In 2018, our country's total population was 126,440,000, and the number of people 65 or older was 35.58 million, which corresponds to 28.1% of the total population. Our country is a super-aging society, and the percentage of people 65 or older will continue to rise. It is estimated to peak in 2042. According to the report "Estimated Future Population of Japan" that the National Institute of Population and Social Security Research Center published in April 2017, the country is in a long-term population decline, and as the overall population declines, those who are 65 and older continues to increase, meaning the ratio of elderly to the total population will continue to rise. By 2036, the ratio of the elderly is expected to reach 33.3% and rise to 38.4% by 2065 [1].

The bodies of elderly people experience physical decline due to aging. Even a trivial matter can end up sending an elderly person into a nursing care facility. In 2016, the average life expectancy in Japan, a country of long lifespans, was 80.98 years for men and 87.14 years for women. However, health problems that affect everyday living mean that as of 2016, men could live normally without restrictions for 72.14 years on average, while women could do so for 74.79 years on average [2]. The gap between life expectancy and healthy life expectancy indicates the amount of time someone is living without good health and with limits on their everyday life. For men, the span of living without good health is 8.84 years. For women it is 12.35 years. Of course, the level of ill health varies greatly from person to person, but within that group, the group of people needing care is included.

The rate of aging is on the rise, as is the ratio of elderly to the total population, which brings up the issue of taking care of the elderly. Because it will be necessary to increase the number of facilities that can accommodate elderly people needing care, it will also be necessary to increase the number of people who can work in those facilities. In 2018, the ratio of job openings to job applicants across all types of work was 1.45 times, and the ratio for caregiving-related work was 3.90 times. The ratio for caregiving was about 2.7 times more than the ratio for all jobs, setting a high bar [3]. According to the Survey of Care Workers published for fiscal 2018 by the nonprofit

Care Work Foundation, there is a shortage of workers engaged in caregiving services. According to the fiscal 2018 survey, 67.2% of the caregivers said they felt that there was a shortage of workers [4]. In the 2013 survey, 56.5% of workers said they experienced a shortage of workers. In the five years beginning in 2013, the rate of shortage continued to increase. In these circumstances, Japan has been trying to compensate by hiring foreigners, but since the percentage of elderly will continue to rise for quite a while, there will be a lot of obstacles in the effort to find sufficient staffing. The Ministry of Health, Labor, and Welfare has been supporting the development and usage of assistive technology and robotics [5]. The aim is to give autonomy to the care receivers, and to lighten the burden on caregivers.

This research focuses on the preservation of safety for care receivers and the lightening of the burden on caregivers, and reports on the monitoring sensors to observe the elderly in nursing care facilities on behalf of the caregivers. Of the elderly in nursing care facilities, some may take abnormal actions and fall from their bed because of dementia or a decline in physical functions. To keep these elderly people from injuring themselves and getting in accidents, caregivers must keep an eye on them, but because they are serving several care receivers at one time, it is not possible to keep an active watch on every individual. If they look away and something happens, there is a danger that they may not be able to protect the safety of the people in the care facility. This is not something that is out of the ordinary. As we know from the way the caregivers feel the effects of the labor shortage mentioned previously, there is a big burden placed on caregivers working at nursing care facilities. This research looks at the effectiveness of monitoring sensors as a way to lessen the strain on both care receivers and caregivers. Up till now, to prevent residents from falling or to detect abnormal behavior, mat sensors [6], bed sensors [7], infrared sensors [8], clip sensors [9] have been used, but all of them have their strong and weak points. Use of these sensors alone cannot assure the safety of the care receivers. In this survey, the Watch Over Sensor (WOS-114N) by King Tsushin Kogyo Co., Ltd. (referred to as "monitoring sensor" hereinafter) is used. These sensors have been placed in multiple nursing care facilities and used to help caregivers monitor care receivers, to verify their usefulness. In detail, we gathered data from the monitoring sensors used on residents of the nursing-care facility, then analyzed that data both quantitatively and qualitatively. By using the monitoring sensor, it was observed that the caregiver won't have to focus solely on one care receiver, but would be able to assist another person or do other work. But depending on the way the monitoring sensor was used and the environment in which it was used, it is difficult to say whether some of the sensors were being used correctly. Through this survey, not only the usefulness of the monitoring sensor, but also problem areas and points for improvement became clear. In the near future, monitoring sensors that have fixed those problem areas and improvement points will monitor the safety of the care receivers and lighten the burden on the caregivers.

2   Method

2.1   Outline

Monitoring sensors have been placed in many nursing-care facilities, and we had the caregivers use the monitoring sensors on the selected care receivers during the survey period. We saved all the data gathered from the monitoring sensors. After the survey period, we analyzed all the data and sorted the places where the sensors were working correctly and where they were not. Then we considered the places where the monitors were not working correctly.

2.2   Survey Period

The period for our research was for 12 months, from 18/12/2018 through 8/1/2020.

2.3   Recording Procedure

In our research, we used the Watch Over Sensor (WOS-114N) by King Tsushin Kogyo Co., Ltd. and gathered data throughout the survey period.

   In our research, sensors were placed in the care receivers' rooms, so that the actions of those people could be observed in real time. However, these monitoring sensors did not use surveillance cameras. In consideration of the care receivers' privacy, their actions were recorded in silhouette, and their movements were able to be viewed. In other words, to observe the care receivers' movements, the monitor showed shadowy figures that made it difficult to identify specific individuals. These silhouette figures looked the same during the day and night through the monitor, which meant there was no restriction on the timing of their usage. Other characteristics are described below (Fig. 1).

   The actions of the subject being monitored could be detected and broken down into different categories such as (1) getting up, (2) jutting out, (3) getting out of bed, (4) standing up, and (5) no movement, and an alarm could go off (Fig. 2). Because of this, the caregiver would know that the care receiver may fall out of bed and can rush to the care receiver, helping to protect the care receiver's safety. The data sent by the monitoring sensor is transmitted over a wireless LAN in the facility and sent to the caregiver's station or to a tablet or a smartphone. During the monitoring, if an action that sets off an alarm is detected, the alarm will ring, but to make sure whether it is a true emergency, they can check the monitor or the tablet. When the alarm sounds, but when the caregiver checks, he or she sees that it is only the care receiver turning in bed, the caregiver can tend to a higher priority care receiver first (Fig. 3). Also, because all of the data can be stored, the caregiver can look back at the actions of the care receiver that were missed. This will help in grasping the characteristics of each care receiver's daily life. Our survey used the data saved for this function.

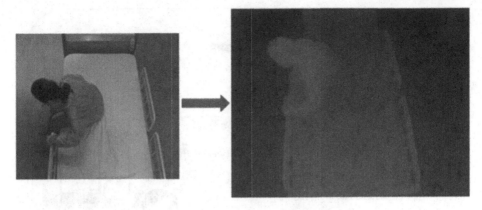

Fig. 1. Actions are recorded in silhouette.

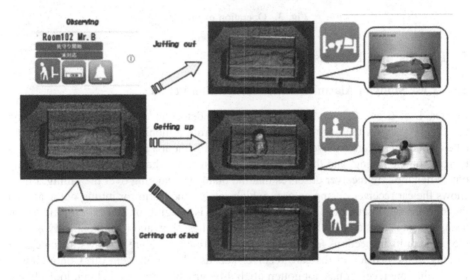

Fig. 2. The actions of the subject being monitored could be detected.

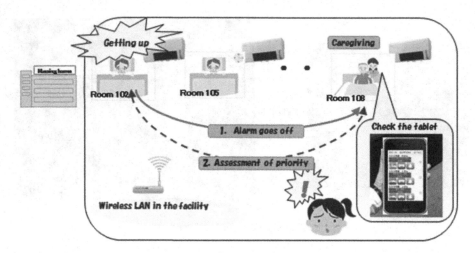

Fig. 3. Operation example.

3 Results and Discussion

3.1 Case Study of Alarms During Observation Period

Figures 4, 5, 6 and 7 indicate video for actual detection of jutting out and getting up. Figure 4 shows the beginning of the video from a monitoring sensor observing a care receiver. The care receiver is lying on the bed without a problem, but the blanket is hanging on the railing, and the alarm went off detecting what it thought to be a jutting out. When the care receiver observes that the blanket is hanging over the railing, Fig. 5 shows the car receiver raising an arm, which sets off the alarm for jutting out again. At the start of the observation, because the blanket is hanging on the railing, the monitoring sensor senses that the height reflects the highest spot, and it automatically adjusts the range of its inspections for jutting out and getting up. Figure 6 shows the caregiver coming to the bedside of the care receiver because the alarm went off. Continuing to Fig. 7, the care receiver has not gotten up, but by grabbing the blanket that looks like it is going to fall, the monitoring sensor detects a getting up action and sounds the alarm. After that, the alarm went off frequently during the night.

Because of detection of jutting out or getting up, the alarm is sounded, and the caregiver can go to the care receiver before she falls out of bed or makes some abnormal movement. Even if a caregiver is looking after several care receivers at the same time, this allows for the care receiver to remain safe. That is one thing that can be said by these series of images. This is the intended usage of the monitoring sensor, but on the other hand, at the start of the observation, the alarm going off unnecessarily may cause problems later for the caregiver. In Fig. 4 at the start of the observation, the care receiver is not engaging in any abnormal actions. But the fact that the alarm continues to go off, but the caregiver does not change its settings shows that in Fig. 5, just by raising an arm, the alarm is set off again. The fact that a care receiver lying on the bed raises an arm is not a particularly dangerous action, but when the alarm goes off, the caregiver has to go to the bedside. The fact that the action is not dangerous, but the alarm still goes off means the caregiver will gradually get used to the situation. The fear is that the caregiver will not come to the bedside. Depending on the condition of the care receiver, it may be necessary to have settings indicating when a person raises their arm. However, as shown in this series of images, it may be necessary for a caregiver to adjust the settings on the alarm to protect the care receiver's safety. That does not happen in this video. It could be because the caregiver does not know how to adjust the settings or that she does not realize that there is a way to adjust the alarm settings on the monitoring sensor. It is necessary to find a method for the caregiver, who does not have spare time to read the manual during work, to quickly and easily understand how to use the sensor.

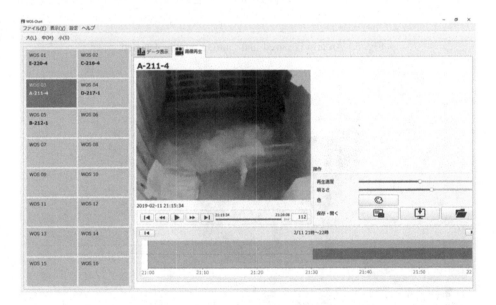

Fig. 4. Beginning point of observation.

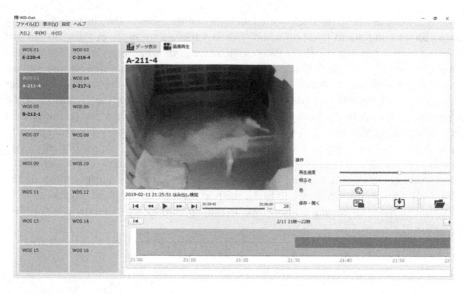

Fig. 5. An arm is raised and "jutting out" is detected.

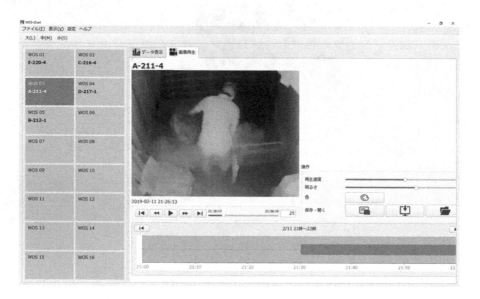

Fig. 6. The caregiver responds.

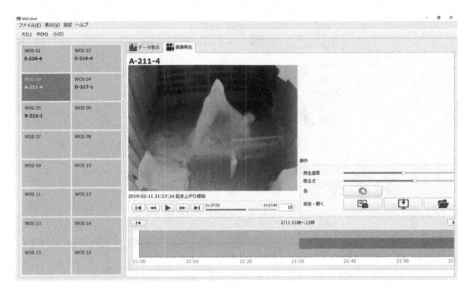

Fig. 7. By raising the blanket, "getting up" is detected.

3.2 Case Study of When Alarm Goes off Unnecessarily Because of the Care Receiver's Movement

In Fig. 8, the observed care receiver does not move, yet "getting up" is detected and the alarm sounds. In the upper left of the Fig. 8 image, there's some interference from a black lump. The monitoring sensor has detected this as the care receiver getting up. The origin of this interference could not be confirmed, but it could be sunlight coming in from the window. In Fig. 9, the care receiver is not in bed, and yet a "getting up" action is detected. This is similar to Fig. 8 in that it looks like the sunlight shining in the window set off the alarm. Looking at the data of this example, we came to understand that as the sunlight shines in at an angle, hitting the window that is being filmed for a short time, creating occasional interference. Even though when confirming the image, it is clear that no one is on the bed, the interference continues to set off the alarm from time to time day and night. The signal to shut off the alarm cannot be found in the data. It's plausible to think that as the alarm continues to go off, it will be neglected or that the alarm will be set so that it cannot be heard. It can be assumed from here that usage of the monitoring sensor could cause an accident. There were also images that were set off as "standing" or "getting up" when a car headlight shone through the window at night. The weak point of the monitoring sensor is that it registers false positives based on rays of light, which means the person installing the monitor must take this into consideration when finding the proper environment to install it. For example, blackout curtains could be used to shut out the interference.

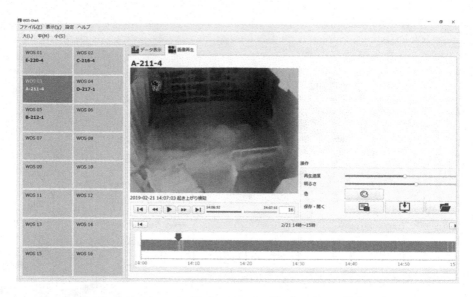

Fig. 8. Interference in the image sets off a "getting up" detection.

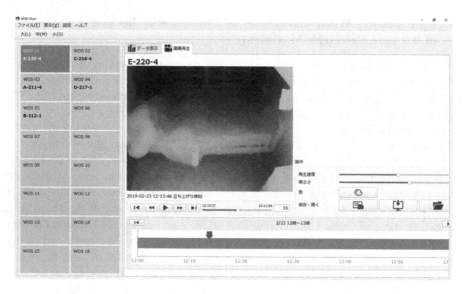

Fig. 9. Interference in the image sets off a "standing up" detection.

3.3 Example of Alarm Sounding for Someone Other Than the Care Receiver

Data acquired from the facility in Fig. 10 shows a translucent partition next to the care receiver's bedside to divide up the room into sections. Looking at Fig. 10, we see the caregiver's reflection in the upper left of the image on the other side of the partition.

The care receiver is lying on the bed without any issues, but the monitoring sensor picks up the image of the caregiver and registers a "getting out of bed" detection. This is not a false positive of the monitoring sensor, but a problem of the environment in which the sensor is set. To eliminate the false positive, the monitoring sensor should be installed as aforementioned explanations on how to avoid environments such as in examples Sects. 3.2 or 3.3.

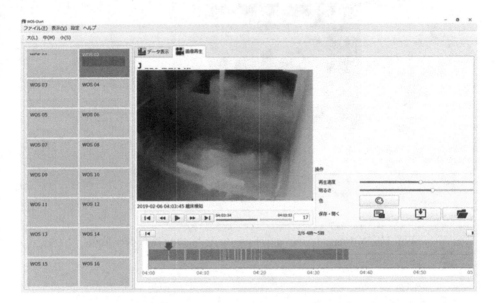

Fig. 10. Caregiver's reflection sets off a "getting out of bed" detection.

3.4 Case Study of Caregiver not Being Sent While Alarm Rings

In the image from Fig. 11, at 4 h 16 min and 40 s, the care receiver gets up in bed and makes a gesture as if searching for footwear on the floor. The monitoring sensor detects a "jutting out" and sounds the alarm, but the caregiver does not visit. Eighteen minutes pass in the images when, at 4 h 34 min and 25 s, the monitoring sensor detects a "getting out of bed" motion and sounds the alarm (Fig. 12). Immediately after that, the caregiver arrives. The reason for the caregiver not coming for a long time despite the alarm sounding is that the caregiver can check the terminal he is caring during work and see why the alarm is sounding. The caregiver can check the smartphone during work to monitor the care receiver. For example, while tending to another care receiver, the alarm goes off and the caregiver can see the images of that care receiver and can make a judgment about the priority of serving the different care receivers. When the caregiver confirmed the images in Fig. 11, the decision was made that it was not an emergency. But after that, when confirming the images of Fig. 12, seeing that it was necessary to rush to the care receiver's bedside, so that she would not fall out of bed, the caregiver was able to act. This is especially useful for caregivers working the night shift who are likely to be shorthanded. It limits the wasted movements of the caregiver and connects to increased safety for the care receiver.

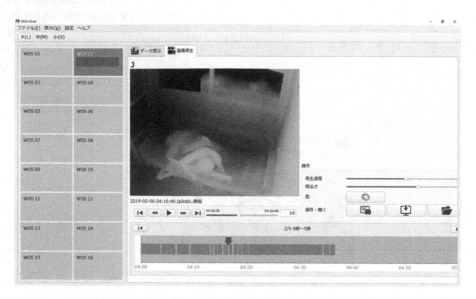

Fig. 11. A dangerous movement results in "jutting out" detection.

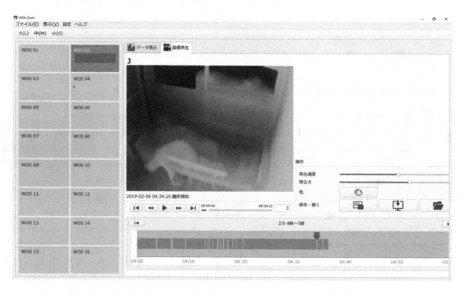

Fig. 12. A dangerous movement results in "getting out of bed" detection.

3.5   Case Study of Caregiver Adjusting the Monitoring Sensor

Figure 13 is the image immediately after observation begins. The image shows the care receiver on the bed with her knees pointing up. Because nothing is detected, the alarm is not going off. However, about 7 s after the observation the images are temporarily suspended. After that, the caregiver comes to the care receiver's bedside and adjusts the care receiver's posture by extending the legs, as seen in Fig. 14. In this example, the caregiver understands that the monitoring sensor needs to be adjusted. Probably, the caregiver checked the images on the smartphone, noticed that the care receiver's knees were extending into the area where a jutting out should be detected, quickly stopped watching and adjusted the care receiver. At the beginning of the observation, the care receiver had her knees up, and the high point of the knees was seen as the baseline, so that the monitoring sensor adjusted accordingly to detect jutting out, getting up, and getting out of bed actions. If the sensor detected the knees in Fig. 13 as the baseline, even if the care receiver tried to get up, it is possible that the alarm for getting up would not go off. This makes it more difficult to keep the care receiver safe. In this example, after adjusting the care receiver's posture, it would be ideal to restart the observation through the monitoring sensor.

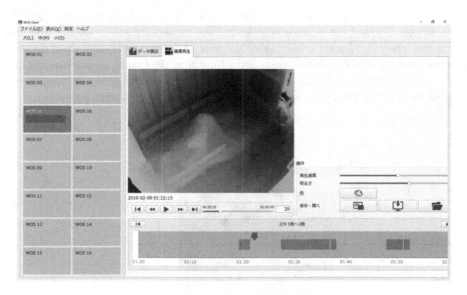

Fig. 13. Knees are up when the observation begins.

Fig. 14. Caregiver makes adjustments.

3.6   Case Study of Alarm Going off for a Long Time

Figure 15 continues images from example Sect. 3.5. The height of the care receiver's knees is adjusted, and the monitor is reset, but the monitoring sensor detects a jutting out action when the blanket droops along the side of the bed. It is clear from the data that the alarm goes off from this point for a long time. But since no adjustments are made, the care receiver is seen through the smartphone as not being in danger, the continuous alarm is annoying, and it may have been set to no longer go off.

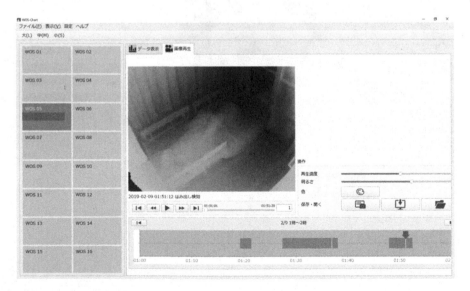

Fig. 15. Blanket's position results in "jutting out" detection.

4 Conclusion

To ensure the safety of care receivers in a nursing-care facility and lighten the burden on caregivers, monitoring sensors are used to verify their usefulness. In some places, the proper use of the monitoring sensors is achievable, but it is clear that for various reasons, unexpected problems arise.

For the monitoring sensors to be used beneficially, it is necessary to explain to the caregiver the proper way to use them. To use the monitoring sensors to observe care receivers, first the range of detection of the monitoring sensors must be set, but there are caregivers who use the sensors without knowing about this function. The proper way to use the monitoring sensors is written in the manual, but the very busy caregivers don't have the time to carefully read the manual while on the job. To solve this problem, the explanations shouldn't be on paper. Instead, a device is needed to correct wrong usage while the sensors are being used.

To use the monitoring sensor functions correctly, it's necessary to prepare ahead of time in an environment that limits interference. This survey indicates that sunlight and car headlights can cause such interference. This is an unexpected situation involving the development of the monitoring sensor, and some improvement is required. Of course, it is important to alert users as to the proper environment in which to use the sensors, but when interference appears in unsuitable environments, the alarm is set off by things other than the care receiver's actions, a function that can filter out the interference should be considered.

This survey found those problems and points for improvement, but also found in the data that proper use of the monitoring sensors connects to the safety of care receivers and the lightening of the burden on caregivers. There is also the thought that to increase the safety of the care receivers, a surveillance camera may be useful. But that infringes on the privacy of the people being observed. The monitoring sensors studied in this survey do not infringe on privacy and also have the advantage of delivering the same quality images both day and night. To take advantage of that strength, improving many of the problems indicated in this survey should allow for better usage of these monitoring sensors.

Acknowledgments. I would like to thank KING TSUSHIN KOGYO CO., LTD for their support, cooperation and expertise. This work was supported by JSPS KAKENHI Grant Number 19H04154 (Research leader Noriaki Kuwahara).

References

1. Cabinet Office, Government of Japan: Annual Report on the Ageing Society, pp. 2–6 (2019)
2. Cabinet Office, Government of Japan: Annual Report on the Ageing Society, pp. 27–33 (2019)
3. Cabinet Office, Government of Japan: Annual Report on the Ageing Society, pp. 34–38 (2019)
4. Care Work Foundation: Results of an actual condition survey of care workers, pp. 1–13 (2019)

5. Ministry of Health, Labour and Welfare: Guide to the development of welfare equipment and nursing care robots, pp. 13–33 (2014)
6. Madokoro, H., Shimoi, N., Sato, K.: Development of non-restraining and QOL sensor systems for bed-leaving prediction. The IEICE Trans. Inf. Syst. **96**(12), 3055–3067 (2013)
7. Hatsukari, T., Shiino, T., Murai, S.: The reduction of tumbling and falling accidents based on a built-in patient alert system in the hospital bed. J. Sci. Labour **88**(3), 94–102 (2012)
8. Kageyama, Y., Machida, Y., Morita, A.: Availability of safety device against overturning at nursing home. Bull. Sch. High-Technol. Hum. Welf. Tokai Univ. **14**, 47–51 (2004)
9. Madokoro, H., Shimoi, N., Sato, K., Li, X.: Prediction of bed-leaving behaviors based on time series feature learning using Elman-type feedback counter propagation networks. Akita Prefect. Univ. Web J. B Results Res. **2**, 154–158 (2015)

A Study of Quantifying Skills of Caregivers Touch to People with Dementia

Haruki Kurase[✉], Noriaki Kuwahara, and Miyuki Iwamoto

Graduate School of Science and Technology, Kyoto Institute of Technology,
Graduate School of Kyoto University, Kyoto, Japan
77.kurase@gmail.com

Abstract. As the global aging population grows so has the need for a care model for the elderly with dementia. Yet, despite this growing urgency, there is currently no established care model for elderly dementia sufferers. Recently, care technology known as 'humanitude', which is shown to be effective for dementia patients, has been attracting increased attention. This technique is empirical. This study focuses on utilizing biosignals to quantitatively evaluate and understand human touch using the humanitude care methodology, for the key purposes of establishing a care model for dementia patients. The present study first investigated the tendencies of biosignals induced by touch in two experiments, and a confirmation experiment. In Experiment 1, the biosignals induced by auditory and visual stimuli were measured. The uniqueness of biosignals induced by non-painful touch with 'non-discomfort' body parts (shoulders, upper arms, back) was examined. In Experiment 2, each participant was touched under a series of conditions. From the results obtained in the visual experiments, it is presumed that EDA response is mainly caused by the surprise emotion. In Experiment 3, a hypothetical evidence experiment was performed with Conditions 5 and 6, in addition to touch Conditions 1–4 [Eyes: Open, Closed: Yes, No]. In summary, it is presumed that the surprise emotion is strongly related to the EDA response of the present experimental results. EDA responses to potential pain were also confirmed. We plan to propose better methods of touch for caregivers based on the findings from biosignal evaluations and surveys conducted in this study.

Keywords: Touch · Elderly people with dementia · Biosignals

1 Introduction

Human touch or physical contact is important, but often ignored. Touch includes an emotional element, and the stimulus obtained from the sense of touch may be recognized as pleasant or unpleasant. Touch also promotes interpersonal affinity and coordination. Social touch is known to have a beneficial effect on physical and mental health.

While it has been shown that non-human primates use social touch to maintain and strengthen their social structure, the role of social touch in human relationships based on different gender, affiliation, and kinship remains unknown [1]. People with a close societal affinity (such as siblings) tend to be allowed a wider range of physical contact.

© Springer Nature Switzerland AG 2020
V. G. Duffy (Ed.): HCII 2020, LNCS 12198, pp. 547–557, 2020.
https://doi.org/10.1007/978-3-030-49904-4_40

Socially, women were allowed to come into contact with more areas of the body than men are. Touch is a powerful tool for conveying positive emotions. We conclude that the emotional ties of an individual are closely related to the physical patterns that allow social touch [1]. C-Tactile (CT) afferents: Tactile receptors found on non-conductive (i.e. hairy) skin that conduct slowly. C-fibers convey pressure, velocity, and temperature information typically through the type of fiber that allows pain [2]. Although the involvement of CT seems to be able to increase the specificity of emotions that can be conveyed socially via touch, the benefit is sensual arousal rather than other tenser emotions. It appears to be particularly relevant to desire and conveyance of desire [3]. Tactile contact behavior (i.e., social touch) is certainly lacking in comparison to other forms of social interaction, such as eye contact, that occurs between people. Woman have been shown to be more likely to make mutual eye contact with others for longer than man [4]. According to research on dementia, in Japan, one in four elderly people has a risk of developing dementia or has already shown signs of dementia. The most risk factor of dementia is aging, so it's becoming more serious social problem. Dementia is a condition in which intellectual functions that have developed normally are continuously reduced, and multiple cognitive deficits affects daily and social life. In the face of the current situation, 'humanitude' care method for dementia is attracting increased attention from practitioners [5].

Humanitude is a comprehensive care technique that combines the techniques created by two French people, Gineste and Marescotti, through years of experience in care under the philosophy of caregiving [6]. Humanitude is both a philosophy of care that focuses on the bond between people and the relationship with the other person, assuming that the caregiver is the same person, and a method to realize the caregiver's care attitude [7]. Although these have been empirically shown to be effective, few studies have shown quantitatively whether humanitude is actually effective in people with dementia. In this way, there are several studies that evaluate the emotions and perceived comfort/discomfort recalled when a person is touched by an object, as well as the area of the body touched (if the area was a 'discomfort' area) and the age/relationship of the person at the time when the touch occurred. However, although human touch has been suggested many times as a way to maintain good relationships, to date, few studies have evaluated human touch. In most cases, there are many studies investigating the emotions that people recall when they touch an object and the feelings they feel when they are touched by a robot. The reason that there are few studies on human touch with people is due to various barriers such as ethical issues.

The ageing society is considered to be a current issue worldwide. Ageing societies exhibit an increase in the number of elderly people needing nursing care, coupled with decrease in the number of younger working people, calling for more efficient care models. It is projected that the number of dementia suffers will increase relative to ageing population growth, and therefore establish an efficient care model for those dementia sufferers is equally pressing. Unlike healthy elderly people, as carers cannot communicate with dementia patients, it is difficult to care for those people with dementia by using ordinary care techniques. Therefore, by properly understanding human touch based on biosignals, we can understand the correct method of human touch for people with dementia. We believe that this will help establish a care model for dementia. We have begun conducting a series of experiments to understand the specificities of the biosignals induced when a person is touched by measuring the human biosignals and investigating how each responds under each particular condition.

In this study, we focused only on the EDA response. The first experiment, comprised of a series hearing and vision experiments, in which the EDA response to auditory and visual stimuli was observed. In the hearing experiment, we investigated the fluctuation of biosignals when two types of rain sound (quiet and intense) were heard. For visual experiments, we used flash movies. No noticeable change in EDA was confirmed in the hearing experiment. However, visual experiments showed a marked increase in EDA. This is presumed to be caused by the surprise or fear emotion. In the experiment, all subjects answered that surprise was unpleasant. This suggests that surprise and fear emotions are one of the factors causing an increase in EDA. The second experiment was carried out under six different touch conditions. The touch was given on body parts (shoulder, back, upper arm) which the participants had answered there was no discomfort. The conditions under which the participants were touched were as follows; Condition 1 [Eyes: Close, Prior notice: No]; Condition 2 [Eye: Close, Prior notice: Yes]; Condition 3 [Eyes: Open, Prior notice: No]; and Condition 4 [Eyes: Open, Prior notice: Yes].

The results showed that the response of EDA was suppressed as a whole when there was prior notice. In addition, when the eyes were open and there was no prior notice, the reaction was less than when there was prior notice. This is presumed to be related to the open field of view. In the third experiment, a verification experiment was performed to verify the hypothesis generated from the results obtained in Experiments 1 and 2. The touch Conditions 1 to 4 performed in Experiment 2 and the new Conditions 5 and 6 were performed. Condition 5 was [Eyes: Open, Closed: Yes, Prior notice: No], and the touch was performed with the implementer reflected in the field of view. The Condition 6 was [Eyes: Open, Closed: Yes, Prior notice: Yes], and the condition was implemented in a state where the implementer was reflected in the field of view. The parts and methods of touching were selected so that the participants did not feel discomforted.

These results suggest that surprise emotion is strongly related to the EDA response. This time, the EDA response was confirmed with 'non-unpleasant' form of touch to 'non-discomfort' body parts. The EDA response was due to the surprise emotion and is presumed to be an unpleasant EDA response. It is presumed that these results can be used as an index for evaluating human touch based on biosignals in not only caring for healthy patients but also caring for patients with dementia.

2   Methods

2.1   Experiment 1 – Measurement of Biosignal Induced by Auditory and Visual Stimuli

In this first experiment, we observed EDA responses elicited by auditory and visual stimuli. EDA refers to the sweating obtained from biosignals. An Emaptica E4 wristband, which measures biosignals such as sweating, heart rate, and body temperature, was strapped to the left wrist of participants while they were sat in a chair in a resting position to prevent noises from entering the device.

Participants. Experiment 1 sample group comprised of 3 healthy persons, one male and two females. The male was 30 years of age, and one female was 21 years old and the other was 27 years old.

Experimental Equipment and Stimulation. The equipment used for the experiment was Empatica E4 Wristband (Fig. 1). The measurement site was the inside of the left wrist. The measuring device was attached to the left wrist like a wristband.

Fig. 1. E4 wristband

Table 1. Experimental condition

No.	Stimulus	Eyes open/close	Visibility	Prior notice
1	Sounds and videos	Open and Close	No	Not applicable

Participants were given auditory and visual stimuli. The auditory stimulus was the sound of rain (quiet and intense). A flash movie was used for visual stimulus, ('surprise' movie (Table 1)).

Procedure. Participants wore an E4 Wristband on their left wrist and sat rested in a chair until the biosignal returned as normal. In the auditory test, they were asked to close their eyes and focus on the sound, and in the visual test they were told to focus on the video. Participants were instructed to sit down on their chairs with their palms down and their left arm on the table in a comfortable position. The tester played the sound after confirming that the biosignal had stabilized. In the visual experiment, after confirming that the biosignal was stable, the video was played.

2.2   Experiment 2 – Measuring Biological Signals When Touching the Body

Experiment 2 observed differences in biosignals when the conditions of human touch with the participants were changed (Table 2). The human touch for Conditions 1 to 4 were performed from behind the participants. The body parts where it was indicated that there was no discomfort (shoulder/back/upper arm) were touched at a painless intensity.

In this experiment, differences in EDA response were confirmed by the presence or absence of prior notice. Research is underway to understand the relationships between touch with objects, the areas of body allowed to be touched, and human relationships [8].

Table 2. Experimental condition

No.	Stimulus	Eyes open/close	Visibility	Prior notice
1	Touch to Shoulder, Back, neck and second arm	Close	No	No
2	Same as above	Close	No	Yes
3	Same as above	Open	No	No
4	Same as above	Open	No	Yes

Participants. Experiment 1 sample group comprised of 3 healthy persons, one male and two females. The male was 30 years of age, and one female was 21 years old and the other was 27 years old.

Experimental Equipment and Stimulation. The equipment used for the experiment was an Empatica E4 Wristband (Fig. 1). The measurement site was the inside of the left wrist. The measuring instrument was attached to the left wrist like a wristband. Participants undertook a preliminary experiment to determine levels of comfort and discomfort prior to the experiment. In Experiment 2, the touch stimulus was applied to the shoulder, back, and upper arm at a painless intensity with the palm of the hand, whereby it had been indicated that no discomfort was felt by the participant.

Procedure. Participants wore an E4 Wristband on their left wrist and sat rested in a chair until the biosignals returned as normal. Participants were instructed to sit down on their chairs with their palms down and their left arm on the table in a comfortable position. The tester confirmed that the biosignals had stabilized before beginning to touch the participant. During the experiment, the touch was performed under four different touch conditions (Table 2). Touch Conditions 1–4 were performed with touch from behind the participant. Under Conditions 1 [Eyes: Close, Prior notice: Yes] and 2 [Eyes: Close, Prior notice: Yes], the participants were touched on their shoulders and back with their eyes closed. Under Condition 3 [Eyes: Open, Prior notice: Yes] and 4 [Eyes: Open, Prior notice: Yes] the participants were touched in a similar manner to when their eyes were opened.

2.3 Experiment 3 – Confirmation Experiment for Healthy Elderly People

In Experiment 3, the participants were touched under the same touch conditions as in Experiment 2, in addition to two new conditions. A hypothetical evidence experiment of the hypothesis raised in Experiment 2 was conducted. The touch was given from behind the participant for Conditions 1 to 4, and in a state of being in view for Conditions 5 and 6. Participants were touched in non-discomfort areas (shoulders, back, upper arms) with a painless intensity. In this experiment, the purpose was to confirm the hypothesis raised in Experiment 2. In Experiment 2, it was hypothesized that the presence of the prior notice suppressed the EDA response caused from the surprise emotion. Experiment 3 aimed to investigate whether the response of EDA obtained so far could be obtained from other people, and whether the same results could be obtained for 65-year-old elderly people as those in their early 30 s or 20 s. Further, touch under the additional Conditions 5 and 6 was performed.

Participant. The sample group for Experiment 3 consisted of a healthy elderly male in his 60 s (Male: 65).

Experimental Equipment and Stimulation. The device used for the experiment was Empatica E4 Wristband (Fig. 1). The measurement site was the inside of the left wrist. The measuring instrument was attached to the left wrist like a wristband. Touch was given under Conditions 1 to 4 as performed in Experiment 2 (Table 2), as well as the additional Conditions 5 and 6 (Table 3). Conditions 5 and 6 were carried out with visibility. The touch stimulus touched the non-unpleasant shoulder, back, and upper arm body parts with an open palm at a painless intensity.

Table 3. Experimental condition

No.	Stimulus	Eyes open/close	Visibility	Prior notice
1	Touch to Shoulder, Back, neck and second arm	Close	No	No
2	Same as above	Close	No	Yes
3	Same as above	Open	No	No
4	Same as above	Open	No	Yes
5	Same as above	Open	Yes	No
6	Same as above	Open	Yes	Yes

Procedure. Participants wore an E4 Wristband on their left wrist and sat rested in a chair until the biosignals returned as normal. Participants were instructed to sit down on their chairs with their palms down and their left arm on the table in a comfortable position. The tester confirmed that the biosignal had stabilized before beginning to touch the participants. In Experiment 3, touch was given under conditions 1 to 4 performed in Experiment 2 (Table 2). For Condition 5 [Eyes: Open, Closed: Yes, Prior notice: No] and condition 6 [Eyes: Open, Closed: Yes, Prior notice: Yes], the touch was implemented with implementer in the participants field of view.

3 Results and Discussion

3.1 Results and Discussion-Experiment 1

The EDA response elicited by auditory stimuli in the experiments did not show any obvious fluctuations. Participants replied that the sound of rain was pleasant.

Participants who watched the video containing the 'surprise' content, which aimed to induce a sense of surprise, in the visual experiment showed significant fluctuations in EDA (Fig. 2).

Participants were discomforted by this 'surprise' video. Since EDA rises when surprise is felt, it is presumed that the body experiences physically discomfort from this emotion. At this time, they also experiences a senses of anxiety and fear, and it was confirmed that the EDA value also increased when the emotions such as fear and anxiety were present. In the future, we will investigate EDA response elicited by these emotions. In Experiment 1, it was found that the EDA value did not fluctuate when the participant was in a relaxed state (not discomforted), and that the EDA fluctuated greatly when surprise or fear was felt. From this, it is presumed that the sound of rain, in which no change in EDA was observed, relaxed the subject and brought him/her to a resting state. It is further presumed that the video including 'surprise' content caused the participant to feel physically stressed from the element of surprise as it was answered that he/she felt discomforted.

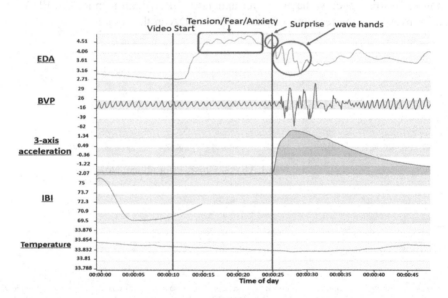

Fig. 2. Biosignals when watching a video that contains 'surprise' content. In this study, we focus on the reaction of EDA.

3.2   Results and Discussion-Experiment 2

With prior notice, the overall EDA response was reduced. In the case of Condition 1, the reaction of EDA was remarkably high. However, in the case of Condition 3, the reaction of EDA was either minimal or no longer noticeable. This is presumed to be related to the open field of view. Participant questionnaire respondents stated they felt more secure when their eyes were open compared to when they were closed. The participant expressed surprise and discomfort when touched suddenly. From the above, it is presumed that the reason why the response of EDA was less for Condition 3 than Condition 1 is that the sense of security due to the open view alleviated the sense of surprise.

In the case of the Condition 2, there were cases where the reaction was either minimal or no noticeable EDA response was observed. This led to the hypothesis that prior notice reduces EDA. The result was similar to the result of the Condition 4. Figures 3 and 4 show the EDA response under each touch condition. In Experiment 2, the response of EDA caused by touch with participants is predominantly related to surprise, and surprise emotions which is thought to have an unpleasant element. It is estimated that the user feels some discomfort. Specifically, this experiment confirmed that EDA responds even when the patient has potential pain such as abdominal pain. In other words, it can be said that EDA responds even when pain occurs.

From the above, surprise and pain are presumed to be the main causes of EDA response. At this stage, we have not yet understood how pain responds to EDA, and plan to investigate the response of pain-specific EDA in the future.

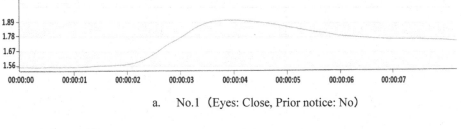

a.   No.1 (Eyes: Close, Prior notice: No)

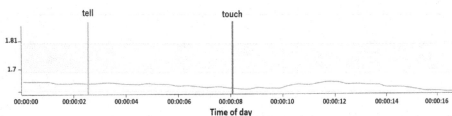

b.   No.2 [Eyes: Close, Prior notice: Yes]

Fig. 3. Experimental condition, a. No.1, b. No.2

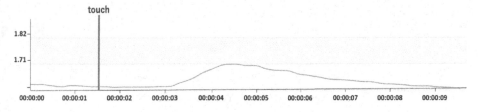

a.   No.3 [Eyes: Open, Prior notice: No]

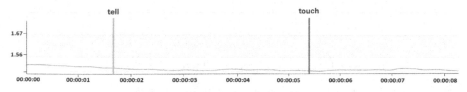

b.   No.4 [Eyes: Open, Prior notice: Yes)

Fig. 4. Experimental condition, a. No.3, b.No.4

3.3   Results and Discussion-Experiment 3

The results obtained from Experiment 3 were consistent with the results obtained from Experiments 1 and 2 so far. In the case of Condition 1, the result of the reaction of EDA was remarkably high, and the result was similar to that of experiment 2.

Next, in the case of Condition 2, no noticeable EDA response was observed. This was also consistent with the results obtained in Experiment 2. In the case of Condition 3, although the EDA response of the participants was confirmed, the EDA response was less than in Condition 1. This was also consistent with the results obtained in Experiment 2. Condition 4 results matched the results from Experiment 2. Regarding Conditions 5 and 6 added this time, no EDA response was confirmed regardless of the presence or absence of prior notice (Fig. 5).

The result of Experiment 3 supported the hypothesis that the presence of the prior notice suppressed the reaction of EDA caused by feeling surprised. In addition, since the results of Experiments 5 and 6 allowed the participants to confirm the presence of the practitioner, a sense of security was generated, which is considered to be the reason why EDA response was not present.

At this stage, while it is not possible to confirm proof of the hypothesis, due to the limited number of samples, it is believed that the result has increased the credibility of the hypothesis.

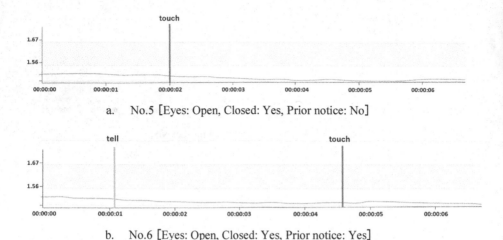

a.   No.5 [Eyes: Open, Closed: Yes, Prior notice: No]

b.   No.6 [Eyes: Open, Closed: Yes, Prior notice: Yes]

Fig. 5.   Experimental condition, a. No.5, b. No.6

4   Conclusion

4.1   Conclusion

In conclusion, it suggested that the EDA tends to respond to touch with humans. Experiments revealed differences in biosignals between the case of prior notice and the case of no prior notice. These results suggest that the response of EDA caused by touch with participants is primarily due to the sense of surprise. EDA response was confirmed not only for surprise but also for fear. In addition, it was confirmed through this experiment that EDA responds even when the patient has potential pain such as abdominal pain. This suggests that EDA will respond if pain occurs.

4.2   Future

In the future, we will work to increase the number of samples in the experiments we have performed so far and to solve any new questions that have emerged in this experiment. I want to investigate the EDA response elicited when certain emotions such as anxiety and fear are felt. If the emotional state of the patient can be estimated from variances in EDA response, caused from each emotion, we believe that it will be useful not only in nursing care but also in all aspects of human care. Next, the difference in the biosignals associated with pain. I want to investigate the response of EDA to pain. However, these "pain" experiments are high hurdles and are considered difficult to implement. In this experiment, it was confirmed that EDA responds to pain, so it is thought that understanding the response of EDA for each pain makes it possible to gain understanding of the physical condition of a patient who cannot communicate. We believe that if this is achieved, we will be able to notice patients' abnormalities immediately. There are various barriers to human touch with humans, and this is an area where progress is unlikely to progress any further. However, in the future, if we can understand the biosignals recalled by human touch, we believe that nursing care technology will take a further leap forward.

References

1. Juulia, T., Suvilehtoa, F.: Topography of social touching depends on emotional bonds between humans. PNAS **112**, 13811–13816 (2015)
2. Schirmer, A., Ralph Adolphs, F.: Emotion perception from face, voice, and touch: comparisons and convergence. Trends Cogn. Sci. **21**, 216–228 (2017)
3. Louise, P., Kirscha, F.: Reading the mind in the touch: neurophysiological specificity in the communication of emotions by touch. Neuropsychologia **116**, 136–149 (2018)
4. Gallace, A., Spence, C.: The science of interpersonal touch: an overview. Neurosci. Biobehav. Rev. **34**, 246–259 (2010)
5. Nakazawa, A., Mitsuzumi, Yu., Watanabe, Y., Kurazume, R., Yoshikawa, S., Honda, M.: First-person video analysis for evaluating skill level in the *Humanitude* tender-care technique. J. Intell. Robot. Syst. **98**(1), 103–118 (2019). https://doi.org/10.1007/s10846-019-01052-8
6. Biquanda, S., Zittelb, B.: Care giving and nursing, work conditions and humanitude. Work **41**, 1828–1831 (2012)
7. Casa da Misericórdia, S. et al.: Implementation of the Humanitude Care Methodology: contribution to the quality of health care. Rev. Latino-Am. Enfermagem, **27** (2019)
8. Juulia, T.F.: Cross-cultural similarity in relationship-specific social touching. Proc. Biol. Sci. **286**, 2019 (1901)

Use of Technologies for Supporting Dementia Care

Noriaki Kuwahara[1(✉)] and Kiyoshi Yasuda[2]

[1] Kyoto Institute of Technology, Kyoto, Japan
nkuwahar@kit.ac.jp
[2] Kyoto Prefectural University of Medicine, Kyoto, Japan

Abstract. Since 2003, the authors of this report have been researching assistive information and communication technology in the everyday lives of elderly people suffering from dementia or higher brain dysfunctions. The original project was part of the "Project on Networked Interaction Therapy for People with Dementia (Sept. 2003 – March 2008)" under the auspices of the Advanced Telecommunication Research Institute (ATR) and Intelligent Robotics Communication Laboratories. During this research, we received in no small way backlash from caregivers, especially professional caregivers, about the usage of information and communications technology and engineering technology in general. We sensed that currently resistance to the use of technology has been decreasing. In this paper, the authors will review the engineering technology that caregivers have been involved with over the past 10-plus years and discuss what caregivers need from engineering researchers in an attempt to help engineers work well with caregivers and other specialists.

keywords: Dementia care · Assistive Technology

1 Introduction

Japan is a rapidly aging society, and accordingly, the rapid rise of elderly people with dementia has become an urgent issue in society. According to the Ministry of Health, Labor and Welfare, the percentage of the overall population that is 65 or older is expected to reach 30.3%, or 36.57 million people by 2025 [1], and the number of elderly with dementia is estimated to be more than 7 million. That accounts for about 1 in 5 elderly people, which means an estimated 5.8% of Japan's total population will be people 65 or older with dementia. This reality means that preventive methods, care and support for dementia patients is necessary. However, on the other hand, the shrinking labor force caused by a falling birthrate gives rise to the problem of a lack of caregivers. In a press release form the Ministry of Health, Labor and Welfare in 2015, the estimated demand for caregivers in 2025 is 2.53 million, but the estimated supply of those caregivers is 2.15 million. There is an estimated gap of about 380,000 people between supply and demand. This shows that sooner or later, a limit on individual caregivers will be reached and that the introduction of robots, artificial intelligence, and other engineering technology into the caregiving sector is unavoidable. Within that sector, it is no exaggeration to say that the time for technology to help with patients with

© Springer Nature Switzerland AG 2020
V. G. Duffy (Ed.): HCII 2020, LNCS 12198, pp. 558–568, 2020.
https://doi.org/10.1007/978-3-030-49904-4_41

dementia is now or never. The issue of rapid aging has become a global problem. Within that, dementia is a universal issue that does not stop at the border, and its complexity is only going to increase. Caregivers often suffer from depression and burnout because of the verbal abuse, violence, wandering and incontinence (BPSD) of dementia patients. This may lead to mental issues among caregivers.

Since 2003, the authors of this report have been researching assistive information and communication technology in the everyday lives of elderly people suffering from dementia or higher brain dysfunctions. The original project was part of the "Project on Networked Interaction Therapy for People with Dementia (Sept. 2003 – March 2008)" under the auspices of the Advanced Telecommunication Research Institute (ATR) and Intelligent Robotics Communication Laboratories. During this research, we received in no small way backlash from caregivers, especially professional caregivers, about the usage of information and communications technology and engineering technology in general. We sensed that currently resistance to the use of technology has been decreasing. In this paper, the authors will review the engineering technology that caregivers have been involved with over the past 10-plus years and discuss what caregivers need from engineering researchers in an attempt to help engineers work well with caregivers and other specialists.

2 Research Trends on Assistive Technology for Dementia

In 2017, a comprehensive review of the literature [2] related to assistive technologies for dementia care was undertaken. This report took 617 papers and 167 additional sources of information reviewed and by accounting for duplication, narrowed it down to 517 data sources. It separated them by the number of reports per year and the technology category, then conducted a detailed analysis of their purposes. It turns out that publications up to 2005 were very scarce, but they began increasing year by year from 2006. Compared with publications put out between 2006 and 2010, the number put out between 2011 and 2015 more than doubled. Of the technologies being used, distributed systems accounted for nearly half. It was also clear that use of robots was becoming more common. As for the reasons for the technology use, 28% was for ADL, or helping dementia patients live independently, 19% was for monitoring, 16% was for physical assistance and cognitive function support. There is expectation that in the future, technologies supporting people with dementia will increase in number and variety. We concentrated on research and development focused on ADL for people with dementia and cognitive function support.

3 Results from Our Research Group

In this section, we look at small reports since 2003 about collaboration with caregivers, examine the limited successes, and describe the factors that helped as well as the points that should be reflected on.

3.1 Survey on Caregiver's Impressions of Assistive Technologies

To begin research into research and development of technologies that will assist those with dementia or higher brain dysfunctions in their daily lives, we conducted a survey where we interviewed groups of caregivers and other interested parties and heard opinions and impressions about what sort of assistive technologies should be developed [3].

As a result, we received three typical answers.

(1) Machines used in care do not evoke a sense of compassion with care receivers.
(2) Communication is difficult with the machines, so dialogue is lost from the care.
(3) The machines don't give off any warmth. There is meaning to care done by hand.

From the next section, we would like to show the bias in some assistive technologies and the response to that bias.

3.2 Is the Feeling of Compassion for the Care Receiver Lost Through the Use of Technologies?

Speech therapists Yasuda and others at the Chiba Rosai Hospital were collaborators in the research and development of information therapy interfaces. They used dolls to send messages and music promoting eating to patients who were thought to have developed eating disorders because of dementia. They reported on examples of improved nutrition [4]. Conditions at the time of intervention are shown in Fig. 1.

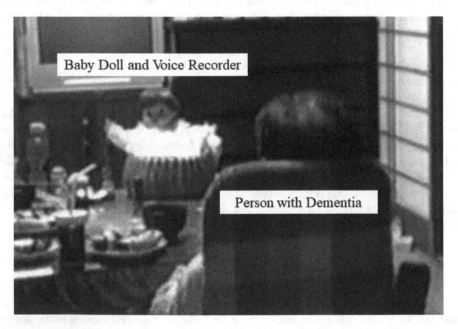

Fig. 1. Scene depicting intervention with baby doll and voice recorder

This woman only ate 20–30% of the food given to her. She was showing signs of malnutrition. Yasuda believes that depression brought on by dementia is the cause of the eating disorder. At first, the thought was to raise her spirits during mealtime by playing music. Also, it was clear that the woman showed a lot of affection for the doll shown in Fig. 1. Through a voice recorder, the doll gave a message encouraging the woman to eat while playing music. During mealtime, these messages would come from the doll's backside. After continuing this for two weeks, the woman was eating more than 50% of the food given to her, and her nutritional status improved. Also, the woman became more mentally calm, and her interactions with family members improved. This pioneering research is known as Human Agent Interaction (HAI).

Next, Yasuda devised a reminiscence video based on patient's memories as a kind of self-reminiscence therapy to prevent the behavioral and psychological symptoms of dementia (BPSD), which proved effective with many patients [5]. The reminiscence video is made by volunteers, who use a handycam to film photos gathered in the patient's photo albums, making a slide-show-like video. Kuwahara worked with Yasuda's team to create reminiscence videos by using digital technology that would bring about interest from dementia patients. They found that for the video to be effective, narration was important. The reminiscence video was digitized, and they developed a semi-automatic system to incorporate zoom, pan, and other video techniques along with narration, and background music [6]. Figure 2 shows a video of memories that was made using this system.

Fig. 2. Scene depicting intervention with digital reminiscence video

This patient sustained frontal injuries that spurred the onset of traumatic dementia. Once the wound healed, he was released from the hospital. But after leaving the hospital, he experienced severe BPSD at home. Yasuda tried to deliver care through a reminiscence video. Immediately after the reminiscence video was installed, this patient who hadn't smiled since leaving the hospital and was typically in a bad mood would smile and was observed enjoying watching the video. Family members who lived with him could not hide their surprise.

One piece of knowledge we obtained from this research is that the use of engineering technology in caregiving does not necessarily mean a loss of compassion.

While a caregiver always wants to offer compassion through care, the severe reality of some dementia care can often rob the caregiver of that ability. Engineering technology softens the edges of the severity, allowing those who offer care the ability to do so with compassion. It may be a stretch to call the use of dolls and videos in this research engineering technology, but these devices can solve a caregiver's problems quite nicely when installed. Also, the effort can be repeated by simply playing the voice recorder or the video again. The success of this research was brought about by the effectiveness and simplicity of technology that can be seen with the naked eye.

3.3   Is Communication Lost from Nursing Care Through the Use of Technologies?

Around 2006, in collaboration with NTT and others, the usefulness of a remote listening device service for dementia patients using a video phone was looked into. A video-phone device provided by NTT was used. It not only transmitted video, but also provided digital reminiscence therapy and other functions and activated conversations between the patient and volunteers. Their effectiveness was inspected through verification tests [7]. Figure 3 shows the interfaces a volunteer listening remotely would see. While checking the living conditions of the dementia patient in the upper right image, the volunteer can use the photograph function to show memory-provoking photographs that can lead to topics of conversation.

Fig. 3. Screen shot of video phone when remote active listening was performed

The results showed an increase in the dementia patient starting conversations, lessening the burden on the active listening volunteer. Companies and organizations that participated in the verification tests had very high expectations for remote active listening services. However, they were unable to create a detailed business model, and the service did not end up being provided. One of the big obstacles proved to be that to use the remote active listening service, a caregiver would have to be at the side of the care receiver, making it necessary for the caregiver to stay there. A big obstacle was the need for nursing care to use the service.

However, Yasuda and team are using free video services such as Skype to get remote active listening volunteers involved in speaking with at-home dementia patients. Through this research, we found that some engineering technologies play an important role by not taking away dialogue opportunities from the person receiving care, but actually increasing those opportunities.

3.4   Is Care Only Meaningful When Performed by a Person?

From around 2015 in collaboration with NTT, we conducted test verifications to see if a communication robot could be effective in recreation activities at a care facility for dementia patients [8]. The system allows for various different recreation programs to be downloaded from the cloud and have a communication robot operate the recreation activity. Figure 4 offers an overview of the system.

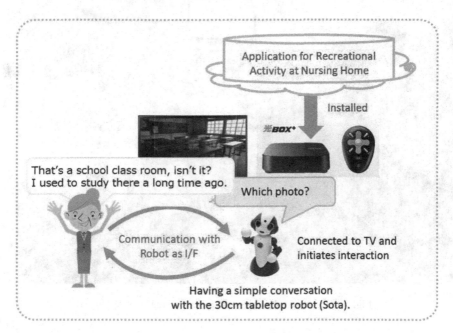

Fig. 4. Overview of recreation service system with communication robot

The results showed that dementia patients showed affection for the robot during recreation and participated with enthusiasm. Also, the variety and quality of the movements of the dementia patients during the recreation improved greatly. This also lightened the burden on the caregiver when it comes to operating a recreation program. The care receivers were able to enjoy the recreation activity, making it possible for deeper engagement with the caregiver when it comes to recreation. This evaluation was done using a person-centered care evaluation method known as Dementia Care Mapping (DCM). Figure 5 shows the place in the caregiving facility where the communication robot is used in recreation activities. As can be seen in the figure, the caregiver's line of sight is the same as those receiving care. In other words, everyone is turned toward the recreation being run by the robot and the contents that are being provided, enjoying the recreation together in a situation that was not possible earlier.

In this verification test, the caregiver really liked the robot. Also, the operation didn't take any extra work. By just turning a switch on the TV and the robot, the recreation began. It fit very nicely into the care facility's routines. Using engineering technology, they were able to focus on what was important. By letting the robot do what it could do, the quality of care was greatly improved.

Fig. 5. Scene of robot-let recreation in caregiving facility

4   Ongoing Project of Our Research Group

Figure 6 shows the stance of our research group when it comes to research. The object of our research, as shown in the center circle of the figure, is elderly or disabled people, including people with dementia. The goal is to improve the quality of life (QOL) of these people through research and development of assistive technologies.

We implement robotic and media technology that has been planned and designed and install a research and development system on site. As a result, if a problem is found after evaluation, action is taken to improve the system, and a new implementation is planned and designed. Objective and universal evaluations are undertaken through data gathering from biological measurements and behavior measurement technology. Our goal is to be able to make automatic judgments through a foundation of machine learning and deep learning.

In Sect. 3, we introduced intervention technologies. Evaluations often require human involvement. Information pulled from a behavior observation index and nursing records showed the burden of BPSD and attempts to find coping time. Also, in the robot recreation research, the reliability of DCM was very high, and the evaluation of the qualifications of Mapper was done by three people. The target evaluation of dementia patients was two hours, and activities were coded at five-minute intervals. The quality was evaluated in seven grades, and it was a very laborious process. We are making efforts to use this information in research and development through objective and universal evaluations using mechanisms for automatic judgments.

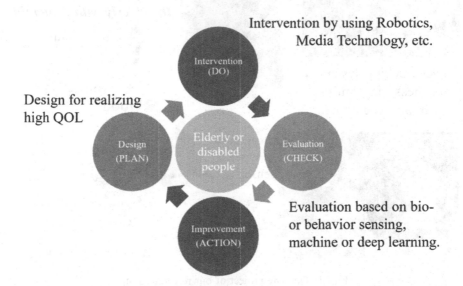

Fig. 6. Research and development of our laboratory

Figure 7 shows an overview of this. The upper left is the balloon-shaped drone developed by Ota and his team at the University of Tokyo [9]. In recent years, some caregiving facilities install cameras in the public spaces like a recreation room. If any sort of trouble develops, whether it is with the caregiver or the resident or a force majeure, there will be evidence. This balloon-shaped drone includes a small camera. The stationary camera (with a 360-degree range) can detect the interaction between the caregiver and the resident. It uses a propeller to move and can record the resident's expressions and store it in a database. Where the balloon-shaped drone goes and who it records can all be controlled.

In the lower left of Fig. 7, a plush doll robot developed by Yonezawa at Kansai University, and Yamazoe and his team at Ritsumeikan University is displayed [10]. It has soft pressure sensors inside of it, and it detects the movements of the resident, inferring whether it wants to hug the doll, or stroke it, while also measuring the resident internally. The objective here is for private monitoring in the resident's room without the use of a camera. The figure in the center is mainly implemented by the author and allows for research into the brain waves, heartbeat, and other biological measurements. The biological signals captured by the spectrogram are processed through a neural net. This sort of data can be used to make a large data set. Through deep learning, this system activates research and development to objectively evaluate the quality of caregiving.

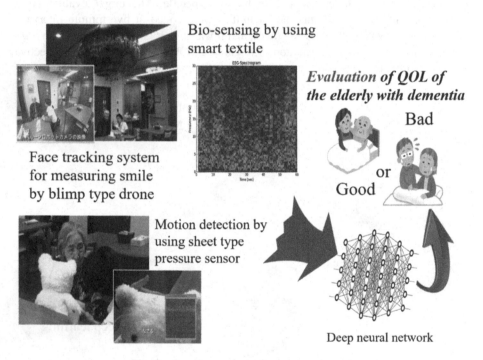

Fig. 7. Ongoing project of our research group

5   Discussion and Conclusion

Today's Japan is experiencing a shrinking birthrate and rapid aging. The limit of human caregiving has been reached. It is clear that communication technology, robotics, artificial intelligence, and other engineering technology must be aggressively used in this sector. Today, the bias caregivers have against engineering technology has been lessening greatly during our more than 10 years researching the caregiving sector. However, there are various hurdles to overcome for caregivers to begin using engineering technology. The important points for overcoming these hurdles is whether we can see the effects and whether the technology fits nicely into the caregiver's routine. One more topic is that within the caregiving sector, there are rising expectations for engineering technology, but there is no market for it. If caregiving devices that are made with the objective of offering physical assistance are covered by long-term nursing insurance, the lessened financial burden would make it possible to use them, our research shows that it will be difficult for cognitive function support and emotional support to be covered by that insurance. In the end, the issue is who will bear the burden. The reminiscence memories and remote active listening service we introduced in Sect. 3 have only gotten to the volunteer phase. We hear that the recreation robot service has been launched, but it still remains to be seen at what scale it will be used in care facilities. When these issues become clear, these developments will be able to assist Japan's rapidly aging society.

Other areas of East Asia such as China and South Korea are facing the same issue of a shrinking birthrate. That is also affecting other regions around the world. We assume that engineering technology for caregiving is being looked into in these areas as well. We hope that we can share the research we have done so far to help caregivers and engineering researchers.

References

1. https://www.mhlw.go.jp/stf/houdou/0000088998.html. (in Japanese)
2. Ienca, M., et al.: Intelligent assistive technology for Alzheimer's disease and other dementias: a systematic review. J. Alzheimer's Dis. **56**(4), 1301–1340 (2017)
3. Kuwahara, N., Kuwabara, K., Utsumi, A., Yasuda, K., Tetsutani, N.: Networked interaction therapy: relieving stress in memory-impaired people and their family members. In: IEEE-EBMS (2004)
4. Yasuda, K., Beckman, B., Yoneda, M.Y.H., Iwamoto, A., Nakamura, T.: Successful guidance by automatic output of music and verbal messages for daily behavioural disturbances of three individuals with dementia. Neuropsychol. Rehabil. **16**(1), 66–82 (2006)
5. Yasuda, K., Kuwabara, K., Kuwahara, N., Abe, S., Tetsutani, N.: Effectiveness of personalized reminiscence photo videos for individuals with dementia. Neuropsychol. Rehabil. **19**(4), 603–619 (2009)
6. Kuwahara, N., Yasuda, K., Tetsutani, N., Morimoto, K.: Remote assistance for people with dementia at home using reminiscence systems and a schedule prompter. Int. J. Comput. Healthc. **1**(2), 126–143 (2010)
7. Kuwahara, N., Abe, S., Yasuda, K., Kuwabara, K.: Networked reminiscence therapy for individuals with dementia by using photo and video sharing. In: Assets 2006: Proceedings of the 8th International ACM SIGACCESS Conference on Computers and Accessibility, October 2006, pp. 125–132 (2006)
8. Doi, T., Kuwahara, N., Morimoto, K.: Assessing the use of communication robots for recreational activities at nursing homes based on dementia care mapping (DCM). In: Duffy, V. (ed.) DHM 2016. LNCS, vol. 9745, pp. 203–211. Springer, Cham (2016). https://doi.org/10.1007/978-3-319-40247-5_21

9. Srisamosorn, V., Kuwahara, N., Yamashita, A., Ogata, T., Ota, J.: Design of face tracking system using fixed 360-degree cameras and flying blimp for health care evaluation. In: Proceedings of the 4th International Conference on Serviceology, Tokyo, Japan, pp. 63–66 (2016)
10. Yonezawa, T., Yamazoe, H.: Analyses of textile pressure-map sensor data of a stuffed toy for understanding human emotional physical contact. In: HAI 2018: Proceedings of the 6th International Conference on Human-Agent Interaction, December 2018, pp. 191–198 (2018)
11. Fangmeng, Z., Peijia, L., Iwamoto, M., Kuwahara, N.: Emotional changes detection for dementia people with spectrograms from physiological signals. Int. J. Adv. Comput. Sci. Appl. (IJACSA) 9(10), 49–54 (2018)

Towards Practical Use of Bedside Sensing/Voice-Calling System for Preventing Falls

Norihisa Miyake[✉], Kazumi Kumagai, Seiki Tokunaga,
and Mihoko Otake-Matsuura[✉]

Center for Advanced Intelligence Project, RIKEN, Nihonbashi 1-Chome Mitsui
Bldg. 15F, 1-4-1 Nihonbashi, Chuo-Ku, Tokyo 103-0027, Japan
{norihisa.miyake,mihoko.otake}@riken.jp

Abstract. The authors have been studying a bedside sensing/voice-calling system for older adults to prevent falls. The basic tasks of the system are as follows: i) monitoring the behavior of an older adult on a bed, ii) voice-calling the older adult by using a bedside robot agent when detecting any activity that leads to leaving the bed, iii) letting the older adult to postpone leaving the bed with the voice-call, and iv) launching nurse calls to allow nurses/caregivers to attend to the older adult, before the older adult leaves the bed.

First, the hardware design and function of the voice-calling agent were confirmed from a safety viewpoint. Second, the content of the voice call was studied in terms of an acceptability. Lastly, the integrated system was introduced into hospitals and care facilities to examine its serviceability. Nevertheless, it is important to consider the reliability and flexibility of the system in meeting its various use conditions, before it can be introduced in real medical/care environments. Moreover, adequate attention should be given to the usability of the sensing/voice-calling system for operators, such as nurses/caregivers.

This paper deals with the design detail of the bedside sensing/voice-calling system, with an emphasis on its reliability and flexibility. First, the background and basic concept of the research are introduced, and an outline of the system is presented. Second, the mechanism of the robot agent installed in the vicinity of the bed is detailed. Third, the controller hardware and software architectures are described. Regarding the controller software, i) the receipt of data from sensors, ii) analysis of the data to detect the behavior of the person on the bed, and iii) control of the robot agent to issue appropriate voice-call contents are explained. Finally, the preliminary use test results of the system, which were obtained in an experimental environment and a hospital, to see the response of older adults, are briefly discussed.

Keywords: Bedside agent · Fall prevention · Assistive robotics · Monitoring

© Springer Nature Switzerland AG 2020
V. G. Duffy (Ed.): HCII 2020, LNCS 12198, pp. 569–580, 2020.
https://doi.org/10.1007/978-3-030-49904-4_42

1 Introduction

In many countries, including Japan, the aging rate of the population is rising, and the number of older adults needing care or assistance is increasing accordingly [1]. Robotic devices designed to assist these older adults with their daily living activities are thus needed. As the word "bedridden" implies, leaving one's bed is one of the most important daily living activities required to maintain a person's physical functions. However, accidents, such as falls, occur near beds where older adults spend considerable time during the day and night [2]. Fall accidents are the most frequent incidents in hospitals in Japan, and the number of such incidents has been rising because of an increase in the average age of hospital inpatients [3, 4]. Designing a safe bed environment is thus one of the most vital issues in hospitals and care facilities.

There are various approaches to preventing patient falls. Physical means, such as the placement of bedside rails to suppress a patient from leaving their bed, however, are considered medical restraint and should be avoided. This has led the authors to the idea of non-physical solution: the proposed sensing/voice-calling system, which is designed to be placed at the bedside.

There are various systems for monitoring a patient's status, such as their posture or motion, which can be interpreted as a precursor to leaving the bed. The most widely used device is the pressure-mat-type sensor, which detects a patient's position on the bed or near the bedside. The sensor can be connected to the nurse call system to notify about the patient's status, thus allowing nurses to visit the patient when necessary. Systems that use infrared or ultrasonic sensors to measure the motion of a patient have been developed, and experimental introduction of such systems to care facilities and hospitals have been reported. Systems that use force and/or pressure sensors to detect the position and/or movement of a patient have been introduced in hospitals and care facilities as well [5–7]. These systems aim to relieve caregivers' burden by providing patients' status information.

There are various robotic agents for older adults, although they are mostly for communication or therapeutic purposes, and it seems that no such agent has been designed to monitor a patient's status [8, 9].

The authors' main motivation in this research is to develop a monitoring system of a person's status on or near their bed, to prevent them from falling, which will benefit not only caregivers but also patients. From this point of view, the proposed system is designed as an active system that communicates with a person needing care. A robotic agent is selected as the most suitable solution for this purpose, because of the intimacy and sense of security it can convey to the person being cared for.

The authors have been studying this type of system and developed a prototype model to learn the robot mechanism safety, content acceptability, and system serviceability [10]. Given that the functionality of the proposed system has been studied, this paper deals with the next step, which is the development of a system with adequate reliability for use in a long-term verification experiment in hospitals and care facilities, and flexibility for responding to various user requirements.

2   Basic Concept

The proposed bedside sensing/voice-calling system with a robotic agent monitors a person's behavior using sensors to provide caregivers with the person's status information. In addition, it sends voice calls to the person through the robotic agent to postpone behaviors that may lead to falls. A schematic diagram of this monitoring agent and the outline of the system are shown in Fig. 1.

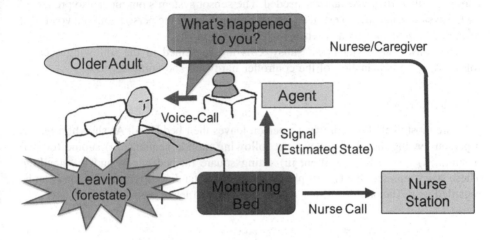

Fig. 1. Bedside sensing/voice-calling system with a robotic agent

In this system, falls are prevented by human caregivers' physical assistance, and the robot agent sends voice-calls to remind the person to wait until the caregivers' arrival. Usually, a nurse call system is used when a patient needs help. Responding to nurse calls by immediately going to patient's wards is a top-priority task for nurses. Thus, fall accidents can be prevented if nurses can visit patients before they leave their beds. Therefore, keeping patients from leaving their beds, at least until nurses reach their wards, is quite beneficial [11]. From this point of view, a system that detects patient activity leading to leaving the bed, launches nurse calls, and prevents patients from leaving their beds with voice-calls would be helpful. Even though the effect of the postponed time span is limited, such a system is beneficial for both nurses and patients, because a patient's chances of falling due to unattended movement can be reduced.

Voice-calling is important in nursing/caring environments, as it enables patients to communicate and make their intention known to staff [12]. An agent equipped with voice-calling capability can as well be used for communication purposes; it can serve as a daily conversation partner of a patient. The expected users of such a system are patients who can notice voice-calls and are at a high risk of falling if they attempt to leave their beds unassisted.

3 System Overview

3.1 Outline of the System

As shown in Fig. 1, the overall system consists of a sensor system and a robot agent; the former is installed on the bed and detect the posture/motion of a person on the bed, whereas the latter is placed near the bed and performs voice-calling. The sensor system is connected to the nurse call system; together, they notify nurses/caregivers about the person's status when assistance is needed. The sensor system's output is also processed by the system controller to estimate the posture/motion of the person, and the voice-call of the agent is then activated when such help is needed.

The sensor and robot agent subsystems are presented in the following section, followed by an explanation of the controller hardware and software.

3.2 Bed Sensor

Falls are most likely to occur when a person leaves their bed [2, 5]. As shown in Fig. 2, a person leaving their bed follows the following motion sequence: i) supine (dorsal) position, ii) long sitting position, iii) sitting square (at bed edge), and iv) standing. These states represent the typical phases that lead to standing up from a bed and can be regarded as predictors of whether a person intends to leave their bed.

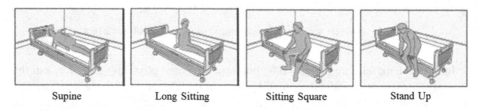

| Supine | Long Sitting | Sitting Square | Stand Up |

Fig. 2. Motion sequence of getting out of bed [6]

The product called "Fall Prevention Alarm System", uses force sensors that are equipped with bed actuators for back lifting and frame lifting to detect the above phases of the process of leaving a bed [6, 7]. The commonly used pressure-mat-type sensors can also be used; multiple sensors are placed on a patient's chest/back, waist/hip, and the edge of the mattress on the bed, as in the authors' previous work [10]. Details about the method of estimating a person's posture/status are explained in Sect. 4.2 (controller software).

3.3 Robot Agent

Figure 3 shows the developed novel robot agent, which is based on the prototype called "Side-Bot" from the authors' previous work [10].

The main features of the robot agent are as follows: i) approximately 180 mm height, 110 mm width and depth, and 180 g weight, ii) acceptable appearance for older adults and nurses, iii) 1 degree-of-freedom for nodding head pitch motion, with a rotation angle of 45° and a safety feature preventing the robot from pinching the user's fingers, iv) a speaker and a microphone that communicate via Bluetooth and Bluetooth Low Energy(BLE), v) RGB LEDs embedded in the face for producing facial expression of emotions, vi) a push switch (on/off state) embedded in the torso enabling the user to communicate their intention to nurses, via Bluetooth, vii) a power switch for safely managing the internal state of the agent. The reasons for incorporating these features are explained below.

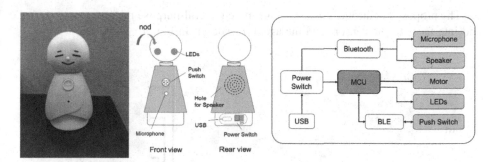

Fig. 3. Bedside robot agent

1) The size and weight of the agent are designed to prevent user injury when the robot is dropped and to discourage the user from putting the robot in the mouth, on the basis of the authors' previous work [10].
2) The importance of the agent's appearance and outer design for the acceptance of older adults and nurses have been confirmed through the previous work [10].
3) The capability of nodding is added as a means of interaction and to provide a feeling of closeness to users [13].
4) The microphone is added to recognize the timing of a user's reaction, including their utterance, although voice recognition technology is not used this time.
5) The LEDs are mounted near the cheeks to represent a variety of facial expressions.
6) The push switch is prepared to provide an intuitive physical interaction with a user, such as a substitute for a conventional nurse call button, but not limited to the particular purpose, depending on the use cases.
7) The power switch is provided for robust power management, such as sudden cable disconnections, in hospital and care facility environments.

4 Controller

4.1 Controller Hardware

The bedside sensing/voice-calling system's controller is required to have the following functions.

1) Estimating the behavior and posture of the person on the bed, according to the on/off signals of the pressure-mat-type sensors.
2) Enabling the input of various sensors, including the pressure-mat-type sensors, to know the person's sleep/awake status and timing of utterance and to estimate the environmental conditions, such as the on/off state of the lighting and temperature in the room.
3) Controlling the robot agent's functions, such as the nodding motion, on/off state of the LEDs, and voice-calling, including the conduct of daily conversations, by using a speaker installed inside of the robot agent.

The proposed controller consists of a simple general-purpose microprocessor board and interfaces to the sensors and the agent, as shown in Fig. 4.

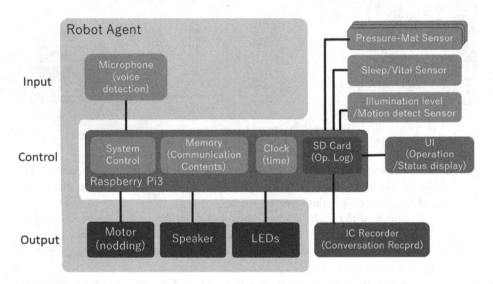

Fig. 4. Controller hardware

A Raspberry Pi is used as the core for the controller. The inputs for the controller appear on the upper part of Fig. 4. The on/off signal of the pressure-mat type sensors are connected using General Purpose Input/Outputs (GPIOs), which are the standard interface for nurse call systems. A sleep/vital sensor, such as a pneumatic pressure sensor [14, 15], illumination level sensor, and motion detection sensor can be connected to the controller.

The outputs for the controller appear on the lower part of Fig. 4. The robot agent's motor for its head nodding, LEDs, voice-calling speaker, and microphone, mounted on the robot's body, are connected to the controller using the Bluetooth interface. The controller can control a couple of robot agents. Additionally, the IC recorder can be attached and switched from the controller when voice recording is needed during experiments.

4.2 Controller Software

The functional structure of the software for the system is shown in Fig. 5. The procedure is divided into the following sub-processes: i) Sensor reading: Data from the
sensors are input and then filtered to reduce the noise in the sensor signals, ii) State
estimation: The filtered sensor data and their alteration are used to estimate the person's
state and state transition, iii) Action generation: Appropriate robot action, namely,
voice-calling content, nodding motion, and LED on/off pattern, is generated based on
the estimated state of the person, iv) Robot control: The corresponding action command is sued to the robot agent. These sub-processes are detailed below.

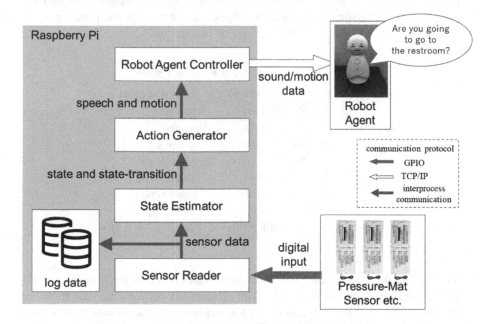

Fig. 5. Controller software architecture

1) Sensor Reading

In this sample case, three pressure-mat type sensors are used. They are placed on a
patient's chest/back (S_1), waist/hip (S_2), and the edge of the bed (S_3). The mat
sensor outputs "1" when the mat is pressed and outputs "0" otherwise. The sensors
are connected to the MCU (Raspberry Pi) via GPIOs.

The Sensor Reader module obtains data from the pressure-mat sensors 10 times per
second. A moving average filter, for a period of Tm (ex. 1 [sec]), is applied to each
sensor output for noise reduction to obtain the current sensor value $Si(t)$. The
average of the filtered data $Si(t)$ for the duration of Tr (ex. 5 [sec]) is updated as the
sensor's reference value $Si\_r(t)$. The module continuously saves the data as the log
data and sends them to the State Estimator module, where the sensor reference
value $Si\_r(t)$ is compared with its current (filtered) value $Si(t)$ to evaluate its
relative variance.

2) State Estimation

The relationship between the sensor reference values and the states that express the person's posture (Fig. 2) is defined in advance. The State Estimator module estimates the person's posture on the bed based on the filtered data, $Si(t)$ and $Si\_r(t-Tm)$. The estimation process can be simplified by giving each sensor datum, $Si\_r(t)$ or $Si(t)$, a value of 1 (on) or 0 (off). In such a case, a bit pattern composed of each sensor value as bit (3-i) (2^{3-i} bit) can be defined as a combined sensor pattern. It can be interpreted considering the person's posture on the bed, as shown in Table 1. Note that the pattern C4 and C5 do not usually occur, although these are included in the Estimator in consideration of special cases, such as a posture in which the person's hips are floating (supporting most of the person's weight with shoulder and feet), or the person is lying near the edge of the bed (where the pressure on the mat sensor is not sufficient to turn the sensor output "on").

Table 1. Sensor pattern and a person's state

Pattern name	Sensor pattern (S1-S2-S3)	Estimated posture
C7	ON-ON-ON (111)	Supine
C6	ON-ON-OFF (110)	Supine
C5	ON-OFF-ON (101)	Quasi-Supine 1
C4	ON-OFF-OFF (100)	Quasi-Supine 2
C3	OFF-ON-ON (011)	Long Sitting
C2	OFF-ON-OFF (010)	Long Sitting
C1	OFF-OFF-ON (001)	Sitting Square
C0	OFF-OFF-OFF (000)	Standing Up (Left)

The module also estimates the transition of the states based on the time sequence of the sensor data, $Si(t)$ and $Si\_r(t-Tm)$. The relationship between the state transition and the change in the state is also defined in advance, and the module estimates the transition based on this relationship. The module can also receive sleep sensor data to turn the below action on and off according to the person's sleep/awake conditions.

The State Estimator module sends the estimated state and the estimated state transition to the Action Generator module. If no transitions are detected, then the duration of such condition is counted, and a signal that means "no state-transition" is sent as the estimated result.

3) Action Generation

The Action Generator module monitors the state and the state transition send by the State Estimator module. When a state transition is detected, this module generates the behavior of the robot according to the state transition, the sleep/awake status, and the time obtained from the clock. The module then sends the signal to the robot agent controller to enable the robot to act as desired. The possible motions, contents of the utterances, and LED colors of the agent's face are generated by this module.

For example, when the system detects a state transition, such as "the person is standing up from the bed", the Action Generator module selects the color of the LEDs and the voice-call content. It then sends the corresponding signal to the robot controller. Although the last state before a person leaves their bed is "sitting square" at the edge of the bed, "long sitting" is the first state in leaving the bed and can thus be treated as for estate information. Providing such information in advance to nurse/caregivers is important for preventing certain types of patients, such as those who are agile in motion, from falling, because it can prompt nurses/caregivers to visit a patient's bedside before the patient leaves their bed. This type of adjustment according to the patient's attribute is also the role of the Action Generator.

4) Robot Agent Control

The Robot Agent Controller contains the defined motion, the voice-call contents, and the color patterns of the LEDs. The contents of the voice-call are prepared as sound files. The possible motions are defined as the time sequences of the target angles of the motor. The colors of the LEDs are defined by changing the RGB values. The Robot Agent Controller plays the file selected by the Action Generator module to deliver voice-calls, execute motions, and show colors as ordered.

5 Preliminary Experiments

5.1 Interview with Nurses and Older Adults

A preliminary interview was conducted with nurses and older adults at the hospital where experiments utilizing the proposed system are planned. The objectives of the interview were to confirm the acceptability of the robot agent for both nurses and older adults, and to learn their impression toward the robot agent. First, the concept and purpose of the system were explained to the nurses of the patients who will participate in the substantiating experiment, and the nurses' comments were collected. The following are their comments.

1) Patients should be familiarized with the robot agent beforehand, so they are not surprised when abruptly addressed by the speaking robot.
2) Patients may want to hold or embrace the robot when they feel an attachment to it.
3) Patients may expect the robot to verbalize their thoughts for them.
4) The robot agent should not make voice-calls from behind the patients.
5) It would be helpful if the robot agent is applicable for patients with dementia.

The authors have started the experiments with 12 older adult patients to determine any difficulty in listening and evaluate the intelligibility of the voice-calling contents.

5.2 User Study with Older Adults

A user study was conducted to determine the impression of the robot agent left on the participants and to see how the participants reacted to the robot agent's behaviors. In this experiment, the system estimated the posture of each participant (standing up, sitting down and so forth) based on the pressure-mat sensor data, and voice-calls were made to the participant according to their posture change. After interacting with the robot, each participant was asked to assess the suitability of the robot's behavior by answering a questionnaire.

Currently, a user study with some healthy older adults is in progress; so far, it has been found that the participants notice and recognize the robot voice-call, and have good impressions of the robot agent.

1) User Study Protocol

First, the motion required for the participants were made simpler than those on a bed: i) standing up from a chair, ii) walking a meter away from the chair and then returning to the chair, and iii) sitting on the chair. These motion changes were monitored by two pressure-mat sensors. One of the mats was placed on the seat of the chair and the other was placed at the feet of the chair. The participants were not required to answer the robot's voice-calls.

The robot spoke to participants whenever the system detected the following motion changes: A) standing up from the chair, B) leaving the chair, C) returning to the vicinity of the chair, and D) sitting on the chair. The voice-call contents corresponding to these motion changes are shown below in the same order as the above motion changes.

A) What happened?

B) Is there any problem?

C) Welcome back.

D) I was waiting for you. Let's start talking.

2) Interview Contents

The participants were asked about the likeability, perceived intelligence, and perceived safety of the robot agent. A robot designed to support older adults has to be reliable and "friendly" and should give users a feeling of security and mental safety. Moreover, the appropriateness of the robot's utterances and their characteristics, such as volume and speed of talking, timing of the voice-call corresponding to the motion or the change in posture of the participants, participants' awareness of the voice-call, and the contents of the utterances, was assessed. The authors aimed to clarify the standard utterances that could appropriately attract the attention of a user who is trying to move with intention.

3) Participant Reaction Example

The robot's utterances were found to be mostly appropriate in the assessment. Although most of the participants did not stop when the robot voice-called them, because they were asked to do a series of motion: standing up, walking, walking back, and sitting on the chair, they noticed the voice-call of the robot and replied while moving.

6   Conclusion

The authors developed a novel bedside monitoring/voice-calling system based on a previously created prototype [10]. The system monitors a person's status on a bed. It prolongs the person's action of leaving their bed through voice-calling, motion and LEDs to give nurses/caregivers time to physically attend to the patient, thus preventing the patient from falling. The outline and design detail of the robot agent, the controller, and the control algorithms are explained in this paper.

The newly developed system is intended to improve the system's reliability for use in a long-term verification experiment at hospitals and care facilities, and flexibility for responding to various user requirements.

Considerations about the reliability and flexibility in the design phase are introduced in this work. Actual experiments using this developed system have recently been launched, and data and findings have been obtained from the experiments. Although results are yet to be found, the participants noticed and recognized the voice-call, and replied to the call of the robot agent.

The authors are planning to introduce this system in hospitals to perform experiments with a large number of participants to further investigate the voice-call contents, timing and other related factors, such as the tone and speed of voice-calling, with respect to the participants' attribute, thus clarifying the appropriate specification of this type of system.

Acknowledgments. The authors would like to thank Mr. Terukuni Yasuda at EcoNaviSta Company for his cooperation.

This research is mainly supported by Japan Agency for Medical Research and Development (AMED) Grant Number JP19he2002014, and partially supported by JSPS KAKENHI Grant Number JP19H01138.

References

1. Cabinet Office of Japan: Annual Report on the Aging Society. (Summary) FY2018 (2018). http://www8.cao.go.jp/kourei/english/annualreport/2018/pdf/cover.pdf
2. Hughes, R.G. (ed.): Patient Safety and Quality: An Evidence- Based Handbook for Nurses, AHRQ Publication No. 08-0043, Agency for Healthcare Research and Quality, Rockville (2008)
3. Centers for Disease Control and Prevention: WISQARS leading causes of nonfatal injury reports. https://webappa.cdc.gov/sasweb/ncipc/nfilead.html. Accessed 18 Feb 2020
4. Japan Council for Quality Health Care: Project to Collect Medical Near-miss/Adverse Event Information 2017 Annual Report (2018). http://www.med-safe.jp/pdf/year_report_english_2017.pdf
5. Daielsen, A., Torresen, J.: Recognizing bedside events using thermal and ultrasonic readings. Sensors **17**(6) (2017)
6. Paramount Bed Co. Ltd.: Fall Prevention Alarm System. https://www.paramount.co.jp/english/product/detail/index/20/84. Accessed 18 Feb 2020
7. Miyake, N., Hatsukari, T.: Care beds and related assist systems. Instrumentaion Control **56**(5), 371–376 (2017)

8. Fujita, Y.: Personal Robot PaPeRo. J. Rob. Mechatron. **14**(1), 60–63 (2002)
9. Wada, K., Shibata, T.: Social effects of therapy in a care house, In: Proceedings of the IEEE International Conference on Robotics and Automation, Rome, Italy, pp. 1250–1255 (2007)
10. Miyake, N., Shibukawa, S., Masaki, H., Otake-Matsuura, M.: User-oriented design of active monitoring bedside agent for older adults to prevent falls. J. Intell. Rob. Syst. (2019). https://doi.org/10.1007/s10846-019-01050-w
11. Potter, P., Grayson, D., et al.: Mapping the nursing process. J. Nurs. Adm. **34**(2), 101–109 (2004)
12. York, T., MacAlister, D.: Hospital and Healthcare Security. Elsevier (2015)
13. Sidner, C., Lee, C.: The effect of head-nod recognition in human-robot conversation. In: Proceedings of the 1st ACM SIGCHI/SIGART Conference on Human-Robot Interaction, Salt Lake City, USA, pp. 290–296 (2006)
14. Paramount Bed Co. Ltd.: Nemuri SCAN. https://www.paramount.co.jp/english/product/detail/index/20/96. Accessed 18 Feb 2020
15. EcoNaviSta Co. Ltd.: Life Rhythm Navi Plus Doctor. http://info.liferhythmnavi.com/. Accessed 18 Feb 2020

Usability Assessment of Augmented Reality-Based Pedestrian Navigation Aid

Liu Tang[1] and Jia Zhou[2(✉)]

[1] Department of Industrial Engineering, Chongqing University,
Chongqing, China
[2] School of Management Science and Real Estate, Chongqing University,
Chongqing, China
zhoujia07@gmail.com

Abstract. This study aimed to explore the usability problems of augmented reality (AR)-based pedestrian navigation aid. A field experiment was conducted to investigate the performance and experience of young and older adults when they used two common functions (virtual navigator and auxiliary map) of AR-based navigation aid. Success rate, navigation error and speed variation were measured. A total of 28 younger adults and older adults participated in this experiment. The results showed that almost all participants could complete navigation tasks successfully. Presenting virtual navigator and auxiliary map would result in more navigation errors for participants. In addition, the effect of virtual navigator on the navigation error was related to road condition. Presenting virtual navigator would decrease the navigation error in simple road condition and increase navigation error in complex road condition. Furthermore, older adults preferred AR-based navigation aid than young adults. Finally, 11 usability problems were collected in this study.

Keywords: Navigation · Augmented reality · Usability · Older adults

1 Introduction

Older adults rely more on walking for their daily journeys. However, as people age, their cognitive, perceptual and motor abilities decline. These abilities affect people navigating, as navigation requires people to perceive and integrate spatial information from the environment [4, 16]. Data showed that 53.58% of the lost population from 2016 to 2019 were elderly in China, and older adults had the higher risk of getting lost [3]. Therefore, it is essential to provide an adaptive navigation aid for older adults to avoid them getting lost.

With the development of mobile and location-based technology, mobile navigation aids have become one of the methods to help pedestrians navigate. In the fourth quarter of 2017, the users of using mobile navigation aid in China has reached 707 million and would continue to grow [7]. With the development of augmented reality technology, AR has been used in pedestrian navigation. Some studies have shown that AR could reduce the cognitive working load of the older adults in switching attention between the real world and information sources [9]. Mulloni et al. [13] believed that AR-based

© Springer Nature Switzerland AG 2020
V. G. Duffy (Ed.): HCII 2020, LNCS 12198, pp. 581–591, 2020.
https://doi.org/10.1007/978-3-030-49904-4_43

navigation systems were usually used at decision points, which could lead to its potential benefits by limiting the attention sharing of the elderly [17]. Considering to these advantages, AR-based pedestrian navigation aid may be beneficial to older adults. However, some study showed that older adults spent more time and had higher rate of navigation errors using AR-based navigation aid than using voice or digital map [12, 15]. In general, whether AR-based navigation aid is useful and usable for older adults still unknown. Therefore, the purpose of this study was aimed to investigate the usability and functionalities of AR-based pedestrian navigation aid.

2 Literature Review

Quantity of researches showed that navigation performance was influenced by individual characteristics, including age, gender, perceptual, and cognitive ability, which maybe benefit or hamper navigation [2, 10]. It has been shown in many studies that spatial ability was the major factor in determining performance. People with high spatial ability performed better than people with low spatial ability [2, 19]. However, as people aging, people's spatial ability declined and needed more time to navigate [16]. Three types of spatial knowledge were required during navigating in a new environment: landmark knowledge, route knowledge and configuralknowledge [18]. Older adults needed more time to learn and elaborate spatial knowledge than young adults, and they had problems in use of configural knowledge [8, 16]. Therefore, using overview map could not improve their navigation performance. Even though, older adults were likely to use overview map, as people felt secure [16] and ensured that they are on the right direction or path by using map.

As a new navigation method, AR-based navigation aid superimposes position and orientation information in real world. In this way, user could not be distracted when they are always staring at the screen [1]. However, AR-based navigation had worse navigation performance, higher cognitive working load and lower system usability comparing with other type of navigation aids, such as voice and digital map [12, 15]. One reason possibly was the participants had no previous experience with AR technology [6]. In addition, the discontinuous and inaccurate tracking of AR-based navigation aid could make users make wrong decisions at intersections [13]. The design of virtual navigation objects, such as their color, also affected user performance and experience, as brightness and screen-glare affected the visibility of virtual navigation objects when they were superimposed on the real world [5, 12].

3 Methodology

3.1 Equipment and Material

Three criteria were used to choose the AR-based navigation aid application: the application should have overview map and text instruction, which are essential functions for users; the application should be stable to use; the application should be accessible. Finally, Baidu Map application with version 10.15.0.915 which has AR-based navigation function was used in this study. Baidu Map APP is a commercial application developed by Baidu to provide navigation aid for pedestrians and drivers and has the highest usage rate in Chinese navigation aid application market.

The interface of AR-based navigation aid consists of three main functions: virtual route, virtual navigator and auxiliary map. Virtual route is a blue line and the basic function of this tool. Virtual navigator is a cartoon character that users can choose to use it if they want. Auxiliary map is an overview map that shows user's current location, destination and surrounding landmark. Figure 1 is the interfaces of the AR-based navigation aid we used in this study.

In this experiment, we used a smart phone, Huawei honor 8 with Android 6.0, to install the application. A camera, Sony FDR-AX40, was used to record the process.

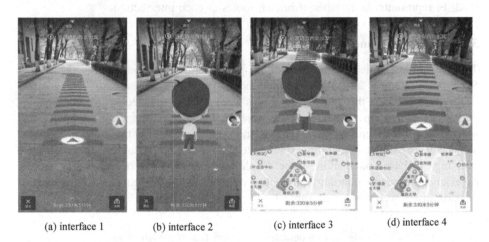

| (a) interface 1 | (b) interface 2 | (c) interface 3 | (d) interface 4 |

Fig. 1. Screenshots of AR-based navigation aid interface. (a) pedestrian was guided only by virtual route. (b) pedestrian was guided by virtual route and virtual navigator. (c) pedestrian was guided by virtual route, virtual navigator and auxiliary map. (d) pedestrian was guided by virtual route and auxiliary map.

3.2   Variables

The independent variables were virtual navigator presentation and auxiliary map presentation, both of which were within-subject variables. Virtual navigator presentation had two levels: with and without virtual navigator in AR-based navigation aid interface. The auxiliary map also had two levels: with and without auxiliary map in the navigation aid interface. Therefore, there were four types of navigation aid interfaces in this study, as shown in Fig. 1.

The dependent variables were user performance and satisfaction. There were three measures of user performance: success rate, navigation error and speed variation. Successful task was considered as participants competed tasks without any help of experimenter. A navigation error was participants deviated from the right route indicated by the navigation aid. Speed variation was defined as the difference between speed of participants using AR-based navigation aid minus the speed of without using navigation aid.

Covariates included demographic variables and road complexity. The demographic variables included: age, prefer walking speed (PWS). Road complexity was related to the length of road where participants passed, the number of intersections and the number of branch routes at each intersection. the formula of calculating road complexity was shown as (1).

$$road\ complexity = \frac{\sum_{i=1}^{n} log_2(Fi)}{L} \tag{1}$$

Note: L is the length of whole road; n represents the number of intersections in the road; Fi represents the number of branch routes at each intersection.

3.3   Participants and Tasks

To examine age difference, a total of 28 participants, 14 young adults (M = 23.8, SD = 0.939, Rang = 22–25) and 14 older adults (M = 67.6, SD = 4.484, Rang = 61–76) were recruited in this study. Age groups were gender-balanced, with 7 females and 7 males in each group. All young adults were students from Chongqing University, and older adults were recruited from campus and communities near the college. Disabled subjects were excluded from this experiment. Only one young adult had the experience of using AR-based navigation aid before. Mostly participants (26 out of 28) had the experience of using technology products (computer and smart phone). Characteristics of participants were shown in Table 1.

Table 1. Demographic characteristics of participants

Variable	Category	Num.		%
		Older adults	Young adults	
Education	Primary school	12	0	42.9
	Junior high school	1	0	3.6
	Senior high school	1	0	3.6
	Bachelor or above	0	14	50.0
Navigation aid using experience	Used	8	14	78.6
	Never used	6	0	21.4

Four different routes were predefined in this study, and each participant needed to navigate in the four routes by using different AR-based navigation aid interface, as shown in Table 2. As some of the participants were familiar with the campus, we did not tell them the destination of each routes and emphasized that they should strictly follow the instructions of the navigation aid.

Table 2. Details of four routes

Route	Number of intersections	Total number of branch routes	Distance	Interface of navigation aid
Route 1	4	8	220 m	Interface 1
Route 2	4	8	450 m	Interface 2
Route 3	6	13	290 m	Interface 3
Route 4	4	11	360 m	Interface 4

3.4 Procedure

The experiment required approximately 50 min. First, experimenter briefly introduced the experiment procedure and asked participants to complete a basic questionnaire about their background and the experience in using navigation aid. Second, we tested the PWS of each participant and showed participants a demonstration of think-aloud. In formal experiment, participants were asked to navigate in 4 routes by using AR-based navigation aid, while experimenter recorded participant's thought and navigation process by using camera. Then, participants needed to complete a Post Study System Usability Questionnaire (PSSUQ) which used a five-point Likert scale and was carefully translated into Chinese [14]. Finally, a brief interview was conducted to collect participant' s attitudes towards the AR-based navigation aid.

4 Results and Discussion

4.1 Performance

Success Rate. Results showed that almost all participants could reach to the destinations by using AR-based navigation aid, with a success rate of 97.32%. Only two older adults failed to reach the destination in three navigation tasks. One of them navigated to an air-raid shelter where was no GPS signal, and said she did not know what to do next. Another participant made multiple navigation errors and finally abandoned the experiment.

Navigation Error. The average number of navigation errors was 1.08 (SD = 1.23). Older adults made more errors (M = 1.42, SD = 1.564) than young adults (M = 0.79, SD = 0.801). However, no significant difference was observed between older adults and young adults.

The data was analyzed by using two-way repeated ANOVA model. Three covariates were included in the model. Prior to the analysis, we performed a regression line homogeneity test. Significant interaction effect (F = 68.9083, p < 0.01) between road complexity and virtual navigator presentation was observed. Therefore, we took road complexity as an independent variable and divided it into two levels: simple and complex.

The results showed that there was a main effect of virtual navigator presentation on navigation error ($F = 4.538$, $p < 0.05$), as shown in Fig. 2 (a). Participants had higher navigation error when virtual navigator was presented than when virtual navigator was not presented in navigation aid interface. Older adults had more navigation errors when presenting or not presenting virtual navigator than young adults, while the difference between them was not statistically significant. Possible reasons are that processing the navigation information provided by the virtual navigator required higher perceptual speed which is declined with age [11] and presenting the virtual navigator increased the cognitive working load of the participants.

A main effect of auxiliary map presentation on navigation error was also observed ($F = 28.128$, $p < 0.01$). Presenting the auxiliary map made the number of errors increased by 61.53%. Older adults showed significant difference between navigating with auxiliary map and without auxiliary map ($F = 20.54$, $p < 0.01$), while no significant difference was fond on young adults. The possible reasons may be related to user's cognitive working load and spatial ability. When the auxiliary map was presented, participants needed to match it with real route, virtual routes, which increased their cognitive working load. In addition, older adults had difficulty using overview map, for their declined spatial ability [16]. What is more, young adults were familiar with overview map, as they used it in their daily life.

Interactive effect between virtual navigator and road condition on navigation errors was observed ($F = 53.112$, $p < 0.05$), as shown in Fig. 2 (c). In simple road condition, presenting virtual navigator could reduce navigation errors ($F = 30.61$, $p < 0.01$). However, in complex road condition, presenting virtual navigator would significantly increase navigation error ($F = 53.78$, $p < 0.01$). In addition, we fond navigation errors often occurred in where road conditions were complex (e.g., an intersection with four branches or roundabout). One possible reason is that presenting virtual navigator in complex road required more attention from participants and increased their cognitive working load.

Speed Variation. Speed variation was used to measure the degree of hesitation of participants during using AR-based navigation aid. There was no significant difference between virtual navigator and auxiliary map on speed variation. Participants seldom stopped during navigation tasks. When unsure which branch to choose at an intersection, participants would continue to walk and choose one of branch routes to try. Even if they made an error, they could quickly start navigating again. However, the covariate of PWS had a significant difference ($F = 20.1992$, $p < 0.01$) on speed variation. The bigger the PWS, the smaller the speed variation.

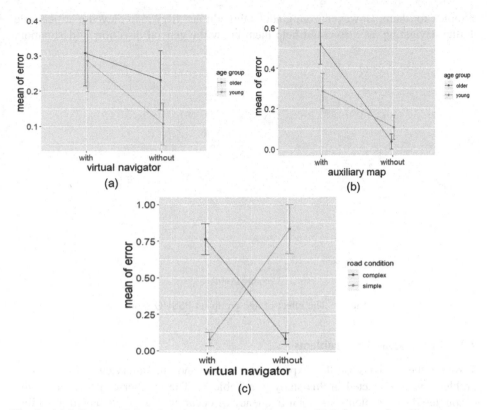

Fig. 2. (a) Influence of virtual navigator on navigation error. (b) Influence of auxiliary map on navigation error. (c) Interactive effect between virtual navigator and road condition on navigation error.

4.2   Satisfaction

The PSSUQ and interview were analyzed. The average PSSUQ score of all participants on AR-based navigation aid was 78.7 (SD = 19.81), and there was a significant difference between older and young adults (F = 16.48, p < 0.01), as shown in Fig. 3. Although older adults had more errors in navigation tasks, they had higher positive feedback (M = 90.81, SD = 10.46) than young adults (M = 66.58, SD = 19.74). During the interview, participants were asked their general feeling about the aid and problems they encountered. Most of older adults thought the aid was easy to learn and use than other types of navigation aids, such as paper map. However, young adults said they preferred to use 2D or 3D digital map rather than AR-based navigation aid, as they always got confused when the virtual route did not match the real route and they thought the auxiliary map was too small to see.

What is more, we fond older and young adults had different opinions towards auxiliary map. Older adults said they seldom used auxiliary map during navigating because they were unfamiliar with overview map, and the map was too small and complex for them. However, young adults thought auxiliary map played a critical role during navigating, as map could help them know the general direction of destination.

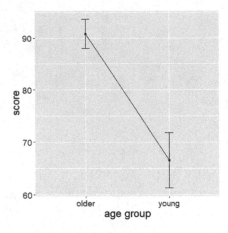

Fig. 3. The effect of age group on PSSUQ score

4.3   List of Usability Problems

Through the analysis of the experimental video and the interviews, 11 usability problems were collected in this study (see Table 3). The number of participants who encountered the problems and total frequency of occurrence were countered. Usability problems were determined according to the following criteria: 1) participants expressed some negative effects, or treated something as problems; 2) participants felt confused; 3) participants made mistakes; 4) participants stopped the navigation tasks. Through statistical analysis, we found that the change delay of virtual route instruction is the most frequency problem participants encountered, which caused participants to deviate from the correct route or stop. In addition, most of participants were confused by the instructions of virtual navigator, virtual route and voice, especially at intersections.

Table 3. List of usability problems with AR-based navigation aid

Usability problems	Participants number	Total number	Average
Instruction of virtual route changed delay at intersection	14	27	1.93
Participants could not understand some instructions of the virtual navigator	13	22	1.69
Participants could not understand the meaning of the virtual route in straight road	4	6	1.5
Participants were confused by the instruction of virtual route at intersections	21	30	1.43

(continued)

Table 3. (*continued*)

Usability problems	Participants number	Total number	Average
Participants were confused by the voice instructions at intersection	24	32	1.33
Participants misunderstood what it meant when a virtual route was a curve	6	8	1.33
While the participants were walking, the virtual navigator was stationary and the participants had no sense of movement	3	3	1
The change of virtual route was too abrupt for participants to respond	2	2	1
The auxiliary map was too small for the subjects to see clearly	3	3	1
The routes on the auxiliary map was not matched to virtual route, which caused participants deviated from the correct route	2	2	1
There were no other indications when the GPS signal was not accuracy	2	2	1

5   Conclusion

This study explored the usability problems of AR-based navigation aid in a field experiment. Participants' performance and satisfaction were investigated. In general, participants could successfully reach to destinations by using AR-based navigation aid. Therefore, it is useful to use AR-based navigation aid. However, despite the high success rate, participants still made many navigation errors, especially older adults. In addition, presenting virtual navigator and auxiliary map would increase the navigation errors, so we suggested that it is better to avoid the use of virtual navigator and auxiliary map for older adults, as too many instruction information would increase their cognitive working load. For young adults, it is necessary to present auxiliary map for them to ensure their sense of control.

From this study, we collected some of usability problems. AR-based navigation aid instruction needs to be more responsive at intersections to avoid users deviating from the correct route or waiting for the change of instructions. In addition, participants could hardly match the instructions of virtual route and virtual navigator with real route, especially when there were multiple branches in the same direction at an intersection. Therefore, it is important to consider the design of AR-based navigation aid at complex intersections.

Acknowledgement.   This work was supported by funding from Chongqing Municipal Natural Science Foundation (cstc2016jcyjA0406) and the National Natural Science Foundation of China (Grants no. 71661167006).

References

1. Amirian, P., Basiri, A.: Landmark-based pedestrian navigation using augmented reality and machine learning. In: Gartner, G., Jobst, M., Huang, H. (eds.) Progress in Cartography. LNGC, pp. 451–465. Springer, Cham (2016). https://doi.org/10.1007/978-3-319-19602-2_27
2. Arning, K., Ziefle, M.: Effects of age, cognitive, and personal factors on PDA menu navigation performance. Behav. Inf. Tech. **28**(3), 251–268 (2009). https://doi.org/10.1080/01449290701679395
3. Chinanews: Lost population data report: adults have the highest rate of lost population (2019). https://baijiahao.baidu.com/s?id=16399267900098671309&wfr=spider&for=pc
4. Czaja, S.J., et al.: Factors predicting the use of technology: Findings from the center for research and education on aging and technology enhancement (create). Psychol. Aging **21**(2), 333–352 (2006). https://doi.org/10.1037/0882-7974.21.2.333
5. Dey, A., Billinghurst, M., Lindeman, R.W., Swan, J.E.: A systematic review of 10 years of augmented reality usability studies: 2005 to 2014. Front. Robot. AI **5** (2018). https://doi.org/10.3389/frobt.2018.00037
6. Huang, H., Schmidt, M., Gartner, G.: Spatial knowledge acquisition with mobile maps, augmented reality and voice in the context of gps-based pedestrian navigation: results from a field test. Cartogr. Geogr. Inf. Sci. **39**(2), 107–116 (2012). https://doi.org/10.1559/15230406392107
7. iiMedia Research: 2017–2018 China mobile map market research report (n.d.). https://www.iimedia.cn/c400/60970.html
8. Kausler, D.H.: Learning and Memory in Normal Aging. Academic Press, San Diego (1994)
9. Kim, S., Dey, A.K.: Simulated augmented reality windshield display as a cognitive mapping aid for elder driver navigation. In: Proceedings of the 27th International Conference on Human Factors in Computing Systems - CHI 2009, vol. 133 (2009). https://doi.org/10.1145/1518701.1518724
10. Kirasic, K.C.: Age differences in adults' spatial abilities, learning environmental layout, and wayfinding behavior. Spat. Cogn. Comput. **2**(2), 117–134 (2000). https://doi.org/10.1023/A:1011445624332
11. Li, Q., Luximon, Y.: The effects of 3D interface metaphor on older adults' mobile navigation performance and subjective evaluation. Int. J. Ind. Ergon. **72**, 35–44 (2019). https://doi.org/10.1016/j.ergon.2019.04.001
12. Montuwy, A., Cahour, B., Dommes, A.: Older pedestrians navigating with ar glasses and bone conduction headset. In: Extended Abstracts of the 2018 CHI Conference on Human Factors in Computing Systems - CHI 2018, pp. 1–6 (2018). https://doi.org/10.1145/3170427.3188503
13. Mulloni, A., Seichter, H., Schmalstieg, D.: User experiences with augmented reality aided navigation on phones. In: 10th IEEE International Symposium on Mixed and Augmented Reality, pp. 229–230 (2011). https://doi.org/10.1109/ISMAR.2011.6092390
14. Ouyang, X., Zhou, J.: How to help older adults move the focus on a smart TV? Exploring the effects of arrow hints and element size consistency. Int. J. Hum. Comput. Inter. 1–17 (2018). https://doi.org/10.1080/10447318.2018.1534346
15. Rehrl, K., Häusler, E., Steinmann, R., Leitinger, S., Bell, D., Weber, M.: Pedestrian navigation with augmented reality, voice and digital map: results from a field study assessing performance and user experience. In: Gartner, G., Ortag, F. (eds.) Advances in Location-Based Services, pp. 3–20. Springer, Heidelberg (2012). https://doi.org/10.1007/978-3-642-24198-7_1

16. Sjölinder, M., Höök, K., Nilsson, L.-G., Andersson, G.: Age differences and the acquisition of spatial knowledge in a three-dimensional environment: Evaluating the use of an overview map as a navigation aid. Int. J. Hum Comput Stud. **63**(6), 537–564 (2005). https://doi.org/10.1016/j.ijhcs.2005.04.024

17. Tang, A., Owen, C., Biocca, F., Mou, W.: Comparative effectiveness of augmented reality in object assembly. In: Proceedings of the Conference on Human Factors in Computing Systems - CHI 2003, vol. 73 (2003). https://doi.org/10.1145/642611.642626

18. Thorndyke, P.W., Stasz, C.: Individual differences in procedures for knowledge acquisition from maps. Cogn. Psychol. **12**(1), 137–175 (1980). https://doi.org/10.1016/0010-0285(80)90006-7

19. Ziefle, M., Bay, S.: How to overcome disorientation in mobile phone menus: a comparison of two different types of navigation aids. Hum. Comput. Interac. **21**(4), 393–433 (2006). https://doi.org/10.1207/s15327051hci2104_2

Extracting and Evaluating Personal Interests with Dialogue Agent

Yuki Tokuda[1(✉)], Shota Nakatani[1], Sachio Saiki[1], Masahide Nakamura[1,2],
and Kiyoshi Yasuda[3]

[1] Graduate School of System Informatics Kobe University,
1–1 Rokkodai, Nada-ku, Kobe 657–8501, Japan
{tokup,shota-n}@ws.cs.kobe-u.ac.jp, sachio@carp.kobe-u.ac.jp,
masa-n@cs.kobe-u.ac.jp
[2] Riken AIP, 1–4–1 Nihon-bashi, Chuo-ku, Tokyo 103–0027, Japan
[3] Osaka Institute of Technology, Omiya 2–16, Asahi-ku, Osaka 535–8585, Japan
fwkk5911@mb.infoweb.ne.jp

Abstract. In order to realize a continuous conversation between a dialog agent and a user, it is important to generate topics that are close to the user. In this paper, we propose a method for extracting and evaluating the concept "Personal Interests" that users are interested in through dialogue with a virtual agent (VA). In the proposed method, the VA first talks about a certain genre, asks the user for interests in that genre, and asks the user to talk about episodes about each interest. In addition, the system extracts the personal knowledge "Personal Ontology" from the user's answer, and built and stores that in the form of Linked Data. The extracted interests are evaluated based on three criteria P1 (length of the episode), P2 (the number of concepts included in the episode), and P3 (the number of reference sources of the concepts), and calculate the level of interest in each concept. We implemented a prototype of the proposed method and performed a subject experiment to extract and evaluate personal interests. As a result, it was found that the scores calculated by the criterion P1 and the criterion P2 correlated with the actual interest level of the user. In addition, it was suggested that the criterion P3 could discover new concerns from other concepts included in the episode.

Keywords: Linked data · Personal ontology · Home care · Virtual agent · Personal interests

1 Introduction

Japan is facing a hyper-aging society. According to the Cabinet Office, while the total population of Japan is decreasing, the proportion of the elderly population is rising. The elderly population is predicated to account for 33.3% of the total. Also, the number of people with dementia (PWD) will reach 7 million in 2025, where one-fifth of five elderly people in Japan will suffer from dementia [5].

© Springer Nature Switzerland AG 2020
V. G. Duffy (Ed.): HCII 2020, LNCS 12198, pp. 592–608, 2020.
https://doi.org/10.1007/978-3-030-49904-4_44

Against this background, effective and sustainable support for the elderly and the PWD is needed.

Validation therapy [6] and reminiscence [11] are known as a non-drug therapy for symptoms of dementia. Validaticon therapy is a care method that recognizes the meaning behind the PWD's confused behaviors and unrealistic behaviors, and calms them by showing the correspondence between acceptance and empathy. Reminiscence is a care method that looks back on the past experience, and responds empathically and receptively to the process to improve the psychological stability of the PWD. In these care methods, continuous conversation between the care provider and the patient is important. However, it is difficult economically and timely for specialists to provide counseling on a daily basis. In addition, the transition of home care has been progressing recently, and the burden on family care has also increased.

Among them, our research group proposes a system that enables a PWD to communicate at any time at home using a **virtual agent (VA)**, which is a robot program capable of voice dialogue [10]. The technical challenges to realize continuous dialogue with VA is how to **generate dialogues that is close to the person**. So far, we have proposed a method to generate topics related to the individual based on the life history of the user [8], and a method to topical events and trends according to user's age.

We also define life history and birth year as **Personal Ontology**. We have developed a system that has VA ask users questions and dynamically generate personal ontology based on their answers [7]. This system saves the built Personal Ontology in the form of Linked Data [4], which is a set of *langle* subject, predicate, and object triples *rangle*. Furthermore, this system connects Personal Ontology to external knowledge by linking with Linked Open Data (LOD)[3], and acquires related knowledge to expand the topic. However, in the current system, only the part that builds Personal Ontology by dialogue is implemented. The task of creating a dialogue close to the individual by using the generated Personal Ontology is a future work. In order to generate attractive dialogues for users, it is important to find the concepts of particular interest from the large amount of concepts accumulated in Personal Ontology.

Therefore, in this research, we propose a method for finding concepts of particular interest to users from individual ontology accumulated in dialogue with VA. In this paper, we define interest as "the emotions and directions in which an individual wants to be more involved in a certain matter", and call matters and concepts that an individual is particularly interested in **Personal Interests**. Then, we extract individual interests through dialogue with VA, and extract the feelings for each interest to evaluate the degree of each interest. More specifically, the proposed method consists of the following two parts.

(A1) Extraction of Personal Interests: We have VA ask questions about personal preferences and have the user answer. Build Personal Ontology in the form of LinkedData from the answer based on the method of previous research [7].

(A2) Evaluation of Personal Interests: For each concept in the personal ontology constructed in LinkedData format, we evaluate the degree of interest of the user based on the following three criteria.

P1: The larger the number of characters in answer 2, the more the user is interested in C1.

P2: The greater the number of concepts C2 included in Answer 2, the more the user is interested in C1.

P3: When there are multiple links to C2, the user is interested in C2.

We implemented the proposed method as a dialog scenario using the preceding system, and conducted an experiment in which seven subjects interacted with VA. In the dialogue scenario, VA asks the user questions about five genres: food, sports, places and scenery, hobbies, and "others," and the user answers the questions by voice. The system analyzes the answer by speech recognition and text analysis, and builds a personal ontology in LinkedData format.

We analyzed the constructed LinkedData and calculated the degree of interest of each concept based on P1, P2, and P3. After the experiment, we conducted a questionnaire for each subject and asked them to answer their interest in the extracted concepts. Finally, we performed a correlation analysis between the score calculated by the proposed method and the degree of interest in the questionnaire. The analysis showed a high correlation between the degree of interest in the questionnaire and the calculated score. As a result, it was found that the proposed method was effective in extracting and specifying personal interests.

2   Preliminary

2.1   Communication System for PWD at Home

Our research group has developed a **virtual care giver (VCG)** system that provides communication care through dialogues for the elderly at home and those with dementia [7]. Figure 1 shows the VCG screen. We have realized dialogues with a home user by using a virtual agent (VA) that can communicate by voice in VCG. VCG can be used as a dialogue partner for PWD regardless of time, and can be expected to reduce the burden on human caregivers.

In order to realize a continuous dialogue between the PWD and VA, it is necessary to provide **topics close to individuals**. In previous research, we proposed a method of dynamically generating topics that are close to individuals using **Life History** and Linked Open Data (LOD) [8].

2.2   Linked Data, Linked Open Data (LOD)

Linked Data [4] is data that is linked by means of links made meaningful using Web technology. Linked Data is one of the technical components for realizing the Semantic Web, and is described in the Resource Description Framework (RDF) that structurally represents arbitrary information on the Web as **resources**.

Fig. 1. VirtualCareGiver

Opened Linked Data as open data and shared on the Internet is called *Linked Open Data (LOD)*. By linking the published data, it is possible to form a huge knowledge database on the Web.

In the RDF model, data is represented by triples that combine three elements: subject, predicate, and object. In some cases, the subject and object are represented by ellipses (resources), and the predicates are represented by directed graphs, which are represented by arrows (links) connecting the two ellipses. However, the object can be a string constant (literal) instead of a URI, in which case the object is represented by a rectangle.

Figure 2 shows an RDF graph example. The URI can be abbreviated by using the namespace prefix. In this figure, dbpedia-ja: Tokyo means http://ja.dbpedia. org/resource/Tokyo. In this example, the figure shows two things: "dbpedia-ja: The URI of Tokyo indicates Tokyo" and "The country where Tokyo is located is Japan".

2.3   Building of Personal Ontology Based on Dialogue with VA [7]

In our previous study [7], we named individuals' knowledge needed to generate topics closely related to individuals as **Personal Ontology**. Then, we extended the VCG system and realized a method of dynamically building and managing Personal Ontology in the form of LinkedData through dialogue with VA.

More specifically, the individual ontology is represented by triples of the three elements described in 2.2. For example, ⟨"Tokuda", "Favorite thing", "Board game"⟩ represents a personal ontology that "The favorite thing of user "Tokuda" is a board game."

PREFIX dbpedia: <http://dbpedia.org/resource/>
PREFIX dbpedia-owl: <http://dbpedia.org/ontology/>
PREFIX rdfs: <https://www.w3.org/2000/01/rdf-schema#>

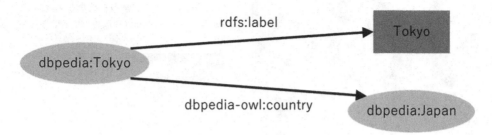

Fig. 2. RDF graph example

As a method of building an Personal Ontology, VA asks U about P and generates a question that asks O from U. For example, when the VA asks, "What do you like about Tokuda?" and the user answers, "I like board games", the system generates a Personal Ontolopy ⟨*"Tokuda"*, *"FavoriteThings"*, *"BoardGame"*⟩. It is also possible to ask places and people as questions.

When ⟨U, P, O⟩ is created, the system converts this to RDF format and represents this as LinkedData. Specifically, we define U as a resource representing a user, O as a resource representing information about the user, and P as a link representing the relationship between the user and information. Also, the system uses http://cs27.org/personal-ontology/resource/ and http://cs27.org/personal-ontology/rproperty/ as the namespace URI, with the prefix written as ex: and ex-prop:. We use these to describe ex: *uid* rdfs: label *"U"* and ex: *uid* ex-prop: P ex: O to obtain *"U's P is O"*. The converted RDF data is stored in a dedicated database called **RDF store**.

From the implementation of the above system and subject experiments, it has been found that when the response from the user to the question from the VA is grammatically correct and the speech recognition and syntax analysis are successful, a personal ontology can be automatically generated. However, in the current system, only the generation and accumulation of Personal Ontology is performed, and the part to generate continuous ontology using these is a future task.

2.4   Personal Interests

In the system under development, we basically assume that the VA interacts by providing topics. At this time, if the topic provided by VA is not interested in the user, continuous conversation cannot be expected. In addition, it is important to know what the individual has **interests** in personal care because of the necessity of close conversation with the individual for dementia care.

In this paper, we define interests as "the emotions and directions of trying to have greater involvement in a certain matter", and call "the matter or concept that an individual is interested in" **Personal Interests**. For example, for an individual who likes travel and travels many times a year, it is presumed that "travel" is the individual's Personal Interests. Also, from the definition of interest, Personal Interests are not necessarily hobbies or interests, and individuals who have "spent at home" or "pain in the feet" as Personal Interests are also conceivable.

3   Proposed Method

In this research, we extend the system described in 2.3 and propose a method to discover Personal Interests based on Personal Ontology obtained by interacting with VA. The proposed method consists of A1: Extraction of Personal Interests and A2: Evaluation of Personal Interests.

3.1   A1: Extraction of Personal Interests

In A1, VA asks the user questions and extracts Personal Interests. The VA introduces a certain genre and asks the user to answer the concerns of the genre. In addition, we collect the data necessary for "A2: Evaluation of personal interests" by asking the user to tell the episodes of each interest appearing in the answer. We build and store the user's answer in the LinkedData format as a Personal Ontology based on the method of previous research described in 2.3.

Step 1 Obtain User ID (uid): VA first asks for the user's name and uses it to create the user's resource U and the identifier uid. In the construction of the following individual ontology, uid refers to U.

Step 2 Obtain Personal Interests: VA talks about the genres defined in the system in advance and asks the user to find out what may be the subject of Personal Interest. First, VA talks about the genre P and asks the user U, "U, are you interested in P?" When the user answers "Yes", the VA asks "What is U's P?" And accepts the user U's interests in the genre P by free answer. The VA then asks, "Tell me anything else," and gets as much user response as possible. The answer obtained at this time is called **Answer 1**. The system extracts **noun phrases** included in Answer 1 and uses them as candidates for interest. VA asks the user whether the extracted noun phrase is correct, and if so, repeats the question. If there is no mistake, generate $\langle U, P, C1 \rangle$ for the concept C1 represented by each extracted noun phrase, and use it as a Personal Ontology.

Step 3 Obtain Episode: By asking the user to answer **episodes** for Personal Interests extracted from Answer 1 in Step 2, we collect their thoughts and feelings. Specifically, for each concept C1 extracted as personal interests from Answer 1, VA asked "Please tell me the episode about C1 of U" and have the user answer in free form. The answer obtained at this time is called **Answer 2**. The system extracts noun phrases included in Answer 2 and extracts nouns from the noun phrases. Then, after confirming that there are no mistakes as in Step 2, the system generates Personal Ontology $langle C1, episode, C2 rangle$. When there are other candidates of interest, the system conducts similar dialogues and collect episodes.

Step 4 Convert Personal Ontology to Linked Data: The system converts the Personal Ontology generated in Steps 2 and 3 into RDF format and manages it as LinkedData. Conversion to RDF is performed by the method described in 2.3. Since resources should be referenced by URIs based on **words**, when O contains multiple words, they are split into words and converted into resources, and these are grouped by blank nodes . Also, O as the original text is connected to the same group as the label. This makes it possible to refer to resources for each word while maintaining O information. In addition, the system keeps **original text of Answer 1 and Answer 2** from users as comments in RDF so that the source of personal ontology can be traced at any time. We describe a specific procedure for converting a personal ontology obtained from a user's answer (answer 1 or answer 2) into RDF.

1) Create a blank node $B0$ and set $B0$ as the root node of Personal Ontology obtained from the answer.
2) To save the answer text, create a literal $L0$ corresponding to the answer text, and create a link from $B0$ to $L0$ with $rdf : comment$ as a predicate.
3) For each concept C in each Personal Ontology $\langle U, P, C \rangle$ (or $\langle C1, "episode", C \rangle$), create a literal $L1$ corresponding to C. Also, create the words $C_1, C_2, ..., C_n$ are extracted from C, and the corresponding resources $R_1, R_2, ..., R_n$ (when they do not already exist). Create a blank node $B1$ that groups them.
4) Create a link of the predicate $rdf : label$ from $B1$ to $L1$. Also, create a link of the each predicate R_i from $B1$ to rdf_i.
5) Create a link of the predicate rdf_1 from $B0$ to $B1$.

By the above procedure, a tree of Personal Interests and a tree of episodes related to each interest are generated from each of Answer 1 and 2. Then, the system connect these trees hierarchically.

6) Create a resource corresponding to user U, a predicate on genre P, and a predicate "episode" (when they do not exist).
7) For the root node $B0$ of tree $T1$ obtained from Answer 1, create a link of predicate P from U to $B0$.

8) For each concept C in the tree $T1$, we define a blank node $B1$ that groups C. We also define the root node $B0'$ of the tree $T2$ obtained from the episode (Answer 2) about C. At this time,create a link of the predicate *episode* from $B1$ to $B0'$.

As an example, the Personal Ontology obtained from Answer 1 of Step 2 "I like udon (Japanese noodle food)" is converted to RDF format as follows.

```
_:B00 rdfs:comment "Ilikeudon" .
_:B00 rdf:_1 _:B01 .
_:B01 rdfs:label "udon" .
_:B01 rdf:_1 ex:udon .
```

In addition, from the answer 2 of Step 3 "I came to eat often in the cafeteria since I entered the university", the system generates the following RDF,

```
_:B10 rdfs:comment "I came to eat often in the cafeteria since I entered the
university" .
_:B10 rdf:_1 _:B11 .
_:B10 rdf:_2 _:B12 .
_:B11 rdfs:label "university" .
_:B11 rdf:_1 ex:univsersity .
_:B12 rdfs:label "cafeteria" .
_:B12 rdf:_1 ex:cafeteria .
```

The link that connects them is generated as follows.

```
ex:uid rdfs:label "Tokuda" .
ex:uid ex-prop:favoritefoods _:B00 .
_:B01 ex:"episode" _:B10.
```

3.2   A2: Evaluation of Personal Interests

A2 is the phase in which we evaluate the personal interests extracted in A1 and thereby identify the concepts of particular interest to the user. In A1, the system first identified the user's interests in a certain genre from Answer 1 in terms of noun phrases, and then had the user asks the episode (Answer 2) about each interest (C1). Therefore, Answer 2 is a great clue to the user's interest in C1. In A2, the system analyzes the **structure** of Personal Ontology based on the following three **Criteria P1, P2, P3** and evaluates the degree of interest in each concept in the ontology.

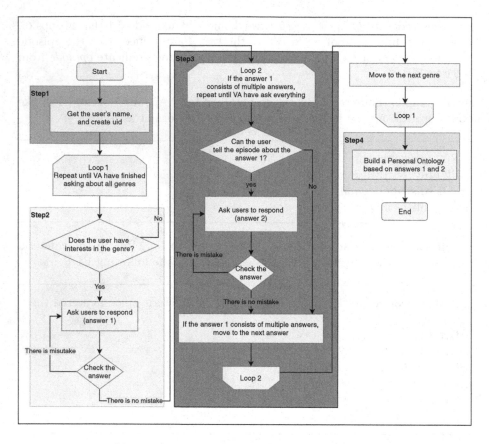

Fig. 3. Extraction of Personal Interests flowchart

P1: The more characters in the episode (Answer 2) about C1, the more the user is interested in C1.

P2: The more concepts included in the episode (Answer 2) about C1, the more the user is interested in C1.

P3: When there are multiple links to a C2 resource, the user is implicitly interested in the C2.

3.3   Evaluation of Personal Interests by P1

P1 is an evaluation criterion that "the more the number of characters in an episode related to an interest, the stronger the interest in that". This is based on the hypothesis that "people will tell more about their interests". We use **episode number of characters** as a specific evaluation scale for criterion P1.

In Linked Data of personal ontology constructed in A1, the original text of the episode exists as a literal linked by $rdf : comment$. By counting the number of characters, the system calculates the interest level score (called **P1 score**) of the concept $C1$ as the link source of the episode. The system evaluates that the higher the P1 score, the higher the interest in the concept.

Evaluation of Personal Interests by P2. P2 is an evaluation criterion that "the more episodes of an interest include more concepts, the stronger the interest is in that". This is based on the hypothesis that "interests are accompanied by more knowledge and experience, so more concepts will appear in the episode." In P2, the evaluation criterion is calculated using **number of concepts appearing in the episode**.

In Personal Ontology Linked Data constructed in A1, concepts that appear in episodes exist as resources in a tree linked by *episode*. By counting these numbers, the system calculates the interest level score (called **P2 score**) of the concept $C1$ from which the episode is linked. The system evaluates that the higher the P2 score, the higher the interest in the concept.

Evaluation of Personal Interests by P3. P3 is an evaluation criterion that "when a concept has many links from another, the concept is an implicit Personal Interest". This is based on the hypothesis that "what the user is interested in will unconsciously say that in various contexts." The specific evaluation scale of P3 uses **number of link sources of concept**.

In Linked Data of Personal Ontology constructed in A1, the presence of multiple link sources in the resource corresponding to a C2 indicates that C2 has appeared in various contexts. Therefore, the number of links entering the resource is defined as the interest level score of $C2$ (called **P3 score**). The system evaluates that the higher the P3 score, the higher the interest in the concept or the concept.

4 Implementation

We implemented a prototype system for extracting and evaluating personal interests proposed in 3. The extraction of Personal Interests in A1 was realized by reusing and expanding the system of previous research. Specifically, for the interaction between the VA and the user in Steps 1 to 3, we implemented a new dialog scenario with the VA on the preceding system. We also added new functions to the predecessor system regarding the extraction of ontology and conversion to linked data.

The technology used for implementation is as follows.

- **Infrastructure system:** Java, Virtual Care Giver [7], MMDAgent [9]
- **Dialogue scenario:** Ruby
- **Server:** Apache Tomcat, Apache Axis2 (Web-API)
- **Linked Data processing:** Apache Jena [1], Apache Jena Fuseki
- **Natural language processing:** COTOHA API [2], kuromoji-ipadic-neologd

We used the predecessor system as the base system, and implemented the dialog scenario in Ruby. We used the Apache Jena framework and the Fuseki RDF store to efficiently manage and accumulate linked data of personal ontology. We used the COTOHA API to parse the user's answer by natural language processing and extract phrases in noun units, and kuromoji-ipadic-neologd to morphologically analyze words and extract named entities.

This time, the evaluation part of Personal Interests of A2 visualized the RDF generated by the system in the form of a graph and evaluated that by manual analysis.

5   Evaluation Experiment

In order to confirm the effectiveness of the proposed method, we conducted an experiment in which subjects were asked to interact with the implemented system and whether or not personal interests could be extracted and evaluated.

5.1   Purpose and Method of Experiment

The purpose of the experiment is to confirm whether the Personal Interests extracted and evaluated by the proposed method are actually the interests of the individual. In the experiment, we first evaluate the Personal Interests extracted from the dialogue with the VA using the P1-P3 scores. Next, we ask the subjects to answer the questionnaire to what extent they are interested in each of the extracted personal interests. Finally, we analyze the correlation between the P1-P3 score and the questionnaire results.

A total of seven subjects participated in the experiment: five men in their twenties, one woman in their twenties, and one man in their forties. We conducted experiments using the system implemented between January 15 and 20, 2020. We used a wireless headset (Logicool G G533) as a device for dialogue with VA in order to reduce noise during speech recognition and increase the sound insulation of conversation. This time, five categories of personal interests were used: food, sports, places and scenes, hobbies, and other favorite things. VA asked questions according to the procedure described in 3.1, and asked the subjects to answer their interests in each genre and episodes related to them.

After the experiment, we conducted a questionnaire survey to determine how much interest the subjects actually had in the concepts extracted by the dialogue. Since this time the experiment was asking for "likes and things", we set evaluation on the 7 levels of "dislike" as 1, "normal" as 3, "like" as 5, and "extremely like" as 7. We asked the subjects to evaluate the degree of interest in each concept in seven levels of evaluation. In addition, if they felt that the concept was inappropriate as an object of interest, we asked subjects answer 0 (not applicable). As a supplementary survey, we asked subjects to rate their interest in the genres of interest "food", "sports", and "places and scenery". We conducted the survey using Google Forms.

5.2 Analysis Method

Since the P1, P2 and P3 scores have different application ranges, we classified the concepts extracted by the dialogue between the subject and the system as follows. In each classification, we analyze the correlation between the evaluation value by the proposed method and the answer value of the questionnaire.

- **Target C1:** Concepts extracted directly as concerns in Answer 1 of Step 2 of A1. We analyze the correlation between the evaluation value by the P1 and P2 scores and the evaluation value by subjects.
- **Taget C2:** Concepts that appeared in the episode of interest in Answer 2 of Step 3 of A1. We analyze the correlation between the evaluation value by the P3 score and the evaluation value by subjects.
- **Target C3:** Concepts corresponding to the genre of interest. We evaluate by the total value of P1 and P2 scores of all interests in the genre, and analyze the correlation with the evaluation value by subjects.

5.3 Experimental Result

Table 1 shows the results. This table shows the correlation coefficient between the interest level score of the concept extracted by the system for each subject and the interest level evaluation by the subjects. We perform correlation analysis for each subject because the length of the episode, the number of concepts, and the subjectivity in the questionnaire evaluation vary greatly depending on the subject. Values in bold indicate places where high correlation is observed.

First, for subject C1, relatively high correlations are seen for subjects U2, U3, U4, U5, and U7. In other words, it is found that the number of characters in an episode and the number of concepts included in the episode for a particular interest are related to the degree of interest in the individual. On the other hand, there is no negative correlation for subject U1 and no correlation for U6. The reason is discussed in 5.4. In addition, the correlation value between the P3 score and the degree of interest of the individual is positive for the subject C2, but there is almost no correlation except for the subject U4. This is due to the fact that among the nouns extracted from Answer 2 by the system, a very large number of nouns with a P3 score of 1 are extracted, and they contain a considerable number of potential interests. On the other hand, there are many nouns that are evaluated by users as inappropriate (0 not applicable). We perform a more detailed analysis considering these in 5.4.

Target C3 is to check whether the sum of the P1 and P2 scores of interests in each genre is related to the degree of interest in that genre. This is not for the evaluation of interests but for the genre, so it is out of the scope of the original proposed method, but we perform correlation analysis as a supplementary analysis. From the results of the rightmost two columns in the table 1, there is a high correlation among subjects U2, U4, U5, U6, and U7. Subject U1 has no correlation, and subject U3 has a negative correlation.

5.4   Consideration

Effectiveness and Limitations of Criteria P1 and P2 for Target C1.
Regarding the concept of Target C1, the P1 score and the P2 score showed
relatively high correlations for five subjects except U1 and U6. Therefore, we
consider that the Criteria P1 and P2 are effective, although limited, as criteria
for measuring the level of personal interest.

We analyze the case of U4 where there is a significant difference between
the P1 and P2 scores. Figure 4 plots the P1 score, P2 score, and questionnaire
evaluation value for the subject U4's six interests. The P2 score is normalized
based on the P1 score to make the scales uniform. We consider why the P1 score
did not correlate well in the U4 case. First, regarding the place genres "Kobe"
and "Kyoto", the evaluation by the questionnaire shows the same degree of
interest, but there is a large difference in the length of the episodes (P1 score).
On the other hand, the number of concepts in an episode (P2 score) is not so

Table 1. Correlation between extracted concept score and subjects evaluation

uid	Target C1		Target C2	Target C3	
	P1 score	P2 score	P3 score	P1 score	P2 score
U1	−0.562	−0.715	0.193	0.118	0.300
U2	**0.841**	**0.630**	0.313	**0.983**	**0.908**
U3	**0.565**	**0.543**	0.115	−0.636	−0.866
U4	0.333	**0.822**	0.499	**0.960**	**0.986**
U5	**0.548**	**0.589**	0.277	**0.716**	**0.715**
U6	0.083	−0.034	0.216	**0.688**	**0.633**
U7	**0.806**	**0.750**	0.166	**0.969**	**0.894**

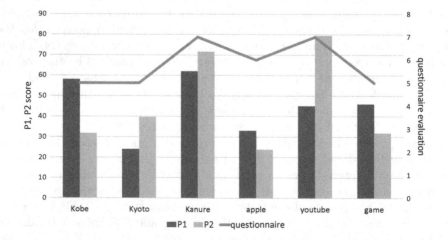

Fig. 4. P1, P2 score and questionnaire evaluation of subject U4

different. In many cases, the length of the episode is proportional to the number of concepts, but in this case, the number of concepts that appear is smaller than that of Kobe. In the comparison between the food genres "apple" and "cannure", both P1 and P2 scores reflect the actual questionnaire evaluation. Although there is a large difference in the questionnaire results between the hobby genre "youtube" and "game", there is no difference in the P1 score. This is due to the difference in the amount of information per unit character that words have. In the episode of "game", frequently there are words with a large number of characters such as "Breath of The Wild" and "switch". On the other hand, answers about the concept "youtube" often used words with short characters such as "Jikitsu", "Toki", "Hima" (a very short word in Japanese). Although there is a large difference in the number of concepts in the P2 score, there is no difference in the number of characters in the P1 score.

In order to find out why the scores did not correlate with subjects U1 and U6, we interviewed the subjects after the experiment. As a result, a cause is found. The cause is that "we couldn't extract enough interest and its episodes." Subjects said they could not externalize their thoughts in words well due to inexperience in dialogue with VA. At the beginning of the dialogue, the subject commented, "I didn't know how much to talk about.", "I was impatient to answer immediately. I wanted to talk more, but I couldn't talk much at that moment.".

Effectiveness and Limitations of Criteria P3 in Subject C2. We consider why there is little correlation between P3 score and individual interest level for the concept of target C2. Table 2 shows the frequency of questionnaire evaluation values for all subjects for each P3 score value obtained in the experiment. Each row in the table shows how many points the subject rated for a concept with a certain P3 score. From this table it can be seen that concepts with P3 score of 1 make up the majority of all samples, including a significant number of potential personal interests (questionnaire ratings 6, 7). This **data bias** greatly affects the correlation coefficient.

In order to remove this bias, we analyze **ratio** of the questionnaire response value for each class of P3 score. Figure 5 shows a graph of the percentage of questionnaire response values for each concept class with P3 scores of 1, 2, 3, and 4. It can be seen that as the P3 score increases, the proportion of concepts with a particularly high degree of interest (questionnaire evaluation 6, 7 points) increases. Therefore, we think that it is reasonable to think that the interpretation of the criterion P3 is not "the higher the P3 score, the higher the level of individual interest in those concepts", but "the higher the P3 score, the higher the personal interest in those concepts".

In addition, in the Table 2, there are many concepts that are not considered to be of interest (question evaluation 0 points). These are pronouns such as "place" and "this", and nouns indicating time such as "recent" and "around". It is concepts that appeared frequently in ordinary conversations, but could not be of interest by itself. There are also concepts where language analysis did not work well such as "eat" and "like". Improvement of these non-essential concepts

Table 2. Frequency of questionnaire response value for each P3 score

	Questionnaire							
P3 score	0	1	2	3	4	5	6	7
1	150	3	3	9	19	73	46	49
2	21	0	0	1	2	14	13	17
3	2	0	0	1	0	2	6	4
4	3	0	0	0	0	0	1	3
5	1	0	0	0	1	0	0	2
6	0	0	0	0	0	0	1	0
7	0	0	0	0	0	0	0	0
8	0	0	0	0	0	0	0	0
9	0	0	0	0	0	0	1	0
10	0	0	0	0	0	0	1	0

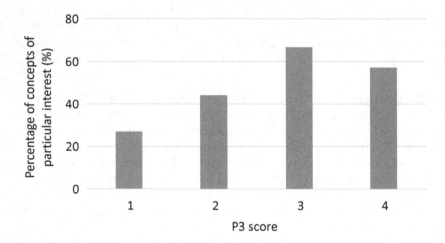

Fig. 5. Percentage of concepts of high interest for each P3 score

can be expected by creating a dictionary of words (stop words) to be excluded and filtering them when extracting ontology.

Discussion on Target C3. The analysis for the target C3 is a supplementary result that analyzes whether the degree of interest in the genre can be characterized by the sum of the evaluation scores of the interests in that genre. As a result, P1 score and P2 score showed high correlation in cases other than subjects U1 and U3. The effectiveness of the genre is limited due to the small number of samples of interest in the genre. However, by accumulating data and understanding which genre an individual is interested in, it can be useful for strategies to select topics from which genres.

6   Conclusion

In this paper, we propose a method for extracting and evaluating the concept "Personal Interests" that users interest in through dialogue with a virtual agent (VA). In the proposed method, VA first introduce into a genre, ask topics in the genre , and ask the user talk episodes about each genre. In the proposed method, we extract the personal knowledge "Personal Ontology" from the user's answer, and built and store that in the form of Linked Data. The extracted interests are evaluated based on the three criteria P1 (length of the episode), P2 (the number of concepts included in the episode), and P3 (the number of reference sources of the concepts), and the level of interest in each concept Is calculated as a numerical value.

We implemented the prototype of the proposed method by reusing and extending the preceding system. We conducted an experiment to extract and evaluate personal interests in seven subjects using the implemented prototype. As a result, it was found that the scores calculated by the criterion P1 and criterion P2 correlated with the actual interest level of the person. It was also suggested that the criterion P3 could discover new concerns from other concepts included in the episode.

Future tasks include improving the issues of the proposed method that were clarified in experiments, such as the problem of the familiarity with dialogue with VA and the problem of accuracy of concept extraction. While improving these, we will refine the personal interest evaluation unit and implement this in a complete system. Furthermore, it is important to evaluate the receptivity and satisfaction of the system by applying and experimenting with the proposed system for the elderly at home and persons with dementia.

Acknowledgements. This research was partially supported by JSPS KAKENHI Grant Numbers JP19H01138, JP17H00731, JP18H03242, JP18H03342, JP19H04154, JP19K02973.

References

1. Apache jena. https://jena.apache.org/. Accessed 12 Feb 2020
2. Cotoha api. https://api.ce-cotoha.com/contents/index.html. Accessed 12 Feb 2020
3. Linked open data - w3c egovernment wiki. https://www.w3.org/egov/wiki/Linked_Open_Data. Accessed 12 Feb 2020
4. Berners-Lee, T.: Linked data - design issues (2009). https://www.w3.org/DesignIssues/LinkedData.html
5. Cabinet office, G.o.J.: annual report on the aging society (2019). http://wwwa.cao.go.jp/. Accessed 13 Nov 2019
6. Feil, N.: The validation Breakthrough: Simple Techniques for Communicating with People with" Alzheimer's-type Dementia". Health Professions Press, Towson (1993)
7. Nakatani, S., Saiki, S., Nakamura, M., Yasuda, K.: Implementation and evaluation of personal ontology building system with virtual agent. In: Duffy, V.G. (ed.) HCII 2019. LNCS, vol. 11582, pp. 391–403. Springer, Cham (2019). https://doi.org/10.1007/978-3-030-22219-2_30

8. Sakakibara, S., Saiki, S., Nakamura, M., Yasuda, K.: Generating personalized dialogue towards daily counseling system for home dementia care. In: Duffy, V.G. (ed.) DHM 2017. LNCS, vol. 10287, pp. 161–172. Springer, Cham (2017). https://doi.org/10.1007/978-3-319-58466-9_16
9. Tokuda, K., Lee, A., Oura, K., Yamamoto, D.: Mmdagent: Toolkit for building voice interaction sytstems (2018). http://www.mmdagent.jp/
10. Tokunaga, S., Tamamizu, K., Saiki, S., Nakamura, M., Yasuda, K.: VirtualCare-Giver: personalized smart elderly care. Int. J. Softw. Innov. (IJSI) 5(1), 30–43 (2016). https://doi.org/10.4018/IJSI.2017010103. http://www.igi-global.com/journals/ abstract-announcement/158780
11. Woods, B., O'Philbin, L., Farrell, E.M., Spector, A.E., Orrell, M.: Reminiscence therapy for dementia. Cochrane Database Syst. Rev. (3) (2018)

Basic Study of Wall-Projected Humanitude Agent for Pre-care Multimodal Interaction

Xin Wan[1] and Tomoko Yonezawa[2]

[1] Kansai University Graduated School, Takatsuki, Osaka, Japan
k805631@kansai-u.ac.jp
[2] Kansai University, Takatsuki, Osaka, Japan
yone@kansai-u.ac.jp

Abstract. In this paper, we propose an agent system that is projected on a wall and that provides a pre-care multimodal interaction with a user by adopting Humanitude method. It was expected that not only human's care but also robot's care using Humanitude smoothen the introductory interaction before the dementia elderly cares. We selected the two steps of Humanitude, "look into their eyes" and "touch them". The agent first moves into the user's field of view corresponding to her/his facing direction to make eye contact, and next approaches to the user (to the virtual camera), and touches on the user by an air cannon. We verified whether the proposed agent system brings about familiarity, reliability, presence, and naturalness by subjective evaluation and found the effectiveness of the movement, approachability action, and touch of the agent.

Keywords: Multimodal interaction · Wall-projected virtual nursing agent · Support for the dementia elderly · Humanitude care · Introduction before care

1 Introduction

Recently, the aging population with fewer children is growing, especially in Japan, and the number of elderly people with dementia is increasing, which is expected to become a serious problem in the future [2]. There is still a caregiver shortage, although the number of caregivers is increasing. Moreover, due to peripheral symptoms (Behavioral and Psychological Symptoms of Dementia, psychiatric symptoms, and behavioral abnormalities) of dementia, caregivers must spend more time and labor than general nurses. Such problematic behaviors are caused when elderly individuals with dementia feel fear and anxiety, etc. In addition, it is difficult to support not only physical aspects but also the mental aspects of dementia patients due to the caregiver shortage.

To solve these problems, in the information technology field, studies on observation systems and labor support robots have been conducted; these robots could possibly replace caregivers [9,11]. On the other hand, there is a nursing care technique for elderly dementia patients called Humanitude care, introduced by

V. G. Duffy (Ed.): HCII 2020, LNCS 12198, pp. 609–621, 2020.
https://doi.org/10.1007/978-3-030-49904-4_45

Geneste et al. [4], which has been developed for care acceptance with consensus and consent. The care technique requires multimodal communication, which consists of four guidelines: "look into their eyes", "talk to them", "touch them", and "help them to stand up". This technique has been evaluated to be effective for patients with dementia in the medical field [5].

Furthermore, various studies on virtual agents have been conducted, aiming at communication opportunities different from observation systems and nursing robots [1,8,13]. Such research indicated that nonverbal multimodal interaction is an indispensable method to communicate information between the agent and the human. Therefore, we propose implementing the Humanitude technique in the virtual agent to support daily life communication with elderly people who have dementia.

In this study, we aim to study an agent with multimodal interaction adopting the actions of "look into their eyes" and "touch them" from the guidelines of Humanitude. Eye contact and physical contact are expected to build reliability. For daily support implementation, a prototype system adopts projection onto a wall surface. The effects of promoting acceptance of the care, stress reduction, and mental stability of elderly people with dementia are expected when the proposed system with Humanitude techniques is applied in their daily lives. The agent is expected to provide relief and to be trusted.

This research focuses on smoothing the pre-care interaction for acceptable systems like the preparation attitude of nursing caregivers. In this paper, we aim to clarify the effectiveness of 1-1) the agent's movement corresponding to the direction in which the user is facing to look into his or her eyes, 1–2) the agent's approximate movement (visual effect as closing) to communicate, and 2) the tactile stimuli on the user's arm to simulate the agent's touch on the user's impression of familiarity, reliability, presence, and naturalness.

2   Related Research

There have been many proposals on communicative nursing agents for dementia patients and elderly individuals. Sakakibara et al. [14] proposed a daily counseling system for dementia patients. The system adopted an interactive virtual agent with supporting images and movies of an appropriate topic that corresponds to the participants' age to stimulate their memories. Huang et al. [7] proposed an autonomous virtual agent that can serve as a companion for dementia patients to help users recall memories. The virtual agent can generate a nod action and back channeling while communicating with the user. An evaluation experiment of this conversational agent showed that the patients felt pleasure communicating with the agent and paid more attention to the agent. Yasuda et al. [16] developed an agent system to serve as a conversation partner for individuals with dementia and proposed that the agent participate as a presenter of conversation topics for the multiparty interaction.

Human beings may be strongly influenced by the appearance and behavior of the object, assuming that it has an internal state and "mind" when interacting with the object [3,10]. Therefore, the embodiment and multimodal interaction should be considered. Many studies on gaze and contact interaction have been proposed. Yoshida et al. [18] proposed an agent with motion-parallax 3DCG to express gaze at real objects and eye contact with users. Their results showed that the accuracy of these expressions made the agent approachable. Rajap et al. [12] examined the impressions of a "sidelong glance" of a lifelike agent as a combinatorial nonverbal behavior. They showed that the "sidelong glance" conveys "friendliness" and "dominance" to users. They also proposed a comprehensive affection model of agent behaviors to help design lifelike agent behaviors.

Yamada et al. [15] conducted an experiment on the multimodal comprehensive methodology Humanitude in an acute care hospital [6] and showed that the care approach Humanitude decreased BPSD and was successful regarding patients' acceptance of care.

Consequently, we aim to realize a multimodal virtual agent that alternates human caregivers in acquiring elderly people's acceptance and consent before care is offered. We especially focused on the steps of "look into their eyes" and "touch them" from the Humanitude guidelines, before "talk to them".

In this paper, we investigated whether the attitude of the pre-care Humanitude agent was appropriate. Thus, the effectiveness of the movement (horizontal and depth directions) of looking into the user's eyes and providing physical touch from the viewpoint adopted in our proposed method was that the user felt familiarity, reliability, presence, and naturalness in the agent when evaluating its impression.

3   Proposed System

3.1   System Overview

We propose a Humanitude-attitude agent system. As pre-care preparation, the agent visually expresses horizontal movement to look into the user's eyes and approach the user.

The agent was projected on a wall surface by a LC projector. To "look into the user's eyes", the agent horizontally moved corresponding to the user's face direction. To perform the approximation movement (visual effect as closing) before the physical touch, the image of the agent was gradually enlarged. Next, an air cannon device provided tactile stimuli; however, to adjust the strength and position of the device, the experimental system was equipped with a portable air pump directed toward the user's right arm from behind a cardboard single-leaf screen.

3.2   System Configuration

The agent system consists of a visual stimuli section that shows the agent's behavioral appearance and a tactile stimuli section that simulates the agent's physical contact.

3.3   Visual Stimulus Section

In this system, the agent is drawn using the Processing 3.3 program[1]. The agent is projected on the wall surface by a projector (RICOH PJ WX4141). The agent's horizontal movement corresponds to the user's face direction with a 3-s delay. The animation of the movement is smoothed to refrain from discontinuous movement from the detected face direction.

The agent's presence is embodied with a simple animation character (Fig. 3) with its face, body, hands, and legs. The background space of the agent includes a wall, floor, and ceiling with depth, as though the space is continuously matched to the user's real world space. The agent's walk is expressed by changing the length of the agent's legs alternately. The agent first moves into the user's field of view. Once eye contact between the agent and the user is established, the agent approaches the user from the current position in the virtual space. In this phase, the agent moves to the user's side (lower depth value) in the virtual space, displayed as if the agent is gradually enlarged on the wall surface.

To track the user's face direction for the horizontal movement, the face image of the user is acquired by the webcam (Microsoft LifeCam Cinema 720p HD Webcam), and the face direction data acquired by faceAPI[2] are sent to Processing via the User Datagram Protocol. Thus, the agent moves in the horizontal direction and the vertical (depth) direction of the wall screen based on the user's face direction and the positional relationship between the user and the agent.

3.4   Tactile Stimuli Section

The physical contact is simulated by an air cannon blowing wind onto user's skin on his or her upper arm. The tactile stimuli were tentatively designed to initiate 3 s after the agent enters into the user's personal space to make it approachable.

4   Experiments

4.1   Purpose

We verified what kind of feelings the participants have and what kind of feelings the agent provided by the movement of the virtual agent entering the participants' field of view, its gradual approach toward the participants, and the tactile stimuli.

We believe the effective elements in the experiment can help to build a virtual agent that obtains the user's consent before pre-care communication.

---

[1] http://processing.org.
[2] https://www.seeingmachines.com/product/faceapi/.

4.2 Hypotheses

The following hypotheses were established with regard to the sense of familiarity, reliability, presence, naturalness, and unpleasantness induced by the agent.

H1: The user feels familiarity with the agent, which moves corresponding to the user's face direction, approaches him or her, and simulates physical contact.

H2: The user feels reliability from the agent, which moves corresponding to the user's face direction, approaches him or her, and simulates physical contact.

H3: The user feels the presence of the agent, which moves corresponding to the user's face direction, approaches him or her, and simulates physical contact.

H4: The user feels the naturalness of the agent, which moves corresponding to the user's face direction, approaches him or her, and simulates physical contact.

H5: The user does not feel unpleasantness from the agent, which moves corresponding to the user's face direction, approaches him or her, and simulates physical contact.

4.3 Participants

The experiment involved 30 Japanese participants between the ages of 21 and 30 (16 males and 14 females).

4.4 Conditions

We prepared a within-subject experiment with 3 factors, and each factor had 2 levels: Factor A) horizontal movement (A1: corresponding to the user's face orientation, A2: without referencing face orientation), B) approachability (B1: approach, B2: without approach), and C) tactile stimuli (C1: with, C2: without). All conditions of the experiment are shown in Figs. 3, 4, and 5. The order of conditions was counterbalanced.

4.5 Experimental System

For simulation of physical contact, a preliminary investigation was conducted with 5 participants using a portable air pump compared to an air cannon. Based on the results, a portable air pump was selected for our experiment to carry out the above conditions in the Wizard of Oz method. A laser pointer was mounted on the portable air pump outlet so that the experimenter could visually understand the target position of airflow on the participant's right upper arm. To simulate the physical contact by the agent from the front, the airflow was emitted from 60° to the right from the center of the participants within 3 s. The air pump was controlled from behind the board screen.

4.6   Experimental Environment

The experimental environment was set as shown in Fig. 3. The projector was placed at a distance of 48 cm from the wall to present the visual stimulus of the experiment, connected to the PC of the experimenter. A webcam was placed at a distance of 65 cm from the wall to obtain participants' face direction data. A chair for the participants was put in a fixed position at a distance of 1 m from the wall. The PC for the experiment was placed on one desk for the experimenter, which was put on the right of the participant. In this experiment, we placed a cardboard screen so that the participants could not see the experimenter. A hole (width: 13 cm, height: 8 cm) was drilled in the cardboard screen for the portable air pump to provide the tactile stimuli. A desk to the left of the participants was used for filling out questionnaires.

4.7   Procedures

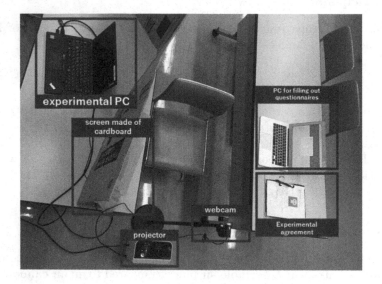

Fig. 1. Experimental environment

We first guided the participant to sit on the chair prepared for the experiment, then instructed the participant that the agent projected on the wall is used for caring for elderly individuals with dementia. Next, we instructed the participant to consider the scene as he or she met the agent for the first time.

Before starting the experimental session, the participant rolled up his or her right-arm sleeve before inserting his or her arms into the hole in the cardboard screen. We adjusted the position of the webcam to take a frontal view of the participant's face to obtain the accurate face direction data (Fig. 1).

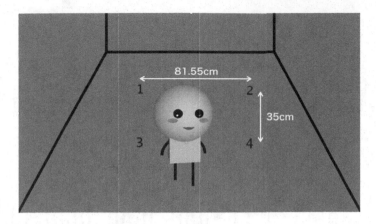

Fig. 2. Wall-projected agents

Then, the experimenter instructed the participant to turn his or her face toward numbers from 1 to 4 in random order. The numbers around the agent are shown in Fig. 2. The experiment was conducted after the participant practiced once.

The stimuli were presented corresponding to the experimental conditions after starting the experimental sessions, including tactile stimuli produced by the Wizard of Oz method. Finally, a questionnaire with 21 evaluation items was filled out to evaluate the system after each experimental condition.

The above procedure was repeated for each experimental condition in the counterbalanced order.

4.8   Evaluation Items

The participants evaluated the following statements on a five-point scale where 5 = relevant, 4 = somewhat relevant, 3 = neutral 2 = somewhat not relevant, and 1 = not relevant for the mean opinion score (MOS) method. Q1–Q4 are the evaluation items related to the familiarity of the agent. Q5–Q14 are the evaluation items related to the reliability of the agent. Q16–Q15 are the evaluation items related to the sense of presence of the agent. Q17–Q19 are the evaluation items related to the naturalness of the agent. Q20–Q21 are the evaluation items related to an uncomfortable or disgusting feeling about the agent.

Q1 You felt familiar with the agent.
Q2 You became familiar with the agent.
Q3 The agent was kind to you.
Q4 You felt kindness toward the agent.
Q5 You felt that you were respected and esteemed by the agent.
Q6 You had respect and esteem for the agent.
Q7 You were relieved by the way the agent moved.
Q8 The agent responded politely.

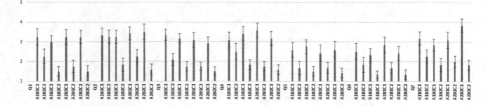

Fig. 3. Mean and SD of subjective evaluation Q1–Q7

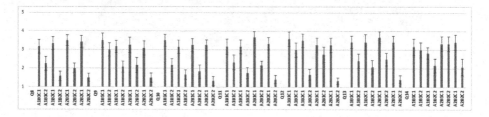

Fig. 4. Mean and SD of subjective evaluation Q8–Q15

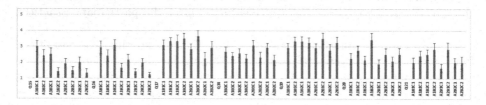

Fig. 5. Mean and SD of subjective evaluation Q15–Q21

Q9 You felt that the agent had emotions.
Q10 You felt that the agent liked you.
Q11 You liked this agent.
Q12 You felt that the agent was interested in you.
Q13 You became interested in the agent.
Q14 You felt intention in the behavior of the agent.
Q15 You felt that the agent was in real space.
Q16 You felt that the agent was with you.
Q17 You felt uncomfortable with the behavior of the agent.
Q18 You felt that the behavior of the agent was natural.
Q19 You felt that the behavior of the agent was unnatural.
Q20 You felt uncomfortable being with the agent.
Q21 You felt disgusted with the agent.

4.9   Experimental Results

Figure 3, 4, and 5 show the results of the MOS for each condition (the standard deviations are shown by bars plotted). Table 1 shows the results of an analysis of variance (ANOVA), with a significance level of 0.05.

Table 1. Result of ANOVA in experiment

	A		B		C		Interaction	Simple main effects for significant interactions
	F	p	F	p	F	p		
Q1	1.061	0.311	5.925	0.021*	81.516	<.01*	ABC	B(a1, c2), C(a1, b1), C(a1, b2), C(a2, b1), C(a2, b2)
Q2	3.928	0.057	5.634	0.025*	64.525	<.01*	None	None
Q3	0.280	0.601	6.026	0.020*	55.450	<.01*	None	None
Q4	0.665	0.421	3.452	0.073	72.406	<.01*	None	None
Q5	1.749	0.196	0.083	0.774	49.826	<.01*	BC	B(c2), C(b1), C(b2)
Q6	1.441	0.239	0.192	0.664	36.296	<.01*	BC	C(b1), C(b2)
Q7	2.573	0.119	0.000	1.000	44.777	<.01*	BC	C(b1), C(b2)
Q8	0.226	0.637	1.804	0.189	80.029	<.01*	BC	B(c2), C(b1), C(b2)
Q9	12.429	<.01*	16.812	<.01*	41.062	<.01*	BC	B(c2), C(b1), C(b2)
Q10	0.319	0.576	3.290	0.080	78.449	<.01*	BC	B(c2), C(b1), C(b2)
Q11	0.703	0.408	3.085	0.089	54.695	<.01*	None	None
Q12	3.702	0.064	20.983	<.01*	62.896	<.01*	BC	B(c2), C(b1), C(b2)
Q13	0.273	0.605	11.210	<.01*	50.765	<.01*	BC	B(c2), C(b1), C(b2)
Q14	0.380	0.542	25.032	<.01*	32.186	<.01*	BC	B(c2), C(b1), C(b2)
Q15	8.471	<01*	10.201	<.01*	18.939	<.01*	BC	B(c2), C(b1), C(b2)
Q16	10.821	<.01*	1.790	0.191	25.551	<.01*	BC	B(c2), C(b1), C(b2)
Q17	2.303	0.139	6.787	0.014*	15.041	<.01*	None	None
Q18	2.228	0.146	0.272	0.606	16.988	<.01*	BC	C(b1), C(b2)
Q19	0.954	0.336	1.620	0.213	12.560	<.01*	None	None
Q20	10.137	<.01*	0.340	0.564	14.470	<.01*	AC	A(c2), C(a1), C(a2)
Q21	6.431	0.017*	0.016	0.900	7.782	<.01*	None	None

*: p<0.05

First, there were significant results by Factors B and C in almost all of the questionnaires on the familiarity, Q1–Q4. It was conjectured that the familiarity to the user would be expressed by the approach and the touch independently. Q1 also showed a significant result in the interactions among Factors A, B, and C. In the simple main effect, the results showed that B1 (with the approaching action) received a higher score than B2 (without approach) in the conditions combining A1 and C2 (moving according to the user's face direction without tactile stimuli). There were also higher scores for C1 (with tactile stimulation) when the conditions were combined with all levels of Factors A and B.

There were significant results regarding Factor C in Q5–14, which are related to reliability. As can be seen in Fig. 3 and 4, the conditions combined with C1 showed higher scores than C2. There were also significant results regarding all the factors in Q9. We believe that the tactile stimuli can create reliability independently. In particular, they can make the user feel that the agent has emotion when Factor A, B, or C appears independently. Furthermore, Table 1 shows significant results in the interactions in Q5–Q14, except for Q11. In the simple main effect of interaction between Factors B and C, the results showed that B1 (with the approaching action) received a higher score than B2 (without approach) when conditions were combined with C2 (without tactile stimuli). The conditions in which C1 (tactile stimulation) was combined with both B1 and B2 showed better results than C2.

Q15 and 16 are the items related to the presence of the agent. There were significant results by all the factors in Q15, and there were significant results by Factors A and C in Q16. There were significant results in the interactions between Factors B and C in Q15–Q16. Regarding the simple main effect, the results showed that B1·(approaching action) received higher scores than B2 in the conditions combined with C2 (without tactile stimulation). It was conjectured that the agent's approach could provide the impression of the agent's presence, especially when the agent does not touch the user.

There was a significant result by Factor C in Q17–Q19, which are related to naturalness from negative items. The results showed that C2 (without tactile stimulation) received higher scores than C1. It is considered that touch communicates naturalness to the user. Here, in Q17, there were significant differences by Factors B and C. The uncomfortable feeling is unintentionally generated by the expressions. There were also significant results in the interactions between Factors B and C. Regarding the simple main effect, the results showed that B1 (approaching action) received higher scores in the conditions combining C2 (without tactile stimulation). It was conjectured that the agent's approach would provide an impression of naturalness to the user.

There were significant results by Factors A and C in Q20–Q21 related to uncomfortable feelings. There were also significant results in the interactions between Factors A and C. Regarding the simple main effect, it was conjectured that the agent would make the user feel unpleasant when it horizontally moved corresponding to the user's face direction without tactile stimuli, and that the user could feel unpleasant without touch regardless of the agent's horizontal movement.

5   Discussion

In this study, we aimed at smoothing the pre-care interaction between elderly users and the agent using the Humanitude method. We tried to promote familiarity, reliability, and the realization of the agent's presence in the pre-care multimodal interaction by its movement corresponding to the user's face direction, its approach toward the user, and its touch. We conducted an experiment to examine the proposed method.

First, there was a result showing that the agent's approach and touch conveyed familiarity, trust, and presence to users and that the agent's movement corresponding to the user's face direction conveyed trust and presence. In other words, it is conjectured that the agent's expression approachability and touch can induce the user to willing to cooperate during pre-care. It is expected that the physical relationship/state between the agent and the user draw the user's attention to establish rapport before the pre-care talk.

On the other hand, the agent's horizontal movement corresponding to the user's face direction decreased the evaluation of familiarity. Because the movement followed the user's detected face direction with a floating-like movement without gait, there might have been an adaptation gap [15], or the motion might have been interpreted as though the agent was always aware of the user and followed his or her field of view. However, this weakness would not affect the total design because the system aims at drawing the user's attention to the agent's presence at first and because the purpose of the movement according to the face direction of the user is for the agent to enter the user's field of view.

Next, according to the result of the simple main effect of the interaction, the feeling of relief was decreased based on the horizontal movement corresponding to the user's face direction without the agent's approach. It is considered that the agent, which the user saw for the first time and which entered the user's field of view many times in the distance, induced feelings of familiarity due to the uncertainty of the agent's intention.

At the same time, the feeling of presence beside the user increased with horizontal movement and without approach. We believe the movement provided an impression of cuddling.

The simple use of the horizontal movement corresponding to the user's face, the action of approaching the user, or the tactile stimuli were effective in inducing feelings of familiarity, reliability, and presence. On the other hand, the action of approach did not show any significance when combined with the tactile stimuli. Based on the results, it is conjectured that the tactile stimuli and the visual approaching action have similar effectiveness and that the tactile stimuli generated stronger impressions of interaction than the approach. At the same time, the approaching action would give an impression of naturalness as an introduction before the touch. Independent verification in the future is required to confirm this hypothesis.

There was no significance of naturalness by the single use of the three factors. That is to say, there was no negative effect of the elements in the proposed method. To provide more familiar and natural presence, we should examine the timing, speed, and smoothness of the agent's movement for its appropriate behaviors. The naturalness of tactile stimuli using airflow should be discussed through comparison with other tactile stimuli, such as pressure [17], vibration, etc.

6 Conclusion

In this study, we aimed to realize a multimodal interactive care agent adopting the Humanitude technique to support elderly people with dementia. In this paper, we introduced and examined our proposed agent, which exhibits "look into the user's eyes" and "touch them" actions to smoothen the pre-care interaction.

To verify the effectiveness of the proposed method, we evaluated the agent's behaviors: horizontal movement, approaching action, and physical contact corresponding to the user's face direction to investigate familiarity, reliability, presence, and naturalness. The results showed that the agent can provide the user with confidence in the agent and express its presence by moving, approaching, and physically contacting the user corresponding to the user's interaction phase.

In the future, we should examine the appropriate timing and speed for the agent's movement. The tactile stimuli should be discussed in comparison with other contemporary methods. The total design of the system should be considered with a whole flow from the introductive multimodal expression to the pre-care talk given to the user. The effectiveness corresponding to the care/communication content should be examined and appropriately redesigned for a total daily support system.

Acknowledgment. This research is supported in part by JSPS KAKENHI 25700021, 19H04154, and 18K11383.

References

1. Bickmore, T.W., Caruso, L., Clough-Gorr, K., Heeren, T.: 'It's just like you talk to a friend' relational agents for older adults. Interact. Comput. **17**(6), 711–735 (2005)
2. Catindig, J.A.S., Venketasubramanian, N., Ikram, M.K., Chen, C.: Epidemiology of dementia in Asia: insights on prevalence, trends and novel risk factors. J. Neurol. Sci. **321**(1–2), 11–16 (2012)
3. Duffy, B.R.: Anthropomorphism and robotics. The Society for the Study of Artificial Intelligence and the Simulation of Behaviour, 20 (2002)
4. Gineste, Y., Pellissier, J.: Humanitude: comprendre la vieillesse, prendre soin des Hommes vieux (think old age, caregiving for old men). Armand Colin (2007). (in French)
5. Honda, M., Mori, M., Hayashi, S., Moriya, K., Marescotti, R., Gineste, Y.: The effectiveness of French origin dementia care method; humanitude to acute care hospitals in Japan. Eur. Geriatr. Med. **4**, S207 (2013)
6. Honda, M., Ito, M., Ishikawa, S., Takebayashi, Y., Tierney Jr., L.: Reduction of behavioral psychological symptoms of dementia by multimodal comprehensive care for vulnerable geriatric patients in an acute care hospital: a case series. Case Rep. Med. **2016**, 4813196 (2016). https://doi.org/10.1155/2016/4813196
7. Huang, H.H.: Toward a memory assistant companion for the individuals with mild memory impairment. In: 2012 IEEE 11th International Conference on Cognitive Informatics and Cognitive Computin, pp. 295–299. IEEE (2012)

8. Kanai, Y., Osawa, H., Imai, M.: Interaction with an agent in blended reality. In: Proceedings of the 8th ACM/IEEE international conference on Human-robot interaction, pp. 153–154. IEEE Press (2013)
9. Kaneko, K., Harada, K., Kanehiro, F., Miyamori, G., Akachi, K.: Humanoid robot HRP-3. In: 2008 IEEE/RSJ International Conference on Intelligent Robots and Systems, pp. 2471–2478. IEEE (2008)
10. Levillain, F., Zibetti, E.: Behavioral objects: the rise of the evocative machines. J. Hum. Rob. Interact. 6(1), 4–24 (2017)
11. Nakamichi, D., Nishio, S.: Effect of agency to teleoperated communication robot by semi-autonomous nod (2016)
12. Rajap, P., Nakadai, S., Nishi, M., Yuasa, M., Mukawa, N.: Impression design of a life-like agent by its appearance, facial expressions, and gaze behaviors-analysis of agent's sidelong glance. In: 2007 IEEE International Conference on Systems, Man and Cybernetics, pp. 2630–2635. IEEE (2007)
13. Russo, A., et al.: Dialogue systems and conversational agents for patients with dementia: the human-robot interaction. Rejuvenation Res. 22(2), 109–120 (2019)
14. Sakakibara, S., Saiki, S., Nakamura, M., Yasuda, K.: Generating personalized dialogue towards daily counseling system for home dementia care. In: Duffy, V.G. (ed.) DHM 2017. LNCS, vol. 10287, pp. 161–172. Springer, Cham (2017). https://doi.org/10.1007/978-3-319-58466-9_16
15. Yamada, S., Yamaguchi, T.: Mutual adaptation of mind mappings between a human and a life-like agent. J. Jpn. Soc. Fuzzy Theory Intell. Inf. 17(3), 289–297 (2005)
16. Yasuda, K., Aoe, J.i., Fuketa, M.: Development of an agent system for conversing with individuals with dementia. In: Proceedings of the 27th Annual Conference of the Japanese Society for Artificial Intelligence, p. 3C1IOS1b2 (2013)
17. Yonezawa, T., Yamazoe, H.: Wearable partner agent with anthropomorphic physical contact with awareness of user's clothing and posture. In: Proceedings of the 2013 International Symposium on Wearable Computers, pp. 77–80. ACM (2013)
18. Yoshida, N., Yonezawa, T.: SCoViA: effectiveness of spatial communicative virtual agent based on motion parallax. In: Proceedings of the 1st International Conference on Human-Agent Interaction (iHAI 2013), II-2-p7 (2013)

Partner Agent Showing Continuous and Preceding Daily Activities for Users' Behavior Modification

Tomoko Yonezawa[1]([⊠]) [iD], Naoto Yoshida[2] [iD], Keiichiro Nagao[1], and Xin Wan[1] [iD]

[1] Kansai University, Takatsuki, Osaka 569-1095, Japan
yone@kansai-u.ac.jp
[2] Nagoya University, Nagoya, Aichi 464-8601, Japan
yoshida@cmc.is.i.nagoya-u.ac.jp

Abstract. In this research, we aimed to support improvement in users' daily lives by behavior modification for people who cannot self-manage their daily activities, such as bed-making, cleaning, tidying, and sleeping. We focused on the preceding behaviors of others who get along with users to encourage them to act on daily matter. Our proposed system adopts an anthropomorphic animation agent that shows its own activities in daily life to users to stimulate their incentives to follow actions of the agent as a familiar and ambient presence. We conducted a series of four-day experiments to investigate whether the preceding behaviors of the agent were repeated and continuously affected users' spontaneous actions. From the results, we suggest that the proposed system has a possibility to induce daily activities of users that will ultimately become spontaneous.

Keywords: Daily activities · Preceding behaviors · Virtual agent · Behavior modification

1 Introduction

Our daily lives involve many things we have to do. If people neglect to clean, tidy up, arrange their living spaces, and manage their time in daily life, they suffer losses to quality of life. Lazy lifestyles cause various problems, including pressure on the living space due to scattering of things, waste of time that could be used meaningfully, and mental pressure from tasks to do later. To improve quality of life, we need to do our daily activities without accumulating them.

Not only children with autism spectrum disorder [1] or attention–deficit disorder [2,3] have difficulty in their daily lives from lacking sufficient social and time management skills; there are adult people who lost or never acquired such the skills. Here, especially for elderly people with dementia, various daily activities are difficult to accomplish constantly and continuously. Many patients lose their motivation of daily tasks such as operation of brushing their teeth or bathing. From

© Springer Nature Switzerland AG 2020
V. G. Duffy (Ed.): HCII 2020, LNCS 12198, pp. 622–637, 2020.
https://doi.org/10.1007/978-3-030-49904-4_46

the viewpoint of rehabilitation, such activities are considered to be very important because the activities stimulate the patients and trigger their next actions.

To draw the patients' interests and motivation toward activities, we considered suggesting or guiding them on activities in direct/indirect ways through families and other familiar people; however, direct suggestions sometimes happen to generate their resistance or rebound. To induce elderly people with dementia in a natural and smooth way, using indirect guidance has been considered effective.

The second point is who should provide the guidance or suggestion. Even if a familiar person were to suggest the next activities to do, the elderly person in question would be annoyed and would ultimately disregard the person. It is presumed that elderly people with dementia become social withdrawal to prevent from sad or shameful emotions occurred by scolding and indication by the people surrounding them. Artificial reminders are one solutions, as there are alarm systems based on dosing schedules. Such systems cannot become effective or be continuously used unless a user understands or feels their necessity. The system should not only notify users on the next activities, but should try to persuade them on the activities' merits and stimulate or elevate the motivation. On the other hand, interactive systems are controllable according to the user's state.

Motivation stimulation using gamification, which is called serious games [4,5], and social motivation [6] are considered effective. In their daily activities, children sometimes play simple games with rewards in the form of snacks and so forth; however, most elderly people do not prefer childish stimulation. Accordingly, we focused on the second type of stimulation: social motivation [6]. When one considers Maslow's hierarchy of needs theory [7], humans are expected to do harmonious and unifying actions with others to satisfy social needs of belonging to a group; overheard communication [8] is known as an indirect inducer of a listener's actions.

Based on this perspective, the preceding activities of other people shown to a target person have possibilities to lead that person's actions. We thus focused on the preceding behavior of others as both a trigger of conforming behavior [9,10] and a sample case that showed the merits of an activity.

Here, we focused on anthropomorphic agents from the viewpoint of 1) human-like persuasion, 2) an appropriate level of the sense of distance, and 3) sympathetic interaction. In this research, we propose an anthropomorphic animation agent, that shows its own activities in daily life to users and stimulate their incentives to follow the actions of the agent as a familiar and ambient presence alongside them. From the viewpoint of social motivation and syntonic activities, anthropomorphic agents that show the state of their daily activities to users are considered effective stimulants of user's incentives to act.

Feedback reflecting users' behavior generates a higher effect on motivation [11] and satisfies their social needs. Consequently, we adopted camera-based user observation to detect users' daily activities, such as tidying. In addition, emotional feedback also has a strong effect on human motivation [12,13]. On that subject, we adopted the agent's smiles to correspond to the user's daily-life activities that follow to the agent's behavior.

We investigated the effect of the agent's preceding behavior on promoting users' spontaneous activities with a series of four-day experiments. The aim of the experiment was to confirm not only a short-term effect but also a long-term behavior modification.

2   Related Research

First, we describe the flow that promotes users' behavior modification through a famous Japanese maxim by Isoroku Yamamoto, which reads, "Show them, tell them, have them do it, and then praise them; otherwise, people won't do anything." There is a series of flows for making a person to act: 1) show examples, 2) encourage the person's understanding of methods and purposes, 3) encourage practice experience, and 4) improve behavioral motivation by reward. As a distinctive point in this maxim, we focused on the step of showing the instructor's example behavior before telling how and why to do the activity. Direct persuasion to do an activity at the beginning may reduce a person's motivation toward the activity.

Suzuki et al. [14] discussed the possibility that an agent would diminish a user's motivation for behavior by a forced feeling imposed by directly persuading the user to act. To improve users' behavioral motivation, they proposed presenting persuasion scenes where one agent persuaded another, which could indirectly show a third party viewpoint. They expected their method to reduce the psychological load on the user; however, it is necessary to pay attention to the linguistic persuasion of the agent's scripts with cognitive loads [15–17], so it is difficult to provide the user intuitive interpretation.

On the other hand, there are several studies on co-eating agents [18,19]. Inoue et al. [18] described the possibility of a user finding it easy to eat at a scene where an agent starts to eat first and the user's dining is promoted. Their research showed the possibility of triggering user's behavior by an agent's preceding behavior (nonverbal expression) without linguistic explanation. Accordingly, we designed a series of activities for an agent, showing its preceding behavior at first before encouraging action by users in the subsequent steps.

According to an effective process for customary behaviors advocated by Weinschenk (Fig. 1-A) [20], we designed a process (Fig. 1-B) in which an agent shows preceding behavior and a user follows the behavior. The agent represents preceding behaviors to the user based on triggers of the user's existing habits.

Furthermore, we also focused on improvement of the user's behavioral motivation in line with the second flow mentioned above. We aimed at improving the user's behavioral motivation by smiling of the agent [21], which implies an empathic attitude [22–24] and positive encouragement. Additionally, the system shows preceding behaviors triggered by the user's unconscious behaviors to avoid interfering with the user's concentration on the other tasks [25]. The system expresses the agent's preceding behavior and smiles only when user switches behaviors [26] or focuses on the agent to avoid the interruption [27]. We expected such an ambient presence to continuously encourage the user with a hands-off attitude.

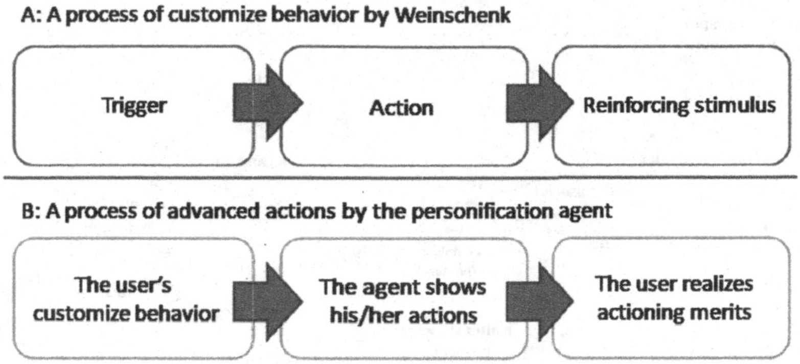

A: A process of customize behavior by Weinschenk

| Trigger | → | Action | → | Reinforcing stimulus |

B: A process of advanced actions by the personification agent

| The user's customize behavior | → | The agent shows his/her actions | → | The user realizes actioning merits |

Fig. 1. Weinschenk's effective process for customary behaviors [20] and our proposed process

3 System Implementation

3.1 Overview of System

In our proposed system, an agent shows preceding behavior of daily activity as an indirect promotion of behavior modification. The agent's behavior is triggered by the user's habitual activity; for example, the agent's bed-making behavior is triggered when the user leaves a bed. In this implementation, we adopted three triggers for the system to ascertain: 1) whether the user enters the room, 2) whether the user sits on the work desk, and 3) whether the user closes the window of the main task at the end of the PC work. We chose these triggers to show the agent's behaviors of 1) operating a vacuum cleaner, 2) checking the schedule, 3-1) cleaning up the desk, and 3-2) discarding the dust around the desk, all of which preceded the user's activities. In addition, we aimed to habituate users' daily activities by continuously promoting spontaneous behavior.

The system consists of 1) a user task state recognition section, 2) an animation control section presenting an agent, 3) a voice synthesis section for the agent's utterance, and 4) a text display section. Figure 2 shows the system flow, and Fig. 3 shows the system view. The system flow simply consists of a) a recognition of the user's state (Fig. 2-A) and b) an agent presentation (Fig. 2-B) outputting animation and information to the user. The agent presentation part (b) includes 2) the animation control, 3) voice synthesis, and 4) text display sections.

An animation that includes the agent's daily activities, living environment, and facial expression is displayed on the PC monitor corresponding to both the user's behavior and his or her state of attention to the agent. Speech of the agent is read aloud by the speech synthesis software, SofTalk[1], and its script text is displayed on the PC screen in a speech balloon. To detect the state of the user, the system processes 1) facial detection of the user through OpenCV and

---

[1] softalk: free software to synthesize characteristic speech voice. http://www.gigafree. net/media/record/softalk.html.

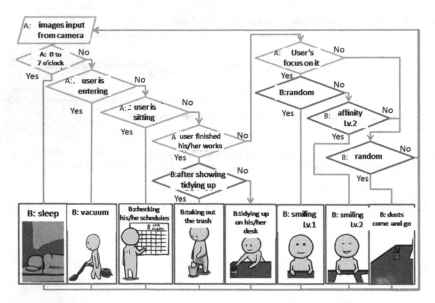

Fig. 2. System flow

Haar-like features, 2) motion detection of the user through optical flow, and 3) on/off detection of the light in the room with respect to the image of the PC's built-in camera set at the upper part of the monitor. Furthermore, the system also detects 4) the PC's processing situation controlled by the user based on observation of the external windows and the active window using the Windows API. These functions are implemented in C++.

Because such a system resides on the terminal as an ambient task, the agent is always reactive to user's situations as something closely tied to their lives. To avoid the system occupying the display area during other work by the user, the display window of the agent becomes inactive when an external window is used by the user.

3.2 Designs for Preceding Behavior of Agent

Since people can conduct daily activities without competition with other tasks by managing their overall daily schedules, the agent shows as though it is checking the schedule at the beginning of the user's activities for a day. From the viewpoint of working efficiency, the system displays an animation of the agent vacuuming its room after detecting that the user has entered the room, and the system displays an animation of the agent confirming its schedules again after detecting that the user has sat down at the working desk.

At the end of the work, people should clean up the top of the desk and throw away the garbage or tidy up for the next use. Accordingly, the system displays an animation of the agent cleaning up the desk and dumping the trash after detecting that the user has finished working.

Fig. 3. System view

Figure 4 shows the animation views of the agent's preceding behaviors: 1) confirming its daily schedule (Fig. 4-A), 2-a) cleaning with a vacuum cleaner (Fig. 4-B), 2-b) cleaning on the desk (Fig. 4-C), and 2-c) disposing of garbage in the basket (Fig. 4-D). In order to prevent user misunderstanding of its behavior, the agent utters and shows scripts about its actions. Finally, the agent shows how it feels the merits of acting with a positive expression.

3.3   Situation Recognition of User

In this configuration, the system currently detects 1) lighting state, 2) seating state of the user, and 3) working state of the user in the work room. The system uses brightness changes in the camera image for detecting that a user has turned the light on. For seating recognition, it uses motion and face detection. When the system detects a user's face after detecting motion, it recognizes that the user has come to the front of the PC and sat down. To recognize the user's working state or end of work, the system detects the state of external windows in the PC.

3.4   Agent's Smiles as Degree of Affinity

The agent smiles at the user to increase affinity. To show the relationship of gradually becoming closer to the user, the quantity of facial expressions of the agent increases according to the number of times the user has looked at the agent. At first, the system shows only a smile Lv.1 (Fig. 5-A) with the degree of affinity Lv.1. When the user looks at the agent a number of times exceeding a certain threshold number, the degree of affinity Lv.2 is obtained. At that point, the smile Lv.2 (Fig. 5-B) is presented (Table 1) in addition to the smile Lv.1. To avoid the user's recognition of the agent as a mechanical presence, the agent's smile is performed randomly when the user looks at it. Table 1 also shows the probability of the agent smiling. The degree of affinity is increased by the number

Fig. 4. Agent's preceding behavior

of times the user looks at the agent, with the tenth look raising the degree of affinity from Lv.1 to Lv.2.

Table 1. Smile probability according to affinity degree

	Affinity Lv.1	Affinity Lv.2	Affinity Lv.3
Smile Lv.	Lv.1 (40%)	Lv.1 (40%)	Lv.1 (40%)
	–	Lv.2 (80%)	Lv.2 (80%)
	–	–	Lv.3 (100%)

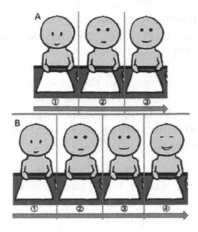

Fig. 5. Two types of agent's smiles

3.5   Space-Sharing Expressions

To make the user recognize the agent as a communal, living personality sharing the living space, it is necessary to express interactions of sharing the space by use of animated expressions. Accordingly, we prepared two types of interactions; when the user stays awake during the designated sleeping time of the agent (for example, from 24 o'clock to 7 o'clock), the system shows animations as though the light of the user space is leaking into the agent space (see Fig. 6), and when the user does not vacuum the room for a long time, the system shows animations simulating dust movement from the user space to the agent space (see Fig. 7).

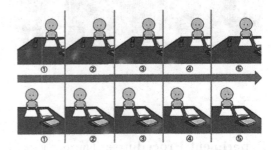

Fig. 6. Expression of light leakage from the user area

Fig. 7. Expression of dust comes and goes

4   Evaluation: Effect of Agent's Continuous Preceding Behavior on Users' Spontaneous Daily Activity

We conducted the following experiment to verify the effect of the proposed agent's continuous preceding behavior on user's spontaneous daily activity and its habituation.

Experimental Hypothesis: We hypothesized the following items.

Hypothesis 1: The agent's preceding behaviors can induce users' activities.

Hypothesis 2-1: The continuous stimuli of the agent's preceding behaviors enable users' daily activities even when the system stops the stimuli.

Hypothesis 2-2: Direct instruction of the agent can only induce users' activities when they are being instructed to do the activity. That is, direct instruction cannot provide continuous effects on users' spontaneous activities.

Hypothesis 3: Instruction from the agent is recognized as bothersome by users and reduces their motivations.

Conditions: The experiment was conducted with six conditions (three levels for a between-subject factor [Factor A] and two levels for a within-subject factor [Factor B]. Factor A, the agent's behavior, had three levels: [A1] showing preceding behaviors, [A2] instructing users' action, and [A3] promoting no action. The factor B, before and after measurements of the agent's promotion, had two levels: [b1] before the promotion (first day) and [b2] after the promotion (fourth day) in the flow of the experiment.

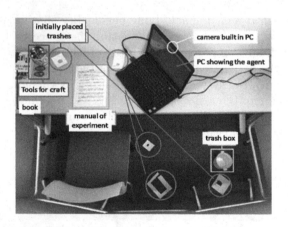

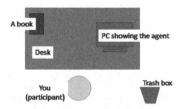

Fig. 8. Experimental environment

Fig. 9. Instruction figure of objects around participants

Experiment Procedures: The participants in this experiment were 16 university students ranging from 21 to 23 years old (13 males and 3 females). The experimental environment is shown in Fig. 8. As an initial state, there were a book, an instruction manual for experiment, and two pieces of garbage on the desk, and there were a trash box and three pieces of garbage on the floor. A PC on which the proposed system was installed was set on the desk. A trash box was placed at a distance of about 75 cm from the right foot of the chair, in a place where participants could not extend their hands. The situations of the participants during the experiment were observed from the PC's built-in camera and another camera was installed under the desk in a position invisible

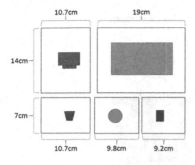

Fig. 10. Parts in the paper craft-works task

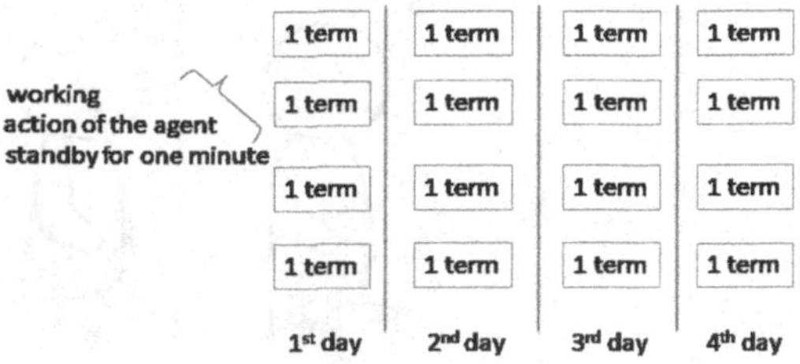

Fig. 11. Flow and schedule of four-day experiment

to the participants. We instructed the participants that we would capture the experimental scenes using cameras and obtained their consent beforehand.

In the experiment, we seated the participants on the chair in front of the desk and instructed them to do the following tasks: 1) check a sample figure shown on the PC as in Fig. 9; 2) cut the paper craftworks, as in Fig. 10; and 3) stick the parts on an A4 paper. After finishing the task, the participants closed the PC window that showed the task instructions, moved to a chair outside of the experimental area, and took a one-minute break. During the break, the experimenter measured the trash weight.

The above sequences are defined as one experimental term. Four experimental terms were conducted in one day, and the experiment continued for four days. Thus, the total number of experimental terms was 16, as shown in Fig. 11. During the tasks, the agent was always displayed on the PC and showed the same tasks to the users (Fig. 12-C). On the second and third days, when the participants closed the instruction window, agent behaviors were shown according to the following experimental conditions: A1, preceding behavior of throwing garbage into the trash box, as in Fig. 12-A; A2, indicating direct instruction with the agent's script, such as saying, "Please throw garbage into the trash," as in Fig. 12-B; and A3, continuing the agent's paperwork task, as in Fig. 12-C. On the first and fourth days, the agent behavior of A3 was displayed in all conditions.

Procedures of Subjective and Objective Evaluation: As observable data, we measured the number of times participants discarded trash in one day (four-term works), the ratio of the discarded garbage into the whole trash at the end of the fourth term, and the total amount of garbage generated from the initial placement to the end of the fourth task. After all the experiments, the participants answered the following statements using a five-point scale (5: very relevant, 4: somewhat relevant, 3: neutral, 2: somewhat irrelevant, 1: irrelevant):

Q1 Discarding trash was bothersome.
Q2 Discarding trash was necessary.
Q3 You felt the benefits of discarding trash.
Q4 You made an effort to discard trash.

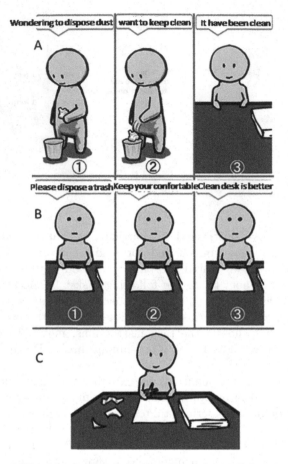

Fig. 12. Agent's behaviors for each condition

Q5 You did not like to discard trash.
Q6 You felt uncomfortable with the agent
Q7 The agent was burdensome.

Analyses of Number of Times and Amount of Garbage: Table 2 shows the analysis of variance (ANOVA) of the number of times users disposed of trash and the ratio of discarded trash. Figure 13 shows the average number of times users disposed trash, and Fig. 14 shows the average ratio of the discarded trash.

From Table 2, we confirmed a significant difference in the number of times in Factor A: a significant difference between A1 and A2 resulted from the multiple comparisons. The number of times users discarded trash increased in A1 compared to in A2. We also confirmed a significant difference in the number of times in Factor B. The number of times users discarded trash and the amount of trash increased in B2 (after the experiment) compared to in B1 (before the experiment).

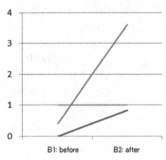

Fig. 13. Number of times (trash disposal)

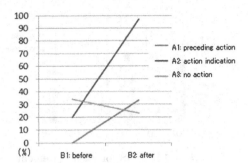

Fig. 14. Ratio of discarded trash

Table 2. ANOVA results for garbage discard

Factor A			Factor B			
F(2, 13)	p	Multi.comp.: A	F(1)	p	Simple Effects	Multi.comp.: A(b2)
I	4.12	0.04*	a2-a1	15.8	<.01	A(b2)*, B(a2)*	a2-{a1, a3}
II	2.57	0.11	–	9.70	=.01	A(b2)*, B(a1)+, B(a2)*	a2-{a1, a3}

*: p < .05, +: p < .10, Multi.comp.: multiple comparisons I: number of time, II: ratio of the discarded amount

Next, we discuss the interaction between Factors A and B. We found significant differences between A1-A2 and A2-A3 with the level B2, whereby the number of times users discarded trash increased in A2 compared to in A1 and A3. We also found a significant difference in Factor B with the level A2, in that the number of times users discarded trash increased in B2 compared to in B1. These results suggest that instruction from the agent increased the number of trash disposal occurrences.

Next, from the multiple comparisons of the amount of discarded trash in Factor A with the level B2, we confirmed significant differences between A2 and, both A1 and A3, such that the amount of discarded trash was increased in A2 compared to in A1 and A3. In addition, from the significant difference of factor B with the level A2, the average amount of discarded trash increased in B2 compared to in B1. Furthermore, with the level A1, we found a significant tendency (p < .10) in Factor B, and so there was a possibility that the amount of discarded trash increased in B2 over that in B1. These results suggest that the agent's preceding behaviors and instructions may have increased the amount of discarded trash.

MOS Results: Figure 15 shows the results of mean opinion scores (MOS), and Table 3 shows ANOVA results of MOS. No significant differences were found in the ANOVA results in all questions.

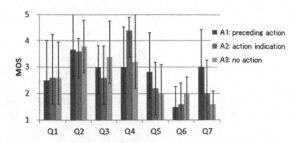

Fig. 15. MOS for each statement

Table 3. ANOVA results for MOS

	F(2, 13)	p
Q1	0.00	0.99
Q2	0.03	0.97
Q3	0.51	0.61
Q4	1.22	0.32
Q5	0.58	0.57
Q6	0.55	0.59
Q7	1.78	0.21

5   Discussion

From analysis of the results of the amount of discarded garbage in Table 2 and Fig. 14, we confirmed the strong effect of direct indication, although there was a weak tendency of the preceding behavior to increase the discarded trash. Here we considered that the immediate effect was stronger when the agent directly indicated what to do to the user, and that the agent still has a possibility to induce users' trash disposal actions by showing a scene of the agent discarding trash. In addition, the resulting comparison of B1 and B2 suggests the possibility that the induced effects persist even in the scenes where no subsequent preceding behaviors are presented, as the B2 level did not show the preceding behaviors. Thus, hypotheses 1 and 2 were both weakly supported.

Furthermore, from the camera image, it is evident that participants in the A1 level, whereby the agent indicated its preceding behavior, threw the trash into the basket at the end of their work. By its continuous preceding behavior, the agent could possibly induce users to spontaneously discard garbage at the end of a task.

Regarding the result of only a significant tendency for the effect of the preceding behavior, we conjecture that an agent with preceding behavior but no other interaction might not be recognized as a social, interactive presence. In contrast, direct indication obviously demonstrates the agent's ability to talk to the user. Here, gaze and facial expression are known as effective tools for agents to induce user behaviors [22]. From the viewpoint of the agent's social presence, interactive experiences and engagement [28] should be built beforehand to make the agent be recognized for its social existence at first.

Although there was no significant difference in subjective evaluation, we conjecture that the subjects did not want to discard garbage, even with the preceding behavior of the agent. To avoid a negative response to such behavior-inducing activity and to improve users' motivation, it is necessary to express the agent's positive attitude through such means as smiles immediately after a user's activities. We did not evaluate the emotional rewards in this paper, but this interaction would increase positive effects in establishing the engagement between the user and the agent.

On the other hand, there are the results against hypothesis 2. From the frequency/amount of trash being discarded, we observed that direct instructions to the participants after the tasks could continue to induce user's activities afterwards even without further instruction (B2). Moreover, there are results against hypothesis 3. The participants did not feel annoyed by the agent's instructions, which also did not decrease the behavioral motivation. We should verify the continued effectiveness of both direct indication and indirect preceding behavior after a week or a month.

Although we did not obtain significant differences in the subjective evaluations, the results suggest that the agent's preceding behaviors might be more annoying than its instructions. The agent's preceding behaviors may be perceived as a tacit pressure requesting activities of the user. It is also worth considering that anxiety about embarrassment or error [24] due to uncertainty in using the system has become one cause of annoyance. To solve these problems, we believe that it is necessary to depict the agent's behavior as though it is independent of users' daily lives to some extent.

6   Conclusion

In this paper, we discussed basic research on our proposed ambient agent, which promotes users' spontaneous activities in daily life by showing activities of its own that precede the users' as triggers to stimulate users' incentive to follow the action of the agent. The agent should become a familiar and ambient presence alongside the user. To improve the user's behaviors, it also smiles according to the user's attention and daily activities based on the agent's expression of affinity toward the user. We designed an agent system that does not require conscious inputs from the user to avoid forced feelings and get users to accept the agent as a resident system.

From the results of the evaluation, there was a tendency for the agent to lead to user activities by showing its own preceding behaviors. There was also a tendency for the agent to promote customary behaviors of users by continuously showing behavior, even when the agent would subsequently stop representing preceding behavior. These results also appeared in the direct indication conditions; however, the long-term verification would reveal differences between two types of the agent's expressions.

For future work, to establish habits that users enjoy, we should evaluate the effects of smiling or showing cooperative behaviors as the reward-strengthening stimuli when users' actions in daily life action precede the agent's activities. It is also necessary to consider the psychological effect of the agent's syntonic actions following to the user's activities on the sense of affinity. As future developments in the system implementations, the system may adopt multiple output devices such as wall projection, to be alongside the user all day. Built-in sensors in smart houses are expected to be of use for recognizing more behaviors by the user. The system design, development, and evaluation for elderly people should be also considered from the viewpoint of ways to indirectly induce people without making them stressed or uncomfortable. Especially for people with dementia, daily support should be provided continuously without interfering in their spontaneous activities.

Acknowledgments. This research was supported in part by JSPS Kakenhi 25700021, 19H04154, 19K12090, and 18K11383.

References

1. Emily, G., Grace, I.: Family quality of life and ASD: the role of child adaptive functioning and behavior problems. Autism Res. **8**(2), 199–213 (2015)
2. Leo, J.: Attention deficit disorder. Skeptic (Altadena, CA) **8**(1), 63 (2000)
3. Kelly, K., Ramundo, P.: You Mean I'm Not Lazy, Stupid or Crazy?!: The Classic Self-help Book for Adults with Attention Deficit Disorder. Simon and Schuster (2006)
4. Michael, D.R., Chen, S.: Serious Games: Games That Educate Train and Info, Course Technology. Muska & Lipman/Premier-Trade (2005)
5. Nakajima, T., Lehdonvirta, V., Tokunaga, E., Ayabe, M., Kimura, H., Okuda, Y.: Lifestyle ubiquitous gaming: making daily lives more plesurable. In: 13th IEEE International Conference on Embedded and Real-Time Computing Systems and Applications, RTCSA 2007, pp. 257–266. IEEE, August 2007
6. Cofer, C.N., Appley, M.H.: Motivation: Theory and Research (1964)
7. Maslow, A.H.: The farther reaches of human nature. Viking Adult (1971)
8. Walster, E., Festinger, L.: The effectiveness of "overheard" persuasive communications. J. Abnorm. Soc. Psychol. **65**(6), 395–402 (1962)
9. Appley, M.H., Moeller, G.: Conforming behavior and personality variables in college women. J. Abnorm. Soc. Psychol. **66**(3), 284 (1963)
10. Balsa, A.I., Homer, J.F., French, M.T., Norton, E.C.: Alcohol use and popularity: social payoffs from conforming to peers' behavior. J. Res. Adolesc. **21**(3), 559–568 (2011)
11. Nakajima, T., Lehdonvirta, V., Tokunaga, E., Kimura, H.: Reflecting human behavior to motivate desirable lifestyle. In: Proceedings of the 7th ACM conference on Designing Interactive Systems, pp. 405–414. ACM, February 2008
12. Terzis, V., Moridis, C.N., Economides, A.A.: The effect of emotional feedback on behavioral intention to use computer based assessment. Comput. Educ. **59**(2), 710–721 (2012)
13. Beale, R., Creed, C.: Affective interaction: how emotional agents affect users. Int. J. Hum. Comput. Stud. **67**, 755–776 (2009)
14. Suzuki, S.V., Yamada, S.: Persuasion through overheard communication by life-like agents. In: Proceedings of IEEE/WIC/ACM International Conference on Intelligent Agent Technology, pp. 225–231, September 2004
15. Plass, J.L., Moreno, R., Brunken, R.: Cognitive Load Theory. Cambridge University Press, Cambridge (2010)
16. Tabbers, H.K., Martens, R.L., Merrienboer, J.J.: Multimedia instructions and cognitive load theory: effects of modality and cueing. Br. J. Educ. Psychol. **74**(1), 71–81 (2004)

17. Paas, F., Renkl, A., Sweller, J.: Cognitive load theory and instructional design: recent developments. Educ. Psychol. **38**(1), 1–4 (2003)
18. Inoue, T., Shiobara, T.: A dining agent system for comfortable meal to a solo diner. IPSJ Trans. Digit. Contents **2**(2), 29–37 (2014). (In Japanese)
19. Liu, R., Inoue, T.: Application of an anthropomorphic dining agent to idea generation. In: Proceedings of the 2014 ACM International Joint Conference on Pervasive and Ubiquitous Computing: Adjunct Publication, pp. 607–612. ACM, September 2014
20. Weinchenk, S.: How to get people to do stuff: master the art and science of persuasion and motivation. New Riders (2013)
21. Rajap, P., Nakadai, S., Nishi, M., Yuasa, M., Mukawa, N.: Impression design of a life-like agent by its appearance, facial expressions, and gaze behaviors-analysis of agent's sidelong glance. In: 2007 IEEE International Conference on Systems, Man and Cybernetics, pp. 2630–2635 (2007)
22. Yuasa, M., Tokunaga, H., Mukawa, N.: Autonomous turn-taking agent system based on behavior model. In: HCII 2009 Proceedings Part III, pp. 19–24 (2009)
23. Yuasa, M., Yasumura, Y., Nitta, K.: Giving advice in negotiation using physiological information. In: IEEE International Conference on Systems, Man, and Cybernetics, vol. 1, pp. 248–253 (2000)
24. Takeuchi, Y., Katagiri, Y.: Establishing affinity relationships toward agents: effects of sympathetic agent behaviors toward human responses. in: WET ICE 1999, pp. 253–258 (1999)
25. Fukayama, A., Ohno, T., Mukawa, N., Sawaki, M., Hagita, N.: Messages embedded in gaze of interface agents – impression management with agent's gaze. In: Proceedings of the SIGCHI Conference on Human Factors in Computing Systems (CHI 2002), pp. 41–48. ACM, New York (2002)
26. Tanaka, T., Fujita, K.: Study of user interruptibility estimation based on focused application switching. In: Proceedings of the ACM 2011 Conference on Computer Supported Cooperative Work, CSCW 2011, pp. 721–724. ACM, New York (2011)
27. Tanaka, T., Fujita, K.: Secretary agent for mediating interaction initiation. In: Proceedings of Human Agent Interaction 2013, II-2-p5 (2013)
28. Glas, N., Pelachaud, C.: Definitions of engagement in human-agent interaction. In: 2015 International Conference on Affective Computing and Intelligent Interaction (ACII), pp. 944–949, September 2015

Author Index

Printed in the United States
By Bookmasters